Behavioral Economics

Edward Cartwright

Routledge
Taylor & Francis Group

LONDON AND NEW YORK

First published 2011
by Routledge
2 Park Square, Milton Park, Abingdon, Oxon OX14 4RN

Simultaneously published in the USA and Canada
by Routledge
711 Third Avenue, New York, NY 10017

Routledge is an imprint of the Taylor & Francis Group, an informa business

British Library Cataloguing in Publication Data
A catalogue record for this book is available from the British Library

Library of Congress Cataloging in Publication Data
A catalog record has been requested for this book

ISBN: 978-0-415-57309-2 (hbk)
ISBN: 978-0-415-57312-2 (pbk)
ISBN: 978-0-203-81686-8 (ebk)

Typeset in Times
by RefineCatch Limited, Bungay, Suffolk

Printed and bound in Great Britain by
CPI Antony Rowe, Chippenham, Wiltshire

Dedicated to Kerry, Robert and Anna

Contents

PART IV
Welfare and policy **391**

Preface

The origins of this book are four or five years ago when I started teaching a course called *Strategy and Games* to first year undergraduates. The idea of the course was to illustrate through classroom experiments some of the basic ideas of economics and game theory. In teaching that course my interest and knowledge of behavioral economics grew a lot; as did my frustration at the limited resources available to students wanting to learn more about this fascinating area of economics. Eventually, I decided it was time to write this book.

My basic objective when writing the book was to convey both the excitement and the importance of behavioral economics. I wanted to explain the basic principles, ideas and results of behavioral economics and show how fascinating they are. I also wanted to illustrate through applications why behavioral economics is fundamentally important in understanding the world around us. I wanted a book that was accessible to a general reader, not just those trained in economics, and/or comfortable with algebra. You can be the judge of whether I achieved what I set out to do.

I could not have written this book without those who have contributed to the literature on behavioral economics and given me such great material to work with. Particular thanks are due to those who made my job so easy by writing papers over many years that, when put together, gave very clear insights into economic behavior. I would love to thank these people publicly, but in writing their names it would probably be all too obvious which names I do not mention. I will, therefore, reserve my thanks for now. I just hope to have done justice to the great work out there. I should also make clear that the opinions expressed in this book are mine, and not necessarily those of the researchers whose work I refer to. Any mistakes are mine as well.

I can be a lot freer in the thanks for my wife Anna, who has helped so much in writing this book. On a personal level she has been patient and supportive while I wrote it. On a practical level, she is my greatest critic, never happy until everything is explained as fully and clearly as possible; she is also a great source of new ideas and new ways of thinking about old ideas. I should also thank all the students and colleagues connected with the Strategy and Games course, for teaching me so much. Finally, I want to give a big thanks to Myrna Wooders who, as well as being a fantastic person to know, has long been, and continues to be, a great inspiration and mentor.

Part I

Introduction

1 An introduction to behavioral economics

However beautiful the strategy, you should occasionally look at the results.

Sir Winston Churchill

It seems natural to start the book by asking, what is behavioral economics? That's a tough question, but I will give you three answers. You might think that this is two too many, but if we put all three together, we get a definition of behavioral economics that I am happy with. So, here's the first answer:

> Behavioral economics is about understanding economic behavior and its consequences. It's about understanding why someone buys a hotdog, goes to work, saves for retirement, gives to charity, gets a qualification, sells an old car, gambles on a horse race, cannot quit smoking, etc. It's also about understanding whether people make good or bad choices, and could be helped to make better choices.

I like this definition, because I want to know the answer to all those questions. The problem is that we end up with far too broad a definition to be very useful. So, we need something a bit different.

For that something different, we can use the fact that economists already have a fantastic model with which to try and understand economic behavior and its consequences. You can find this model in any economics textbook, and it gives us a beautiful story of how things *might* work. We can, for example, derive demand and supply curves, solve for equilibrium prices and quantities, and design mechanisms or policy to increase efficiency and social welfare.

The potential problem with this **standard economic model** is that it is based on some strong assumptions. For example, it assumes people can be approximated by a **homo economicus** who is rational, calculating and selfish, has unlimited computational capacity, and never makes systematic mistakes. It also assumes market institutions work and so, for instance, prices should converge, as if by magic, to equilibrium. There is no obvious reason why humans can be well approximated by homo economicus, or why market institutions should work. This leads to my second definition:

> Behavioral economics is about testing the standard economic model on humans, seeing when it works and when it does not, and asking whether it can be tweaked, or given an overhaul, to better fit what we observe.

This is a more practical and specific definition, but it does leave open the question of how we are going to test and tweak the model. After all, surely economists have been testing the model all along? Well, unfortunately, the standard economic model is flexible enough that it can be manipulated to explain just about any anomaly we ever observe, and we somehow need to step out of this trap. That leads to my third and final definition:

> Behavioral economics is about applying insights from laboratory experiments, psychology, and other social sciences in economics.

We will, therefore, be guided by the evidence on human behavior and psychology, both in testing and in tweaking or overhauling the standard economic model. In short, we will replace homo economicus with homo sapiens.

If you combine all three definitions, I think we can strike a nice balance. Behavioral economics is about working constructively with the standard economic model to get a better understanding of economic behavior. The objective is definitely not to criticize the standard economic model, or accentuate the negatives. Testing the standard model is a means to an end, and that end is to understand economic behavior as best we can.

Behavioral economics has really come of age in the last 40 years or so. Various things could have happened when we started to put the standard economic model to the test. The model could have worked perfectly; that would have been fantastic news for economics, but not so exciting for the future of behavioral economics. At the other extreme, the model could have proved useless; that would be bad news all round (except for those who like to poke fun at economics). What has actually happened is an exciting mix in which the model sometimes seems to work very well, sometimes work very badly, but most of the time is not far off, and with a bit of tweaking gets a lot better.

This is exciting because it means that behavioral economics can teach us a lot. It can tell us when the standard economic model does a good job and when not, and it can tell us how to change the model to get a better fit with reality. That is progress, and that is why behavioral economics is revolutionizing economics and our ability to understand economic behavior. In this book I hope to talk you through some of the main results and insights of behavioral economics in order that you can see for yourself how exciting and informative it is.

This chapter will set the scene a little by introducing some basic ideas and concepts, before previewing the rest of the book.

1.1 The history and controversies of behavioral economics

Behavioral economics has an interesting and checkered history. I will not delve too deeply into that history here, but an overview is useful because it will allow me to expand on the motivations behind behavioral economics, as well as explain some of the controversies and debates that surround it. These controversies and debates still rumble on, and so it is helpful to have some understanding of them before you see what behavioral economics has to offer.

It is difficult to say when behavioral economics began, but I am going to credit Adam Smith with being its founder. Any student of economics should be familiar with Adam Smith's book *An Inquiry into the Causes of the Wealth of Nations*, first published in 1776. In that book Smith famously explained the invisible hand of the market. Less well known to most economists is a book that Smith first published in 1759, called *The Theory of Moral Sentiments*. It was actually in this book that the invisible hand first made an appearance. More interesting, for our purpose, is how Smith explains in the book that people are not motivated solely by self-interest, but also feel a natural sympathy with others, and have a natural sense of virtue.

In short, in *The Theory of Moral Sentiments*, Smith talks about many things that in the last 30 years or so have become major issues in behavioral economics. For example, a theme through many parts of the book is the importance of reward and punishment (something we will pick up on in chapter seven). Another theme is the influence of custom and fashion (which we will pick up in chapter five). In my mind Smith comfortably does enough to be the father of behavioral economics. The intriguing question is why did we have to wait over 200 years for the ideas that he talked about to be taken seriously by economists?

That turns out to be slightly the wrong question, because psychology did go hand-in-hand with economics for a long time after Adam Smith. Early economists gave much weight to emotions, impulses, stimulus, morals and the like. For example, the law of diminishing marginal utility, one of the most fundamental principles of the standard economic model was based on psychological ideas and economists would often appeal to the work of psychologists in supporting and developing their work. At the beginning of the twentieth century, however, economics turned away from psychology, and behavioral economics, if we can call it that, disappeared for over half a century.

This shift was initiated by Vilfredo Pareto. In a letter dated 1897 Pareto writes: 'Pure political economy has therefore a great interest in relying as little as possible on the domain of psychology'. This is presumably why, when he published a paper in 1900 outlining a new approach to the theory of choice, he claims as one of its main achievements that 'every psychological analysis is eliminated' (these quotes taken from Bruni and Sugden 2007). Why would we want to rid economics of psychology, and how is it possible to do so?

It is easier to start with the latter question. Psychology can be taken out of economics by focusing on choice rather than desire. Instead of trying to work out why people do things, we can make inferences basely solely on what they do. To quote again from Pareto: 'I am not interested in the reason why man is indifferent between [one thing and another]: I notice the pure and naked fact'. This approach makes a lot of sense, because it allowed Pareto, and subsequent economists, to abstract away from difficult psychological questions and develop a mathematical theory of rational choice.

Indeed, asking, as Pareto did, what happens if people are rational is a good, logical thing to do because it provides a natural benchmark to work with. The same could be said of asking, as Adam Smith did in discussing the invisible hand, what happens if people are selfish. Assuming for mathematical convenience that people are rational and selfish clearly does not, however, mean that people actually are rational or selfish. Adam Smith clearly recognized this, and Pareto did so too by distinguishing when rational choice should or should not be expected to approximate what people do.

The problem is that these caveats can easily be forgotten in the beauty or simplicity of the argument. Adam Smith's conjecture that someone, 'by pursuing his own interest, frequently promotes that of the society more effectually than when he intends to promote it' is truly intriguing. Similarly, Pareto's new theory of choice seemed widely applicable. In the face of such appeal and convenience it became easy to overlook the fact that people are neither rational nor selfish; homo economicus became king, and economics became very distant from psychology.

Interestingly, homo economicus became ever cleverer as the twentieth century progressed, Pareto's caveats long since forgotten. The assumption of rational expectations, for instance, meant that homo economicus knew far more about the workings of the economy than any economist. As behavioral economist Richard Thaler wrote, while behavioral economics was still in its relative infancy (1990: 203):

> The problem seems to be that while economists have gotten increasingly sophisticated and clever, consumers have remained decidedly human. This leaves open the question of whose behavior we are trying to model. Along these lines, at an NBER conference a couple of years ago I explained the difference between my models and Robert Barro's by saying that he assumes the agents in his model are as smart as he is, while I portray people as being as dumb as I am.

In my mind, to assume people are like rational and selfish homo economicus is the most natural, objective place to begin thinking about modeling economic behavior. Indeed, in many of the chapters that follow I will start by asking what a selfish, rational person would do, and so you will hopefully see why it's a good place to start. The crucial point, though, is that it is the start point and not the end point. It is the best way to start thinking about modeling economic behavior but not necessarily the best way to model economic behavior. A crucial distinction!

The standard economic model does, though, march ever onwards, and behavioral economics has so far done relatively little to quell the tide. Many economists continue to derive ever more complicated and elaborate results based on the standard economic model. Whether these results are any use in understanding what happens on planet Earth, I am not so sure. That's why we need behavioral economics, and that's why the time would inevitably come for behavioral economics to be reborn.

1.1.1 Behavioral economics is reborn

From the 1960s onwards, psychology gradually did make a return to economics. I would suggest four distinct elements to its comeback. Let's look at each in turn.

The first element I would call the 'you cannot be serious attack', and give the main credit to Herbert Simon. Simon seriously questioned the sense of approximating people by homo economicus. For example, in a paper published in 1955, he solves for how a rational person should behave before stating: 'My first empirical proposition is that there is a complete lack of evidence that, in actual human choice situations of any complexity, these computations can be, or are in fact, performed.' Instead, Simon suggested looking at the information and computational capacities that humans do possess, and using this as the starting point for economic models. Recognizing the limitations faced by humans led to the term 'bounded rationality.'

Simon won the Nobel Prize in Economics in 1978 for his 'pioneering research into the decision-making process within economic organizations'. His calls, however, to replace homo economicus with something more human-like fell largely on deaf ears. Symptomatic of this was Herbert Simon leaving the Graduate School of Industrial Administration at Carnegie Mellon University for the psychology department. In his autobiography (Simon 1991) he writes: 'My economist friends have long since given up on me, consigning me to psychology or some other distant wasteland.'

One thing notably lacking in much of what Simon wrote was proof that homo economicus is not a good approximation of how people behave. He may have thought this was obvious, many do, but the lack of any formal proof made it easy for economists to ignore his work. The same could not be said of the second element I want to talk about. I will call this the 'your assumptions are wrong attack', and give the main credit to Daniel Kahneman and Amos Tversky. The approach here is one of demonstrating that people really are very different to homo economicus. One way to make the point is to get people, including economists, to answer simple questions such as this (which I took from Thaler and Sunstein 2007):

> A bat and ball cost $1.10 in total. The bat costs $1.00 more than the ball. How much does the ball cost?

If you said ten cents, then you are like most people, but need to think again, because the answer is five. Here's another famous example from Tversky and Kahneman (1983):

Bill is 34 years old. He is intelligent, but unimaginative, compulsive, and generally lifeless. In school, he was strong in mathematics but weak in social studies and humanities.

Rank the following eight statements from most probable to least probable:
Bill is a physician who plays poker for a hobby.
Bill is an architect.
Bill is an accountant.
Bill plays jazz for a hobby.
Bill surfs for a hobby.
Bill is a reporter.
Bill is an accountant who plays jazz for a hobby.
Bill climbs mountains for a hobby.

If you are like most then you said it is more likely Bill is an accountant, than Bill is an accountant who plays jazz for a hobby, than Bill plays jazz for a hobby. Now, how can it be more likely that Bill is an accountant who plays jazz, than Bill plays jazz? It cannot.

If most people make mistakes like this, how we can possibly expect them to do the complex calculations that homo economicus routinely does. With this, and many other examples, very clear evidence was provided that people are not like homo economicus, or at least not like the version assumed in the standard economic model. Different assumptions, therefore, seemed sensible. To quote from a paper Kahneman and Tversky published in 1981 (p 453):

> The definition of rationality has been much debated, but there is general agreement that rational choices should satisfy some elementary requirements of consistency and coherence. In this article we describe decision problems in which people systematically violate the requirements of consistency and coherence, and we trace these violations to the psychological principles that govern the perception of decision problems and the evaluation of options.

Daniel Kahneman won the Nobel Prize in Economics in 2002 for 'having integrated insights from psychological research into economic science, especially concerning human judgment and decision-making under uncertainty'. Even so, I am not so sure his work, and that of others in a similar vein, was ultimately that crucial in the comeback of psychology. That's because the attack was still too easy to dodge for economists confident in the standard economic model. After all, was it not obvious that people are not like homo economicus? The real issue is whether models in which people are approximated by homo economicus made good predictions. The early work of Kahneman, Tversky and others had less to say on this issue.

To illustrate the point we can get to the third element, which I will call the 'markets work revelation' and give the main credit to Vernon Smith. Starting in 1955 Smith performed a series of experiments to see whether basic predictions of the standard economic model about markets would prove correct. We will look at these experiments in more detail in the next chapter, but basically the predictions proved good. A stunning result! Maybe, therefore, it does not matter if people are not like homo economicus; the standard economic model can still work.

These initial experiments led to a continuing line of research on market institutions that to my mind provide the most important results to have come out of behavioral economics, and Vernon Smith did win the Nobel Prize in Economics in 2002 'for having established laboratory experiments as a tool in empirical economic analysis, especially in the study of alternative market mechanisms'. I am still though reluctant to think this work had too much of a hand in the comeback of psychology. That's because, while moving beyond the standard economic model, it largely confirmed the standard economic model was getting something right. Why, therefore, would we need behavioral economics?

While all three of the elements I have discussed so far were instrumental in the comeback of behavioral economics, you have probably guessed by now that it is to the last element I would give most importance. This final element I will call the 'what equilibrium to choose problem', and give the main credit to Reinhard Selten. The problem became apparent with the rapid progress of game theory in the 1950s and 1960s. Game theory looks to capture behavior in strategic situations, and meant the demands on homo economicus became ever more stringent. Not only should he or she be selfish, rational, more clever than any economist, and the like, homo economicus also needs to be telepathic (and even that is not enough). Basically, in strategic situations, it usually becomes ambiguous what homo economicus should do; it is ambiguous what the rational thing to do is.

The technical way to express this problem is to say that there are multiple equilibria. Somehow we need to try and say which of the equilibria 'makes more sense' or 'seems more likely to occur'. That's a bit like throwing darts at a dartboard while blindfold. To have any chance of success it makes sense to question how people might think or reason in such strategic situations and observe what people do when they play games. In other words, it made sense to draw a little on psychology and to run controlled experiments.

In the late 1950s Selten did begin running experiments. These first experiments were primarily concerned with industrial economics and ultimately led to important theoretical ideas like subgame perfection, something we will look at in chapter six. The main thing, though, was that experiments increasingly became seen as a useful way to learn more about economic behavior. To quote from an autobiographical sketch by Selten (1994), 'More and more I came to the conclusion that purely speculative approaches like that of our paper of 1962 are of limited value. The structure of boundedly rational economic behavior cannot be invented in the armchair, it must be explored experimentally.'

Selten won the Nobel Prize in Economics in 1994 together with John Nash and John Harsanyi 'for their pioneering analysis of equilibria in the theory of non-cooperative games'. More than anything else I think that game theory was instrumental in the rebirth of behavioral economics. That's because it meant the next logical step in developing the standard economic model was to draw from psychology and use experiments. The standard economic model had hit a dead end and behavioral economics was needed to move it forward.

If we put together these four different elements in the rebirth of behavioral economics, it is no surprise that it has made a strong comeback. Behavioral economics has the potential to improve our understanding of economic behavior from so many different angles, and this eventually shone through. (Before moving on, it would be remiss of me not to mention that it did so through the work of many more than just the five people I gave credit above.)

1.1.2 The different faces of behavioral economics

In suggesting, as I just have, that there were four distinct elements in the rebirth of behavioral economics, it is not too surprising that behavioral economics is somewhat splintered into subtly different sub-fields. In this book I am going to use a very broad and encompassing notion of behavioral economics that tries to cut across any arbitrary divisions. Divisions do exist, however, and it is worth knowing something about these, and some terms used to describe them that you may come across.

I will start with the notion of **bounded rationality** that we already came across in talking about Herbert Simon. The idea here is to recognize the constraints people face, in terms of computational capacity, memory, information, time, and the like. We should not, for instance, assume that homo economicus can do mathematical calculations a human cannot do, or can remember more things that a human can. This sounds clear enough, but there are two quite different ways in which the idea has been put into practice.

Today, the term bounded rationality is commonly reserved for work in which the constraints people face are explicitly modeled. The approach is thus one of solving for what a rational person will do if she has, say, limited memory. For instance, what password should Anna use on her computer if she knows she might forget it? With this approach it is still assumed that people can be approximated by a selfish and rational homo economicus; just one with a bit less memory and mathematical ability. Such an approach is prone to something called the infinite regress problem, that I will talk about in the next chapter, but does give us an idea of how a person can optimally cope with their limitations, or bounded rationality.

This common usage of the term is somewhat removed from what Herbert Simon originally envisaged. More in keeping with his work is the idea of **simple heuristics that make us smart**. This approach starts with the idea that people use heuristics, or 'rules of thumb', to make decisions. For example, Anna might use the same password whenever she is asked to give a password; this way she is less likely to forget the password for her computer. Whether or not heuristics like this are optimal is not really considered important. More important is to find what heuristics people do use, and to think about the consequences.

This approach most naturally fits with the work of psychologists, like Kahneman and Tversky. Heuristics, however, tend to come with biases, and sometimes it's the bias that gets more of the headlines. For example, a reasonable heuristic in repetitive situations is: 'do what I did last time'. Anna, for instance, might always go grocery shopping in the same store. Sensible though this may be, it can lead to a **status quo bias** in which she fails to change her behavior 'often enough'. Maybe she keeps going to the same store even though a cheaper and better store opened nearer to her house. Such biases usually go by the name **cognitive biases**.

Cognitive biases are simplest to see in well designed experiments, and experiments have long been the most common form of research method in psychology. In economics the story is a bit different with experiments basically unheard of until the early ones involving Vernon Smith and Selten. Since then they have become progressively more common, but the proportion of academic economists who have run an experiment is still way below the corresponding proportion of psychologists. Where I work at the University of Kent, for example, I estimate the respective proportions at 20 percent and 100 percent. This means one still often sees the term **experimental economics** as referring to any economic research based on experiments.

As more and more economists use experimental methods, however, the term experimental economics becomes ever more non-descriptive. Experiments are now being used in very different ways and in very different subject areas. Sometimes, for instance, as with the market experiments of Vernon Smith, the focus is on institutions or aggregate behavior and there may be relatively little interest in individual behavior. Other times, as with the experiments of Selten, there is a greater focus on individual behavior and testing theories of individual behavior. Experiments have also been run across the subject boundaries of economics from game theory to macroeconomics.

The contrasts between game theory and bounded rationality on the one side and experimental economics and research on cognitive biases on the other can be quite stark. As far as I am concerned, however, it is all behavioral economics. Good behavioral economics can involve theoretical research with no experiments. It can also involve experimental research with little or no theory. It seems natural, therefore, to split things according to subject of investigation and not method of investigation, and that's how I will do things in this book, trying to mix theory and experiment. It's notable, however, that big gaps do still exist between theory and experiment, and sometimes these gaps are hard to bridge.

Before I finish, a few more terms you may come across seem worth mentioning. I will start with economic psychology. In principle, **economic psychology** is a sub-discipline of psychology that deals with the psychology of economic decision-making. For example, it might ask what cognitive processes were used in deciding to buy this book. The difference between behavioral economics and economic psychology is sometimes a little subtle, and I will come back to the difference shortly. But it seems fair to say that a lot of what has historically been called behavioral economics would probably be more appropriately called economic psychology. The trouble is that behavioral economics needs to draw heavily on economic psychology, and that's why the dividing line becomes a bit blurred. It's also why a lot of what I am going to talk about would probably be more appropriately called economic psychology.

The next term I want to mention is behavioral finance. As the name suggests, **behavioral finance** is, in principle, a subset of behavioral economics that deals with financial decision-making and financial behavior. I say 'in principle' because in reality behavioral finance has taken on something of a life of its own. While I will not give a specific treatment of behavioral finance here, I will cover key issues and results. Indeed, many of the applications I will look at will be from behavioral finance, and I will also mention key issues in behavioral finance such as the validity of the efficient market hypothesis.

Finally, I want to introduce neuro-economics. **Neuro-economics** gets its own chapter in the book, and so probably needs little mention here. But I will mention that it is the latest development in behavioral economics, and brings neuroscience to bear on economics. It seems safe to say that neuro-economics has contributed more to neuroscience than it has to economics, so far. For that reason it remains somewhat controversial, but only time will tell whether it can significantly advance economics. And behavioral economics is not short of controversy, as I now want to explain.

1.1.3 Debate and controversy

Yes, behavioral economics does have its controversy and disputes. Economists question whether we need behavioral economics, and whether we need economic experiments. Behavioral economists question the methods and techniques of others, such as the need for neuro-economics. There is nothing unusual in academics disagreeing, but it can be useful to know something about the disagreements. Here are four interesting debates for you to think about, both now and while you read through the book.

Let's start with the big question, one that I talked about a little in tracing the decline and rebirth of behavioral economics:

> Is it enough to assume people can be approximated by homo economicus, or do we need psychologically grounded assumptions?

Common sense might suggest that we do need psychologically grounded assumptions. The **methodology of positive economics**, advocated by Milton Friedman, suggests things are not so obvious. The basis of this methodology is that a model and theory should be judged on its predictions and not its assumptions. Friedman (1953: 40–41) writes:

> One confusion that has been particularly rife and has done much damage is confusion about the role of "assumptions" in economic analysis. A meaningful scientific hypothesis or theory typically asserts that certain forces are, and other forces are not, important in understanding a particular class of phenomena. . . .
>
> Such a theory cannot be tested by comparing its "assumptions" directly with "reality." Indeed, there is no meaningful way in which this can be done.

Complete "realism" is clearly unattainable, and the question whether a theory is realistic "enough" can be settled only by seeing whether it yields predictions that are good enough for the purpose in hand or that are better than predictions from alternative theories.

That people are not like homo economicus is not, therefore, reason to *assume* they are not like homo economicus. We need to look at the predictions. To illustrate this distinction, suppose we see Anna go in to the bookstore and are interested in whether she will buy this book. We come up with two models of what she does; call them the 'cognitive model' and the 'choice model'. Suppose that the cognitive model better describes the thought processes that Anna will go through when deciding to buy the book. Suppose that the choice model better predicts whether or not Anna will buy the book. Which model is better?

You might say that this is a trick question, because something that better describes her thought processes should better predict what she does. Unfortunately, however, the need to use models that are tractable abstractions from a complex reality makes it common to face such a dilemma. So, you do need to make your choice!

To a psychologist, the cognitive model is surely best, because it gives a better description of what Anna was thinking; this is good economic psychology. To an economist, the choice model is surely best because we get a more accurate economic prediction; this is good behavioral economics. It is not so obvious, therefore, that psychologically grounded assumptions are better for economics, and we will see examples in this book where models with psychological grounded assumptions do a lot worse than the standard economic model.

Search though we might, therefore, for the 'perfect model' that combines the best elements of both the cognitive and choice model, we may not find it. Behavioral economics needs to prove itself by coming up with good economic predictions, and better predictions than that of the standard economic model.

This leads on to the second debate I want to talk about:

> Should more emphasis be put on things the standard economic model does well or badly?

An interesting example of this debate playing itself out came after the Behavioral Foundations of Economic Theory conference held in 1985. The conference organizers stressed 'a growing body of evidence – mainly of an experimental nature – that has documented systematic departures from the dictates of rational economic behavior' (Hogarth and Reder 1987). Vernon Smith (1991), who was present at the conference, preferred to stress 'a growing body of evidence that is consistent with the implications of rational models'! Previously, in 1988, Smith wrote that 'Our scientific advance is handicapped by our failure to pursue the exciting implications of the fact that things sometimes work better than we had a right to expect from our abstract interpretations of theory'.

It is clear that the argument carries on to this day. Some behavioral economists prefer to emphasize the good, and some the bad. Why no agreement? One reason is probably the distinction between assumptions and predictions. Behavioral economists from an economics background, like Vernon Smith, have usually been the ones emphasizing what the standard economic model does well, and that's possibly because they more naturally focus on the predictions, not the assumptions. Those coming from a psychology background seem more prone to emphasize what the standard economic does badly, possibly because they more naturally focus on the limitations of the assumptions. If the assumptions of the standard economic model are pretty bad but the predictions are often pretty good then we can see why there may be grounds for disagreement.

This is far from the end of the story, however, because people can also disagree how to evaluate predictions. This partly stems from how far people are prepared to push the standard model. As game theorist and experimental economist Ken Binmore (2008: F249) explains:

> At one end of the spectrum, there are conservative experimenters who defend traditional economic theory by looking at situations in which it predicts fairly well. At the other end of the spectrum, there are radical experimenters who seek to show that traditional economic theory does not work at all by looking at situations in which its predictions fail.

Even on relatively safe ground, however, there can be disagreement. To see why, consider this question:

> What should we conclude if the standard economic model only predicts well what experienced people do, i.e. people familiar with a task or decision?

This turns out to be a tough question to answer. The problem is that in many instances we find that the standard economic model gives a poor prediction of what happens the first time someone faces a particular situation, but a much better prediction the fourth, fifth, sixth time they face the same situation. This is the **discovered preference hypothesis,** that the standard economic model is a good predictor if people have had ample opportunity to learn from experience.

There is debate over the validity of the discovered preference hypothesis, and we shall see situations where no amount of experience helps the standard economic model predict well. This, however, gets us back to a half-full or half-empty debate. More interesting is to ask what we should conclude if the discovered preference hypothesis is correct. This will depend on whether people have ample opportunity to learn from experience in most of the things we are interested in. Arguably they do not because there are many important things that a person only does once or few times in their life, like retiring, choosing a career, buying a house, and so on. We want to be able to predict what will happen in these situations too, so maybe the standard economic model is not so great after all?

I shall conveniently avoid that question and finish with a much easier one:

> Should behavioral economics look to rewrite economics from a psychological perspective, or adapt the standard economic model to take account of psychological insight?

Some would probably like to start from scratch, and scrap the standard economic model. Maybe that is what you expected of behavioral economics. This is not, however, what behavioral economics is about. Behavioral economics is very much about working with the standard economic model, whether it is a good predictor or not. That's because, as mentioned earlier, it is the natural starting point. Daniel Kahneman writes, for example, about his work with Tversky that: 'The rational-agent model was our starting point and the main source of our null hypotheses.' To quote from two other leading behavioral economists, Colin Camerer and George Loewenstein (2003): 'At the core of behavioral economics is the conviction that increasing the realism of the psychological underpinnings of economic analysis will improve economics on its own terms.'

1.2 Some background on behavioral economics methods

We have already seen that behavioral economics involves both theory and experiment. In this section I want to briefly sketch a little more about the methods of behavioral economics and in particular give some background on economic experiments. Before doing so, I want to make clear that my objective is not to explain how to run experiments, or to perform statistical tests on the experimental data. These warrant books on their own and there are lots of good books out there (see the further reading at the end of the chapter). All I want to do is explain enough that you will be able to follow the rest of this book. That means, in particular, getting straight some terminology that I am going to use.

Rather than talk abstractly about experiments and theory I thought it would be more interesting to talk through some research that I did (with Federica Alberti and Anna Stepanova) while writing this book. This will give me chance to introduce all the concepts you need at this stage. Other concepts will be introduced as and when needed or relevant in 'research methods boxes' that you will find throughout the book.

I will use the term **study** for a particular piece of research. The objective of our study was to see whether the amount of money people are endowed with in a threshold public good game has any affect on their ability to coordinate. That might not make much sense at this point but do not worry because it should make more sense shortly. A study may be part of a more general **project**. Our ongoing project is to see how people can better coordinate in threshold public good games. The main part of this study involved running experiments, and so I will talk about that first.

1.2.1 Some background on experiments

To run an experiment we need people who are willing to take part. Those that do are given the title **subject** or participant. In order to recruit subjects we sent emails and placed adverts and eventually got the 120 volunteers we needed. Most of these were students at the University of Kent. Each subject was asked to come to a particular **experimental session** and we ran six sessions in all, with 20 people invited to come to each session. (We actually invited a few more, because the chance that 20 students will turn up on time in the right place is clearly quite small.) All the sessions took place in a computer lab at the University.

When the subjects arrived, after a brief introduction, they were each allocated to a computer. After this there was no talking until the experiment ended, and a subject could only see their own computer screen. Things were, therefore, completely anonymous, and subjects were reassured this would be the case. Beside their computer each subject would find an instruction sheet, which read something like this:

> In this experiment you will make decisions, and earn an amount of money that depends on what you and others choose. The money will be given to you at the end of the experiment in an envelope. Only you will know how much money you earned.
>
> You have been organised into groups of five. Each group will consist of the same five people for the duration of the experiment. The experiment will last for 25 rounds. In each period you will be required to make a decision, and your total earnings will depend on your decisions in all rounds.
>
> At the beginning of every round you, and all other members of your group, will receive 55 tokens. Each of you must decide, on your own, how many of the 55 tokens to allocate to a group account.
>
> If the total number of tokens allocated to the group account is 125 or more then you will each receive an additional 50 tokens.
>
> If the total number of tokens allocated to the group account is less than 125 then you will receive no additional tokens but will get back any tokens you allocated to the group account.
>
> So, at the end of the round:
>
> If the total number of tokens allocated to the group account ≥ 125
>
> your earnings = initial 55 tokens – tokens allocated to group account + additional 50 tokens.
>
> If the total number of tokens allocated to the group account < 125, your earnings = initial 55 tokens.
>
> At the end of the session, you will be asked to fill in a short questionnaire. You will be paid in cash the total amount that you earned for all rounds in the session plus £2. Each token will be worth 0.5p.

Once all subjects had read the instructions the experiment would commence with everything taking place on computer (using an experimental economics program called z-tree). So, the first thing that would happen is each subject was asked to input how many tokens they wanted to allocate to the group account. To illustrate, in group one, subject one input 25, subject two input zero, and subjects three to five input 50, 25, and 10. The total number allocated was, therefore, 110 which was short of the 125 target. The subjects were told this and told their earnings were 55. That was the end of round one.

The same happened in rounds two to 25. This did not take long and so the experiment was over after around 30 to 45 minutes. Once the last round had finished we worked out how much money each subject had earned and paid them in cash. The average subject earned around £10, which is not bad for 30 minutes.

One thing I do want to highlight is that, in an experiment, subjects are typically asked to do the same thing several times. In this case they were asked to play the same threshold public good game 25 times. There are various reasons for doing this of which the main one is to see how people learn with experience. For instance, the group I have just talked about were short of the target in round one and we might wonder how they will respond. In fact the total number of tokens allocated in round two went up to 161, well above the target. As you may have seen by now the term **round** keeps track of how far subjects have progressed through the experiment. (The word period is also used, but I will try and avoid this because we will use period for something slightly different.)

Hopefully, this gives you some idea what a threshold public good game is (we are going to talk about them in more detail in chapter six). Hopefully, it also gives you some idea what an experiment is, and what it's like to take part in one. But what were we hoping to get out of this experiment?

The primary thing of interest in a threshold public good game is whether group members give enough to the group account to reach the threshold of 125. If this seems all a little abstract, then imagine five housemates who want to buy a new TV that costs $125. Between them they need to find enough to buy the TV or they go without. Broadly speaking, it is in their interests to reach the threshold, but there are good reasons why they may fall short. From prior research we know groups can be quite unsuccessful at reaching the threshold.

The specific question that motivated our study was whether groups will be more successful at achieving the threshold if they have more tokens to start with. The instructions above correspond to the case where subjects got 55 tokens, which you can think of as each housemate having $55 of spending money. What if they have $30 or $70; will they be any more or less successful at reaching the threshold?

This is relatively easy to test with experiments, because we can just give some groups 55 tokens to start with, some 30, some 70 and record how often groups reach the threshold. That's basically what we did. The term **experimental treatment** is used to distinguish these different versions of the experiment. We had five treatments, but I will just focus on the three of them that I have already mentioned. These are summarized in Figure 1.1, and correspond to subjects having 55, 30 or 70 tokens.

It's common to have one treatment called the **baseline treatment,** which serves as a reference point for comparison. In our study the treatment where subjects got

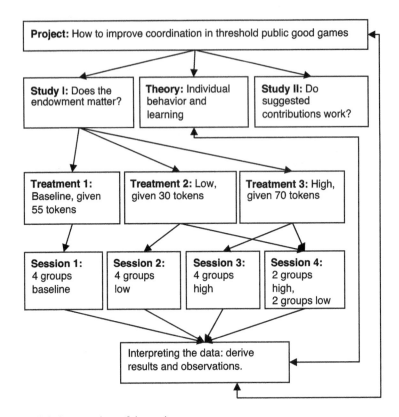

Figure 1.1 An overview of the project.

55 tokens was the baseline. We chose this as the baseline because it had already been used many times by other researchers. We thus have an expectation of what should happen in this treatment, and can more easily relate our results to the results of other researchers. This is invaluable in making good scientific progress and so the baseline does typically correspond to a treatment that has already been done in previous studies.

One thing I do want to make clear is the distinction between experimental session and experimental treatment. **Experimental session** refers to a particular instance in time and space when an experiment was run; for instance, we had a 2.00 pm session on Friday 29 January. Experimental treatment refers to a specific version of the experiment used; for instance, we had the baseline treatment where subjects got 55 tokens. Session and treatment are quite different. You might have, as we did, one session with multiple treatments or multiple sessions with the same treatment. In session four, for example, we had four groups, two of which were in the high treatment so subjects in these groups got 70 tokens, and two were in the low treatment so subjects got 30 tokens.

Another thing I want to mention is deception. In psychology it is not unknown to see **deception** in experiments, meaning the experimenter basically lies to subjects about what they are doing. (Afterwards they are told that they were lied to.) This is a definite no-no in economics, where we are not allowed to deceive subjects in any way. So, if the instructions say there will be 25 rounds, or say one token is worth 0.5p, then it really is so. That subjects cannot be deceived does not, however, mean that they have to be told everything. Indeed, a basic requirement of most experiments is that they be **single blind,** meaning subjects are not biased by knowing too much. For instance, we did not want the subjects in our experiment to know that the objective of our study was to vary the number of tokens given. If they knew this, it might have biased how they behaved. So, while subjects cannot be deceived, they can be given a minimum amount of information.

Before moving on to look at theory I should point out that the experiment I have described above is not untypical, but experiments do vary considerably. For example, some experiments are done with pen and paper rather than via computer. Some do not involve interaction between subjects in any way. Others allow subjects to communicate with each other, possibly via computer chat. Some use schoolchildren as subjects, or experienced financial traders. Some are done outside the lab in a supermarket, or at a sports show. There are many other possibilities, and I will talk about some of these as and when we get to them.

1.2.2 *Some background on theory*

Experiments are not much use without some theory behind them. So, I also want to give a little background information about basic theoretical concepts we are going to need. Let's start by thinking what someone called Edward does when he is in the experiment described above. To keep things simple, imagine for now that there is only one round.

All Edward has to do is to decide how many tokens to allocate to the group account. He can choose any integer between 0 and 55. We call this the **set of actions** or **set of possible options**, and he needs to pick one action or choose one option from this set. An **action** thus describes what he does, for instance 'allocate 20 tokens to the group account'.

I now want to contrast action with strategy. You can think of a **strategy** as a description of how Edward decides what action to choose. To explain what this means it's useful to talk briefly about a second study we are currently working on. In this study, one person in the group will be allowed to suggest how much others should allocate to the group account, before others do choose how much to allocate. If Edward is not the one giving the suggestion then his set of actions is the same as before; he needs to choose an integer between 0 and 55. His strategy can, however, be conditional on what was suggested. For instance, his strategy might be 'allocate as many tokens as was suggested'. With this strategy his action will be 'allocate 20 tokens' if the suggestion is to allocate 20 tokens but 'allocate 25 tokens' if the suggestion was to allocate 25, and so on.

Actions and strategies are, therefore, different and you might have noticed that actions are observable but strategies need not be. For instance, we observe how many tokens Edward gave but generally speaking will not know how many tokens he would have given if, say, the suggestion had been different.

The next thing to introduce is the payoff function. Edward's **payoff function** says what payoff he will get for any possible combination of strategies he and everyone else uses. For instance, if everyone allocates 20 to the group account, his payoff is 55. There are various different notations for the payoff function. One is to write $u_E(s_1, s_2, s_3, s_4, s_5)$ for Edward's payoff as a function of the strategies of the five group members, including him. Another is to write $u_E(s_E, s_{-E})$ for his payoff as a function of his strategy and the strategy of others. The payoff function in the experiment we are looking at is:

$$u_E(s_E, s_{-E}) = \begin{cases} 55 - s_E + 50 & \text{if } s_1 + s_2 + s_3 + s_4 + s_5 \geq 125 \\ 55 & \text{if } s_1 + s_2 + s_3 + s_4 + s_5 < 125 \end{cases}$$

For simplicity, it's not uncommon, as I have just done, to substitute action for strategy when working out the payoff function.

One slightly troublesome thing is the interpretation of payoff. Payoff can be thought of as something objective like an amount of money earned. It is typically more useful, however, to think of payoff as equivalent to utility, which is a subjective measure of happiness (we'll get to it in chapters two and ten). These two definitions differ because doubling, say, the amount of money earned need not lead to a doubling in the amount of increased happiness. The norm, though, is to equate payoff function and utility function, and I shall do the same here. I will, at least, point out that this is done mainly for convenience rather than any good economic reason!

If we have a group of people and know the set of actions and strategies and payoff function of each person, then we have a **game**. To keep game theorists happy, we should call what happens in any one round the **stage game** or **base game** or **constituent game**. So, the stage game in our experiment was the threshold public good game. The whole experiment, i.e. the 25 rounds, constitute the **game**. The reason to make this distinction is that someone may want to make their action in round two conditional on what happened in round one, and so on. For instance a strategy might be 'if we reached the threshold in round one I will allocate the same number of tokens to the group account in round two'.

Normally, the distinction between stage game and game is a bit over the top, but it can be useful if the stage game changes at some point during the experiment. For example, we shall see experiments where subjects play one stage game for ten rounds and then a different stage game for ten rounds.

The final concepts I want to talk about are possible outcomes of a game. Two particularly important concepts are Pareto efficiency and Nash equilibrium. Let's do Pareto efficiency first. We say that an outcome is **Pareto efficient** if no one could be made better off without making someone worse off. To see why this is interesting, imagine an outcome that was not Pareto efficient. Then we would be able to do something that made at least one person better off and no one worse off. This looks like a good thing to do. In the threshold public good game, if everyone were to allocate 25 tokens to the group account, everyone would get a payoff of 80 tokens. This is Pareto efficient. If everyone were to allocate zero tokens to the group account, they would get a payoff of 55. This is not Pareto efficient. Pareto efficiency is thus one way to formalize the idea of something that is desirable versus something that is not.

Contrast this with Nash equilibrium. A **Nash equilibrium** is a strategy for each person such that no one could change their strategy and increase their own payoff. Again, imagine this were not the case. Then someone can change their strategy and increase their payoff. We might expect them to do so. A formulation you might come across is that Nash equilibrium requires:

$$u_i(s_i, s_{-i}) \geq u_i(s, s_{-i})$$

for any person i where s_i is the strategy they do choose, and s is any other strategy they might have chosen. In the threshold public good game, everyone allocating 25 tokens to the group account is a Nash equilibrium. Everyone allocating 24 tokens to the group account is not a Nash equilibrium because the total will fall short of the threshold by five, and if one person were to give 29 rather than 25, their payoff would increase.

Interestingly, everyone allocating zero tokens to the group account is also a Nash equilibrium, because no one person on their own can do anything to reach the threshold. This illustrates that a Nash equilibrium need not be Pareto efficient. It's also true that a Pareto-efficient outcome need not be a Nash equilibrium (see if you can find an example in the threshold public good game). Nash equilibrium and Pareto efficient are, thus, two very different things.

I will finish this section by making a connection with some of the ideas I talked about in the last section. In many ways the Nash equilibrium is the epitome of the standard economic model. Homo economicus would never do anything other than play a Nash equilibrium. But there can be many Nash equilibria. I have already shown you that there are at least two in the threshold public good game, and there are actually many more. The standard economic model has essentially nothing to say about which of these homo economicus will choose. That renders it pretty useless and on its own motivates behavioral economics (for me at least). Experiments can help us to understand what happens when people do play such game, and this can give us the clues to improve our theoretical ability to model economic behavior, and better understand how people reason and learn.

1.3 How to use this book

To put things in some context I should give a brief preview of the rest of the book. Before I do that, I want to talk a little about my approach in writing this book.

As I said in the preface, my objective in writing the book was to explain the basic principles, ideas and results of behavioral economics and also illustrate through applications how these can help us understand the world around us. This will be reflected in the make-up of each chapter. The first half of each chapter will be dedicated to explaining the basic principles, ideas and results, while the second half will give various applications. Hopefully, this will give a nice mix of theory and practice.

The approach I have taken throughout is to pick a few experiments and theoretical papers that I think best illustrate the more general lessons that have been learnt. I like this approach because it gives me a chance to look in a bit more detail at some studies and give a better flavor of what behavioral economics is all about. One downside is that it can give the impression that our knowledge hangs on the results of one or two experiments or theoretical examples (that you might spot a potential flaw in). Sometimes this impression would not be far wrong, but for the most part it is a long way off. Most of the ideas I will talk about in this book are robust. In terms of experiments, that primarily means the results have been replicated in many other similar studies. In terms of theoretical examples this means the examples can be generalized to give the same conclusions. The further reading, at the end of each chapter, gives you chance to check this and explore things in a bit more depth.

To make the book as accessible as possible, I have tried to keep algebra and notation to the minimum. Algebra, though, is part and parcel of behavioral economics, so a few equations are unavoidable to get a full grasp of the main issues. I also do not like discriminating against those who do like a bit of algebra. So, sometimes you will see [Extra] written, which is a cue that the rest of the paragraph will contain some algebra but can be skipped without missing anything. Finally, I have little time for the politically correct issue of whether to use he or she, or she or he. So, each chapter will be based on one or two characters and the language will reflect the sex of those characters. The fact that the characters share the same names as my wife and colleagues is pure coincidence.

And now to preview what will follow. The book will be split into three further parts, of which the next part will be by far the biggest, looking at what behavior we observe and how we can model it. It begins, in chapter two, with an introduction to heuristics and context effects. The main message I want you to get from this chapter is that people can be influenced in a systematic way by the context or setting in which choices are made. This might seem obvious enough, but is quite a big step away from the standard economic model.

In chapter three I will look at choice with risk, and in chapter four at choice over time. The basic approach in both chapters will be the same: to start with a simple and standard way to model behavior, namely expected utility and exponential discounting, and then to propose various modifications to the model so that we can better fit the behavior we observe. This will bring us to some of the more important concepts in behavioral economics like prospect theory and time inconsistency.

A theme throughout chapters two to four will be the importance of reference dependence and context. In particular, we shall see that behavior often depends on whether outcomes are perceived as a loss or gain relative to some reference point. We shall also see that the reference point a person has in mind can change a lot depending on the context.

In chapters five and six the focus switches to how people use information. In chapter five the focus will be on how people can learn from the information around them, including that they get from other people. In chapter six the focus will be on learning and behavior in interactive situations, where it's necessary to predict the behavior of others. I think the basic message that comes out of these two chapters is that people are clever and do learn, but also struggle to cope with more complex situations. We are going to see, for example, some worrying biases in how people learn from new information.

Chapter seven continues the theme of chapter six in looking at interactive situations, but has a very different focus. The focus here will be on looking at whether people are selfish, and if not, how we can model this. We shall see that it is necessary to take account of people's preferences for fair and just outcomes and there are various ways we can do this. One of the more important lessons from this chapter will be the heterogeneity of behavior. We'll see that some people give, some not, and what is considered fair or just can vary from one person to the next and one context to the next.

The next part of the book will consist of two chapters that look at the origins of behavior. That is, we shall try to answer questions like, why people are risk averse, loss averse, value fairness and so on. Chapter eight will focus on the role of evolution and culture in shaping economic behavior. Chapter nine will look at neuro-economics and recent attempts to see what is going on in the brain as people make economic decisions. We'll see that an evolutionary and neuroscience perspective provides some fascinating insights to economic behavior, and really do tell us something about why people are risk averse and the like.

In the final part of the book my focus will primarily be on whether behavioral economics can help us do something useful in improving the happiness of people. In chapter ten I will look at what makes people happy and whether they know what makes them happy. We are going to see that people do not always do the thing that would make them happiest, and may be willing to pre-commit or delegate choice to others. It's clear, however, that people still desire some choice or self determination.

Chapter eleven follows this up by looking at how behavioral economics can help inform policy. I will look at both the design of institutions, and policies aimed more at individual incentives. Making the world a better place is always easy on paper, but I am going to argue that behavioral economics does give us some nice tools to improve policy for the better.

1.4 Further reading

Many have given good introductions to what behavioral economics is all about: Mullainathan and Thaler (2000), Camerer (2003) and Camerer and Loewenstein (2004) is a small selection. The excellent review articles by Conlisk (1996), Rabin

(1998) and DellaVigna (2009) are also worth a mention at this point. For more on the methodology of experiments the books by Cassar and Friedman (2004) and Bardsley et al. (2010) are recommended. For more on the history of behavioral and experimental economics, see Roth (1995), Sent (2004) and Bruni and Sugden (2007).

1.5 Review questions

1.1 Why is the standard economic model a good thing, and why is it a bad thing, in trying to understand economic behavior?

1.2 Why do we need to run economic experiments?

1.3 Why does a heuristic usually come hand in hand with a cognitive bias? Should we emphasize how clever people are for having good heuristics, or how dumb they are for being biased?

1.4 Why does is make sense to mix up experimental treatments and sessions, i.e. to have multiple treatments in each session and multiple sessions for each treatment?

1.5 Is it good that experiments usually involve students as subjects?

1.6 What are the objectives of behavioral economics?

1.7 What are the objectives of studying the standard economic model?

Part II
Economic behavior

2 Simple heuristics for complex choices

Rule No. 1 is never lose money. Rule No. 2 is never forget rule number one.

Warren Buffet

Even the most innocuous of economic choices are in principle very complicated. For example consider a shopper in a grocery store looking at rows of breakfast cereal and deciding which one to buy. Should she buy the cereal she usually buys? Should she try a new cereal the store has just introduced? Should she buy the cereal on special offer? Will the cereal she usually buys be on special offer next week? Will it be cheaper in another store? Should she be tempted by the cereal with the chance to win a holiday in the Caribbean?

Clearly, most of us do not spend much time considering all these issues. Indeed, most of us simply buy the cereal that we usually buy. That way we can make a quick decision that will probably keep us happy. This is an example of a heuristic. A **heuristic** is any 'rule of thumb' or simple rule of behavior by which a person solves a problem. The shopper can solve their problem of what cereal to buy with the heuristic 'buy what I usually do'. Almost all the economic decisions we make are based on such heuristics, otherwise life would get far too complicated. This means we need to know how heuristics work and what their consequences can be.

Heuristics, and the biases they give rise to, are going to be a recurring theme throughout the book, and are the primary focus of this chapter. I will start by giving some examples, but the main thing I want to do is provide some structure for how we can think about the consequences of heuristics. In doing this we shall come across some of the key concepts and ideas in behavioral economics.

2.1 Utility and search

I will start by taking up the story of a shopper called Anna in a grocery store deciding what breakfast cereal to buy. There is a large selection of potential choices, all with different characteristics, but we will narrow things down to the four listed in Table 2.1. How can she decide what to buy?

The standard way of thinking about this in economics is to assume that Anna has a **utility function** that says how much utility she gets from particular combinations

Table 2.1 Cereals for sale, and their characteristics, where 1 = low, 2 = medium and 3 = high

Product	Price	Taste quality	Health quality
Budget	$1	1	1
Nutty	$3	2	2
Honey	$4	3	2
Superior	$6	3	3

of money, and goods. In this context we would write $u(x, TQ, HQ)$ as the utility she gets from having money x and a cereal with taste quality TQ and health quality HQ. One important point to note is that in the standard description, utility should be a function of money wealth, and so when evaluating each choice we need to focus on how much money Anna will have after buying the cereal. To illustrate, Table 2.2 works through an example where she initially has $100 and her utility function is

$$u(x, TQ, HQ) = 20\sqrt{x} + 2TQ + HQ.$$

She can buy no cereal, keep wealth $100 and have utility 200, or pay $1 for Budget, have wealth $99 and utility 202, and so on.

You might be wondering what it means to say that Anna's utility is 200, or 204. The interpretation we should give to utility is crucial but ultimately very tricky and so, on the basis that we have plenty of other things to worry about at this stage, I am going to dodge that question for now. In chapter ten we will look at it in some detail. In the meantime you can think of utility as a general measure of happiness or satisfaction. So, more utility is better, and Anna wants to choose the cereal with highest utility. We are also not going to get far unless we think in terms of **cardinal utility**. What this means is that the differences in utility should mean something. So, we can say things like: 'Honey is better than Budget by the same amount as Budget is better than no cereal.'

In the example we can see that Honey offers the highest utility and so looks like the best choice. It does so because it offers the best trade-off of quality for price. Anna is willing to pay the extra $1 to $4 that Honey costs over other choices in order to improve the taste and health quality, but is not willing to pay a further

Table 2.2 The utility of each cereal if initial wealth is $100

Choice	Wealth	TQ	HQ	Utility
No cereal	$100	0	0	200
Budget	$99	1	1	202
Nutty	$97	2	2	203
Honey	$96	3	2	204
Superior	$94	3	3	203

$2 to get the highest quality. We have, therefore, a prediction of what Anna should buy: she should buy Honey.

This is fine, if she knows what maximizes her utility. Realistically, however, she probably will not know. Maybe she has never tried Budget or Superior, or maybe she did try them once but has forgotten what they tasted like, her preferences have changed, or the manufacturers have subsequently improved the quality.

This lack of knowledge is crucial, and means that it is not enough for us to say Anna should do the thing that maximizes her utility. She does not know what that is, and so we need to delve a little deeper. Two things that become relevant when we do so are search and choice arbitrariness. I will look at each in turn.

2.1.1 How to search

If Anna does not know the quality of goods, or her utility function, then she can gather more information in order to become better informed, we call this search. A **search heuristic** specifies what Anna should do in order to become better informed. There are lots of possible search heuristics and I shall look at five to give you some idea of what they, and heuristics in general, look like.

The most obvious search heuristic is to 'try everything'. For example, Anna could try a different cereal every week until she has tried them all, and then subsequently buy the one she liked most. This does mean she will end up knowing a lot about cereals. The process will, however, be potentially costly. To see why, suppose that in the first week she tries Honey and can tell that she likes it a lot. If she sticks to her heuristic then in subsequent weeks she will have to buy and try cereals that are not going to give her as much utility. She would have been better off just sticking with Honey (if you will excuse the pun).

In this case search proves costly in terms of **forgone utility**. Search can also be costly in terms of time and money. A good search heuristic needs to trade off the benefits of acquiring more information with these costs. Characterizing optimal, or good, search algorithms has a long history in mathematics, computer science and economics. Optimal search algorithms are, however, typically very complicated, so we need to think what search heuristics people could realistically use that come close to the optimum. Three such heuristics are satisficing, elimination by aspects and directed cognition.

The basic idea behind **satisficing** is that a person sets some **aspiration level** for what they are looking for, and continues to search until they find something above the aspiration level. For example, Anna may decide she wants something that tastes good and is reasonably healthy. This determines her aspiration level, and she will keep on trying cereals until she tries Honey or Superior. Satisficing relaxes the objective from finding the optimal choice, to merely finding a choice that is good enough. This means a person may not end up with the best, but they will end up with something relatively good, while avoiding the costs of excessive search. If Anna, for instance, tries Superior before Honey, then she will never get to know how good Honey is, but she might also avoid knowing how bad Budget is.

How close satisficing comes to the optimum will depend on the aspiration level. This is where satisficing does become slightly more complicated, because it is not trivial what the aspiration level should be, or how it should change. If, for example, Anna's aspiration is to find a cereal costing less than $7, then she may end up with Budget; the aspiration level looks too low. If her aspiration is to find a very tasty and healthy cereal for less than $5 then she will be disappointed because no such cereal exists; the aspiration level looks too high. Anna will need, therefore, to set the aspiration level appropriately and revise it as she goes along, it's just not clear how exactly she will do so.

An alternative that partly addresses this problem is that of directed cognition. The idea behind **directed cognition** is that a person treats each chance to gather information as if it is the last such chance before they have to make a choice. Typically, it will not actually be their last chance. Directed cognition simplifies Anna's task, because she does not need to forward plan. To illustrate, suppose she knows only the characteristics of Nutty. Using directed cognition she should ask herself, shall I try one alternative cereal, and if so, which one? This is a much simpler question than would be needed with forward planning. With forward planning there are many more permutations that need to be considered, such as, shall I try Budget, and if that tastes nice try Honey, and if not try Superior, and then Honey?

The final search heuristic I want to look at, for now, is that of elimination by aspects. The basic idea of **elimination by aspects** is to consider the aspects of possible choices one by one and sequentially eliminate choices that fall below some aspiration level. For example, if Anna's aspirations are to buy a medium taste and health quality cereal for under $5, then on the price aspect she would eliminate Superior, and on the quality aspects eliminate Budget. This would leave a choice between Honey and Nutty.

Elimination by aspects is different from the previous two heuristics in that it compares across aspects, such as price, rather than across choices, such as Honey or Nutty. Conceptually it is simpler to compare across aspects because there is likely to be a simple ordering from best, e.g. least expensive, to worst, most expensive. The problem is that comparing across aspects presupposes that the person has information about all the possible choices. With aspects like price and health quality this is plausible because the prices and ingredients will be displayed on the box. With an aspect like taste quality it is difficult to know the differences without trying them all. Elimination by aspects can, therefore, only take us so far in explaining search, but it does offer vital clues on how a person can chose what to try next and what to not try at all.

The three heuristics we have discussed should be seen as complementary rather than alternatives, as summarized in Table 2.3. Satisficing, for instance, suggests how long Anna should search, but offers no clues as to what she should try. Directed cognition has less to say about how long to search, but can offer clues as what to try next. Together, therefore, they give us a picture of how people might search. In general, no one heuristic is ever going to be perfect and so we can expect people to use different combinations of heuristics for different tasks.

Table 2.3 Five search heuristics with a very brief statement of how they can help with search

Heuristic	What it does well	What it does not do so well
Try them all	Make the person well informed	Minimize the cost of search
Satisficing	Say when to stop search	Say what choice to try next
Directed cognition	Suggest what choice to try next	Give a forward looking plan of search
Elimination by aspects	Say what choices not to try	Say when to stop searching
Search for x minutes	Give certainty how long search will last	React to success or failure in search

Indeed, they may have a heuristic to say what heuristic to use (see Research Methods 2.1).

Research Methods 2.1

The infinite regress problem

We began talking about Anna's problem of 'what cereal to choose' and suggested she should choose the cereal that maximized her utility. Having noted that she will probably not know what cereal maximizes her utility, we got the additional problem 'how to find out what cereal maximizes utility'. This has to be a harder problem to solve than the original one, but, we have not finished yet. That is because there are lots of ways to search for information about preferences, so we get a further additional problem, 'how to find out, how to find out what cereal maximizes utility'. I could go on: 'how to find out, how to find out, how to find out . . .', and so on.

More generally, finding the optimal answer to a problem involves finding the optimal way to find the optimal answer, and the optimal way to find the optimal way, and so on. This is known as the **infinite regress problem**. Clearly, if Anna, or anyone else, is going to make a decision, they need some way to break the loop. Heuristics and intuition (which we shall get to shortly) are one way to do this because they provide simple rules to make decisions. That answer is not, however, entirely satisfactory, because Anna will need heuristics to choose what heuristic to use, and then we are back in the cycle again!

In short, the problem is not going to go away, and so we need to be aware of it when we try to model behaviour. Behavioral economists have primarily focussed on basic heuristics, i.e. heuristics designed to solve a specific problem. Some attention, but much less, has been given to heuristics for choosing heuristics, and we will get to them in later chapters. The problem of how people choose heuristics for choosing heuristics is ignored, but in chapter eight I will suggest that evolution might do that job.

To get a feel for how people do search we can look at the results of a study by Gabaix et al. (2006). In the study, subjects were asked to choose between eight options where the payoff of each option was the sum of ten numbers. One of the numbers was visible, but to find the value of each of the other nine numbers the subjects had to click on the screen. To relate this back to our earlier example, imagine that the price is visible, but to find the health quality Anna has to pick up the box and look up the ingredients. A software called mouselab can track what information subjects chose to look up and give us some idea how subjects searched (see Research Methods 6.1).

There are lots of things we can look at in the data in terms of how much information subjects choose to look up, what sequence they choose to look it up, and so on. One way to see if subjects were using a particular heuristic is to compare how much information subjects should have looked up about each choice, if they were using, say, directed cognition, and how much information they did look up. This measures how well the search heuristic fits observed search behavior. A second thing we can do is see how well the search heuristic fits the final choice made. This measures how well the search heuristic fits observed choice behavior.

Figure 2.1 summarizes the results Gabaix et al. found. We see that directed cognition does a good job of fitting how subjects search, while elimination by aspects does less well. In terms of fitting choice, all algorithms do roughly as well as each other, and the choice is what we would have expected around 50 percent of the time. A 50 percent success rate at predicting what subjects will choose is

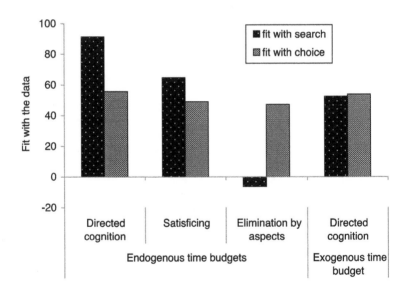

Figure 2.1 How well search heuristics fit the observed search and choices in a search experiment. The fit is measured relative to what could have been expected by chance. Directed cognition and satisficing give the best fit.

Source: Gabaix et al. (2006).

much better than we could have done by guessing (remember there were eight possible choices), but still not as high as we might like. It looks like we are missing something.

One thing that becomes apparent is that subjects were not as selective in what information they looked for as the three heuristics suggested they should have been. In different ways they looked up both too much and too little. First, the too much: if one choice ranks poorly on the visible aspect, then it pays to not search for other information about that choice. For example, if Superior is too expensive, then there is little point in looking at the health quality. Subjects tended to look up more information than we might expect in such instances (see Research Methods 2.2). Next, the too little: it does not matter how long the search has gone on, if the search has not yet uncovered something useful, it pays to carry on searching. Subjects, however, seemed to stop searching if they have looked up a lot of information, even if that information had not been very informative.

Research Methods 2.2

How long should an experiment take?

One slightly troublesome issue in running experiments is how much time to give subjects to make decisions.

On a practical level this issue is important if we do not want some subjects to be delayed by others. In particular, it immediately becomes apparent when running an experiment that some people take a lot longer to make decisions than others. If the experiment can only proceed when each subject has made a decision this can leave some subjects twiddling their thumbs for a long while. On the one hand this may be good if it means some subjects spend a bit more time thinking about the experiment. On the other hand it can lead to boredom and less thinking about the experiment.

On a theoretical level it may be important how much time subjects have if we are interested in the consequences of time pressure. Time is very relevant in search and so important to take into account. Gabaix et al. do this by comparing an exogenous and endogenous time budget. In an exogenous time budget treatment, subjects are given a fixed amount of time they can look at a particular set of eight choices. In an endogenous time budget treatment, subjects are given 25 minutes to look at as many sets of eight choices as they wish.

This distinction turns out to be potentially informative. In particular, subjects were more selective what information they looked up with an endogenous than exogenous budget. So, the low success at predicting search with an exogenous time budget (see figure 2.1) may reflect subjects having too much time. Optimally, they should have found out more information about the current best looking choices but maybe they had already made up their mind and so were filling in time.

Putting these observations together suggests a fifth search heuristic: a person decides how much time to spend on search and then searches for that long. This may mean that Anna would search too long, if she initially tried something she liked, or search too little, if she has yet to try anything she really likes.

But it does mean search will last a definite length of time, and this may be a useful thing.

There are many more possible search heuristics and many more studies (see the suggested reading) that look at how people do search. We will, however, come back to search elsewhere in the book, notably chapter five, and so I will leave the issue for now. The main thing I wanted you to see at this stage is how people can use simple (or not so simple) heuristics to solve complex search problems. Hopefully, this gives you some idea how people can search effectively, and gives some feel for what heuristics in general look like. Now I want to look at choice arbitrariness which raises some quite different issues.

2.1.2 *Choice arbitrariness*

In the process of search, Anna is going to face some fairly arbitrary choices. That's because she does not yet know what maximizes her utility but still has to choose something. For example, she may have narrowed her choice to Nutty or Honey and there is no real reason to try one ahead of the other. Which one to try first? Her choice will be arbitrary, and she might as well toss a coin to decide. Arbitrary does not, however, have to mean random. For instance, Anna might be attracted by the bright red packaging of Honey, the '50 percent off' sticker on Nutty, or choose Budget because she just saw it advertised on TV. In each of these cases choice is systematic. The crucial thing is that choice is influenced by factors that just happened to be like that and could have been different, this is **choice arbitrariness**. Let's look at some examples.

I will start by looking at the difference between conflicting and non-conflicting choices. We say a set of choices are **conflicting** if one choice is better on one aspect and a different choice better on some other aspect. For example, Budget is better on the price aspect but Superior is better on the health quality aspect, and so these are conflicting choices. A set of choices are **non-conflicting** if one choice is better on all aspects. For example, if Superior were on sale for $0.50 then there would be a non-conflicting choice.

To illustrate the potential consequences of conflicting versus non-conflicting choice, consider this example from a study by Tversky and Shafir (1992). Subjects were asked to imagine they want to buy a CD player, and walk past a shop with a one-day clearance sale. Some subjects were given the conflicting choices of a Sony player for $99 and a top of the range Aiwa player for $169. Some were given the non-conflicting choice of the Sony player for $99 or an inferior Aiwa player for $105. Others were just given the option of the Sony player for $99. All subjects were asked whether they would buy one of the players or wait and learn more about the models. Figure 2.2 summarizes the choices made.

We see that more people buy the Sony when the choice is non-conflicting than when it is conflicting. Also, more choose the Sony when the choice is non-conflicting than when there is no choice at all. This latter observation violates the **regularity condition** of choice that an increase in the number of available options

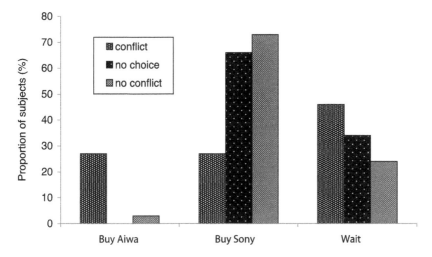

Figure 2.2 The decision subjects made when the choice is conflicting or non-conflicting, compared to when there is no choice. Subjects were more likely to wait the more conflicting the choice.

Source: Shafir et al. (1993).

should not increase the share buying a particular option. It seems that the presence of an inferior option increased the likelihood of buying the Sony.

What we have just seen suggests that one alterative can look more or less desirable depending on what it is compared to. A slightly different possibility is that particular aspects of an alternative can look more or less desirable depending on what they are compared to. To illustrate, let's suppose Anna has narrowed her choice to either Nutty or Honey and there are only three cereals on display: Nutty, Honey, and one of Budget or Superior. Honey looks relatively cheap when contrasted with Superior but relatively expensive when contrasted with Budget. She might, therefore, be more likely to buy Honey when it is contrasted with Superior. This would be an example of tradeoff contrast. The **tradeoff contrast hypothesis** is that a product with a desirable quality will appear cheaper if contrasted with a product where that desirable quality is more expensive.

A study by Simonson and Tversky (1992) shows the relevance of tradeoff contrast. In one part of the study, subjects were asked to choose between coupons and cash, where each coupon could be redeemed for books or CDs at local stores. In a background stage subjects were exposed to choices where a coupon cost either $15 or $5. After this they were all exposed to the same choices where a coupon cost $10. Figure 2.3 summarizes the results. The first choice offered to subjects was $47 and five coupons, or $37 and six coupons (the extra coupon costing $10). We see that those exposed to a background stage where coupons cost $15 were more likely to choose the extra coupon, while those exposed to a background stage where coupons cost $5 were not. This is consistent with the

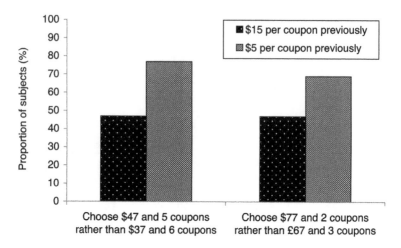

Figure 2.3 Whether subjects prefer an extra coupon to $10 depends on whether they were exposed to a background stage where coupons cost $15 or $5.

Source: Simonson and Tversky (1992).

tradeoff contrast hypothesis; the $10 coupon looks cheap, or expensive, depending on whether coupons previously cost $15, or $5.

Let us now go back to the scenario where there are two or three cereals on display out of Budget, Nutty and Honey. Budget has the advantage of being cheap, Honey has the advantage of being tasty, but Nutty strikes a good compromise. Maybe, therefore, Anna will buy Nutty because it's 'in the middle'. If true this means the shopper should be more likely to buy Nutty when all three cereals are on display than just two. This would be an example of **extremeness aversion with comprise**. There is another possibility. It may be that the presence of Honey or Budget on display emphasizes the importance of quality. So, the presence of Honey on display increases the likelihood Anna will buy Nutty, but the presence of Budget on display decreases the likelihood Anna will buy Nutty, because she switches to Honey. This would be an example of **extremeness aversion with polarization**. Table 2.4 distinguishes these possible effects with examples.

To give an example of extremeness aversion we can return to the study of Simonson and Tversky, and a different scenario. Subjects were given information about three radio cassette players, a mid-quality Emerson, mid-quality Sony and top-quality Sony. In Figure 2.4 we see the proportion that chose the mid-quality Sony. Adding the top-quality Sony decreases the proportion choosing the mid-quality Sony compared to the Emerson. Also, adding the Emerson increases the proportion choosing the mid-quality Sony compared to the top-quality Sony. This is an example of extremeness aversion with polarization. It is also a second example violating the regularity condition.

In the next example we push extremeness aversion a bit farther. First, imagine that Anna asks herself 'What cereal shall I buy?'. She might say Superior because

Table 2.4 Examples of how Anna's choice may be influence by the three psychological effects

Psychological effect	Example of what Sarah may choose
Tradeoff contrast	If choices are Budget, Nutty and Honey buys Nutty. If choices are Nutty, Honey and superior buys Honey.
Extremeness aversion with compromise	If choices are Nutty and Honey buys Honey. If choices are Budget and Nutty buys Budget. If choices are Budget, Nutty and Honey buys Nutty.
Extremeness aversion with polarization	If choices are Nutty and Honey buys Nutty. If choices are Budget and Nutty buys Budget. If choices are Budget, Nutty and Honey buys Honey.

it is more extreme, higher quality. Now imagine she asks herself 'What cereal shall I not buy?' She might say Superior because it is more extreme, more expensive. In both cases the fact that Superior is more extreme makes it more salient. That means it is the first thing she considers, and so might be the first thing she accepts and/or rejects. This can lead to a **choose-reject discrepancy** where a person chooses the same thing whether asked what she wants or what she does not want.

Here is an example from a study by Shafir et al. (1993). Subjects were given two choices for a vacation. Spot A was relatively neutral: average weather, average beaches, average nightlife etc. Spot B was more extreme: lots of sunshine, gorgeous beaches, very strong winds, no nightlife. Some subjects were asked which they would prefer to book. Other subjects were told they have a provisional booking at each location and now have to decide which to cancel. In Figure 2.5 we see that

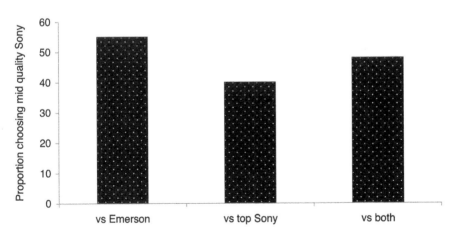

Figure 2.4 The proportion choosing a mid-level Sony radio, cassette player when the alternative was an Emerson player, a top-quality Sony player, or both the Emerson and Sony. We observe extremeness aversion with polarization.

Source: Simonson and Tversky (1992).

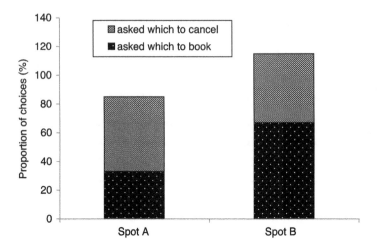

Figure 2.5 The proportion who choose spot A and B to book and to cancel. Both columns should add up to 100 percent, because if say 30 percent prefer spot A, 70 percent should reject spot A.

Source: Shafir et al. (1993).

most subjects preferred spot B over A but were equally split on whether to cancel A or B. Overall the proportion of choices for spot B exceeded 100 percent. This basically means that some people would both prefer spot B and want to cancel spot B!

To motivate a final example, suppose that on going into the grocery store Anna is stopped and asked to do a survey. One question they ask is whether she would be willing to pay $8 for a new cereal they are trialing. After that, Superior may look relatively cheap at $6. If the question had said $4, then maybe Superior would look expensive. This is an example of an **anchoring effect** where a person's choice is influenced by some prior cue or anchor. This might look like a trade-off contrast. In trade-off contrast, however, two or more different products are compared, while with the anchoring effect, a person's thoughts on a particular product are influenced by some prior event.

To illustrate how the anchoring effect can happen, we shall look at part of a study by Ariely et al. (2003). Subjects were first asked whether they would buy a box of Belgian chocolates, and some other items, for more than the last two digits of their social security number. For example, if the last two digits are 25 they are asked whether they would pay more than $25. They were then asked how much they would be willing to pay. The last two digits of a social security number are random, but did matter, as we see in Figure 2.6. On average those asked whether they were willing to pay, say, $55 subsequently said they were willing to pay a higher price than those who were asked to pay, say, $15.

The five psychological effects we have looked at are the consequences of choice heuristics. Heuristics like 'pick the one in the middle' or 'pick the most extreme'. They result in choice arbitrariness. Put another way, they cause **context effects**, a

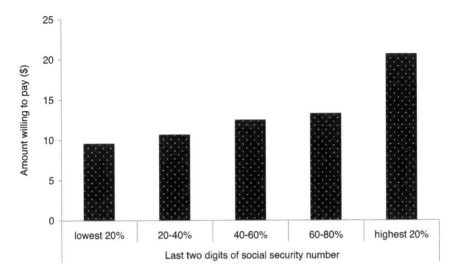

Figure 2.6 The amount subjects were willing to pay for a box of chocolates was higher for those with a higher social security number.

Source: Ariely et al. (2003).

general name I shall give to any external factors, like the other choices on offer, that influence choice. Recall that this all comes about because people are unlikely to know what maximizes their utility. We should expect, therefore, context effects in just about any economic choice a person ever makes. This means choice arbitrariness and context effects are important. Important enough, that I shall devote the next section to trying to understand them in more detail.

Before doing that I want to make one point clear. Some would have you believe that things like trade-off contrast and extremeness aversion are evidence of people not being rational and not being like homo economicus. This is not true. In a complicated world where there are lots of decisions to make it may be optimal to 'pick the one in the middle' or 'pick the most salient' or 'be influenced by the other choices on offer'. We are not, therefore, going to spend time wondering whether such things are evidence for or against the standard economic model. Indeed, even the more bizarre affects, like choice being influenced by the last two digits of a social security number, can be consistent with rational behavior. Such affects just mean that the heuristics people use are not always well adapted to some of the things experimenters have us do in the lab!

2.2 Mental accounting and framing

What I want to do now is question why context effects exist: why is it that external factors can influence the choice someone makes? A good starting point is to focus on a subset of context effects called framing effects.

Framing effects are where essentially equivalent descriptions of the same thing lead to different choices. That some people would choose to go to spot B for their vacation but also choose to not go to spot B for their vacation is an example of a framing effect: what people chose is dependent on the way the question was asked, or framed. If we can explain why people choose different things when offered the same set of choices, it should be simple to see why they may choose different things when offered a slightly different set of choices.

To understand why we observe framing (and context) effects I want you to look at the simple classification of cognitive processes summarized in Figure 2.7. (In chapter nine we will revisit this classification to see how accurate it is and see that, while not perfect, it is more than good enough for our purposes.) The classification suggests that when we initially see something, perception and intuition kick in automatically to give us impressions of what we are looking at. This process happens spontaneously and the person has no or very little control over it. Anna, for example, may make a choice purely based on intuition. More generally, however, particularly for the kind of choices of interest in economics, she might use reasoning to think through options and make a more deliberate, informed judgment. In this case she will use reasoning processes.

Now, here's the key thing we learn from this classification: even if Anna does use reasoning, her initial perception and intuition will inevitably influence the starting point for her subsequent reasoning. Initial perceptions and intuition will, therefore, matter and how a choice is framed will likely effect perception and intuition which will in turn affect reasoning. We saw this happen when explaining trade-off contrast. If someone was led to think a coupon costs $15 then being asked to pay $10 will be perceived as a good deal and maybe one worth taking. If they were led to think it costs $5, then it looks like a bad deal.

That context and framing influence perception and intuition, which influences reasoning, is one of the most important ideas in behavioral economics. Homo economicus only ever uses reasoning, and so recognizing the role played by perception and intuition gives us a completely different perspective on why people behave the way they do than we would get with the standard economic model. Furthermore, this explanation of context and framing effects means that they are inevitable, and not just a quirk of some experiment. Every time a person makes a choice, that

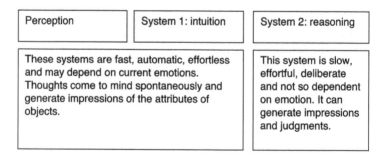

Figure 2.7 A representation of different brain processes.

choice has to be framed in a particular way, and how it is framed will likely affect perception, intuition, reasoning and the choice made. If we want to understand economic behavior we therefore need to understand framing effects. What I want to do now is explain why this means we need to understand reference points.

2.2.1 Reference-dependent utility

Some attributes of an object are more **accessible** than others when we first perceive it. Such **natural assessments** of an object include size, distance, loudness, temperature, similarity, and whether it is good or bad. Importantly, a natural assessment will usually be a relative rather than absolute one. It is far more natural for us to say what is bigger, longer, louder, hotter and better, without knowing the exact volume, length, temperature etc. To be able to judge relative magnitude we need some standard of comparison, and this is called the **reference point** or **reference level**.

To illustrate why the distinction between absolute and relative can be important for economic behavior consider this question, taken from Kahneman (2003):

> Two persons get their monthly report from a broker. Carol is told that her wealth went from $4 to $3 million dollars. Amanda is told that her wealth went from $1 to $1.1 million dollars. Who is happier?

As we have already discussed, the standard in economics is to measure utility using a utility function $u(x)$ where x is money and the more money, the higher is utility. The answer, therefore, should be that Carol is happier because $u(\$3\ million) > u(\$1.1\ million)$. Things, however, do not seem quite this simple, because many of us may be tempted to think that Amanda would be the happier. She might be the happier because her wealth is bigger than before, while Carol's is smaller than before.

This example suggests we need to take seriously the distinction between relative and absolute measures. The simplest way to do this is to suppose some reference point about which outcomes are measured. So, we can use a utility function or **value function** $v(x - r)$ that measures the utility of outcome x relative to some reference point r. If the reference point is $r = 0$ then the value function will coincide with the original formulation, but if r is different, say wealth last year, then we get something different. Setting r as wealth last year we see that Carol would get $v(-\$1\ million)$ and Amanda would get $v(\$0.1\ million)$. With this formulation it seems that Amanda should be happier because $v(\$0.1\ million) > v(-\$1\ million)$.

Now Amanda is happier. Things still seem, however, a little incomplete because Carol does have more money than Amanda. A more general formulation is the **reference dependent utility function:**

$$u^r(x) = \eta u(x) + v(x - r)$$

where η is some parameter and r is the reference point. Total utility is now a weighted sum of utility from total wealth and the utility from a relative gain or loss. With this we can capture Carol being potentially happier because she has more wealth and potentially less happy because her wealth has decreased.

Judging things relative to a reference point raises the important distinction between gains and losses. Intuitively there is something distinctly different about being above the reference point, a gain, or being below the reference point, a loss. A large amount of evidence, which we shall get to shortly, backs this up and points towards something called loss aversion. Someone is **loss averse** if a loss causes a bigger fall in utility than a similar sized gain causes an increase in utility. In terms of the value function loss aversion implies that $v(-g) < -v(g)$ for any $g > 0$. Basically, losses are worse than gains are good.

We are going to see that reference dependence and loss aversion have big implications for economic behavior. Before we look at this in more detail I want to briefly preview why reference dependence is so important.

At first glance it might look as though we have just rewritten the utility function to include an extra parameter r called the reference point. If this were the case then economists could carry on modeling utility and utility maximization the way they traditionally have done and not a great deal would need to change. This is not how it is! That's because the reference point a person uses when making a particular decision can be relatively arbitrary and will likely be determined by perception and intuition. In other words the reference point can depend on the context, causing important framing and context effects. This is why reference dependence is more than just adding a parameter to the utility function. The ways in which the reference point can depend on context will be a recurring theme in the rest of this chapter and those to follow.

2.2.2 The endowment effect

One important consequence of reference dependence and loss aversion is the endowment effect. To explain what this is, we shall look at a study by List (2004). The study was conducted on the floor of a sports card show in the US. Subjects were recruited throughout the day and completed a short survey, before being asked to choose whether they would like to take a coffee mug or chocolate bar as reward for doing the survey. Both the mug and chocolate bar retailed at around $6. The key thing about the experiment was to vary the perception of ownership. Some people were physically given a mug and told they could swap for a chocolate bar, some were given the chocolate bar and told they could swap for a mug, others were either given both or neither and asked to choose.

Figure 2.8 details the proportion of subjects who chose the mug. Look first at the non-dealers, who were people attending the show. Here we see the same has been observed in many other experiments: those given the chocolate bar do not want to swap for a mug, and those given a mug do not want to swap for a chocolate bar. It is highly unlikely that this is just an accident of giving chocolate to those who like chocolate and mugs to those who like coffee. Instead it seems that people are biased by physically having the good in their hand, a framing effect. This is clear from the 'both' and 'neither' cases, where approximately 50 percent swap.

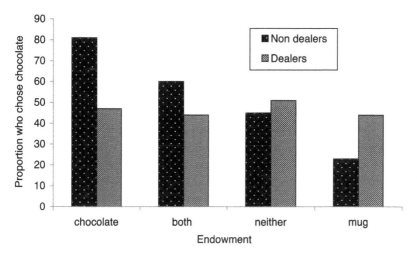

Figure 2.8 Whether subjects chose chocolate depended on the endowment. Those given chocolate were more likely to choose chocolate and those given a mug to choose the mug.

Source: List (2004).

That people value more highly goods that they have some ownership over is called the **endowment effect**. Interestingly, the effect appears less pronounced for people who are more experienced in trading goods. To see this look at what dealers, people with booths at the show, did. Dealers had more market experience in trading (sports cards) than non-dealers, and show no signs of being biased.

One way to explain the endowment effect is through reference dependence and loss aversion. If Anna has the coffee mug in her hand then she may feel that she already owns that coffee mug. To give it away would be a loss. By contrast, if she does not have the chocolate bar in her hand then she feels no sense of ownership over it. To get the chocolate would be a gain. We have suggested that losses are weighted more heavily than gains. If so, Anna would be reluctant to swap the mug in her hand for a chocolate bar, even if she would have marginally preferred a chocolate bar.

If the endowment effect shows up in people who randomly possess for a few seconds a mug they probably do not want, then economists need to take it seriously, because ownership and trading of goods is at the heart of economics.

One curious thing is why we observe the endowment effect, because it does not seem to improve the decision made in this example. In some situations the endowment effect may be beneficial, as we shall see when we talk about housing and saving. In those situations where it is not, we should expect more experienced people to have learned to avoid it. This is what we generally do observe, although not always to such an extent as in the study by List. Interestingly, however, people may redirect the endowment effect, rather than suppress it, by appreciating opportunity cost. To someone familiar with the concept of opportunity cost, to keep the coffee mug in your hand is a loss, because of the value that can be got from swapping the mug. The distinction between what is a loss and what is a gain can thus be blurred. In this way the endowment effect is lessened and we get our first suggestion that the reference point depends on the person and context.

2.2.3 Willingness to pay or accept

One place the endowment effect does show up is contingent valuation. **Contingent valuation** is an often-used technique to get people to reveal how much they value things like health, safety or the environment. Two basic methods of contingent valuation are willingness to pay (WTP) and willingness to accept (WTA). In the first, **willingness to pay**, people are asked how much money they would be willing to pay to get an extra unit of some good; that is, they are asked how much they would pay to consume $c + 1$ rather than c units of the good. In the second, **willingness to accept**, people are asked how much money they would be willing to accept for having one unit less of the good; that is, they are asked how much they would accept to consume c rather than $c + 1$ units. In both cases we get a valuation on the $c + 1$st unit of the good.

Given what we know of loss aversion and the endowment effect, we should not be surprised that WTA and WTP can lead to different valuations. WTP makes the person think of losing money and they may not be willing to pay much, i.e. lose a lot of money, to get an extra unit of the good. WTA, by contrast, makes the person think of losing the good, and they may want a lot of money to compensate for getting less of the good. This is consistent with what we do observe. The valuation of a good based on willingness to accept typically exceeds one based on willingness to pay, and this difference can be large. This is a **violation of procedural invariance**, in that the answer we get to a question depends on the procedure we use to find the answer, a specific form of framing effect.

To illustrate, Figure 2.9 provides some data from a study by Bateman et al. (2005) in which subjects were asked to put a contingent valuation on ten chocolates. For now, just focus on the WTA and WTP. The WTA valuation is around 60 percent more than the WTP valuation. This difference is a problem for anyone who wants to obtain a reliable estimate of the value people put on goods. Should they use the WTP or WTA measure?

It also raises some fundamental questions about how people value goods. That's because when talking about the endowment effect it is natural to have in mind physical ownership of a good. So, we think of the subject owning a mug or owning a box of chocolates, if only for a few seconds. The WTA and WTP measures, however, get subjects to think about potentially owning a good and this seems enough to trigger an endowment effect and shift the reference point.

One place this becomes relevant is in thinking through the **no loss in buying hypothesis**. The idea behind this hypothesis is that when people are deciding whether to buy a good, they mentally deduct money from their current income and then decide whether to gain the good or (re)gain the money they would spend

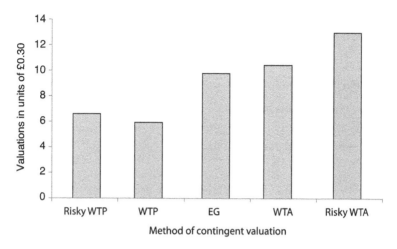

Figure 2.9 The valuation put on ten chocolates. The WTP exceeds the WTA but not the EG.

Source: Bateman et al. (2005).

buying the good. For example, if Anna usually buys Honey cereal for $4 then she feels no loss in spending $4 buying Honey because she expected to pay $4. We can rephrase this in terms of the reference point. Is the reference point current income, and so buying Honey involves a loss of $4, or is it current income minus the amount needed to buy Honey, meaning that not buying the good involves regaining $4?

For me, it is more natural to think of the latter. For example, I might say that 'Anna's reference point for Honey is $4'. What I really mean is that Anna expects to spend $4 on Honey, and so has mentally deducted that from her wealth to give a reference point of wealth minus $4. The study by Bateman et al., however (see Research Methods 2.3) put the no loss in buying hypothesis to the test and found little support for it. What to make of this result?

The no loss in buying hypothesis essentially assumes people take account of the opportunity cost of money, as we suggested experienced traders might do to avoid the endowment effect. This suggests that experience is important. If people are inexperienced in a particular task, which is likely when finding the WTP and WTA of goods the person rarely if ever buys, then buying may be interpreted as a loss. By contrast, if people are more experienced in a task, like Anna buying Honey every week, then buying may not be interpreted as a loss, unless the price is more than she expected.

The interesting thing this illustrates is that it can be quite ambiguous what a person thinks they own or do not own, or what is counted as a gain or a loss. For instance, when Anna walks into the grocery store, does she own $4, or the box of

Honey that she expects to buy for $4? That depends on how she thinks. That means it's somewhat arbitrary and subject to perception, intuition and framing. Will this matter?

Research Methods 2.3

Adversarial Collaboration

Often, observed behavior can be explained by two or more competing theories, with no way to distinguish between the theories using existing data. That means we need a more nuanced experiment to try and evaluate one theorem over another. Typically, such experiments are done by researchers who historically have supported one side of the debate. Typically, they find data that supports their side of the debate. This may be for pure reasons, such as confirmation bias which we shall explain in chapter five, or for less pure reasons, such as wanting to further their career. Either way it does not often seem the most constructive way to do things.

An alternative is adversarial collaboration. This is where researchers on both sides of a debate get together and jointly design and evaluate an experiment to test respective theories. In the Bateman et al. study, a team, loosely based at the University of East Anglia, joined with Daniel Kahneman to explore the no loss in buying hypothesis. Given that both sides are given equal chances to influence the design of the experiment and look at and evaluate the data, the conclusions should be free of systematic bias. This seems, therefore, a much more constructive way of doing things.

For completeness we should briefly explain what the researchers did do. A third valuation method is **equivalent gain** (EG), in which a person is asked the smallest amount of money that would be equivalent to one more unit of the good. Like WTA, this question asks about consuming c rather than $c + 1$ units of the good. The difference is the endowment point. In WTA the person should feel as though they are endowed with $c + 1$ units and are being asked to give up a unit. With EG the person should feel as though they are endowed with c units and have a choice between more money or an extra unit of the good.

All agree that WTA will exceed EG. The more interesting question is whether EG exceeds WTP. If giving up money in exchange for a good is counted as a loss then EG should exceed WTP, if it is considered a foregone gain then EG and WTP should be equal. This seems to provide a simple test. What happens, however, if WTA is a 'lot bigger' than EG and EG only 'slightly bigger' than WTP? This is the kind of thing open to different interpretations. So, valuation methods called risky WTP and risky WTA are also used. For reasons we will skip, this gives a test of the no loss in buying hypothesis:

if $\dfrac{EG}{WTP} > 1$ and $\dfrac{WTP}{risky\ WTP} = 1$ evidence that exhange is a loss of money

if $\dfrac{EG}{WTP} = 1$ and $\dfrac{WTP}{risky\ WTP} > 1$ evidence that exchange is a foregone gain of money

Other checks that things are working well include that risky WTA equals the WTA. The data, summarized in Figure 2.9, suggest that exchange is a loss of money.

2.2.4 Transaction utility

If reference dependence fundamentally effects how much we value goods, as loss aversion and the endowment effect suggest it does, then it should influence our decisions to buy or not. To illustrate, suppose that Anna is on holiday and wants to buy Nutty, so goes into the local grocery store. How much should she be willing to pay? There are two things worth considering. First is the maximum she is willing to pay for a box, ignoring any possible psychological effects. Let's suppose that she likes Nutty a lot, so this is $8. Next is the reference point, and given that she normally pays $3, we can start with a reference point of $r = \$3$. Remember what this actually means is 'the reference point is wealth minus $3'.

We can then distinguish between acquisition and transaction utility. **Acquisition utility** measures the net gain from buying something for less than it is valued, so in this case is $v(8 - p)$. **Transaction utility** measures the net gain or loss from buying something for less or more than expected, so is $v(r - p)$. The total value from buying the box of cereal is therefore $v(8 - p) + v(3 - p)$. If $p = \$2$ then she will feel a double gain, she buys something she likes and pays less than she expected to! If $p = \$4$ then she will probably buy but will feel a loss of paying more than she expected. If $p = \$6$ then she will probably not buy because the loss from 'paying too much' exceeds the gain from buying the cereal she likes.

Transaction utility is the key thing here in that it captures how Anna may feel good about buying a bargain, or bad about being charged too much. This can influence whether or not she buys Nutty, but this in itself is not so fundamental. What is fundamental is that the reference point she has will likely depend on perception and intuition. Whether she perceives Nutty as a bargain or a rip off will depend on the context. Another example from Thaler (2008) illustrates:

> You are lying on the beach on a hot day. All you have to drink is water. For the last hour you have been thinking about how much you would enjoy a nice cold bottle of your favorite brand of beer. A companion gets up to go make a phone call and offers to bring back a beer from the only nearby place where beer is sold, a fancy resort hotel. He says that the beer might be expensive and so asks how much you are willing to pay for the beer. . . . What price do you tell him?
>
> Now, substitute 'a small, run-down grocery store' instead of 'a fancy resort hotel'.

People surveyed by Thaler said they would pay on average $2.65 in the fancy hotel, and $1.50 in the store. The difference probably reflects concerns for fairness, which we shall look at in chapter seven, but the key point is that there is a difference. The reference point, and thus the perception of what is a bargain or a rip-off depended on the context. The reference point by which transaction utility is judged can seemingly change quite easily. We are back to framing effects and choice arbitrariness. Someone might buy a beer from a fancy resort hotel but not from a small, run-down grocery store, even if it's the same beer at the same price.

The notion of transaction utility may seem intuitive, but we do hit a snag. Anna might have a reference price for Nutty, or beer, but it is unlikely she has a reference price for everything she might buy. It is also unlikely she knows for sure what things she is going to buy. It is even more unlikely she keeps track of each gain or loss of transaction utility when buying 100 or more different products in a grocery store. We have, therefore, some work to do in order to apply the notion of transaction utility.

2.2.5 Narrow framing

It could be that Anna enters the grocery store with a reference point for various things she might buy, like 'I will probably spend $3 on Nutty'. More likely, however, is that Anna has an expectation of how much she should spend in the grocery store, or how much she should spend a week on food. The important reference point will thus be something like '$200 a week on food'. If Nutty is cheaper than $3, then great, but that will soon be counteracted if apples are more expensive than usual. What matters most is the final total at the checkout.

What's happening here is that things are being grouped together, or not, so that Anna can keep track of what is going on and whether she is spending more or less than she wanted. She can keep track of this on individual items, like a box of Honey, and in terms of the total amount she spends in the store.

This process of grouping things not only brings some things together but also separates those that end up in different groups. This can cause **narrow framing,** wherein a choice or outcome is seen in isolation rather than being integrated with other things. For instance, spending on food items might be seen as separate from spending on leisure. Here's another example:

> Question one. Imagine that you have decided to see a play where admission costs $10 per ticket. As you enter the theater you discover that you have lost a $10 bill. Would you pay $10 to watch the play?
>
> Question two. Imagine that you have bought the ticket to see a play where admission costs $10. As you enter the theatre, you discover you have lost the ticket and there is no way to recover it. Would you pay $10 for another ticket?

Tversky and Kahneman (1981) report that 88 percent of subjects asked question one said they would pay, but only 46 percent asked question two said they would pay. In both cases the loss is $10, so where the loss comes from clearly matters.

To capture such things we can introduce mental accounting. **Mental accounting** is the process of coding, categorizing and evaluating choices and outcomes. The primary component of mental accounting is to put any spending or income into separate accounts for specific purposes. For example, Anna might have a 'go to the theatre account', a 'loose change account', and a 'food account'. Outcomes will be perceived and experienced relative to the particular account that is brought to mind. Losing a $10 bill brings to mind the loose change account, whereas losing the theatre ticket brings to mind the theatre account. Losing the $10 bill has, therefore, no implications for the theatre account, and so should not influence Anna's choice to go to the theatre; she expected to pay $10 and so should still pay $10 to watch, she just might look to save $10 somewhere else to bring the loose change account back below the reference point. By contrast, losing the ticket does matter for the theatre account; she expected to watch for no extra cost but now has to pay an additional $10. This makes the cost to go to the theatre feel like $20 and that may put her off going.

A pertinent question is how narrowly defined accounts are. For example, is there a 'theatre account', an 'entertainment account', or just a general 'current spending account'? To get some idea, we can look at a study by Heath and Soll (1996). In the study, subjects were asked how their spending would likely be affected by a related purchase, a gift, or an unrelated purchase. For instance, subjects were asked whether they would purchase a $25 theatre ticket if they had (a, related purchase) already bought a $50 sports ticket, or (b, gift) been given for free a sports ticket worth $50, or (c, unrelated purchase) heard of a flu epidemic and had to spend $50 on a flu inoculation. Of particular interest are people who answer no, yes and yes. That they answer yes to (b) and (c) means they would be willing to go to both the theatre and sports event and can afford to do so even if they have already spent $50. That they answer no to (a) is evidence of narrow framing.

Table 2.5 summarizes what proportion of subjects answered no, yes, yes for various combinations of the good being purchased and the related purchase. For instance, 38 percent did so for our example question of buying a theatre ticket after having purchased a sports ticket. We see that a high proportion of subjects did say no, yes, yes and so there is evidence of narrow framing. By comparing goods we can also see how narrowly defined mental budgets appeared to be. The

Table 2.5 The proportion of subjects (%) who answered no, yes, yes to purchasing a good when the alternative was a related purchase, gift, or unrelated purchase. The numbers in bold indicate that the related purchase was not considered in the same mental account as the good being purchased

The 'related' purchase	The good being purchased		
	Theatre ticket (entertainment)	*Chinese take away (food)*	*Sweatshirt (clothes)*
Sports ticket	38	**12**	**12**
Boat tour	41	**16**	6
Party snacks	21	12	6
Salmon	21	24	0
Dinner out	32	32	6
Wine	15	18	3
Jeans	**0**	0	12
Watch	15	3	9
Costume	38	9	9

Source: Heath and Soll (1996).

combinations in bold were considered by subjects to not be related purchases. For example, buying a sweatshirt was not considered related to buying a sports ticket. In these cases the proportion of no, yes, yes answers goes down. This suggests that mental accounts can be quite narrowly defined. Spending on a sweatshirt does not come out of the same account as spending on a sports ticket, boat tour, party snacks, etc.

More generally, the evidence does suggest that people use mental accounts to keep track of income and spending, and that gains or losses are coded relative to an account reference point. One interesting thing about this is that we now have two dimensions to the arbitrariness of the reference point. There is the question of what reference point will be brought to mind; will Anna think of the 'Nutty is usually $3' reference point or the 'I should spend $200 on food' reference point; will the person on the beach think of the '$2 for beer is expensive' reference point or the 'I have $8 loose change' reference point? There is then the question of what level the reference point should be: a person might pay $2.50 from a fancy resort hotel but only $1.50 from a small, run-down grocery store. This gives lots of room for perception and intuition to matter. No wonder we get framing effects and choice arbitrariness. But can we go even further?

2.2.6 Hedonic editing

So far we have primarily been thinking of a person responding to external factors beyond their control that influence perceptions, intuition, the reference point and possibly behavior. Mental accounting, however, suggests that people may have some control of such factors. Anna can potentially choose what mental accounts she has, the reference point for each account, and how she codes gains and losses.

To illustrate, suppose that Anna buys one box of Nutty for herself and a box of Superior for her son. She goes to the shop and fortunately finds that both are in a half-price sale. This means she gains $1.50 on the box of Nutty and $3 on the box of Superior. This could be coded as two separate gains or as one big gain. If the outcomes are **segregated** they are valued separately to give $v(\$1.50) + v(\$3)$. If they are **integrated** they are combined together to give $v(\$4.50)$. We are going to show in the next chapter that the value function is probably concave, which means that $v(\$1.50) + v(\$3) > v(\$4.50)$. Thus, it would be better for Anna to segregate the gains in her mind.

Suppose that a month later, the sale long over, Anna goes to the store and finds that the prices of the Nutty and Superior have increased by 50 percent. This means she needs to spend an extra $1.50 on Nutty and $3.00 on Superior. Segregating these losses gives $v(-\$1.50) + v(-\$3)$, while integrating the losses gives $v(-\$4.50)$. We shall show the value function is probably convex in losses, which mean that $v(-\$1.50) + v(-\$3) < v(-\$4.50)$. This means that Anna would do best to integrate losses.

So, if Anna has a choice how to code gains and losses, then: multiple gains should be segregated, multiple losses should be combined, and gains should be used to cancel small losses. Does such integration and segregation make sense? Intuitively it does seem to, as an example by Thaler (2008) illustrates:

Mr A was given tickets to some lotteries. He won $50 in one lottery and $25 in the other. Mr B was given a ticket for another lottery and won $75. Who was happier?

Most people say that B will be happier. As Thaler suggests, 'Moral: don't wrap all the Christmas presents in one box'! We call this process of categorizing gains or losses as **hedonic editing**. It suggests that people can partly manipulate how they perceive or interpret things in order to make themselves feel better. Another way to do this is choice bracketing.

2.2.7 Choice bracketing

The focus in this final section is on the coding of losses and gains over time. Often there is a delay between paying for a good and consuming it, or consuming it and paying. For example, Anna might buy some frozen food she does not expect to eat for a month or two, but also might put everything on credit, meaning that she does not need to pay for a month or two. Such things mean that losses and gains will appear in accounts at different points in time. People can choose how narrowly or broadly they want to group together events spread over time, an example of **choice bracketing**.

I will look first at the implications of a delay between paying and consumption, using a study by Shafir and Thaler (2006) to illustrate. They first asked subscribers to a wine newsletter how they would think about giving away as a gift, drinking, or dropping and breaking, a bottle of wine that cost $20 and now sells for $75. Figure 2.10 summarizes the results. Overall we see a fairly mixed response. Many,

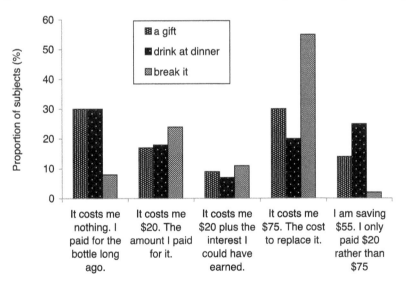

Figure 2.10 How subjects valued a bottle of wine that cost $20 and is now worth $75 depending on whether they drank it, gave it as a gift, or broke it.

Source: Shafir and Thaler (2006).

however, thought that giving away or drinking the bottle of wine costs them nothing, or even saves them money. This suggests the cost must be accounted for when the bottle is bought. Further questioning, however, suggested that when buying the wine, most framed the purchase as an investment rather than a cost. This motivates the title of Shafir and Thaler's paper, 'Invest now, drink later, spend never'. It is as if delayed consumption allows people to frame the initial purchase as an investment which has depreciated by the time the consumption takes place. This is a convenient way to never feel any loss! Only if the bottle is broken does the loss become apparent.

We can next look at what happens when there is a delay between consumption and paying, with a study by Siemens (2007). In the study, subjects were paid $5 for doing a 30-minute survey. All subjects were given the $5 immediately. What differed was when they did the study. Some did it immediately, some three days later, some a week later and some two weeks later. Having finished the survey, subjects were asked what they thought about the task. Figure 2.11 summarizes the results. We see a fairly clear and consistent drop-off in perceived satisfaction, fairness and willingness to do the task again, the more the delay between getting the $5 and doing the survey.

Both these studies give a consistent picture in which the costs and benefits, or losses and gains, diminish over time. So, the cost of buying the wine is forgotten by the time it is drunk, and the gain of $5 is forgotten by the time the task has to be done.

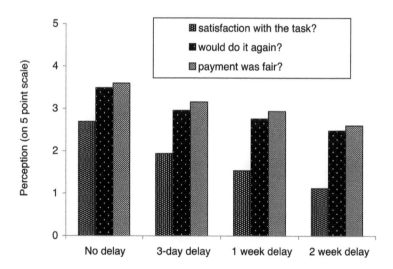

Figure 2.11 How subjects felt about a task depending on how long they did it after getting paid. Answers measured on a five point scale from unpleasant, definitely would not, extremely unfair (1) to pleasant, definitely would, extremely fair payment (5).

Source: Siemens (2007).

One interesting thing to take from this is that we now have a third dimension to the arbitrariness of the reference point. Namely, how far forward or back a person looks. For instance, Anna's entertainment account could be '$50 a week', or'$200 a month'. The former option means she will probably only go to one event a week. The latter option allows her to attend a few events one week if she makes up for that with subsequent weeks of abstinence. What time frame comes to mind at any one time will likely depend on her perception and intuition of the situation.

Hopefully, by now you have got the idea that reference points matter and are somewhat arbitrary. They are likely to depend on the context and the way that someone perceives a particular situation. This is a very important idea to keep in mind as you read through the rest of the book.

2.3 Summary

We have already covered a lot of important ideas, so it's high time that I put things into context with a short summary.

I started with the observation that saying someone should maximize her utility does not get us far if, as seems reasonable, she does not know what maximizes her utility. This lack of knowledge means she needs to search for more information about what she likes and dislikes. It also means that her choices will be somewhat arbitrary until she becomes better informed. Indeed, her choice can be influenced by all sorts of external factors including the way things are framed. We called these context effects.

I then argued that people focus more on relative rather than absolute judgments. In terms of economic behavior this means there will be a focus on gains or losses relative to some reference point. People seem particularly averse to losses, resulting in things like the endowment effect.

We then saw that the reference point can be a very subjective thing. It is essentially what someone expected or thought would or should happen and the person is free to think different things. She is also free to change the viewpoint from, say, what will happen this week to what will happen this month.

One step up from this is a person using 'creative accounting' to manipulate the reference point or viewpoint to increase their utility. This we called hedonic editing. Most of the time, however, the reference point will probably be influenced by subconscious processes like intuition and perception. So, context influences perception and intuition, which influences the reference point, which influences choice. Framing matters and the reference point matters!

That there are context effects and that framing matters might seem obvious, particularly if you have studied some psychology, but it does mean a fairly funda-mental departure from the standard economic model. Specifically, there are two new and fundamental things we need to add to the model: (i) that utility depends on outcomes relative to some reference point, and (ii) that the reference point and choice will depend on the context in which the decision is made in somewhat arbitrary ways. The first thing is relatively easy to add to the model, the second less so. But, we will see more on that in the next chapter. What I want to do now is look through some applications where heuristics, search and reference dependence have a role to play.

2.4 Demand, supply and markets

Through much of this chapter I have used the example of Anna in the grocery store choosing a breakfast cereal. This is illustrative of a **market** where potential buyers of a good, such as Anna, interact with people who are collectively willing to provide that good (the owners and workers of the store, farm that supplies the wheat for the cereal etc.). Markets are at the heart of economics, so they seem an apt place to begin looking at applications of what we have learned.

It's easiest to start with an laboratory market. The standard way to create a market in the experimental lab begins by randomly allocating subjects to the role of buyer or seller. Each buyer is given a card that has written on the value to him or her of buying one unit of a fictitious good that will be traded in the experiment. Each seller is given a card that has written on the value to him or her of selling one unit of the good. Different subjects are given different values and only they know their value. Buyers and sellers are then able to interact and do a deal. The profit of a buyer is her value minus the price she bought for. The profit of a seller is the price she sold for minus her value. So, in principle, buyers want to buy as cheap as possible and sellers to sell as dear as possible.

If we know the values of all sellers and buyers we can derive a demand and supply curve. To illustrate, suppose that the values given to buyers and sellers are as in Table 2.6. For example, one buyer is given a value $2.30 meaning that if she bought for $2 she would make a profit of $0.30. To derive the **supply curve** we have to look at all possible prices and ask how many sellers would sell at each price. If the price is less than $1.50 then no one should sell. If the price is between $1.50 and $2 then there is one person who should sell, namely the seller with value $1.50. If the price is between $2 and $2.50 then there are two people who should sell, namely the sellers with value $1.50 and $2. Carrying this on we obtain the supply curve in figure 2.12. To derive the **demand curve** we have to look at all possible prices and ask how many buyers would buy at each price. If the price is more than $3.10 then no one should buy. If the price is between $2.80 and $3.10

Table 2.6 The number of sellers and buyers before and after a shift in demand

Type	Distribution of values
Sellers	There are five sellers with values $1.50, $2, $2.50, $2.50 and $3.
Buyers	There are five buyers with values $1.80, $2.30, $2.60, $2.80 and $3.10.
Buyers after change	There are five buyers with values $1.50, $1.70, $2.20, $2.20 and $3.

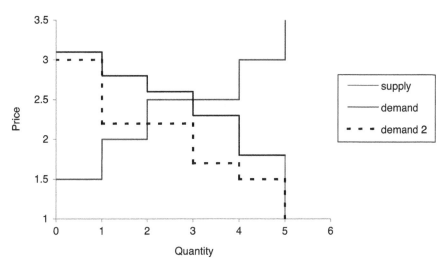

Figure 2.12 The demand and supply curves before and after a shift in demand.

then there is one person who should buy, namely the buyer with value $3.10. Carrying this on we obtain the demand curve.

Demand and supply curves are one of the most basic ideas in economics, and these curves are no different to those you may be familiar with. For instance, the demand curve must slope down and the supply curve slope up. (You might be used to smooth curves rather than the stepped ones drawn here, but this is just because it is usually more convenient to think of a smooth curve.) The **market equilibrium price** and **quantity** is where demand equals supply. In the example, that is where price is $2.50 and quantity is three. In practice this means we should expect there to be three trades, each at a price of $2.50. If we change the demand curve we see that the equilibrium price drops to $2.20 and the equilibrium quantity to two. Thus, a shift in demand and supply should change the market price in a predictable way.

One remarkable thing about market equilibrium is that total profit is maximized at the equilibrium. Table 2.7 illustrates how this works by contrasting the equilibrium with two other possible set of trades. In equilibrium there are three trades at $2.50 and total profit is $2.50. In the second scenario all ten people trade and make a profit but total profit is only $1.10. There are lots of other possible combinations of trades we should check but none will give as high a profit as the equilibrium. This is an illustration of the celebrated **First Fundamental Theorem of Welfare Economics,** that any market equilibrium is Pareto efficient. Notice, however, the equilibrium need not be 'fair'. For instance, one seller makes $1 while several sellers would make $0.

This stylized example illustrates why demand and supply analysis is so fundamentally important in economics: it is a tool to predict what may happen in markets, and should tell us what the most efficient outcome is.

Table 2.7 The market is most efficient in equilibrium as evidenced by the high total profit

	Trades			Profit		
	Buyer value	Seller value	Price	Buyer	Seller	Total
Equilibrium	$3.10	$1.50	$2.50	$0.60	$1.00	$1.60
	$2.80	$2.00	$2.50	$0.30	$0.50	$0.80
	$2.60	$2.50	$2.50	$0.10	$0.00	$0.10
						$2.50
Maximum trades	$1.80	$1.50	$1.65	$0.15	$0.15	$0.30
	$2.30	$2.00	$2.15	$0.15	$0.15	$0.30
	$2.60	$2.50	$2.55	$0.05	$0.05	$0.10
	$2.80	$2.50	$2.65	$0.15	$0.15	$0.30
	$3.10	$3.00	$3.05	$0.05	$0.05	$0.10
						$1.10
Maximum seller profit	$3.10	$1.50	$2.79	$0.31	$1.29	$1.60
	$2.80	$2.00	$2.79	$0.01	$0.79	$0.80
						$2.40

One thing we have not done is specify how people interact in order to make trades. Three of the more common ways we observe are:

1 A **negotiated price institution** where buyers and sellers are free to talk to each other and try to do a deal. This is similar to bartering in a local market.

2 A **double auction institution** where buyers submit bids of what they are willing to pay and sellers submit asks of what they are willing to sell for. All bids and asks are displayed on a screen for all to see. A buyer can buy by accepting the lowest ask price. A seller can sell by accepting the highest bid price. This institution is used in most financial, commodity and currency markets.

3 A **posted offer institution** where each seller displays a take it or leave it price. Buyers can go to any seller and agree to trade at the displayed price. This institution is what we are familiar with when we go to the grocery store or most shops.

That is enough background information. I now want to get on and look at some data on how markets work. I will start with markets in the experimental lab and progressively work towards real markets.

2.4.1 Double auction markets in the lab

All three of the institutions above have been used in the laboratory but the double auction is most common, so I will start by looking at that.

In the one of the earliest economic experimental studies, Vernon Smith (1962) ran ten experimental double auction markets. Each market was repeated up to six periods and had different demand and supply curves. Figure 2.13 summarizes

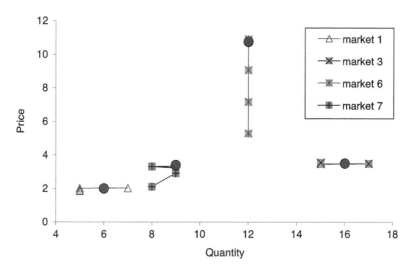

Figure 2.13 Convergence of market price and quantity to equilibrium in four double
auction markets. The circles show the equilibrium.

Source: Smith (1962).

the data from four of the sessions. For each market the equilibrium price is represented by a circle. We can then see the observed quantity and average price over
the periods.

Market six is the easiest to explain, because there we see the average price
increase over the periods from 5.29 in period one to 7.17, 9.06 and finally 10.9 in
period four. The quantity traded is 12 in every period. The equilibrium price was
10.75 and quantity was 12, and so by period four the market was trading at equilibrium. In the other three sessions I have plotted there is not much to see, and the
same could be said of all of the sessions run in the study, but that's the beautiful
thing! The average price and average quantity traded were remarkably close to the
market equilibrium in all periods.

The closeness between market and observed prices also holds when demand
and supply are changed from period to period. This is illustrated in Figure 2.14
where the equilibrium and average price are plotted for a market that lasted 15
periods with the equilibrium price changing each period. The match between
equilibrium and observed average prices is nearly perfect!

Basically, the average price and quantity observed in experimental double
auction markets almost always get close to the market equilibrium with repeated
trading, and typically start close. The price and quantity also change as predicted
by changes in demand and supply.

This is a fantastic result. It suggests that demand and supply are reliable predictors of what will happen in a market, which is good news for economists. It also

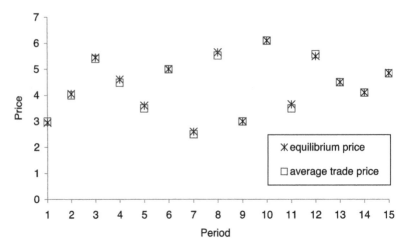

Figure 2.14 The equilibrium price and average price traded in a market that lasted 15
periods.

Source: Smith (2002).

suggests that markets are a great way to allocate resources, which is good news for
everyone. Indeed, this result goes further than the First Fundamental Theorem of
Welfare Economics, because the Theorem is agnostic about how prices will be
determined, but the double auction gives us an institution to determine prices and
achieve efficiency.

The efficiency of double auction markets is arguably the most important lesson
so far from behavioral economics. That double auction markets do work so well
is because subjects only need use simple heuristics. Recall that the only thing a
subject knows at the start is her own value to buy or sell. So she simply needs to
buy for less or sell for more than her value to make a profit, and this is something
very familiar to most of us (see Research Methods 2.4).

Research Methods 2.4

Intelligent Institutions or People?

There are broadly two reasons why double auction markets work: subjects are very
clever, or double auction markets are very clever. It is probably a bit of both. To
illustrate why, we can look at a study by Gode and Sunder (1993) They compared
what happens in double auction markets if choices are made by 'zero-intelligence'
computer programs rather than human subjects.

They use two versions of zero intelligence. In the first, each trader randomly generated bids or offers, and so there was no sense to behavior at all. This really does look

like a zero-intelligence trader. In the second, each trader randomly generated bids or offers, but would never do a deal that would lose them money. So a seller never sold for less than value, and a buyer never sold for more than value. I will call this a 'don't sell at a loss' trader. Table 2.8 gives a snapshot of the results by comparing the efficiency of markets with humans to those with zero-intelligence traders. The main result is that 'don't sell at a loss' seems enough to get high efficiency.

Table 2.8 The market efficiency of five experimental markets, comparing human participants to zero-intelligent traders

Participants	Market efficiency (%) in market				
	1	*2*	*3*	*4*	*5*
Zero intelligence	90.0	90.0	76.7	48.8	86.0
Don't sell at a loss	99.9	99.2	99.0	98.2	97.1
Human	99.7	99.1	100.0	99.1	90.2

Source: Gode and Sunder (1993)

How should we interpret this result? It would appear to demonstrate the relevance of heuristics because the simple, 'don't sell at a loss' heuristic is enough to achieve market efficiency. We need to be a little careful, however, to distinguish institutions from individuals. This is because an individual trader may want to use something more subtle than this heuristic, and there was good evidence that human subjects did do that. The main lesson, therefore, is that some institutions can work well even if people use only the most basic of heuristics. This does not imply that people do use only the most basic of heuristics, but it does mean that institutions can be clever, and potentially make up for a lack of subtlety in people's strategy or behavior.

Having given the good news, it is time for some of the bad. Markets are not always so efficient, for a variety of reasons. In chapter five we shall see how efficiency can decrease if buyers and sellers have some uncertainty about the value of the good. Here I shall look at a host of other reasons efficiency may be less, starting with a brief look at posted offer markets.

2.4.2 Posted offer markets and market power

To give an illustration of what happens in posted offer markets I will look at a study by Ketcham, Smith and Williams (1984). Figure 2.15 summarizes the differences between prices and quantities observed in double auction and posted offer markets averaged over the 12 experimental markets of the study. As expected, in the double auction price and quantity converged over the periods towards the equilibrium. The same cannot be said in the posted offer market. In this case prices stayed consistently above the equilibrium and quantity below the equilibrium, and there is no evidence that this would change if the market were to be repeated more times.

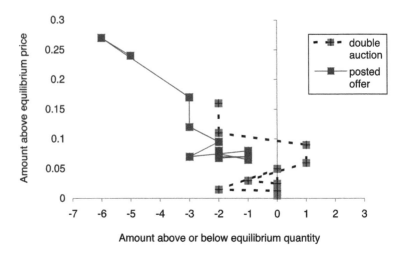

Figure 2.15 The deviation from equilibrium price and quantity in experimental double
auction and posted offer markets.

Source: Smith (2002).

It is not too much of a surprise that we do not always see convergence to the
market equilibrium in posted offer markets. This is because suppliers have an
incentive to try and keep the price high. To illustrate, we can look back at the third
set of possible trades in Table 2.7. In this case the price is pushed above the equilibrium and while total profit is less than at equilibrium the profit of sellers is
higher than at equilibrium, $2.08 compared to $1.50. Things are not so simple
because sellers do not share the profit so have an incentive to compete amongst
each other for their share of the profit. The basic incentive to push prices
higher exists, however, and a posted offer market gives sellers more possibility to
do so.

Sellers can keep prices high because they have the power to set prices. They can
signal to each other from one period to the next through the prices they offer and
potentially collude on higher prices. Prices are, therefore, higher because sellers
have market power.

More generally, we observe that market power can move the price away from
the market equilibrium.

2.4.3 *The law of one price*

The final institution to look at is negotiated price. In looking at this type of market
it is pertinent to mention the law of one price. The **law of one price** is that all
items should be sold at the same price in market equilibrium. For instance, in
Figure 2.12 we predict all items are sold at $2.50. In a double auction this is what
we typically do see, and this is not surprising, given that all buyers and sellers

automatically have access to the same information. If we consider institutions where buyers and/or sellers have to search for information, then things change.

We can illustrate by looking at a negotiated price market from one of the first ever recorded economic experiments by Chamberlin (1948). Recall that in this institution, buyers and sellers move around the room, interact personally, and try to do a deal on a one-to-one basis. This makes it possible that people on one side of the room could be agreeing a different price to people on the other side of the room. Figure 2.16 summarizes what happened in the market. The equilibrium price was 5.7 but we can see that the actually prices traded vary considerably from as low as 4 to as high as 7.2. The law of one price does not hold in this market. Interestingly, however, the average price comes out at 5.3, which is not that far from the equilibrium.

This large variation of individual prices but an average price close to the equilibrium is what we typically observe in this type of market. So, demand and supply are still reliable predictors of what will happen in the market but are not so reliable a predictor of what will happen in a specific transaction. Why?

The person who sold at $4 and the person who bought at $7.20 could have come together and agreed a price of $5.60. This would mean both make an extra profit of $1.60 and would mean the traded price would have been a lot closer to the equilibrium. Why did they not do that? Presumably they never met to talk about this possibility. Both could have searched a bit longer, or harder, for a better deal. The problem is that such search is costly, not only in time and effort, but also in potentially missing out on a good deal. For example, selling at $4 might look like

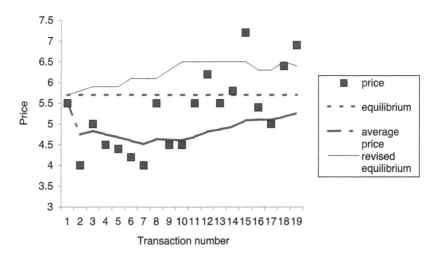

Figure 2.16 The prices traded in an negotiated price market. The prices vary a lot but the average ends up close to equilibrium. As trades are being done and buyers and sellers leave the market, the demand and supply curve changes, so we should concentrate more on the revised equilibrium price than equilibrium price.

Source: Chamberlin (1948).

a good deal to the seller, remember he or she has no idea what the market demand is, so should they risk losing that deal to search for a better one? Potentially not, and so search costs and reference points are a good reason we should not expect to see the law of one price.

Search costs are clearly relevant in many markets. You might have an idea what the price of a textbook is, but you cannot know for sure the price of different sellers without a little bit of effort. This means we should not be surprised to see variation in prices for an identical good that is sold at more than one location. This is the case irrespective of the institution used to sell the good. To illustrate this, Pratt, Wise and Zeckhauser (1979) randomly opened the Yellow Pages of the Boston telephone directory to select 39 products, and then rang all the advertised sellers for each product to see how much they charged. Figure 2.17 illustrates the large variability in prices across sellers. The maximum price was often twice that of the minimum.

The data in Figure 2.17 is arranged in order of increasing price. Carnations are cheapest, with a price of $0.33, and a boat the most expensive, with a price of $602.87. One slightly curious thing is that the relative variability in price does not decline for more expensive items. To better understand why this is curious, consider this question:

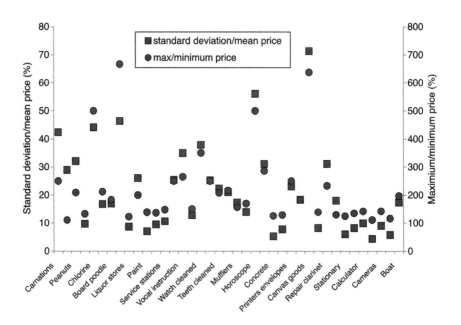

Figure 2.17 The law of one price does not hold in many markets. The standard deviation in price is typically more than 10 to 20 percent of the mean price. The maximum price is typically twice or more the minimum price available.

Source: Pratt, Wise and Zeckhauser (1979).

You are about to purchase a jacket for $125 and a calculator for $15. The salesman tells you that the calculator is $5 cheaper at another branch of the store 20 minutes' drive away. Would you make the trip to the other store?

Now imagine the jacket costs $15 and the calculator $125.

Tversky and Kahneman (1981) report how 68 percent of those they surveyed would make the trip to save $5 on an item costing $15 but only 29 percent would make the trip to save $5 on something costing $125. Either way, the person will save $5 and so it is slightly strange that it matters whether the saving is on a cheap or expensive item. Put another way, however, the person will save 33 percent in the one case and 4 percent in the other, so if we have a heuristic that says 4 percent is not a good saving but 33 percent is, then things become easier to explain.

Now let's return to search costs. There is no reason to suppose the cost of search depends on the price of the item being sold. So, if someone puts the same effort into searching for a $1 saving on all goods, we should see less variability in the relative price of expensive items. We do not see this. If someone puts the same effort into searching for a 1 percent saving on all goods, then the variability in relative prices should not depend on the price of the good. This is what we do seem to observe.

This focus on relative rather than absolute savings is the first indication we have seen in this section that framing and perceptions can influence a person's willingness to trade. What I want to do now is look at two specific markets where we might expect a bit more evidence that framing and perceptions matter.

2.5 Reference dependence, labor supply and housing

The story told in the previous section is largely one where it is obvious if someone has made a profit, and so gains and losses are easy to calculate. The buyer wants to sell for less than she values the good, and the seller wants to sell for more than the cost of the good. In some markets that story is all we need, but in others it misses something, because it may not be obvious what counts as a gain or a loss, or selling at a profit. In other words, it may not be clear what the relevant reference point is and this can have implications for how the market works. I shall illustrate by looking at labor supply and the housing market.

2.5.1 Labor supply

In the labor market it is natural to think of people deciding how many hours they want to work at the going wage. For example, if Anna is an accountant then she needs to decide how many clients to take on, whether to work full-time or part-time, and so on. Anna may have a reference level of hours that she wants to work, or a reference level of income that she wants to earn. This reference level could be determined by a variety of things, but what has previously happened, or what friends and peers are doing, are two likely candidates. Before we look at some data it is useful to have a model of labor supply to see how the reference level may matter.

The standard way of modeling labor supply is to think of the utility function $u(x, H)$ which depends on wealth x and the number of hours spent working H. To measure the benefit of working we need the hourly wage rate w. Anna trades wealth for leisure time and if we solve for the optimal amount of hours she should work we get a condition like:

$$-\frac{du}{dH} = w\frac{du}{dx}. \tag{2.1}$$

This means that the disutility from an extra hour of work should be offset by the utility she gets from the money earned by working an extra hour.

Figure 2.18 gives two examples of how Anna's utility may change as she works more or less. The marginal disutility of working is assumed to increase the more she works in both examples. What differs is that in one she has a reference level for working eight hours a day. This causes a big change in the disutility of working at eight hours. Anna is relatively happy to continue work if she has worked less than eight hours, but is relatively unhappy to continue work if she has already worked more than eight hours. Consequently, equation (2.1) is likely to be satisfied when she works eight hours and labor supply is likely to be insensitive to changes in the wage.

The story when there is a target level of income is relatively similar. Figure 2.19 illustrates what may happen if Anna has $10,000 in wealth and wants to increase her income by $160. Extra income is worth relatively more when she has earned

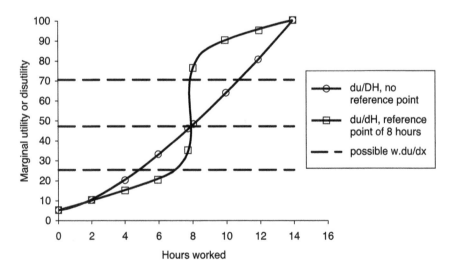

Figure 2.18 Two possible utility functions. If there is a reference level of eight hours work the utility function becomes S-shaped and the number of hours worked will not change much as the wage changes.

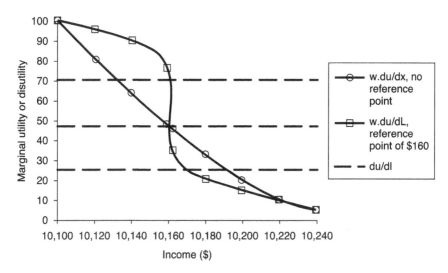

Figure 2.19 If there is a reference level of earning $160 the utility function becomes S-shaped. An increase in wages will cause a decrease in hours worked because the target of $160 can be achieved more easily.

less that the target than when she is above the target. Consequently, amount earned will be relatively insensitive to changes in the disutility of working. The number of hours worked would, however, change if the wage rate changes. A higher wage would mean Anna can work less hours and still reach her target, while a lower wage would mean Anna needs to work more hours to reach the target.

In practice we might expect that Anna has both a target income and target number of hours she wants to work. This comes out in the first set of data I want to look at. The people who arguably have most control over how many hours they work are self-employed workers. An example that has attracted some interest amongst economists is that of taxicab drivers. Many taxicab drivers lease a cab from a taxi leasing company and keep any money they make from fares or tips, net of fuel costs. By choosing when to start and end the shift, and how many breaks to have, the driver has complete control over how long he works and some control over his income. In New York City, taxicab drivers are required to fill out trip sheets which record details on all the trips done during a shift, including times, locations and fares. The trip sheets are a great source of data to look at labor supply. To illustrate, I will look at a study by Farber (2005, 2008) of 21 New York City taxicab drivers working in 1999 and 2000.

What we can focus on is the probability that a driver ends his shift at a particular point in time. Things that might influence that decision are the hours already worked, income already earned, and things like the weather and time of day. Demand for taxicabs varies a lot across days and within the course of a day, meaning that the wage rate *w* will fluctuate a lot day to day and during the day. We saw that if drivers focus on a reference level of hours they want to work, fluctuations in the wage should make little difference to the number of hours they work. By contrast, if drivers focus on a target level of income, changes in the wage should affect hours worked.

To see what does happen we can estimate the probability that a driver will stop after each trip. Figure 2.20 summarizes what we get from estimating this probability. It shows the change in the probability that a driver ends his shift, compared to if he has worked nine hours and earned $150–175. We see that drivers are far more likely to stop after having worked ten or more hours. By contrast, income earned has very little effect. [Extra] These probabilities were estimated by writing the probability that driver i on day j will stop after trip t by:

$$P_{ijt} = \Phi(X_{ijt}\beta)$$

where Φ is the cumulative normal distribution and $X_{ijt}\beta$ is a term that includes things like the number of hours worked and the time of day.

Figure 2.20 suggests that drivers primarily stop after having worked a certain number of hours, and not after reaching a target level of income. Clearly, this is consistent with a reference level of hours worked (but see review question 2.9). It does not, however, completely rule out there being a subsidiary target level of income. To check this, we can plug a target income into the equation we estimate and see whether we get a better fit with the data. Doing this suggests that drivers do indeed have a target level of income. Somewhat strangely, however, we also find that the target fluctuates a lot from day to day. In particular, the mean target was

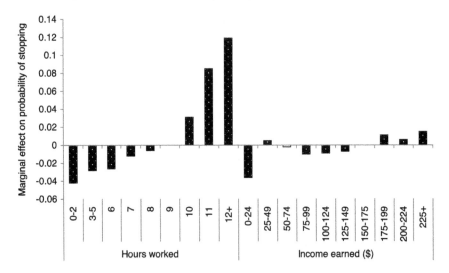

Figure 2.20 The probability that a driver stops his shift compared to when he has worked nine hours and earned $150–175. Drivers were significantly more likely to stop if they had worked ten or more hours. The decision to stop was not influenced much by income already earned.

Source: Farber (2005).

$196 but the standard error $91. So, a driver might have a target income of $120 one day, $250 the next, and so on. It is not so easy to interpret what this means.

[Extra] To check whether drivers do have a target income, we can slightly change the equation estimated to:

$$P_{ijt} = \begin{cases} \Phi\left(X_{ijt}\beta + \delta\right) \text{ if } y_{ijt} \geq r_{ij} \\ \Phi\left(X_{ijt}\beta\right) \text{ if } y_{ijt} < r_{ij} \end{cases}.$$

where r_{ij} is a reference level of income for driver i on day j and y_{ijt} is current income. If current income is above the reference point, $y_{ijt} \geq r_{ij}$, then the larger is δ, the higher the probability the driver will stop. Term δ therefore measures the potential importance of a target level of income. We can assume that the reference point is determined by:

$$r_{ij} = R_i + \varepsilon_{ij}$$

where R_i is the average reference level of driver i, which may fluctuate day to day. On estimating δ, R_i and β it turns out that δ is significantly greater than zero and so there does appear to be a target level of income.

The overall picture we get from the taxicab data is that drivers might have a target level of income, but the number of hours they have worked seems a more dominant factor. I now want to look at some data that gives a slightly different perspective. Most workers do not have as much flexibility as these taxi drivers in how many hours a day they work. Often choices are restricted to a more discrete choice of whether to work full-time or part-time, or to work at all, but this still raises some interesting issues. For instance, Figure 2.21 plots the growth in labor force participation of women in the US and UK since the Second World War. Clearly there is a significant rise in the number of women choosing to work. Why?

If we look at equation 2.1, then either the wage increased, the utility of money increased, or the disutility of working decreased. Changes in wages and the disutility of work can account for a lot of the increase in participation. For example, lower fertility and the growth of the service sector are two reasons why the disutility of work could have decreased for women. I want to focus more, however, on the possibility that the utility of money has changed. Why would it have? If people want to earn a similar amount to friends and family then the fact that some women enter employment (because of the higher wages and decreased disutility of work) could spur other women to enter employment so as to not fall behind.

Neumark and Postlewaite (1998) explore this possibility with data on a sample of US women who become of employable age in the 1980s. They question whether a women is more likely to work if her sister-in-law works, or if her sister's husband earns more than her husband.

[Extra] To see how this is done, let P_{it} denote the probability women i is employed at time t. To see whether a women is more likely to work if her sister-in-law also works we can fit equation

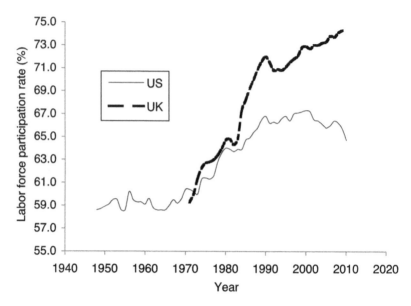

Figure 2.21 The participation rate of women aged 16 and above in the US and UK.

Sources: Bureau of Labor Statistics and Office for National Statistics.

$$P_{it} = \Lambda(X_{it}\beta + \gamma SL)$$

where $X_{it}\beta$ captures things like education, Λ is the logistic cumulative probability distribution and SL is one or zero depending on whether the sister-in-law works. The bigger is γ the more likely a women will work if her sister-in-law works. To see whether a women is more likely to work if her sister's husband earns more than her husband we can fit

$$P_{it} = \Lambda(X_{it}\beta + \gamma HM)$$

where HM is one or zero depending on whether the sister's husband earns more.

Figure 2.22 summarizes the main results. We see that a women's choice to work or not did seem to be significantly affected by what her sister or sister-in-law was doing. She was more likely to work if her sister-in-law worked, and a lot more likely to work if her sister worked and her sister's husband earned more than her husband! This is consistent with a person, or family, being influenced by a reference level of income that depends on what others are earning.

We have now seen evidence that workers can have a reference level of hours they want to work and a reference or target level of income they want to earn. This is important in understanding individual labor supply but also important in

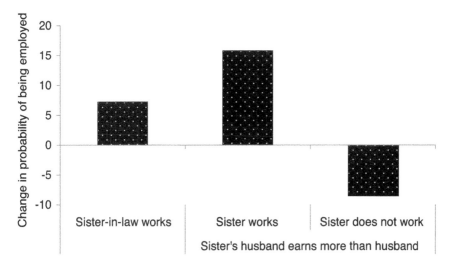

Figure 2.22 The change in probability of a women being in employment depends on whether her sister-in-law works and her sister's husband earns more or not than her husband.

Source: Neumark and Postlewaite (1998).

understanding how the labor market works. That's because the reference point will partly determine what is counted as a gain or loss and so also partly determine the equilibrium price and quantity. We see this in the large increase in the number of women working, and in the price of a taxicab in the middle of the night.

2.5.2 *The housing market*

The second market I want to look at is the housing market. Buying property is one of the bigger decisions most people will make in their life and can be thought of as both a consumption and investment decision. People want somewhere nice to live, but are also aware that the value of a house can increase or decrease, and the more it increases the better. Figure 2.23 plots the average property price and number of sales by month in England and Wales between January 1995 and December 2009. The price clearly increases over this time, but not without periods of decline. Knowing when to sell or buy, and what price to ask or bid are financially important and complicated decisions. But what is an appropriate reference point to say what is a gain or loss?

Let's look first at what price Anna might want to sell her flat. She could use two natural reference prices: the price that other similar properties are selling for, and the price she originally paid for it. For instance, selling for less than she originally paid might be interpreted as a loss, while selling for more is interpreted as a gain. To see the implications of this, suppose that Anna bought her flat for $80,000

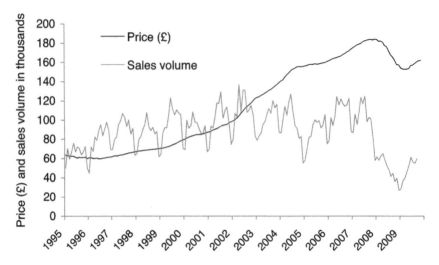

Figure 2.23 The average selling price of residential property and sales volume in England
and Wales.

Source: Land Registry.

while John bought an almost identical flat for $100,000. Both are looking to sell,
and the price of other similar flats is $90,000. For Anna, selling at $90,000
feels like a gain, so she might be happy to sell at this price, or maybe even slightly
less. For John, selling at $90,000 feels like a loss. Loss aversion might mean he
tries selling his flat at something like $95,000, or even decides to not sell his flat
at all.

A study by Genesove and Mayer (2001) puts this prediction to the test with data
from downtown Boston in the 1990s. They use data from over 5,000 apartments
put up for sale between 1990 and 1997. Most importantly they have data on the
price someone bought an apartment for and the price they first listed it when
trying to sell. They also have estimates of market value and any outstanding loan
at sale. This latter number is important to rule out people being reluctant to sell
below the price they paid because they have to repay the loan used for purchase.

What Genesove and Mayer find is that someone, like John, who is expected to
make a loss, does ask for a higher price and has to wait longer to sell, but does sell
at a higher price. It seems, therefore, that sellers may be averse to selling a house
for less than they paid for it. This helps us better understand the housing market.
In particular, one puzzling thing we observe in housing data, and that can be seen
in Figure 2.23, is that sales volume falls during a slump in prices. If prices fall, we
might expect demand to pick up, not fall. This becomes easier to explain once
we account for loss aversion. If prices fall, and people are unwilling to sell at a
loss, then we can predict less property being put up for sale and prices being above
what they should be. This clearly suggests lower sales.

What is less clear is whether loss aversion benefits a potential seller or not. To put the magnitude of loss aversion into context, we can plug in the numbers estimated by Genesove and Mayer into the Anna and John example. Anna would have asked for $90,000 and sold for this after around 60 days. John would have tried to recoup 25–35 percent of his 'loss' and so would have asked for around $93,000 and actually recouped 3 to 18 percent of the loss by selling for say $91,000. He would have had to have waited around 6 percent longer, but this only equates to an extra four days. It seems as though John does not do so badly!

It is not as simple as that, however, because people who sell, also typically buy. A slump in the market may be a good opportunity to sell, even if at a loss, and upsize to a more expensive property. Someone who does not want to sell at a loss could miss this opportunity. Or perhaps they need to do a bit of hedonic editing and alter their reference point to focus on the gain they can make on the property they will buy, rather than the loss on the property they will sell.

This brings us on to the buyers. What price should someone be willing to pay for property? The price of similar property may be the most natural reference point in this case. A nice way to see whether it is, is to follow people who relocate from one area of the country to another. To illustrate, suppose Anna currently lives in an area where a good apartment costs $90,000 and she is going to relocate due to work. If, where she is moving, apartments cost around $70,000, they will look cheap, but if they average $120,000 they will look expensive. Reference dependence suggests that she might be happy to buy something for less than $90,000 but be averse to spending anything more than $90,000.

A study by Simonsohn and Loewenstein (2006) puts this prediction to the test by looking at data on people in the US relocating between 1983 and 1993. They question whether the average rent or house price in the location a person moved from significantly affects the price they pay where they move to. They find that it does matter. A 10 percent difference in the median rent or property price at the location moved from causes an increase of around 2 percent in the rent paid or purchase price at destination. You might say that this could be because of preferences or something else. They also find, however, that when people move for a second time, this time the same area, any differences disappear. It seems, therefore, as if the reference point readjusts as people live in the area for some time. Reference dependence does, therefore, really matter.

2.6 The Behavioral Life Cycle Hypothesis

Having spent some time looking at markets I now want to move on to another of the more important and controversial ideas in economics, the life cycle hypothesis. The **life cycle hypothesis** comes in various different guises but the basic idea is relatively simple: a person should take a long-term view about their future income and smooth consumption over their lifetime to maximize expected utility. Figure 2.24 gives a stylized illustration of the model. We see that income goes through large variation over the lifecycle, as Anna earns little when a student, has increased income as she works and gets promoted, and then little income again

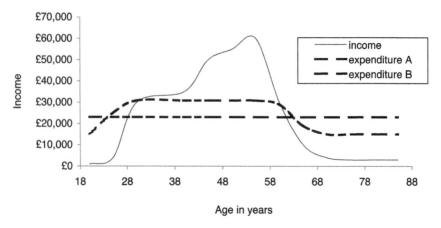

Figure 2.24 An illustration of consumption smoothing. Income varies a lot with age but consumption can be completely smoothed, as in schedule A, or partly smoothed, as in schedule B.

when she retires. Presumably she will want her standard of living and consumption to be more stable than this (something we shall discuss in chapter four). Consequently she may smooth consumption by borrowing in her student years, saving during her working years, and using her savings during retirement. Smoothing consumption completely would give schedule A. More realistic is something like schedule B. where consumption does change with age because, for example, of having children.

Rather than rely on the stylized illustration in Figure 2.24 we can look at some actual data. When we look at consumption over the lifetime we typically find an inverted U shape like that in Figure 2.25. This inverted U shape has been observed in different countries, and for all types of workers, education background etc. An alternative view is obtained by looking at consumption over calendar time. Figure 2.26 shows what typically happens when we do this. It is very noticeable that consumption is cyclical and changes by as much as 11 percent from trough to peak. Unsurprisingly, these cycles coincide with the business cycle.

Figures 2.25 and 2.26 do not look very consistent with the life cycle hypothesis. Instead it seems as though consumption tracks income with little sign of consumption smoothing. If we factor in the effects of children and a desire to be prudent, or to not want to spend uncertain and unearned future income, then we could argue that the data in Figures 2.25 and 2.26 is consistent with the life cycle hypothesis. But, that essentially amounts to arguing that the optimal thing is to not smooth consumption! This seems an unsatisfactory conclusion.

A more realistic perspective is to acknowledge that people undeniably do smooth consumption over their lifetime by saving for retirement, borrowing when a student, or borrowing to buy a first home. But they do not smooth consumption

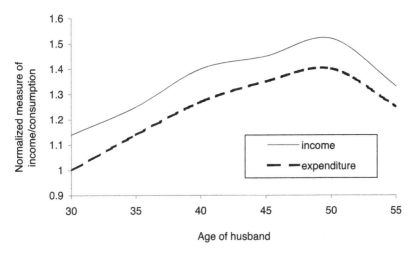

Figure 2.25 An inverse U-shaped consumption and income pattern derived from UK couples with a husband born between 1936 and 1943. Cyclical and growth effects are removed from the data.

Source: Browning and Crossley (2001).

as much as we might expect because consumption seems to track current income more closely and be more sensitive to macroeconomic cycles than would seem reasonable. We need to try and understand why this is the case. One potential contributory factor is mental accounting.

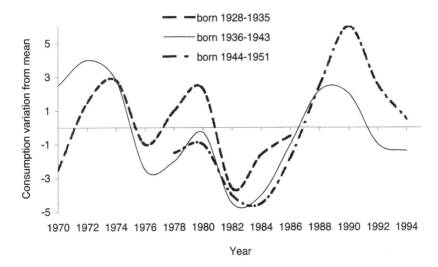

Figure 2.26 Consumption patterns over time derived from UK data.

Source: Browning and Crossley (2001).

2.6.1 *Fungibility and mental accounting*

Mental accounting and narrow framing are very important in thinking about the life cycle hypothesis. That's because the life cycle hypothesis assumes **fungibility**, meaning that all money is treated the same, no matter where it came from. If people keep mental accounts then money is likely to be segregated according to how it was obtained and so is not fungibile.

To illustrate, consider these three scenarios:

> You have been given a special bonus at work, meaning you will receive $200 a month over the next year.
> You have been given a special bonus at work, meaning you will receive a lump sum payment of $2,400.
> You have been told of a distant relative who has left you an after-tax inheritance of $2,400, but you will not receive the money for five years.

In all three scenarios your wealth will increase by $2,400. Fungibility requires that the use to which you put this extra money should not depend on where it came from. You should just think how you will spend the $2,400 over the rest of your lifetime. In reality things seem different, as the results of a study by Shefrin and Thaler (1998) illustrate. Figure 2.27 shows a stark difference in how much of the extra $2,400 people said they would consume over the following year. If the money can from the regular payment people planned to consume half of it in one year, but if it came from a future inheritance would spend none of it.

Broadly speaking we can think that households keep in mind three basic mental accounts, a current income account, an asset account, and a future income account.

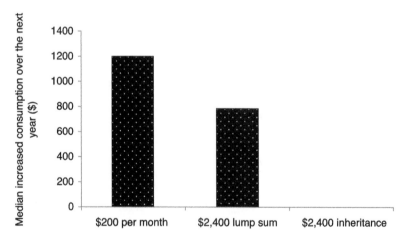

Figure 2.27 The amount of the $2,400 subjects thought they would spend in the next year. The origin of the money significantly affects the amount subjects expected to spend.

Source: Shefrin and Thaler (1998).

The **current income account** is for day-to-day spending. We would expect that the **marginal propensity to consume** from this account, or the proportion of the money spent, is relatively high, because the money is there to be spent. The **asset account** is for saving and investing for things like retirement or a new house. We would expect a much lower marginal propensity to consume from this account. Indeed, its purpose maybe to commit the household to save adequately. Finally, the **future income account** includes predictable future income such as from a pension, inheritance or expected salary increases. The marginal propensity to consume from this account is likely to be very low if people are reluctant to spend income they do not have.

These predicted differences in the marginal propensity to consume are not consistent with fungibility. They are, however, consistent with the data in Figure 2.27. A regular payment of $200 a month is more likely to be added to the current income account. A lump sum payment may be saved in the asset account. The inheritance is clearly put in the future income account. This can help explain the decreasing marginal propensity to consume.

Fortunately we have a wealth of expenditure data with which to move beyond hypothetical surveys to real choices. I will look at three examples.

The first example concerns a tax rebate in the US in 2001. Most US households over a ten-week period received a rebate of either $300 or $600. The rebate could have been predicted because the policy was widely publicized and was part of a long-term change in tax policy. There was, therefore, a gap between a person knowing they would get $300 or $600 and actually getting the money. Fungibility requires that people should start spending the money as soon as they know they will get it, and not when they actually get it (unless they have insufficient money). Mental accounting would suggest that receipt of the money moves it from the future income account to either the current income or asset account and so the money is treated differently once it is received.

Johnson et al. (2006) looked at expenditure data on what households did with the money, and paid particular attention to whether receiving the rebate made any difference to spending. Figure 2.28 shows the change in spending in the three months after the rebate arrived compared to the three months before the rebate. Different households received the money at different times, so there is no possibility this difference is due to some seasonal effect. It looks like receipt of the money did make a difference to spending. This is consistent with mental accounting, not fungibility.

Another interesting thing about this rebate is that what households did with it seemed slightly at odds with what they planned to do with it. For example, Shapiro and Slemrod (2003) surveyed households about what they planned to do with the rebate. Only 22 percent of those surveyed expected to spend the rebate. Most expected to pay back debt. This suggests that households planned to put the money in the asset account. This is seemingly confirmed by Agarwal et al. (2008), who showed that households did initially 'save' the money by paying off debt, such as credit card debt. Soon after, however, their spending rose.

We can pick up on this distinction between the current and asset account in the second example I will look at. In this example the focus is on Israeli recipients of

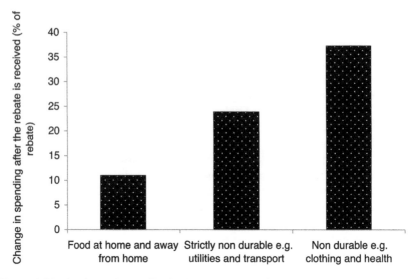

Figure 2.28 The change in spending in the three months after receiving the rebate compared
to the three months before receiving the rebate.

Source: Johnson et al. (2006).

German restitution payments in the late 1950s. Families received a lump sum
'windfall payment' of varying amounts. Landsberger (1966) looked at what
people did with the money and compared it to normal spending. The results are
summarized in Figure 2.29. The difference between the marginal propensity to
consume from normal income and the windfall is large. As with the tax rebate this
suggests a lack of fungibility. More interesting is how the size of the windfall
seemed to matter in terms of how much a family spent of the money. A small
payment was spent twice over, while a large payment was primarily saved. This
illustrates how the amount of money can matter in terms of what mental account
it is put into. A small windfall is added to the current account and a big windfall
added to the savings account.

The final example I want to look is very different to the previous two. It demonstrates how accounts can be more narrowly defined than the three accounts I have
mentioned so far. Often, money is given for a specific reason. For example, child
benefit is given to families with children. Fungibility would suggest that households should ignore the reason they got the money. Mental accounting suggests
they may not. Kooreman (2000) looks at data from the Dutch child benefit system
from 1978 to 1994. Over these years various changes to the benefit system allow
us to try and estimate whether child benefit is used to buy things for children. In
the study, the focus was put on the amount spent on clothing in families with one
child. Figure 2.30 summarizes the main finding. The marginal propensity to

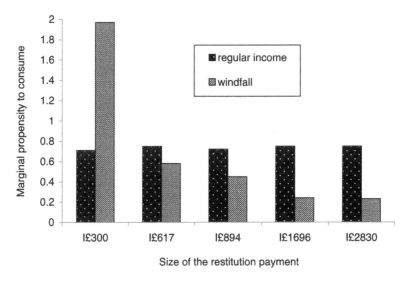

Figure 2.29 The marginal propensity to consume the windfall gain compared to normal income of Israeli recipients of German restitution payments.

Source: Landsberger (1966).

consume child clothing out of child benefit was much larger than that from other income. By contrast, the marginal propensity to consume adult clothing out of child benefit is much less than that from other income. It seems that child benefit was spent on the child.

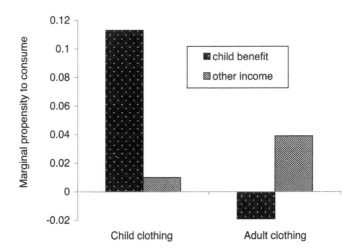

Figure 2.30 The marginal propensity to consume clothing our of normal income and child benefit.

Source: Kooreman (2000).

All three of these examples show a lack of fungibility. Households treat money differently depending on where it comes from, how much it was, and for what purpose it was given. There are lots of other examples I could give to demonstrate the same basic conclusion (see review question 2.11). Given what we saw, however, in section 2.2 it should could as no surprise. If people keep mental accounts then it is natural that money should not easily flow from one account to the next. The question we need to get back to is what implications this has for the life cycle hypothesis?

One thing we have seen is that people seem reluctant to spend future unearned income. Only when they got the money did households spend the tax rebate and restitution payment. We know, more generally, that people do spend unearned income. Student debt and families taking out a mortgage to buy a house are ample evidence of this. The point is, however, that people may spend less of their unearned income than the life cycle hypothesis might suggest they should. Given that most people get increasing amounts of money through their lifetime this would mean spending tracks income more than would be predicted by the life cycle hypothesis. This is what we observe.

2.7 Saving for the future

One particularly important aspect of the life cycle hypothesis is saving. People need to save enough for retirement, to buy a house, or new car, and so on. A survey of faculty and staff at the University of Southern California by Benartzi and Thaler (1999) found that 58 percent spent less than one hour determining their contribution rate and investment decisions to a savings plan. This is presumably quite typical, but these are important, complicated decisions, and so it is slightly worrying that so little time is spent making them. Put another way, however, people must be using simple heuristics to help them make decisions so quickly. Maybe these heuristics help them make the right decisions?

To illustrate the heuristics we do observe, Figure 2.31 plots the distribution of contribution rates of those joining a large retirement savings plan in 2001 or 2002. The contribution rate is the proportion of income that people allocate to the savings plan. Three heuristics are apparent in this data. First is to **pick a multiple of five** as seen in the notable spikes at 5, 10 and 15 percent. Second is to **pick the maximum allowed**. In 2001 the maximum allowed in this contribution plan was 16 percent, but in 2002 the maximum was increased to 100 percent. We can see that this caused a big fall in the proportion choosing 16 percent or more. Finally, in most contribution plans, the employer will match the contribution of an employer up to some limit. The third heuristic is to **pick the maximum to get a full employer match**. In this plan that maximum was 6 percent, explaining why so many chose this contribution rate.

With these three heuristics we can get a good feel for why the contribution rate is distributed as in Figure 2.31. Next I want to look in a bit more detail at one important kind of heuristic we have not seen yet.

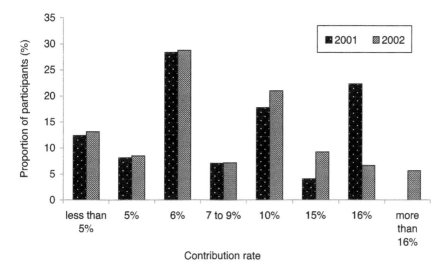

Figure 2.31 The contribution rate of people enrolled in a large defined contribution plan.
Source: Benartzi and Thaler (2007).

2.7.1 Let's diversify

As well as deciding how much to save, an investor also needs to decide where to save, or invest. The typical contribution retirement savings plan will give the saver a set of funds or investment opportunities that they can invest the money into. For example, Benartzi and Thaler (2001) look at a database from the Money Market Directories that covers 170 retirement savings plans with 1.56 million participants. The average number of investment options available in a plan was around six to seven. For example, a plan might allow participants to split investments between an equity, international equity, corporate bonds, balanced growth, government bonds and money market funds.

Deciding where to invest is a complex choice. One option is to use a simple **diversification strategy**, called the 1/n heuristic. The **1/n heuristic** is to split the amount to be saved or invested equally among the available funds. A simple heuristic, but one that leaves the saver exposed to any bias in the options on offer. For example, compare a plan that has three equity options and one money option to one with two equity options and two money options. In the first someone using the 1/n heuristic would invest 75 percent in equity and in the second they would invest 50 percent. That's a big difference.

Do we observe people using the 1/n heuristic? Benartzi and Thaler categorized the investment plans in their data as having a low, medium or high proportion of equity fund options. Figure 2.32 compares the proportion of equity fund options with the proportion invested in equities. We can immediately see that things are not as simple as the 1/n heuristic would suggest because the proportion invested is

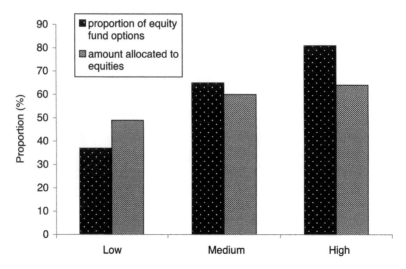

Figure 2.32 The proportion of funds that were based on equities and the proportion of savings that savers invested in equity. Those in plans with more equity funds invested more in equity.

Source: Benartzi and Thaler (2001).

more consistent across plans than the proportion of equity fund options offered. Even so those in a plan with a larger number of equity fund options do invest significantly more in equities.

It is hard to justify such a systematic difference in investments without people being biased by the options they have to choose from. To illustrate this further Benartzi and Thaler analyze data from a specific company. The company is interesting because at the end of 1994 and 1996 the fund options available to investors were changed. Figure 2.33 charts the change in investment patterns over time. In 1994 four new fund options were made available. In 1996 the bond fund was withdrawn. You can see that by the end of 1997 investments are quite evenly split amongst the remaining possible funds. The remarkable thing about this is that it means there was a huge shift in exposure to equity funds. In 1993 only 18 percent of investments were in equity but by 1997 that has rise to 76 percent. It is highly unlikely that this shift is because of a change in preferences or the optimal portfolio!

2.7.2 Let's not diversify

The 1/n heuristic makes most sense if n is not very large, i.e. the number of options is small. What if the number of options is large? Then we might get a **conditional 1/n heuristic** of picking a small number of funds and dividing investments equally amongst these.

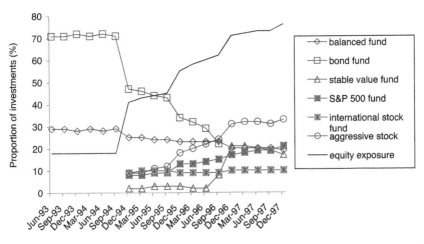

Figure 2.33 The proportion of investments in each fund of a companies' contribution savings plan. In 1994 new funds are added and in 1996 the bond fund withdrawn. The amount invested in equities increases a lot as a consequence.

Source: Benartzi and Thaler (2001).

Huberman and Jiang (2006) looked at the investment decisions of over half a million participants of defined contribution plans in 2001. Figure 2.34 compares the number of funds participants chose to invest in versus the number of funds offered. The majority of participants were in plans with over ten funds to choose from. Despite this, the majority of participants chose to invest in only one to five of the possible funds. Investors were clearly, therefore, selective in where they invested, consistent with the first part of the conditional 1/n heuristic.

To check the second part of the conditional 1/n heuristic we need to see how participants allocated their investments between the funds they did invest in. This is not simple to do, because the value of funds goes up or down over time, and so even if an investor did split her investments equally across funds initially, it may not look this way a few years later. To compensate for this, Huberman and Jian look at new participants. Figure 2.35 summarizes for each choice of number of funds the proportion of new participants that invest consistent with the 1/n heuristic. We see that a high proportion of those investing in two, four, five and ten funds do seem to use the 1/n heuristic. Intuitively this makes sense because then 1/n is a round number. Figure 2.35 is misleading as to the total proportion who use the 1/n heuristic because we need to factor in the proportion of participants who chose one, two, and three funds etc. Doing this we find that over 70 percent of participants behaved consistent with a conditional 1/n heuristic.

Figure 2.32 suggested investors may be biased towards investing in equity if the proportion of equity funds offered is high. It was clear, however, that the differences in investments chosen were smaller than those of investments offered. Huberman and Jiang draw a similar conclusion, finding only a small positive

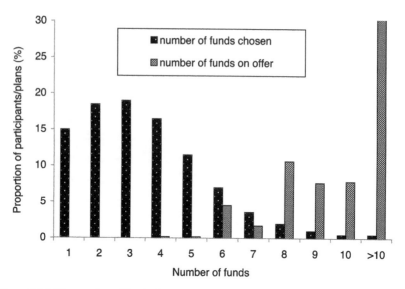

Figure 2.34 The number of funds that savers invest in and are on offer in a large sample of defined contribution plans. A typical plan offers ten or more funds. Most savers invest in one to five funds.

Source: Huberman and Jiang (2006).

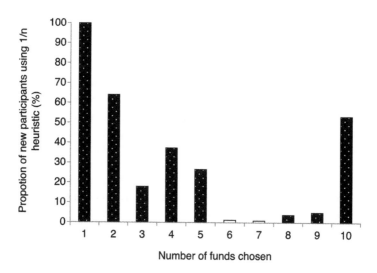

Figure 2.35 The proportion of new participants that behave consistent with the conditional 1/n heuristic, i.e. split their investments equally between the funds they invest in.

Source: Huberman and Jiang (2006).

correlation between the number of equity funds offered and the number chosen. One possibility is that when the number of offered funds is small, as in Figure 2.33, investors are biased by the number of equity funds on offer, but if the number of funds is large investors are not so biased by the proportion of equity funds.

Whether this is true or not, the picture we get is one of investors using simple heuristics to make complex choices. What's not so clear is whether these heuristics are optimal for the investor. It's hard to believe that, by some happy co-incidence, a contribution rate of 10 percent, or a split of 75 to 25 percent between equities and money, is optimal. Maybe, however, a contribution rate of 10 percent is nearly as good as the true optimum of, say, 9.34 or 11.28 percent? Maybe it is not so bad that investors increase their exposure to equity because of a change in the funds on offer? These are important questions, and so we will come back to them in subsequent chapters.

2.8 Further reading

There is an overlap between this chapter and the next in terms of further reading for sections 2.1 and 2.2. That said, the papers by Tversky and Kahneman (1981, 1986), Kahneman and Tversky (1983), Rabin (1998), Kahneman (2003) and Thaler (2008) are particularly worth a look. One issue I covered relatively briefly is search; the paper by Schunk (2009) provides an interesting recent addition to the literature connecting search with loss aversion. For more on markets the papers by Vernon Smith (2002, 2003) are a good starting point. For more on the life cycle hypothesis and savings you could start with Shefrin and Thaler (1998), Thaler (1990), Browning and Crossley (2001) and Benartzi and Thaler (2007).

2.9 Review Questions

2.1   If you wanted to find a new mobile phone, outfit, car, house, job, how would you search for one?

2.2   Why might a company wanting to advertise a product be interested in the trade-off contrast hypothesis and extremeness aversion?

2.3   Is it possible Anna could be influenced by both trade-off contrast and extremeness aversion simultaneously?

2.4   Why is time important in reference dependent utility? Compare how happy Carol and Amanda will feel the day they get the report from their broker, the next day, after a month etc.

2.5   List all the heuristics that have appeared in the chapter?

2.6   Argue that, if true, the 'no loss in buying' hypothesis means the WTP valuation is more reliable than the WTA valuation

2.7   Why would we expect EG to be greater than WTA?

2.8   Suppose someone's willingness to pay for a good is $10 and there reference point is $20. If the good is $13 will they buy it? What does this tell us about sales and 'bargain buys'?

2.9 Does the fact a taxi driver works nine hours a day mean he has a reference level of hours he wants to work? [Hint: it could be that his utility function just becomes steep at nine hours. A reference level of hours worked should be determined by some exogenous factor such as how many hours his friends work. But, is it always possible to distinguish exogenous factors from his preferences?]

2.10 Using search, contrast effects and reference dependence suggest why a person who lives in an area where apartments cost around $200,000 may be reluctant to buy when she moves to an area where apartments cost around $300,000.

2.11 Suppose that Anna owns her own house and house prices go up. Should she spend more? Now, suppose she has money invested in the stock market and share prices go down. Should she spend less?

3   Choice with risk

The safest way to double your money is to fold it over once and put it in your pocket.

Kin Hubbard

Economic choices are almost always made with some uncertainty as to what the outcome will be. A person buys groceries without knowing for sure how tasty they will be. He buys a new car without knowing how it will perform or how long it will last, a plane ticket without knowing whether the plane will be delayed, house insurance because he does not know whether his house will be burgled, and invests in shares without knowing whether they will increase or decrease in value. In the last chapter we saw that uncertainty can lead to choice arbitrariness and all the consequences that entails. What I want to do in this chapter is look in more detail at some other important consequences of risk.

Before we get started there is one distinction I need to explain. We say that someone faces a **situation of risk** if they know what could happen and how likely it is. An example would be someone who bets $10 on the toss of a coin; they know that there is a 50–50 chance it could be heads or tails, and if it's heads they win $10 and if it's tails they lose $10. We say that someone faces a **situation of uncertainty** if they do not know some of the possible outcomes and/or how likely they are. An example would be someone booking a plane ticket, who is unlikely to know all the possible delays or problems that could happen to change his experience of the flight.

Most of the situations we face are ones of uncertainty. Even the toss of a coin could be biased in many different ways. It is, however, more difficult to model situations of uncertainty than ones of risk, and without knowing the consequences of risk we cannot get very far thinking about uncertainty. It is traditional, therefore, to focus on situations of risk, and that is what I shall do in this chapter. That makes our task manageable and, as we shall see, still gives us a lot to think about. But do not be too disappointed, because in chapters five and nine we will come back to look at choice with uncertainty.

3.1 Expected utility

To illustrate some of the issues, imagine someone called Alan deciding whether or not to insure his car. Table 3.1 summarizes the choice he has to make. This is a choice with risk, because he cannot know for sure whether the car will be stolen, will be in an accident, or he will be asked to prove he has insurance. He begins with $20 in money and his car is worth an additional $50 (you can multiply these numbers by a $1,000 if you wish). Full insurance costs $9 and guarantees his final wealth will be $61 = 20 + 50 − 9. Insurance against theft costs only $6 but does not insure against an accident. No insurance costs nothing but leaves him vulnerable to theft, an accident, or being fined $40 by the police for having no insurance. Should he insure his car?

More generally we shall be interested in things called prospects. A **prospect** is a list of probabilities that things will happen, together with the monetary payoff if they do happen. In the insurance example there are three prospects. The 'full insurance prospect' gives probability one of having $61. We can write this as (1, $61). The 'insurance against theft prospect' gives probability 0.95 of $64 and 0.05 of $14. We can write this as (0.95, $64; 0.05, $14). Finally, the 'no insurance prospect' gives probability 0.1 of $20, 0.1 of $30 and 0.8 of $70, which we write as (0.1, $20; 0.1, $30; 0.8, $70). In general we would summarize a **prospect** with the list $(p_1, x_1; p_2, x_2; \ldots; p_n, x_n)$ where p_i is the probability of getting monetary payoff x_i.

The reason we are interested in prospects is that this is what a person must choose. In the insurance example Alan must decide whether to choose the 'full insurance', 'insurance against theft' or 'no insurance prospect'. We need, therefore a model of how people choose prospects. The standard way to do this is to use expected utility.

To calculate expected utility we make use of a utility function u that translates money into utility. This is the same utility function as we saw in the last chapter, it is just that, to make life easier for ourselves, we ignore things other than money. So, if Alan has x in money his utility is $u(x)$. The **expected utility of a prospect** $A = (p_1, x_1; p_2, x_2; \ldots; p_n, x_n)$ is then found using the formula:

$$U(A) = \sum_{i=1}^{n} p_i u(x_i). \tag{3.1}$$

Table 3.1 The possible consequences of Alan buying insurance

	Car is stolen	Car is in an accident	Stopped by police	No theft, accident, or police.
Probability	0.05	0.05	0.10	0.80
Final wealth if buys full insurance	$61	$61	$61	$61
Insurance against theft	$64	$14	$64	$64
No insurance	$20	$20	$30	$70

We can then predict that people will choose the prospect with the highest expected utility. This gives us a simple way to predict choice with risk.

To see how this works in the insurance example I shall contrast the choices Alan would make for three different possible utility functions. Table 3.2 provides the numbers and Figure 3.1 plots them. With a linear function we see that insurance against theft gives the highest expected utility. If the utility function is sufficiently concave, then full insurance gives the highest expected utility, and if it is sufficiently convex, no insurance gives the highest expected utility.

The example illustrates how the prospect that gives highest expected utility will depend on the shape of the utility function. To explain why, I should first define the **expected value of a prospect A** as:

$$V(A) = \sum_{i=1}^{n} p_i x_i.$$
(3.2)

Table 3.2 Alan's expected utility depends on his utility function

Utility function	Expected utility if chose			Predicted choice
	full insurance	insurance for theft	no insurance	
Linear: $u(x) = x$	61.0	61.5	61.0	insurance for theft
Concave: $u(x) = 10\sqrt{x}$	78.1	77.9	76.9	full insurance
Convex: $u(x) = x^2/50$	74.4	78.0	81.0	no insurance

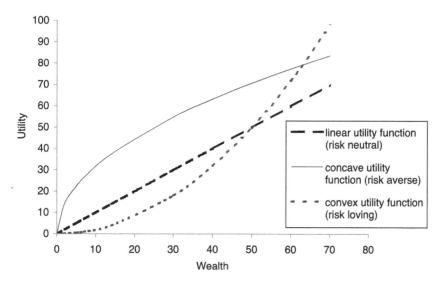

Figure 3.1 Three possible utility functions: one is concave which would imply Alan is risk averse, and one convex which would imply Alan is risk loving.

Table 3.3 The expected value and risk of different choices

	Expected value	Minimum possible	Maximum possible	Probability wealth below expected value
Full insurance	$61	$61	$61	0.00
Insurance against theft	$61.5	$14	$64	0.05
No insurance	$61	$20	$70	0.20

The only difference between equations (3.1) and (3.2) is that we do not transform monetary payoffs into utility payoffs. This means we obtain expected monetary payoff rather than expected utility payoff. In the example, insurance for theft has the highest expected value. It is not clear, however, that choosing the prospect with the highest expected value is best. This is because Alan will want to also take into account the riskiness of the prospect.

The relevant trade-offs are illustrated in Table 3.3. With full insurance Alan knows his payoff will be $61. There is no risk, and Alan might like this. Indeed he might like it so much he is willing to sacrifice $0.50 of expected value to get it. In this case we would say that he is risk averse. Someone is **risk averse** if they prefer a certain amount of money to a prospect with the same expected value; they would rather avoid risk. Going to the other extreme, it may be that Alan likes to gamble and prefers to choose no insurance because that is where the risk is highest. In this case we would say that he is risk loving. Someone is **risk loving** if they prefer a risky prospect to the expected value of the prospect for sure; they would prefer risk.

Whether or not Alan is risk averse or risk loving will depend in a simple way on the curvature of his utility function. If his utility function is concave, Alan loses relatively more if his wealth goes down than he gains if his wealth goes up, so he would rather not risk a loss for a gain, and he is risk averse. If his utility function is convex, then he loses relatively less if his wealth goes down than he gains if his wealth goes up, so he would risk a loss for a gain and he is risk loving. The curvature of the utility function tells us, therefore, a lot.

There are two commonly used ways to measure this: one measures **absolute risk aversion** and the other **relative risk aversion**. It's not so important you know exactly what these are, but for completeness the formulas are:

$$\text{absolute risk aversion: } r_u^a = -\frac{u''(x)}{u'(x)}; \text{relative risk aversion: } r_u^r = -x\frac{u''(x)}{u'(x)}$$

where $u'(x)$ denotes the derivate and $u''(x)$ the second derivate of $u(x)$. If Alan is risk neutral then $u(x) = x$ and so $r_u^a, r_u^r = 0$ but if he is risk averse $r_u^a, r_u^r > 0$, and the more risk averse he is, the larger is r_u^a and r_u^r. Various methods can be used to measure risk aversion (see Research Methods 3.1).

Economists like things simple, and so two utility functions are of particular note because they imply respectively **constant absolute risk aversion** (CARA) or **constant relative risk aversion** (CRRA). It's even less important you know what these are, but here they are:

$$\text{CARA: } u(x) = -e^{-r_u^a x}; \quad \text{CRRA: } u(x) = \frac{x^{1-r_u^r}}{1-r_u^r}$$

The beauty of the CARA or CRRA functions is that we only need to know one number, the level of risk aversion, and then we can model choice with risk, because we know what the utility function is and can use expected utility to find what maximizes utility. No wonder expected utility has become the standard way of modeling choice with risk: If we know Alan's level of risk aversion then we can predict his choice over any set of risky prospects!

Research Methods 3.1

Measuring risk aversion

Given the risk inherent in many economic choices it is important to know the level of risk aversion, even if our primary interest is not how a person reacts to risk. There are lots of methods that have been used to measure risk aversion and we will see many of them as we go through the rest of the chapter. The basic idea behind most methods is the same: choices are observed and fed into either the CARA or CRRA utility function to estimate the parameter r_u^a or r_u^r. The differences between methods are the choices observed. Needless to say the experimental laboratory is one setting that has been used. In this case we look at prospects with relatively small amounts of money. Empirical settings where we can measure risk aversion include asset and insurance markets. In this case we can observe choices over prospects with both relatively small and large amounts of money (see section 3.7).

An intriguing and slightly different way to measure risk aversion was suggested by Chetty (2006). This method does not use choices over prospects but instead looks to directly estimate the curvature of the $u(x)$ function. This is, after all, what we need to calculate r_u^a or r_u^r, because the more curved is $u(x)$ the more risk averse a person is. The curvature of $u(x)$ is estimated by looking at labor supply. To explain how this works: the more curved is $u(x)$ the quicker a person becomes relatively satiated with money, that is, has enough money to not want more; if someone is satiated with money then they will not want to risk losing money to gain more, they are risk averse, and have no desire to increase their income, so can work less if the wage rate increases. By looking at how people react to changes in wages we can therefore estimate risk aversion.

The problem economists face is that different studies have given very different estimates for the level of risk aversion, and we are not talking small differences. For example, Chetty estimates that r_u^r must be less than two but we shall see estimates later in this chapter as high as 1,000. This suggests that there is no real measure of risk aversion just measures that are appropriate for particular situations.

Expected utility does give us, therefore, a very simple and transparent way to model and understand how people make choices when there is risk. Maybe, however, it is a bit too simple. Is it possible to capture all the things that can influence choice, and that we are interested in predicting and modeling, in just one number? The only way to find out is to look at some data and see. To get us started on this I am going to give a series of examples that suggest expected utility cannot explain everything we typically observe. These examples will serve as a precursor to us thinking more generally about how to move beyond expected utility. As we go through the examples, I would strongly encourage you to 'play along' and think what you would choose and why.

3.1.1 The Allais Paradox

Consider the prospects in Table 3.4. When asked to choose between prospects A and B, most people choose prospect B. When asked to choose between prospects C and D, most people choose prospect C. This seems entirely sensible but is not consistent with expected utility theory; the **Allais Paradox**.

To see why this is a paradox, first observe that prospect C is obtained from prospect A, and prospect D is obtained from prospect B, by removing a 0.66 chance of winning $2,400. Now, if Alan chooses B over A (and put $u(0) = 0$),

$$u(2,400) > 0.33u(2,500) + 0.66u(2,400)$$

which (removing the 0.66 chance of winning $2,400) means that

$$0.34u(2,400) > 0.33u(2,500). \tag{3.3}$$

If, however, he chooses prospect C over D:

$$0.33u(2,500) > 0.34u(2,400). \tag{3.4}$$

Equations (3.3) and (3.4) cannot both be true.

So, what causes the Allais Paradox? There is a sense in which removing the 0.66 chance of winning $2,400 matters more for prospect B than A because changing a sure thing to a risk matters more than changing a risk to a risk. Generalizing from this, the evidence suggests that people favor outcomes that are perceived certain rather than probable or possible. This is called the **certainty effect**.

Interestingly, the certainty effect can be relevant even if outcomes are not theoretically certain. To illustrate, consider Table 3.5, with four more prospects. Most people choose prospect F over E and prospect G over H. This is again inconsistent with expected utility theory. It does seem consistent with a certainty effect because

Table 3.4 The Allais Paradox. Many people prefer B to A and C to D

Prospect	Amount with probability of outcome		
A	$2,500 with probability 0.33	$2,400 prob. 0.66	$0 prob. 0.01
B	$2,400 for sure.		
C	$2,500 with probability 0.33		$0 with probability 0.67
D	$2,400 with probability 0.34		$0 with probability 0.66

Table 3.5 The near certainty effect. Many people choose F over E and G over H

Prospect	Amount with probability of outcome	
E	$6,000 with probability 0.45	$0 otherwise
F	$3,000 with probability 0.9	$0 otherwise
G	$6,000 with probability 0.001	$0 otherwise
H	$3,000 with probability 0.002	$0 otherwise

a 0.9 chance might look relatively certain compared to a 0.45 chance. What is perceived as certain can thus depend on the context.

3.1.2 Risk aversion

Next consider the prospects in Table 3.6. Anyone who prefers prospect I to prospects J to N is risk averse. They prefer $0 for sure to a prospect with expected value greater than $0. The further we go down the list of prospects, the more risk averse someone would have to be to prefer prospect I. Many people choose prospect I over prospect J (see Research Methods 3.2). More generally, many people display risk aversion for relatively small gambles.

This, in itself, is consistent with expected utility. The problem comes when we try to infer what such a choice implies a person would do when choosing amongst prospects with bigger stakes.

Research Methods 3.2

Money or something else

Experimental subjects are almost always given financial incentives. This means at the end of the experiment they are given cash, and the knowledge that they will be given cash is supposed to be incentive enough to think about their choices. For economists this is easy to justify, because money is a unit of exchange and easily substituted for other goods. Maybe, however, subjects would behave differently if the incentive were something other than money? We have already encountered an experiment that gave chocolates as well as money, but this does not really answer the question of interest here. What we need is an experiment where subjects are provided a monetary incentive in one treatment and a different incentive in another treatment.

Harrison, List and Towe (2007) did such a study on risk aversion. The study was done at the Central Florida Coin Show and involved subjects choosing amongst prospects that had either monetary or coin outcomes. In a monetary treatment the possible prize was money and in a coin treatment it was a collectable coin. The coins that could be won had a retail value of $40, $125, $200 and $350. The money prizes were set to match these amounts.

Harrison et al. found very similar estimates of risk aversion whether subjects chose over prospects with a monetary or coin prize. The answer to our question, at least on the basis of this study, would, therefore, be that subjects did not behave differently when the incentive was something other than money. There is, however, one important caveat to this conclusion.

Two versions of the coin treatment were considered in the study. In one, the grade of the coins that could be won was clear to subjects, and in the other it was not. The grading is important in determining the value of the coin. When the grade of coin is clear someone who knows about coins would be able to give a relatively accurate value of the coin. When the grade is not clear the valuation would be more uncertain. Harrison et al. find that risk attitudes are the same whether the prize is money or a coin of known grade. When the grade was not clear subjects were more risk averse.

This suggests that people may be more risk averse if there is background uncertainty about the value of possible outcomes. This also suggests that estimates of risk aversion based on monetary incentives may understate risk aversion for the many contexts where people do face background uncertain. Note that we could only know this by using non-monetary prizes. That is because there cannot be background uncertainty in a monetary prize: for instance, a subject in the US has a pretty good idea what a $10 note is worth.

To explain, suppose that Alan has a wealth of $100 and prefers prospect I to prospect K. This means that:

$$u(100) > 0.5u(0) + 0.5u(225).$$

If $u(0) = 0$ and $u(100) = 100$, it must be that $u(225) < 200$. Knowing that Alan prefers prospect I to prospect K thus tells us something about the utility he gets from having wealth $225. Now, suppose that Alan has a wealth of $225 and still prefers prospect I to prospect K. We can then infer something about the utility he gets from having wealth $350, see below. Continuing in this way we get a picture of what the utility function must be like if Alan continues to prefer prospect I to K for higher and higher levels of wealth. Figure 3.2 gives such a picture.

[Extra] I should explain how to get this picture. Let us say that $u(225) = 199$, and so Alan just prefers prospect I to K when his wealth is $100. If Alan has wealth of $225 and would still prefer prospect I to prospect K:

$$u(225) > 0.5u(125) + 0.5u(350).$$

Table 3.6 Prospects that can lead to extreme risk aversion

Prospect	Amount with probability of outcome	
I	$0 for sure	
J	$100 loss with probability 0.5	$105 gain otherwise
K	$100 loss with probability 0.5	$125 gain otherwise
L	$100 loss with probability 0.5	$200 gain otherwise
M	$225 loss with probability 0.5	$375 gain otherwise
N	$600 loss with probability 0.5	$36 million gain

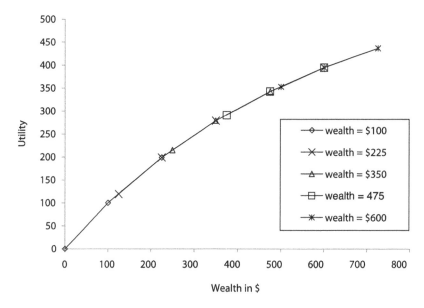

Figure 3.2 What we can infer about the utility function of someone who prefers prospect I to prospect K for increasing levels of wealth?

We do not know $u(125)$ but we do know that $u(100) = 100$ and $u(225) = 199$ so can infer that $u(125) > 119$. This means $u(350) \leq 279$. Suppose that $u(350) = 279$. Now imagine that Alan has wealth of $350 and would still prefer prospect I to prospect K. This means that:

$$u(350) > 0.5u(250) + 0.5u(475).$$

Again, we do not know $u(250)$, but we can infer that $u(250) > 215$, so $u(475) \leq 343$. We can go on and on doing this.

The key point to notice in Figure 3.2 is how the utility function has already curved a lot. Going from $0 to $100 is worth 100 utility, but going from $600 to $700 is worth only 40 utility. We need the utility function to bend like this for low levels of wealth in order to understand why Alan would prefer prospect I. The problem is that once we have started bending it, we have to carry on bending it. This relative bending of the utility function has implications for bigger gambles. To illustrate, if $u(225) = 199$, and, if you carry on the reasoning above, you should find that $u(600) < 400$. Consequently, if Alan had a wealth level of $225 he would prefer prospect I to prospect M. This may well be the case, but we see that the difference between the relative gain and loss has increased quite a lot. If we were to look at realistic wealth levels of $50,000 to $300,000, then this effect would become very pronounced.

To demonstrate, Table 3.7 details the amount of money Alan would need as potential gain in order to take on a 50–50 gamble, if he had a wealth level of

Table 3.7 The amount a person would need to gain on a 50–50 bet to take the bet if risk averse for small gambles

Potential loss	Potential gain needed to take the bet if	
	Prefers prospect I to J	*Prefers prospect I to K*
$400	$420	$1,250
$600	$730	$36,000,000,000
$800	$1,050	$90,000,000,000
$1,000	$1,570	$160,000,000,000
$20,000	$71,799,110	$540,000,000,000,000,000,000

Source: Rabin (2000).

$290,000 and would prefer prospect I to J or K, for any level of wealth below $300,000. By this stage we see that the differences between relative gain and loss have become huge, implausibly huge. For example, it must be that anyone who would prefer prospect I to prospect K must prefer prospect I to prospect N. This is possible, but seems highly unlikely, suggesting that expected utility cannot explain risk aversion for small gambles (see Research Methods 3.3).

Research Methods 3.3

Risk aversion and incentives in the lab

In many economic experiments we are interested in something other than attitudes to risk. The outcome may, however, inherently be risky. For example, in chapters six and seven we shall look at behavior in strategic contexts where one person's payoff will depend on what others do. Our focus will be on things like a person's ability to predict what another will do, or his desire to be fair. His payoff will, however, depend on what another subject does, and so there is an element of risk. This complicates things. For example, we shall have to try and determine whether he gave something to another to be fair or because he is risk averse. What we would like is that the subject's choice does not depend on his attitude to risk.

If subjects are risk neutral then the problem goes away. If, however, subjects are risk averse (or risk loving) then things are not so simple. One potential solution is to frame choices in a slightly different way. Instead of asking subjects to make choices that might increase their payoff from, say, $5 to $10 we can offer them choices that increase the probability of winning, say, $100 from 0.05 to 0.10. If a subject maximizes expected utility then this approach should make attitudes to risk irrelevant. If, however, the subject maximizes expected utility, then risk aversion should not matter anyway for the small sums of money in a typical experiment. It is not clear, therefore, how much such alternative framings really help.

Indeed, there seems to be no simple way to disentangle the consequences of risk and uncertainty from other things we might be interested in. This means we need to be mindful of attitudes to risk in interpreting any experimental results.

3.1.3 Risk loving for losses

The next set of prospects are in Table 3.8. Most people choose prospect P rather than O, and prospect Q rather than R. This suggests that people are risk averse for gains, preferring the $3,000 for sure, but risk loving for gambles, preferring to gamble on losing $0.

Such choices are theoretically possible while maximizing expected utility, but only by pushing things to the limit. Recall that utility should be measured according to the absolute level of wealth. So, we would need that when asked to choose amongst these options a person's current wealth just happened to be at a point where the utility function is concave for higher levels of wealth, and convex for lower levels of wealth. This is possible but seems a bit too much of a coincidence. More plausible, particularly given what we saw in the last chapter, is that choices are made, in part, by measuring relative deviations from current wealth. This is called the **reflection effect**.

To illustrate the possible consequences of the reflection effect consider the next set of prospects given in Table 3.9. In principle prospect S is equivalent to U and prospect T equivalent to V. Despite this, most people chose prospect T rather than prospect S and prospect U rather than prospect V. This can be explained by the reflection effect. In prospect T the $500 is perceived as a gain, while in prospect V the $500 is perceived as a loss.

3.1.4 When expected utility will work

Expected utility provides a brilliantly simple way to model choice with risk. We have already seen, however, that it can be a bit too simple to capture all we observe.

Table 3.8 Prospects with gains and losses. Many prefer P to O and Q to R

Prospect	Amount with probability of outcome	
O	$4,000 with probability 0.8	$0 otherwise
P	$3,000 for sure	
Q	$4,000 loss with probability 0.8	$0 otherwise
R	$3,000 loss for sure	

Table 3.9 Framing of losses versus gains. Many prefer T over S and U over V

Prospect	Preliminary stage given	Subsequently get amount with probability of outcome	
S	$1,000	$1,000 gain with probability 0.5	$0 otherwise
T		$500 for sure	
U	$2,000	$1,000 loss with probability 0.5	$0 otherwise
V		$500 loss for sure	

No model will work all the time and so this is no great surprise, and it does not mean that we should ditch expected utility. If you want a model that can reliably capture how a person behaves for particular types of gamble, then expected utility may be good enough. If, though, you want a single model that can capture all the risky choices a person may make, whether it be big or small gambles, gambles with losses or with gains, then expected utility is probably not good enough. It is natural, therefore, to look for a model that can do a better job. A useful first step in doing this is to question when expected utility does provide a good model of choice. This can hopefully help pinpoint what expected utility misses.

The first thing we need for expected utility to work well is transitivity. **Preferences are transitive** if for any three prospects X, Y and Z,

$$\text{if } X \geq Y \text{ and } Y \geq Z \text{ then } X \geq Z$$

where the notation $X \geq Y$ means prospect X is preferred to or indifferent to prospect Y. In other words, there should be a natural ordering to preferences with a best, X in this case, and worst, Z.

The second thing we need is independence. **Preferences satisfy independence** if for any three prospects X, Y and Z,

$$\text{if } X \geq Y \text{ then } (p, X; 1-p, Z) \geq (p, Y; 1-p, Z)$$

for any number p between zero and one. In other words, if Alan prefers prospect X to Y then he must also prefer a prospect that mixes X with some other prospect Z to one that mixes Y with the same prospect Z.

If preferences satisfy independence and transitivity (as well as two other properties of completeness and continuity) then preferences and choice can be modeled using expected utility. Expected utility would then be the best way to model choice. This is useful to know in trying to work out why expected utility may not work so well and in the following sections I shall take up in turn the possibility that preferences do not satisfy transitivity and that they do not satisfy independence. With this we shall see how to adapt expected utility to better account for choice with risk.

3.2 Independence and fanning out

I want to start this section by revisiting the Allais Paradox. To help us understand the paradox we can use a probability triangle diagram like that in Figure 3.3. On the horizontal axis we measure the probability of having $0, and on the vertical axis we measure the probability of having $2,500. Any point in the triangle is a prospect. This becomes clear by plotting on the four prospects in the Allais Paradox. Prospect B guarantees $2,400 for sure so goes at the bottom left corner where $p_1 = p_3 = 0$. Prospect A gives $0 with probability 0.01 and $2,500 with probability 0.33 so goes where $p_1 = 0.01$ and $p_3 = 0.33$. We can also plot on prospects C and D. Drawing this diagram makes clear that prospects C and D are similar to A and B but 'moved across' by adding a 0.66 chance of getting $0.

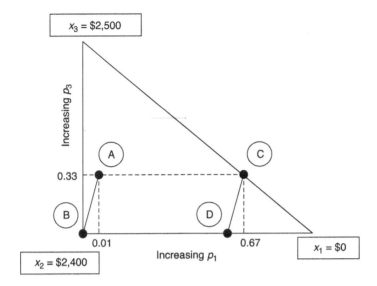

Figure 3.3 A probability triangle diagram of the Allais paradox. The horizontal axis is the probability of winning $0 and the vertical axis the probability of winning $2,500. The other possibility is to win $2,400.

What we now want to start to do is representing preferences on the probability triangle diagram. While we are doing this I want to clarify two different notions of utility. First, there is **outcome utility**. This is the utility we talked about in the previous chapter and can capture with the function u. It tells us the utility Alan will get from a particular outcome such as winning $0, $2,400 and $2,500. Next is the **utility of a prospect**. You can think of this as the utility Alan gets from a prospect before he knows the outcome of that prospect. We capture this with the function U and to understand the Allais Paradox we need to know the utility of prospects A to D. Expected utility is one way of getting at this, see equation (3.1), but we now want to consider alternatives.

If we know the utility that Alan would get from any possible prospect, then we can start to draw indifference curves in the probability triangle diagram. An **indifference curve** should show prospects that give the same utility. So, all we need to do is fix a level of utility, and find the prospects, that is points in the probability triangle diagram, that give this utility. Figure 3.4 illustrates what indifference curves may look like. Indifference curves will likely slope up because a higher probability of the worse outcome $0 needs to be offset by a higher probability of the best outcome $2,500. This also means that the steepness of the indifference curves measures attitude to risk. The more risk averse someone is, the more the probability of getting $2,500 has to increase to compensate for any increase in the probability of getting $0. Thus, the steeper the indifference curve, the greater the risk aversion.

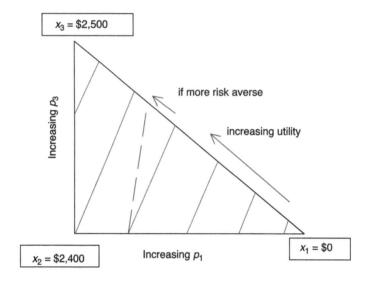

Figure 3.4 Indifference curves in a probability triangle diagram. The steeper the indifference curve the more risk averse.

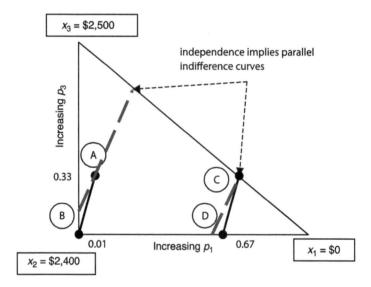

Figure 3.5 The Allais paradox. If preferences satisfy independence the person should prefer either A and C or B and D.

It turns out that if preferences satisfy independence then the indifference curves must be straight parallel lines like those in Figure 3.4. Figure 3.5 illustrates the implications of this by combining parallel indifference curves with the four prospects. If the lines between prospects A and B, and C and D are parallel, and the indifference curves are also parallel, then Alan should choose either A and C or B and D. As I have drawn it he would choose A and C. Recall, however, that most people chose B and C. This is the paradox.

From this we learn two things. First, the Allais Paradox is probably caused by preferences not satisfying independence. Second, to explain the Allais Paradox we will need indifference curves that are not parallel but instead **fan out** like those in Figure 3.6. The key thing about fanning out is that indifference curves get steeper the closer to the vertical axis, meaning that people are more risk averse the closer they get to being guaranteed $2,400 or more. This is consistent with the certainty effect and can explain why someone prefers B over A and C over D.

There are lots of ways that have been suggested for how to model the fanning out of indifference curves. Basically, if we want indifference curves to fan out then we can write down an equation for the utility of prospects that will give us what we want. More constructive is to develop models based on some intuition for why indifference curves might fan out. I shall look at two such models, one with disappointment and one with rank dependent expected utility. In section 3.3 we shall look at other, more radical models that also cause fanning out.

3.2.1 Disappointment

One explanation for why Alan might dislike prospect A in the Allais Paradox is that if he chooses A and gets a payoff of zero he will likely be very disappointed

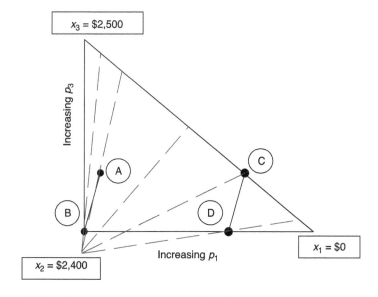

Figure 3.6 The Allais paradox can be explained by the fanning out of indifference curves where indifference curves get stepper the closer the person is to being guaranteed $2,400 or more.

(you might want to substitute some stronger word here). Such disappointment can be avoided by choosing prospect B and getting a guaranteed high payoff. A way to capture such disappointment and its consequences was proposed by Loomes and Sugden (1986).

The basic idea is to measure outcome utility relative to some prior expectation of what utility will be. If outcome utility is below the expected level then Alan experiences **disappointment**. If the outcome utility is above the expected level then he experiences **elation**. Elation and disappointment are captured by some function D. So, if the outcome is x his utility will be $u(x) + D(u(x) - prior)$, the outcome utility plus or minus elation or disappointment. The utility of a prospect X is then written:

$$U(X) = \sum_{i=1}^{n} p_i[u(x_i) + D(u(x_i) - prior)].$$

This is the same as expected utility but taking into account disappointment and elation of being below or above the prior expectation. The prior expectation can be context specific but a natural candidate is the expected utility of a prospect, calculated using equation (3.1). It is also natural to impose assumptions on D including that $D(g) \geq 0$ if $g > 0$ and $D(l) \leq 0$ if $l < 0$ so elation is good and disappointment bad.

To demonstrate the implications of disappointment, we can work through the Allais Paradox. Suppose that $u(x) = x$ and

$$D(g) = \begin{cases} \theta g^2 \text{ for any } g > 0 \\ -\theta l^2 \text{ for any } l < 0 \end{cases} \tag{3.5}$$

where $\theta \geq 0$ measures the importance of disappointment. Table 3.10 details the utility of each prospect for different values of θ. When $\theta = 0$ we have a standard expected utility model and Alan would choose prospect A over B and C over D. If disappointment is given weight $\theta = 0.0002$ we see that prospect B becomes preferred to prospect A. Why? The expected utility of prospect A is \$2,409 and so if he gets \$0 his disappointment is $1,161 = 2409^2\theta$ which is relatively large. For example, the elation he feels if he gets \$2,500 is only $1.66 = 91^2\theta$. These numbers must be weighted by the probability they will happen, because he will only be disappointed with probability 0.01. Even so, we get a net effect of $-0.01 \times 2409^2\theta - 0.66 \times 9^2\theta + 0.33 \times 91^2\theta = -11$. This is enough to just swing things in favor of prospect B.

The small probability of being very disappointed if he chooses prospect A can be enough for Alan to prefer prospect B. The Allais Paradox can thus be caused by people avoiding potential disappointment. If we plot the indifference curves when $\theta = 0.0002$, we find that they do indeed fan out similarly to in Figure 3.6.

Disappointment provides, therefore, a plausible explanation of the Allais Paradox and fanning out. It can also point to other things we might want to be aware of. For example, if we increase the weight given to disappointment we can get indifference curves with weirder shapes. Figure 3.7 illustrates what happens

Table 3.10 The Allais Paradox can be explained by disappointment. If $\theta = 0$ prospect A is preferred to B and C to D. If $\theta = 0.0002$ prospect B is preferred to A and C to D

Prospect	Utility of the prospect		Value of D(.)			Net D(.)
	$\theta = 0$	$\theta = 0.0002$	if $0	if $2,400	if $2,500	
A	2,409	2,398	−1,161	−0	+2	−11
B	2,400	2,400	–	0	–	0
C	825	919	−136	–	+561	+94
D	816	899	−133	+502	–	+83

when $\theta = 0.002$. There is still a preference for prospects B and C but the indifference curves are no longer fanning out. In fact we obtain, counter-intuitively, that an increase in p_1, the probability of getting $0, can increase the utility of a prospect! The explanation is that when p_1 is relatively large, Alan is not so disappointed if he gets $0, because he expected it. He might, therefore, prefer less chance of winning because this means less disappointment if he does not win. Maybe not so counter intuitive after all?

3.2.2 Rank dependent expected utility

A model of disappointment deviates from expected utility by changing how utility is perceived. An alternative possibility is to change how probabilities are perceived. This is the approach taken by rank dependent expected utility. I should

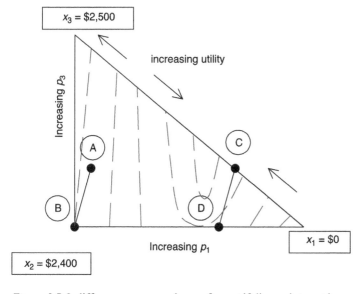

Figure 3.7 Indifference curves no longer fan out if disappointment is very strong.

probably warn you, before launching into the explanation, that the primary virtue of rank dependent expected utility is that it works. It's not so intuitive why it works, so a little bit of faith is needed.

One crucial component we need is a function π that **weights probabilities**. A commonly used function is:

$$\pi(p) = \frac{p^{\gamma}}{(p^{\gamma} + (1-p)^{\gamma})^{\frac{1}{\gamma}}}$$

where γ is some number between zero and one. The main reason for using this function is that it gives the nice S-shaped probability weights illustrated in Figure 3.8. You can see that if $\gamma = 1$ then $\pi(p) = p$, and so there is essentially no weighting of probabilities. When γ is less than one, there are two things that happen: First, there is an **overweighting of small probabilities,** in the sense that a small probability is given a relatively bigger weight. Second, there is an underweighting of large probabilities. We will come back later to why we would want these two things.

Now that we know how to weight probabilities, we can find the utility of a prospect. The first thing we need to do is rank the outcomes so that x_1 is the worst outcome and x_n is the best. For now we shall assume that $x_1 \geq 0$, and so the worst outcome is not a loss. The **rank dependent expected utility** of a prospect X is then given by:

$$U(X) = \sum_{i=1}^{n} w_i u(x_i). \tag{3.6}$$

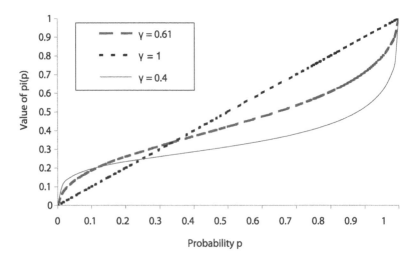

Figure 3.8 An illustration of probability weighting.

where the **decision weights** are:

$$w_i = \pi(p_i + \ldots + p_n) - \pi(p_{i+1} + \ldots + p_n)$$

for all i. In interpretation, $\pi(p_i + \ldots + p_n)$ is the weighted probability of getting an outcome equal to or better than i, and $\pi(p_{i+1} + \ldots + p_n)$ is the weighted probability of an outcome better than i.

Rank dependent expected utility is easy enough to work out if we know u and π. It's slightly harder to know why it works or why we would want to do it. I can though try to provide some intuition. If $\pi(p) = p$ then $w_i = p_i$ and we have standard expected utility. More generally, decision weights allow us to capture pessimism and optimism. To illustrate, consider prospect $X = (0.5, \$0; 0.5, \$100)$ where Alan has a 50–50 chance of winning \$100. The decision weights will be $w_1 = 1 - \pi(0.5)$ and $w_2 = \pi(0.5)$. If $\pi(0.5) < 0.5$ then $w_1 > w_2$. This suggests Alan is **pessimistic** because he puts a higher decision weight on the worse outcome. If $\pi(0.5) > 0.5$ then $w_1 < w_2$. This suggests Alan is **optimistic** because he puts a higher decision weight on the best outcome. Figure 3.8 illustrates that with the weighting given by equation (3.6) we primarily observe pessimism with a little bit of optimism over small probabilities.

To illustrate rank dependent expected utility, Table 3.11 works through the Allais Paradox when $u(x) = x$. We can see that for the most part the weighting of probabilities has little effect. The important exception is prospect A where the 0.01 probability of the worse outcome is increased in decision weight to 0.088. This is pessimism and is enough to make prospect B be preferred to prospect A. The Allais Paradox could thus be explained by pessimism and the overweighting of a small probability of getting \$0.

For completeness we should have a look at the indifference curves we get in the probability triangle diagram. Figure 3.9 illustrates what they look like. They are not as exciting as with disappointment, but even here we see that the story is not as simple as fanning out. The indifference curves have an S shape.

My focus throughout this section has been on the Allais Paradox, but hopefully you can see that there is enough intuition behind the models of disappointment and rank dependent utility that we should be able to meaningfully apply them more generally. Indeed, given that both models capture something intuitively

Table 3.11 Rank dependent utility and the Allais paradox, when $u(x) = x$. If $\gamma = 0$ prospect A is preferred to B and C to D. If $\gamma = 0.61$ prospect B is preferred to A and C to D

Prospect	If $\gamma = 1$				If $\gamma = 0.61$			
	w1	w2	w3	Utility	w1	w2	w3	Utility
A	0.01	0.66	0.33	2409	0.088	0.577	0.334	2221
B	0	1	0	2400	0	1	0	2400
C	0.67	0	0.33	825	0.666	0	0.334	836
D	0.66	0.34	0	816	0.661	0.339	0	815

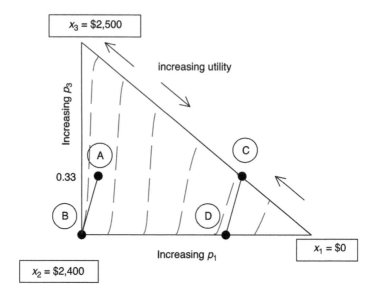

Figure 3.9 Indifference curves in the Allais Paradox with rank dependent utility.

appealing, a next step is to combine them together and try to account for things other than the Allais Paradox. This is the direction we shall take in the next section.

3.3 Reference dependence and prospect theory

A theme through much of the previous chapter was the relevance of reference points and a potential asymmetry between losses and gains. I now want to show how we can extend that to choice with risk. Doing so brings us to **prospect theory** (see Research Methods 3.4). Prospect theory can be as general or as specific as one wants it to be. Given that I have already talked about reference dependence a fair bit in the previous chapter, I am going to focus on a specific formulation of the theory here.

Research Methods 3.4

The development of an idea

In 1979 Kahneman and Tversky published a paper on 'Prospect theory: an analysis of decision under risk'. This paper went on to become one of the most cited papers in economics, and prospect theory became arguably behavioral economics' most well known idea.

The first half of the 1979 paper was a critique of expected utility. Kahneman and Tversky used hypothetical choice problems to demonstrate phenomena (like the

Allais Paradox) that violated expected utility theory. The second part proposed a
theory that could explain these phenomena and, therefore, provide a better account
of decision making with risk. The theory consisted of two parts, an editing phase in
which prospects would be organized and reformulated, and then an evaluation phase
where probabilities are weighted and the value of a prospect evaluated. The editing
phase could account for things like framing effects and the evaluation phase for
things like loss aversion.

The theory originally proposed by Kahneman and Tversky in 1979 was hard to
apply. It was formulated only for prospects with two outcomes, and essentially set
out what properties a model of decision making with risk should have, rather than
proposing a specific model. In 1992 a second paper was published that proposed a
parameterized model of prospect theory that could more easily be applied. This is
commonly referred to as second generation prospect theory. The key step was to
make use of rank dependent weighting of probabilities.

The second generation model was simpler and focused on the evaluation phase,
with the editing phase almost completely forgotten. This lack of an editing phase left
it unclear what the reference point should be. Recent models address this by allowing
for a changing and probabilistic reference point. This is commonly referred to as third
generation prospect theory, and brings the attention back a little on the editing phase.

Combined together, this work pointed out the shortcomings of standard economics
while also, crucially, proposing something else that might work instead. That is
progress, and prospect theory has rightly become a celebrated idea.

Unsurprisingly, one key ingredient of prospect theory is a reference point about
which outcomes are judged. We then talk of gains or losses relative to the reference point. If x is final wealth and r is the reference level of wealth then $x \geq r$ is a
gain and $x < r$ is a loss. Outcomes are judged relative to the reference point using
utility function or value function:

$$v(x) = \begin{cases} (x-r)^\alpha & \text{if } x \geq r \\ -\lambda(r-x)^\beta & \text{if } x < r \end{cases} \tag{3.7}$$

where α, β and λ are parameters. In interpretation this value function is exactly the
same as that I talked about in the previous chapter. The only difference is that I
have now given a specific functional form for what it might look like.

The thing we do need to do, that we did not do in the last chapter, is think about
risk. To do this we shall use rank dependent expected utility. One slight twist is
that when weighting probabilities, we should distinguish gains from losses. So,
when we rank outcomes from worst x_1 to best x_n, we also need to distinguish
outcomes that are losses, say x_1 to x_L, and gains x_{L+1} to x_n. Gains are then given
decision weight:

$$w_i = \pi^g(p_i + \ldots + p_n) - \pi^g(p_{i+1} + \ldots + p_n)$$

as before, and losses are given decision weight:

$$w_i = \pi^l(p_1 + \ldots + p_i) - \pi^l(p_1 + \ldots + p_{i-1})$$

Where

$$\pi^g(p) = \frac{p^\gamma}{(p^\gamma + (1-p)^\gamma)^{\frac{1}{\gamma}}}, \quad \pi^l(p) = \frac{p^\delta}{(p^\delta + (1-p)^\delta)^{\frac{1}{\delta}}}$$

are the probability weights for gains and losses. This formulation might look a little messy, but it is just a natural extension of what we did before to capture the asymmetry whereby gains are good and losses are bad.

With equations (3.6), (3.7) and this weighting of probabilities, we can work out easily enough the utility of any prospect, if we know r, α, β, λ, γ and δ. The overriding motivation for this formulation is that it is relatively simple but has the potential to explain what we observe. For instance, if $\lambda > 1$ then we capture loss aversion because losses are given more weight than gains. If $1 > \alpha$, $\beta > 0$ then we capture risk aversion over gains and risk loving over losses. Finally, if γ, $\delta < 1$ then we can capture the certainty effect.

But, to see whether this formulation really does work we need to go and estimate the parameters λ, α, β, γ and δ. Tversky and Kahneman (1992) did this by recruiting 25 graduate students from Berkeley and Stanford and having them choose amongst a series of prospects. Before giving the headline numbers I want to point out that these estimates are based on the median responses and we should not ignore the possibility that different subjects behave very differently. Now, for the headline numbers: they were $\lambda = 2.25$, α, $\beta = 0.88$, $\gamma = 0.61$ and $\delta = 0.69$. Thankfully, these numbers are consistent with what we needed to capture loss aversion and the like.

Figure 3.10 plots the utility function for parameters $\lambda = 2.25$ and α, $\beta = 0.88$. The asymmetry between losses and gains is apparent, and comes from losses being given over twice the weight of gains. You might also notice, however, that there is not much curvature to the utility function. It is marginally concave for gains and convex for losses, but this is quite hard to see. This is because the estimates of α, $\beta = 0.88$ are close enough to one for the utility function to be nearly linear above and below the x axis. Indeed, to simplify things, it is not uncommon to use α, $\beta = 1$.

This lack of curvature might suggest that we are going to struggle to explain risk aversion over small gambles. The utility function in Figure 3.10, for example, is a lot flatter than that in Figure 3.2. Loss aversion, however, can help us out. That's because the kink in the utility function at zero means that the utility function curves a lot when we compare negative and positive amounts. Loss aversion can, for example, explain why Alan would prefer prospect I in Table 3.6 to prospect J. This line of thinking does raise some questions, that I will come back to, about what the reference point should be and what should be coded as a gain and a loss. For now though let's focus on the good news: prospect theory has allowed us to capture everything we came across in sections 3.1.1 to 3.1.4.

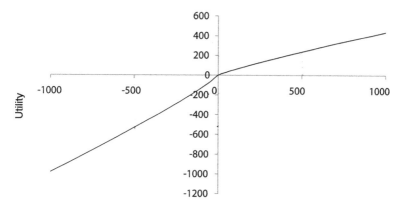

Figure 3.10 A prospect theory utility function for money with parameters $\lambda = 2.25$, α, $\beta = 0.88$, $\gamma = 0.61$ and $\delta = 0.69$.

3.3.1 Reference dependent utility

To put prospect theory in context we can write down a more general model that includes as special cases all the models we have seen so far. This extends the reference dependent utility function I introduced in the previous chapter. The **rank dependent, reference dependent expected utility** of a prospect X is:

$$U(X) = \sum_{i=1}^{n} w_i [\eta u(x_i) + h(x_i, r)] \tag{3.8}$$

where h is some function that depends on a reference point r and η is some parameter. The three special cases we have looked at can be explained as follows.

If $\eta = 1$, $w_i = p_i$ and h is the same as the disappointment function D in equation (3.5) then we have a model of disappointment. In this case there is no weighting of probabilities but there is disappointment or elation if the utility of the outcome is above or below the prior expected level of utility.

If $\eta = 1$ and $h(x, r) = 0$ for all x then we have rank dependent expected utility. If $w_i = p_i$ then this reduces to expected utility. Another way to get at the same thing is have $\eta = 0$, $u(r) = 0$ and h the same as the utility function u. In this case outcomes are not judged relative to a reference level but there is weighting of probabilities.

Finally, if $\eta = 0$ and h is the same as the value function v in equation (3.7) then we have prospect theory. In this case utility is determined by the loss or gain relative to the reference point, and there is weighting of probabilities.

The reference dependent utility function (3.8) gives us, therefore, a framework to compare models. We see that they are all different, and all point to different ways that we might want to move beyond expected utility. This is summarized in

Table 3.12 How disappointment theory, rank dependent expected utility and prospect theory differ from expected utility

Model	Differences to expected utility
Disappointment	There is disappointment or elation if the utility of the outcome is below or above the prior expectation.
Rank dependent utility	There is weighting or probabilities to take account of pessimism or optimism.
Prospect theory	There is weighting of probabilities, and the utility of the outcome is determined solely by the gain or loss relative to the reference point.

Table 3.12. Clearly, when we combine the three models we also obtain a very general model to think about choice with risk. The model, however, is probably a bit too general to be very practical. So, in practice it is necessary to start thinking about narrowing things down a little by asking what features are most important or most important in particular contexts.

That is an exercise I leave for you to think about because what I want to do now is focus on two things that we looked at in some detail in the last chapter but are worth briefly revisiting here. First, equation (3.8) is going to depend crucially on reference point r, and so we need to think about that. Second, attitudes to risk will depend on how potential risks are bracketed or perceived relative to existing risk.

3.3.2 The reference point and expectations

We have seen so far, in this chapter, three candidates for the reference point, they are the current level of wealth (prospect theory), zero wealth (expected and rank dependent expected utility), and the expected utility of the prospect (disappointment theory). In the last chapter we looked at other things that might influence the reference point, such as the no loss in buying hypothesis, and said that these things primarily reflected expectations. For instance, if Anna expected to pay $3 for a box of Nutty cereal, then paying $3 for a box was not counted as a loss. In choice with risk, expectations of what may happen can become even more important.

To illustrate the implications of expectations lets return to the insurance example and consider the choice between full insurance and insurance against theft. Recall that the insurance against theft is prospect $AT = (0.05, \$14; 0.95, \$64)$, full insurance is prospect $FI = (1, \$61)$, and Alan's wealth is $70. Suppose that Alan has the reference dependent utility function:

$$u^r(x) = \begin{cases} 10\sqrt{x} + (x - r) & \text{if } x \geq r \\ 10\sqrt{x} - 2.25(r - x) & \text{if } x < r \end{cases}$$

where r is the reference point. I shall now contrast three scenarios worked through in Table 3.13.

First, suppose that it was a complete surprise to Alan that he was asked to make this choice, and once he has the made the choice he will immediately find out the outcome. For example, the renewal letter arrives in the post when he is not expecting it, he needs to reply that day, and the next day he will find out whether his son is going to use the car. This sounds a bit contrived but is the scenario that most closely fits what we have been analyzing so far, and happens in a typical experiment. In this case the current level of wealth seems the most relevant reference point. Paying for insurance is thus seen as a loss, and Alan would prefer insurance against theft.

Next suppose, more realistically, that Alan was still surprised to get the renewal letter but will only have to pay for the insurance after some delay and will not find out the outcome, i.e. whether the car is in an accident, for some time. In this case it makes sense for the reference level to be the expected outcome of the prospect Alan chooses, because he will have time to change his expectations of wealth before anything happens. His reference point will thus depend on what he chooses. In this case Alan will prefer full insurance because buy the time he pays for it he will not think of it as a loss. With insurance against theft, by contrast, he could still lose if the car is in an accident.

Finally, suppose that Alan was expecting the renewal letter. He presumably had some expectation what he would choose and has already factored this into his reference point. The reference point will, therefore, depend on whether he expected to choose insurance against theft or full insurance. In both cases he prefers full insurance. We see, however, that full insurance looks relatively better if he expected to buy full insurance and insurance against theft looks relatively better if he expected to buy insurance against theft. This can lead to self-fulfilling expectations where the thing Alan expected to choose looks better because he expected to choose it.

Two general points are apparent in this example. First, whether or not Alan expected to face risk will influence how he deals with that risk. For instance, he is

Table 3.13 How the utility of Alan will depend on his expectations. The expected utility from gains and losses measures the expected utility from gains and losses relative to the reference point

Framing	Reference point	Expected utility from gains and losses		Reference dependent utility	
		AT	FI	AT	FI
Unexpected choice, immediate outcome	$70	−19.1	−20.3	58.8	57.9
Unexpected choice, delayed outcome, chooses AT	$61.5	−3.0	–	74.9	
Unexpected choice, delayed outcome, chooses FI	$61	–	0.0	–	77.9
Expected choice of AT	$61.5	−3.0	−1.1	74.9	77.0
Expected choice of FI	$61	−2.4	0.0	75.4	77.9

not willing to pay for full insurance when the renewal letter was a surprise, but is when the renewal letter was expected. Second, if risk was expected, the optimal choice can depend on what Alan expected to choose. Kőszegi and Rabin (2007) capture this with the idea of a **personal equilibrium**. The expected choice of full insurance is a personal equilibrium because it makes sense for Alan to choose full insurance if he expected to choose it. The expected choice of insurance against theft is not a personal equilibrium because Alan would want to choose full insurance even if he expected to choose insurance against theft.

The picture we get is one where expectations and context can matter a lot in determining the reference point and hence the perception of gains and losses. This naturally builds on the things we talked about in the previous chapter, but the presence of risk adds even more things in the mix. There is even more ambiguity about how things will be perceived and what the reference point may be. This clearly raises some challenges in trying to model choice with risk. One small part of meeting this challenge is asking how people might perceive interrelated gambles.

Research Methods 3.5

TV game shows

The objective in most economic experiments is complete anonymity. The exact opposite is probably a TV game show where contestants make choices in front of millions of viewers. TV game shows can, therefore, provide an interesting alternative to the economic experiment, particularly as the stakes are typically a lot higher.

Post et al. (2008) are one of several researchers to study the show 'Deal or no deal?'. In the game a contestant has to choose one of 26 briefcases. Each briefcase contains an amount of money from €0.01 to €5,000,000 (in the Dutch edition). Having chosen a briefcase the contestant is sequentially told what is in the other briefcases, and given a walk away offer. If he or she continues to turn down the offers they eventually get to see how much money is in the briefcase they first chose, and they can keep it! The walk away offer depends on the expected value of the remaining suitcases.

The issue Post et al. focus on is whether choice is path dependent. Specifically, did the contestants' risk attitudes change as they began to see what was in briefcases? They find that they did. Contestants became less risk averse when either high amounts (which is unlucky) or low amounts (which is lucky) were in the briefcases they did not choose. For example, one contestant called Frank was unlucky but carried on gambling, eventually rejecting a sure €6,000 in favor of a 50/50 gamble of €10 or €10,000. He won €10. A second contestant, Susanne, was lucky and rejected a sure €125,000 to eventually win €150,000. It is doubtful we would see such risk taking without the prior process of sequentially seeing what was in other briefcases.

Post et al. show that such behavior can be explained by prospect theory with a reference point based largely on prior expectations of the likely prize.

3.3.3 Combined gambles

Most people are constantly exposed to existing risks because they have money invested in the stock market, might lose their job, have already bought a lottery ticket etc. This raises interesting issues about how a person should evaluate a new risk.

To get us started I will demonstrate that it may be in Alan's interest to take on a small gamble, as a form of diversification, if he is exposed to existing risk. Consider the prospects in Table 3.14. Suppose that Alan is already committed to prospect X, because, say, he has money invested in the stock market. He now needs to decide whether to take on prospect Y or Z. As you can see, the outcome of prospects may be revealed now or in one week's time. Suppose that his current wealth is $20,000 and his utility function is:

$$u^r(x) = \begin{cases} x - 20,000 & \text{if } x \geq 20,000 \\ -2(20,000 - x) & \text{if } x < 20,000. \end{cases}$$

With these preferences Alan would not prefer prospect Y or Z to prospect W. More relevant, however, is to compare prospect Z with prospect X, because both will be resolved in a week's time. If he chooses prospect Z then this should be combined with the existing prospect X to give a combined prospect X + Z. It turns out that prospect X + Z is preferred to prospect X.

The key point of the example is that Alan should choose prospect Z if he is already exposed to prospect X. That's because any new risk should be considered in the light of existing risk. This holds more generally than this simple example. People should be less risk averse over prospects for small amounts of money if they are already exposed to risk.

Another thing the example illustrates is how the delay before knowing the outcome of a prospect should influence choice, if there are existing risks. Alan would do well to choose prospect W rather than Y, but also choose prospect Z. Or should he? If there is no escape from being told the outcome of prospect Y imme-diately then, yes, he should choose prospect W rather than Y. Suppose, however, he could somehow arrange that he will not be told the outcome of prospect Y until

Table 3.14 Risk aversion for small gambles is less if there is existing risk. Alan is already exposed to prospect X and so by choosing prospect Z would obtain prospect X + Z which is preferred to prospect X

Prospect	Probability and value	Timing	Expected utility
W	(1, $0)	now	0
X	(0.5, –$10,000; 0.5, $30,000)	one week	5,000
Y	(0.5, –$500; 0.5, $550)	now	–225
Z	(0.5, –$500; 0.5, $550)	one week	–225
X + Z	(0.25, –$10,500; 0.25, –$9,450; 0.25; $29,500; 0.25, $30,550)	one week	5037.5

one week's time. Then he should do this. This brings to the fore the question of how often a person should choose to observe the outcome of prospects. If Alan is loss averse it may be beneficial for him to delay or combine finding the outcomes of existing prospects so as to avoid too much 'bad news'.

These issues of how to combine prospects are the same as those we looked at in chapter two in terms of mental accounting, hedonic editing, narrow framing and the like.

A pertinent question is whether people do take existing risks, and delay, into account. Narrow framing would suggest they do not, but we also know there is a question of how narrowly people like to bracket things together. I will come back to some evidence on this later when looking at investing the stock market. In the meantime, here are two things for you to think about. Let's start with the puzzle of low stock market participation. Historically, though things have changed now, relatively few people invested in the stock market. If people are risk averse this may seem reasonable. If, however, we take into account all the other risks that people were exposed to, such as becoming unemployed, being in an accident etc, then it becomes much harder to explain such low participation. This suggests narrow framing. On the other hand, it is not unknown for people to delay opening a letter that may bring bad news until they can also open a letter that will hopeful have good news!

3.4 Preference reversals

Recall that in section 3.1.4 I said expected utility should be appropriate if preferences satisfy independence and transitivity. Up until now our focus has primarily been on independence. For instance, preferences consistent with reference dependent expected utility need not satisfy independence but must satisfy transitivity. What I want to do now is change focus a little by questioning whether preferences satisfy transitivity. The way that we can tackle this question is by revisiting the disparity between willingness to accept and willingness to pay, that we first looked at in the previous chapter.

Research Methods 3.6

Behavioral economics' longest saga

Preference reversals have created a lot of debate over the years. Things got started with work by Lichtenstein and Slovic published in the late 1960s and early 1970s. Most widely cited is a paper they published in 1971, entitled 'Reversals of preferences between bids and choices in gambling decisions'. Since then debate has continued unabated about whether preference reversals are real, what causes them, whether they disappear with experience, and so forth.

One interesting aspect of the debate has been the different methods used to think about the issue. Psychologists have largely focused on the issue of procedural invariance, but then there are lots of different ways to model and explain procedural invariance that have been suggested. Some economists have focused on whether preference reversals are real, questioning whether the experimental methods used are reliable enough. Others have pointed out that preference reversals could be obtained by a violation of the independence axiom, and others, as we shall see, that they can be obtained by a violation of the transitivity axiom. A more recent literature has looked at what happens if the willingness to accept is elicited from markets, and subjects have chance to learn over time.

This mix of approaches looks fantastic, but can end up seeming a little antagonistic. On times it seems as though the debate is one in which some argue preference reversals are not real and others respond by showing they are. This is good because it has given us sufficient evidence to suggest preference reversals really are real. It can, however, detract slightly from some of the more subtle underlying issues that tend to get muddled together. For example, we need to ask if the willingness to accept a sure thing is different to the willingness to pay, and if so why? How does willingness to accept or pay change for risky prospects? How does willingness to accept or pay change when we use different methods, e.g. markets to elicit choices? Why can we observe cyclical choices in experiments when the willingness to accept or pay is not considered at all?

Look at the prospects in Table 3.15. Prospects AA and AB have the same expected value but get there in different ways: the **P bet** offers a high probability of winning a low payoff and the **$ bet** a low probability of winning a high payoff. Suppose that we elicit the willingness to accept for each of the prospects. You can refer back to the last chapter for a definition of willingness to accept, but basically we shall ask Alan the minimum amount of money he or she would accept rather than have prospect AA, or prospect AB and shall interpret this as the price Alan puts on the prospect. Subsequently we can ask Alan what he would rather choose, prospect AA or prospect AB.

Figure 3.11 summarizes the results of a study by Tversky, Slovic and Kahneman (1990) where subjects were asked to do this. Many put a higher price on the $ bet than the P bet, but then choose the P bet over the $ bet. This is an example of a **preference reversal**. Another example is to value the P bet more than the $ bet yet choose the $ bet over the P bet. This is rarer.

Preference reversals are puzzling. To see why, suppose that Alan prices the $ bet at $9 and the P bet at $7 and also says he would choose the P bet over the $ bet. You could sell him the $ bet for $9, then offer to swap that for the P bet, and

---

Table 3.15 Prospects that can lead to a preference reversal. Many value the $ bet higher than the P bet but choose the P bet over the $ bet

Prospect	Amount with probability of outcome	
AA, the '$ bet'	$100 gain with probability 0.08	$0 otherwise
AB, the 'P bet'	$10 with probability 0.8	$0 otherwise
AC, sure thing	$8 with probability one	

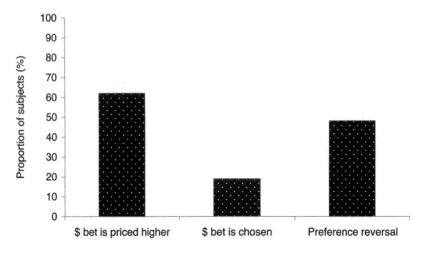

Figure 3.11 The proportion of subjects who price the $ bet higher, choose the $ bet, and exhibit a preference reversal.

Source: Tversky et al. (1990).

then buy the P bet off him for $7. We are back where we started, except you are $2 richer and he is $2 poorer. It looks like a good deal for you!

Because they are so puzzling, many have questioned whether preference reversals really exist. The evidence, however, suggests they definitely do exist (see Research Methods 3.6 and 3.7). The more important question, therefore, is why do they exist? It might be because preferences are non-transitive. After all, it looks like Alan has preferences $AA \geq AC$ and $AC \geq AB$ yet $AB \geq AA$. These preferences would be non-transitive. We saw enough in the last chapter, however, about framing effects and procedural invariance to suggest that this might be the cause. Maybe Alan perceives prospects differently depending on how they are presented to him. We need to think about both of these possibilities.

Research Methods 3.7

Do incentives matter?

A perennial issue in experimental economics is how to incentivize subjects to make the choices that really capture their preferences. For example, when asking a subject to state a willingness to accept for a $ bet, how can we be sure he tells us what he would really want?

In psychology it is common to ask subjects hypothetical questions, and so a subject is asked about his willingness to accept, knowing that his answer is ultimately not going to matter. Economists are generally skeptical about such an approach and prefer monetary incentives. So, having asked the subject his willingness to accept a real game is played. For example, we could generate a random number between 0 and 10. If the random number is above his willingness to accept he gets to keep that amount of money, e.g. if his minimum willingness to accept is $8 and the number comes up 9, he gets $9. If the random number is below his willingness to accept, the $ bet is played out and he either wins $100 or gets $0. Knowing that this game will happen should get a subject to reveal his true willingness to accept.

A study by Berg, Dickhaut and Rietz (2010) looks back over the many studies on preference reversals and tries to pick out whether it matters what the incentives are for subjects. In some studies choices are hypothetical and in others monetary incentives are provided that should get subjects to reveal their true preferences. In an intermediate category subjects are given monetary incentives but the procedure used may not get subjects to reveal their true preferences. Figure 3.12 summarizes some of their data. It turns out that the overall preference reversal rate does not change much if there is truth revealing incentives: it does go down but not a significant amount. This might suggest that incentives do not matter much.

If we look a little deeper, however, we do see that incentives start to matter. This is most apparent when comparing the $ bet reversal rate (the percentage of those subjects who priced the $ bet higher and subsequently chose the P bet) and the P bet reversal rate (the percentage of those subjects who priced the P bet higher and subsequently chose the $ bet). With non-truth revealing preferences there is a systematic tendency for more $ bet reversal than P bet reversals. With truth revealing preferences this disappears. This is important, because a systematic tendency for reversals of one kind and not another suggests something we can model and explain. If reversals are non-systematic they could be just due to mistakes or errors.

This study is not going to close the debate on preference reversals. We now have lots of evidence that there are systematic tendencies in preference reversals even

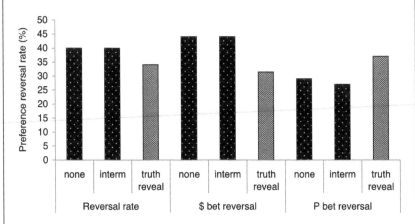

Figure 3.12 Whether the rate of preference reversal differs if there are no, truth revealing, or intermediate incentives. The overall reversal rate does not significantly change but the rate of $ and P reversals becomes more similar.

Source: Berg, Dickhaut and Rietz (2010).

with truth revealing preferences. The study is also not going to close the debate on whether incentives matter (and we shall return to this issue a few times in the rest of the book). The study does, however, illustrate the care needed in running and interpreting experimental results. The incentives subjects are given do matter, but possibly in quite subtle ways that are not immediately apparent.

3.4.1 Procedural invariance

When describing prospect theory we focused on something Kahneman and Tversky called the **evaluation phase** and ignored the editing phase (see Research Methods 3.4). The editing phase is, though, important. In the **editing phase** Alan will organize and reformulate prospects to make them simpler to understand. This can consist of various operations. For example, in a coding phase he classifies outcomes as gains or losses. In a simplification phase he may round probabilities and outcomes up or down. It is basically a combination of mental accounting and the use of simplifying heuristics.

This editing and reformulating of prospects means that the way in which prospects are presented to Alan can affect his interpretation of them. We already saw this in Table 3.9 where a different framing of the same prospect meant that outcomes were coded differently as gains or losses. A similar type of thing could explain preference reversals, because there is a big difference between asking Alan to price a prospect and asking him to choose between the prospect and another.

To pursue this possibility further, Tversky et al. also included the sure thing prospect AC (see Table 3.15) and asked subjects whether they would prefer prospect AA or AC and prospect AB or AC. To see why this is useful suppose that Alan chose prospect AB over AA while pricing prospect AA more than $8 and prospect AB less than $8. This is a preference reversal. Table 3.16 summarizes the four possible things that can happen when Alan is asked to think about prospect AC. For instance, if he chooses prospect AA over AC and AC over AB then it looks as though his preferences are intransitive. If, by contrast, he chooses prospect AC over both AB and AA, then it looks as though his preferences are transitive but he just put too high a price on $ bet, prospect AA.

Table 3.16 The four possible explanations for the preference reversal and the number of choices fitting each explanation. The sample is restricted to those who chose AB > AA, and price AA > $8 > price AB

Explanation	Choices	Times observed
Intransitivity	$AA > AC$ and $AC > AB$	10.0%
Overpricing of $ bet, AA	$AC > AA$ and $AC > AB$	65.5%
Underpricing of P bet, AB	$AC > AA$ and $AB > AC$	6.1%
Both overpricing of $ bet and underpricing of P bet	$AC > AA$ and $AB > AC$	18.4%

Source: Tversky et al. (2000).

I have also put in Table 3.16 the percentage of choices in each category. We see that most preference reversals in this study could be explained by an overpricing of the $ bet. Only 10 percent of preference reversals suggested intransitive preferences. It is plausible, therefore, that preference reversals are caused, in large part, by procedural invariance. To back this up it would be nice to have a good explanation for why there is procedural invariance. Two context effects that seem relevant are scale compatibility and the prominence effect.

Scale compatibility is where the importance of one aspect of an option, e.g. the probability or money that can be earned on a prospect, is enhanced by compatibility with the decision a person is asked to make. So, when Alan is asked to put a price on the $ bet his attention is drawn to the relatively large payoff, causing him to overprice it. The **prominence effect** is where one aspect of an option becomes more prominent depending on the task. For example, the probabilities in a prospect may become more prominent when Alan is comparing prospects. So, when asked to choose between the P bet and the $ bet he may focus on the higher probability of the P bet.

Procedural invariance clearly seems relevant in explaining why we observe preference reversals. But, have we done enough yet to completely rule out intransitive preferences?

3.4.2 Regret theory

In the study by Tversky et al. around 10 percent of choices were suggestive of intransitive preferences. This might seem a relatively small percentage. If we think in a different way, however, we can get a much bigger percentage. For example, Loomes, Starmer and Sugden (1991) asked subjects to choose amongst several prospects like those in Table 3.15 and found that only 36 percent of subjects always made choices consistent with transitive preferences. Most subjects, therefore, made choices suggestive of intransitive preferences, some of the time.

You may be skeptical of this approach. Is it not a case of asking subjects to choose amongst so many prospects that they eventually make a mistake, but we interpret it as them having intransitive preferences? It is probably not. The main evidence that it is not is the fact that subjects were far more likely to choose $AA >
AC, AC > AB$ and $AB > AA$ than $AA > AB, AB > AC$ and $AC > AA$. If subjects were making random mistakes we should not see such a systematic tendency for one set of choices. It seems, therefore, that preferences can be intransitive.

None of the models we have considered so far can lead to intransitive preferences (although I will come back to prospect theory later), so we need something new. One possibility is **regret theory**. Regret theory is most easy to apply when comparing two prospects, so, let's compare prospects AA and AB from Table 3.15.

The key to regret theory is a function $R(x, y)$ that assigns a number to any pair of payoffs x and y. In interpretation $R(x, y)$ is the **regret** or **rejoice** Alan experiences from getting payoff x if he would have got payoff y by choosing the other prospect. One slight complication is that by choosing, say, prospect AA, Alan will generally speaking not know what his payoff would have been if he had chosen AB. We can get around this by thinking of distinct states of the world and saying what the outcome would be in each state of the world, ordering outcomes according to payoffs, as in Figure 3.13. So, for example, there is 0.08 chance he will rejoice $R(100,10)$, a 0.72 chance he will regret $R(0,10)$, and a 0.2 chance he will have no regret $R(0,0)$. We then say that prospect AA is preferred to AB if $0.08R(100,10) + 0.72R(0,10) + 0.2R(0,0) > 0$. That is, prospect AA is preferred if the expected rejoice exceeds the expected regret.

Generalizing from this example, given any two prospects X and Y we can distinguish possible states of the world (in the example there were three). We then say that:

$$X \geq Y \text{ if and only if } \sum_i p_i R(x_i, y_i) > 0$$

where i are possible states of the world and x_i and y_i are the outcomes of the respective prospects. Three assumptions are natural for the function R: (i) $R(x, y) = -R(y, x)$ implying regret is the opposite of rejoice. This also implies $R(0,0) = 0$. (ii) $R(x, y) > R(z, y)$ if $x > y$, implying that regret and rejoice are increasing in the difference in outcomes. (iii) $R(x, z) > R(x, y) + R(y, z)$ if $x > z > y > 0$, implying that a large difference in outcomes is regretted or rejoiced more than two smaller differences combined.

Of primary interest for us is to see whether and why regret can lead to non-transitive preferences. The short story is that it can, and in particular preferences $AA > AC$, $AC > AB$ and $AB > AA$ are consistent with regret theory while choices $AA > AB$, $AB > AC$ and $AC > AA$ are not. Remember, it was the first type of choices that are most often observed, so this is a really nice result.

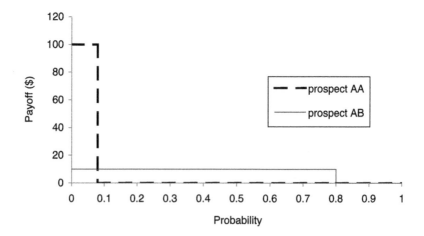

Figure 3.13 The expected regret and rejoice from choosing prospect AA rather than AB.

[Extra] If you want the slightly longer story then here it is. Applying regret theory we get:

$AA \geq AB$ if and only if $0.08R(100,10) + 0.72R(0,10) > 0$.
$AC \geq AA$ if and only if $0.08R(8,100) + 0.92R(8,0) > 0$.
$AB \geq AC$ if and only if $0.8R(10,8) + 0.2R(0,8) > 0$.

Now, let's consider whether it is possible that $AA > AB$, $AB > AC$ and $AC > AA$. Using symmetry we know that $0.92R(8,0) + 0.2R(0,8) = 0.72R(8,0)$. It will also be convenient to write $0.8R(10,8) = 0.08R(10,8) + 0.72R(10,8)$. Doing this, we require the following to hold:

$$0.08[R(100,10) + R(8,100) + R(10,8)] + 0.72[R(0,10) + R(8,0) + R(10,8)] > 0.$$

We can rewrite this as:

$$0.08[R(100,10) + R(10,8) - R(100,8)] + 0.72[R(8,0) + R(10,8) - R(10,0)] > 0.$$

If we now apply condition (iii) we see that this is not possible (use $x = 100$, $y = 10$, $z = 8$ and $x = 10$, $y = 8$, $z = 0$). So, we cannot get preferences $AA > AB$, $AB > AC$ and $AC > AA$. In showing this, however, we have shown that we can get preferences $AB > AA$, $AA > AC$ and $AC > AB$.

Regret theory can explain why we observe non-transitive choices and can explain why we observe some choice cycles and not others. The intuition behind this is regret aversion. Risk aversion could easily explain why prospect AB is preferred to AA and prospect AC is preferred to AB. What we need to do is explain why prospect AA is preferred to AC. That Alan would regret not having a gamble on prospect AA and potentially missing out on $92 is one possible explanation, and we can think of this as **regret aversion**. Regret theory does, therefore, give a plausible explanation for why preferences may be non-transitive.

3.4.3 Prospect theory and preference reversals

For a final plausible explanation of preference reversals I am going to revisit prospect theory. To make this work we are going to rethink what the reference point might be if someone is endowed with a risky prospect.

Suppose that Alan is asked the minimum price for which he will give up the $ bet, prospect AA. Given that he is being asked to sell prospect AA it makes sense, recalling the endowment effect, to think of that as his reference point. The problem is how to interpret a risky prospect as a reference point. What does it mean to say the reference point is $100 with probability 0.08 and $0 with probability 0.92? The simplest way to deal with this is to say that if he accepts some amount of money, say, $9 then with probability 0.08 he will be down $91 on his reference point and with probability 0.92 he will be up $9. This is quite similar to regret and rejoice.

The minimum price he is willing to sell the $ bet, prospect AA, will then be where the expected gain equals the expected loss. Putting this into the standard prospect theory model with parameters $\lambda = 2.25$, $\alpha = 0.5$, $\gamma = 0.61$ and $\delta = 0.69$ gives a selling price of $16.7. If we do the same for the P bet, prospect AB, we get a selling price of $9.7. So, the $ bet is priced above the P bet.

[Extra] To see how we can get these numbers let p_{AA} denote the price Alan puts on the $ bet. Setting the gains equal to the losses gives:

$$\pi^g(0.92) \times p_{AA}{}^\alpha = \lambda\pi^l(0.08) \times (100 - p_{AA})^\alpha.$$

Using parameters $\lambda = 2.25$, $\alpha = 0.5$, $\gamma = 0.61$ and $\delta = 0.69$ implies that:

$$0.74p_{AA}{}^{0.5} = 2.25 \times 0.15 \times (100 - p_{AA})^{0.5}.$$

Squaring both sides gives:

$$0.55p_{AA} = 0.11(100 - p_{AA})$$

and $p_{AA} = \$16.7$ works. So, he would be willing to sell the $ bet for $16.7. Using the same logic for the P bet, prospect AB, we get he would sell for p_{AB} where:

$$\pi^g(0.2) \times p_{AB}{}^\alpha = \lambda\pi^l(0.8) \times (10 - p_{AB})^\alpha.$$

Working through the algebra gives $p_{AB} = \$9.7$.

Finally, we can ask whether he should choose prospect AA or prospect AB. In this case the relevant reference point would appear to be his current wealth. So, he chooses the P bet if:

$$\pi^g(0.08) \times 100^{0.5} < \pi^g(0.8) \times 10^{0.5}.$$

If you work this out it comes to $1.5 < 2.1$, which it clearly is. So he would choose the P bet.

To recap, Alan priced the $ bet above the P bet and yet would choose the P bet over the $ bet. We have a preference reversal! Furthermore, we have done so because of an overpricing of the $ bet, consistent with the data in Table 3.16. Basically, Alan would be reluctant to sell the $ bet both because of the overweighting of the small probability of winning, and the large potential loss from selling a prospect that could have yielded him a high payoff.

Thus, prospect theory provides another plausible explanation for preference reversals. Is this explanation procedural invariance or intransitive preferences? I would say it is a bit of both. Framing is clearly relevant here because the explanation relies on Alan perceiving that he does or does not have ownership of a prospect. The explanation also, however, captures something of preferences; Alan puts a higher price on the $ bet because he does not want to regret missing out on a potentially big win.

3.4.4 Why preference reversals matter

We have seen that a combination of things seem to come together to make preference reversals a reality. But, why is it important that we observe preferences reversals? We saw in the last chapter that choice can depend on context effects for a host of different reasons; have we not just seen a further example of this? I want to finish this section by arguing that preference reversals go beyond being just another context effect.

To motivate the point let's think back to the last chapter and Anna deciding what cereal to buy. According to Table 2.2 she would maximize her utility by choosing the honey cereal. Maybe her preferences will change, but at that point in time the best thing she could do would be to buy honey. The problem is, she may not know that this is the best thing to do, and because of context effects choose something different. For instance, if she is attracted to the bright red packaging of superior she might choose that. This does not change the fact that honey was what she should have chosen.

Now, let's think about Alan deciding what insurance to buy. Maybe we can say that full insurance is definitely the best thing for him to choose but because of context effects he might choose something else. This would be analogous to the story with Anna. If, however, his preferences are intransitive we get a quite different picture. Suppose, for example, that Alan prefers full insurance to no insurance, $FI \geq NI$, prefers no insurance to insurance against theft, $NI \geq AT$, and insurance against theft to full insurance, $AT \geq FI$. This does not seem so crazy.

With such preference it should come as no surprise that Alan's choice would depend on context effects. There is, however, a deeper issue here of what is best for Alan. Whatever choice he makes we can find a choice that he seemingly prefers! There is no best thing he can do. This kind of thing plays havoc with the standard economic model. It also raises some interesting policy questions concerning what is in Alan's best interest. Intransitive preferences and preference reversals, therefore, matter and raise some fundamental questions. In choice with risk they might also be not so uncommon.

3.5 Summary

We started with the idea that the utility of a prospect is equal to the expected utility of the prospect. This is the standard way of modeling choice with risk in economics and is a simple, transparent way of doing so. It must be a good way to do so if preferences are transitive and satisfy independence.

We subsequently saw evidence that expected utility is a bit too simple to capture all we observe. The Allais Paradox, risk aversion for small gambles, risk-loving behavior over losses, and preference reversals are all hard to reconcile with expected utility. This motivated adapting how we model choice with risk.

One thing we considered was to take account of disappointment and elation when measuring the utility of a prospect. A second possibility was to weight probabilities to take account of pessimism and optimism. This is enough to explain the Allais Paradox.

We subsequently looked at prospect theory and reference dependent utility and showed this can explain all the other deviations from expected utility we looked at. We also saw how the presence of risk suggests additional reasons, to those we looked at in the previous chapter, why the reference point can depend on context effects and expectations of what might happen are particularly important.

Finally we looked at preference reversals and the possibility that preferences are intransitive. Regret theory is one way to explain this.

There can be no denying that the things we have looked at in this chapter so far can give us a much better understanding of choice with risk. The one minor problem is that we have lots of different ways of thinking that individually make sense and can explain a lot, but not everything. For example, rank dependent expected utility can explain the Allais Paradox but not preference reversals. Regret theory can explain preference reversals but not why someone would be risk loving over losses. On this score, prospect theory looks like a clear winner because it can explain all we have seen. Arguably, however, this is only because we have the flexibility to change the reference point to something that works. The search still goes on, therefore, for a unified theory of choice with risk. Until we have such a theory it's important to think carefully which model or way of thinking is the one best adapted to the question of interest.

3.6   Financial trading

The first application I want to look at in this chapter is financial trading. Investing in stocks and shares is clearly an inherently risky business and so the models and ideas we have developed in this chapter should be able to tell us something useful about it. To illustrate that they can I have picked out three inter-related things to talk about, the equity premium puzzle, disposition effect and ostrich effect. A particular reason for choosing these three things is that in looking at them we not only learn something useful about investor behavior, but also need to think more about the importance of time and risk, an issue we only briefly looked at in section 3.3.3.

3.6.1   The equity premium puzzle

The **equity premium puzzle** is that the real rate of return on stocks is much higher than the return on 'safer assets' like treasury bills. Figure 3.14 gives some data to illustrate the size of these differences. Such differences in annual return can multiply to huge differences over a few years. For example, $1 invested in stocks in the US in 1926 would have been worth over $2,500 by the year 2000, while the same amount invested in treasury bills would have been worth less than $20. Given such numbers, why would anyone invest in treasury bills?

The obvious answer would be that investors are risk averse and so only invest in stocks, the riskier of the two, if the average return is higher. The equity premium

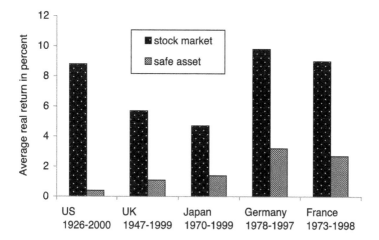

Figure 3.14 The equity premium puzzle. The average annual return on money invested stock exceeds that invested in a safe asset like treasury bills.

Source: Mehra and Prescott (2003).

that we observe could not, however, be explained solely by risk aversion, because to do so would require a coefficient of relative risk aversion of around 30, which is implausibly high. We need a different explanation. An explanation that does work is loss aversion and prospect theory. To make it work, however, we are going to have to think about one complicating factor, time.

The prices of stocks are changing minute by minute during a working day and in principle an investor could change his investments at any time. There is, therefore, no definite moment in time where the outcome of investing in the stock market is known. Instead, an investor must choose how long to leave his investments before he evaluates how they are doing. We call this length of time the **evaluation period**. It seems sensible to assume that the investor gets utility when he evaluates his investments at the end of each evaluation period. For example, Alan might check how his investments are doing every Friday morning and it's then that he perceives any loss or gain.

The evaluation period is going to be crucial. To explain why, it is easiest to work through an example. In Figure 3.15 I have plotted the value over time of $100 invested in two hypothetical assets. In any month the risky asset could fall or rise by $10 while the safe asset grows by a steady $1. If we just look at the value of the investment, in the top half of the figure, then the risky asset looks a clear winner. Things, however, are not so simple when we look at the investor's utility.

Let's look first at the case where the evaluation period is one month and Alan invested in the risky asset. In the first month the value of the asset went up $10. If we plug a gain of $10 into the prospect theory equation (3.7) with values $\alpha = 0.88$ then we get a utility of $10^{0.88} = 7.6$. The same thing happened at the end of month two. What about at the end of month three? In the third month the asset fell in value by $10. If we plug a loss of $10 into equation (3.7) with values $\lambda = 2.25$ and $\beta = 0.88$ then we get a utility of $-2.25 \times 10^{0.88} = -17.1$. This is bad, and bad enough to wipe out the positive utility of the previous two months. Given Alan's loss aversion, his cumulative utility after three months would have been higher if he had invested in the safe asset and avoided this loss. The same can be said after eighteen months.

Now suppose the evaluation period is six months. At the end of every six months the value of the risky asset has gone up. Consequently, the cumulative utility from the risky asset works out to be a lot higher than that from the safe asset.

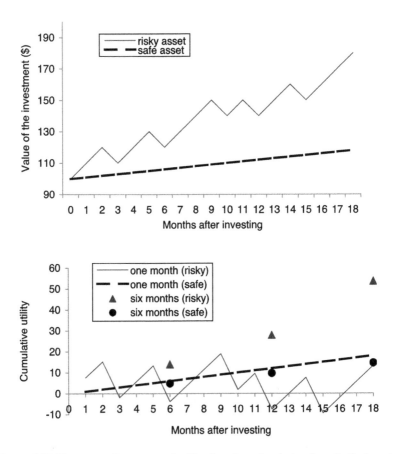

Figure 3.15 The returns in money and utility from investing in two hypothetical assets. If the evaluation period is one month the investor gets more cumulative utility from the safe asset because he avoids the frequent falls in the risky asset. If the evaluation period is six months the investor gets more cumulative utility from the risky asset.

What we see in this example is how the volatility of a risky asset can make it undesirable for someone who is loss averse, even if the overall returns are high. For every month the investment goes down in value there needs to be three months of gain to compensate Alan for the disutility of a bad month. This effect is lessened by lengthening the evaluation period. The longer the evaluation period the less chance the investment will have decreased in value and so the less chance Alan feels a loss. This means there should be an evaluation period where he is relatively indifferent between the risky and safe asset.

Benartzi and Thaler (1995) asked how long the evaluation period would have to be to explain the equity premium we do observe. That is, how long the evaluation period would have to be to make the expected utility on safe assets the same as on stocks. They evaluate this by simulating the utility an investor would have got from investing in US stocks, bonds or treasury bills for various time intervals between 1926 and 1990. As in our stylized example they find that with an evaluation period of one month estimated utility would be higher from investing in safe assets, while with an evaluation period of 18 months it would be higher from stocks. The point where the estimated utility from safe assets and stocks are equal is an evaluation period of 12 months.

The estimate of 12 months is remarkably plausible! It does seem intuitive that ordinary investors might use a one-year period to evaluate returns on investments. Managers of pension and investment funds might also be evaluated on their year-by-year performance. We have, therefore, an explanation for an equity premium. This explanation is based on people being both loss averse and **myopic** in the sense that the evaluation period is shorter than it could be.

3.6.2 The disposition effect

Our next puzzle is why investors prefer to sell stocks that are trading at a gain and hold on to stocks trading at a loss. To explain, suppose Alan sells a stock on a particular day. We can ask whether there was a **realized gain** – the stocks were sold for more than was paid for them – or a **realized loss** – the stocks were sold for less than was paid for them. We can also look at all the other stocks in his portfolio that are not sold and ask whether there was a **paper gain** – the stocks could have been sold for more than was paid for them – or a **paper loss** – the stocks could only have been sold for less than was paid for them. Next we calculate two ratios:

$$\text{proportion of gains realized} = \frac{\text{number of realized gains}}{\text{number of realized gains} + \text{number of paper gains}}$$

$$\text{proportion of losses realized} = \frac{\text{number of realized losses}}{\text{number of realized losses} + \text{number of paper losses}}$$

The **disposition effect** is that the proportion of gains realized is significantly greater than the proportion of losses realized. In other words, investors prefer to sell stocks that will give them a realized gain than to sell stocks that will give them a realized loss. To give some numbers we can look at a study by Odean (1998), who analyzed the trading activity from 1987 to 1993 of 10,000 households who held accounts at a large brokerage firm. He found that the proportion of gains realized was 0.148 and the proportion of losses realized only 0.098.

You might be thinking that the disposition effect is just good investing. For example, if a stock has gone up in price, meaning realized gains, maybe it will subsequently fall in price, so does it makes sense to realize the gain? Unfortunately the evidence suggests otherwise. Odean found, for instance, that stocks that were sold for a realized gain earned on average 3.4 percent more over the subsequent year than stocks that were not sold for a realized loss. Again, we need a different explanation. Given that prospect theory did so well at explaining the equity premium puzzle maybe it can work again?

I shall stick with a very similar story to that we used to think about the equity premium puzzle. So, imagine assets that every month either go up or down in value. At the end of the year Alan will evaluate his portfolio. The utility he feels at that point depends on the gain or loss on his portfolio and is consistent with the prospect theory equation (3.7) with $\lambda = 2.25$ and $\alpha, \beta = 0.88$. Up to now, everything is the same as when we looked at the equity premium puzzle. Here is the new thing: during the year Alan can check how his portfolio is doing and buy or sell assets if he wishes to. When he checks how his investments are doing he does not feel any loss or gain; that only comes at the end of the evaluation period.

Now, suppose that Alan checks how his investments are doing six months into the year. If his investments have gone down during the first six months then, because of loss aversion, he will be very eager to regain those losses before the evaluation period ends. By contrast, if his investments have gone up during the first six months then he may be keen to guarantee those gains to avoid any loss. This looks like a possible explanation for the disposition effect, but we need to check that (see Research Methods 3.8). Barberis and Xiong (2010) do that by working out the optimal strategy of an investor in such a situation, and then simulate asset prices to calculate the proportion of gains realized and losses realized we would expect to see.

Figure 3.16 plots some of the data from the study. Recall that we are trying to explain why the proportion of gains realized is larger than the proportion of losses realized. Figure 3.16 suggests that prospect theory will actually give us the opposite! For the most part we predict that the proportion of losses realized should exceed the proportion of gains realized.

To try and understand why we obtain this result we can work through an example illustrated in Figure 3.17. Suppose that Alan will evaluate his portfolio after 12 months and check it once after six months (the $T = 2$ case in Figure 3.16). He is only interested in one asset, which starts the year at price $25 and every six months either goes up in value by $5 or down by $2.50. Alan buys two shares at the start of the year, investing $50. We need to ask what he will do after six months if the price has gone up and down.

First, suppose that it has gone up. This means he is at point G in Figure 3.17. He could sell at this point and be guaranteed a gain by the end of the year, but why

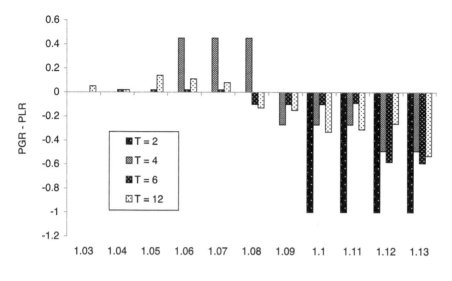

Figure 3.16 The proportion of gains realized (PGR) minus the proportion of losses realized (PLR) in simulated investments. T is the number of times the investor looks up his portfolio during the evaluation period. The disposition effect is that the proportion of gains realized exceeds the proportion of losses realized. Prospect theory appears to give the opposite.

Source: Barberis and Xiong (2010).

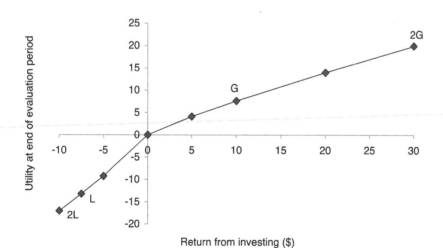

Figure 3.17 Why prospect theory does not cause the disposition effect. If the investor is at point G after six months, he should increase his investment and aim for 2G. If the investor is at point L after six months, he should decrease his investment to make sure he does no worse than 2L.

stop there? He could buy two more shares, be still guaranteed to not make a loss, and have the chance to be at point 2G if the price goes up again. It turns out that if he was willing to invest at the start of the year (when there was the chance of making a loss), then he must want to increase his investment at this stage (now that he is guaranteed not to make a loss).

Now, suppose the price has gone down after six months. This means he is at point L. He would like to regain his losses, but also wants to avoid further losses. This is possible by selling one share and keeping the other. If the price goes up then he will be back to zero by the end of the year and if the price goes down a second time he will at least only be at point 2L with losses of $7.50. Again, this will be the optimal thing to do.

We see through this example that prospect theory fails to explain the disposition effect on both counts. If Alan had realized gains then he should increase his investment, and if he had realized losses he should decrease his investment. You might say this result is dependent on the asymmetry whereby the price of the asset increases by more than it decreases. This, however, is what we do tend to observe about asset prices. Furthermore, if Alan was willing to invest at all, despite his loss and risk aversion, then there must have been this asymmetry, because he will only invest in stocks that are more likely to go up than down.

Prospect theory does not, therefore, seem a convincing explanation for the disposition effect. Indeed, it suggests we have even more of a puzzle to solve than we might have first imagined. Not all hope is lost, because we might argue that the investor will feel a loss or gain in utility every time he looks at the value of his portfolio and not just at the end of the evaluation period. Perhaps, however, it is better to accept reality. Prospect theory was able to explain the equity premium puzzle without any trouble, but raises more questions about the disposition effect than it solves. In chapter five we shall come back and try to answer these questions.

3.6.3 The ostrich effect

In both the previous puzzles, time has played a pivotal role. First, we looked at the evaluation period over which gains and losses are judged. Then, we looked at how often an investor may check up on and trade within the evaluation period. The point I shall pick up on now is that the evaluation period and frequency of trade are not only pivotal but also typically chosen by the investor. This raises the issue of how often Alan should pay attention to his investments.

To get some insight on this issue imagine that Alan periodically hears news about the performance of the stock market. This news gives him some idea what may be happening to his investments. It is only by looking up his investments, however, that he can definitively find out what has happened to them. What should he do after he has watched the news?

If he only feels the loss or gain of investing when he evaluates his investments at the end of the year then he should look up his investments, because he has got nothing to lose. Realistically, however, he is going to feel something when he checks on his investments, even if the biggest effect is at the end of the evaluation

---

Research Methods 3.8

Don't always trust intuition

Ronald Reagan once said: 'One definition of an economist is somebody who sees something happen in practice and wonders if it will work in theory.' A nice quote which sums up a lot of what economics is about. Many question whether this formalism is of any use, as clear in a second quote, from Alfred Knopf: 'An economist is a man who states the obvious in terms of the incomprehensible.' This study by Barberis and Xiong is one illustration of why economists believe it is good to check that things work in theory.

Prospect theory was an intuitive solution to the disposition effect. If a stock has risen in value it takes an investor to the concave risk averse area of her utility function and if it falls in value it takes her to the convex risk-loving area of her utility function. Consequently, he should take more risks on stocks that have fallen in value than gained in value. It was so intuitive an explanation it became the most commonly mentioned explanation for the disposition effect. Barberis and Xiong took on the task of checking the explanation does work in theory (to make the obvious incomprehensible). Their conclusion was that prospect theory is not so great an explanation for the disposition effect. Sometimes, therefore, intuition and common sense can lead us astray. That's why it's important to write down models and check things really do work like they seem to.

---

period. We can distinguish, therefore, two effects. First, there is an **impact effect** whereby looking up his investments makes it more likely he will feel the gain or loss on his investments. Second, there is a **reference point updating effect** whereby he is more likely to change the reference point by which he will evaluate his investments at the end of the evaluation period.

These two effects work in opposite directions. If the news is good then the investor would be tempted to look up his investments and feel happy about the gain he is likely to observe. But, he would also be reluctant to see the gain, increase his reference point and subsequently be more likely to experience a loss relative to this higher reference point. There are similar trade-offs if the news is bad. Intuitively, however, the reasons to look up the investments after good news seem a bit stronger than those to look up after bad news. This suggests the **ostrich effect,** whereby the investor is more likely to look up his investments following good news rather than bad.

A study by Karlsson, Loewenstein and Seppi (2005) looked at data from Norway and Sweden on how often investors do look up their investments. They compare the daily number of investors who look up their portfolio to the performance of the relevant stock market index in the previous week. Figure 3.18 summarizes the data and shows that there did indeed appear to be an ostrich effect. When the stock market index was going up (good news), investors were more likely to look up their investments than when it was flat or going down (neutral or bad news).

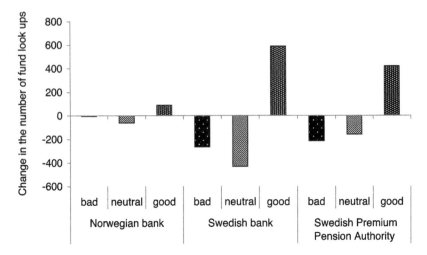

Figure 3.18 The change in the number of investors looking up their investments depending on whether the stock market was up, down or neutral over the previous week.

Source: Karlsson et al. (2005).

The consequences of an ostrich effect are interesting to hypothesize about. In discussing the equity premium puzzle, we suggested investors may have too short an evaluation period. The ostrich effect partly alleviates this. In discussing the disposition effect we suggested that investors may not do the best thing when they look up a portfolio with gains and losses. The ostrich effect may be a way to avoid this. Selective attention may, therefore, be a good way of managing loss aversion and the like? I leave you to think about that.

3.7 Insurance

I started this chapter with the example of Alan buying insurance, so it seems apt to finish by looking at some real data on insurance. One basic observation is that people seem to want insurance. Most people buy at least one of the following: house insurance, life insurance, car insurance, health insurance, travel insurance etc. In some instances this is because insurance is compulsory, but that can only explain so much. It seems, therefore, that people like insurance, and this clearly suggests that people are risk averse for big gambles. This should be no surprise, given that we observe risk aversion for small gambles, and so it is not too hard to explain why people might want insurance.

What I will focus on, therefore, is a more subtle question of how much insurance people choose to have. One particularly interesting issue is that of the deductible. The **deductible** is the amount of any insurance claim that a person would have to pay themselves. So, for example, if Alan's car is involved in an accident with total damage of $2,000 and his deductible is $500, then Alan pays the first $500 and the insurance company the remaining $1,500.

Insurance companies typically give some choice of deductible and a policy with a lower deductible will have a higher premium. In choosing the level of deductible, Alan faces a clear trade-off: by spending, say, $10 more in premium he will have to pay, say, $100, less if he makes a claim. The choice of deductible is, therefore, a nice thing to look at. It can give us a picture of how people choose insurance and also give us some general insights on choice with risk.

Sydnor (2010) looked at a sample of 50,000 standard policies from a large home insurance provider in the US. Customers could choose a deductible of $1,000, $500, $250 or $100. Table 3.17 summarizes some of the data and shows that the majority chose the $500 or $250 deductible. The exact amount of premium would depend on the house value, location etc, but on average people paid around $100 or $150 extra to lower the deductible.

There was evidence, which we cannot see in Table 3.17, that households were price sensitive, in the sense that those buying the $250 deductible paid on average less extra premium than those who chose the $500 deductible would have had to do. Even so, the amount that households spent to lower the deductible looks high. We can say this with some confidence because we know the actual claim rate of the customers and so know the amount they would have benefited from the lower deductible. The costs of the deductible do not seem to justify the benefits, and the estimated level of risk aversion to justify such choices is way above what is plausible.

How can we explain the preference for a lower deductible? One likely factor is an over-estimation of the likelihood of making a claim. If the claim rate is 20 percent then the estimates of risk aversion come down to below 10. This, in itself, is still not enough, however, because an expected claim rate of 20 percent would be too pessimistic and a coefficient of risk aversion of 10 is still too high. A second likely factor is loss aversion.

Care is needed, however, in applying loss aversion to insurance because paying the premium might be interpreted as a loss. It can, therefore, become even harder to explain why someone would incur for sure the loss of, say $100, to lower the

Table 3.17 Choice of deductible on home insurance. Few households chose the $1,000 deductible, but this is hard to explain using expected utility because it requires extreme levels of risk aversion

Deductible	Proportion who chose it	Average extra premium	Claim rate	Expected saving with $1,000 deductible	Lower bound on risk aversion using CRRA
$1,000	17.0%	$0	2.5%	–	–
$500	47.6%	$100	4.3%	$80	1,719
$250	35.0%	$159	4.9%	$127	4,000
$100	0.3%	$243	4.7%	–	–

Source: Syndor (2010).

probability they will subsequently lose $500. Indeed, this would directly contradict the evidence that people are risk loving over losses. One way out of this puzzle is to apply the 'no loss in buying' hypothesis that we looked at in the last chapter. Recall that this hypothesis says giving up money to buy something is perceived as a foregone gain rather than loss. So, spending an extra $100 on insurance is not perceived as a loss. Recall also the example in section 3.3.2.

If we accept the 'no loss in buying' hypothesis and apply the standard formulation of prospect theory with $\lambda = 2.25$, α, $\beta = 0.88$ and $\gamma = 0.61$ we find that a 4 percent claim rate would be weighted as 12 percent and a person would pay $110 for a $500 deductible. A combination of loss aversion and overestimating the probability of making a claim can easily, therefore, explain the choices of deductible. Prospect theory again comes up trumps.

Things may not be quite so simple, however. To give a first hint why, we can look at a study by Cohen and Einav (2007). They looked at the deductible choices of over 100,000 individuals buying car insurance in Israel between 1994 and 1999. Again people could choose from four deductible levels, called regular, low, high or very high. This time the premium and deductible were percentages of the premium and deductible for the regular premium. For example, someone opting for a low deductible paid multiple 1.06 of the regular premium and got multiple 0.6 of the regular deductible. Table 3.18 gives some numbers to compare with those of Table 3.17.

The financial trade-offs that people faced were roughly similar to those of the previous study, with one notable exception, namely the claim rate is much higher. Unfortunately, it is difficult to calculate a precise estimate of risk aversion from the data. If we focus on the fact that the vast majority of people chose the regular deductible, and not the high or very high deductible, then we would obtain high estimates of risk aversion, similar to those in the study by Syndor, and too high to be plausible. Cohen and Einav noted, however, that customers may not have been informed about the high and very high deductible options when deciding what to do. In this case we should focus on the fact that people chose the regular and not the low deductible. Doing this, we find low and plausible estimates of risk aversion of less than four.

Table 3.18 Deductible choice in Israeli car insurance. (Monetary amounts were converted from the actual New Israel Shekels by dividing by 3.5, the average exchange rate over the period.)

Deductible chosen	Average deductible	Proportion who chose it	Extra premium	Claim rate
very high	$1,075	0.5%	0	13.3%
high	$745	0.6%	$69	12.8%
regular	$415	81.1%	$182	23.2%
low	$250	17.8%	$237	30.1%

Source: Cohen and Einav (2007).

We are simply unable to tell from this data what the attitudes to risk were. That, in itself, though is informative because it emphasizes that other things will likely influence the insurance decision. Indeed, Syndor also found considerable inertia, with people choosing the same deductible as they did in the past. To carry on this story we need to look at choice over time, which is the focus of the next chapter.

3.8 Further reading

The survey paper by Starmer (2000) is a great place to start. Much of the material in this chapter owes its origins to the work of Robert Sugden and co-authors. Some of the relevant papers are Loomes and Sugden (1982, 1983, 1986), Loomes, Starmer and Sugden (1991) and Schmidt, Starmer and Sugden (2008). Most of the rest of the material owes its origins to Kahneman and Tversky, including their 1979 and 1992 papers I mentioned earlier (much of the suggested reading for chapter two is relevant here as well). I also want to mention Rabin (2000), who first appreciated the issues in section 3.1.2, and on the issue of measuring risk aversion the paper by Holt and Laury (2002) is a useful reference.

3.9 Review questions

3.1   Explain why the indifference curves in a probability triangle diagram are straight lines if preferences satisfy expected utility theory. [Hint, we can write the expected utility of a prospect as $U(x) = p_1 u(x_1) + (1 - p_2 - p_3)u(x_2) + p_3 u(x_3)$.]

3.2   Show why it is inconsistent with expected utility that most people choose prospect F over E and prospect G over H, when the prospects are as in Table 3.5.

3.3   Using the model of disappointment with $\theta = 0.002$ consider the following three prospects, $A = (0.5, \$2,400; 0.5, \$0)$, $B = (0.7, \$2,400; 0.3; \$0)$ and $C = (0.3, \$2,400; 0.7; \$0)$. Work out the utility of each prospect and comment on the result.

3.4   Using prospect theory say whether a person would prefer prospect I or prospects J to N from Table 3.6.

3.5   In 1963 Paul Samuelson wrote about a colleague who said that he would turn down the prospect $(0.5, -\$100; 0.5, \$200)$ but would accept 100 such prospects. Suppose that his utility function is $u(x) = x - w$ if $x \geq w$ and $u(x) = -2.5(w - x)$ if $w > x$ where w is his wealth. Show why he turned down the prospect? Now, imagine two prospects will be done in turn and he will adjust his wealth level after each prospect. Show that he should turn down the two prospects? Finally, imagine that he only adjusts his wealth level after seeing the outcome of both prospects. Should he take on the two prospects? Should he take on 100 prospects?

3.6   What do you think is the relevant reference point of a prospect? How might the certainty effect be related to reference dependence?

3.7   One set of prospects considered by Loomes et al. (1991) was the following, $A = (0, \$10; 0.6, \$4)$, $B = (0.7, \$7.50; 0.3, \$1)$ and $C = (1, \$5)$. What would you choose between A and B, B and C, and A and C? How can regret theory help us explain choices in this case?

3.8 What would happen to the equity premium if investors were less loss averse or the evaluation period was longer? How often should you evaluate your investments?

3.9 I argued in section 3.7 that, applying the standard formulation of prospect theory with $\lambda = 2.25$, $\beta = 0.88$ and $\gamma = 0.61$, a person would pay $110 for an extra deductible of $500 if the claim rate was 4 percent. How much would a person be willing to pay to reduce the deductible by $165 if the claim rate is 25 percent? Comment on the numbers in Table 3.18.

3.10 Is expected utility theory of any practical revelance?

4 Choosing when to act

The only way to get rid of a temptation is to yield to it.
I can resist everything except temptation.

Oscar Wilde

Time is important in most economic decisions because the choices we make will have future consequences. Should a person do the shopping today, or tomorrow? Should she buy a new TV, or save for retirement? Should she look for a new job? Should she go to university and get a qualification? Should she eat healthily and join a gym? The answer to all these questions involves weighing future benefits and costs with present benefits and costs. We need to think about how people do that, and that's the focus of this chapter.

4.1 Exponential discounting

To illustrate some of the issues, consider Maria planning when to do her homework. The homework was set on Friday and must be handed in on Monday morning. She can do it on Friday, Saturday, Sunday or Monday. Table 4.1 gives her day-by-day utility, depending on when she does the homework. For example, if she does it on Friday she pays a cost on Friday, gets to enjoy Saturday and Sunday, and on Monday gets to know how well she did. Doing the homework on a weekend is more costly but also means she does it better. When should Maria do the homework?

Clearly she has to weigh up the benefits and costs of doing the homework on each possible day. Before we see how she might do this, it is worth introducing some general notation for thinking about choice over time. We can think of time as running from period one to period T. In the example, period one is Friday and period $T = 4$ is Monday. Maria needs to plan what she will do in each period between now and T, and given a plan, she can work out what her utility will be in each period. We can think of the utility in a period as determined by the same utility function that we came across in chapters two and three, and I will use u_t to denote the utility in period t. (Just to clarify, in some parts of the book I have used u_i to denote the utility of person i, but not in this chapter.) In the example, a plan

Table 4.1 The day-by-day utility for Maria of doing her homework on different days

Plan	Utility on			
	Friday	Saturday	Sunday	Monday
Do it Friday	−5	5	10	4
Do it Saturday	0	−5	10	10
Do it Sunday	0	5	−5	10
Do it Monday	0	5	10	−5

is when to do the homework, and we see, for example, that the utility in period three is $u_3 = 10$ if Maria plans to do the homework on Friday.

To try and model Maria's choice we can use an **inter-temporal utility function** that combines utility from each period to one measure of overall utility. The simplest way to do this would be to just add together the utility from each time period. Generally, however, she might want to **discount**, that is give less weight to future utility. This suggests a **utility function with exponential discounting**. The inter-temporal utility of getting u_1 in period 1, u_2 in period 2, and so on is then:

$$u^T(u_1, u_2, ..., u_T) = u_1 + \delta u_2 + \delta^2 u_3 + ..., +\delta^{T-1}u_T = \sum_{t=1}^{T}\delta^{t-1}u_t \qquad (4.1)$$

where δ is a number called the **discount factor**. Inter-temporal utility is, therefore, a simple weighted sum of the utility in each period. If $\delta < 1$ then less weight is given to the utility in a period the further away that period is. So, the smaller is δ the more future utility is discounted.

If we know the utility in each period of each plan then we can work out the inter-temporal utility of each plan. A prediction would be that Maria should choose the plan with highest inter-temporal utility. Table 4.2 illustrates what happens when we do this for three different discount factors. We can see that the higher is δ, the more impatient Maria becomes. If $\delta = 1$ she is willing to sacrifice an enjoyable Saturday in order to get a higher mark on Monday. If $\delta = 0.7$, she is more impatient to enjoy herself and does not do the homework until Monday.

Exponential discounting is a very simple way to model choice over time. All we need to know is the discount factor, and then we can easily predict choice. For that reason exponential discounting is by far the most common way used in economics to model choice over time. What we need to do is ask whether it is sophisticated enough to capture all the things we observe. Before we do that, it is important we fully understand what the model and, in particular, the discount factor, implies and so there are a couple of things I want to mention.

The first thing I want you to think about is the units of measurement: a period and utility. Maria's choice is going to have a stream of future consequences and we somehow need to measure those consequences. What I have done is split the future into days and say what her utility will be on each day, but there is inevitably

Table 4.2 The inter-temporal utility of each plan for three different discount factors

Plan	inter-temporal utility		
	$\delta = 1$	$\delta = 0.9$	$\delta = 0.7$
Do it Friday	14	10.5	4.7
Do it Saturday	15	10.9	4.8
Do it Sunday	10	7.7	4.5
Do it Monday	10	9.0	6.7

something arbitrary about how we split things up. For instance, I could have split into hours and said what her utility will be in each hour, or seconds, etc. One sensible approach is to split things up as Maria perceives them, and so, if she thinks in terms of what will happen each day, then that is how we should split things. How Maria perceives things will, however, likely depend on the context. This is already enough to suggest important context effects.

The second thing I want to clarify is the distinction between discount factor and discount rate. If the **discount factor** is 0.8, then '$10's worth of utility' next period is equivalent to $8 today. More generally, $10 next period is equivalent to δ10 today. The smaller the discount factor, the more impatient Maria is. Given a discount factor δ we can work out a **discount rate** ρ using the relation:

$$\delta = \frac{1}{1+\rho} \text{ or } \rho = \frac{1-\delta}{\delta}.$$

For example if the discount factor is 0.8 then the discount rate is 0.25. In interpretation a discount rate of 0.25 means Maria would require an interest rate of 25 percent to delay until next period. So, instead of $8 today she would want $1.25 \times \$8 = \$10$ next period. The higher the discount rate, the more impatient she is. It does not matter whether we use discount rate or discount factor, and so to be consistent I will use discount factor throughout this book. If you follow up the further reading, however, expect many to use the term discount rate. [Extra] If you are wondering why the name 'exponential discounting': in continuous time, equation (4.1) becomes:

$$u^T = \int_0^T e^{-\rho t} u_t$$

where ρ is the discount rate.

4.1.1 The discount factor

To better understand exponential discounting we need to see what values for the discount factor seem most appropriate. In the experimental lab the discount factor can be estimated by giving subjects questions of the form: 'Would you prefer $100 today or $150 in a year's time?' If they answer $100 today then the discount factor is smaller than 0.66 (but see review question 4.1!). I want to look now at a study by Benzion, Rapoport and Yagil (1989), where subjects were asked questions a bit like this. More precisely, subjects were asked questions of the four basic types given below. As you look through these questions, please think what your answer would be.

- **Postpone receipt**: You have just earned $200 but have the possibility to delay receiving it one year. How much money would you need to get after a year in order to want to delay payment?
- **Postpone payment**: You need to pay back a debt of $200 but have the possibility to delay payment one year. How much money would you be willing to pay back after a year if payment is delayed?
- **Expedite receipt**: You will get $200 in one year but have the chance to receive the money immediately. How much money would you accept now rather than have to wait a year?
- **Expedite payment**: You need to pay back a debt of $200 in one year but can pay it now. How much would you be willing to pay now rather than pay off the debt after one year?

In specific questions the time period was changed from six months to four years and the amount of money from $40 to $5,000. Figure 4.1 summarizes the implied annual discount factor we get from subject's responses to each question. There is a lot to look at in Figure 4.1. One thing, however, stands out immediately and that's that the discount factor appears to depend a lot on context. We can see this in how the discount factor varies a lot depending on the length of time, amount of money, payment versus receipt, and expedite versus postpone.

In looking in a little more detail at Figure 4.1 I want to point out five things. First, notice that the discount factor is relatively low, around 0.8–0.9, suggesting the subjects were relatively impatient. Next, notice that the discount factor is higher the longer it is necessary to wait, suggesting **short-term impatience**. For example, subjects wanted on average almost as much compensation to postpone receipt six months as to postpone four years. A third thing to note is that the larger the sum of money, the larger the estimated discount factor, suggesting people are more patient for larger amounts. This is called the **absolute magnitude effect**.

Next I want to compare payment versus receipt and loss versus gain. If you look from top to bottom in Figure 4.1, then you can see a **gain-loss asymmetry** where the estimated discount factor is smaller for gains than for losses. For example, the discount factor is higher in the case of postponing payment (which would require a loss of money) than for postponing receipt (which would involve a gain of money). Similarly, the discount factor is higher in the case of expediting receipt (which would require a loss of money) than for expediting payment (which would involve a gain of money). This is consistent with loss aversion because it suggests subjects were reluctant to lose money in order to postpone or expedite.

The final thing I want you to do is compare postponing versus expediting. If you look from left to right in Figure 4.1 then you can see a **delay-speed up**

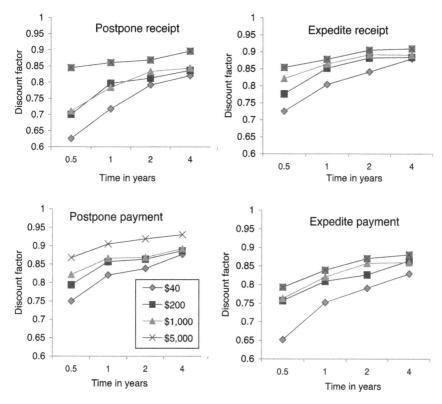

Figure 4.1 Estimated discount factors for four types of choices.

Source: Benzion et al. (1989).

asymmetry where the estimated discount factor is higher to postpone than to expedite payment and higher to expedite than postpone receipt. This is because subjects were willing to pay relatively less money to postpone a payment than they demanded to expedite payment. Similarly, they demanded relatively more to postpone receipt than they were willing to pay to expedite receipt.

To really work well, exponential discounting requires that the discount factor should not change depending on context. In other words, in Figure 4.1 we should see overlaying horizontal lines all at the same discount factor. We clearly do not, and this is not good news for anyone wanting to use exponential discounting. By now, however, you should be getting used to the idea that context matters. Indeed, the gain–loss asymmetry is consistent with loss aversion, and the delay–speed up asymmetry suggestive of mental accounting.

The existence of such large context effects does not mean that exponential discounting is necessarily a bad way to model choice. What it does mean is that we have to be very careful in thinking what the appropriate discount factor should be for a particular situation. There is no such thing as 'Maria's discount factor'.

Instead, Maria will likely have different discount factors for different things. For example, she might be impatient to repay $10 she lent from one friend, but more patient to get back a CD she lent to another friend. Before we explore the implications of this there is one more important context effect we have yet to consider.

Research Methods 4.1

Empirical versus lab evidence

Inter-temporal choice is one area where the experimental lab does seem inadequate to answer many of the questions we are interested in, because we want to know how people trade-off money over relatively large time periods. How can we create delay over relatively large time periods in the experimental lab? One option is to use hypothetical scenarios, as in the Benzion et al. study. This, however, leads to the objection that subjects are not making real choices. If we do use real choices then we cannot realistically delay payment beyond a few months, and certainly not years. It is also questionable whether subjects would find delayed payment credible.

This means that empirical studies in which we observe people making choices with long-term trade-offs are very useful. We can illustrate with a study by Warner and Pleeter (2001). In 1992 the US Department of Defence needed to reduce the size of the US military. They offered selected servicemen two possible packages for leaving the military: (a) a lump sum payment of around $25,000 for privates and NCOs, and $50,000 for officers; (b) an annuity that would pay some fraction of current basic pay for twice the length the person had worked for the military.

Serviceman had, therefore, the choice between a one-off payment and deferred payments. For a particular serviceman it is possible to work out the discount factor such that the serviceman should be indifferent between the two options. Formally, we find the δ^* such that:

$$LS(1 - T_{LS}) = \sum_{t=1}^{2YOS} \delta^{*t-1} A(1 - T_A)$$

where LS is the lump sum payment, A the annuity payment, YOS the years of service and T the respective tax rates. A serviceman should choose the lump sum payment if and only if they are more impatient that is implied by δ^*, i.e. only if their discount factor is $\delta < \delta^*$. With data on what a person did choose and by calculating δ^* we can therefore estimate a person's discount factor. This is what Warner and Pleeter do. Estimates of the mean discount rate were around 0.85.

The estimate of 0.85 is consistent with what we see in Figure 4.1, which provides reassurance that the numbers obtained from the study by Benzion et al. are not unrealistic. I think this nicely illustrates how empirical studies can complement experimental studies. Experimental studies allow us to investigate relatively easily the comparative statics of changing things like the amount of money and time frame. This is simply not possible with empirical studies because events such as the US military downsizing are rare and only give a point estimate of the discount factor. Empirical studies do though serve as a useful check that results obtained in the lab are meaningful.

4.1.2 The utility of sequences

Imagine now that instead of asking someone whether they would prefer $100 today or $150 in a year's time, we ask them whether they would prefer $100 today and $150 in a year's time, or $150 today and $100 in a year's time. This gets us thinking how people interpret **sequences** of events. To illustrate how people tend to respond to such questions I will look at how subjects answered two questions asked in a study by Loewenstein and Prelec (1993).

In the first question people were asked to imagine two planned trips to a city they once lived in but do not plan to visit again after these two trips. During one trip they need to visit an aunt they do not like, and in the other visit friends they do like. Those asked were given three scenarios for when the trips might be (e.g. one this weekend and the other in 26 weeks) and asked to say who they would rather visit first. The results are in Figure 4.2.

One thing to pick out from Figure 4.2 is a **preference for an improving sequence** in which subjects visit the aunt first and then friends later. This might seem natural but is the opposite of what exponential discounting would predict. If someone uses exponential discounting, with a discount factor less than one, then they would maximize their inter-temporal utility by visiting the friends first because they are impatient for higher utility. This impatience does become apparent when the gap between the trips is made bigger because subjects then wanted to visit friends first.

In the second question I want to look at people who were asked to choose when over the next three weeks they would like to eat out at restaurants called

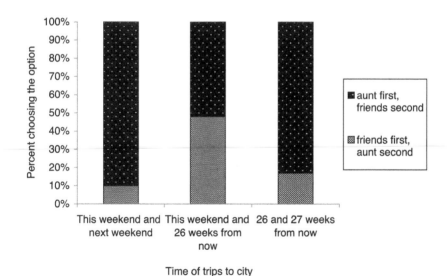

Figure 4.2 Choice of when to visit an aunt and friends. If the two trips were close together, most subjects chose to visit the aunt first. If the two trips were far apart more subjects chose to visit friends first.

Source: Loewenstein and Prelec (1993).

Table 4.3 Choice of when to eat at a restaurant. When asked to choose between options A and B, most subjects prefer to delay eating at Fancy French restaurant. When asked to choose between options C and D, most subjects prefer not to delay eating at Fancy French restaurant.

Option	This weekend	Next weekend	Two weekends away	choices
A	Fancy French	eat at home	eat at home	16%
B	eat at home	Fancy French	eat at home	84%
C	Fancy French	eat at home	Fancy Lobster	54%
D	eat at home	Fancy French	Fancy Lobster	46%

Source: Loewenstein and Prelec (1993).

Fancy French and Fancy Lobster. The results are in Table 4.3. When asked to choose between options A and B, we see the same preference for an improving sequence that we saw for the previous question. When asked to choose between options C and D, however, many subjects preferred to spread the good events over the sequence. Again, this might seem natural, but is not consistent with exponential discounting. This switch in choices should not happen because the utility in period three should not affect the optimal choice in periods one and two. It clearly may do.

Overall, therefore, we see a preference for improving sequences coupled with a preference for spreading events evenly throughout the sequence. None of this seems consistent with exponential discounting. The only way to make it consistent is to distinguish sequences from disjoint events. This can work. For instance we could say that the relevant time period for deciding when to visit the aunt and friends is one month. If, therefore, the two trips are consecutive weekends they should be bundled together and seen as a sequence, while if they are 26 weeks away they should be seen as disjoint events and discounted. Table 4.4 illustrates how this might work to explain what we see in Figure 4.2.

Table 4.4 Maria deciding when to visit an aunt and friends. Events in weeks one to four and weeks 24 to 28 are bundled together as a sequence. Events in weeks 24 to 28 are seen as disjoint from those in weeks one to four and discounted with a factor of 0.8.

Events		Inter-temporal utility
Weeks 1–4	*Week 24–28*	
Visit aunt then friends		10
Visit friends then aunt		5
Visit aunt		0
Visit friends		15
Visit aunt	Visit friends	12
Visit friends	Visit aunt	15
	Visit aunt then friends	8
	Visit friends then aunt	4

This approach works perfectly if we can distinguish a length of time and say that events happening over a shorter period of time are a sequence and everything happening over a larger period of time are separate events. In general, however, this is not going to be easy, because we need to know how the person perceives things. Does Maria perceive the events before she hands in her homework as separate, or a sequence? Will she be thinking, 'Today I want to play sport so other things can wait till tomorrow', or 'If I do my homework today then tomorrow I can go out and play sport'? It will likely affect her choice, but it is not obvious how she might think. There is certainly no simple rule to say when something is a sequence or not. It is more likely to depend on the context.

Clearly, context will matter in think about and modeling inter-temporal choice. What I want to do now is question what the implications of this may be, and whether we need a different model to that of exponential discounting in order to capture it.

4.2 Hyperbolic discounting

We clearly see in Figure 4.1 that the discount factor is larger for longer time intervals. This means that people are impatient over the short term but more patient over the long term. To give another example, in a study by Thaler (1981), subjects were asked the amount of money they would require in one month, one year or ten years to make them indifferent to receiving $15 now. The average responses of $20, $50 and $100 seem entirely sensible, but imply an annual discount factor of 0.22, 0.45 and 0.84 respectively. Relatively speaking, therefore, subjects were asking a lot to wait one month but not very much to wait ten years. Such decreasing impatience is called **hyperbolic discounting**.

One way to capture hyperbolic discounting is to modify the model of exponential discounting and allow for different discount factors in different periods. In equation (4.1) we assume exponential discounting where payment in t time periods from now is discounted by an amount:

$$D(t) = \delta^{t-1}.$$

One of many possible alternatives is to assume:

$$D(t) = \frac{1}{1 + \alpha t} \tag{4.2}$$

where α is a parameter that can capture changes in the discount factor over time. I will call this a **model of hyperbolic discounting**. In either case equation (4.1) is generalized to:

$$U^T(x_1, x_2, ..., x_T) = \sum_{t=1}^{T} D(t) \, x_t. \tag{4.3}$$

To illustrate, Figure 4.3 plots $D(t)$ and the annualized discount factor assuming exponential discounting with factor $\delta = 0.85$ and hyperbolic discounting with

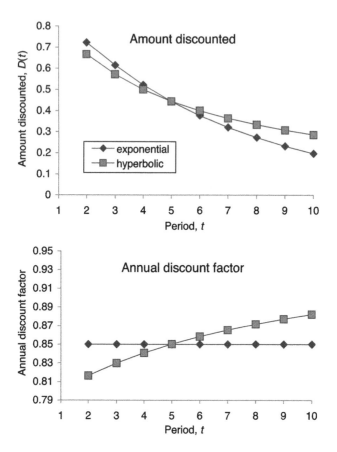

Figure 4.3 Hyperbolic discounting compared to exponential discounting. With hyperbolic discounting the discount factor is lower for shorter time periods.

$\alpha = 0.25$. We see that hyperbolic discounting does give a higher discount factor for longer periods and looks a bit more like what we saw in Figure 4.1.

We are, therefore, able to accommodate a changing discount factor without too much change to a standard exponential discounting model. But are we really capturing decreasing impatience? To explain why we might not be, consider the following set of choices:

Do you want $100 today or $110 tomorrow?

Do you want $100 in 30 days or $110 in 31 days?

When asked such questions, many people choose the $100 today and $110 in 31 days. This can be consistent with a model of hyperbolic discounting. The potential problem comes if we ask the same question after 30 days and get the same answer. That is, suppose Maria says she would prefer $110 in 31 days to $100 in 30 days, but then after 30 days says that she prefers $100 today to $110 tomorrow. This is not consistent with a model of hyperbolic discounting, because the model requires choices to be consistent over time. Maria should not change her mind. If she says that she prefers $110 in 31 days' time to $100 today then after 30 days she should still prefer $110 tomorrow to $100 today.

[Extra] To illustrate this with some numbers, let me first explain why it can be consistent with a model of hyperbolic discounting to choose the $100 today and $110 in 31 days' time. Suppose the time period is a day and $D(2) = 0.9$, $D(30) = 0.85$ and $D(31) = 0.84$. Then $110 tomorrow is worth $99 today, $100 in 30 days is worth $85 today and $110 in 31 days is worth $92.4 today, so it makes sense to choose $100 today and $110 in 31 days' time. What happens after 30 days? Given that $D(30) = 0.85$ and $D(31) = 0.84$ we should, after 30 days, calculate a revised discount factor of $D(2) = 0.99$. With this value of $D(2)$ it is optimal to choose the $110 tomorrow rather than $100 today.

It seems plausible that someone who chooses the $100 today and $110 in 31 days might also choose the $100 today and $110 in 31 days when asked 30 days later. We need, therefore, a different model to that of hyperbolic discounting.

4.2.1 Quasi-hyperbolic discounting

With exponential and hyperbolic discounting, a time period should be interpreted as a specific date. For instance, in the homework example we thought of period one as Friday and period four as Monday. If today is Friday then the discount factors $D(t)$ are specific to that day, and on Saturday we need to update them. For example, if $D(2) = 0.9$ and $D(3) = 0.9$ on Friday then, Maria does not discount between Saturday and Sunday, and on Saturday we should get $D(2) = 1$. Consequently, in a model of hyperbolic discounting, decreasing impatience means that a person gets less impatient as they get older, even if only by a few days.

An alternative interpretation of decreasing impatience is that a person is more impatient for short-term gains relative to long-term gains, and this has nothing to do with age. We can capture this by interpreting $D(2) = 0.9$ and $D(3) = 0.9$ as constant over time and showing how much future amounts are discounted relative to today. So, if today is Friday then $D(2) = 0.9$ and if today is Saturday then $D(2) = 0.9$. In this interpretation Maria chooses the $100 today because she is always impatient for a possible immediate gain. The distinction is illustrated in Figure 4.4.

If it makes more sense to think of the discount factor as relative to today rather than calendar time we say there are **present-biased preferences**. In this case Maria does not postpone her homework today, or choose the $100 today, because today is Friday 1 May and on Friday 1 May she is impatient; she is always impatient for immediate gains.

To model present biased preferences we can reuse equation (4.2) but now interpret t as how many time periods from today rather than a specific point in time. But, we still need to capture decreasing impatience. A simple way to do this is to use a model of **quasi-hyperbolic discounting** or (β,δ)-**preferences** where:

Time consistent preferences, e.g. a model of hyperbolic discounting

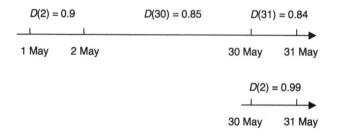

Present biased preferences, e.g. a model of quasi-hyperbolic discounting

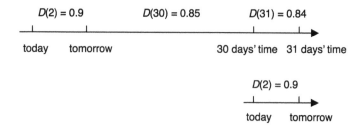

Figure 4.4 The difference between time consistent and present biased preferences. In the model of hyperbolic discounting, period refers to a specific moment of calendar time. In the model of quasi-hyperbolic discounting, period refers to a delay from now.

$$U^T(x_1, x_2, ..., x_T) = x_1 + \beta \sum_{t=2}^{T} \delta^{t-1} x_t. \tag{4.4}$$

where β is some number between zero and one. The β is crucial here because it measures **present bias**. If $\beta = 1$ then there is no bias and equation (4.4) is equivalent to (4.1). If $\beta < 1$ then more weight is given to today than to the future. This means there is a present bias and decreasing impatience. For instance, if $\beta = 0.7$ and $\delta = 0.99$ then $110 in 31 days is always preferred to $100 in 30 days but $100 today is always preferred to $110 tomorrow.

To see how (β, δ) preferences work, we can return to the example of Maria deciding when to do her homework. Table 4.5 summarizes the payoffs that she gets if she does or does not have a present bias. First, look at what happens if $\beta = 1$ and so she does not have a present bias: On Friday, she should plan to do her homework on Saturday and on Saturday she also thinks this way and so would do the homework. The same is true when $\beta = 0.9$. Next, look what happens if $\beta = 0.8$ and so the present bias is relatively large. On Friday she would plan to do the homework on Saturday. The interesting thing is that when Saturday comes she would rather do it on Monday.

Table 4.5 Quasi-hyperbolic discounting in the homework example. If the present bias is high, Maria plans to do the homework on Saturday, but on Saturday would rather do it Monday.

Plan	$\beta = 1, \delta = 0.9$		$\beta = 0.9, \delta = 0.9$		$\beta = 0.8, \delta = 0.9$	
	On Friday	Saturday	On Friday	Saturday	On Friday	Saturday
Do it Friday	10.5	–	9.0	–	7.4	–
Saturday	10.9	12.1	9.8	10.4	8.7	8.7
Do it Sunday	7.7	8.6	7.0	8.2	6.2	7.9
Monday	9.0	10.0	8.1	9.5	7.2	9.0

We say that there is a **time inconsistency** if someone plans to do something in the future but subsequently changes her mind. Planning to do the homework on Saturday but then on Saturday deciding to do it Monday, and planning to wait an extra day for $110 but when the time comes taking the $100, are examples of time inconsistency. There cannot be time inconsistency in a model of exponential or hyperbolic discounting, but there can be in a model of quasi-hyperbolic discounting. Time inconsistency is potentially very important in terms of welfare and policy because it suggests people plan to do something but then end up doing something else. I am, therefore, going to spend some time on the issue in chapters ten and eleven when we look at welfare and policy. At this point I want to show you how time inconsistency can have important consequences for behavior.

4.2.2 The consequences of time inconsistency

The consequences of time inconsistency will depend on whether people know they are time inconsistent or not. For example, does Maria realize on Friday, that if she plans to do the homework Saturday, when Saturday comes she might think differently? This could clearly be important in deciding what she does do on the Friday.

We say that someone is **naïve** if they are unaware that they have present-biased preferences. In this case, Maria would plan on Friday to do the homework Saturday and not expect to think differently on Saturday. By contrast, we say that someone is **sophisticated** if they know that they have present-biased preferences. In this case Maria will realize on Friday that if she leaves the homework until Saturday she will probably end up doing it Monday.

I'll look first at what happens if Maria is naïve. It's easiest to start with cases where the costs of an activity precede the benefits, as in the homework example. We saw in the example, that on Friday Maria will expect to do the homework on Saturday, but on Saturday might decide to do it Monday. This means that she can end up doing the homework later than she expected and later than she would have done without a present bias. To delay doing something in this way is called **procrastination**. Maria procrastinates because she puts off doing the costly thing. What happens if the benefits come before the costs?

To help illustrate, I will use a second example. Imagine, it costs $10 to go to the movies and Maria only has $11 spending money. There are movies on Friday, Saturday and Sunday. Table 4.6 shows that she will prefer the movie on Sunday to that on Saturday to that on Friday. Table 4.7 summarizes her inter-temporal utility (these tables can be compared to 4.1 and 4.5). If Maria has time-consistent preferences then she would plan go to the movie on Sunday. If she has present-biased preferences then on Friday she would to plan to go on Sunday but on Saturday would change her mind and go that day. Again we see a time inconsistency. The difference is that this time Maria does something earlier than she expected and earlier that she would have done with no present bias. To bring forward something in this way we can call to **preproperate**.

In both the homework and movie example, Maria is impatient for benefits. In the homework example this causes her to put off something that is costly. In the movie example it causes her to do early something that is pleasurable. Will someone who is sophisticated and knows they are time inconsistent avoid such problems? The answer is a bit surprising.

The surprise is not in the homework example. If Maria knows that on Saturday she will delay until Monday, then on Friday she knows the real choice is between doing her homework now, giving utility 7.4, or on Monday, giving utility 7.2. So, she will do the homework on Friday and behave as if time consistent. Being sophisticated thus allows Maria to avoid any time inconsistency. So far, so good. But what above the movie example? In this case Maria knows that if she does not go on Friday she will go on Saturday. On Friday she therefore knows that the real choice is between going today or tomorrow. She will go today. Being

Table 4.6 Payoffs from Maria going to watch a movie

	Payoff on		
Plan	Friday	Saturday	Sunday
Go on Friday	5	0	0
Go on Saturday	0	6	0
Go on Sunday	0	0	8

Table 4.7 Inter-temporal utility in the movie example with time-consistent and present-biased preferences

	$\beta = 1, \delta = 0.9$		$\beta = 0.8, \delta = 0.9$	
Plan	On Friday	On Saturday	On Friday	On Saturday
Go on Friday	5.0	–	5.0	–
Go on Saturday	5.4	6.0	4.3	6.0
Go on Sunday	6.5	7.2	5.2	5.8

sophisticated, therefore, means that Maria preproperates more than if she was naïve! She knows that she will not be able to resist going to the movies and so goes even earlier.

Table 4.8 summarizes the choices made. We see that in the case of delayed benefits sophistication helps overcome the problems associated with present bias, but in the case of delayed costs it makes things worse. It is not obvious what is better or worse in terms of utility because it is not clear whether to take into account the present bias or not. What we do see, however, is that a present bias has important implications for choice, even if someone is sophisticated.

The movie example shows that being sophisticated can make things worse because Maria anticipates her future present bias. This, however, misses part of the story. That is because someone who is sophisticated may use **commitment** to constrain her future choice. For instance, Maria could pre-order her movie ticket on Friday for Sunday. She would be willing to pay to do such a thing because it means she is committed to making the best choice. If she was naïve, she would see no need to do so. Someone who is sophisticated will thus be looking for ways that they can commit and avoid future temptation.

4.2.3 Temptation and self-control

The model of quasi-hyperbolic discounting is a nice simple model that has allowed us to capture important aspects of inter-temporal choice. One thing that it does not capture so well is the potential benefits of commitment. An approach suggested by Gul and Pesendorfer (2001) provides us with a more elegant way to capture this. To illustrate how it works I will continue the homework example.

On Saturday Maria can either do the homework or play sport. What I want you to imagine now is the possibility that on Friday Maria can commit to what she will do on Saturday. So, she can commit to doing the homework or to playing sport by, for example, arranging things with friends. This means that on Friday Maria has three choices: commit to doing the homework Saturday, commit to playing sport Saturday, or not commit and decide what to do on Saturday.

If Maria has time-consistent preferences then the possibility to commit is irrelevant. If she thinks it is best to do the homework on Saturday then she will be indifferent between committing to do the homework on Saturday and not

Table 4.8 A summary of the two examples: choice and utility (calculated as inter-temporal payoff on Friday with no present bias)

	Delayed benefits (homework)		Delayed costs (movie)	
	Choice	*Payoff*	*Choice*	*Payoff*
Time consistent	Saturday	10.9	Sunday	6.5
Sophisticated	Saturday	10.9	Friday	5.0
Naive	Monday	9	Saturday	5.4

committing because she will do the homework on Saturday either way. If Maria has present-biased preferences then things are different.

If Maria thinks it is best she does the homework on Saturday but knows that on Saturday she may not do it then it may be good for her to commit on the Friday to doing the homework Saturday. What's interesting is that we can now distinguish two distinct reasons for her to commit: Most obvious is that Maria knows on Saturday she will choose to play sport and wants to stop this happening. Looking back at Table 4.5 this makes sense if $\beta = 0.8$. The second possibility is that Maria knows she would do the homework on Saturday but only after overcoming the temptation to play sport. That is, she would do the homework but only after exercising **self-control,** which is psychologically costly. She may be able to avoid this cost by committing on Friday to do the homework Saturday. This fits the case where $\beta = 0.9$.

We can formalize this in a simple model. We already have u_2 to measure the utility of Maria on Saturday. If she does her homework she gets utility $u_2(H) = -5$, and if she plays sport she gets utility $u_2(S) = 5$. We are now going to add to this a cost of temptation. The cost of temptation should reflect Maria's psychological cost of not doing something she might have wanted to do. So, let $m(H)$ denote the **temptation** to do homework and $m(S)$ the temptation to do sport. The **cost of temptation** from doing action a is then calculated as follows:

$$C(a) = m(a) - max_{b=H,S}m(b).$$

For instance, if the temptation to do sport is greater than that of doing homework, then $m(S) \geq m(H)$ and so the cost of temptation from doing the homework is $C(H) = m(H) - m(S)$. This is the psychological cost of doing the homework when Maria would rather being playing sport.

What if we add together Maria's basic utility plus the cost of temptation? Then we get that if she has not committed on Friday to do something on Saturday, her overall utility on Saturday can be of two forms. First Maria could exercise self control and so the payoff from not committing includes the cost of overcoming temptation. We can write this,

$$u_2^m(H,S) = max_{a=H,S}\{u(a) + m(a)\} - max_{b=H,S}m(b). \tag{4.5}$$

Or, it could be that Maria has not exercised self control and so chooses the action that gives highest utility. We can write this,

$$u_2^m(H,S) = max_{a=H,S}u(a) \text{ subject to } m(a) \geq max_{b=H,S}m(b). \tag{4.6}$$

We can, therefore, distinguish the two reasons that Maria may want to commit.

Equations (4.5) and (4.6) might look a little over the top for what we need. The neat thing, though, is that if Maria would want to pre-commit we can say for certain that her overall utility must be like that in (4.5) or (4.6). More generally, if someone wants to be able to pre-commit then we must be able to represent their preferences with a utility function u and temptation function m like this (see research methods 4.2). This means that a desire to pre-commit must come hand in hand with temptation.

Research Methods 4.2

Axioms and behavior

Gul and Pesendorfer analyzed a much more general setting than that we have discussed here and obtained a stronger result than I have suggested so far. They showed that preferences satisfy four 'intuitive' axioms if and only if preferences can be represented by functions like u,m and $u,^m$. As well as being a beautiful mathematical result this is also an interesting illustration of the axiomatic approach to modelling choice.

In an axiomatic approach a researcher basically questions what properties of preferences are consistent with a particular way of modelling choice. Gul and Pesendorfer look at four axioms. Informally these are that preferences (i) be complete and transitive, (ii) be continuous, (iii) satisfy independence, in the sense that a third option would not change the choice between two others, and (iv) satisfy a preference for commitment, meaning that if someone would rather they did one action rather than another then they prefer to commit to doing that action. Their results show that if you think a person's preferences satisfy these axioms then you have to think functions u,m and u^m are a good way to model choice. Similarly, if you think u,m and u^m are a good way to model choice then you have to think these axioms are reasonable.

The axiomatic approach has a very long history in economics. In principle, it seems entirely consistent with behavioural economics in trying to match plausible assumptions on preferences with observed choices. In reality, something of a divide has emerged between behavioural economics and the axiomatic approach. This is probably because axioms that seemed sensible have not held up to scrutiny in the experimental laboratory, transitivity being one example. The axiomatic approach does, however, give definitive answers about when ways of modelling choice are appropriate and so clearly does have its place, as Gul and Pesendorfer show.

To illustrate, Table 4.9 follows through what Maria's preferences may look like. If there is no present bias, then there is no temptation, and so it is natural to think that $m(S) = m(H) = 0$. It does not matter whether she commits or not. If there is a relatively small present bias, $\beta = 0.9$, then Maria will do the homework on Saturday. If she does not pre-commit, however, she will have a cost of temptation. If $m(S) = 0.5$ and $m(H) = 0$ then by pre-committing to do her homework she can avoid the cost of this temptation and increase the utility she gets on Saturday. If there is a larger present bias, $\beta = 0.8$, then Maria will delay doing the homework unless she commits to doing it Saturday. This is motive enough to commit.

This model allows us to nicely capture the benefits of commitment. In particular, it illustrates how someone may make consistent choices yet still desire commitment, in order to avoid the psychological costs of temptation. Altogether,

Table 4.9 The utility of Maria on Saturday. The basic utility u^T is the same as in Table 4.5, the temptation is given by m and the overall utility, taking into account the cost of temptation, is given by u^{T^m}. By committing to the homework she avoids the cost of temptation when $\beta = 0.9$ and avoids procrastinating when $\beta = 0.8$.

	$\beta = 1, \delta = 0.9$			$\beta = 0.9, \delta = 0.9$			$\beta = 0.8, \delta = 0.9$		
	u^T	m	u^{T^m}	u^T	m	u^{T^m}	u^T	m	u^{T^m}
Committed to homework	12.1	0	12.1	10.4	0	10.4	8.7	0	8.7
Committed to sport	10.0	0	10.0	9.5	0.5	9.5	9.0	0.5	9.0
Decide on Saturday	12.1	–	12.1	10.4	–	9.9	9.0	–	9.0

therefore, we now have some useful ways to model decreasing impatience and present bias. We have, however, only addressed one of the issues raised in section 4.1. Now, it is time to consider some of the others.

4.3 Loss aversion and sequences

What I want to do now is look back on things like the delay–speed up asymmetry and see if we can better understand them. In doing so, I will draw heavily on work by Loewenstein and Prelec (1992, 1993).

4.3.1 Reference dependence

We can begin by applying the idea of reference dependence to inter-temporal choice. This means writing the inter-temporal utility function as:

$$u^T(x_1, x_2, ..., x_T) = \sum_{t=1}^{T} D(t)v(x_t - r_t)$$

where $D(t)$ is the discount factor, $v(x)$ is some value function and r_t is the reference point in period t. We shall not say much about the discount factor because everything we did in section 4.2 is relevant here. Our focus, therefore, will be on the value function.

As we saw in chapters two and three, the most important thing about the value function is that it measures consumption relative to some reference point. So, instead of thinking of x_t as the payoff in period t we need to think of $x_t - r_t$ as the loss or gain relative to the reference point. This raises familiar questions about what the reference point should be, but we can assume for now that the reference point is current income. What does the value function need to look like for us to capture the behavior I talked about in section 4.1.1?

To answer that question, suppose that Maria is indifferent between getting $q now rather than $y > q in some future period t. This means $v(q) = D(t)v(y)$. Recall that the **gain–loss asymmetry** implies she should be relatively reluctant to post-pone payment compared to postponing receipt. So, she should prefer to pay $q now instead of having to pay $y in period t. For instance, if she is indifferent between getting $10 today or $11 tomorrow, she would prefer to pay $10 today than $11 tomorrow. This means $v(-q) > D(t)v(-y)$. The gain-loss asymmetry requires, therefore, that:

$$\frac{v(q)}{v(y)} < \frac{v(-q)}{v(-y)}. \tag{4.7}$$

Recall that the **absolute magnitude effect** means the larger the amount the more patient she is. So, Maria should prefer getting αy in period t rather than αq now, if $\alpha > 1$ captures some proportional increase in the amounts to be paid. This means that $v(\alpha q) < D(t)v(\alpha y)$. The absolute magnitude effect requires, therefore, that:

$$\frac{v(q)}{v(y)} > \frac{v(\alpha q)}{v(\alpha y)}. \tag{4.8}$$

Finally, we come to the **delay–speed up asymmetry**. Speed up is naturally thought of as expediting a receipt, in order to get $q > 0 now rather than $y > 0 in some future period t. One can think of the reference level as zero now and $y in the future. By expediting the receipt Maria loses, therefore, $y in the future but gains $q now. If she is indifferent between doing this, then $-D(t)v(-y) = v(q)$. We can estimate a discount factor for speeding up t periods using $q = \delta^{speed\ up} y$ to give:

$$\delta^{speed\ up} = \frac{q}{y} = \frac{v^{-1}(-D(t)v(-y))}{y}.$$

Delay is naturally thought of as delaying a receipt so as to get $y > 0 at some future period t rather than $q > 0 now. This time we can think of the reference level as $q now and zero in the future. By delaying receipt Maria loses $q now but gains $y in the future. If she is indifferent to do this, then $-D(t)v(y) = v(-q)$. We can estimate a discount factor for delaying t periods using $q = \delta^{delay} y$ to give:

$$\delta^{delay} = \frac{q}{y} - \frac{v^{-1}(-D(t)v(y))}{y}.$$

Suppose we compare these two discount factors and for simplicity assume that $D(t) = 1$. Then, $\delta^{speed\ up} > \delta^{delay}$ if:

$$v^{-1}(-v(-y)) > -v^{-1}(-v(y)).$$

If you stare at this long enough you might see that we require $-v(-y) > v(y)$. But, this is what we get with loss aversion. So, all we need to explain the delay-speed up asymmetry is loss aversion.

A model with reference dependent preferences can, therefore, capture a lot of the things we observe in inter-temporal choice. Unfortunately, things do not work out as perfectly as we might hope, because the formula for the value function we looked at in chapter three, see equation (3.7), does not satisfy either relations (4.7) or (4.8)! But, we could easily tweak it and sort that out. As in chapters two and three, therefore, reference dependence helps a lot in understanding behavior.

As you might expect, however, by now we do need to think a bit more about the reference point. To illustrate why let's return to the homework example and suppose Maria must do the homework Saturday or Monday. Furthermore, suppose that it is rare for homework to be set over the weekend, and so this is not her reference point. Instead, her reference point is to doing something on Saturday. One possibility is that on a Saturday she usually plays sport. Another is that she usually has to visit an aunt she does not like. This gives the reference dependent utility in Table 4.10.

Irrespective of the reference point Maria faces the same trade-off between a relatively large drop in utility on Saturday, a difference of 10, for a gain on Monday, a difference of 15. The reference point will matter in how she perceives this trade-off. Let's go through each reference point in turn. If she normally plays sport on Saturday, then doing the homework on Saturday will feel like a loss. This might make her reluctant to do the homework. If:

$$D(2)v(-10) + D(4)v(10) < D(4)v(-5)$$

Table 4.10 The homework example with reference dependent preferences. If the reference point is to play sport, doing the homework on Saturday feels like a loss, but if the reference point is to visit an aunt, doing the homework Saturday feels like a gain.

	Utility on		
	Saturday	Sunday	Monday
Payoff x_t if do homework Saturday	−5	10	10
Payoff x_t if do homework Monday	5	10	−5
Reference point is to play sport			
Reference payoff r_t	5	10	0
Reference dependent utility if do homework Saturday	−10	0	10
If do homework Monday	0	0	−5
Reference point is to visit aunt			
Reference payoff r_t	−10	10	0
Reference dependent utility if do homework Saturday	5	0	10
If do homework Monday	15	0	−5

then she will leave the homework until Monday. If she normally visits her aunt on Saturday then doing the homework on Saturday will feel like a gain. This might make her more likely to the homework. If:

$$D(2)v(5) + D(4)v(10) > D(2)v(15) + D(4)v(-5)$$

then she would want to do the homework on Saturday.

To focus on the issue at hand, suppose that $D(2) = D(4) = 1$. Then we need to know whether $v(-10) + v(10) < v(-5)$ and whether $v(5) + v(10) > v(15) + v(-5)$. These equations may or may not be satisfied but suppose, by way of illustration, that $v(5) = 3, v(10) = 5, v(15) = 6, v(-5) = -7$ and $v(-10) = -13$. Then she would not do her homework on Saturday if the reference point is playing sport, but she would do her homework on Saturday if the reference point is to visit her aunt. The reference point and context can, therefore, influence behavior.

4.3.2 Preferences for sequences

What I want to look at next is how to model preferences over sequences. For now we shall ignore the question of when a set of events is viewed as a sequence rather than separate. So, what we need to do is measure the overall utility of a sequence of payoffs such as $\{x_1, x_2, \ldots, x_T\}$.

One way we do so is to compare this sequence with one that gives the same payoff in each period. That is we compare the actual sequence to the smoothed sequence $\{\bar{x}, \bar{x} \ldots, \bar{x}\}$ where:

$$\bar{x} = \frac{1}{T} \sum_{t=1}^{T} x_t.$$

For every period t let:

$$d_t = t\bar{x} - \sum_{t=1}^{t} x_i$$

be the difference in utility, up to and including period t, between the smoothed sequence and actual sequence. We then get a nice way to think about the utility of a sequence by saying utility is given by:

$$u^q(\{x_1, x_2, \ldots, x_T\}) = \sum_{t=1}^{T} x_t + \beta \sum_{t=1}^{T} d_t + \sigma \sum_{t=1}^{T} |d_t|. \tag{4.9}$$

To see why this is a nice way to think about things I need to introduce two further concepts.

We say that the **anticipated utility** of receiving sequence $\{x_1, x_2, \ldots, x_T\}$ is given by:

$$AU = \sum_{t=1}^{T} (t-1)x_t.$$

The story is that if Maria is going to receive payoff x_t in period t then she spends $t-1$ periods anticipating this. So, she gets $(t-1)x_t$ anticipated utility. Summing this over all periods gives total anticipated utility.

Following a similar logic we say that the **recollected utility** of the sequence is:

$$RU = \sum_{t=1}^{T} (T-t)x_t.$$

If Maria received payoff x_t in period t then she has $T-t$ periods to recollect it, and so gets $(T-1)x_t$ recollected utility.

A bit or rearranging shows that:

$$\sum_{t=1}^{T} d_t = 0.5(AU - RU).$$

So, positive values of Σd_t are associated with more anticipated than recollected utility. This means that a high Σd_t goes hand in hand with an improving sequence in which the x_t's increase with t.

Now we can go back to equation (4.9) and make some sense of it. We can see that a $\beta > 0$ means a preference for an improving sequence and a $\beta < 0$ a preference for a worsening sequence. We also see that $\sigma < 0$ indicates a preference for a smoothed sequence while $\sigma > 0$ indicates a preference for a one-sided sequence. To illustrate what this means Table 4.11 has some example sequences. If σ is small and β positive then Maria would prefer sequence C with lots of anticipation utility. If σ is negative and β positive then she may prefer sequence E which still has anticipation utility but is more smoothed over time.

Table 4.11 Preference over sequences of outcomes with the anticipated and recollected utility

	Period					AU	RU	Σd_t
	1	*2*	*3*	*4*	*5*			
Sequence A	1	1	1	1	1	10	10	0
Sequence B	5	0	0	0	0	0	20	−10
Sequence C	0	0	0	0	5	20	0	10
Sequence D	2	1	1	1	0	6	14	−4
Sequence E	0	1	1	1	2	14	6	4
Sequence F	2	0	1	0	2	10	10	0

Table 4.12 Preferences over sequences in the homework example

Plan	Payoff on				AU	RU	Σd_t
	Friday	Saturday	Sunday	Monday			
Do it Friday	−5	5	10	4	37	5	16
Do it Saturday	0	−5	10	10	45	0	22.5
Do it Sunday	0	5	−5	10	25	5	10
Do it Monday	0	5	10	−5	10	20	−5

The evidence we looked at in section 4.1.2 would suggest that $\beta > 0$ and $\sigma < 0$. With the help of Table 4.12 we can see what this means in the homework example. Doing the homework Saturday gives the most improving sequence, but not a very smooth one. To do the homework on Friday or Sunday may, therefore, be optimal. Indeed, if σ is very negative, Monday may be optimal as it gives the most smooth sequence.

The homework example brings us back to the troubling question of when period payoffs are seen as part a sequence and when they are not. Will Maria think of the weekend as one sequence of events, or think of each day as separate from another? We see now that this might affect her choice. Unfortunately, there is no simple rule as to when a person will think of periods as separate or part of a sequence. The further apart are two events then the more likely it intuitively seems that they will be seen as two separate events rather than a sequence of events. This logic can only take us so far, however, as we shall see shortly in looking at habit formation.

4.4 Summary

I began by looking at a utility function with exponential discounting. The basic idea here is that inter-temporal utility, and choice, can by captured by assuming people discount the future at a constant rate. If true, this would make our life easier. Unfortunately, we saw that preferences seem to depend a lot on context and exponential discounting is not well placed to pick this up. For example, we observe, things like a gain–loss asymmetry, delay–speed up asymmetry, absolute magnitude effect and preference for improving sequences.

In looking at alternatives to exponential discounting we focused first on the fact that people seem impatient for short term game. We saw that there are two distinct ways to think about this. We can think in terms of a model of hyperbolic discounting with time consistent preferences, or we can think in terms of quasi-hyperbolic discounting with time-inconsistent or present-biased preferences. The latter looked the better way to go.

A present bias, and time inconsistency, raises some interesting possibilities. A person may procrastinate by putting off doing something costly, preproperate by doing early something pleasant, or fight to overcome temptation. What happens can depend on whether the person is naïve or sophisticated in knowing about their present bias.

We next added reference dependence and loss aversion to the mix and showed this can explain things like the delay–speed up asymmetry and gain–loss asymmetry. We also saw that perceptions of the reference point can influence choice.

Finally, we looked at how we can capture the utility from a sequence of events using anticipated and recollected utility.

A recurring theme in chapters two and three was that context mattered. It would influence perceptions which would then influence choice because of things like the reference point. In thinking about inter-temporal choice we can come up with many other good reasons context will matter. For instance, whether someone perceives a series of events as a sequence or separated can have a huge impact on behavior; in the one they are impatient for gain and in the other they want to delay for the future. Context effects will be less of a theme in the rest of the book (although they will crop up again in chapter seven). So, before we move on I do want to emphasize their importance.

Most economic choices involve choice arbitrariness, risk and time, all mixed up together. The potential context effects are, therefore, huge and behavior will depend a lot on the context, and perceptions of the context. It's vital to be aware of and try to account for this. It's a key part of being a behavioral economist. What this means in practice is questioning things like, what is the reference point, and what is a loss or a gain, in the different contexts you are interested in understanding. This is a matter of judgment.

4.5 Borrowing and saving

In chapter two we spent some time looking at the life cycle hypothesis and saving. Clearly these are inter-temporal issues and so it is natural to think back to them now we have a means to model inter-temporal choice. In doing so there are two new issues I want to pick out: habit formation and consumer debt.

4.5.1 Saving equals growth or growth equals saving?

A high saving rate usually goes together with a high growth rate. What is not so clear is why. A standard life cycle model of consumption predicts that higher expected income should lead to less saving, because the higher expected income means less income needs to be saved now in order to smooth future consumption. The prediction, therefore, would be that high saving causes high growth, and not the other way around. A lot of evidence, however, tends to suggest that things do go the other way around. It seems that high growth tends to proceed and cause high saving.

Habit formation is one possible way to account for this, as shown by Carroll, Overland and Weil (2000). I am going to look at habit in more detail in chapter ten, but the basics are all we need here. In a **model of habit formation** the utility of today's consumption depends on past consumption. One possible reason for this is that a person wants to maintain consumption at past levels. They have got used to a certain standard of living and would rather keep to, or improve upon, that standard. This fits with the idea that people want an improving sequence. People want to see their income and standard of living improving and not getting worse.

To capture this assume that Maria has a habit level of consumption h. The habit evolves over time according to:

$$\frac{dh}{dt} = \rho(c - h)$$

where c is consumption and ρ determines to what extent habit depends on the recent past. The larger ρ is, then the more quickly Maria's habits adapt to recent consumption.

A simple utility function we could use would be:

$$u(c,\ h) = \frac{c}{h^\gamma}$$

where γ measures the importance of habit. If $\gamma = 0$ then habits are irrelevant and we have a standard model where utility depends on consumption. If $\gamma = 1$ then utility depends only on whether consumption is more or less than the habit level. For intermediate γ utility depends on both the absolute level of consumption and whether it is more or less than the habit level. For example, if $\gamma = 0.5$ then consumption of two with a habit level of one gives the same utility as if both consumption and the habit level are four.

It is possible to show, with some reasonable assumptions, that savings will increase with income if and only if the importance of habit γ is sufficiently large. Thus, habit can cause high savings if there is a high growth rate of income. The intuition for this is that a habit level of consumption means less reason to devote any increase in income to consumption. As long as consumption is above the habit level and the standard of living is rising Maria will get relatively high utility. So, she does best to increase her consumption slowly over time and always have a rising standard of living. What she would not want to do is devote all the increased income to consumption. This would risk a subsequent fall in consumption below her new habit level with a consequent fall in living standards and utility.

Table 4.13 illustrates how this may work. We can see that income is going to increase over the four periods and can compare a smoothed consumption schedule A to an increasing schedule B. The increasing schedule gives higher utility because Maria does relatively well compared to what she has become used to. It also guards against any potential fall in the income she might get in period four.

We see, therefore, that habit and a preference for an improving sequence can explain why people save rather than spend even if they expect future income growth. That people may think about their lifetime earnings as a sequence also highlights the problems of trying to distinguish when events are seen as separated

Table 4.13 Two sequences of consumption compared in a model of habit formation. Consumption schedule B gives the highest utility.

Table $\rho = 0.5$

	Period				Total utility
	1	*2*	*3*	*4*	
Income	15	15	30	100	
Consumption A	40	40	40	40	
Habit A	15.0	27.5	33.75	36.9	
Utility A	10.3	7.6	6.9	6.6	31.4
Consumption B	25	35	45	55	
Habit B	15.0	20.0	27.5	36.0	
Utility B	6.5	7.8	8.6	9.1	32.0

rather than a sequence. Here we are thinking of someone potentially seeing year to year earnings as a sequence!

4.5.2 Why save when you have debts?

One of the more puzzling aspects of saving behavior is that many people borrow on credit cards at a high interest rate to buy consumer goods, while simultaneously saving for the future at lower interest rates. To give some figures, in March 2009, US consumer debt, made up primarily of credit card debt, was about $950 billion, and around 14 percent of disposable income went to paying off this debt. At the same time the savings rate was around 4 percent of disposable income. One might argue that some people are saving while others are borrowing, but this does not seem to be the case, many people are both saving and borrowing. Why?

In trying to explain this puzzle the key thing to recognize is that people typically borrow for the short term, i.e. to buy a new dress, while save for the long term, i.e. to buy a new house or retire. This distinction between short term and long term leads naturally to thoughts of quasi-hyperbolic discounting and time-inconsistency. Several studies have indeed shown that this can help explain what is going on. For example, Laibson, Repetto and Tobacman (2007) try fitting the (β, δ) preferences model to data from US households. Having taken account of risk attitudes, they find that the model with parameters $\beta = 0.90$ and $\delta = 0.96$ fits the data well. This equates to a long-run discount rate of 4.1 percent and a short term rate of 14.6 percent.

Why does a model with (β, δ)-preferences work? First, a consumer with a long-run discount rate of 4.1 percent would be happy to save over the long term at a savings rate of say 5 percent per year. Second, a consumer with a short-term discount rate of 14.6 percent would be happy to borrow money to buy something now if she can pay that back at a rate of say 14 percent per year. Basically, the consumer wants to save but because of time inconsistency may also be unwilling to wait to buy that new dress.

Clearly banks and credit card companies can profit from this. This brings us nicely on to the next topic.

4.6 Exploiting time inconsistency

We have seen that present-biased preferences and time inconsistency can result in someone procrastinating. They keep on delaying something they need to do. Could a company exploit this? To see why this question is pertinent I am going to look at a study by Della Vigna and Malmendier (2006). The study was published with the title 'Paying not to go to the gym', which somewhat gives away the punch line.

4.6.1 Time inconsistency and consumer behavior

DellaVigna and Malmendier look at attendance data for over 7,000 health club members at three health clubs in New England between April 1997 and July 2000. People going to the gym had four basic options: (i) pay $12 per visit, (ii) pay $100 every 10 visits, (iii) sign a monthly contract with a fee of around $85 per month, and (iv) sign an annual contract with a fee of around $850. One difference between the monthly and annual contract is that the monthly contract was automatically renewed, while the annual contract was not. Those on a monthly contract could cancel at any time, but needed to do so in person or writing. Those on an annual contract needed to sign up again at the end of the term, or their membership would stop.

This difference between the monthly and annual contract is a difference of what happens if the member does nothing, or in the **default position**. The default position with a monthly contract is that a member needs to **opt-out** of being a member. With the annual contract a member needs to **opt-in** to being a member. Why should we worry about this distinction? Possibly we should not, because it costs very little to make a phone call, or write a letter, to opt-in or opt-out. There is, however, potential for time inconsistency. A person may want to cancel, or rejoin, but put it off until tomorrow, and then put it off until the next day, and so on. Similarly, a person may think they will go to the gym often, but typically find some excuse to go tomorrow rather than today. Let's look at the data.

Any of the four payment options could make sense to a particular consumer. They may go rarely, so the pay per visit makes sense; they may know they will go often, so the annual contract makes sense; or they may be unsure how often they will go, so prefer the flexibility of the monthly option. The interesting question is whether consumers do choose the option that is best for them. The study finds that basically they do not. To give a first illustration of this, Figure 4.5 plots the average price per attendance of new members. We see that in the first six months of membership the average cost per visit was relatively high. Indeed, 80 percent of monthly members would have been better off paying for every ten visits.

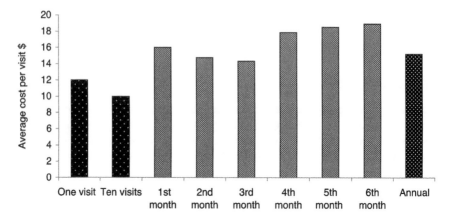

Figure 4.5 Average cost per visit to the gym for the first six months of monthly member-
      ship or year of annual membership. Monthly members pay on average more per
      visit than if they had paid per visit.

Source: DellaVigna and Malmendier (2006).

Figure 4.5 is suggestive of customers not choosing the best option, but does not capture the whole picture. That is because we need to see whether people learn and readjust. It may have been optimal for someone to sign a monthly contract but then switch to paying per visit once they realized how much (or little) they used the gym. There is little evidence, however, of readjustment. This is particularly the case for those on the monthly contract. Many monthly members appeared to consistently overestimate their future usage and put off cancelling their membership. Particularly telling is the average lag of over two months between the last time a person attends the gym and the moment they cancel membership! Such a delay is costly. Looking over the whole period of membership the average loss for someone on the monthly contract was $614. For those on the annual contract it was just $1.

In trying to make sense of these results, DellaVigna and Malmendier suggest the most likely explanations are overestimation of future usage, time inconsistency and naivety. A model of naïve consumers with (β, δ)-preferences where $\beta = 0.7$ and $\delta = 0.9995$ can explain the data, including the average delay of over two months in cancellation.

4.6.2 *Firm pricing*

In the gym example the loss made by a consumer on the monthly contract was the firm's gain. This raises the question of whether firms use a pricing strategy that maximizes the profit they can make from consumers. To answer this question we first need to know how firms should price if consumers have a present bias. To do so I will work through a model of gym membership based on that by Della Vigna and Malmendier (2004).

There are three periods. In period one the gym proposes a **two-part tariff** (L, p) that consists of a **lump sum membership fee** L and a **user fee** p that is paid every visit. If Maria joins the gym then in period two she pays the membership fee and decides whether or not to use the gym. If she uses the gym then she pays the user fee p plus some personal cost to attend c. Maria does not know the personal cost until after joining. If she does go to the gym then in period three she receives some benefit B. Figure 4.6 summarizes what happens. The key to the model are the delays: There is a delay between joining and using the gym, so Maria needs to predict future usage when joining. There is also a delay between using the gym and benefitting from having used the gym.

This delay gives scope for present bias to matter. So, let's assume that Maria has (β, δ) preferences but thinks she has $(\hat{\beta}, \delta)$ preferences. If $\hat{\beta} > \beta$ then she has a present bias but underestimates the strength of the bias.

To see what Maria will do we first need to imagine that we are in period one and Maria is predicting what she will do in period two. She expects that when period two comes she will think the payoff from using the gym is $\delta\hat{\beta}B - p - c$, the discounted benefit minus the cost. She, thus, expects that she will use the gym if $c < \delta\hat{\beta}B - p$. From the perspective of period one the benefit from using the gym is $\delta\beta(\delta B - p - c)$. So, if Maria signs the contract she should expect net benefit:

$$NB = \delta\beta\left(-L + \int_0^{\delta\hat{\beta}B-p}(\delta B - p - c)dc\right). \tag{4.10}$$

The integral term captures her uncertainty about what the personal cost of using the gym could be.

The next thing we need to do is question what Maria will actually do in period two. She will only use the gym if $c < \delta\beta B - p$. If, therefore, $\hat{\beta} > \beta$ she is biased in

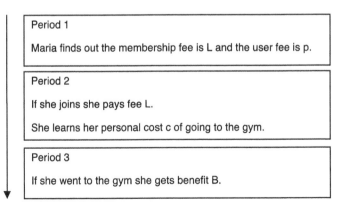

Period 1

Maria finds out the membership fee is L and the user fee is p.

Period 2

If she joins she pays fee L.

She learns her personal cost c of going to the gym.

Period 3

If she went to the gym she gets benefit B.

Figure 4.6 The timeline of the model of gym pricing.

overestimating her likelihood of going to the gym, and because of this overestimates the benefits of joining the gym. This is consistent with what we saw in Figure 4.5.

Now we can consider the firm. Suppose, the firm pays production cost K whenever anyone joins and per-unit cost a if anyone uses the gym. They know that a consumer will use the gym in period two if $c < \delta\beta B - p$. The objective of the firm is to choose L and p to maximize profits,

$$max_{L,p}\left(L - K + \int_0^{\delta\beta B - p}(p-a)\,dc\right).$$

The one caveat is that the net benefit NB must be greater than zero, or no one would join. If you solve this maximization problem (see below) then the optimal price is:

$$p = a - \delta B(1 - \hat{\beta}) - \delta B(\hat{\beta} - \beta). \tag{4.11}$$

I'll look at this in three stages, summarized in Table 4.14.

If customers have no present bias, $\beta = 1$, the firm should set the per usage fee equal to the cost, $p = a$. This result should be familiar to those who have studied price discrimination. The optimal thing for the gym to do is charge as high a membership fee as customers will pay and then make zero profit from customer use.

Table 4.14 The consequences of optimal pricing in the gym example with present-biased preferences

Preferences	Consumer	Firm
No present bias, $\beta = 1$.	Correctly predicts when will use the gym.	Makes a profit on membership fees. Makes no profit when members use the gym.
Present bias and sophisticated, $\beta = \hat{\beta}$.	Knows will possibly not use the gym because of present bias.	Needs to charge a lower user fee to attract customers. Makes a loss when people use the gym but this is compensated for by a higher lump sum fee. Does not profit from consumer's present bias.
Present bias and naïve, $\beta < 1$ and $\hat{\beta} = 1$.	Does not realize will possibly not go to the gym because of a present bias.	Charges a lower use fee to exploit customers. Makes a loss when people use the gym but this is compensated for by a higher lump sum fee and some customers not using the gym. Profits from consumer's naivety.

If customers do have a present bias, $\beta < 1$, then the firm should set the per usage fee below the cost, $p < a$. That means the gym makes a loss every time a customer uses the gym! Why would that make sense? It depends on whether the customer is sophisticated or naïve. If Maria is sophisticated, she knows that, because of her present bias, she may put off going to the gym. Thus, she wants something that makes it more likely she will go. A lower user fee serves that purpose. Maria would, therefore, be willing to pay a higher membership fee in order to have a lower usage fee. The gym does not profit from Maria having a present bias, but it does need to charge different prices.

If Maria is naïve then she may overestimate how much she will use the gym. The lower the usage fee the more she thinks she will use the gym, and the higher the membership fee she is willing to pay. In this case the gym can profit from Maria's present bias. By offering a low usage fee it can charge a high membership fee and gain on people who join but subsequently do not use the gym. The larger is the naivety of consumers the more profit the gym can make.

[Extra] To see how to get equation (4.11): If we set $NB = 0$, we can substitute in for L from equation (4.10) to rewrite the firms problem as:

$$max_p \left(\int_0^{\delta\hat{\beta}B-p} (\delta B - p - c)\,dc - K + \int_0^{\delta\beta B-p} (p-a)\,dc \right).$$

This can be rewritten:

$$max_p \left(\int_0^{\delta\hat{\beta}B-p} (\delta B - a - c)\,dc - K + \int_{\delta\beta B-p}^{\delta\hat{\beta}B-p} (\delta B - p - c)\,dc \right).$$

and:

$$max_p \left((\delta\beta B - p)(\delta B - a) + \delta B(\hat{\beta} - \beta)(\delta B - p) - K - \int_0^{\delta\hat{\beta}B-p} c\,dc \right).$$

Evaluating the last integral and differentiating with respect to p gives the result!

There are two important lessons from this simple model. First, firms should take account of present bias when setting an optimal price. This is particularly pertinent if consumers are sophisticated. In this case, the firm cannot profit from the present bias but does need to price differently to make the same profits as without a present bias. Second, firms can profit by exploiting naïve consumers. They can charge a high membership fee and offer a low usage fee, knowing that some customers will not take advantage of the lower usage fee.

The data that we have for gym membership would suggest that firms are aware of this. The user fee for members was zero, which must be below the gym's per unit cost. We also did see underuse of the gym. Let's look at another example.

4.6.3 Choosing the correct calling plan

If the title of DellaVigna and Malmendier's paper, 'Paying not to go to the gym', gave away the punchline, the title of a paper by Miravete (2003), 'Choosing the wrong calling plan?' leaves things more open.

Miravete looks at consumer's choice of telephone calling plans following a tariff change by company South Central Bell in 1986. Customers had the choice between a flat-rate tariff of $18.70 per month, or a measured tariff of $14.02 per month plus call charges. Such choices (and utility payments in general) are often suggested as fertile ground for present bias. That's because it may be best for a customer to switch tariff, and she may know that, but delays doing it because of present bias. This study aimed to put that anecdotal hunch to the test.

Key to the study was a survey of 5,000 customers that included questions on expected telephone usage. If we know how much customers expected to use the telephone then we can hope to identify customers who should have expected the other tariff would be less costly, but did not switch.

Around 30 percent of the consumers surveyed chose the measured option and 70 percent stayed with the flat rate. So, did consumers make the correct choice, and more importantly, did they switch if it looked like they had initially made a wrong choice? Table 4.15 provides some relevant data to see what happened. There was a high proportion of people over/under-estimating the number of calls they would make. This should feed through to some making the wrong choice of calling plan. Of interest to us is how many of those who were in the wrong plan in October switched by December to the better plan. Overall, around 40 percent of customers were in the wrong plan in October, falling to 33 percent in December. There is also evidence that those with the most to gain from switching were the ones to switch.

This study gives an interesting contrast to the one on gym membership. Recall, that with gym membership it was those opting for the 'flat' monthly tariff that were most often making the wrong choice. In this telephone example those choosing the flat rate are on average making the right choice. It is those choosing

Table 4.15 Choices of calling plan, estimates of usage, and the proportion of customers making the wrong choice

Choice in October	Flat	Flat	Measured	Measured
Choice in December	Flat	Measured	Flat	Measured
Number of customers	953	43	41	375
Under-estimated calls by 20% or more	26%	28%	32%	33%
Over-estimated calls by 20% or more	59%	49%	61%	49%
Made wrong choice in October	11%	44%	100%	57%
Made wrong choice in December	6%	7%	0%	67%

Source: Miravete (2003).

the 'variable' per-use tariff that are most often making the wrong choice. It would be hard, therefore, to argue that people are on average biased towards a flat versus variable tariff or vice-versa. It just seems that people are bad at predicting future usage and therefore end up making the wrong choice.

Present bias can give a plausible explanation for all of this: People might over-estimate how much they will use the gym and under-estimate how much they will use the telephone because of time-inconsistency. Furthermore, they may put off changing plan once they have realized its wrong because of procrastination. Present bias gives us a good story, but is it the whole story?

Probably not: in the gym case those who are paying too much do eventually change their membership. Similarly, in the telephone case the number of customers choosing the wrong tariff does fall over time. What appears to be time-inconsistency and procrastination may, therefore, just be people taking time to learn their preferences and make the best choice. This is not to say that present bias is not important, it is just to highlight that other things are clearly going on as well. These other things will be a theme of the next two chapters as we look at how people interpret new information and how they learn over time.

4.7 Further reading

The survey article by Frederick, Loewenstein and O'Donoghue (2002) is a good place to start. The papers by O'Donoghue and Matthew Rabin (1999, 2000, 2002) are recommended reading on time inconsistency. As is the pioneering article by Strotz (1956). Note that we will return to time inconsistency in chapter eleven and so much of the further reading there is also relevant here. For an interesting look at the desire for wages to increase over time see Frank and Hutchens (1993). For more on applying behavioral economics in industrial organization see Ellison (2006).

4.8 Review questions

4.1   Inter-temporal utility (as defined in equation 4.1) is about measuring streams of utility over time. To make life easier for themselves, however, economists normally think about streams of money over time. This should be ok if we think in terms of, say, '$10's worth of utility', but could be problematic if we really mean 'a $10 note'. To illustrate, if someone says they are indifferent between $150 in one year's time to $100 today, what is the discount factor, when the utility function is $u(x) = x$ and $u(x) = \sqrt{x}$ and x is money? Think about the implications of this.

4.2   Explain the difference between time-consistent and present biased preferences. Why is this distinction not important in a model of exponential discounting?

4.3   In section 4.3 I showed that $\delta^{speed\,up} > \delta^{delay}$ in the case of a receipt. Show that $\delta^{speed\,up} < \delta^{delay}$ in the case of a payment?

4.4   Looking back at Table 4.10, what would happen if Maria's reference point was to do her homework on Saturday, and what if it was to do it on Monday?

How is this related to the concept of personal equilibrium we looked at in the last chapter?

4.5   Looking back over this chapter and the previous two, come up with examples of context effects.

4.6   What is the expression for $D(t)$ with quasi-hyperbolic discounting?

4.7   What context effects do you think makes it more likely someone will think of a series of events as a sequence rather than separated?

4.8   What are the implications of habit formation for the life cycle hypothesis?

4.9   What is the relationship between a model of habit formation and reference dependent utility?

4.10 Why do many firms, like gyms, charge a two-part tariff with a zero user fee?

4.11 Is there a difference between firm's exploiting a customer's bias, and changing their strategy to take account of a customer's bias?

4.12 What strategy can firm's use to take account of other cognitive biases and heuristics we have looked at like loss aversion and risk aversion?

4.13 How can people over-estimating how much they will use the gym and under-estimating how much they will use the telephone both be caused by time inconsistency?

5 Learning from new information

He is accelerating all the time. That last lap was run in 64 seconds compared to the one before in 62 seconds.

John Coleman, sports commentator

A theme in chapters two and three was uncertainty and risk. For instance, in chapter two I talked about Anna not knowing whether she would prefer the Nutty breakfast cereal or the Honey cereal. In chapter three I talked about Alan deciding whether or not to fully insure his car without knowing whether his car would be stolen. New information should remove some of this uncertainty. For example, if Anna tastes the breakfast cereals, or Alan finds out the number of cars stolen in his area in recent years, then they should be able to make more informed decisions. This looks like a good thing.

It should, therefore, be a good thing that we are continually bombarded with new information, from the TV, radio, internet, newspapers, friends, family, colleagues, and our own experiences! New information is only useful, however, if it is used wisely. It is clear that it can influence behavior in significant ways. Why else would firms spend so much money on advertisements? Why else would someone ask friends, or look on the internet, for advice before making a decision? What we need to think about is how wisely people use new information and the consequences this has for how they behave. That will be the focus of this chapter.

5.1 Bayesian updating and choice with uncertainty

Imagine someone called John, who is thinking of buying a new car and has narrowed it down to two choices, a 'Sporty' car or 'Comfort' car. Either car is approximately the same price but John does not know which will give him higher utility. In the process of deciding he tries to become better informed by asking his friends, doing a test drive, searching for advice on the internet, and so on. What should he do with this new information?

The benchmark for what he should be doing is **Bayesian updating**. Let p denote the **prior probability** John puts on the Sporty giving the higher utility. Any new information he gets we call a **signal**. For example, a signal might be his friend saying 'buy the Comfort' or him doing a test drive and 'liking the Sporty'. Let θ denote the **signal precision** or probability he would got the signal if Sporty does give the higher utility. The value of θ should capture things like the trust that John puts in his friends opinion or expertise, or how relevant he thinks a test drive is. If John uses **Bayes rule** then the **posterior probability** he should put on the Sporty giving the higher utility is:

$$\Pr(\text{Sporty is best} \mid \text{signal}) = \frac{\theta p}{\theta p + (1-\theta)(1-p)}. \tag{5.1}$$

For example, if John started relatively indifferent between the two, say $p = 0.4$, but his friend said that Sporty is better and he trusts his friend's opinion, say $\theta = 0.9$, then he should put posterior probability 0.86 on the Sporty being better for him. This new information changes his beliefs and in doing so may change his behavior from buying the Comfort to buying the Sporty.

Bayesian updating is what John should do if he wants to make the most informed decision. Every new piece of information he gets, it makes sense to use Bayes rule. We have, therefore, a prediction for how John should use any new information. Bayes updating can, however, be a bit more complicated than equation (5.1) might suggest. To explain why, it is useful to relate John's choice to what we did in chapters two and three.

We can think of John as not knowing what car will give him highest utility and so he searches for more information to become better informed. He is never going to be completely sure what is best, but new information allows him to update his beliefs and eventually make a more informed decision. Throughout this process John is making risky choices, particularly when he finally buys a car. For example, we can think of there being a 'Sporty prospect' and a 'Comfort prospect' where each prospect details the possible outcomes from buying that car. New information allows John to change the numbers in one or more of the prospects. For example, if he test drives the Comfort he can update the Comfort prospect. By updating the Comfort prospect he can then update his beliefs the Comfort is best. Table 5.1 illustrates how this might work in practice when John test drives the Comfort.

Framing things in this way we can see two potential issues. First, it becomes complicated to update beliefs. When I introduced Bayes updating, the focus was on the probability the Sporty is best for John. Now, we are starting to get down to finer details about each car. This seems natural but means that John has some work to do in order to turn new information into updated beliefs. He has to update his beliefs about the merits of each car, and then update his belief about which car is best. This can easily get quite complicated. Can John realistically be expected to do it? We will get back to that question in section 5.2.

A second issue is that of ambiguity and uncertainty. At the start of chapter three I mentioned the distinction between risk and uncertainty and you might recall that if a person has a choice with uncertainty then they may not know the probability of possible outcomes. John can presumably predict that he could like the Comfort,

Table 5.1 John updates his beliefs after a test drive. The Comfort is best if it is worth $12,000. Initially he puts probability 0.7 on this being the case so Sporty is best with probability 0.3. He test drives the Comfort and did not like it. This lowers the probability he puts on the Comfort being worth $12,000 down to 0.6

Event	John's opinion	Summary
Initial prior	The Sporty is worth $10,000 with probability 0.9 and $9,000 with probability 0.1.	Sporty is best with probability 0.3.
	The Comfort is worth $12,000 with probability 0.7 and $4,000 with probability 0.3.	
Test drives the Comfort and gets signal 'did not like the Comfort'	The signal precision, i.e. probability this would happen if the Comfort is worth 12, is 0.39.	Sporty is best with probability 0.4.
	He updates his beliefs about the Comfort to being worth $12,000 with probability 0.6 and $4,000 with probability 0.4.	

not like the Comfort, and so on. What would be much harder for him to do is put specific numbers on, say, the probability that he will like the Comfort, and the value he would put on it if he did like it. This means that John's choice of car is a choice with uncertainty. It also means we need to think about where the numbers in Table 5.1 could come from because without them we cannot possibly expect John to use Bayesian updating. We need, therefore to think about choice with uncertainty.

5.1.1 Models of choice with uncertainty

I shall start by talking about a relatively simple example to illustrate the most important issues, and then relate things back to John buying a car. Imagine a box containing ten balls. One of the balls is going to be drawn randomly from the box, and you have to bet on what color the ball will be. If you get it correct you win $2. Now contrast these two different possibilities:

Box 1: Contains five red balls and five black balls.
Box 2: Contains an unknown number of red balls and black balls. It could be zero red and ten black, ten red and zero black, or anything in between.
    What box would you rather bet on?

Box 1 provides a simple choice with risk like that we looked at in chapter three. If John bets on black he faces the prospect (0.5, $2; 0.5, $0), so with a 50 percent chance he will be correct and win the $2. His expected utility is then:

$$U(\text{black}) = 0.5u(w + 2) + 0.5u(w)$$

where w is his wealth. What about box 2? This time I cannot write down the prospect because I cannot say what probability John has of winning if he bets on black. The probabilities are **ambiguous**. If the probabilities are ambiguous then we cannot work out John's expected utility, use prospect theory, or do anything else we did in chapter three. We need something new.

The simplest thing we can do is use **subjective expected utility** in which we go with what John thinks will happen. If John thinks that box two will contain four red balls and six black balls then his subjective probability of drawing a black ball is 0.6 and his subjective expected utility is:

$$U(black) = 0.6u(w + 2) + 0.4u(w)$$

That looks like a simple solution! The problem is that John could have any beliefs he wanted and not be wrong. He could think none of the balls are black, all of them are black, and we have no way to tie down what his beliefs should be, or are likely to be.

Consider now another possible box:

> Box 3: A number between zero and ten will be randomly drawn and determine the number of red balls in the box. The rest of the ten balls will be black.

Does this box provide a choice with risk or with uncertainty? The correct answer is that it provides a choice with risk. It does, however, look different to box one. That's because it involves a compound lottery. A **compound lottery** is when there are two or more consecutive lotteries to determine the outcome. Box three is a compound lottery because there is a lottery to determine how many balls in the box, and then a lottery when John comes to pick a ball. Just to confuse, the final stage, where John picks a ball, is typically called the **first order lottery** or **second stage lottery**. The preliminary stage, where the number of balls in the box is determined, is called the **second order lottery** or **first stage lottery**. Two stages are enough in this case but there can be three or more stages.

To try and capture the lottery of box three we could write down one long prospect (0.09, \$2; 0.09, (0.9, \$2; 0.1; \$0); 0.09, (0.8, \$2; 0.2, \$2); . . .) where we recognize there is a one in eleven chance all the balls are black and John wins \$2, a one in eleven chance nine of the balls are black and John wins \$2 with probability 0.9, and so on. This looks a bit messy. We could, therefore, try **reducing the compound lottery** to a simple lottery. To do this we work out the overall probability that a ball will be black or red. If you do this you should find that there is a 50 percent chance a ball will be black and a 50 percent chance it will be red. This suggests betting on black with box three gives the same prospect (0.5, \$2; 0.5, \$0) as it did with box one!

It is not clear, however, that we should be reducing compound lotteries to a simple lottery. For instance we could do something called **recursive expected utility** and work out the expected utility of each lottery and compound them together. To do this, we start with the first order lottery where John picks a color.

If there is one black ball and nine black balls his expected utility of betting on black is:

$U(black|$ one black$) = 0.1u(w + 2) + 0.9u(w)$.

We need to do this for all possible combinations of black and red balls. We then go to the second order lottery where the number of balls is determined. For reasons we do not need to worry about, Kilbanoff, Marinacci and Mukerji (2005) show that his expected utility can be written:

$U(black) = 0.09\phi(U(black|no\ black)) + 0.09\phi(U(black|one\ black)) + \ldots$

where ϕ is some function that captures preferences over second order lotteries.

The key to this way of doing things is that we may want to distinguish risk attitudes towards first and second order lotteries. In particular, there are good arguments for why John may be more risk averse in a second order lottery than a first order lottery. If so, that means we should not be reducing compound lotteries but instead using recursive expected utility. It also means that John will be more reluctant to bet on box three than box one because he essentially does not like compound lotteries.

It is now interesting to go back and look again at box two. When the probabilities are ambiguous, as they are in box two, it seems more natural to think in terms of a compound lottery. That is, it seems natural to think of John having subjective beliefs about an additional stage in which balls are added to the box. For example, he might put subjective probability 0.5 on there being five red and five black balls, and probability 0.25 that all the balls are black, and so on. It may, therefore, be most apt to use **recursive subjective expected utility** to think about choice with uncertainty. To see whether that is the case we need to look at some data.

5.1.2 The Ellsberg Paradox

I am going to look at the results of a study by Halevy (2007). In the study, subjects were asked to bet on boxes one to three, and a fourth box:

> Box 4: A fair coin will be tossed to determine whether all the balls in the box are black, or all of them are red.

The interesting thing about box four is that all risk is resolved in the first stage. So, we have box one where risk is resolved in the second stage, box four where it is resolved in the first stage, and box three which is a true compound lottery. If people are more risk averse about second order risk, we should be able to pick this up.

In the study, rather than just have subjects bet on a color, subjects were given the chance to sell bets by saying the amount they were willing to accept to forgo

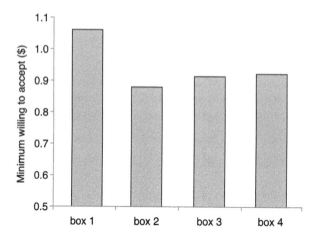

Figure 5.1 The willingness to sell a bet on each of the boxes. The Ellsberg Paradox is why subjects want less to sell a bet on box two than on box one.

Source: Halevy (2007).

the bet. Figure 5.1 plots the average, minimum amount subjects were willing to accept. Remember they would win $2 if they won the bet, so a risk neutral person would want $1. The most important thing to pick out is the greater willingness to sell a bet on box two than a bet on box one. This difference was first pointed out by Ellsberg (1961), and so goes by the name of the **Ellsberg Paradox**. (For another Ellsberg Paradox, see review question 5.2.) The Paradox is why people do not like betting on box two. It seems that people are **ambiguity averse** in preferring a choice with risk to one with uncertainty. The results for boxes three and four suggest, however, we need to qualify this somewhat because subjects also seem averse to a second order lottery.

To delve a little deeper, Halevy looks at the choices of individual subjects and tries to classify those choices. Table 5.2 summarizes his findings. Let's go through the table row by row.

First, there were subjects willing to sell a bet on any box at the same price. They did not seem to be bothered by ambiguity or a second order lottery and so their choices seem consistent with subjective expected utility maximization.

Second are those who were more willing to sell a bet on box four than on box three than on box one. These subjects seemed to be risk averse about a second order lottery and so their choices are most consistent with recursive expected utility.

Third are those who are willing to sell a bet on boxes one and four at the same price but more willing to sell a bet on box three. It does not look as though these subjects are risk averse about a second order lottery, otherwise they would be more willing to sell a bet on box four. Instead, it seems they disliked the

Table 5.2 The proportion of subjects fitting each model of preferences and the average willingness to sell

Model of preferences	Proportion of subjects	Willingness to accept to forgo bet			
		box 1	box 2	box 3	box 4
Subjective expected utility	19.2%	1.03	1.03	1.03	1.03
Recursive expected utility	40.3%	1.04	0.78	0.96	0.79
Recursive non-expected utility	39.4%	1.11	0.91	0.85	1.07
Maxmin expected utility	0.1%	0.90	0.80	0.90	0.90

Source: Halevy (2007).

compounding of lotteries necessary with box three. I will not go into the details, but this is consistent with recursive non-expected utility in which a person uses rank dependent utility (as introduced in chapter three).

Finally, we come to those who simply do not like ambiguity. In his original paper Ellsberg suggested that when there is ambiguity, people are pessimistic and go with the worst thing that can happen. Hence we get a story of maximizing the minimum. Only one subject in this study behaved like that in being more willing to sell box two, but not boxes three or four.

Let's go back now and think about John deciding what car to buy. First of all, we now know that we should view the numbers in Table 5.1 as John's subjective beliefs about what he thinks might happen. We can also now see that it is natural to think of his choice as a compound lottery where, say, the quality of each car is determined in a second order lottery and the car he would most prefer is determined in a first order lottery.

The subjective nature of John's beliefs means it will be very hard for us to know why John would choose one car over another and whether he made the best choice. We do see, however, in Table 5.2 that the majority of people do not seem to like compound lotteries, or are ambiguity averse. This does have clear implications: John may be reluctant to gamble on which car is best, and so put off buying a car; he should also be eager to become better informed about each car in order to reduce the ambiguity or second order risk he faces. It is this last possibility I want to focus on first.

5.2 Two cognitive biases

If John does not like ambiguity or second order risk then he needs to become better informed, and so he should be on the look-out for new information. What we need to ask is whether he will use that information wisely. Will he, for example, use Bayes rule? To do so, would be quite complicated and so it would not be a huge surprise to see some mistakes and biases in how he does interpret new information. In this section I will look at two of the more common biases we do seem to observe: the confirmatory bias and law of small numbers.

5.2.1 Confirmatory bias

Suppose John asks his friend's advice and is told: 'The Comfort is a great car, but the Sporty more eco-friendly.' This may be useful information, but it is not obvious how John should interpret it. The basic problem is that the information is ambiguous, in the sense that any interpretation of it will be subjective, and different people might interpret it in different ways. Some might focus on 'the Comfort is a great car' and others on 'the Sporty is more eco-friendly'.

This ambiguity is common in a lot of information we get and can easily lead to a biased interpretation of information. We say that there is **confirmatory bias** if a person has a tendency to interpret ambiguous, new information as consistent with his initial beliefs and opinions. Two psychology studies will help illustrate.

In a study by Lord, Ross and Lepper (1979), subjects were asked to read two reports on the deterrent effect of the death penalty and then asked to use their own 'evaluative powers' in thinking whether the reports provided support for or against the death penalty. They were initially given a brief description of the first report and asked questions about their attitudes and change in attitudes having seen the report. They were then given a more detailed description and asked questions about how well they thought the research in the report had been conducted and how convincing it was. The whole process was then repeated for the second report.

Some weeks before doing this experiment, subjects had filled in a questionnaire where half of the subjects invited to the experiment had appeared proponents of capital punishment and the other half opponents. The reports given to subjects could also be classified as having a pro- or anti-deterrence conclusion.

The main results of the experiment are summarized in Table 5.3. We see that brief descriptions of a study do change attitudes in the way we would expect.

Table 5.3 Evidence of confirmatory bias in attitudes to capital punishment. Mean evaluations on a −8 to +8 scale where +8 meant convincing and well done and −8 not convincing and not well done

Question	Report	Evaluation	
		Proponents	Opponents
Brief description changes my attitude to capital punishment	Pro-deterrence	1.3	0.4
	Anti-deterrence	−0.7	−0.9
How convincing the research was	Pro-deterrence	1.4	−2.1
	Anti-deterrence	−1.8	0.1
How well the research was conducted	Pro-deterrence	1.5	−2.1
	Anti-deterrence	−1.6	−0.3
Detailed description changes my attitude to capital punishment	Pro-deterrence	0.8	−0.9
	Anti-deterrence	0.7	−0.8

Source: Lord, Ross and Lepper (1979).

After a detailed description, however, attitudes diverge. Proponents of the death penalty rate pro-deterrence studies as convincing and well-conducted, while anti-deterrence studies are not convincing or well-conducted. Vice-versa for opponents. Thus, subjects had a tendency to rate positively evidence that was consistent with their opinion, and rate negatively evidence inconsistent with their opinion! This is **confirmatory bias**. The consequence is a **polarization of attitudes** with proponents of the death penalty becoming more in favor and opponents less in favor, despite having read the same evidence.

In the second study by Darley and Gross (1983), subjects were asked to evaluate the academic capabilities of a fourth-grade child. All subjects were given some basic information about the child. Half of the subjects were given the impression she was from a low-income background and the other half that she was from a middle-class background. Half of the subjects then watched a video of the child answering questions. The video was designed to be relatively uninformative of the child's ability. Subjects were finally asked to evaluate the child's capabilities.

The results of the experiment are summarized in Table 5.4. We see that those who did not see the video and believed she was from a middle class background have a higher expectation of ability than those who believed she was from a low income background. Whether or not this might be justifiable is not our main concern. Of interest to us is that watching the video lowered perceptions of ability if the child was believed to be from a low income background but increased perceptions of ability if she was believed to be from a middle-class background. How subjects interpreted the same video depended, therefore, on initial information about the child. Those primed to think she might be low ability had their belief confirmed by the video, and those primed to think she might be high ability had this different belief confirmed by the same video! This is confirmatory bias.

In neither of these studies were subjects asked to make economic choices. Clearly, however, confirmatory bias can potentially influence economic behavior. If John was favoring the Comfort then confirmatory bias suggests the main thing he will take from his friends advice is 'the Comfort is a great car'. This could

Table 5.4 Evidence of confirmatory bias in assessing the ability of a child. Predicted grade placement goes down after watching a video if the child was perceived to be from a low income background, and goes up if she was perceived to be from a middle-class background

Watched the video or not?	Information provided	Grade level placement in		
		Mathematics	Reading	Liberal arts
Did not	Low income	3.98	3.90	3.85
	Middle class	4.30	4.29	4.03
Did	Low income	3.79	3.71	3.04
	Middle class	4.83	4.67	4.10

Source: Darley and Gross (1983).

mean he is over-confident when making his choice. To explore this further it is useful to have a model and for that I will turn to the work of Rabin and Schrag (1999).

5.2.2 A model of confirmatory bias

Imagine that every week John reads a magazine or looks up some review on the internet and gets a signal of which car is better. The signals are correct with probability $\theta \in (0.5,1)$. So, if the Comfort is best for John then with probability θ a review will suggest the Comfort is best, and with probability $1 - \theta$ it will suggest the Sporty is best.

To capture confirmatory bias we assume that John does not always correctly interpret signals. To see how this works, suppose that he currently believes the Comfort is best. If he reads a review that suggests the Comfort is best, he always correctly interprets the review as supportive of the Comfort. But, if he reads a review that suggests the Sporty is best, he incorrectly interprets the review as supportive of the Comfort with probability q. This captures confirmatory bias because John has a bias to interpret information as consistent with his prior belief. If he thinks that the Comfort is best, he is likely to think a review is supportive of the Comfort even though it is not. Similarly, if his prior belief is that the Sporty is best, he is likely to think a review is supportive of the Sporty even though it is not. The larger is q then the larger the bias. If $q = 0$ there is no bias because all signals are correctly interpreted. If $q = 1$ then there is complete bias because whatever John reads he will think is supportive of what he believes.

Suppose John uses Bayes rule based on the signals he thinks he has received. If he started indifferent between the two, and after t weeks thinks he has read S_t reviews supportive of Sporty and C_t reviews supportive of Comfort, then his posterior belief should be:

$$prob(\text{Sporty is best} \mid S_t, C_t) = \frac{\theta^{S_t}(1-\theta)^{C_t}}{\theta^{S_t}(1-\theta)^{C_t} + (1-\theta)^{S_t}\theta^{C_t}}.$$

What are the consequences of confirmatory bias?

We can first look at whether it leads to John having wrong beliefs more often. By wrong beliefs I mean he thinks one car is better when actually the other car is better. Table 5.5 details the proportion of times he has the wrong belief after reading 10 or 100 reviews. Remember that if $q = 0$ there is no confirmatory bias and so we see the unbiased probability of John being wrong. Confirmatory bias has two consequences: (i) John has wrong beliefs more often, as seen by the larger proportion of errors as q increases. (ii) He does not correct these beliefs over time, as seen by the error rates being similar after reading 100 reviews and 10 reviews the higher is q.

We can see that these two effects combine to make wrong beliefs much more likely. To get some intuition for why this is the case suppose that the Sporty is the

Table 5.5 The probability of an incorrect belief after reading 10, 100 reviews. The higher is the confirmatory bias q, the higher the probability John has wrong beliefs and the less difference it makes if he reads more reviews

q	θ			
	0.6	0.7	0.8	0.9
0	25%, 2%	7%, 0%	2%, 0%	0%, 0%
0.1	25%, 5%	10%, 0%	2%, 0%	1%, 0%
0.3	32%, 27%	13%, 5%	6%, 0%	2%, 0%
0.5	35%, 34%	20%, 18%	9%, 7%	5%, 3%
0.7	36%, 36%	24%, 24%	15%, 15%	7%, 7%
0.9	40%, 40%	27%, 27%	19%, 19%	10%, 10%

best car for John and he receives signals C,C,S,C,S,S,S so the first two review are supportive of the Comfort, the next of the Sporty, and so on. If John has no confirmatory bias he will correctly think that three reports are supportive of the Comfort and four of the Sporty, and four beats three, so overall the Sporty looks best. If he has confirmatory bias, however, he may become biased by the first few reports that are supportive of the Comfort. Specifically, he will correctly think the first, second and fourth reviews were supportive of the Comfort. So, he only needs to wrongly think one of the third, fifth, sixth or seventh reviews were supportive of the Comfort and he will have wrong beliefs. The higher is q the more this becomes expected.

Confirmatory bias can, therefore, lead John astray. This means we might want to be careful of anything he tells us. Suppose, for instance, that John tells you that 'I think the Comfort is best because 11 of the 15 reviews I have read are supportive of the Comfort'. What should you believe if you suspect confirmatory bias? It is possible to show that, you should believe John is correct but be less confident than he is. For instance, if he says that 11 of the 15 reviews he has read are supportive of the Comfort then it would be sensible for you to think that around nine or ten were actually supportive. This is because the confirmatory bias will, on average, make him overestimate the number of times he read a supportive review.

Next suppose that John tells you: 'The Comfort is best, but I have recently read some reviews supportive of the Sporty,' or he says: 'The Comfort is best but I used to think the Sporty was.' In the first case you should probably put less faith in his belief, because there are signs that confirmatory bias is causing him to overestimate Comfort. Indeed, if there is a strong confirmatory bias, the fact that he has recently read some reviews supportive of the Sporty might imply you should think the Sporty is best. In the second case, we have cause to be confident in John's belief. That he recently changed his mind, despite confirmatory bias, suggests you should be more confident than John is that the Sporty is best.

Things are now starting to get a bit messy and complicated. Indeed we now see that John should be thinking about the confirmatory bias of the people writing the reviews that he is reading! The main point, however, is simple: confirmatory bias means people may not correctly interpret new information, and so we may want to be skeptical of what they say they have learnt.

5.2.3 Law of small numbers

Suppose, continuing the previous thread, that John tells you 75 percent of the reviews he has read are supportive of the Comfort. If you do not suspect confirmatory bias, how should you interpret this information?

A Bayesian updater wouldn't do anything without asking first: how big was the sample size? That three out of four reviews are supportive of the Comfort should be much less persuasive than hearing that 15 out of 20 reviews were supportive. For instance, if $\theta = 0.6$ a Bayesian updater would put probability 0.69 on the Comfort being best for John in the first case, and 0.98 in the latter.

There is evidence, however, that many people fail to recognize the importance of sample size and expect small samples to be more representative of the population than they likely are. This is the **law of small numbers**. There are two sides to the law of small numbers that we need to look at. I'll start with something called the gambler's fallacy.

If John expects a small sample to be representative of the population then he may expect random events to be self-correcting. For example, if ten tosses of a coin have been heads, there may be a tendency to think the next one 'must be tails'. This is known as the **gambler's fallacy**. We see interesting evidence for the gambler's fallacy in betting on lottery numbers. To illustrate, I will look at studies by Clotfelter and Cook (1991) and Terrell (1994) which analyzed data from the state lotteries of Maryland and New Jersey. In both lotteries a better must correctly guess a three-digit winning number. In Maryland any winner gets $500. In New Jersey a prize fund is split between all those who guess the right number, meaning that a person wins more the fewer guess the winning number.

In both Maryland and New Jersey there was clear evidence of people betting less on a number that had recently won. This is consistent with the gambler's fallacy: 'if number 525 has just won it cannot win again'. In Maryland the gambler's fallacy does not affect expected winnings because all numbers are equally likely and every winner gets $500. In New Jersey, however, it does matter, because winnings are higher the fewer pick the number. If others are unlikely to pick a number that has just won then that it is actually a good number to pick.

Table 5.6 demonstrates that winners in New Jersey did indeed get more when betting on numbers that had recently won. The difference is large, with a person choosing a number that won in the previous week winning on average $89, or 34 percent more than the average winner! The gambler's fallacy thus lowered a person's expected winnings. This suggests we should see less evidence of the gambler's fallacy in New Jersey, where it did reduce earnings, than in Maryland, where it could not. Table 5.6 partly supports this by estimating the payout there would have been in Maryland if winners were paid as in New Jersey. There we see slightly larger differences in potential winnings, but only slightly larger. That the

Table 5.6 Payouts to winners in state lotteries. Less people bet on numbers that have just won, so the payout is higher in New Jersey, where the winnings are shared, and would be higher in Maryland, if the winnings were shared

Winning number repeating	Average payout in New Jersey	Estimated average payout in Maryland
Within 1 week	$349	$396
Between 1 and 2 weeks	$349	–
Between 2 and 3 weeks	$308	–
Between 3 and 8 weeks	$301	$382
Not within 8 weeks	$260	$289

Source: Terrell (1994).

gambler's fallacy would reduce winnings did not, therefore, seem to make much difference to the strength of the bias.

The flip side the gambler's fallacy is the **hot hand fallacy**. Here there is an expectation that streaks will continue, and it has particularly come to be associated with professional sport. For instance, a footballer or basketball player who is 'on form' or 'on a roll' is expected to keep on shooting well.

In a famous study Gilovich et al. (1985) put the hot hand fallacy to the test by looking at the performance of professional and college basketball players. This included following the fortunes of the Philadelphia 76ers during the 1980–81 season. As Table 5.7 shows, supporters and players expressed a belief in a hot hand. They thought that a player would be more likely to make a shot if he had just made one. The data on actual performance painted a different picture. There was no evidence for a hot hand. This study has now been replicated in other sports, with similar results. Sports fans, it seems, are not good at judging whether a sequence is random or not!

At first sight, the gambler's fallacy seems very different to the hot hand fallacy. In the one 'five heads means the next must be tails' while in the other 'five successes must mean he will be successful again'. It is important, therefore, to understand why the gambler's fallacy and hot hand fallacy can both result from

Table 5.7 Evidence (or lack of it) for the hot hand fallacy. Supporters and players expected performance in the recent past to be a predictor of future performance. It was not

	Probability of making a field goal shot	
	If just missed one	If just made one
What supporters expected	42%	61%
What players expected	50%	63%
What the data says	54%	51%

Source: Gilovich et al. (1985).

the same law of small numbers. The key difference is whether the probability of each outcome is known.

The gambler's fallacy can occur when the probability of the outcome is known. It occurs if someone trying to predict the next draw from a sequence expects a small sequence to match the known probability. For example, we know that a fair coin has a 50 percent chance of landing heads, and so John might expect 50 percent of coin tosses to be heads. This means he would think five heads in a row is unlikely, and likely to be balanced out by a subsequent tail. Similarly, a lottery number should not occur two weeks in a row.

The hot hand fallacy can occur when there is uncertainty over the probability of the outcomes and someone trying to predict the probability of the next draw expects a small sequence to be a good predictor of what will happen next. So, a basketball shooter who has got five in a row must be on form and likely to get the next. Similarly if John has read four reviews in a row supportive of Comfort, he might expect the next one will also be supportive of Comfort.

One interesting way to illustrate how these two fallacies can fit together is to look at sequences of random events, such as coin flips. Here are three possible sequences of coin flips. Which do you think are really generated by a coin?

hhTThTThhhTTThhTTThTThTTTTThhhhhThTThThTTThThhTTTh
hTThhhTThTThThhThTTThhThhhThTThhThTTThhThhTTThThhT
hhhhhTThThhTThhhhhhhhThTTThTThhTThThhTTThThhhhhhTT

The top and bottom really were random and the middle one a figment of my imagination. To try and understand why you might think the middle one is random it is useful to use the **proportion of alternations**. For a sequence of n signals you need to count the number of **streaks**, or unbroken sub-sequences, r and then calculate:

$$\text{proportion of alternations} = \frac{r-1}{n-1}.$$

If the sequence is random, the proportion should be 0.5 and in the top and bottom sequences it is 0.49 and 0.43. The evidence, however, is that many people think sequences with a proportion of around 0.6 are actually random, and in the middle sequence it is 0.59.

That we expect the proportion of alternations to be high is consistent with the gambler's fallacy; we do not expect five heads in a row. That we think sequences with a low proportion of alternations cannot be random is consistent with the hot hand fallacy; if we do see five heads in a row then the coin cannot be fair. (Basketball fans may be interested to know that Gilovich et al. (1985) found the proportion of alternations of professional basket players was very close to that expected if the sequence of hits and misses was random.)

In looking at the consequences of the law of small numbers it is useful to have a model. Again we turn to Mathew Rabin (2002).

5.2.4 *A model of the law of small numbers*

Imagine again John reading car reviews. As before, let θ be the probability that a review is supportive of the Comfort and $1 - \theta$ the probability a review is supportive of the Sporty. John wants to know θ because then he can better know what car is best.

First, let's think about the gambler's fallacy. In this case it is most apt to think that John is confident that he knows θ. The bias comes when he tries to predict what a review will say. We can capture this by assuming that John thinks signals are randomly drawn **without replacement** from a box containing N balls. On θN of the balls are written 'Comfort is best' and on $(1 - \theta)N$ are written 'Sporty is best'. I have emphasized the 'without replacement' because that is what causes the bias. If you substitute 'with replacement' then there would be no bias. To see why, suppose that $N = 2$ and John thinks $\theta = 0.5$. Then John thinks the box contains one review supportive of Sporty and one supportive of Comfort. So, if he reads a review supportive of Sporty he would think the next report must be supportive of Comfort. If $N = 4$ then there are two reviews supportive of Sporty and two supportive of Comfort. If he reads a review supportive of Sporty he would think there is a two in three chance the next report will be supportive of the Comfort.

This nicely captures the gambler's fallacy because John expects that a sample of size N will be representative. The smaller is N then the more biased he is. There is, however, a problem with the model: what happens when he has read more reviews than there are balls in the box? To overcome this we assume that the box is replaced after he reads every other review. This makes the model work in a way that we can still capture the gambler's fallacy. Can it also capture the hot hand fallacy?

To capture the hot hand fallacy we need to add some uncertainty about θ. Suppose that John thinks $\theta = 0.25$, 0.5 or 0.75 are equally likely. He then reads two reviews in a row that are supportive of the Comfort. How will he update his beliefs about θ? Table 5.8 compares what he will think if he is unbiased and biased. We see that when he is biased he ends up overestimating the probability reviews are supportive of Comfort. Indeed, he infers it is impossible that reviews are more likely supportive of Sporty. This example is representative of what will

Table 5.8 Beliefs when there is the law of small numbers. If John is biased he overestimates the significance of two C signals

		θ		
		0.25	*0.5*	*0.75*
The likelihood of two C signals	unbiased, N large	0.0625	0.25	0.5625
	biased, N = 4	0	0.166	0.495
Updated beliefs after two C signals	unbiased, N large	0.071	0.286	0.643
	biased, N = 4	0	0.251	0.749

happen more generally. John will overestimate how much he can learn from reading a small number of reviews. This is the hot hand fallacy.

One implication of the law of small numbers is that John's beliefs are too sensitive to the signals he gets. Whether he reads good reviews about the Comfort or the Sporty will lead to a bigger swing in his beliefs than is justified. This can have a knock-on effect in how much variation he perceives in the quality of cars. For example, suppose he compares other pairs of cars besides Sporty and Comfort. If $\theta = 0.5$ for all the pairs then in around half of the pairs he is likely to read two reviews supportive of one of the cars. The hot hand fallacy means that John will read too much into this and come away believing there is more variation in cars than there actually is. In other words, some cars are naturally going to have a run of bad or good reviews, but John will over-interpret this as due to differences in quality rather than chance.

5.2.5 Generating random sequences

One interesting implication of the law of small numbers is that people may be bad at generating random sequences. For example, Rapoport and Budescu (1997) asked subjects to imagine a sequence of 150 draws with replacement from a deck of cards with five black and five red cards, and call aloud the sequence. Table 5.9 summarizes how subjects were biased towards switching too often and balancing out the sequence. If the sequence really is random, the probability of calling out black should always be 50 percent. We see, however, that subjects called out black more often if they had just called out red, and called out black less often if they had recently called out black more often.

It might seem a bit artificial to ask a person to generate a random sequence, there are, however, strategic situations where this is a useful skill. One such setting is competitive sports, where a player wants to keep an opponent guessing. For example, in tennis a server does not want his opponent to be able to predict where in the court he will serve. Similarly, in football or hockey a penalty-taker does not want the goalkeeper to know which side he will shoot. We might think that professional sportsman would learn to generate random sequences when competing. Do they?

One study, by Walker and Wooders (2001), looked at serving in ten important tennis matches, and analyzed how often players served left versus right. There are

Table 5.9 Probability of calling out a sequence of blacks and red in a deck of cards with five back and five red cards

Last few calls	Probability of calling out black
Red	58.5%
Black, red	46.0%
Black, black, red	38.0%
Black, black, black, . . .	29.8%

Source: Rabin (2002).

two things that it is interesting to check with the data: whether a player was serving left and right with a probability that maximized his chance of winning, and whether sequences of serves were random. They found that players did serve left and right with appropriate probabilities but, on average, there was too much switching for the sequences to be random. To illustrate, Table 5.10 summarizes the famous 1982 Wimbledon final between Jimmy Connors and John McEnroe. Connors won the match, but that would be hard to guess from the data! McEnroe wins roughly as many points to the left and right, showing that he was serving left and right with the correct probability. He also had an appropriate number of streaks (or proportion of alternations) indicating the sequence of serves looked random. Connors, by contrast, should have served more to the right from the ad court and more to the left from the deuce court than he did. He also had too many streaks for the sequence to look random, suggesting he was switching from left to right too often.

We see, therefore, that learning and experience does not necessarily mean that people can generate random sequences. It does seem clear, however, that people become better at generating random sequences with experience. For example, Walker and Wooders compared the performance of the tennis players with subjects in a previous lab experiment and the data from the tennis players was starkly different from that of the lab subjects. Less clear is whether people experienced at generating random sequences in one setting, e.g. a tennis game, are able to carry that skill over to a different setting, e.g. a game of poker.

5.2.6 Do biases matter?

To briefly summarize what we have seen in this section, it is helpful to first recall how Bayesian updating requires both correctly interpreting signals and updating probabilities according to Bayes rule. Confirmatory bias means that people are biased in interpreting signals. The law of small numbers means that people do not update probabilities according to Bayes rule. Overall, therefore, we get a somewhat pessimistic picture of people's ability to use new information appropriately.

Table 5.10 Data from the 1982 Wimbledon final. If maximizing their payoff, players should win approximately as many points to the left and right. A high number of streaks tells us if players were switching from left to right more often than a random sequence

Player	Court	Serves			Points won		Streaks	
		total	left	right	left	right	number	prob. if random
Connors	Ad	78	41%	59%	50%	70%	49	0.001
	Deuce	91	84%	16%	67%	53%	31	0.042
McEnroe	Ad	71	45%	55%	72%	62%	36	0.563
	Deuce	79	44%	56%	69%	68%	36	0.848

Source: Walker and Wooders 2001.

And the bad news does not stop there, because there are many other biases that I have not mentioned here (some of which we shall see later).

Do such biases matter? Some important consequences of the biases we have seen include: (1) overconfidence and wrong beliefs; (2) a belief that there is more variation in a population than there actually is; (3) a polarization of views despite people seeing similar information. These look like pretty important things. For example, overconfidence can cause John to make a relatively uninformed choice of car and not choose the car that is best for him. Polarization can lead to prejudice and discrimination. It is clear, therefore, that we do need to take seriously possible biases in interpreting new information. This will become clear when we look at health care and the stock market later in this chapter.

5.3 Learning from others

One issue that we need to consider in a bit more detail is how to interpret information that comes from other people. Often this is how we get new information, for example, John asking his friend or reading a magazine review. The complication that I want us to think about is that John only sees the choice or decision of the other person and not the reason for that choice. For example, if John sees a friend driving the Sporty car then he can never really know why his friend chose it. Instead he has to try and infer his friend's motives and then ask whether this tells him anything useful.

When trying to infer motives many complicating questions arise, such as: (i) how biased is my friend? (ii) does he have similar preferences or tastes to me? and (iii) is he deliberately trying to manipulate me? We need to have some answers to such questions.

5.3.1 To conform or not

To get us started, imagine that John test drives both the Sporty and Comfort and decides he prefers the Sporty. Before he makes a final decision, however, goes out and looks at what others are driving. If he sees lots of others driving Comfort should he change his mind?

To answer that question it is useful to work though a simple model. Suppose that everyone has the same preferences. So, either the Comfort is the best car for everyone or the Sporty is best car for everyone. Let β be the probability that Comfort is the best. Before anyone buys a car they test drive both of them and form an independent opinion of which car is best. If Comfort really is the best car there is a θ_C chance a person will prefer Comfort on the test drive, and if Sporty is the best car there is a θ_S chance they will prefer Sporty on the test drive. To see what happens I will set $\beta = 0.5$ and $\theta_C = \theta_S = 0.67$ and work through the possible choices. Table 5.11 summarizes what is going on.

Anna is first to buy a car. She has no choice but to buy the car she preferred on the test drive. Imagine she preferred the Comfort and bought it.

Alan is the next to buy a car. He does the test drive and sees that Anna has bought the Comfort. If he preferred the Comfort on the test drive then he has an

Table 5.11 An information cascade. Anna and Alan both prefer Comfort when they test drive it, so buy it. Emma preferred Sporty but can see the other two have bought Comfort so also buys Comfort. Same for John. If three friends each prefer the Sporty, their three signals outweigh the two choices of Anna and Alan

	Order to buy a car					
	1st	*2nd*	*3rd*	*4th*	*5th to 9th*	*10th*
Person	Anna	Alan	Emma	John	–	3 friends
Signal	Comfort	Comfort	Sporty	Sporty	–	3 Sporty
Choice	Comfort	Comfort	Comfort	Comfort	Comfort	Sporty

easy choice. If he preferred the Sporty he has a more difficult choice. It makes sense, however, to choose the Sporty. Imagine he actually preferred the Comfort and bought it.

The choice of both Anna and Alan tells a lot about what car they preferred on the test drive. In particular, it should be possible to infer their signal from their choice. If Anna buys the Comfort she must have preferred the Comfort on the test drive. If Alan buys the Sporty he must have preferred that. This means that observing what they bought is useful information.

Emma is the third person to buy a car. She can see that two people have bought the Comfort and from this infers that two people must have preferred the Comfort on the test drive. What does that mean? Even if Emma does a test drive and prefers the Sporty, it is still two against one in favor of the Comfort. Using Bayes rule these two observations should outweigh her one signal. She should choose Comfort.

Irrespective of what she thinks about the test drive, Emma should choose Comfort. This means that she should ignore her own signal and her choice tells us nothing about her signal. We call this an **information cascade**. The same is true of John and all those after him. They should buy Comfort.

Finally, suppose that three friends decide to all buy a car simultaneously. They each test drive the cars and say what they prefer. Imagine that all three preferred the Sporty. Do these three signals that Sporty is best outweigh seeing nine people driving Comfort? Yes, they do, because the friends should know that they cannot infer anything from Emma and John buying Comfort. They only bought Comfort because Anna and Alan did. So, it is three signals versus two observations and they should buy the Sporty.

What we see here is that an information cascade can be **fragile**. That three, four, five or more bought Comfort conveys no new information. Thus, someone with a more precise signal may want to go with their signal rather than what others have been observed doing.

What can we learn from this model? First of all we see that a person's choice may convey a lot of information about what they know. This is the case for Anna, Alan, and the three friends. We also see, however, that a person's choice may convey very little information about what they know, because they are conforming to others. This is the case for Emma and John. It is very important, therefore, to try and work out how much information someone's choice conveys before drawing too many inferences from it. In practice this can be complicated to do, particularly if $\theta_C \neq \theta_S$ or different people have different θs. But more important for us to start questioning how people do behave when faced with such situations.

5.3.2 Cascade experiments

There have now been a variety of experimental studies to see whether information cascades happen as predicted. Anderson and Holt (1997) were one of the first to do so and Figure 5.2 summarizes some of their results. There are two things these results try to pick up. The first is whether subjects got as good a payoff as they could have done if they had used Bayes rule. This is measured by actual efficiency. When $\theta_S = \theta_C = 0.67$ we see that subjects were pretty close to using Bayes rule, but in the more complicated game where $\theta_S = 0.86$, $\theta_C = 0.71$ there is a bigger gap. The next question is whether subjects did better than they would have done just following their own signal. This is measured by private efficiency. We see that in both cases subjects did a lot better than they would have done from just following their own signal. It is clear from this, and other studies, that people do learn from observing others, because actual efficiency is above private efficiency, but not everyone uses Bayes rule, because actual efficiency is not 100 percent.

If John knows that others are likely to be biased in some way then he should rethink what choices say about signals. For example, if he suspects that Emma

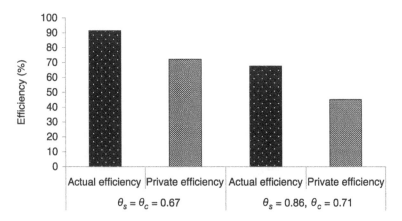

Figure 5.2 A cascade experiment. The payoff subjects got relative to what they would have got if they had followed Bayes rule, actual efficiency, and the payoff they would have got if they had followed their own signal relative to that they would have got with Bayes rule, private efficiency.

Source: Anderson and Holt (1997).

will follow her own signal, and ignore that Anna and Alan chose Comfort, then her choice is more informative than it would be if she was following Bayes rule. We can test whether subjects do take this into account by looking at choices relative to the **empirical optimum** (see Research Methods 5.1). For example, we can look at all situations where a subject has signals and has observed three others choosing C. On average, does a subject in this situation get a higher payoff choosing S or C? We call the answer the empirical optimum and then ask how many subjects follow the optimum.

Research Methods 5.1

Empirical optima versus Nash equilibrium

A Nash equilibrium details a strategy for each person such that it is optimal for a person to follow his strategy if all other people follow theirs. That is, it consists of a strategy s_i for each person such that she can do no better,

$$u_i(s_i, s_{-i}) \geq u_i(x, s_{-i})$$

by playing another strategy x if others play strategies s_{-i}. In a cascade experiment there is one Nash equilibrium and so it is simple to say whether a subject behaved consistent with the Nash equilibrium.

The problem is that if one person does not behave consistent with Nash equilibrium, because of some bias, then it may no longer be optimal for others to follow their Nash equilibrium strategy. For example, Anna is supposed to buy the car she preferred on the test drive. If she randomly decides what to buy, then it is optimal for others to ignore what she does. So, if Anna does not follow her Nash equilibrium strategy neither should anyone else!

This makes it difficult to judge whether people are behaving optimally. Does a person deviate from his Nash equilibrium strategy because he is biased or because he expects others to be biased?

This will be a recurring question over the next few chapters and calculating the **empirical optimum strategy** is one way to address it. First we calculate the strategies that others typically follow. Denote by e_i the strategy the person usually plays. We then ask whether person i is maximizing his payoff,

$$u_i(e_i, e_{-i}) \geq u_i(x, e_{-i})$$

given that others are playing e_{-i}. If yes, then we say that i is playing the empirical optimum strategy. If all people play the empirical optimum strategy we get back to a Nash equilibrium.

Weizsäcker (2010) did this for a collection of previous experimental data (see Research Methods 5.2) and the results are summarized in Table 5.12. Let's focus first on the choice rate. This tells us that on those occasions where subjects would have maximized their expected payoff by not following their own signal they did

Table 5.12 Did subjects play the empirical optimal strategy in cascade experiments? The choice rate tell us the percentage of times subjects did play the optimal strategy. The success rate tells us the percentage of times they chose the best option

Some possible scenarios	Choice rate	Success rate	
		Actual	Empirical optima
Should not follow own signal	44%	53%	64%
Should follow own signal	91%	73%	75%
Signal different to majority choice	–	54%	–
Signal same as majority	–	89%	–
Signal different to what many and all have previously chosen	–	73%	–

Source: Weizsäcker (2010).

so only 44 percent of the time. The conclusion is, therefore, clear: subjects followed their own signal more often than they should have done. By looking at the success rate we can see how much this lowers their payoff. When it is optimal for them to not follow their own signal they choose the best option 53 percent of the time, but if they were to follow the empirical optimal strategy they would choose the best option 64 percent of the time.

This drop in success rate shows that subjects did not learn enough from what others were doing. The second part of Table 5.12 shows us that subjects were only successful in learning from others if a lot had all chosen the same thing. Put another way, for the average subject to not follow his signal there needed to be a more than 67 percent chance that not following his signal was optimal. This should have been 50 percent. We need to ask why subjects were reluctant to learn more from the choices of others.

Research Methods 5.2

Meta-data analysis

A typical experimental study will involve around 50 to 150 participants. If each participant makes between 10 and 20 decisions, this gives 500 to 3,000 data points. This should give enough statistical power to test some important hypothesis but not all. Ideally we would want more data points and more variety of locations and subjects. One way around this is to be a bit more inventive in recruiting subjects, for example, using the internet or newspapers. Another way is to compile meta-data sets in which results from similar studies are combined together. This is what Weizsäcker (2010) did for his study. The results from 13 cascade experiments, including Anderson and Holt (1997), were combined to give almost 30,000 data points. With such a large data set it is possible to ask questions that cannot be asked with a single study.

5.3.3 What happened to conformity?

The basic conclusion from the cascade experiments is that subjects follow their own signal more often than they should. This is interesting because it seemingly goes against psychological evidence that people tend to conform to the choices of others more than they should. In famous experiments by Soloman Asch, for instance, subjects given a very simple visual task seemingly conformed to the choices of others (see Research Methods 5.3). So, what role does conformity play?

Research Methods 5.3

Deception in experiments

In chapter one I briefly talked about the issue of deception. In economic experiments, everything that subjects are told should be true (but there might be things they are not told). In a psychology experiment it is not considered so bad to mislead or deceive subjects about the true experiment. This is apparent in the Asch experiments.

In these experiments subjects were asked to say which of three lines was the same length as a fourth. In a control experiment only one subject ever gave a wrong answer, so this was a very simple task. In the real experiment there were a number of **confederate**s, people told what to do by the experimenter, and one subject. In turn, the confederates would say which line they thought was the same length, and then the subject would say. The subject did not know that the others were confederates and had been told what to do by the experimenter. On some occasions the confederates were told to give the wrong answer, with the objective of seeing whether the subject would conform to the obviously wrong choice of others. Three-quarters of subjects did do so at least once during the experiment.

The deception in this experiment was to give the impression the confederates were other subjects. Economists do not like deception for a number of reasons. A most basic concern is whether choices will be reliable if the subject fears deception and/or the situation appears implausible. In the Asch experiments it is simply not possible that a string of people would have given the wrong answer. The subject is, thus, faced with a non-credible situation that can create a sense of discomfort and unease because 'something is not right'. How reliable are choices made in such a context? The study by Goeree and Yariv does not raise such a concern because all choices are made by subjects.

A study by Goeree and Yariv (2010) shows that conformity does matter. In their study, subjects had to choose between S and C, as in a cascade experiment, but without seeing any signal with informative information. Specifically, the first three subjects make their choice seeing only the choices of those before them. This would equate to Anna, Alan and Emma choosing without the benefit of a test drive. They seemingly have no option but to randomly choose a car. Subsequent subjects were then given the choice to see a private informative signal or to see the choices made by those who had not received a signal. So, John could either do a test drive or find out what Anna, Alan and Emma had chosen.

If a subject's objective is to choose the best option then this is a simple choice, they should get the informative signal. As Figure 5.3 shows, however, this is not what a significant proportion of subjects did. Two treatments were considered. In the first, a subject is paid solely for choosing the best option. In this case 34/50 percent of subjects chose to see what others did and 84/88 percent of those copied the majority choice. In the second treatment, subjects were paid if the majority of subjects choose the best option. Here there is at least some rationale for looking at other's choices in order to go against the majority and balance out the uninformed choices of others. We see, however, that most subjects still conformed to the majority choice. The end result of this was lower success rates. In the high stakes treatment subjects missed out on an average of $16.80 each, compared to the optimal strategy!

Overall, therefore, we get a mixed picture: the cascade experiments suggest people often overweight private information, while this study, and others, suggest people conform too much to the choices of others. These two things need not be incompatible but just how much choices are determined by own information, or those of others remains a very open question that I leave you to think about.

5.3.4 Signalling games

Before we finish this section there is one important complication I want to mention. In the cascade experiments Anna, Alan and everyone else has no incentive other than to try and buy what they think is the best car. Sometimes, however, a person may have an incentive to try and influence others through her actions. For instance,

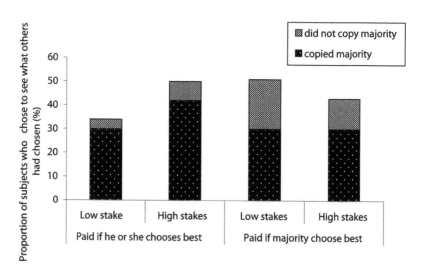

Figure 5.3 The proportion of subjects who chose to see what others had done and then copied or not the majority.

Source: Goeree and Yariv (2010).

if Maria's job is to sell Comfort cars then it is not a surprise she drives one. It would also not be a surprise if she says to John that 'it is a fantastic car, far better than Sporty'. She might be telling the truth, but she clearly has an incentive to say such a thing, even if it is not the truth.

To model such situations we can use a signaling game. The basic idea of a **signaling game** is that one person, called a **sender**, does some action, like say how wonderful the Comfort car is, and another person, called the **receiver**, tries to infer information from that, like how good Comfort really is. Signaling games are very useful for modeling strategic interaction, and so we shall come across them a few times in the next couple of chapters. Here I shall look at one study by Brandts and Holt (1992) to illustrate the issues that arise.

Rather than talk of car saleswomen I want you to imagine signaling in the labor market. Figure 5.4 schematically depicts the game in a game tree. It looks a bit messy but is not that bad if we think one stage at a time. Start at the middle. Chance decides whether the worker, John, is low ability or high ability. John then chooses how hard to work in his education. He can work hard and get A grades, taking him to the left of Figure 5.4, or work less hard and get B grades, taking him to the right of Figure 5.4. Knowing the grades of John, but not knowing his innate ability, the employer, Anna, must decide whether to give John an executive job or a manual job. The numbers give the payoffs to John and Anna for any combination of decisions.

The payoffs mean that, ceteris paribus, John prefers the executive job to the manual job, but prefers to get A grades when high ability and B grades when low ability. Anna would like to put a low-ability worker in a manual job and a high-ability worker in an executive job.

What makes the game interesting is that John knows whether he is high or low ability but Anna does not. She would like to know and so has to try and infer

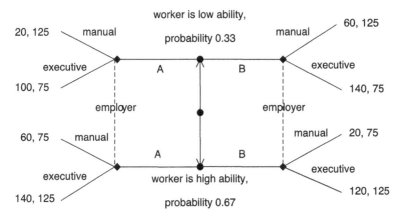

Figure 5.4 The game tree of a signaling game. Chance decides the type of the worker. The worker then chooses A or B and the employer manual or executive. The worker knows his type but the employer does not.

something from John's actions. John, however, has an incentive to appear as though he is high-skilled. He potentially, therefore, has an incentive to mislead. It is this incentive to mislead that has been absent from everything we have done so far in this chapter.

There are two Nash equilibria in this game, one given the technical name of intuitive and the other unintuitive. The **intuitive equilibrium** is that John works hard and gets an A grade whether he is high or low ability and is then given an executive job. If John did get a B grade he would be given a manual job. The **unintuitive equilibrium** is that John works less hard and gets a B grade whether he is high or low ability and is given an executive job. If John did get an A grade he would be given a manual job.

In both cases there is **pooling,** in the sense that John will do the same irrespective of his type. This means that the employer will not be able to distinguish whether John is high or low ability. The reason that one of the equilibrium is called intuitive and the other unintuitive should, hopefully, need little explanation. It seems far more natural that John should have to sacrifice a little when he is of the low ability, undesirable type, than when he is of the high ability, desirable type. A priori, however, we cannot rule out the unintuitive equilibrium.

Table 5.13 summarizes results from the study by Brandts and Holt in which subjects played this and similar games. In the top row we see that subjects did not initially play either the intuitive or unintuitive equilibrium. Instead, high-ability workers chose A and low-ability workers chose B. Employers, however, did behave consistently with the intuitive equilibrium by assigning workers with an A grade to executive jobs and those with a B grade to manual jobs. Workers learnt from this, and by rounds 9–12 both types of worker were choosing A.

In some subsequent experiments the payoffs of the game were revised to make workers more indifferent whether they chose A or B but to give employers more incentive to predict worker type. One objective was to see whether the unintuitive equilibrium would ever emerge. To see whether it did, we look to the bottom two rows of Table 5.13. Intriguingly we do see that most workers choose B and

Table 5.13 Play in a signaling game. In the standard game behavior converges towards an intuitive equilibrium. In the revised game behavior is closer to that of the unintuitive equilibrium

Game	Round	Worker choice given type		Employer choice given worker choice	
		A if high	*A if low*	*exec. if A*	*manual if B*
Standard game	1–4	100%	21%	98%	74%
Standard game	9–12	100%	75%	98%	60%
Revised game	1–6	39%	52%	45%	15%
Revised game	7–12	15%	38%	56%	13%

Source: Brandts and Holt (1992).

high-ability workers are less likely to choose A than low-ability workers. This is consistent with the unintuitive equilibrium. Employer behavior is not, however, consistent because those getting an A grade are still more likely to be allocated an executive job. We do not, therefore, see the unintuitive equilibrium, but are far from seeing the intuitive equilibrium either.

This study by Brandts and Holt illustrates some the more general lessons that have emerged from looking at signaling games. The most important lesson is that people do seem to behave strategically and expect others to behave strategically. For instance, the low-ability worker may work hard to get A grades and appear high-ability, but the employer will probably realize this and be skeptical whether those with A grades are high-ability. Similarly, the car salesman may say 'Comfort is best', even if she knows it is not, but the buyer is likely to be skeptical of such claims.

It seems, however, that people do need a bit of experience before they start behaving strategically. At first, the employer may think that all those with A grades must be hard-working, and John may believe the car salesman's claims. With experience they learn to be more skeptical. One consequence of such learning is that it becomes hard to predict what will happen. We can predict people will learn but we cannot predict quite what they will learn, because that could depend on all sorts of random things. This makes is hard to know for sure whether the intuitive or unintuitive equilibrium will be the one to emerge in a particular situation.

In the next chapter we shall explore these issues of strategy and learning in a lot more detail. The key thing I want you to see at this point is how complicated it can be to try and infer information from someone's actions, particularly if there is an incentive for them to mislead. Things get even more complicated when we realize that confirmatory bias, the law of small numbers and conformity are clearly relevant in signaling games. For example, an employer who has some workers who got A grades and some B grades might suffer from confirmatory bias, and think those with A grades are more productive than they really are. Also, because of the law of small numbers, and a few bad experiences with workers who got B grades, he may only hire those with A grades. Learning from new information is complicated, and learning from what others do is even more complicated!

5.4 Summary

We started by looking at Bayes updating as the most appropriate way to learn from new information.

I next suggested that choices often involve compound lotteries or ambiguity. This led us to look at recursive expected utility and ambiguity aversion. We saw that most people seem to be averse to ambiguity and/or second order risk. This means people should be eager to get new information.

We saw, however, that people can be biased in how they interpret new information. Confirmatory bias means someone can misinterpret new information and the law of small numbers means they can infer too much from new information.

Next, we saw that people can also be biased when learning from what others do. In some situations people seem to learn less from others than they could have done, and in other situations they conform more to others than seems sensible.

Finally, we saw that if one person has the incentive to mislead another, then we can use a signaling game to capture this but things quickly can become quite complex. So, it becomes hard to know how a person should interpret new information.

Overall, this presents a somewhat depressing picture of how wisely people use new information. Are things that bad? On the one hand I think they are; the assumption that people use Bayes rule I would comfortably put as the dodgiest assumption in the standard economic model. On the other hand things are probably not so bad; in particular, people can still make good choices even if they do not use information wisely. One reason for this is the aversion to ambiguity and second order risk. Such an aversion may mean people simply avoid making choices when they are poorly informed and we saw some evidence for this in chapters two and four.

5.5 Health care

Health care is one area of life where information is fundamentally important. To see why, let's think about the decisions that are made. A patient will decide things like: whether to take out private medical insurance, whether to seek treatment if ill, where to go for treatment, what to tell the doctor or nurse, whether to follow their recommendations and whether to seek a second opinion. Doctors and other medical practitioners decide things like: which patients to prioritize, what tests to perform, what treatments to recommend, and what to tell a patient. Each of these decisions requires good use of available information, and the stakes could not be higher because lives are involved. What evidence do we have that patients and practitioners do make these decisions wisely? I will look at patients first and practitioners second.

5.5.1 Patients

Recent years have seen dramatic increases in the amount of information available to patients in many western countries, the internet being one reason for this. For example, patients in the UK can go to a website (www.nhs.uk), put in their address, and instantly find a wealth of information about doctors and hospitals in their area. Everything is rated, from the quality of hospital food to mortality rates. Similar information is available in the US (www.HospitalCompare.hhs.gov). Do people use such information?

The evidence suggests not. The Kaiser Family Foundation routinely surveys people in the US about attitudes to health care. In the 2008 survey only 30 percent of people had seen information comparing health care providers in the last year and only 14 percent used this information! Instead people were more likely to rely on family and friends, with, an earlier survey finding that, 59 percent think the opinions of family and friends are a good source of information compared to just 36 percent who thought that family and friends do not have enough knowledge and experience to advise. Figure 5.5 gives some more evidence to think about. Here we see a strong, but declining, desire for familiarity rather than higher ratings.

One might argue that family and friends are a potentially good source of information. Again, however, the evidence suggests otherwise. For instance, patients are good at judging aspects of quality such as whether the doctor was respectful, attentive, clear in explaining issues, and had a clean and efficient office. Unfortunately, they are not so good at judging aspects such as whether the doctor supplied appropriate, evidence-based treatment. Also, it seems that patients have high levels of trust in practitioners and are willing to put errors down to things beyond the practitioner's control, even if it be that the practitioner is stressed and overworked.

The evidence does, therefore, point towards the biases that we looked at in section 5.2. For instance, we see evidence for the law of small numbers given that patients are content to rely on past experience and the experience of friends; such experience is likely to be a fairly small sample on which to draw inferences. We see evidence for confirmatory bias in the trust that patients put in practitioners and treatments. If they think their doctor is good or medication is working then ambiguous information may be interpreted in a way to support this belief. The considerable ambiguity of information about health care exasperates these two biases. For instance, if a patient gets better was that because of the medication or nature taking its course? The answer is ambiguous enough that a patient could believe whatever they want.

That we observe the law of small numbers and confirmatory bias is not so surprising. What is more surprising is that patients do have alternative sources of

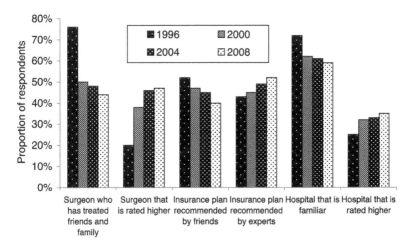

Figure 5.5 Preferences of respondents in surveys of patients in 1996, 2000, 2004 and 2008. Most people prefer things that are familiar or recommended by friends and family, rather than things recommended by experts.

Source: Kaiser Family Foundation (2008).

information that they seem to ignore. Why would patients choose not to use the wealth of information that is available about health care, and is based on large samples and scientifically based experiments?

One possibility is the availability heuristic. The **availability heuristic** could be summarized: if you remember something, it must be important. One consequence of this heuristic is that more vivid and memorable experiences can seem more important. For instance, John is more likely to remember his grandfather living to 100 despite smoking all his life, than the statistics on lung cancer. Similarly, he is more likely to remember the great treatment he got at a hospital, rather than a report showing the average performance of the hospital was poor.

A nice illustration of the availability heuristic is provided by Lichtenstein et al. (1978). In the study they look at whether subjects knew the likely causes of death in the US. In one part of the study subjects were told that on average 50,000 per year die in the US because of motor vehicle accidents and were then asked to say how many they thought died from 40 other possible causes. Table 5.14 gives some

Table 5.14 Approximate number of deaths in the US and estimated number of deaths for different causes

	Actual number	Estimated number	Newspaper inches
Fireworks	6	331	0
Whooping cough	15	171	0
Venomous bite or sting	48	535	0
Tornado	90	688	153.5
Lightning	107	128	0.8
Non-venomous animal	129	298	33.8
Flood	205	863	41.8
Pregnancy, childbirth and abortion	451	1,932	0
Appendicitis	902	880	0
Electrocution	1025	586	42.2
Train collision	1517	793	0
Asthma	1,886	769	1.9
Firearm accident	2,255	1,623	28.2
TB	3,690	966	0
Fire and flames	7,380	3,814	320.7
Drowning	7,380	1,989	247
Leukemia	14,555	2,807	14.8
Homicide	18,860	8,441	5,042.9
Accident falls	17,425	2,585	124.8
Breast cancer	31,160	3,607	0
Diabetes	38,950	2,138	0
Motor vehicle accidents	55,350	50,000	1,440.5
Lung cancer	75,580	9,723	35.9
Heart disease	738,000	25,900	303.4

Source: Lichtenstein et al. (1978)

of the results. There is a primary bias to overestimate the number dying from less likely causes. More interesting is a secondary bias in which two things that actually cause a similar number of deaths are thought to cause very different numbers of deaths. They find that this bias does correlate with things that might influence availability, including newspaper coverage and whether the subject had direct experience of someone dying from the cause.

When put together, the law of small numbers, confirmatory bias and availability heuristic present a depressing picture of how wisely patients may use information and make choices. One particular situation where we do see such biases having negative consequences is health scares. For example, a study published in 1998 in the UK suggested that a vaccine against measles, mumps and rubella (the MMR vaccine) caused autism in children. For one reason or another, this story hit the headlines, and despite all the experts saying that the MMR vaccine was safe, the number of parents who gave their children the vaccine fell dramatically. By 2009 the UK had one of the highest rates of measles in Europe. Given that one in 15 children suffer complications from having measles this is a serious problem that could have been avoided. An inability to correctly interpret new information caused this health scare.

5.5.2 Practitioners

That patients may be biased is not great, but surely we can expect better of medical practitioners? Unfortunately, the evidence here is not good either.

The possibilities for bias are not hard to imagine. For instance, we might imagine a doctor is reluctant to use a treatment that did not save one of his previous patients. More generally, we might imagine a doctor relies more on his own experience with treatments than the results of scientific tests. The law of small numbers, confirmatory bias, and the availability heuristic all come into play again. And now we have a new factor to add into the mix, conformity. If a doctor is in a practice where other doctors use a particular treatment, will he be the one to do something different? But, this is just conjecture. What does the data say?

One thing it is very easy to find data on is whether patients receive the same treatment for the same illness in different parts of the country. To a rough approximation, they should. Often they do not. Table 5.15 gives some examples of the differences in the number of people treated in different areas. Such variation is known as **small area variation**. To give a more specific example, Figure 5.6 summarizes some data from a study by Baicker et al. (2006) into the prevalence of Cesarean sections in different US cities. The variation may not look that big, but given the number of births in these cities, there is no way this could be random variation.

If it is not random variation then what it is? One suggestion is that practitioners in certain areas conform to the norms of their peers or learn from their peers. This can be exaggerated by the education of new doctors if different teaching hospitals emphasize different methods. For instance, Phelps and Mooney (1993) quote a physician from New Haven: 'The academic flavor in Boston, the teaching

Table 5.15 The highest and lowest rates of performing a treatment (per 10,000 people) in different areas of the US

Procedure	Highest rate	Lowest rate
Injection of hemorrhoids	17	0.7
Knee replacement	20	3
Cartoid endarterectomy	23	6
Bypass surgery	23	7
Heart catherization	51	22
Hip replacement	24	8
Appendix removal	5	2
Hernia repair	53	38

Source: McCall (1996).

atmosphere, has a much stronger tradition of bringing people into the hospital .... [When Boston-trained physicians relocate in New Haven] they bring their bad habits with them, but peer pressure changes that.'

Such variation cannot be efficient, because treatment is expensive. So, either patients are getting under-treated in some regions or over-treated in others. In a thorough review published in 2001, the Institute of Medicine gave a fairly damming verdict: 'Americans should be able to count on receiving care that meets their needs and is based on the best scientific knowledge. Yet there is strong evidence that this frequently is not the case.' They do indeed find evidence of under- and over-treatment. They also find that physicians regularly departed from

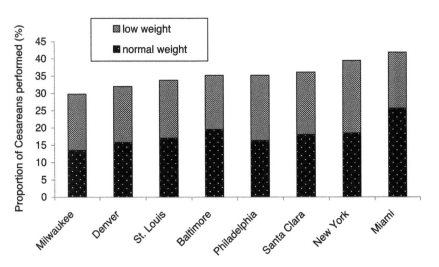

Figure 5.6 Cesarean rates in different counties of the US for normal weight and low weight babies.

Source: Baicker et al. (2006).

best practice in treating conditions like diabetes, depression and asthma, and were reluctant to use drugs widely shown to have improved health outcomes.

My objective is not to scare you about the state of the US health system, or any other health system. But we do need to be realistic. Health care practitioners are no better or worse than anyone else, and so they are likely to be biased in interpreting information. Recognizing this provides a means to progress. If we have the tools to understand biases, and we have seen some in this chapter, then we can potentially mitigate the problems they cause.

5.6 Bubble and bust

Bubbles and crashes are familiar in many markets, like the housing and financial markets. It is headline news when markets crash, and bad news for many. Which is why crashes are often etched into the history books as a black day: 'black Friday' on September 24 1869, 'black Thursday' and 'black Tuesday' on October 24 and 29 1929, 'black Monday' on October 19 1987, 'black Wednesday' on September 16 1992 and 'black week' beginning October 6 2008! What I want to look at in this section is why we get such extreme swings in the prices of goods.

I will primarily focus on stock markets. The **efficient markets hypothesis** says that the price of stock should be equal to its fundamental value. The **fundamental value** is basically the expected future returns from the stock, in the form of dividends. We cannot predict for certain what these future returns will be, and so the fundamental value is uncertain. The share price should, however, take into account all the information available at the time on what it is. It follows that the share price should only change if there is some new information about fundamental value.

So, information is key. Given, therefore, that new information is likely arriving all the time, is it any surprise that prices fluctuate? That turns out to be a tricky question. The consensus, however, is that the fluctuations we observe in share prices seem too large to be caused solely by new information.

To explain: mathematical logic says the fluctuations in the fundamental value must exceed fluctuations in the expectation of the fundamental value. This means that share prices should be less volatile than fundamental value. The intuition for this is that if people do not know all the relevant information, the share price should vary less, on average, than it would have done if they had known everything. What we observe is the opposite. To illustrate, Figure 5.7 plots the price of the S&P 500 index, compared to the estimated fundamental value. Prices clearly fluctuate more than the fundamental value.

There are lots of reasons to question the data in Figure 5.7. For instance, the fundamental value at a particular time is found by looking at the discounted value of dividends that accrues after that time, and we could argue what discount rate should be used. The data also looks at a composite index, rather than individual assets. Even if we take this into account, however, the evidence points to more volatility in share prices than we might expect. We observe **bubbles,** where price exceeds fundamental value, **busts** where price is below fundamental value, as well as sudden rises and falls in prices.

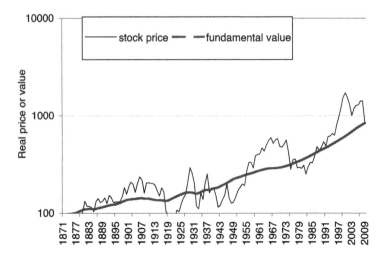

Figure 5.7 Price of the S&P 500 index compared to the estimated fundamental value. The fundamental value at a particular time is calculated by looking at what the dividends were in the following years.

Source: Shiller (2003).

Before we get on to why this happens, it's useful to step into the experimental lab to see whether we observe bubbles and busts there.

5.6.1 Bubbles in the lab

In chapter two we saw that double auction markets appeared to work well in that the price and quantity traded was close to the efficient amount where supply equals demand. In those experiments, subjects were either a buyer or a seller, knew their value for the good, and traded once at a time. This is a good representation of many markets, such as the labor market or new car market, but is not so good a representation of many other markets, such as the stock market. In a stock market we observe traders who sometimes buy and sometimes sell, do not know the value of the good they are trading, and trade over consecutive periods. What happens when we add such things to experimental markets?

To illustrate, I shall look at some results of a study by Smith, Suchanek and Williams (1988) in which subjects took part in experimental markets for an asset. To explain how these experiments worked I will talk though an example with Figure 5.8 to help. There are three subjects or traders. At the start of the experiment each trader is given an initial amount of money and some units of the asset. There are then 15 market periods, lasting at most 240 seconds each. In each period traders can sell any units of the asset they hold, and/or buy units if they have sufficient money. This buying and selling takes place via a double auction. At the end of each period the asset yields a randomly determined amount of money called a

Start of the experiment	Anna is given $2.80 and 4 units of the asset.
	Alan is given $7.60 and 2 units.
	Emma is given $10.00 and 1 unit.
Market period 1	Anna sells a unit to Alan for $4 and Emma for $3.80.
End of period 1	Anna has $10.60 and 2 units of the asset.
	Alan has $3.60 and 3 units. Emma has $6.20 and 2 units.
	The asset yields a dividend of $0.40.
Start of period 2	Anna has $11.40 and 2 units of the asset.
	Alan has $4.80 and 3 units. Emma has $7.00 and 2 units.

Figure 5.8 A description of an experimental asset market that can give rise to bubbles.

dividend. Traders receive this dividend and the next period begins. Thus, traders can accumulate money and assets over the fifteen periods. At the end of the fifteenth period, traders take home any money they have accumulated, and the assets become worthless.

Given that assets will be worthless by the end of the experiment, the primary reason to hold an asset is the dividend it may yield. Suppose that the dividend could be $0.00, $0.08, $0.16 or $0.40 with equal probability. The expected dividend is $0.16 per period and so the expected value of holding the asset in period one is $15 \times \$0.16 = \$2.40$, the expected value in period two is $14 \times \$0.16 = \$2.24$, and so on. By the final period the expected value is just $0.16. The maximum dividend is $0.40 per period and so the maximum value of holding the asset in period one is $15 \times \$0.40 = \$6.00$, the maximum value in period two is $14 \times \$0.40 = \$5.60$, and so on.

Figure 5.9 illustrates what happened in an experimental market the same as we have described but with twelve rather than three subjects. What we see is a spectacular bubble and crash! The price rises in the first eight periods with relatively large amounts of trading. It reaches a price far higher than can be justified by the value of the asset, even on the most optimistic hopes of future dividends. Then, after period ten, the volume of trade slows down and the price crashes towards zero.

What we observe in Figure 5.9 is startling, and to my mind one of the most fascinating insights of behavioral economics to date. This was a very simple market to understand, with a minimal amount of uncertainty. Yet, we observe

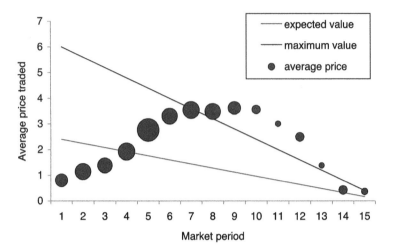

Figure 5.9 A bubble in an experimental asset market. The size of the average price circle
indicates the number of trades done. The efficient markets hypothesis would
suggest average price should track expected value or, at least, not go above
maximum value.

Source: Smith, Suchanek and Williams (1988).

trading at prices well below and well above the fundamental value of the asset. If
we get such bubble and bust in so simple an environment, then no wonder we see
bubble and bust in more complicated financial and goods markets.

You might think that bubbles would stop happening if we change the market
institution. For example, what if we allow **short selling**, where a trader can
sell assets they do not own? Or, what about **futures trading**, where traders can
trade, say, period eight assets ahead of schedule? The basic conclusion seems to
be that institutions sometimes dampen bubbles, but they do not stop them
happening. Bubbles, it seems are hard to stop, even in these simple experimental
markets.

5.6.2 Experience and bubbles

One thing that might stop bubbles happening is experience. When the price
crashed, in Figure 5.9, some of the subjects lost money. Will they be reluctant
to fall for the same trap a second time? Figure 5.10 plots what happened
when nine subjects from the session that generated the data in Figure 5.9
came back to take part in a second asset market (see Research Methods 5.4). As
we can see, the bubble and bust is much reduced. In general, it seems that experience is enough to stop bubbles in some situations. For instance, bubbles are rare if
subjects have taken part in two previous asset markets in the same group. It is

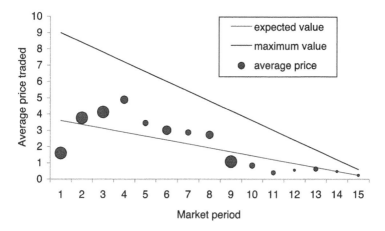

Figure 5.10 The second time the group takes part in an experimental asset market the bubble is much reduced.

Source: Smith, Suchanek and Williams (1988).

clear, however, that experience in itself is not enough to always stop bubbles happening.

Research Methods 5.4

Experienced trader versus experienced group

In most experiments we want subjects who have no prior experience. They have not taken part in the experiment before, they do not know the other subjects, they have not studied the experiment in an economics class, and so on. Sometimes, though it is useful to have something different. For instance, there may be practical reasons for inviting experienced subjects who have, say, some experience of double auctions. That way, it is not necessary to spend so long on the instructions, and still be unsure how much subjects really understood. In the study by Smith et al. all subjects had taken part in a double auction before taking part in this study. More importantly, though, it may be interesting to see how more experienced subjects play the game. There are various ways this can be done, as the study by Smith et al. demonstrates.

In one experimental session, business people from the Tucson community were subjects. In this case subjects were experienced in 'real world' trading.

In some sessions, nine of the twelve who took part in an earlier session took part again. In this case the subjects had experience of trading, and of trading with other people in that group.

In two further sessions, subjects were given experience in an environment where bubbles could not happen before being put in an environment where bubbles could happen. In this case there is experience of the mechanisms of the market but not of the possibility of bubble and bust.

Finally, other sessions involved a combination of inexperienced subjects and subjects who had taken part in at least two previous asset markets and performed well. Here it is possible to combine subjects who had previous experience of bubbles, or no previous experience of bubbles.

There are lots of possible combinations and permutations. All of them are interesting.

To illustrate, I will look at a study by Hussam et al. (2008). Subjects were invited to take part in three experimental sessions. In the first session they were all inexperienced. In the second session everything was kept the same as the first session, both the market and the other subjects. In the third session the market was changed, e.g. the expected dividend was changed, and subjects were put into a new group. So, subjects were given time to learn and then put in a very different environment. Would bubbles reappear in the new environment? As a control it is necessary to have some subjects who interacted together all three sessions. This gives three treatments as shown in Table 5.16.

A snapshot of the results is provided in Figure 5.11. The figure shows what happened in three sessions, one from each treatment, after subjects had become experienced. In the baseline treatment we see no bubble and so it looks like experience does matter. In the rekindle treatment, however, we do see a bubble, and so it seems that bubbles can reappear if the environment changes. This could be due to a change in the market or change in group, and the extreme treatment suggests it is a bit of both. Here we also see a bubble that is as big but lasts less time.

It is a little bit cheeky to give the data from just three sessions, but I chose these sessions, trust me, because they illustrated the more general pattern we observe. Experience in the same environment reduces the duration of bubbles but not their amplitude. Sometimes this is enough to stop bubbles happening but not always. Experience, therefore, does not stop bubbles happening. Indeed nothing seems guaranteed to stop bubbles happening (see Research Methods 5.5).

Table 5.16 The three different treatments in Hussan et al. (2008)

Treatment	1st session	2nd session	3rd session
Baseline	basic market	basic market	basic market, same group
Extreme	extreme market	extreme market	extreme market, same group
Rekindle	basic market	basic market	extreme market, different group

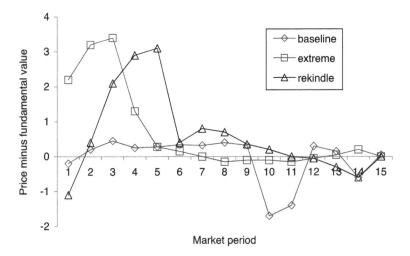

Figure 5.11 The deviation of price from fundamental value when subjects have already experienced two markets. In the baseline market there is no bubble. In the extreme market there is a bubble. In the rekindle market there is a bubble of longer duration.

Source: Hussam et al. (2008).

Research Methods 5.5

Why do experiments?

The experimental work on asset market bubbles provides a good example of why experiments are worth doing. Bubbles and crashes are ubiquitous and matter so we need to know why they happen but trying to discern this from real markets seems like a hopeless task, because they are so complicated. In the experimental laboratory we can simplify down to something that is manageable.

I think to most people it is surprising how easily bubbles can be created in very simple markets, even with experienced traders. It is this surprise that shows why experiments are worth doing. Economics is full of very complicated theories for why we might get bubbles. These might be correct, but we observe bubbles in experiments with markets far too simple for these theories to make sense. So, something more basic is going on. Realizing that seems fundamental to making any progress in truly understanding why bubbles happen.

This logic does, however, only work if the bubbles we get in the laboratory resemble those in real markets. Fortunately, they appear to. For instance Henker and Owen (2008) look at data from the Australian stock exchange and find similarities with the laboratory data.

5.6.3 Explaining bubbles

Having seen bubbles we now need to try and work out why they happen. Let's start by saying that the bubbles we have seen are not necessarily damming evidence against the efficient market hypothesis. That is because the trading price does eventually equal the fundamental value. For instance, it gets there by period 14 in Figure 5.9, period 13 in Figure 5.10, and period 12 in Figure 5.11. So, we could argue that subjects just take time to learn. This is particularly plausible if subjects start with different initial beliefs and it takes time for these beliefs to converge.

There are, however, good reasons to think that bubbles are caused in part by biases in interpreting new information. The law of small numbers would suggest that if the price has gone up three or four periods in a row then it should keep on rising. Confirmatory bias would suggest that if people expect prices to rise they will interpret a slight fluctuation in price as a signal that this is going to happen. Putting these and other biases together gives something called feedback theory. The basic idea of **feedback theory** is that prices rise because people expect them to rise, and they expect them to rise because they have been rising! A rising price translates, therefore, to a rising price.

Feedback theory can explain bubbles, and comes about because people are biased by what they see happening to the price. What it cannot do is explain the crash. Why do prices not keeping on rising? Well, there are only so many investors, and so prices cannot keep on going higher and higher, because eventually no buyers are left. In the laboratory, a crash is usually preceded by a period with less trades, see Figures 5.9 and 5.10. Bubbles, therefore, basically run out of steam. In real markets there is a less pronounced drop off in volume than in the laboratory, presumably because real markets are not going to end after a known 15 periods, but the logic still holds.

To put a bit more substance to the feedback theory I want to finish with an interesting study by Barber and Odean (2007). They looked at data from individual and institutional investors to see whether the news matters. The news might matter because of various reasons but one is the availability heuristic. When choosing where to invest people might remember seeing a stock in the news and choose that one. If stocks get in the news because their price has increased this can cause a feedback of prices rising because prices are rising.

One key to Barber and Odean's empirical strategy is the difference between buying and selling. When investing, the investor has thousands of stocks to choose from, but when he comes to sell, he only has to look at those stocks he has invested in, and these probably number at most one hundred. So, we should expect investors to be more influenced by the news when they buy than when they sell. For institutional investors this is less likely to matter because they can short sell stocks they do not own. More generally, we might expect professional, institutional investors to be less influenced by the news.

If we expect buying to be influenced by the news and selling to not be, then the buy–sell imbalance is a useful measure. For a particular stock on a particular day this is calculated as follows:

$$\text{buy sell imbalance} = \frac{\text{number of buys} - \text{number of sells}}{\text{number of buys and sells}}.$$

Barber and Odean consider various measures of a stock being in the news but we will just consider one: whether the stock appeared on the daily news feed from the Dow Jones News Service on a particular day. Figure 5.12 summarizes the result. We see that for private investors there is a large difference in the buy sell imbalance depending on whether the stock was in the news or not that day. For institutional investors there is no such difference. It would appear, therefore, that people are influenced by what stocks have appeared on the news when deciding where to invest. Interestingly this effect becomes even more pronounced if the stock went down in value that day (i.e. the news was likely to be bad) than if it went up!

That people are more likely to buy stocks that have appeared on the news brings us nicely on to something called the beauty contest, which is where I will begin the next chapter.

5.7 Further reading

Tversky and Kahneman (1974) provide an interesting introduction to the psychology of choice under uncertainty. Camerer and Weber (1992) provide a comprehensive survey of economic research on uncertainty and ambiguity. Rabin

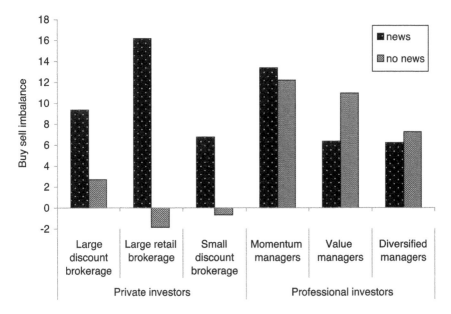

Figure 5.12 The buy–sell imbalance for different types of investors depending on whether the stock appeared in the news or not.

Source: Barber and Odean (2007).

(1998) gives a good overview of many of the biases we have looked at. Oskarsson et al. (2009) provides a comprehensive survey of the literature on the gambler's fallacy and hot hand beliefs. Also worth a read is Kahneman and Tversky (1973). One consequence of the law of small numbers and confirmatory bias can be prejudice and stereotyping. The book by Brown (1995) provides a fascinating and thought provoking introduction to these issues. Bikhchandani et al. (1998) provides an introduction to information cascades. Chapter six by Richard Frank in Diamond and Vartiainen (2007) is a great starting point for more on health care. The book by McCall (1996) is also worth a read. For more on bubbles and stock market movements I would recommend the excellent surveys by Caginalp, Porter and Smith (2000), Porter and Smith (2003) and Shiller (2003).

5.8 Review questions

5.1 Why might people dislike compound lotteries or uncertainty?

5.2 Ellsberg (1961) suggested another box in which there are 90 balls. You know that 30 of the balls are red and the other 60 are some mix of black and yellow. One ball will be randomly drawn from the box. Would you prefer to 'bet the ball is red' or 'bet the ball is black'? Would you prefer to 'bet the ball is red or yellow' or 'bet the ball is black or yellow'? Were your choices consistent with subjective expected utility maximization?

5.3 Why might someone who is ambiguity averse delay making a decision? How does this relate to procrastination because of a present bias?

5.4 There are no experiments to test for confirmatory bias in economic behavior. Design one. And then do one to test for the law of small numbers.

5.5 Why might people be over-influenced by what others do in some situations, and under-influenced in others?

5.6 Can we trust people's opinions? Why might people trust friends over expert advice?

5.7 Consider reasons why confirmatory bias and the law of small numbers may matter in health care.

5.8 How can we address the problems caused by biases in the interpretation of new information in health care, and more generally?

5.9 When should someone buy an asset that is rising in price? When should they sell it?

5.10 Why do we see bubbles and crashes in the housing market?

5.11 What do you think happens if some traders have experience of bubble and crash but some do not?

5.12 How does the buy sell imbalance relate to the ostrich effect?

6 Interacting with others

For it is, so to speak, a game of Snap, of Old Maid, – a pastime in which he is victor who says *Snap* neither too soon nor too late, who passes the Old Maid to his neighbour before the game is over, who secures a chair for himself when the music stops.

John Maynard Keynes, *General Theory of Employment, Interest and Money*

Economics is fundamentally about exchange and interaction between people. We can capture some of that by saying people interact through markets, but a lot of the time that is not enough. We need to think how people interact with each other more directly, and that will be the theme of the next two chapters. In this chapter I want focus on strategic behavior, which primarily means focusing on how people try to predict what others might do. For example, when should a trader sell her investments to ride the bubble but avoid the crash? What route should she take to work to avoid traffic jams? How much effort should she put into keeping her office tidy? And what should she choose for lunch at the canteen? In all these examples, the trader would do best to predict what others will do, whether they are fellow traders or the canteen chef, before making her choice. In this chapter I want to look at how she can do this.

6.1 The beauty contest

In this first section I want to set the scene a little for the rest of the chapter by looking at a game called the beauty contest. In the **simple beauty contest** people are independently asked to say which of six faces is the most beautiful. Anyone who picks the most beautiful face is eligible for a prize. John Maynard Keynes said that this contest was a useful way to think about how stock markets behave. His basic argument was that to pick the most beautiful face is a relatively naïve strategy. More sophisticated is to pick the face you believe most others will pick. This maximizes your chances of winning the prize. The stock market is similar except we substitute beautiful companies for beautiful faces. The fundamental value of a company may, therefore, be less relevant in determining the movement in share price than popularity.

We are going to look in more detail at a slightly different version of the beauty contest. To motivate this version, imagine someone called Emma holds shares in a company called FlyMe. At the moment the share price is increasing, which is great, but it is also well above fundamental value. Emma knows the price is probably going to crash, but she wants to hold on to the shares while the price is still rising. The decision she has to make is how long she is going to hold on to the shares before she sells them.

What she will probably do is track the share price and see what happens. That, however, does not make for a very simple story. So, we are going to assume instead that she has to decide today when she will sell the shares, and after that she cannot change her mind. She could decide to sell them anytime between today, zero days, and 100 days from now. Suppose that everyone else who holds shares in FlyMe also has to make the same decision. When is the optimal time to sell?

The 'it' in the quote with which I started this chapter is 'investing in the stock market'. Keynes explains that a trader needs to be 'neither too soon nor too late', and we saw this when looking at bubbles and crashes in the last chapter. The crucial thing is that what is too soon or too late will depend on others, because the optimal time to sell will depend on how long others delay. A simple way to capture this is to assume that the optimal time to sell depends on the average number of days D that other investors choose to delay.

This is what happens in a **p-Beauty Contest**, where the objective is to be as close as possible to p times the average chosen by others. A p less than one makes most sense, because then Emma does best to wait less than the average, and so is selling before most others. For example, if the average trader delays 30 days and $p = 0.67$, then the optimal delay is 20 days. This way Emma does not sell too early, to avoid the entire rise in price, but sells early enough to avoid the crash. To understand what Emma should do in this game (given that she does not know what others are doing), we need to introduce some basic concepts from game theory.

6.1.1 Strategy and Nash equilibrium

One thing we shall talk a lot about in this chapter is strategy. Recall, see chapter one, that a **strategy** is best thought of as a person's plan of what they will do. In the simple beauty contest, Emma's strategy is which face to choose. In a p-beauty contest Emma's strategy is how long to delay. Emma's payoff will depend on her strategy, and the strategy of others. For example, in a 0.5-beauty contest with n investors, we could write the payoff of Emma as:

$$u_E(s_E, s_{-E}) = 100 - \left| s_E - 0.5 \times \left(\frac{s_1 + s_2 + \dots + s_n}{n} \right) \right|$$

where s_E is her strategy and s_{-E} is a shorthand way of writing down the strategies of everyone but her. She wants, therefore, to be as close as possible to 0.5 times the average, and if she gets it spot-on, her payoff is 100.

One of the most basic concepts in game theory is that of a dominated strategy. To illustrate the idea let's think about the 0.5-beauty contest. Given that investors can delay at most 100 days, the highest the average delay can possible be is 100 days. This means that the highest the optimal delay can possibly be is $0.5 \times 100 = 50$ days. Does it, therefore, make sense for Emma to delay more than 50 days? No; by delaying 50 days she is guaranteed doing at least as well as if she delays 51, 52, or more days. This does not mean she should necessarily want to delay 50 days, but it does mean she would be unwise to delay more than 50 days because the strategy of waiting 50 days dominates any strategy of waiting more than 50 days.

More generally, we say that a strategy l **dominates** a strategy j for Emma if she always gets a higher payoff from l than from j, that is:

$$u_E(l, s_{-E}) > u_E(j, s_{-E})$$

for any s_{-E}. The prediction is that people should not play a dominated strategy. Intuitively, this makes sense because strategy l is guaranteed to give a higher payoff than j, so why play j?

Now, suppose that Emma believes no one would ever play a dominated strategy. For instance, she does not expect anyone to delay more than 50 days in a 0.5-beauty contest. If no one is going to delay more than 50 days then the optimal delay cannot be more than $0.5 \times 50 = 25$ days. This means that delaying 25 days seems better than delaying more than 25 days. We say that the strategy to delay more than 25 days is **one-step dominated** by a strategy to wait 25 days. The one step is there to acknowledge that Emma needed to go through one step of reasoning to get to this. But, why stop there. If Emma believes that no one would ever play a one-step dominated strategy and delay more than 25 days then there is no sense delaying more than 12.5 days. The strategy to delay more than 12.5 days is **two-step dominated** by a strategy to wait 12.5 days.

More generally, we say that strategy j is **one-step dominated** by strategy l for Emma if she always gets a higher payoff from l than from j if no one plays a dominated strategy, that is:

$$u_E(l, s_{-E}) > u_E(j, s_{-E})$$

for all s_{-E} where no one plays a dominated strategy. Two-step dominates, three-step dominates are defined in an analogous way.

Carrying on in this way is called **iterated deletion of dominated strategies**. There is a logic that says people should only play strategies that **survive** iterated deletion of dominated strategies. What strategies survive iterated deletion of dominated strategies in the 0.5-beauty contest? There is only one, and that is to delay zero days. We get, therefore, a very specific prediction of what should happen in this game.

This prediction is an example of a Nash equilibrium. Recall, that a **Nash equilibrium** is a list of strategies s_1 to s_n for each person such that no one could change their strategy and do better. That is,

$$u_i(s_i, s_{-i}) \geq u_i(j, s_{-i})$$

for all people i and any strategy j. A dominated strategy cannot be part of a Nash equilibrium and so, if there is only one strategy that survives iterated deletion of dominated strategies then that strategy must be a Nash equilibrium strategy. In the 0.5-beauty contest, for example the unique Nash equilibrium is that everyone chooses zero.

If, as in the 0.5-beauty contest, there is only one strategy that survives iterated deletion of dominated strategies then we get a nice and simple prediction. Unfortunately, things do not always work out so nicely. Sometimes, eliminating dominated strategies does not get us very far, and we end up with multiple Nash equilibrium. We already came across this in the previous chapter where there was an intuitive and unintuitive equilibrium in a signaling game.

To give another example, think about a 1.5-beauty contest, where it is optimal to choose 1.5 times the average. What should Emma do if everyone else chooses zero? The best she can do is also choose zero, because $0 = 1.5 \times 0$ and she will be spot-on the optimal delay. What should Emma do if everyone else chooses 100 days? The best she can do is also choose 100 because that is as close as she can get to the optimal delay of 150 days. 'Everyone delay zero days' and 'everyone delay 100 days' are both Nash equilibria, and we can tell from this that there is no dominated strategy in this game.

If there are multiple Nash equilibria we get a less precise prediction of what will happen. But, we still get a prediction. The natural question is whether dominance and Nash equilibrium give us good predictions.

6.1.2 Choice and learning in a beauty contest

To recap: in a p-beauty contest, the Nash equilibrium is for everyone to choose zero if $p < 1$, and either for everyone to choose zero or everyone choose 100 if $p > 1$. Is this what people actually do? Figure 6.1 gives some data from a study by Nagel (1995). It shows what numbers subjects chose the first time they played a p-beauty contest. A couple of things stand out from this data. On the one hand it looks a mess, because there is a lot of heterogeneity in what subjects did and very few chose the Nash equilibrium strategy. On the other hand there are clear peaks in the data that change as p varies. So, people are not playing Nash equilibrium but they are seemingly responding in a systematic way to the incentives of the game.

Why does the Nash equilibrium turn out to be such a bad predictor in this game? One thing we can do is to see whether people play dominated strategies or not. Let's say that a person is **type D-0** if they never play a dominated strategy, but may play a one-step dominated strategy. Similarly, someone is a **type D-k** if they never play a k-step dominated strategy, but may play a $k + 1$-step dominated strategy. By looking at Figure 6.1 we can start to work out how many subjects seemed to be of each type. A study by Ho, Camerer and Weigelt (1998) does this in a more structured way by looking at four different beauty

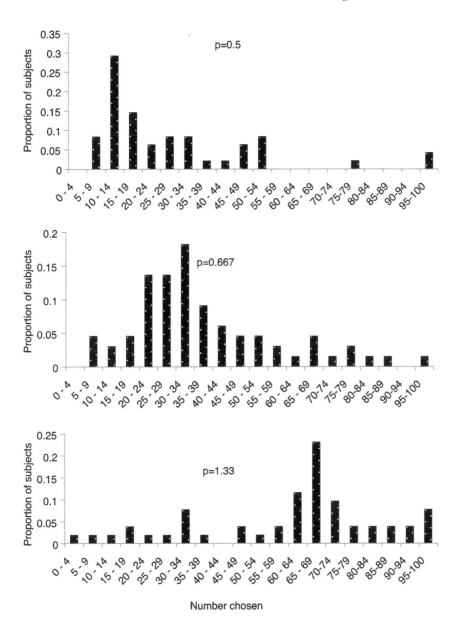

Figure 6.1 Choices the first time subjects play a p-beauty contest.
Source: Nagel (1995).

contests. Their results are summarized in Table 6.1, where lower bounds are put on the proportion of subjects of each type. They are lower bounds because someone who does not realize a strategy is dominated may still not play it, by accident.

Table 6.1 Proportion of subjects of each type in four p-beauty contests

Game	Type						
	played dominated	D-0	D-1	D-2	D-3	D-4 +
$p = 1.3$	15.7%	36.4%	36.1%	11.8%		
$p = 1.1$	4.3%	3.2%	5.1%	9.8%	35.0%	42.6%
$p = 0.9$	4.4%	2.6%	8.4%	6.2%	12.0%	63.4%
$p = 0.7$	15.0%	23.2%	18.9%	12.5%	13.9%	16.5%

Source: Ho et al. (1998).

The results in Table 6.1 are broadly consistent with what we see in many other games. Relatively few people play dominated strategies but most people only go through one, two or three steps of iterated deletion of dominated strategies. To say that people do not play dominated or iterated dominant strategies does, therefore, give us some power to predict what people will do, but we are going to need more than this to fully understand what is going on (see also Research Methods 6.1). For example, looking at Figure 6.1, we have an explanation for why so few people choose more than 50 when $p = 0.5$ or 0.667, or less than 50 when $p = 1.33$. We still do not have an explanation for the choices people did make. This though is arguably natural enough, because the focus in looking at dominated strategies is on what strategies people will not use, and not what they will.

The next issue I want to look at is what happens when the same game is played a second, third and fourth time. Figure 6.2 illustrates what happened in the study by Nagel. There is a clear downward trend in the average number chosen. This suggests that subjects did learn from experience and behavior is converging towards the Nash equilibrium. Nash equilibrium becomes, therefore, a better predictor if people have some experience with the game. Just to illustrate how intriguing this issue can be, in Figure 6.2 I also included data from a no-feedback treatment from a study by Weber (2003). In the experiments by Nagel, subjects were told after each round what the winning number was before they played again. Most subjects guess too high and so lowered their choice next round making things converge towards the Nash equilibrium. In the no-feedback treatment subjects were not told the winning number before playing again. Subjects could not, therefore, have known they guessed too high. Still, however, the choice decreases over the rounds!

This discussion of the beauty contest helps motivate the three key themes I want to focus on in the rest of the chapter. First, I want us to think more about what people do the first time they play a game, like the beauty contest. How can we explain the data in Figure 6.1? Second, I want us to think more about how people learn when playing a game several times. How can we explain the data in Figure 6.2? Third, I want us to think more about the relevance of the Nash equilibrium, particularly in situations when there are multiple Nash equilibria. Once we have done all that we should have a good picture of how people behave in strategic situations.

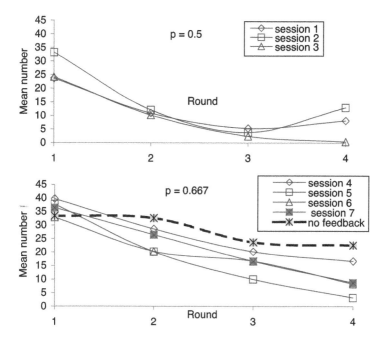

Figure 6.2 The mean number chosen when playing a p-beauty contest four consecutive times, for each of the experimental sessions.

Sources: Nagel (1995) and Weber (2003).

6.2 Playing for the first time

I will begin by looking at how we can model what people do when they play a game for the first time. A useful starting point for doing that is something called level-k thinking.

6.2.1 Level-k thinking

The basic idea behind level-k thinking is that someone, like Emma, forms an expectation of what others will do and tries to be 'one step ahead of them'. In a p-beauty contest this is nice and easy to apply: Emma is assumed to form an expectation of the average delay of others and then guesses p times that average. For example, if she thinks the average will be 50 she will guess $50p$, and if she thinks the average will be $50p$ she will guess $50p^2$.

In a general model of **level-k thinking** we start with people of **type L-0** who are assumed to choose without thinking too much about what others will do. More on this below. We then say that someone like Emma is of **type L-1** if she thinks that all others will be type L-0, and maximizes her payoff given this belief. We say that she is of **type L-k** if she thinks that all others will be type L-$k - 1$, and maximizes her payoff given this belief.

The type L-0s are crucial here because they determine what the L-1 types will do, which determines what the L-2 types will do, and so on. Unfortunately there is no simple rule for saying what the L-0 types will do. Two possibilities are: A **type L-0 randomly chooses** what strategy to choose because they are maybe confused, misunderstood the game, or are simply uninterested. A **type L-0 chooses some salient or focal strategy** such as a Nash equilibrium. In neither case does a type L-0 take account of what others will do. We shall see, however, that a different assumption about type L-0s can lead to very different conclusions about what everyone else will do.

To illustrate we can work through the p-beauty contest with the help of Table 6.2. If type L-0s choose randomly then on average they will choose 50. This means that Emma will choose $50p$ if of type L-1 and $50p^2$ if of type L-2 which equals 25 and 12.5 in a 0.5-beauty contest. Now, suppose, by contrast, the L-0 types choose the Nash equilibrium of 0 or 100. Maybe, for instance, they have just gone to a game theory class and been told this is the equilibrium. Then Emma should also choose the Nash equilibrium, and we get a very different prediction. Clearly some thought needs to go into what the type L-0s will do, and different situations will suggest different ways they might behave. Having done this, however, we have a simple way to make predictions of what people will do. Are these predictions any good?

You may already have noted the spikes in Figure 6.1 at 12.5, 33.33 and 66.67 suggest that we are on the right track. A study by Costa-Gomes and Crawford (2006) provides a more detailed test. In the study, eighty-eight subjects played sixteen two-player guessing games similar to a beauty contest. The sixteen games were chosen to try and distinguish how subjects were reasoning and classified them as type L-k, D-k, someone who plays the Nash equilibrium, or someone who is sophisticated (which I shall explain below). Figure 6.3 summarizes the main results.

We see that many subjects were best classified as type L-1 or L-2. It seems, therefore, that level k-thinking does a relatively good job of capturing what people do. By contrast, no one was best classified as type D-1 or D-2. This is not inconsistent with what I said in section 6.1.2 about dominated strategies, because

Table 6.2 Level-k thinking in the p-beauty contest if type L-0s choose randomly compared to if they choose the Nash equilibrium

Type	Type L-0s choose randomly			Type L-0s choose Nash equilibrium		
	$p = 0.5$	$p = 0.67$	$p = 1.33$	$p = 0.5$	$p = 0.67$	$p = 1.33$
L-0	50	50	50	0	0	100
L-1	25	33.5	66.5	0	0	100
L-2	12.5	22.45	88.44	0	0	100
L-3	6.25	15.03	100	0	0	100

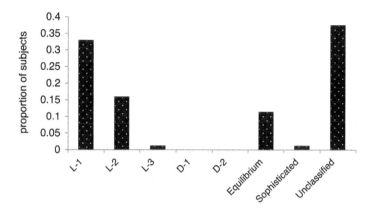

Figure 6.3 Classifying subjects by type after they had played 16 different games. Many subjects were best classified as type L-1 or L-2.

Source: Costa-Gomes and Crawford (2006).

a level-k thinker will never play a dominated strategy. So, we are still correct in saying that most people do not play a dominated strategy we just now have a sharper prediction of what they will play. Before we question more how good a prediction that is I should explain what is meant by someone being sophisticated.

Research Methods 6.1

Seeing how subjects choose

In behavioral economics we are often interested in how people decide what to do. Experiments, however, typically only show us what people do, and not why they did it. It is routine to add questionnaires to the end of an experiment asking subjects why they chose as they did. But it is also routine to ignore such questionnaires as unreliable because subjects may not know why they did what they did. Technology is starting to offer more possibilities.

The study by Costa-Gomes and Crawford used a program called MouseLab that can track where subjects click or put the cursor on the computer screen. This makes it possible to know what subjects would have known when making their choice and what they wanted to know before making their choice. This is useful in trying to understand how people decide, and in Figure 6.3 we report results that make use of this data. More technologically demanding ways of recording what subjects do include eye tracking and brain imaging, but more on that in chapter nine.

6.2.2 Sophisticated beliefs

One slightly concerning aspect of k-step elimination of dominated strategies and level-k thinking is that the higher is k, the worse a person will typically be at predicting what others will do. This is because a k-step thinker believes that all others will be k-step thinkers and a level-k-1 thinker believes that all others are level-k-1 thinkers. The higher k is, the less sensible this might be. For example, in a 0.5-beauty contest if Emma is of type D-3 she would think that no one will choose more than 6.25 and if type L-3 would expect the average choice to be 12.5. These are relatively low numbers. Is it reasonable that Emma expects everyone else to be one level lower than her?

It might be, but equally it might not. Indeed, it seems more intuitive for me that she would expect some to be, say, level-0 thinkers, some to be level-1 thinkers, some to play the Nash equilibrium, and so on. This leads us to the idea of sophisticated and semi-sophisticated types.

To illustrate, we can look at the **cognitive hierarchy model** of Camerer, Ho and Chong (2004). The model starts with type L-0s and L-1s exactly as I defined them above. But, we do need to keep track of how many people are of each type, so let $f(0)$ be the proportion of type L-0s in the population, $f(1)$ be the proportion of type L-1s and $F(1) = f(1) + f(0)$ be the proportion of type L-0s and L-1s.

We then say that someone is of **type C-2** if she expects that proportion $f(0)/F(1)$ of others will be type L-0 and proportion $f(1)/F(1)$ will be type L-1, and maximizes her payoff given this belief. Thus, if Emma is of type C-2 she expects that some will be type L-0 and some will be type L-1. This is different to a type L-2 who expects all others to be type L-1. Furthermore, if of type C-2 she correctly predicts the proportion of type L-0s relative to type L-1s. What she does not do is account for the possible existence of type L-2s, C-2s or beyond.

But, there is no need to stop with a type C-2. Let $f(2)$ is the proportion of type C-2s and $F(2) = f(1) + f(2) + f(3)$ be the proportion of types L-0, L-1 and C-2 in the population. Emma is of **type C-3** if she expects proportion $f(0)/F(2)$ to be type L-0, $f(1)/F(2)$ to be type L-1, proportion $f(2)/F(2)$ to be type C-2 and chooses the optimal strategy given this belief. Continuing in this way we can go define type C-4, and so on. Table 6.3 illustrates how this works in the 0.5-beauty contest.

We can say for sure that if Emma is of type C-3 she will be better at predicting what others will do than someone of type C-2. Similarly, if she is of type C-4 she will be better than someone of type C-3. The higher, therefore, is k, the better Emma is at predicting what others will do, creating a natural cognitive hierarchy.

Table 6.3 Level-k thinking in the 0.5-beauty contest compared to a model of cognitive hierarchy. For example, a type C-2 believes 37.5% of others are type L-0 and 62.5% are type L-1, so chooses 17.19

Level-k thinking		Cognitive hierarchy				
Type	Choice	Type	Proportion	Type C-2 beliefs	Type C-3 beliefs	Choice
L-0	50	L-0	30%	37.5%	33.3%	50
L-1	25	L-1	50%	62.5%	55.6%	25
L-2	12.5	C-2	10%	0%	11.1%	17.19
L-3	6.25	C-3	10%	0%	0%	16.23

Someone of type C-k is, however, still only **semi-sophisticated**, because they fail to predict people at the same (or higher) cognitive level than themselves. The final step is to consider someone who is **sophisticated** and correctly predicts what all others, including other sophisticated people, will do. That is, if Emma is sophisticated, she will correctly predict the proportion of people of type D-k, L-k and C-k, the proportion of people who play the equilibrium, are sophisticated, and so on. This means she will play the empirical Nash equilibrium and best respond to what others are doing (see Research Methods 5.1).

The issue of sophisticated and semi-sophisticated people brings into sharp focus the relative proportions of each type in the population. That's because we need to clarify what it means to correctly predict the proportions of people at lower, or the same, cognitive levels. For Emma to correctly predict the actual proportions would be asking too much, unless she is telepathic! More sensible is that she predicts the average proportions one might expect to see. We need, therefore, to think what these proportions might be.

Camerer, Ho and Chong, suggested that the higher γ is the less likely there are to be people of type C-k. One way to capture this is to assume that:

$$\frac{f(k)}{f(k-1)} \propto \frac{1}{k}.$$

This implies that $f(k)$ is characterized by a Poisson distribution with parameter τ and we can write:

$$f(k) = \frac{e^{-\tau}\tau^k}{k!}.$$

Figure 6.4 illustrates what proportion of people will be of each type for three different values of τ. We see that the higher is the more levels of reasoning the average person is expected to do. To put this in some perspective, if $\tau = 1.5$ then someone of type C-2 would expect 40 percent of others to be type L-0 and 60 percent to be type L-1.

The neat thing about this model is that everything now depends on just one parameter. If we know τ then we know how many people to expect of each type, and if we know how many people to expect of each type we can predict what everyone will do. With just one parameter we can, therefore, estimate the full distribution of choices. Fantastic, if it works!

Camerer, Ho and Chong estimated τ for a variety of games, including the p-beauty contest, and suggested that $\tau = 1.5$ as a reasonable value to assume. Without going into the details, the cognitive hierarchy model with $\tau = 1.5$ does seem to work quite well for some games, and so can give us a very simple and parsimonious way to model choices. For other games the model seems a bit too restrictive and we need to better capture the mix of L-k, D-k, C-k and sophisticated types. This, though, can easily be done by changing assumptions about the distribution of types. We can, therefore, create models that are as simple or complicated as needs dictate.

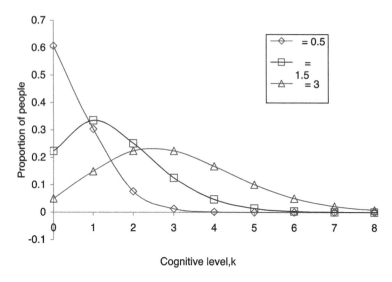

Figure 6.4 The proportion of people at each cognitive level in a cognitive hierarchy model for three difference values of τ. The higher is τ, the more people there are at higher cognitive levels.

Let's not, however, get too carried away just yet. If you look back at Figure 6.3 you will see that the biggest spike is over 'unclassified'. With the notions of type D-k, L-k and C-k we are able to better understand and model what a lot of people seem to be doing but we are still some way from a complete picture. We have also yet to tackle the problem of multiple equilibria. It is to this problem that I now turn.

6.2.3 Focal points

Consider the simple beauty contest that I introduced towards the start of the chapter. Recall that people were asked to pick which of six faces they thought most beautiful and anyone who picked the most popular face was eligible for a prize. If we know that Emma is of type L-k or D-k or sophisticated, can we predict what she will do? Not really, at least, not without doing a bit of work first. That's primarily because there are multiple Nash equilibria.

To explain, in the simple beauty contest, if everyone chooses face two, then the optimal thing Emma can do is choose face two. The same if everyone chooses face one, three etc. There are, therefore, six Nash equilibria (plus some ones we don't need to worry about). Basically, it does not matter to anyone what they choose, they just want to choose the same as everyone else. This is called a **pure coordination game**. If people are not allowed to communicate with each other then it can seem a pretty hopeless task to coordinate in a pure coordination game. Is Emma supposed to just choose one of the six faces at random and hope for the best?

Maybe not, if there exists a focal point. Thomas Schelling highlighted the remarkable power of focal points in his book *The Strategy of Conflict*. For example, Schelling asked people to imagine that they had to meet someone in New York, but are unable to communicate with that person. Where should they go in the hope of meeting? New York is a big city, so this seems like a difficult problem, but most people named the same place, Grand Central Station. As a further example, Schelling asked people to independently choose between the words 'Heads' or 'Tails' trying to match someone else's choice. Most people (36 out of 42) said 'Heads'.

The point Schelling was trying to make is that people are able to coordinate much better than can be due to pure chance. So, Emma does not need to pick a face randomly. But, she does need to know the secret of how to coordinate. There are, at least, three plausible explanations for what this secret is.

The **primary salience hypothesis** is that people choose the option that is most salient to them, and because the same option is salient to many people, people coordinate by accident. For example, people might have said Grand Central Station simply because it is their favorite place in New York. Similarly, Emma can just say which face she thinks is most beautiful and expect to coordinate with others.

The **secondary salience hypothesis** is that people expect others to use primary salience and so choose the option they think will have primary salience for others. For example, if Emma's favorite place in New York is the Yankee Stadium, but she expects the favorite place of most others to be Grand Central Station, then using secondary salience she will choose Grand Central Station. Similarly, if she really likes face three but thinks that others will like face two, she should choose face two.

Secondary salience should sound like level-k thinking. That's because it assumes people will be of type L-1. It does, however, a little bit more than this by tying down what someone of type L-0 will do. Someone of type L-0 is assumed to choose their favorite option, or the option that is primary salient. Recall that when discussing the p-beauty contest we assumed that type L-0s would choose randomly or choose the equilibrium. We now have, therefore, three possible assumptions for what type L-0s might do. What seems most apt to use will likely depend on the context. For instance, it is hard to think of a favorite option in the p-beauty contest.

The third possible secret to coordination is the Schelling salience hypothesis. The **Schelling salience hypothesis** is that people ignore what is primary or secondary salient and look for some key or clue to how to coordinate. For example, Grand Central Station may not be the favorite place of anyone, but somehow stands out as the best choice. Similarly, no one may like face four but it stands out, because, say, it is the only male face. Schelling salience may not look much like level-k thinking but it is not really that different. That's because we can again think of it as assuming people will be of type L-1. The difference now is that someone of type L-0 is assumed to choose the **focal point** or the option that stands out most. We do, of course, need to think what the focal point might be but let us look at some examples first.

In a study by Mehta, Starmer and Sugden (1994) subjects were asked questions like 'Write down any year, past, present, or future', and 'Write down any positive number'. Some subjects were given no incentive to match the choices of others while others were given the objective of trying to match the choices of others. Table 6.4 summarizes the results for two of the questions. The answers of those with no incentive to match should tell us what was primary salient. For example, when asked to 'Write down a year', many chose their year of birth. There is a lot of variety in the answers, and we can infer that coordination due to primary salience would be low. There is much more consistency in the responses of subjects who were given an incentive to match.

These examples illustrate the ability of people to coordinate when needed. That the incentive to coordinate changed responses so much also means we can rule out primary salience as an explanation for coordination. The data points more towards Schelling salience or secondary salience. Distinguishing between these two is, however, much harder. In the 'write down any number' example it looks like Schelling salience is at work, because many chose number one when they had an incentive to coordinate and very few without this incentive. In the pick a year example it is harder to tell. The majority of students chose the then current year 1990 when they had an incentive to coordinate, and so we might think this is a focal point. But, 1990 was also a relatively popular response for those with no incentive to coordinate, so secondary salience also looks plausible.

More generally, it seems that an ability to coordinate can come from either secondary salience or Schelling salience. Which fits better seems to change depending on the context. One thing, however, is clear and that is that the notion of focal point and Schelling salience is compelling. In some situations we are able to coordinate with others because there exists some focal option. If we are going to predict what people do in such situations then we need to be able to predict the focal point. This, though, is no easy task (see Research Methods 6.2).

Table 6.4 The answers subjects gave, and the proportion giving each answer, to two questions. The answers depend on whether the subjects did or did not have an incentive to match with others.

Question	No incentive to match		Incentive to match	
	Response	*Proportion*	*Response*	*Proportion*
'Write down any year'	1971	8.0	1990	61.1
	1990	6.8	2000	11.1
	2000	6.8	1969	5.6
	1968	5.7		
'Write down any positive number'	7	11.4	1	40.0
	2	10.2	7	14.4
	10	5.7	10	13.3
	1	4.5	2	11.1

Source: Mehta, Starmer and Sugden (1994).

Research Methods 6.2

Algebra has limits?

In particular situations it can be 'obvious' to most people what the focal point is. The problem is that, to make good economic predictions, we need to abstract away from particular situations to get a more general model. This is hard to do. It is hard to say in general why and when, 'things stand out' or 'seem obvious'. This presents a particular problem for economists, who have an insatiable desire to capture things in models with equations. The idea of a focal point may be something that equations simply cannot capture. Framing effects may be another. Does this matter?

It should not. Just because we cannot write down a nice equation does not mean we should not take focal points or framing seriously or be able to model them. We just need to be content with a more descriptive theory. Daniel Kahneman commented: 'psychological theories of intuitive thinking cannot match the elegance and precision of formal normative models of belief and choice, but this is just another way of saying the rational models are psychologically unrealistic' (Kahneman 2003: 1449).

Sugden (1995) proposed one means to try and capture focal points by introducing the idea of a **collectively rational recommendation**. The basic idea behind a CRR is to imagine two people being recommended rules by which to make a choice; if one or more of them do not use a recommended rule then they all get strictly less than if they used the rules. To illustrate the concept, consider these three different scenarios:

Scenario A: Emma and Alan are independently handed five discs that are identical except for the numbers one to five written on the underside of the discs. Both are asked to choose one of the discs with the objective of matching the choice of the other. They cannot see the numbers but an independent witness can, and can therefore verify whether they choose the same disc. The discs are presented to each of them in a random order.

In this scenario there is simply no way Emma and Alan can improve their chances of coordinating. For example, if both use the recommendation 'pick the one furthest to the left' the random way that they are presented means the chances of matching are still only 20 percent. In this game any recommendation is a CRR.

Scenario B: Now suppose that the discs have the numbers written visibly on the topside.

In this scenario it is much easier for them to coordinate. For instance, if they both use the recommendation 'choose disc one', then they coordinate for sure. The problem is that they need to coordinate on a recommendation. This means that there is no CRR. For example, recommending they 'choose disc one' cannot be a CRR because they could both ignore the recommendation, use their own rule 'choose disc two' and do just as well.

Scenario C: Finally, suppose that the numbers are written on the non-visible underside but two disks are blue and three are red.

This scenario combines elements of both scenarios A and B. Specifically there is the chance to coordinate (as in Scenario B) using color, but this will not guarantee coordination (as in scenario A) because there is more than one disc of each color. The CRR in this scenario is for both 'to choose a blue disc'. This does not guarantee coordination but does mean a better chance of success than both choosing red. In this scenario blue is a focal choice.

Can we use the concept of a CRR to capture why so many people choose Grand Central Station and Heads? Yes. That is because in many coordination games it turns out that the only CRR is to recommend 'choose the option most frequently mentioned in everyday life'. This is basically because a lot more people are likely to agree on what is the most frequently mentioned option than to agree on what is, say, the tenth or eleventh or 235th most frequently mentioned option. The chances of coordination are thus maximized if everyone chooses the most frequently mentioned. Closely related is the **recognition heuristic** of 'if in doubt, choose the one you recognize, or are most familiar with'. For example, subjects in the Mehta et al. study were also asked to name a mountain, and 89 percent of subjects named Everest.

The notion of a focal point is a hard one to tie down and the concept of a CRR is only going to make sense in some situations. It does, though, give us some insight and pure coordination games are always going to be very tough games to try and predict what people will do, because people are completely indifferent to what they do as long as they coordinate. In games with a bit more structure, where people are not so indifferent to what they do, our task may be a little easier?

6.2.4 Equilibrium refinement

So far we have looked in some detail at the p-beauty contest where there is a unique Nash equilibrium and the simple beauty contest where there are many Nash equilibria and little to choose among them. Between these two extremes there is a limitless supply of different games that are interesting for us to look at. What I want to do here is select two/three of those games to illustrate some concepts that are useful in thinking about how people might behave and reason when playing games.

Let's start by looking at the game depicted in Table 6.5. If you have never seen a matrix game before the idea is very simple. Alan and Emma both need to decide at the same time whether to choose high or low effort. The numbers indicate the possible payoffs. So, if they both choose high effort they get $13 each. In section 6.6 I am going to look in more detail at why these payoffs fit a story of high or low effort. For now, I want you to think what Alan should do.

There are two Nash equilibria in this game (plus another one I will ignore). There is one where they both choose low effort and another where they both choose high effort. You could argue that that the equilibrium where they put in high effort stands out as more salient because it gives a higher payoff. To capture

Table 6.5 A matrix game. For example, if Alan chooses low effort and Emma chooses high effort, Alan gets $7 and Emma gets $0. The Nash equilibrium of low effort is risk dominant and high effort is Pareto dominant

		Emma	
		Low effort	High effort
Alan	low effort	$7, $7	$7, $0
	high effort	$0, $7	$13, $13

this we say that a **Nash equilibrium is Pareto dominant** if it gives a higher payoff to everyone than any other Nash equilibrium. The high effort Nash equilibrium is Pareto dominant in this game. Will Emma and Alan coordinate on the Pareto dominant Nash equilibrium?

If Alan chooses low effort he is guaranteed $7, while if he chooses high effort he could get $13, but might also get $0. If he is worried about getting $0 then he may prefer to play it safe and guarantee himself $7. To capture this we say that a **Nash equilibrium is risk dominant** if each person is choosing the strategy that would maximize their payoff if they cannot predict what others will do. To see how this works, suppose that Alan cannot predict what Emma will do and so says there is a 50 percent chance she will choose high effort and a 50 percent chance she will choose low effort. Given this, his payoff from choosing low effort is $7 and that from high effort is $0.5 \times \$0 + 0.5 \times \$13 = \$6.5$. $7 beats $6.5 and so Alan should choose low effort. The low effort Nash equilibrium is risk dominant.

We see that there are good arguments why Alan should choose high effort, and good arguments why he should low effort. That's the problem of multiple equilibria! In this case there is a tension between the Pareto dominant equilibrium, that gives a high payoff, and the risk dominant equilibrium, that is less risky. It is only by observing what people do that we can hope to pull apart when people favor one or the other. We will come back to that in section 6.6 and look at some data.

I next want us to look at sequential games. In a **sequential game** one person chooses before another. To illustrate we can look at versions of the battle of the sexes game. Figure 6.5 summarizes a standard version. In this case Alan decides whether to buy tickets for the football or ballet. His friend, Emma, sees what tickets he bought and then decides whether to go to the football or ballet. The numbers indicate the respective payoffs with Alan first. You can see that they both want to go together but Alan prefers football and Emma prefers ballet. What should Alan choose?

In this game there are three Nash equilibria. In describing the Nash equilibria we need to be a little careful because, recall, a strategy should be a complete plan of what to do. So, Emma needs to say what she will do if Alan buys football tickets and what she will do if he buys ballet tickets. The simplest strategy is where Emma says: 'If he buys football tickets I go to the football and if he buys ballet tickets I go to the ballet.' If she does this and Alan chooses football, then we have our first Nash equilibrium.

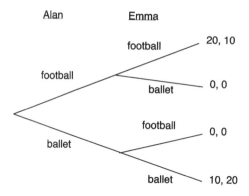

Alan

Emma

football — 20, 10

football

ballet — 0, 0

football — 0, 0

ballet

ballet — 10, 20

Figure 6.5 A sequential battle of the sexes game. Alan chooses to buy football or ballet tickets and then Emma decides whether to go to the football or ballet. For instance, if they both choose football, Alan gets payoff 20 and Emma payoff 10.

In this case it does not really matter what Emma would have done if Alan had bought a ballet ticket. There is, therefore, a second Nash equilibrium where Alan buys a football ticket and Emma says 'I will go to the football if he buys football or ballet tickets'. The final equilibrium is similar. This time Emma says: 'I am going to the ballet whether he buys football or ballet tickets.' You could think of this as a threat that she will go to the ballet. In this case the best thing Alan can do is buy a ballet ticket, and this gives us our third Nash equilibrium. The three equilibria are summarized in Table 6.6.

How can we choose amongst these three equilibria? One of them probably stands out as more sensible. That's the first one where Emma does what Alan does. The second equilibrium seems strange given that Emma would go to the football if Alan buys ballet tickets! The third equilibrium is more intuitive but there is a problem. The threat of Emma to go to the ballet if Alan buys football tickets is not a **credible threat** because she would get a higher payoff going to the football.

One technique we can use to justify the first equilibrium as more sensible is **backward induction**. We start with Emma's choice and ask what it is optimal for her to do. If Alan buys football tickets, it is optimal she chooses football, and if he buys ballet tickets, it is optimal she chooses ballet. We then assume that Alan knows this. If he knows that Emma will choose football if he buys football tickets

Table 6.6 The Nash equilibria in the sequential battle of the sexes

Equilibrium	Alan strategy	Emma's strategy
1	Football	Football if Alan chooses football and ballet if he chooses ballet.
2	Football	Football no matter what Alan chooses.
3	Ballet	Ballet no matter what Alan chooses.

then it is optimal for him to buy football tickets. Another way to describe this is to say that the first equilibrium is **sub-game perfect** because if we look at any part of the game, people are behaving optimally. The first equilibrium is the unique sub-game perfect equilibrium of this game. If we look at the third equilibrium, for instance, Emma is not behaving optimally in the part of the game where we imagine Alan has chosen football.

A complement to backward induction is forward induction. To motivate this, consider a modified battle of the sexes game, like that in Figure 6.6. What I have done is give Emma the option of choosing whether or not to go out with friends before she contacts Alan and asks him if they should go somewhere together. How does this change things? If you use backward induction you will find that there is a unique sub-game perfect Nash equilibrium and that involves Emma going with friends. If she goes with Alan they will end up going to the football and she gets a payoff of 10, which is less than if she goes with friends. This looks like a bad outcome.

What would happen if Emma were to choose to go with Alan? Alan might reason that she could only possibly have chosen to go with him if she expects they will go to ballet. That is the only thing that could justify her choice. If they go to the ballet he gets payoff 10, which is better than he would have got if Emma went with friends. This might, therefore, look like a good deal. This is an example of **forward induction** where we start with the first choice and ask what will happen if a certain choice is made. Forward induction gives a Nash equilibrium where Emma chooses to go with Alan and threatens to choose ballet whether Alan buys football or ballet tickets. The fact that she chose to go with Alan arguably makes the threat more credible.

Hopefully, you are getting the idea that there are lots of ways we can model how people might reason when playing games. Risk dominance, Pareto dominance, backward induction, sub-game perfection and forward induction are just some of the concepts game theorists have dreamt up to deal with the complication of multiple equilibria. In the latter half of this chapter and the next we will look at

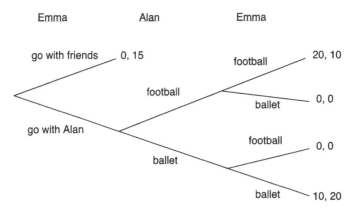

Figure 6.6 A sequential battle of the sexes game with an outside option. Emma decides first whether or not to go with friends or Alan.

lots of examples to see whether these concepts are any good at predicting what people actually do. All the concepts we have looked at so far, though, are called equilibrium refinements (see Research Methods 6.3); to finish I want to give one example of equilibrium selection.

Research Methods 6.3

Equilibrium refinements and selection

If there are multiple Nash equilibria it seems natural to ask if one equilibrium seems more likely to be observed than others. This has led to various suggestions of how to refine and select equilibria.

A Nash equilibrium is **refined** by adding an extra condition that must be satisfied. For example, a sub-game perfect Nash equilibrium is required to be a Nash equilibrium of every possible sub-game of the original game. A Pareto-dominant Nash equilibrium is required to give higher payoffs to everyone than any other Nash equilibrium. Refining the set of Nash equilibria can be done using ideas from behavioral economics. The problem is that there may be multiple or no equilibria that satisfy the refinement. So, the original problem of saying which equilibrium will be observed need not be resolved.

Equilibrium **selection** tackles the problem of multiple equilibria head on by providing an algorithm to select a unique equilibrium for a general class of games. Quantal response equilibrium is one example of this. Clearly this approach provides a specific prediction of what people will do. The problem is that the behavioral justification for the algorithm may have to give way to the analytical need to pick one equilibrium. Put another way, it may be natural to think of multiple or no equilibria as possible outcomes of the game, and equilibrium selection does not allow that.

6.2.5 Nash equilibrium with mistakes

In section 6.1 we saw that Nash equilibrium was a poor predictor of what people would do when they play the p-beauty contest, for the first time. In section 6.2.3 we saw that Nash equilibrium was a slightly better predictor in the simple beauty contest, but still far from perfect. Trust me, we are going to see before too long that Nash equilibrium is not always as bad. Even so, it seems as though we should be looking at deviations from Nash equilibrium. One way to do this is to assume people sometimes make mistakes. There are different ways this can be done but I will focus on one possibility called quantal response equilibrium, for which we need to thank McKelvey and Palfrey (1995).

The basic idea behind **quantal response equilibrium** (QRE) is that people choose their optimal strategy with some error. The main thing we need to know is that at a QRE the probability person i will choose strategy l is given by:

$$\sigma_i^*(l) = \frac{e^{\lambda u_i(l, \sigma_{-i}^*)}}{\sum_j e^{\lambda u_i(j, \sigma_{-i}^*)}} \tag{6.1}$$

for all i and l where λ is a precision parameter that measures the size of errors. This equation looks a bit messy but it does turn out to be a nice way to capture mistakes. That's because: if $\lambda = 0$ then everyone chooses at random, and the larger is λ the less errors people make. If $\lambda = \infty$, then any QRE is a Nash equilibrium.

To illustrate how to find a QRE, consider the matrix game in Table 6.7. The only Nash equilibrium here is what's called a Nash equilibrium in mixed strategies, where Alan and Emma are supposed to randomize what they do. To find the QRE, let p_L denote the probability Emma chooses left and q_U denote the probability Alan chooses up. Plugging this into equation (6.1) we get:

$$q_U = \frac{e^{9\lambda p_L}}{e^{9\lambda p_L} + e^{\lambda(1-p_L)}} \quad \text{and} \quad p_L = \frac{e^{\lambda(1-q_U)}}{e^{\lambda q_U} + e^{\lambda(1-q_U)}}.$$

We now need to find the values of q_U and p_L such that both equations hold. This will depend on λ. For example, if $\lambda = 1$ then we get $q_U = 0.89$ and $p_L = 0.31$ (check it and see). Figure 6.7 plots the values of q_U and p_L for different values of λ.

Table 6.7 A matrix game

		Emma	
		Left	Right
Alan	up	$9, $0	$0, $1
	down	$0, $1	$1, $0

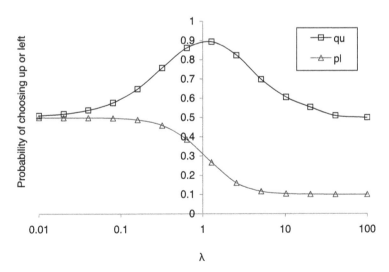

Figure 6.7 The QRE for the game in Table 6.7. The equilibrium depends on λ where a high λ means fewer mistakes are made.

One way to interpret the QRE here is that, because of mistakes, Emma is likely to choose left more often that she would do with the Nash equilibrium. Consequently Alan should play up more often than with the Nash equilibrium. QRE thus gives us a prediction of where Nash equilibrium might go wrong. The really clever thing, however, is that it also gives us a means to select equilibria. This is how it works: if $\lambda = 0$ then there is a unique QRE. The trick is then to increase λ and keep track of how this QRE changes. Doing this gives a unique QRE for each λ and ultimately (when $\lambda = \infty$) selects a unique Nash equilibrium. Analytically this is very neat. Does it work?

McKelvey, Palfrey and Weber (2000) had subjects play the game in Table 6.7 and two others. In these other games the payoffs of Alan and Emma were four times as big. This increase in payoffs does not change the Nash equilibrium but it does change the QRE. Indeed one of the main predictions of QRE is that people should make smaller errors, and be expected to make smaller errors, when payoffs are bigger.

McKelvey, et al. found that QRE did a lot better at predicting what subjects do than Nash equilibrium or an alternative of Nash equilibrium with mistakes. The news was not all good, however. To see why, Figure 6.8 plots the estimated distribution of λ for each of the games. The way to interpret this distribution is that some people make more mistakes than others and the distribution shows the probability a random person is best characterized by the different values of λ. The main concern is that the distribution of λ is different for each game. This makes it hard to apply QRE because we cannot know what the distribution of λ will be for another game we might be interested in.

Let's finish by focusing on the good news. We have now looked at lots of different ways to think about how people might play games. Most of them are

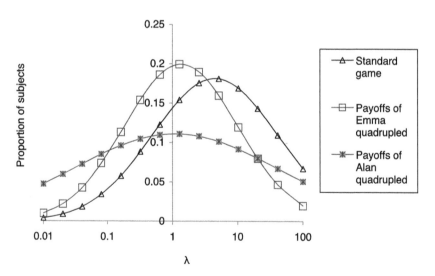

Figure 6.8 The estimated distribution or λ across subjects for each of the three games.
Source: McKelvey, Palfrey and Weber (2000).

complementary. For example, level-k thinking requires us to think what the type L-0s will do and the equilibrium refinements and selections we have looked at give us some clue what they might do. What we need to do now is get a feel for which way of thinking is best for particular game. Before getting started on that, however, I want to look at how people can learn from experience.

[Extra] If you are desperate to know where equation (6.1) comes from, then here is one motivation. Suppose Emma's perception of the payoff she will get is slightly wrong. We denote by $u_E^P(l, s_{-E})$ the payoff she thinks she will get from choosing l if others choose s_{-E}. This will be her actual payoff plus an error, i.e.:

$$u_E^P(l, s_{-E}) = u_E(l, s_{-E}) + \varepsilon_l$$

where ε_l is the size of the error. Suppose that size of the error ε_l is determined randomly according to probability distribution f. If Emma believes others will use strategy σ_{-E} then she will maximize her expected payoff by choosing l if $u_E^P(l, \sigma_{-i}) \geq u_E^P(j, \sigma_{-i})$ or $u_E(l, \sigma_{-E}) + \varepsilon_l \geq u_E(j, \sigma_{-E}) + \varepsilon_j$ for all j. The probability she will choose l is, therefore:

$$\sigma_E^*(l) = \int_{R_l(\sigma_{-E})} f(\varepsilon) d\varepsilon \tag{6.2}$$

where $R_l(\sigma_{-E})$ is the set of errors ε_l for which she would choose strategy l. A QRE is obtained when everyone has correct beliefs of what others will do. That is strategy vector $\sigma^* = (\sigma_1^*, \ldots, \sigma_N^*)$ is a QRE if each σ_i^* satisfies (6.2) with $\sigma_{-i} = \sigma_{-i}^*$. If f is something called the extreme value distribution, then it is possible to derive equation (6.1). The main thing to take from this exercise is that we can justify QRE as a likely outcome if people are uncertain of their payoff function. In chapter two I suggested people may be uncertain of their payoff function, so QRE has an intuitive appeal.

6.3 Learning from experience

I now want to look at what happens if Emma has the chance to play a game a few times and so learn from experience. In this context it is natural to think of the probability that she will play a strategy, because she may, for instance, want to try a new strategy to see what happens, or stick with a strategy that has done well in the past. What we need to determine, therefore, is the probability $P^l(t)$ that Emma will player strategy l the t'th time that she plays a game. There are two key elements to doing this.

First, are initial beliefs. In the previous section we were effectively questioning what $P^l(1)$ is, that is the probability Emma will play each strategy the first time she plays the game. What she plays will depend on her **initial beliefs**. For example, Emma may have no idea what her payoff function is, or prior what others will do, and so chooses a strategy randomly, but is eager to learn from experience. In other situations, she may know her payoff function and having read section 6.2, be sure what strategy she wants to choose. Initial beliefs are important, but primarily the subject of the last section, and so I will not mention them here much. Instead I want to focus on the second element of learning.

Once she has played the game Emma might want to **update her beliefs** and change the probability she chooses each strategy. In modeling how this works it is useful to measure the attractiveness of a strategy. I shall denote by $Q^l(t)$ the **attractiveness of strategy** l for Emma the t'th time that she plays the game. What a learning model needs to do is specify the **learning rule** or **updating rule** whereby we can determine $Q^l(t)$ from $Q^l(t-1)$. That is, we need to know the rule determining how attractive each strategy will look for Emma.

Once we know the learning rule and the attractiveness of each strategy we can then work out the probability Emma will choose each strategy. As you might expect, we will assume more attractive strategies will be more likely to be chosen. The simplest way to do this is to set:

$$p^l(t) = \frac{Q^l(t)}{\sum_j Q^j(t)}.$$

In other words, we assume that Emma chooses a strategy with a probability **proportional to its attractiveness**. This way is simplest but not necessarily best. Other ways include use of an exponential, power or probit formula. For example, using an **exponential** formula we get:

$$p^l(t) = \frac{e^{\omega Q^l(t)}}{\sum_j e^{\omega Q^j(t)}}. \tag{6.3}$$

The parameter ω allows us to vary how sensitive Emma's choice is to the attractiveness of a strategy. The higher is ω the more likely is Emma to choose the strategy with the highest attractiveness.

The focus of this section will mainly be on the learning rule and there are three main models of learning that we need to look at.

6.3.1 Reinforcement learning

Abundant psychological evidence has shown that choices that led to good outcomes in the past are likely to be repeated. This is called the **law of actual effect**. For example, if Emma is playing the 0.5-beauty contest, delays 20 days and does well, then she is likely to delay around 20 days the next time. Models of **reinforcement learning** or **adaptive learning** are designed to capture this. To illustrate how such models work, I shall work through a model based on that of Roth and Erev (1995).

Imagine that the t'th time Emma played a game she chose strategy l and got payoff $u_E(l, s_{-E}(t))$. Also imagine that she has an **aspiration level** of a (which you can think of in the same way as the aspiration level I introduced in chapter two). We then assume that she updates the attractiveness of each strategy using learning rule:

$$Q^j(t+1) \propto \begin{cases} Q^l(t) + [u_E(l, s_{-E}(t)) - a] & \text{if } j = l \\ Q^j(t) & \text{if } j \neq l \end{cases}. \tag{6.4}$$

There are two key things about this rule. First, a strategy can only become more attractive if Emma plays it and it gives a higher payoff than her aspiration level. Second, the higher the payoff above the aspiration level the more attractive it becomes next time.

This means that Emma will tend over time to choose those strategies which she has played in the past and gave her a relatively high payoff. She is less likely to choose those strategies that gave her a relatively low payoff. That looks like a reasonable plan. To see how it works, Table 6.8 illustrates what might happen as Emma plays the 0.5-beauty contest with an aspiration level of 90. Recall that her payoff could be between zero and 100 and an aspiration of 90 means she wants to be within 10 of the optimum. To keep things simple I assume that Emma only considers waiting 20 days or 30 days and the probability of choosing either is proportional to the attractiveness. After playing the game four times she has become more likely to wait 30 days (see also review question 6.5).

This basic model can be adapted in various ways. One interesting extension is **local experimentation**. In this case for every strategy *l* we associate a set of strategies $L(l)$ that we consider near to or similar to *l*. Assuming an aspiration level of zero the updating rule is then modified to:

$$Q^j(t+1) \propto \begin{cases} Q^l(t) + u_E(l, s_{-E}(t)) & \text{if } j = l \\ Q^j(t) + \varepsilon u_E(l, s_{-E}(t)) & \text{if } j \in L(l) \\ Q^j(t) & \text{otherwise} \end{cases}$$

where ε measures the extent of local experimentation. The additional feature this adds is that a strategy becomes more attractive if a nearby strategy earned a high

Table 6.8 Emma using reinforcement learning in the 0.5-beauty contest. Her choice and the optimum are hypothetical, but given this hypothetical experience we can see what happens to the attractiveness and probability of her choosing each strategy

Round	Attractiveness Q^l		Probability of choosing P^l		Outcomes	
	20 days	30 days	20 days	30 days	Chooses	Optimum
1	30	30	0.5	0.5	20	40
2	20	30	0.4	0.6	20	25
3	25	30	0.45	0.55	30	30
4	25	40	0.38	0.62	30	35

payoff. Thus, Emma would be willing to, say, experiment with a delay of 29 days if 30 days has worked in the past.

The main advantage of reinforcement learning is that Emma need only know her own payoff. She just tries things and sees what happens. She does not need to know what others did, what their payoffs were, what payoffs she would have got for doing something else, etc. Reinforcement learning can, therefore, be very generally applied and has a good chance to capture learning when someone is relatively uninformed about a game. If, however, Emma does know something about the game, reinforcement learning gives no scope for her to exploit what she knows. Belief based learning, which I shall look at next, does.

6.3.2 Belief based learning

As well as reflecting on past payoffs it may be appropriate to reflect on the past behavior of others and try to predict what they will do in the future. For example, if it would have been optimal for Emma to delay 25 days last time, then maybe she should delay 25 days next time. Models of **belief based learning** capture this. To illustrate I will work through a model based on that of Cheung and Friedman (1997).

The main thing we need to do is determine Emma's beliefs about what others will do. For example, how long she thinks others will delay. Let $B^c(t)$ denote the probability with which she thinks others will play strategy combination s^c_{-E} the t'th time the game is played. Beliefs will likely depend on what happened in the past and so we assume Emma keeps track of what others have done. Let $\#^c(t)$ denote the number of times that strategy combination s^c_{-E} has been chosen by others in the first t plays of the game. In a p-beauty contest this would require Emma keeping count of the number of times the optimal delay was one day, two days, etc.

If $s_{-E}(t)$ denotes what others did in the t'th game we assume that beliefs are updated using rule

$$B^c(t+1) \propto \begin{cases} \rho \#^c(t) + 1 & \text{if } s_{-E}(t) = s^c_{-E} \\ \rho \#^c(t) & \text{if } s_{-E}(t) \neq s^c_{-E} \end{cases}$$

where ρ is a parameter. To understand this rule it is useful to think about two special cases. If $\rho = 0$ Emma would expect others to do in the future what they did last time. This is called **best reply** or **Cournot**, and means beliefs are based solely on the last time the game was played. If $\rho = 1$ Emma believes the probability a strategy combination will be chosen by others in the future is equal to the relative frequency with which it has been chosen in the past. This is called **fictitious play** and means beliefs are based on the average of what has happened in all plays of the game. The parameter ρ measures, therefore, how far into the past Emma wants to look. The lower is ρ the quicker the past is ignored, or the quicker she forgets. Table 6.9 illustrates what Emma may do in the 0.5-beauty contest when $\rho = 0.5$.

From the beliefs $B^c(t)$ we need to get to attractiveness. We can do this by equating attractiveness with expected payoff. Given beliefs $B^c(t)$, Emma's expected payoff of from choosing strategy l is proportional to:

$$Q^l(t) = \sum_c u_E(l, s^c_{-E}) B^c(t). \tag{6.5}$$

In this case Emma is more likely to choose a strategy that would have been a relatively good strategy to have chosen in the past. If $\rho = 1$ she will choose the strategy that would have been best that last time the game was played. If $\rho = 0$ she will choose the strategy that would have been best averaging over all the times she has played the game. Again, these seem like sensible things to do. [Extra] Equation (6.5) is good enough for our purposes but if we do substitute in for $B^c_i(t)$ we can get the updating rule

$$Q^l(t+1) \propto \rho Q^l(t) \sum_c \#^c(t) + u_E(l, s^c_{-E}(t)). \tag{6.6}$$

Crucial in the model is the value of ρ. In the study by Cheung and Friedman they report experiments that allow us to estimate ρ for different subjects and different games (see Research Methods 6.4 for more on this). The estimates are given in Figure 6.9 (and for completeness I also give estimates from Camerer and Ho (1999) that we shall discuss below). Overall, we see relatively low values of ρ suggesting the average player looks mainly to the recent past. There was, however, a lot of heterogeneity. Of those subjects they could classify Cheung and Friedman estimated 56 percent used Cournot (with $\rho = 0$), 33 percent used fictitious play (with $\rho = 1$), and 11 percent were adaptive (with $\rho \in (0,1)$). Most subjects, therefore, took a short term view but many took a long-term view. Crucially, though the distribution of ρ's was similar across the games considered, which is useful for applying the model to predict what will happen in other games.

Table 6.9 Emma using belief based learning in the 0.5-beauty contest with $\rho = 0.5$. Her beliefs keep track of what has happened in the past. The attractiveness is worked out using equation 6.5. For simplicity I only give the attractiveness of three possible strategies

Round	Beliefs B^c			Attractiveness Q^l			Others' choice
	10	20	30	5	10	15	
1	0	0	0	–	–	–	30
2	0	0	1	90	95	100	20
3	0	1	0.5	140	147.5	145	10
4	1	0.5	0.25	170	168.75	162.5	20

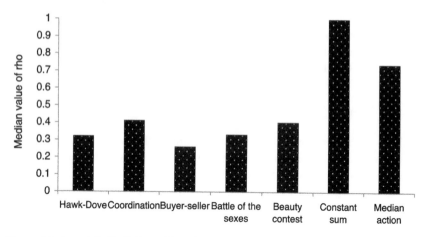

Figure 6.9 A model of belief based learning. Estimates of the median ρ for different matrix games.

Sources: Friedman and Cheung (1997) and Camerer and Ho (1999).

Research Methods 6.4

Estimating learning models

A learning model is typically fitted to experimental data using **maximum likelihood estimation**. Basically, for any given set of parameters it is possible to calculate the likelihood of the experimental data given the particular set of parameters and model. For example, in the EWA model, we can fix values for δ, β, φ, $P^1(0), \ldots, P^K(0)$ and #(0) and then say how likely a particular set of experimental data was, given the EWA model. We then search for the parameters that maximize the (log) likelihood to see how well a model can fit the data.

A real concern when doing this is that some models have more parameters than others and so a priori are likely to have a better chance of fitting the data. Put another way a model with too many parameters may over-fit the data. There are various sophisticated ways to check for such things but a more basic solution is to do an **out of sample forecast**. To do this, maximum likelihood estimates are derived using, say, 70 percent of the data and then the estimated model is used to predict what should happen in the other 30 percent of the data. If the model does a great job of fitting the original 70 percent but a poor job of predicting the other 30 percent then there is evidence of over-fitting.

A related issue is how to capture heterogeneity. To assume that all subjects will have the same parameters seems a little extreme because we might imagine that some people learn more by reinforcement learning and others by belief based learning etc. If, however, we allow different subjects to have different parameter values we are likely to over-fit the data. A **latent class approach** allows there to be one, two, or more, types of people where each person of a particular type is assumed to have the same parameter values. The amount of data should be used to determine how many types seem reasonable. Camerer and Ho consider two latent types, Friedman and Cheung let each individual have different parameters.

Friedman and Cheung also provided interesting insight on the choices of subjects and whether they choose the strategies with highest attractiveness. They use equation (6.3) to estimate choices from attractiveness. Recall that a high ω means someone is more likely to choose attractive strategies. Figure 6.10 gives estimates of ω for two of the games but four different treatments. In a **mean matching experiment** each subject is matched to play every other subject in each round while in a **random experiment** each subject plays one randomly selected subject per round. In a **history experiment** the distribution of past choices in previous rounds is displayed and in a **no history experiment** it is not. In a mean matching and history experiment a subject has relatively more information on what others have done in the past. This should help form beliefs. Consistent with this we see, from the higher ω, that choice was more likely to be informed by beliefs in the mean matching and history experiments.

6.3.3 Experience weighted learning

Reinforcement and belief based learning nicely complement each other. Reinforcement learning means Emma looks at whether a strategy did give a high payoff; with belief based learning she looks whether it would have given a high payoff. Reinforcement learning means Emma updates beliefs about the payoff of each strategy, with belief based learning she updates beliefs about what others will do. Is there any way to combine the two and get the best of both worlds?

Camerer and Ho (1999) showed that this is possible with **experience-weighted attraction learning** or EWA. Similar to a belief based model, we need a variable $\#(t)$ that keeps count of past experience and is updated using rule

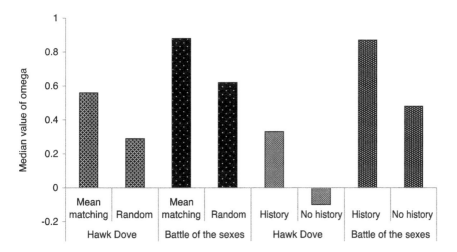

Figure 6.10 Median estimates of ω in a belief based model of learning. The higher ω in situations with mean matching and history suggests subjects were more influenced by what others have done in the past in these situations.

Source: Cheung and Friedman (1997).

$$\#(t) = \beta\#(t-1) + 1$$

where β is some number called the **depreciation rate**. To see how $Q^j(t)$ is updated, suppose that in period t Emma chooses strategy l and others choose $s_{-E}(t)$. She gets payoff $u_E(l, s_{-E}(t))$, but for every other strategy j misses out on the payoff $u_E(j, s_{-E}(t))$ she could have got. Emma is assumed to weight received payoffs by $1 - \delta$ and missed payoffs by δ. The updating rule is then:

$$Q^j(t+1) \propto \begin{cases} \varphi\#(t)Q^l(t) + u_E(l, s_{-E}(t)) & \text{if } j = l \\ \varphi\#(t)Q^j(t) + \delta u_E(j, s_{-E}(t)) & \text{if } j \neq l \end{cases}$$

where φ is some number called the **decay rate**.

This looks a bit complicated but you do not need to worry too much about that because the beauty of the EWA model is its ability to capture reinforcement learning and belief based learning as special cases. It does so primarily through the parameter δ which measures the relative weight given to missed payoffs rather than received payoffs. If $\delta = 0$, $\#(0) = 1$, $\varphi = 1$ and $\beta = 0$, then we obtain a model of reinforcement learning like that in equation to (6.4). That's because when $\delta = 0$ Emma focuses exclusively on the payoff she did receive and ignores the payoffs she missed out on. If $\delta = 1$ and $\beta = \varphi = \rho$ then we obtain a model of belief based learning similar to that of equation (6.6). That's because when $\delta = 1$ Emma focuses equally on the payoff she missed out on compared to the payoff she did receive. If δ is between zero and one we get a mix of reinforcement learning and belief based learning.

Camerer and Ho fitted the EWA model to a variety of data and compared fit to that with reinforcement and belief based learning. Table 6.10 summarizes the estimates they find for the various parameters and Figure 6.11 plots an estimate of goodness of fit. As we would expect, EWA does relatively well. More interesting is how reinforcement learning does relatively well in the beauty contest and

Table 6.10 EWA parameter estimates

Game	Learning	δ	β	φ	ω
Beauty contest	Reinforcement	0	0	1.375	0.223
	Belief based	1	0.402	0.402	0.942
	EWA	0.232	0.941	1.330	2.579
Constant sum	Reinforcement	0	0	0.96–1.01	0.03–0.10
(4 different games)	Belief based	1	0.99–1.00	0.99–1.00	0.46–1.81
	EWA	0.00–0.73	0.93–0.96	0.99–1.04	0.18–0.65
Median action	Reinforcement	0	0	0.930	1.190
	Belief based	1	0.738	0.738	16.726
	EWA	0.853	0.000	0.800	6.827

Source: Camerer and Ho (1999).

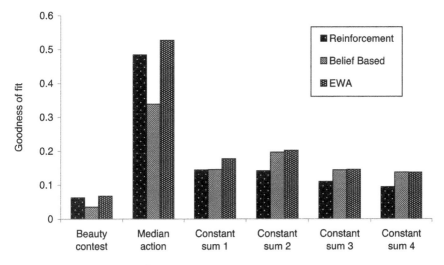

Figure 6.11 The adjusted R^2 for the three different learning models in six games.
Source: Camerer and Ho (1999).

median action game, while belief based learning does better in constant sum games. We can give an ex-post rationalization for this but the main point is that people might learn in different ways in different games, and EWA is well placed to pick this up. Indeed, with the three models of learning we now have we are well placed to better understand how people learn from experience. But is this enough?

6.3.4 Learning and prediction

A model of learning says what Emma will do is conditional on what has happened previously. This is great for looking back and trying to make sense of what she did do. But is it so useful in trying to look forward and predict what she will do? One thing we could do is combine the ideas of sections 6.2 and 6.3, get a prediction of what will happen the first time a game is played, and then use a learning model to see what will happen after say ten plays of the game. But how confident we can be in the answer? Looking back at Tables 6.8 and 6.9, that trace through what happens as Emma learns in the 0.5-beauty contest, we can see that the prediction we will get depends a lot on chance events like what Emma randomly chooses to do.

Another approach is to ask whether play will **converge**, and if so to what. To do this, we ask what happens after people have played the game say 1,000 times. If we always get the same answer then we say that play converges and then use this as a prediction of what will happen. This puts the focus firmly on what will happen in the long run, but maybe it also gives a good prediction of what will happen in short run after, say, ten plays of the game? Unfortunately, this approach does not work so well for the three learning models we have seen so far. That's because play need not converge, and if it does converge, it converges to a Nash equilibrium, and so we are basically just using a kind of equilibrium refinement. There are though alternatives and in this section I will consider three.

I will start with something called **payoff sampling**. Suppose that for each possible strategy, Emma samples the payoff she got from choosing that strategy on, say, six previous occasions. Remember, we are assuming Emma has played the game lots of times and so she can do this. She then chooses the strategy that gave her the highest payoff. This is a type of reinforcement learning and lets us predict what Emma will do. Indeed, we can find a **payoff sampling equilibrium** that tells us the probability she will choose each strategy in the long run if everyone uses payoff sampling.

To illustrate how it works, consider the matrix game in Table 6.11. Suppose that when Alan samples the payoff from choosing up there were U_L times that he got 10 and $6 - U_L$ times he got 0. When he samples the payoff from choosing down he must have got nine all six times. So, he will choose up if $10U_L > 9 \times 6 = 54$. This could only happen if $U_L = 6$. If p_L is the probability that Emma chooses left, this happens with probability p_L^6. So, letting q_U denote the probability that Alan chooses up we get:

$$q_U = prob(U_L = 6) = p_L^6.$$

We can now do the same to derive p_L as a function of q_U. When Emma samples her payoff from choosing left, she gets nine. Suppose that when she samples her payoff from choosing right there were R_U times that she got 18 and $6 - R_U$ times she got eight. She will choose left if $9 \times 6 > 18R_U + 8(6 - R_U)$ or $6 > 10R_U$. This can only be satisfied if $R_U = 0$. Thus:

$$p_L = prob(R_U = 0) = (1 - q_U)^6.$$

We now know the probability Alan chooses up as a function of the probability Emma chooses left, and vice versa. To obtain a payoff sampling equilibrium we look for the point where these two probabilities are consistent. That is, where $q_U = ((1 - q_U)^6)^6$ and $p_L = (1 - p_L^6)^6$. Values $q_U = 0.071$ and $p_L = 0.643$ work. This is a prediction of what Alan and Emma might do.

Before we see how good this prediction is I want to go through the other two possibilities. Next up is **action sampling**. Imagine now that Emma samples what

Table 6.11 A matrix game to illustrate payoff sampling

		Emma	
		Left	*Right*
Alan	up	$10, $9	$0, $18
	down	$9, $9	$9, $8

Alan chose on, say, seven previous occasions. She then chooses the strategy that would have maximized her payoff given what Alan did. This gives a form of belief based learning. By finding an **action sampling equilibrium**, using similar techniques to that we used to find a payoff sampling equilibrium, we get a prediction of what Emma will do. If we work through the game in Table 6.11 then we get the values $q_U = 0.057$ and $p_L = 0.664$.

[Extra] To see where these numbers come from. Alan should choose up if $10p_L > 9$ or $p_L > 0.9$. So, he should choose up if and only if he observed Emma choosing left all seven times he samples. So:

$$q_U = prob(\text{observes left seven times}) = p_L{}^7.$$

Emma should choose left if $9 > 18q_U + 8(1 - q_U)$ or $q_U < 0.1$. So she should choose left if Alan never chose up on the seven times she samples. Thus:

$$p_L = prob(\text{does not observes up}) = (1 - q_U)^7.$$

To obtain an action sampling equilibrium we look for the point where these two probabilities are consistent. That is, $q_U = ((1 - q_U)^7)^7$ and $p_L = (1 - p_L{}^7)^7$. The values $q_U = 0.057$ and $p_L = 0.664$ work this time.

The final possibility I want to look at is called **impulse balance**. What we do here is calculate a **security level** of payoff that Emma can guarantee herself. For instance, in the game in Table 6.11, Emma can guarantee a payoff of $9 by choosing left. Taking into account loss aversion we then say that gains above the security level are treated as less than losses below the security level. For example, we might say that a loss counts twice as much as a gain. Table 6.12 shows what happens when we do this. For instance, if Alan chooses up and Emma chooses right the payoff of $0 is $9 short of the security level and so would feel to Alan like $9 - 2 \times 9 = -9$.

The final thing we do is to say that Emma would have an **impulse** in the direction of a particular strategy if choosing that strategy would have earned a higher payoff. The size of the impulse is given by the payoff difference. Table 6.13 shows the impulses in the example. An impulse of zero means she has no incentive to change strategy, and the higher the number the stronger the impulse to change. There is an **impulse balance equilibrium** if these impulses to change strategy cancel out.

Table 6.12 Transforming the payoffs to take into account loss aversion. Losses relative to the security payoff of $9 count twice as much

		Emma	
		Left	*Right*
Alan	up	10, 9	−9, 18
	down	9, 9	9, 7

Table 6.13 Impulses after taking into account loss aversion. For instance, if Alan chose up and Emma chooses left he has no impulse to change strategy, but if he had chosen down he would have had an impulse of one to change strategy

		Emma	
		Left	Right
Alan	up	0, 9	18, 0
	down	1, 0	0, 2

To see how this works we can work through the example. Given that Emma chooses left with probability p_L and he chooses up with probability q_U Alan's expected impulse from up to down is $18q_U(1 - p_L)$ and his expected impulse from down to up is $(1 - q_U)p_L$. At an impulse balance equilibrium we want these to be the same, so $18q_U(1 - p_L) = (1 - q_U)p_L$, or

$$q_U = \frac{p_L}{18 - 17p_L}.$$

Similarly, Emma's expected impulse from left to right is $9q_U p_L$ and from right to left is $2(1 - q_U)(1 - p_L)$. Setting these equal gives:

$$p_L = \frac{1 - q_U}{3.5q_U + 1}.$$

Solving these two equations gives the equilibrium. In this case $q_U = 0.1$ and $p_L = 0.67$.

Impulse balance combines elements of both reinforcement learning and belief based learning because it favors strategies that give a relatively high payoff. The most appealing thing about it, however, is that it can capture the loss aversion we saw in chapters two and three. It says that people will be drawn away from strategies that are likely to cause a loss. Given the evidence we saw for loss aversion this looks like a great thing to be doing.

The nice thing about payoff sampling equilibrium, action sampling equilibrium and impulse balance equilibrium is that there is only one of them. They give us, therefore, a nice prediction of what should happen in the long run. Furthermore, they are relatively easy to calculate because we do not need to model the learning process itself. But are the predictions any use? In a study by Selten and Chmura (2008) subjects played twelve different games similar to that in Table 6.11. Figure 6.12 gives a measure of how good different equilibria were at fitting the data. A smaller number means a better fit so action sampling, payoff sampling and impulse balance did a much better job than Nash or quantal response equilibrium.

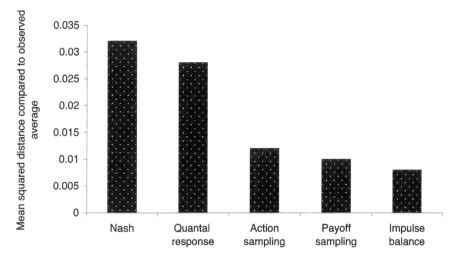

Figure 6.12 Assessing the goodness of fit of various equilibria. The smaller the mean
squared distance compared to the observed average, the better the fit.

Source: Selten and Chmura (2008).

An important question to ask in interpreting these results is how many times
subjects played the games. There were twelve games and a subject played for 200
rounds, so they played each game around sixteen or seventeen times. The results,
though, are the same if we focus on just the first 100 rounds. This is good news
because it means these equilibrium predictions look as though they work even if
people have had little or no chance to learn from experience. That does present
something of a conundrum as to why they work so well, but maybe they just
capture nicely how people reason when playing games. That seems a positive note
upon which to stop with the theory and look at some applications.

6.4 Summary

In trying to understand strategic behavior we started with the notion of Nash
equilibrium and elimination of dominated strategies. A basic premise is that
people should not play dominated strategies. A slightly more involved premise is
that they should play a Nash equilibrium strategy. In some games this gives us a
very nice prediction, in principle, of what people should do because there is a
unique Nash equilibrium or a unique strategy that survives iterated elimination of
dominated strategies.

Evidence on how people behaved in the p-beauty contest was enough to
suggest, however, that Nash equilibrium and elimination of dominated strategies
is not enough to explain behavior. This led us to the ideas of level k-thinking
as well as semi-sophisticated and sophisticated behavior. The focus here is

to model the various ways that people might reason in strategic situations and not 'get as far as' the Nash equilibrium. On a related note we looked at quantal response equilibrium which tries to model what happens if people make mistakes.

In many contexts the notion of Nash equilibrium and elimination of dominated strategies does not get us very far, because there are several Nash equilibria. That means we need to think how people might reason which equilibrium 'makes more sense'. By looking at focal points, risk and Pareto dominance, and backward and forward induction, we have seen that there are various ways to do this.

We then looked at how people might learn with experience, contrasting reinforcement learning and belief based learning. We also looked at how learning models can be used to predict what will happen after people have learnt.

One thing you may have noticed by now is that modeling behavior in strategic contexts is not easy. There is a lot going on, because we have all the choice arbitrariness, risk and uncertainty that we had in chapters two to five compounded by the interdependence between people, and different games raise very different issues. For this reason anyone expecting a unified theory of behavior in strategic contexts is probably going to be disappointed. Sometimes, level-k thinking will work well sometimes not; sometimes, backward induction will work well and sometimes not. This though, is not bad news. We now have lots of different ways to help us think about strategic behavior, and that's a good thing.

6.5 Auctions

A nice example of where strategy matter is auctions. We have already encountered auctions a few times, in chapters two and four, but now I want to look at them in a bit more detail. It seems apt to start by saying that auctions are one of the most important ways that goods are sold. Examples are as diverse as the selling of antique furniture or paintings at Sotheby's, cars, houses, goods on ebay, and government's selling tracts of land for oil drilling. It is important, therefore, that we can understand them well. Here I want to focus on two particularly interesting aspects of auctions, revenue equivalence and the winners curse. In chapter 11 we will look at some other aspects.

6.5.1 Revenue Equivalence

There are various different types of **auction format**. I will look at four of the more common formats here (and a few more in chapter 11).

In an **English auction** the auctioneer starts the bidding at a low price and incrementally increases the price until only one bidder is willing to pay that price. This is the most common auction format and is what you would see, for instance, at Sotheby's.

In a **Dutch auction** the auctioneer starts the bidding at a high price and incrementally lowers the price until someone is willing to buy at that price. This auction gets its name from the way tulips are sold in Holland.

In a **first price sealed bid auction** potential bidders are asked to submit simultaneously and independently the amount they are willing to pay for the item. The highest bidder wins and pays the price he bid. This is a standard format for government tendering.

Finally, in **second price sealed bid auction** everything is the same as the first price sealed bid auction, except the highest bidder only has to pay the price of the second highest bidder. Ebay is a combination of this and an English auction.

A natural question for anyone looking to sell using an auction is which type of auction will maximize the revenue from the sale. Auction theory offers a specific and intriguing answer to this question: the **Revenue Equivalence Theorem** says that in many cases all four auction formats result in the same revenue if bidders behave optimally.

One case where this theorem applies is an **independent, privately known value auction**. In such an auction different bidders may value the item differently, but each bidder knows her own value, and knows her own value does not tell her anything about the likely values of others. This is the situation found in many common auctions such as the auctioning of an antique, car, house or consumer items on eBay. For example, consider a painting up for auction that Emma is thinking of bidding for. She knows that different people will likely value the painting differently, some liking it and some not, but she only knows her own preferences, and not those of others.

If Emma decides she wants the painting, and values it at $1,000, how much should she bid? The optimal way to bid in this type of auction depends on the auction format.

In an English or second price sealed bid auction, she should bid up to the amount she values the item, i.e. $1,000. There is no point bidding more because she might end up paying more than she thinks it's worth. There is no point bidding less because she will only have to pay the amount the second highest bidder is willing to pay, and so cannot gain anything by lowering her bid. For example, if Alan is the second highest bidder at $950 she only has to pay $950 so there would have been no gain in bidding say $980 rather than $1,000.

Things are different in the Dutch and first price sealed bid auctions. Now Emma needs to bid below the amount she values the item, say $980. This is called **shading the bid**. If she does not shade her bid then she can never make any profit, because she will have to pay what she bids. But, she does need to bid high enough to have a good chance of winning. It is quite complicated knowing exactly how much to bid given these competing incentives, but we do not need to worry too much about that.

Let's now go back to the Revenue Equivalence Theorem. We can see now why the English and second price auction should give the same revenue, and the Dutch and first price should give the same revenue. What remains to be shown is that a first price or Dutch auction gives the same revenue as a second price or English auction. In a first price auction Emma needs to shade her bid, and so bids less than she would in a second price auction. If she wins a second price auction, however, she only has to pay the amount bid by the second highest bidder. The neat thing is these two effects cancel each other out: the highest bid in a first price auction will, on average, equal the second highest bid in a second price auction! Thus, all four auctions give the same expected revenue. Well, that's the theory.

Lucking Reiley (1999) put the theory to the test in a field experiment that involved selling 'Magic cards' to online devotees of a game called 'Magic: The Gathering'. Four different collections of cards were independently auctioned using two of the four different auction formats. The results are summarized in Table 6.14. Collections one and two allow us to compare first price and Dutch auctions. We see that the Dutch auctions raised more revenue than the first price auction, with more cards selling for a high price. Collections three and four allow us to compare second price and English auctions. Here we so no significant differences in revenue. Overall, therefore, we see somewhat mixed support for the Revenue Equivalence Theorem. A similar conclusion has been found in laboratory studies, but with different results. Indeed, in the laboratory, first price auctions have been seen to raise more revenue than Dutch auctions, and second price auctions more than English auctions (see Research Methods 6.5).

Anyone selling an item might, therefore, want to think more closely about which auction format to use than the Revenue Equivalence Theorem might suggest. The popularity of the English auction is possibly a signal what many sellers think is best. To progress beyond such conjectures we need to know more about how people typically bid in auctions. We will get some insight into this as we look at the winner's curse.

Table 6.14 Bidding in the Magic game. The Dutch auction appears to raise more revenue than the first price auction. There is no difference between the English and second price

	First price		Dutch		No. of cards sold at higher price		
	Revenue	Bidders	Revenue	Bidders	1st price	Neither	Dutch
Collection 1	$431.25	32	$446.35	56	12	12	63
Collection 2	$327.05	42	$348.45	88	22	5	59
	Second price		English		No. of cards sold at higher price		
	Revenue	Bidders	Revenue	Bidders	2nd price	Neither	English
Collection 3	$85.50	27	$79.50	40	38	8	20
Collection 4	$517.05	43	$600.40	38	24	9	65

Source: Lucking Reiley (1999).

Research Methods 6.5

Field experiments

Given that auctions are so common and easy to take part in, they seem one natural setting for field experiments or source of field data. In this study, Lucking Reiley needed to find a setting flexible enough that he could auction the same things using four different auction formats. The online community of 'Magic: the Gathering' offered such an opportunity because there was already use of the English, first price and Dutch auctions, so only the second price auction would be new to bidders.

The usual potential advantages of field experiments over laboratory experiments are seemingly present in this study, namely, the subjects should be experienced in valuing the items and bidding for them. The results illustrate why this can prove important. That the Dutch auction raised more revenue than a first price auction goes against what has been observed in laboratory experiments. The probable explanation is that more people wanted to take part in the Dutch auction. This, unpredictable, increase in the number of bidders could not have happened in a lab experiment where the number of bidders is fixed by how many subjects the experimenter invites to the lab.

6.5.2 Winner's Curse

Recall that in a privately known value action, Emma knew how much the item was worth to her but not to others. The opposite extreme is a **common value auction**. In this type of auction a bidder will not know how much the item is worth until she has got it, but does know that others will value it as much as her. An example of this would be drilling rights to a tract of land that may or may not have oil. Only having purchased the land and drilled for oil can it be known for sure whether there is oil, but if there is, then any oil company would have wanted to buy the land. A slightly more mundane example would be people entering a charity auction at the local fete not knowing what the mystery winning prize is.

In a privately known value auction the bidder who wins is likely to be the one who most valued the item. For example, the one who most liked the painting. In a common value auction the bidder who wins is likely to be the one who was most optimistic about the value of the item. Optimism is sometimes a dangerous thing. If the bidder is more optimistic than others then she may be too optimistic and may pay more for the item than it is actually worth. This is called the **winner's curse**. Examples of the winner's curse abound. Oil companies have overpaid for land, telephone companies have overpaid for the rights to transmit signals, TV channels have overpaid for the rights to televise sporting events, and many have been disappointed by the prize they won at the local fete.

To look in more detail at why the winner's curse can happen, it is useful to first look at how a person should bid in a common value auction. So, imagine Emma is entering a charity English auction for a prize of unknown value. She likely gets some signal of how much the prize might be worth. From this she gets an initial expectation of the value of the item. For example, she might have an initial expectation the prize is worth \$20. Surely she should bid up to \$20? No. She should reason that if she wins she must have had the most optimistic initial expectation. For example, if she wins bidding \$20 then everyone else must have thought the prize was worth less than \$20. If everyone else thinks the prize is worth less than \$20, maybe she was over optimistic? She should lower her expectations, and so bid up to something less than her initial expected value.

With this we can now list some distinct reasons for why Emma might suffer the winner's curse. (1) She could be a risk loving person who bids high knowing the probability the prize is worth so much is small, but she is happy to take the risk. Ultimately the gamble does not pay off. (2) She bids optimally, and so lowers her bid below her initial expectation, but still proves unlucky because the prize turns out to have a lower value than most expected. (3) She naïvely bids up to her initial expectation and is unlucky. (4) She bids an irrationally high amount. This is most likely in a second price auction if she expects the second highest bid will be relatively low.

I now want to look at two studies. The first, by Crawford and Iriberri (2007), looks to explain the winner's curse using level-k thinking. The focus, therefore, is on the behaviour of inexperienced bidders. The second, by Selten, Abbink and Cox (2005) uses impulse balance and so puts the focus more on learning from experience.

We know that in level-k thinking it is crucial what we assume about type L-0s. Crawford and Iriberri consider two alternatives: First, that type L-0s bid randomly, or second, they bid naively their initial expectation. In different auction formats bidding behavior will differ, but Table 6.15 summarizes the main predictions of level-k thinking by comparing level-k bidding with the equilibrium bidding that would happen if everyone used the optimal strategy, explained above.

Table 6.15 Bidding strategies of a type L-k comparing what happens with two different assumptions about type L-0s

Type	Random	Initial expectation
L-0	Bids randomly	Bids up to her initial expectation
L-1	Bids up to her value, and more than the equilibrium amount. Because type L-0s are bidding randomly, that she wins tells her nothing about the expected values of others. So, she sees no reason to lower her bid.	Bids less than her value, and less than the equilibrium amount. Because type L-0s are bidding more than in equilibrium, she thinks that if she wins she must have been very optimistic about the expected value. So, she lowers her bid to compensate.
L-2	Bids less than her value, and less than the equilibrium amount. Because type L-1s are bidding more than in equilibrium, she thinks that if she wins she must have been very optimistic about the expected value. So, she lowers her bid to compensate.	Bids more than an L-1 type and possibly more than the equilibrium amount. Because type L-1s are bidding less than in equilibrium, she thinks that if she did win she was not necessarily optimistic. So, there is less need to lower her bid.

We see that if people of type L-0 bid randomly then people of type L-0 and L-1 are particularly vulnerable to the winner's curse. If people of type L-0 bid initial expectations then people of type L-0 and L-2 are vulnerable. Figure 6.13 details the percentage of subjects Crawford and Iriberri estimated were of each type in four different auctions. It's fairly clear that the most subjects were classified as being type L-1 with an expectation type L-0s bid randomly. These types are vulnerable to the winner's curse because they naïvely ignore the information that the bids of others convey. They fail to take into account that if they win, they must have been relatively optimistic about the expected value.

If people are vulnerable to the winner's curse because of naïve bidding then we might expect that they should learn with experience. Things are not so simple, however, because Emma, say, could bid 'too much' but be lucky and win a great prize, or bid 'the optimal amount' and be unlucky because the prize is less than everyone expected. This makes it potentially difficult to learn from experience.

The study of Selten et al. uses impulse balance equilibrium and a closely related idea of learning direction theory to try and understand how people do learn when playing auctions several times. The basic idea of **learning direction theory** is that someone goes with their impulse and moves in the direction of improved payoffs. In the context of an auction the person who wins almost certainly bids more than they needed to and so will lower their bid subsequently. The person who does not win might regret not bidding more and so increase their bid subsequently. This gives an interesting contrast between overpaying and a missed opportunity.

Selten et al. find that learning direction theory and impulse balance equilibrium fits well how subjects did behave in their experiments. This means that bids did

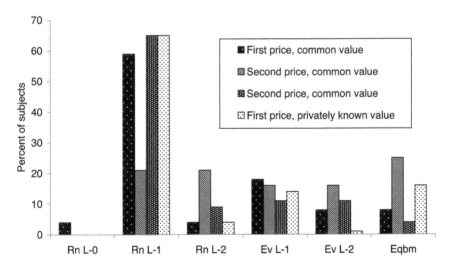

Figure 6.13 Percentage of subjects of each type in four auction experiments. Rn means assuming type L-0s choose randomly and Ev means they choose initial expectation.

Source: Crawford and Iriberri (2007).

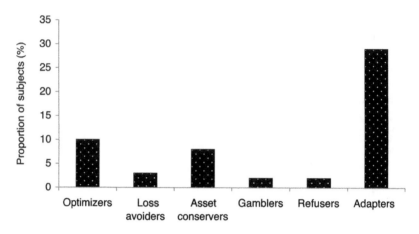

Figure 6.14 Categories of bidder. Adapters behaved consistently with learning direction theory, increasing their bid if they previously missed out and lowering their bid if they previously paid too much.

Source: Selten, Abbink and Cox (2005).

not converge over time to that predicted by equilibrium, but instead tended to fluctuate as subjects overpaid some periods but then regretted not bidding more in other periods. This is despite playing 100 successive auctions. To see this a bit more clearly Figure 6.14 shows what happens if we try to put subjects into categories depending on how they bid. Clearly, a lot of subjects were adapters, and this is the category that most closely fits learning direction theory. Of the other categories gamblers are worth a mention. Gamblers were seemingly interested in high gains and did seem to fall for the gambler's fallacy. If they overpaid one auction they tended to bid more next time, possibly thinking their luck must change.

Such gambling is the opposite of what is predicted by learning direction theory. So, learning direction theory cannot capture what everyone does but it does do a good job of capturing what many do. It also gives us an explanation of why the winner's curse does not disappear with experience. Namely, naïve bidding sometimes pays off, and so people need not realize that it is not the best thing to do.

This is an important point, not only in looking at auctions, because it demonstrates that learning need not converge to Nash equilibrium. The reason it did not do so here is because payoffs were random. If payoffs are going up and down, through good luck and bad luck, quicker than Emma learns the optimal way to bid she might never learn the optimal way to bid. Auctions, therefore, are one area of life where it pays to read the economic textbook and not rely on trial and error!

6.6 Learning to coordinate

To finish this chapter I want to go back and look in a bit more detail at **coordination games**–games where people want to coordinate their strategies to mutual benefit.

Coordination is vital in many areas of life, whether it be the world deciding how to tackle climate change or two friends trying to meet in a crowded cafeteria. So, it is very interesting to look at coordination games and see what we can learn. In section 6.2.3 we saw some evidence that people can coordinate using focal points, and in section 6.2.4 we saw how people might use forward or backward induction to coordinate. In this section I want to ask more generally how well people can coordinate. In doing so we shall look at two very different types of coordination problem.

6.6.1 Weak link games

In a **weak link game** or **minimum effort game** a group of people independently must decide how much effort to put into a group task. Higher effort is costly but the output of the group is determined by the smallest effort that someone puts in. A nice example to illustrate is going somewhere by plane. To get to her destination on time Emma would probably need lots of people to put in effort: the taxi driver to get her to the airport, the pilot to be there, the cleaner to clean the plane, the serviceman to put in the fuel, etc. If anyone puts in low effort Emma may not leave on time. The plane is going nowhere, for instance, if the pilot turns up late.

Table 6.16 gives the payoffs that are usually used in weak link game experiments. In this case people need to choose effort between one and seven. The best thing for the group and the individual, the Pareto dominant Nash equilibrium, is for all members of the group to put in high effort. This gives the highest payoff of 13. The safest thing for the individual, however, the risk dominant Nash equilibrium, is to put in low effort. This guarantees a payoff of 7. Choosing higher effort is risky because it only takes one member of the group to choose low effort for the high effort to be wasted and costly.

The weak link game has the tension between the Pareto dominant and risk dominant Nash equilibrium that we looked at in section 6.2.4. Indeed the payoffs in Table 6.5 are a condensed version of Table 6.16. Ideally we want people to coordinate on the Pareto dominant Nash equilibrium.

Table 6.16 Payoffs in a weak link game

Your choice of effort	*Smallest choice of effort in the group*						
	7	*6*	*5*	*4*	*3*	*2*	*1*
7 (high)	13	11	9	7	5	3	1
6		12	10	8	6	4	2
5			11	9	7	5	3
4				10	8	6	4
3					9	7	5
2						8	6
1 (low)							7

Figure 6.15 gives a fairly typical picture of what happens in a weak link game experiment. In this case there were four players who played together for ten rounds. We see that there was coordination failure. That subject two chose low effort in every round meant that the high effort of subject one, three and four was wasted. Over the rounds the effort of these three subjects falls as they learn effort is not going to pay. Figure 6.16 summarizes some aggregate results from a series

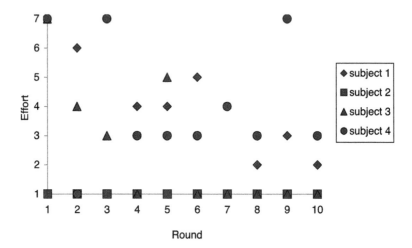

Figure 6.15 An example of coordination failure in a weak link game. That subject two chose an effort level of one meant the high effort of the other three was wasted.

Source: Gillet, Cartwright and van Vugt (2009).

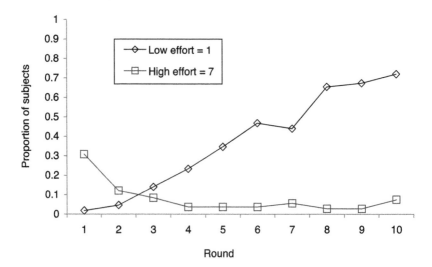

Figure 6.16 The proportion of players choosing one and seven in weak link games. There is a large rise in the proportion choosing low effort.

Source: Van Huyck et al. (1990).

of experiments by van Huyck, Battalio and Beil (1990). The dramatic rise in the proportion of subjects choosing low effort clearly demonstrates coordination failure. Nearly 80 percent of subjects are choosing low effort by round ten!

Such coordination failure is not good. With results like this I would not be betting on Emma's plane leaving on time. So, how can we make things better? Many suggestions have been tried out in the laboratory, with varying degrees of success. I shall look at a series of work done by Brandts and Cooper (see also Research Methods 6.6). First, however, it is useful to get a better idea why there is coordination failure.

Research Methods 6.6

Money versus real effort

A common interpretation of choice in the weak link game is a choice of effort. Experimental subjects, however, are usually asked how much money to give. Do we get different results if subjects are asked to put in effort rather than give money? This is a question about the external validity of weak link game experiments. Bortolotti, Devetag and Ortmann (2009) go some way to answering this question by getting subjects to do a real effort task. Subjects were asked to sort and count, within a given time interval, a bag of one, two, five and ten cent euro coins. Group payment was based on the worst performance in the group. They found that there was significant coordination failure in the first few rounds but increasing coordination over time. This suggests that real effort might be different to money, because of say social norms around working versus shirking. The effort task used was, however, still very particular and so concerns about external validity can never be completely removed. Also, significant coordination failure was still observed, just less than in standard experiments.

To do this we can use the models we looked at in sections 6.2 and 6.3. I will start by looking at initial choices. Costa Gomes, Crawford and Iriberri (2009) looked at how well things like level-k reasoning did at matching first round choices in the weak link game. Figure 6.17 gives the log likelihood of each model which is an estimate of goodness of fit. To give some interpretation to the numbers the first two bars show what numbers we would get with a perfect fit and assuming subjects choose randomly. The clear winner is to that subjects played the Pareto dominant equilibrium of high effort. How can that be? How can people be choosing the Pareto optimum of high effort yet we get coordination failure? The answer is that we need just one person to choose low effort to get coordinate failure. Most subjects do choose high effort but there is typically at least one subject who chooses low effort, as in Figure 6.15. This causes coordination failure.

Next we can look at how subjects learn with experience. Crawford (1995) showed a model of belief learning, similar to that discussed in section 6.3.2, can do a good job of explaining the change in behavior over time. In the model people update their beliefs about what the minimum effort will be over time. A person

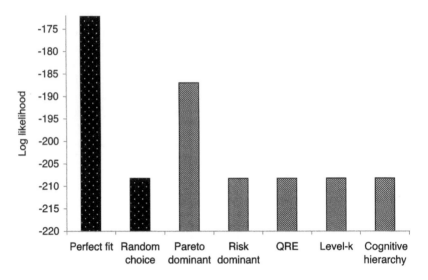

Figure 6.17 How well various models fit data from the weak link game. Perfect fit and random choice given us an upper and lower bound on how good fit could be.

Source: Costa-Gomes et al. (2009).

who expected others to choose high effort but observes low effort will lower her future estimate of expected effort. If less effort is expected from others then she puts in less effort herself. This means that the low effort of one person can drag down the effort of everyone in the group. That's also what we see in Figure 6.15.

The picture we get is one of coordination failure being caused by a small minority of people who choose low effort. Most do try high effort but the one or two people choosing low effort mean this is wasted. That suggests we might be able to overcome coordination failure if we can stop this minority of people choosing low effort.

To see if coordination failure could be overcome, Brandts and Cooper looked at a **turnaround game** in which we can think of a manager trying to get a group of workers to increase effort. In the first ten periods the group play the weak link game and effort typically falls to a low level. In period 11 the manager steps in and tries things to increase effort. For example, the manager can talk to the group and/ or increase the payoff incentives for high effort.

Let's look first look at what happens if the payoff incentives to high effort are changed. Figure 6.18 plots minimum effort from round ten onwards as the bonus from coordinating is increased from six to more than six. The first thing to observe is that effort is low in period ten and does not improve if the bonus remains at six. By contrast, if the bonus is increased, we observe a rise in effort. Interestingly the change in the bonus to eight increases effort more than a change to ten or

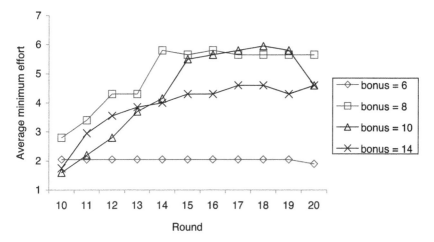

Figure 6.18 The minimum effort in the turnaround game. A change in the bonus to coordination allows groups to escape from low effort.

Source: Brandts and Cooper (2006).

fourteen. So, it is not the size of the incentive that seems to matter, but that incentives were changed.

The most plausible explanation for the increased effort is that the change in incentives provides a focal event around which members of the group can escape from low effort. One critical part of this story is that subjects observe the effort of all members of the group, called **full feedback**. If they only observe the minimum effort in the group, called **limited feedback**, then things do not work so well. This is apparent in Figure 6.19, where we can compare full feedback and limited feedback. With limited feedback the increase in effort is much less. The story we get, therefore, is one where the change in bonus is a focal event around which enough people increase effort to persuade others to increase effort. This time it is the subjects putting in high effort that drags up the effort of others.

Another possibility the manager could use is communication. With one-way communication the manager can talk to the group and try to encourage high effort. With two-way communication members of the group can talk to the manager, and perhaps suggest what might work well, and then the manager talks to the group. Figure 6.19 plots some results that allow us to see how well communication performs (see also Research Methods 6.7). Overall we see that one-way communication was not very successful but two-way communication was. This, however, masked the fact that saying the right thing did usually work. Saying the right thing meant asking for a specific effort level and stressing the benefits of coordination. This did usually lead to an increase in average effort, when coupled with an increase in the bonus.

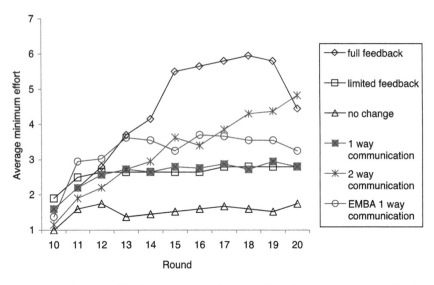

Figure 6.19 Average effort in the turnaround game. It is easier to overcome coordination failure with full feedback than limited feedback, and two-way communication than one-way communication.

Sources: Brandts and Cooper (2007), Cooper (2005).

Research Methods 6.7

Artefactual field experiments

An **artefactual field experiment** is performed in the lab but with subjects likely to have **task specific experience**. A study by Cooper (2005) provides an interesting example by comparing the performance in the turnaround game of undergraduate students to that of managers on an executive MBA program. People on the program had at least ten years' work experience, including five years as managers, and had average annual earnings over $120,000. The main findings of the study were that those on the MBA were very successful at turning things around and did so faster than students. They did so because they knew how to effectively communicate to people in the group better than students. These results offer reassurance that the turnaround game does capture things going on in the workplace.

It is possible, therefore, to get people to coordinate in a weak link game, but is not easy. It will be a similar story for the next type of game I want to look at.

6.6.2 Threshold public good games

The basic idea of a **threshold public good game** is that a good will be provided for the benefit of everyone if and only if people contribute enough to exceed some

threshold. For example, if a church roof needs replacing and doing so costs $100,000, then members of the church somehow need to raise the $100,000 threshold. Or if flatmates have to clean a flat to the standard their landlord requires, between them they need to put in time cleaning the flat to the threshold standard. In this game there is no trade-off between risk dominance and Pareto dominance. The best outcome is that they contribute enough to exceed the threshold. The problem now is a **conflict of interest** over how much each should contribute. For instance, one flatmate may do little to clean the flat, in the hope that another flatmate will do lots.

The main question is whether people can coordinate by contributing enough, despite the conflict of interest. Figure 6.20 gives the results of a typical experiment. In this experiment subjects were put in groups of five, and were given 55 tokens. To produce the public good they needed to contribute between them 125 tokens (see chapter one for more on this). We see that the group was not as good at coordinating as we might have hoped. In nine of the twenty-five rounds the total contribution was less than the threshold and things get worse as time goes on. This is primarily because subjects two, four and five give less and try to free ride on the contributions of the others.

Yet again we see that people are not great at coordinating. Yet again, we need to ask what might help people coordinate better. One thing that might matter is the institution in place to collect contributions. For example, if contributions fall short of the threshold then we might be able to give people a **refund** on their contribution. Sometimes this is not possible, for instance, flatmates cannot get back the time they have spent cleaning. But sometimes it is possible, for instance, the

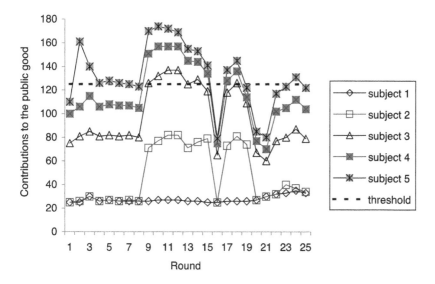

Figure 6.20 A typical threshold public good experiment.

Source: Alberti and Cartwright (2010).

church could give back donations if insufficient funds are raised. Another possibility is to give a **rebate** if contributions exceed the threshold.

Figure 6.21 gives for comparison the success rates of providing the public good observed in various experiments with various institutions. We want the success rate to be 100 percent, meaning that the public good is always provided. In the base case, where there is a refund, no rebate, and contributions are made simultaneously, the success rate is a disappointing 40 to 60 percent. Can we do any better?

The most dramatic drop in the success rate comes from removing the possibility of a refund. In this case the success rate drops to around 20 percent! So, refunds work. The consequences of a rebate seem to depend on the type of rebate. I have given data for two types of rebate in Figure 6.21. With a proportional rebate contributions above the threshold are given back in proportion to how much a person contributed. This does not seem to increase the success rate. What works better is a utilization rebate whereby excess contributions are used in some way to increase the value of the public good. An example of this type of rebate would be the church using any money it raises above the $100,000 to, say, paint the walls. Another thing that seems to work well is sequential choice. In this case people can see contributions as they happen. For example, the church might put a chart on the wall to see how close they are to the target.

I could go on talking about various other institutions that have been looked at, but I think that we have done enough to illustrate the main points. In both the weak link game and the threshold public good game we have seen that it can be a problem to coordinate. We need to understand why, and ask how to make things better. The benefits of doing so could be huge: Emma gets her plane on time, the church gets its new roof, the flat gets cleaned, and much more besides. When looking at the

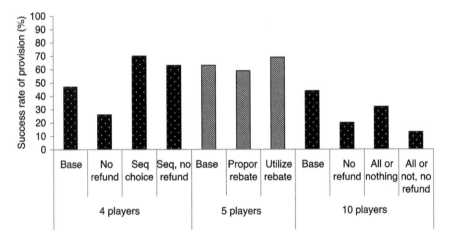

Figure 6.21 Success at providing a threshold public good depends on the institution.

Sources: Croson and Marks (2001), Marks and Croson (1998), Coats et al. (2009) and Cadsby and Maynes (1999).

weak link game I focused on how people within or connected to the group could possibly make things better. When looking at the threshold public good game I have focused on how the broader institution can possibly make things better. Together, therefore, we have a variety of ways that might help people coordinate.

The main lesson, however, seems to be that coordinating is not easy: the best we have seen are success rates of around 70 percent. Which is a depressing way to finish a chapter, but fortunately the next chapter is a bit more optimistic in showing that people can cooperate better than we might have expected.

6.7 Further reading

We have covered a lot of ground in this chapter so there are plenty of sources for further reading. The book by Colin Camerer (2003) is the most natural place to start. Additional material on equilibrium selection and equilibrium refinements can be found in any good game theory textbook, of which there are many. For more on focal points, coordination games, and strategic interaction more generally, the book by Schelling (1990) is definitely recommended. The further reading for chapter eleven contains references to more on auctions. One issue I have ignored is that: people rarely play the same game multiple times, and so more realistically have to learn from their own or others experiences of playing 'similar' games. This raises questions about what is similar, and so on. Case-based decision theory, see Gilboa and Schmeidler (1995), and analogy-based expectation equilibrium, see Jehiel (2005), are two potential ways to deal with this.

6.8 Review questions

6.1   When is the best time to sell an asset as a function of what other investors will do?

6.2   Suppose you are playing the p-beauty contest with a group of people who have only just been told about the game. Is what you have learnt in this chapter any help to you? What about in the simple beauty contest?

6.3   Does it make any difference if people can communicate with each other before playing a game?

6.4   Does risk dominance or Pareto dominance seem more relevant to you in predicting what people will do? What about forward or backward induction?

6.5   Look back at Table 6.8. I assumed an initial attractiveness of 30 for both strategies. What happens if the initial attractiveness of both is 10 or is 100? What has this got to do with initial beliefs?

6.6   Look back at Table 6.9. What would happen if $\rho = 0$ or $\rho = 1$?

6.7   I said that it does not always make sense to set the probability of choosing a strategy proportional to its attractiveness. Can you explain why?

6.8   How can we change the models of reinforcement learning and belief based learning to take account of loss aversion?

6.9   What do you think are the consequences of the law of small numbers and confirmatory bias for learning in games?

6.10 Given what we see in Figures 6.13 and 6.14, which auction format do you think will raise the most revenue?

6.11 Why do you think it matters if there is the possibility of a refund or rebate when contributing to a threshold public good?

6.12 How can leadership help people coordinate in the weak link game and threshold public good game? You might want to think about forward induction.

7　Social preferences

Charity collector: I want you to give me a pound and then I go away and give it to
the orphans.
Merchant banker: Yes.
Charity collector: Well that's it.
Merchant banker: No, no, no. I don't follow this at all. I mean, I don't want to seem
stupid but it looks to me as though I'm a pound down on the whole deal.

Monty Python's merchant banker sketch

You may recall from chapter one me saying that homo economicus is both rational
and selfish. Up until now we have primarily been questioning whether it makes
sense to assume people are as rational as homo economicus. Now it's time to look
at whether it makes sense to assume they are selfish. That people behave as if
selfish is one of the most basic assumptions in the standard economic model. The
evidence suggests, however, that most people do care about others. Why else
would millions of dollars be given to charity every year? Why else would someone
feel envious of a work colleague earning a higher salary than them? If the utility
of one person depends on the utility of another, then we say that there are **social**
or **interdependent preferences**. In this chapter our task is to review the evidence
for social preferences, look at how we can model them, and look at what consequences they can have.

7.1 The experimental evidence for social preferences

There have been literally thousands of experiments suggesting that people
do have social preferences in one shape or another. In this section I am going
to look at a selection of these experiments in order to illustrate the main things
we observe. At this point, I shall not try to explain why people behave as they
do (that comes in sections 7.2, 7.3 and 7.4), but you might want to be asking
yourself this question when you look at the evidence. To try and help you through
the maze of different games I will look at, Table 7.1 gives a basic description of
each game.

Table 7.1 A brief overview of the games I will look at

Game	Stage 1	Stage 2
Dictator game	proposer splits $10	–
Trust game	investor can invest up to $10	proposer can give back to the investor
Gift exchange game	employer pays the worker a wage.	worker chooses how hard to work
Ultimatum game	proposer splits $10	receiver accepts or rejects
Dictator game with third-party punishment.	proposer splits $10	third party can punish proposer
Linear public good game	contribute to a public project	
Linear public good game with punishment	contribute to a public project	can punish others after seeing contributions
Moonlighting game	proposer invests or takes from responder	responder gives or takes from proposer
Ultimatum game with responder competition	proposer splits $10	many receivers can try to accept
Ultimatum game with proposer competition	many proposers say how they would split $10	receiver can accept best offer

7.1.1 The nice side of social preferences

I shall begin with three games that show the nice side of social preferences. That is, they show people voluntarily giving money to others.

The dictator game is an obvious place to start. A **dictator game** involves two people, a proposer and receiver. The **proposer** is given a sum of money, say $10, and asked how much of that $10 he would like to give to the **receiver**. There the game ends! The receiver gets what she is given and the proposer keeps the rest. You may well have played this game yourself in a restaurant you will never visit again. In that case you play the role of proposer, deciding what tip to leave the waiter before you leave the restaurant. If the proposer only cares about his own payoff, then he should simply walk off with the $10 and give nothing to the receiver. What proposers actually do is quite different.

Figure 7.1 summarizes what happened in a series of comparable experiments by Forsythe et al. (1994), Hoffman et al. (1994) and Hoffman et al. (1996). Each treatment varied the way that the game was run (see Research Methods 7.1 for more info), but we can ignore that here. The size of the bubble in the figure indicates what proportion of proposers offered a particular share to the responder, so the larger the bubble, the more offered that amount.

By looking up from zero we can see that lots of proposers did give zero to the receiver; the proportion of subjects varies from around 20 percent in the standard experiments to 60 percent in the double blind experiments. Clearly, however, not everyone gives zero, and lots of proposers did give money to the receiver. The

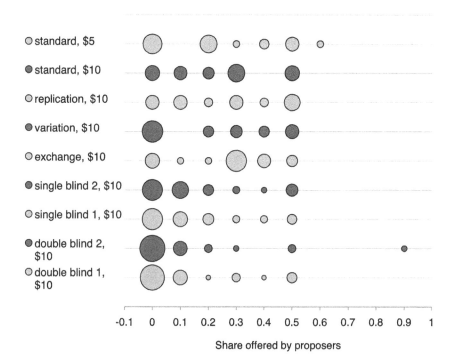

Figure 7.1 The amount that proposers gave in dictator experiments. The size of the bubble indicates the proportion of subjects offering each share. Many do give zero, but the majority give more than zero.

Sources: Forsythe et al. (1994), Hoffman et al. (1994), Hoffman et al. (1996), Camerer (2003).

amount they give varies, but there is always at least some willing to give away half of the money.

Research Methods 7.1

Single and double blind, anonymity versus reality?

The dictator game is a **one-shot** game, in that it is played just once and anonymously. So, in principle there is no point in a subject thinking about reputation or what others, including the researcher, might think about them. In reality, particularly when experiments are done on university campuses with students and faculty, do subjects really behave as if the game is one shot and anonymous? Or does it cross their mind that, 'if I take all the money the researcher will think that I am mean, and he will probably be marking my exam soon'?

In a series of experiments, Hoffman, McCabe, Schachat and Smith varied the **social distance** between subjects and researcher to try and answer such questions.

The results are summarised in Figure 7.1. I shall not explain all the nuances of the different treatments, but here are the basic differences.

In the standard and replication treatments the instructions contain **sharing language** such as 'has been provisionally allocated' $10 and the 'the amount to be divided'. In the variation treatment the sharing language is dropped. In the exchange treatment the game is framed as a seller (the proposer) setting a price which the buyer (receiver) must pay.

In the single blind two treatment, once they have written down their choice, the proposers put any money they will give to the receiver into a sealed envelope along with some blank pieces of paper (so that all envelopes have the same weight/size) and drop this envelope into a box. All proposers put their envelopes into the same box. Receivers randomly pick an envelope from the box. This guarantees anonymity between proposer and receiver and so is called **single blind**. In the single blind one treatment a proposer no longer has to write down their choice but does let the researcher look inside the envelope before it is sealed.

In the double blind two treatment proposers put envelopes into the box and leave. Only then does the researcher look inside the envelopes and record how much was left. This guarantees anonymity between proposer and researcher and so is called **double blind**. In the double blind one treatment the recording of offers is made by a randomly assigned student monitor (not the researcher) and two dummy envelopes containing no money are also put in the box. This means that a receiver who gets $0 cannot know whether there was a proposer who left $0 or they were just unlucky and got a dummy envelope. Anonymity between proposer and receiver and proposer and researcher is maximised.

The further we go down the line, the greater the social distance between the proposer and receiver and the proposer and researcher. This should make the proposers more readily believe the game is one shot and anonymous. Figure 7.1 suggests this is the case, given that we see less giving with more social distance. Note, however, that a significant proportion of proposers still give money, even in the double blind one treatment. Care is also needed in creating too much social distance because it could leave subjects doubting the experiment is real. For example, proposers might start doubting whether there really is a receiver waiting in another room to pick up the envelope!

The next game I want to look at is called the trust game. A **trust game** involves an investor and a proposer. Both investor and proposer are given $10. The **investor** is told that he can give as much of this $10 as he likes to the proposer. Any amount that he gives will be tripled in value before being given to the proposer. The proposer can then give as much money as she likes back to the investor.

As in the dictator game, a proposer who cares only about her own payoff should not give any money back to the investor. Investors, therefore, should not give money to proposers. This, however, results in inefficiency because it misses out on the tripling of money that is possible with investment. To illustrate, if the investor invests $0 then both investor and proposer get $10. If the investor invests all his $10 then the proposer would have $40 (the initial $10 plus the invested $30) and so could easily pay back the investor on his investment.

Figure 7.2 shows what subjects did in a study by Berg, Dickhaut and McCabe (1994). For now, let's ignore the distinction between 'no history' and 'with history'. The squares show the amount that different proposers returned to investors. As in the dictator game, we see that some proposers do keep all the money for themselves but many, the majority, give at least some money back. The circles tell us how much investors gave to responders. The majority of responders were willing to invest at least half their $10 with the proposer. This could be because the investors were happy to give money away to proposers. More realistically, however, it suggests that most investors were willing to trust that proposers would return the investment. An investor who gives to a responder expects the responder will give something back.

This brings into focus what is expected of others and whether others fulfill expectations. The distinction between 'no history' and 'with history' takes this further. In a 'no history' experiment subjects simply got the instructions and played the game. In the 'with history' experiment investors and proposers were told what happened in the earlier experiment (i.e. the 'no history' side). Things could have gone potentially two ways, investors could have been put off investing by seeing that some proposers kept all the money, or investors and proposers could have been influenced by the positive investing and returning. The later effect seemed to come through in the experiment with more money being returned.

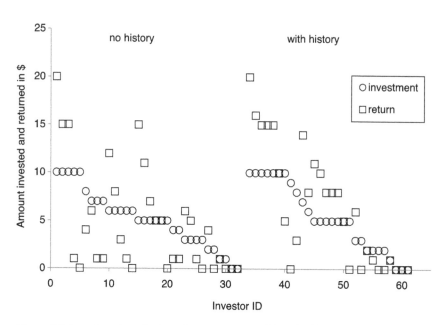

Figure 7.2 Investments and returns in a trust game with and without social history. Most investors do invest something. Many proposers do not give anything back but the majority do give something back.

Source: Berg, Dickhaut and McCabe (1994).

Proposers perhaps better understood that they were given money on the expectation they would give a 'fair' share back.

The third game I want to look at is a gift exchange game. A **gift exchange game** is a slight variant on a trust game. There are two people, often thought of as worker and employer. The employer is given an amount of money, say $10, and chooses how much of this to give to the worker, as a wage. Having observed her wage, the worker chooses how much effort to put into working. Higher effort costs the worker money, but also means the employer receives higher revenues.

Cost and revenue are usually designed in such a way that higher worker effort is mutually beneficial, i.e. the extra effort would earn enough extra revenue that the employer could offer a high enough wage to offset the worker's effort cost. A worker motivated solely by her own monetary payoff would not, however, put in effort, because it is too late to do anything about her wage and so all it would do is lower her payoff. Given this, why should an employer pay a high wage? He should not.

To see what happens in a typical experiment I will look at the results of a study by Gächter and Falk (2002). In this case employers could choose a wage between twenty and 120 and workers choose effort between 0.1 and one. Figure 7.3 plots wages and effort over ten rounds of play. In a one shot experiment workers and

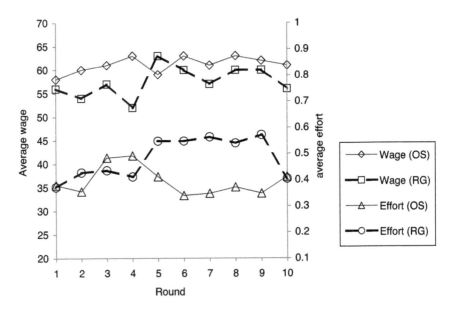

Figure 7.3 Wage and effort levels in a gift exchange experiment comparing one shot (OS) and repeated game (RG). The average wage and average effort are well above the minimum. Effort is higher in the repeated game, but falls in the last round consistent with imitation.

Source: Gächter and Falk (2002).

employers were randomly re-matched each round and so interaction was one shot. In a repeated game experiment the same workers and employers were matched in each round. As in the trust game we see that on average employers were willing to give workers wages above the minimum, and workers reciprocated by choosing effort above the minimum.

To delve a little deeper, in the one shot game, Gächter and Falk classified a worker as a **reciprocator** if there was a positive correlation between the wage they were offered and the effort they chose to make, and an **egoist** if they choose the minimum effort most of the time. They find that 20 percent of workers were egoists and 53 percent were reciprocators. The majority of workers, therefore, reciprocated a high wage by higher effort.

In the repeated game it becomes slightly harder to judge reciprocation, because a worker may want to build a reputation as someone who reciprocates a high wage. This way she can secure a high wage in the future. We could call such a worker an **imitator** because they imitate a reciprocator. How can we tell a reciprocator from an imitator? We look at the last round. In this round an imitator no longer has any need to reciprocate a high wage, so she should choose minimum effort. A genuine reciprocator would still reciprocate a high wage by high effort. Gächter and Falk found that 20 percent of workers were imitators, 21 percent were egoists and 48 percent were reciprocators. What we learn new, therefore, is that some people realize that it may be in their interests to look like someone who gives or reciprocates.

To summarize what we have seen so far: many people are willing to give to others at a cost to themselves, expect others will reciprocate giving, and/or realize it may be in their interests to look like someone who gives. But, don't overlook the fact that many do not give at all.

7.1.2 The nasty side of social preferences

Now it is time to look at a more nasty side of social preferences, people taking money from others.

I will start by looking at the ultimatum game. The **ultimatum game** is a twist on the dictator game. As in the dictator game, a proposer is given a sum of money, say $10, and asked how much of that $10 he would like to give to the receiver. The twist is that the receiver must decide to either accept the offer, in which case the receiver gets what she is given and the proposer keeps the rest, or rejects the offer, in which case both get zero.

If a receiver only cares about her own payoff she should accept any positive offer, because if she rejects the offer she gets zero. To illustrate what typically does happen, Figure 7.4 gives the proportion of subjects who would have rejected offers in experiments by Larrick and Blount (1997). (See Research Methods 7.2 for more on why I chose this study.) Clearly, a large proportion of people were willing to reject offers less than a 50–50 split. The evidence, therefore, is that some people are willing to sacrifice their own monetary payoff to decrease that of others.

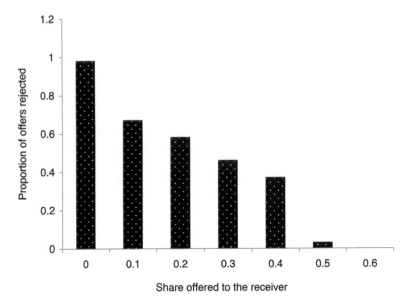

Figure 7.4 The proportion of offers rejected in an ultimatum game. Offers of a 0.5 share or better are rarely rejected, but offers of a less than 0.5 share are often rejected.

Source: Larrick and Blount (1997).

Research Methods 7.2

Finding out what you actually want to know, the strategy method

In the ultimatum game what we are particularly interested in is whether receivers reject or not. This, however, presents a problem: if all of the proposers propose a 50–50 split then we can never know whether or not the receivers would have rejected a low offer. One way around this is the **strategy method,** where responders are asked what they would do in any possible contingency. So, receivers have to say what they would do if they got offered $0, $1, $2, and so on. Only after this do they learn how much they have actually been offered. This way we can learn if a low offer would be rejected by the receiver.

Despite this big advantage, the strategy method is rarely used. I took the results for Figure 7.3 from one study that did use this method. More typical is the **game method,** in which receivers get to see the actual offer made by proposers before deciding what to do.

In principle, the strategy method and game method frame the problem in two different ways so we might expect different behaviour. It could also be argued that the more typical framing in real life is the game method. We get to see, for example, the waiter's service before we decide the tip. The evidence, however, suggests that there is relatively little difference in conclusion depending what method is used. It is also not uncommon to see framing in real life similar to the strategy method. For example, a wage contract might specify what will happen for a variety of different possible effort levels. I am, therefore, at a loss to explain why the strategy method is used so rarely!

The main lesson to be learnt from the ultimatum game is the rejection of positive offers. For completeness, however, we should have a look at what proposers offer. This, though, will not take long because the evidence is relatively easy to summarize, most proposers offer a 50–50 split. Figure 7.5 illustrates some representative experiments. In chapter nine we shall have more to say about the ultimatum game giving across different cultures.

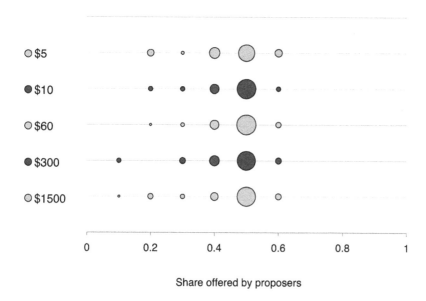

Figure 7.5 The share that proposers gave in ultimatum experiments where the amount of money given to the proposer ranged from $5 to the equivalent of $1,500.

Sources: Forsythe et al. (1994), Slonim and Roth (1998).

Another variant on the dictator game is the **dictator game with third-party punishment**. In this game, two people play the dictator game while being observed by a third person. This third person has no monetary interest in the game, but having observed the game has the option to reduce the payoff of the proposer. Specifically, for every $1 the third person gives up, she can lower the payoff of the proposer by $3. If she only cares about her own payoff there is no reason for the third person to punish. But, many do.

Research Methods 7.3

Does stake size matter?

A guiding rule of economic experiments is that subjects should be paid according to their decisions. Otherwise we cannot be sure that subjects take decisions seriously. But, how much do subjects need to be paid to take things seriously? The evidence seems to be that subjects do need to be paid something, but paying them more does not necessarily make much difference.

To illustrate, Figure 7.5 shows the results from experiments by Slonim and Roth (1998) in Slovakia in which the money at stake was varied between $60 and $1,500. These can be compared with standard experiments of Forsythe et al. (1998) using a stake of $5 and $10. It is clear that stake size had no effect in these experiments for the amount proposers gave. There was evidence that it had an effect on receivers, with them being less likely to reject the higher the stake. The effect, however, was arguably still not large, with the rejection rate falling from 17.1 percent to 12.1 percent to 8.8 percent as the stake size went from $60 to $300 to $1,500.

Figure 7.6 illustrates what happened in a study by Fehr and Fischbacher (2004). Focus first on the dark shaded columns. These show the amount that proposers were punished as a function of the share offered. We see that low offers are

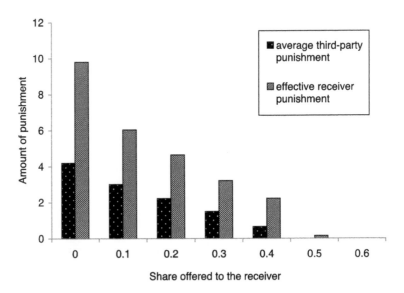

Figure 7.6 Punishment in a dictator game with third-party punishment compared to in the ultimatum game. Third-party observers punish low giving, but not as much as responders do.

Source: Fehr and Fischbacher (2004), Larrick and Blount (1997).

punished by the third-party observer. In fact, roughly 60 percent of observers were willing to punish low offers, and the lower the offer, the more they punished. Many people, therefore, were willing to sacrifice their own payoff to lower that of someone they observe giving too little to someone else. This is a step up from the ultimatum game where people punished people giving little to them. For comparison, the lighter-shaded columns in Figure 7.6 show the effective punishment in the ultimatum game as seen in Figure 7.4. Third-party observers punish less than responders, but still a relatively large amount.

7.1.3 Reciprocity

Having seen something of the nice and nasty sides of social preferences, I am now going to consider two games in which both sides seem to combine: people voluntarily giving money to some and taking from others.

In a **linear public good game** there is a group of n people, typically four, who are each given some money, say $20, and asked how much of this $20 they wish to contribute to a group project. Any money contributed to the group project is multiplied by some multiplier M and shared equally amongst the people in the group. The key to the game is that $1 < M < n$ and so it is good for the group that a person contributes, but not in the material interests of the person to contribute.

For example, if $M = 1.6$ and someone like Anna contributes $1, then each person in the group gets $1.6/4 = $0.4 and the overall return is $1.6. This is clearly better than the $1 contributed. So, the best for the group, or **Pareto efficient** outcome, is that every person contributes everything they have. For each $1 Anna contributes, however, she only gets back $0.4 and so it is not in her material interests to contribute. A person only interested in her own material payoff would, therefore, not contribute to the public project and the **Nash equilibrium** is for no one to contribute anything. Table 7.2 illustrates this trade off.

As a slight aside: In general, we say that there is a **social dilemma** whenever there is a difference between the Pareto efficient outcome, that captures what is

Table 7.2 Some possible payoffs in a four person linear public good game with endowment $20 and multiplier $M = 1.6$. The group payoff is maximized if all people contribute $20. Person 1's payoff is highest if she free-rides by contributing $0 while all others contribute $20

Scenario	Contributions	Payoff of person				Total payoffs
		1	*2*	*3*	*4*	
A	$20, $20, $20, $20	$32	$32	$32	$32	$128
B	$0, $0, $0, $0	$10	$10	$10	$10	$40
C	$0, $20, $20, $20	$44	$24	$24	$24	$116
D	$10, $10, $10, $10	$26	$26	$26	$26	$104
E	$0, $10, $10, $20	$36	$26	$26	$16	$104

best for the group, and the Nash equilibrium, that captures individual incentives. A linear public good game, trust game and gift exchange game are social dilemmas.

Figure 7.7 shows what happened in a study by Fehr and Gächter (2000a). For now, focus on the left hand side of the figure, i.e. the first ten rounds. In a partner treatment the same four people played the game ten times. In a stranger treatment each person is matched with three randomly chosen people each round. In both experiments we see that subjects do contribute in the first round but contributions fall over time. Given what we saw in the dictator game it comes as no surprise that in the first period some subjects contribute zero and some contribute a positive amount. What is new here is the dynamic effect of falling contributions over time. This suggests that giving to others is not done unconditionally. In particular, a subject who contributes, but sees that others did not, has a tendency to lower his or her subsequent contributions. Maybe they do not want to give to the **free-riders** who contribute zero.

Next consider a variant of the game called the **linear public good game with punishment**. The linear public good game is played, as explained above, but then a second stage occurs. In this second stage each person can pay an amount t to punish another person by lowering that person's monetary payoff by \$1. For example if $t = \$0.33$ then by paying \$1 Anna could lower the payoff of three other people by \$1 each or lower the payoff of one person by \$3. Given that punishment is costly and cannot possibly change the contributions which have already been made, no person, who maximizes their own material payoff, should ever punish. Punishment does not, therefore, change the Nash equilibrium or the fact there is a social dilemma.

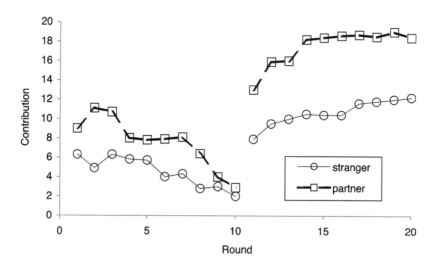

Figure 7.7 Contributions in linear public good games with and without punishment and with stranger and partner matching. Contributions fall over time without punishment and rise with punishment.

Source: Fehr and Gächter (2000a).

Punishment does, however, change what people typically do, as we can see on the right-hand side of Figure 7.7. With punishment there are high and increasing investments over time. Punishment makes a difference because subjects punish those who do not contribute. Figure 7.8 illustrates by plotting the amount of punishment received by a subject depending on how less or more they contributed relative to the average contribution of others in the group. We clearly see that those who contribute less are punished more. This is incentive enough for those who might want to free-ride to contribute.

In the linear public good game with punishment we see people willing to give money to others by contributing, but also taking money from some by punishing. Giving and taking is thus conditional on others' behavior. A game that makes this more explicit is the moonlighting game.

The **moonlighting game** combines various elements of the games considered so far. There are two people, a proposer and responder. Both are given, say, twelve tokens. As in a trust game, the proposer can give up to six tokens to the responder and any tokens given will be tripled in value. The proposer can, however, also take up to six tokens from the responder. Having seen what the proposer has done, the responder can reward the proposer by giving her some of her own tokens. Or, she can punish the proposer by paying to reduce the tokens of the proposer. This game is the most flexible that we have considered so far in that it allows, giving, taking, punishing and rewarding.

The main lesson that we can learn from this experiment is summarized in Figure 7.9 with results from a study by Falk et al. (2008). Of most interest to us,

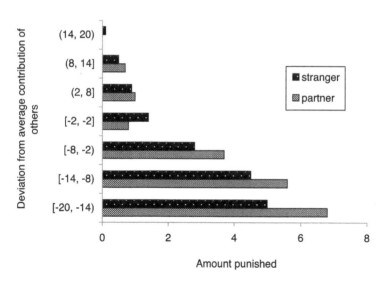

Figure 7.8 The amount of punishment depends on how much the subject contributed relative to the average contribution in the group. Those contributing less than the average are punished more.

Source: Fehr and Gächter (2000a).

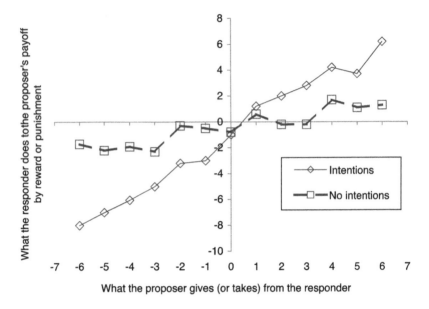

Figure 7.9 Responders' impact on proposers in the moonlighting game. If the proposer gives to the responder, the responder rewards the proposer. If the proposer takes from the responder, the responder punishes the proposer. If the computer randomly decides, the responder neither rewards nor punishes the proposer.

Source: Falk et al. (2008).

at this stage, is the intention treatment. Here, as in the trust game, we see that if a proposer gives money then the responder reciprocates by also giving. As in the ultimatum and public good games, we see that if a proposer offers a low share (takes money), then the responder reciprocates by punishment. In a no-intentions experiment the choice of the proposer is made randomly by a computer, and we see much less evidence of reciprocation. We will come back to this in section 7.3.

7.1.4 Fairness and competition

I want to finish with some experiments showing that in the face of competition, giving can change. To do so, I will revisit the ultimatum game. In an **ultimatum game with responder competition** there is one proposer and many receivers. Once a proposer has made an offer each receiver says whether she would accept the offer. One of those who said she would accept the offer is randomly chosen to actually get the offer. In an **ultimatum game with proposer competition** there are many proposers and one receiver. All proposers make an offer and the receiver can accept or reject the best offer made.

Competition would suggest that offers should be higher with proposer competition and lower with responder competition. Figure 7.10 shows that this was the

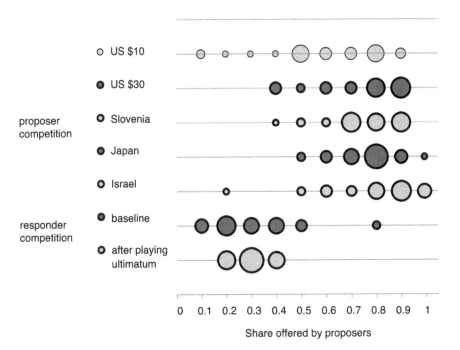

Figure 7.10 The share proposers offer in ultimatum games with competition. Roth et al. find the effects of proposer competition is the same across four countries and Grosskopf finds that responder competition lowers offers even if subjects had played the standard ultimatum game beforehand.

Sources: Roth et al. (1991) and Grosskopf (2003).

case in experiments run by Roth et al. (1991) and Grosskopf (2003). This figure can be compared with Figure 7.5 to see that competition makes a real difference. Interestingly, however, competition does not eradicate giving. For example, with responder competition, offers are less than in the ultimatum game but still well above zero. It would seem, therefore, that proposers still wanted to give something but did give less than in the ultimatum game.

7.1.5 The terminology of reciprocity

I have talked through a lot of different games and results so it seems apt to summarize what we have seen. In doing so, I will introduce some useful terminology. We saw:

- Many people are willing to sacrifice their own monetary payoff to increase that of others (dictator game, trust game, public good game).

- Many people reciprocate the kind action of another to them by kindness of their own (trust game, gift exchange game, moonlighting game). This is **positive reciprocity**.
- Many people reciprocate the unkind action of another to them with punishment (linear public good game, moonlighting game). This is **negative reciprocity**.
- Many people show both positive and negative reciprocity (moonlighting game, linear public good game). This is **strong reciprocity**.
- Many people reciprocate the kind or unkind action of another to someone other than them (dictator game with third-party punishment). This is **indirect reciprocity**.
- There is considerable **heterogeneity** in desires for giving and reciprocity (all experiments) with many giving zero if they have the chance.

The clear picture we get is one of reciprocity, not of altruism or unconditional giving. An important question is whether such behavior is consistent with utility maximization. We know that it is inconsistent with utility maximization if a person cares only about her own payoff. But this does not mean it is inconsistent with utility maximization. Andreoni and Miller (2002) had subjects play a series of modified dictator games and asked whether choices were consistent with utility maximization (see review question 7.3 for more details). They were for all bar three of the 176 subjects.

This is important because it shows that interdependent preferences, reciprocity and the like need not be inconsistent with the standard economic story of utility maximization. Our task now, therefore, is to find a utility function that can capture the type of behavior described above. In doing this, it is useful to distinguish material payoff from utility. You should think of **material payoff** as the utility from money or goods that go directly to the person; so far in the book that is what we have focused on. What we want to allow now is that utility depends on some social component as well as material payoff, giving us social preferences.

7.2 Inequality aversion

Reference dependence was a recurring theme in chapters two, three and four. We saw that the perceptions of an outcome are often determined by whether it was above or below some reference level. We also saw that the reference level can be determined by a multitude of factors such as past experience, an expectation of what would happen, and so on. A very natural reference point, which we only briefly touched upon in section 2.5.1, is what others are getting. For instance, if Alan observes his co-workers getting paid $30 an hour then he might expect to get paid $30 an hour. Similarly, if Anna knows her friend bought a box of Nutty cereal for $4 then she might also expect to pay $4.

If the reference point is what we observe happening to others then doing better than others is a gain while doing worse than others is a loss. Making the argument that people are averse to getting less than others seems easy enough. Making the argument that people positively gain from getting more than others, particularly given the evidence we have seen in section 7.1, is slightly harder to make. We are going to look, therefore, at something called inequality aversion. If a person is **inequality averse** then she gets disutility from earning less than others and, possibly, gets disutility from earning more than others. This means she may be willing to sacrifice some of her material payoff to obtain a more equitable outcome with others.

What are the consequences of inequality aversion? We shall see that inequality aversion can do a good job of explaining the experimental data summarized in section 7.1. For example, if Alan is averse to earning more than others, then he would be willing to propose a positive amount in a dictator or ultimatum game. Similarly, if Anna is averse to earning less than others she would be willing to reject a low offer in the ultimatum game and punish a free-rider in a public good game. To formalize this we need a good model of inequality aversion.

I am going to look at two models. The principal way in which they differ is what information they assume a person has. The first model I will look at is applicable to situations with **incomplete information**, where a person does not know the actions of others. The second model can only be applied in situations with **complete information**, where a person does know the actions of all others. To explain this distinction we can look back at Table 7.2 and contrast scenarios D and E. In a game of incomplete information person two only gets to know her payoff is $26. She can infer that total contributions to the public good must have been 40 and so the average payoff is $26, but she cannot know whether person one was a free-rider or not. In a game of complete information she gets to know individual contributions and so can tell whether person one contributed $10 or $0.

Some settings may naturally be ones of incomplete information and some of complete information. Intuitively this is going to make a difference because person two might think differently about scenarios D and E. That means we need a model for both possibilities.

7.2.1 Inequality aversion with incomplete information

The **Equity, Reciprocity and Competition** (ERC) model was proposed by Bolton and Ockenfels (2000) and is a natural way to capture inequality aversion in settings with incomplete information. I shall explain here a simple, special case of the more general model they propose.

Imagine a group of n people who have played a game and earned material payoffs of $u_1, u_2, \ldots, u_n$. I will focus on one of the people, called Miguel. In calculating the utility of Miguel the first thing we do is work out his **relative share** of the total payoff using equation

$$s_M = \frac{u_M}{\Sigma_j u_j}.$$

The utility of Miguel is then assumed to be:

$$U_M(u_1, ..., u_n) = u_M - \theta_M \left(s_M - \frac{1}{n} \right)^2,$$

where θ_M measures the strength of his inequality aversion.

If Miguel does not care about inequality aversion then $\theta_M = 0$ and his utility is simply his material payoff u_M. If he does care about inequality aversion then he cares about how close his payoff is to the **social reference point** of an equal share. He dislikes earning more or less than the average material payoff of others. The squared term means that the further he is away from the social reference point then the more he dislikes earning more or less than the average. So, he does not mind being too much away from the average but dislikes a lot being a long way from the average.

To better illustrate the model we can work through the experimental games of section 7.1 and show that the model does a good job of fitting what we observe. To simplify matters a little I will equate material payoff with money received, but you need to think whether this is a reasonable thing to do or not.

We can start with the **dictator game**. If the proposer, Miguel, splits the $10 so that he keeps p then his material payoff is p and his utility is:

$$U_M = p - \theta_M \left(\frac{p}{10} - \frac{1}{2} \right)^2.$$

The social reference point in this case is $5 and inequality aversion means he gets disutility from keeping more or less than $5. To be a bit more specific we can maximize utility with respect to p and get equation

$$1 = \frac{2\theta_M}{10} \left(\frac{p}{10} - \frac{1}{2} \right)$$

which can be rearranged to:

$$p = min \left\{ 5 + \frac{50}{\theta_M}, 10 \right\}.$$

He will, therefore, keep at least $5 and if $\theta_M \leq 10$ will keep $10. If $\theta_M > 10$ then he will give some money to the receiver so as to not be earning relatively too much. For example, if $\theta_M = 25$ then he will keep $7 and give $3 to the receiver, consistent with what we see in Figure 7.1.

Extending this to the **ultimatum game** is relatively simple because the proposers have the same utility function as in the dictator game. We only, therefore, need to think about what responders will do and all they can do is accept or reject. Suppose that Anna is the responder. If she accepts her utility will be:

$$U_A = 10 - p - \theta_A \left(\frac{10-p}{10} - \frac{1}{2} \right)^2$$

and if she rejects it will be $U_A = 0$. So, she will accept if:

$$10 - p \geq \theta_A \left(\frac{10-p}{10} - \frac{1}{2} \right)^2$$

which we can rearrange to:

$$\frac{100(10-p)}{(5-p)^2} \geq \theta_A.$$

If $\theta_A = 0$ she will accept any positive offer but the higher is θ_A the higher needs to be the offer before she will accept. For example, if $p = \$9.50$ and so she is offered $\$0.50$ then she will reject if $\theta_A > 2.5$. This is because the material gain of $\$0.50$ is not enough to compensate for the disutility of earning less than Miguel. If she is offered the social reference point of $\$5$ then she will accept for sure.

I will finish looking at the ERC model with the **linear public good game**. Consider first the case without punishment. Going through the equations is a bit tedious. We can, however, argue quite easily that the unique equilibrium will be one where no person contributes. To see why suppose that all people are contributing the same amount, say, c^*. What would happen if someone like Miguel contributes a tiny amount less than c^*? He gains in monetary payoff, because he has lowered his contribution, but he is now earning more than the average payoff, because he is contributing less than others. Recall, however, there is hardly any utility loss from earning a little bit more than the average. So, provided he only contributes a little bit less than others his utility will increase by contributing less.

You can see this in Table 7.3 by comparing scenarios A and F. If Miguel lowers his contribution to $\$19$ he gains $\$0.60$ in material payoff and loses $0.75^2 \theta_M = 0.56 \theta_M$ because of inequality aversion. This is a good deal if $\theta_M \leq 1$. I will leave it to you to work out how high θ_M can be for him to gain from lowering his contribution by $\$0.50$ or $\$0.01$. You should find that he will gain from lowering his contribution a bit. If everyone thinks like this then contributions will drift downwards, either hypothetically or for real, until no one is contributing.

What if we add punishment? Punishment does require complete information about the distribution of payoffs and so we can no longer assume incomplete information. But, let's ignore that and apply the model anyway. Doing so, we find that it can be in everyone's interests to contribute $\$20$ provided two (or more) people are willing to punish. In explaining why I will keep things simple by assuming it costs $t = 0.1$ to punish, and we only want to deter people contributing $\$19$ rather than $\$20$. Suppose that Anna threatens to lower the payoff of anyone who contributes $\$19$ by amount $\$2$. This would cost her $\$0.20$. Also, suppose that Alan threatens to lower the payoff of Anna by $\$2$ if she contributes $\$19$. Will this work?

It will, as illustrated in Table 7.3. We first need to check that the threat of punishment would deter Miguel from lowering his contribution to $19. Comparing scenarios A and G we see that if Miguel contributes $19 and is punished then he loses both in material payoff and relative terms. This is enough to deter him from contributing $19. We next need to check that Anna would be willing to punish. This is slightly trickier but comparing scenarios F and G we see that by punishing, she loses in material terms and gains in relative terms. Provided the utility gain from being closer to the social reference point exceeds the $0.20 cost of punishing then she will want to punish.

If, therefore, there are some people like Anna and Alan who are relatively inequality averse, high contributions can be sustained by the threat of punishment. More generally, we have seen that the ERC model can do a good job of explaining a lot of the evidence we saw in sections 7.1, even in situations of complete information. Before long, however, we shall see that when people do have complete information their utility will likely depend on individual actions in a way the ERC model cannot capture so well. What I want to do now, therefore, is introduce a model better suited to situations of complete information.

7.2.2 Inequality aversion with complete information

Fehr and Schmidt (1999) developed a model of inequality aversion that works when there is complete information. For want of a better name it is usually called the **Fehr-Schmidt model**. As before, imagine a group of n people who have played a game and earned material payoffs of $u_1, u_2, \ldots u_n$. To work out the utility of Miguel we first distinguish between people who earned a higher and lower

Table 7.3 The ERC model and linear public good game. If he will not be punished Miguel gains by contributing $19 (scenario F) rather than $20 (scenario A). If he will be punished (scenario G) he does best to contribute $20. Anna does better to punish Miguel for contributing $19 (scenario G) if she sufficiently dislikes earning less than the social reference point.

Scenario		Person				Reference point
		Anna	*Alan*	*3*	*Miguel*	
A	Contributions	20	20	20	20	
	Material payoff	32	32	32	32	
	Relative to reference point	0	0	0	0	32.00
F	Contributions	20	20	20	19	
	Material payoff	31.6	31.6	31.6	32.6	
	Relative to reference point	−0.25	−0.25	−0.25	+0.75	31.85
G	Contributions	20	20	20	19	
	Material payoff	31.4	31.6	31.6	30.6	
	Relative to reference point	+0.1	+0.3	+0.3	−0.9	31.3

material payoff than him. So, let $H_M = \{j: u_j > u_M\}$ be the set of people who earned more than him and $L_M = \{j: u_j < u_M\}$ be the set of people who earned less. The utility of Miguel is then calculated using:

$$U_M(u_1, \ldots, u_n) = u_M - \alpha_M \frac{1}{n-1} \sum_{j \in H_M} (u_j - u_M) - \beta_M \frac{1}{n-1} \sum_{j \in L_M} (u_M - u_j),$$

where $\beta_M \leq \alpha_M$ are measures of Miguel's inequality aversion.

To explain how this works, let's concentrate first on the α_M bit. This captures Miguel's disutility from earning less than others. For every person who has a higher material payoff than him he suffers a utility loss proportional to the difference in payoff. The higher is α_M the more he dislikes earning less than others. The β_M bit captures his disutility from earning more than others. Again, for every person who has a lower material payoff than him he suffers a utility loss proportional to the difference in payoff. The assumption that $\beta_M \leq \alpha_M$ means that he gets more disutility from earning less than others then he does from earning more than others, which, hopefully, seems intuitive.

To better illustrate the model we can work through the same examples as for the ERC model, starting with the **dictator game**. If Miguel splits the $10 so that he keeps p and the receiver gets $10 - p$ then his utility will be $p - \alpha_M(10 - 2p)$ if $p < \$5$ and $p - \beta_M(2p - 10)$ if $\geq \$5$. Given that $\beta_M \leq \alpha_M$, there is never any incentive for him to give more than $5, so he should maximize $p - \beta_M(2p - 10)$ with respect to p. Consequently, he should give $0 if $\beta_M < 0.5$ and give $5 if $\beta_M \geq 0.5$. This is not exactly what we observe in Figure 7.1, but we do at least see a possible incentive for the proposer to share something.

In the **ultimatum game** proposers again have the same utility function as in the dictator game so we just need to think what receivers will do. Assuming that proposers will at best offer an equal share, i.e. $p \geq \$5$, the utility function of the receiver, Anna, will depend on whether she accepts or rejects. If she accepts she gets $10 - p - \alpha_A(2p - 10)$ and if she rejects gets zero. Thus, Anna will accept if:

$$p < 10 \left(\frac{1 + \alpha_A}{1 + 2\alpha_A} \right).$$

This means that if Anna does not mind earning less than Miguel, $\alpha_A = 0$, she will accept any offer, but if she is more inequality averse, α_A increases, she will only accept offers closer to an equal share. For example, if $\alpha_A = 1$ she will reject anything less than a one-third share.

This possibility of rejection may make the proposer think a little. We know from looking at the dictator game that if $\beta_M \geq 0.5$ Miguel will offer an equal share and this will be accepted. It is slightly trickier to say what he should do if $\beta_M < 0.5$. He would want to offer the minimum amount that will be accepted. The problem is, he is unlikely to know the inequality aversion of Anna and so will not know what this minimum is. Instead, he will have to form some expectation about what the responder will do and offer an appropriate share. He, therefore, faces a risky choice.

Suppose we now add competition. In the **ultimatum game with proposer competition** it is natural to assume that the receiver will accept the best proposal. This means that there will be inequality for sure, because the receiver and one proposer will get a positive material payoff while all other proposers get zero. Given this, the objective of a proposer should be to offer an amount that will be accepted. This way he will at least be earning more than others which is better than earning less than others. If all proposers are aiming to get their offer accepted then they should offer almost all of the money. This is consistent with what we saw in Figure 7.10. I leave you to think about what happens with responder competition.

Finally, we can look at the **linear public good game**. Depending on how inequality averse people are it may or not be an equilibrium to contribute to the public good. Table 7.4 will help illustrate why. Suppose that everyone is contributing \$20. Would Anna want to contribute less? Comparing scenarios A and H we see that for every \$1 she decreases her contribution she gains \$0.60 in material payoff, but increases the gap between her payoff and others by \$1. If she dislikes earning more than others, or more specifically $\beta_A > 0.6$, then she does best to contribute \$20. If she does not mind earning more than others, $\beta_A < 0.6$, then she

Table 7.4 The linear public good game and Fehr-Schmidt model from the perspective of Anna. Anna may not want to contribute less than others (scenarios A and H) but may want to lower her contribution if someone else contributes zero (scenarios I and J). She may also be willing to punish anyone who contributes zero (scenarios I and K)

Scenario		Person			
		Anna	*2*	*3*	*Miguel*
A	Contributions	20	20	20	20
	Material payoff	32	32	32	32
	Relative to others	–	0	0	0
H	Contributions	19	20	20	20
	Material payoff	32.6	31.6	31.6	31.6
	Relative to others	–	+1	+1	+1
I	Contributions	20	20	20	0
	Material payoff	24	24	24	44
	Relative to others	–	0	0	−20
J	Contributions	19	20	20	0
	Material payoff	24.6	23.6	23.6	43.6
	Relative to others	–	+1	+1	−19
K	Contributions	20	20	20	0
	Material payoff	21.5	24	24	19
	Relative to others	–	−2.5	−2.5	+2.5

would contribute $0. We could, therefore, see high or low contributions depending on preferences.

Most realistic, given the heterogeneity we observed in section 7.1, is that some people have a high β and some a low β. This raises the interesting question of how many people it needs to contribute $0 for all those with a high β to also contribute $0. In Table 7.4 we can compare scenarios I and J to see what happens if Anna contributes $20 or $19 and Miguel contributes $0. In this case, when Anna lowers her contribution $1 she gains $0.60 in material payoff, gains by lowering the gap between her and Miguel, but loses by increasing the gap with the other two. Overall she gains if $0.60 + 0.33\alpha_A > 0.67\beta_A$. This means that β_A needs to be at least 1.8 to stop Anna also contributing $0. It only takes, therefore, one person to contribute $0 for it to be likely the other three will too. This is consistent with the falling contributions we observe in Figure 7.7.

[Extra] For those that like a bit of algebra, models of social preferences are fun to play around with. In a linear public good game the task is made a bit easier by the fact that if Anna contributes c_A and Miguel contributes c_M then, irrespective of what else happens, the difference in their material payoffs is $u_A - u_M = c_M - c_A$, the difference in contributions. So, if there are n people each endowed with $20 and contributions are $c_1, c_2, \ldots, c_n$ the utility of Anna will be:

$$U_A = 20 - c_A + m \sum_j c_j - \alpha_A \frac{1}{n-1} \sum_{j \in H_A} (c_A - c_j) - \beta_A \frac{1}{n-1} \sum_{j \in L_A} (c_j - c_A).$$

Now suppose that K people are contributing $0, and the rest are contributing $20, what will Anna want to contribute? If she contributes $20 her utility is:

$$U_A = 20m(n - K) - \alpha_A \frac{20K}{n-1}.$$

If she contributes $0 her utility is:

$$U_A = 20 + 20m(n - 1 - K) - \beta_A \frac{20(n - 1 - k)}{n-1}.$$

So, she does better to contribute $0 if:

$$(1 - m)(n - 1) > \beta_A (n - 1 - K) - \alpha_A K$$

or the proportion of those contributing $0 is:

$$\frac{K}{n-1} > \frac{\beta_A + m - 1}{\alpha_A + \beta_A}.$$

This gives us a measure of how many people will need to not contribute for others to also not contribute.

As you might imagine, adding punishment only complicates the analysis. We shall, therefore, restrict ourselves to showing that it can be an equilibrium for all people to contribute when punishment is allowed. In fact, we shall show it is enough to have just one person willing to punish. Suppose that $\beta_A > 0.6$ and so we know Anna would contribute \$20 if everyone else does. Suppose also that Anna threatens to lower the payoff of anyone who contributes \$0 by \$25 and that this will cost her \$2.50, because $t = 0.1$. Will this work? This size of punishment will clearly deter any person from contributing \$0, but will Anna be willing to pay to punish this much. In Table 7.4 by comparing scenarios I and K we see what happens if she punishes Miguel for contributing \$0. She loses the \$2.50 in material payoff but is now only \$2.50 behind or ahead of the others rather than \$20 behind Miguel. She must be better off if $5\alpha_A - 5/6\beta_A > \$2.50$ and because $\alpha_A \geq \beta_A > 0.6$ we know that this must be the case. She is, therefore, willing to punish Miguel so as to narrow the gap in their material payoffs.

7.2.3 An evaluation of inequality aversion models

Both the ERC and Fehr-Schmidt model do a good job of fitting the experimental data summarized in section 7.1. In particular, they are able to account for cooperation in some contexts, such as a public good game with punishment, and a lack of cooperation in other contexts, such as a public good game without punishment. The models also have the virtue of being relatively simple and easy to apply. The news is not all good, however, because when pushed a bit further both the ERC and Fehr-Schmidt models do a bad job of fitting other data. The models do, therefore, have their limitations and that means we need to think of something other than inequality aversion. Before we do that I want to briefly show that in some situations there are different models of inequality aversion that can outperform the ERC and Fehr Schmidt models.

Engelmann and Strobel (2002) asked subjects to play a variety of **distribution games**. In different games, three of which are given in Table 7.5, person two was able to decide which of the distribution of payoffs A, B, or C should be used. Different models of inequality aversion give different predictions. In the taxation game, for example, the Fehr-Schmidt model predicts option A, while the ERC model predicts option C (but I will leave you to check this).

In the final row of Table 7.5 we have the choices actually made to compare with the predictions. It is clear that the ERC model does a relatively poor job at predicting the data. This would suggest that subjects did take account of the full distribution of payoffs. What seemed to matter most to subjects was maximizing the minimum payoff that any person would receive, which we can think of as a **maximin** notion of fairness. The Fehr Schmidt model can pick up this effect to some extent, because it predicts that a person will get disutility from earning more than others. The model also predicts, however, that a person would be more willing to lower the payoff of those earning more than increase the payoff of those

Table 7.5 Payoffs, predictions and choices in distribution games. Person two gets to choose which distribution of payoffs there should be, A, B, or C

Payoffs	Taxation game			Envy game			Rich game		
	A	B	C	A	B	C	A	B	C
Person 1	8.2	8.8	9.4	16	13	10	11	8	5
Person 2	5.6	5.6	5.6	7	8	9	12	12	12
Person 3	4.6	3.6	2.6	5	3	1	2	3	4
Predictions									
Efficiency	A			A			A		
ERC			C		B	C	A		
F-S	A					C	A		
Maximin	A			A					C
Choices									
Percentage	84	10	6	77	13	10	27	20	53

Source: Engelmann and Strobel (2002).

earning less, and this was not the case in these experiments, particularly the envy game.

In these distribution games an inequality aversion model based on maximin would do a good job of fitting the data. Maximin would, however, do a lousy job of fitting the data for an ultimatum game or public good game, with or without punishment. This illustrates how different strategic settings likely call for different models. That's why we also need look at some models that are not based on inequality aversion.

7.3 Intentions and social norms

In models of inequality aversion people are motivated solely to earn no more and no less than others. To illustrate why this sometimes appears to miss something I will return to the ultimatum game and look at an **ultimatum game with restricted choice**. When I first explained the ultimatum game I said the proposer could propose to split the $10 in any way that he chose. Offers of an $8, $2 split were often rejected, seemingly because of the unequal payoffs. Suppose now that we constrain the proposer to offer either an $8, $2 split or a $10, $0 split. The offer of an $8, $2 split does not look quite so unfair now. But will it still be rejected?

A study by Falk, Fehr and Fischbacher (2003) allows us to answer this. They considered four different games. In each game the proposer must choose between just two possible offers. As Table 7.6 summarizes, one of the offers is always an $8, $2 split. What we want to know his how the perception of an $8, $2 offer changes relative to the other offer a proposer could have made. If a responder cares only about inequality aversion then the other offer should make no difference because she still gets $2 and the proposer $8. We clearly see, however, that it does make a difference. Responders are more likely to reject an $8, $2 split if

Table 7.6 The proportion who offered and the proportion that would reject an $8, $2 split in ultimatum games with restricted choice

Game	Proposer's choices		Interpretation of an $8, $2 offer	Proportion of $8, $2 offers (%)	Proportion would reject an $8, $2 offer
	A	*B*			
(5/5)	$8, $2	$5, $5	unfair	31	44
(2/8)	$8, $2	$2, $8	relatively fair	73	27
(8/2)	$8, $2	$8, $2	no choice	100	18
(10/0)	$8, $2	$10, $0	fair	100	9

Source: Falk, Fehr and Fischbacher 2003.

the proposer could have proposed a $5, $5 split compared to if he could have proposed a $10, $0 split.

These results are not consistent with inequality aversion. Arguably, what is missing is that inequality aversion does not take into account the intentions of proposers. If Miguel offers $8, $2 when he could have offered $10, $0 then he is intending to be fair. If he offers $8, $2 when he could have offered $5, $5 he is intending to be unfair.

We have already seen something similar if you look back to Figure 7.9 and the moonlighting game. You may recall that in the no intentions experiment a computer randomly chose the proposer's offer and in this case responders did little to reward or punish proposers. Again, if a computer generates the offer then there is no intention on the part of proposers, and this seems to matter. We need, therefore, some way to build intentions into a model of fairness.

7.3.1 A model of fairness based on intentions

I shall work through a model of fairness that does take account of intentions. The model is based on the work of Rabin (1993) and Dufwenberg and Kirchsteiger (2004). Unfortunately, the model is not as easy as the inequality aversion models, but if you stick with it, all will hopefully become clear.

Consider Miguel and someone called Federica playing a game. The key thing we want to do is think about what Miguel believes Federica will do, and what Federica believes Miguel will do. **Beliefs** are going to give us a means to think about intentions. Here is why.

Suppose that if Miguel chooses action a_M and Federica chooses action a_F they get material payoffs $u_M(a_M, a_F)$ and $u_F(a_M, a_F)$ respectively. Now, if Miguel believes that Federica will choose action b_F then he should also believe that if he chooses action a_M they will get payoffs $u_M(a_M, b_F)$ and payoff $u_F(a_M, b_F)$. This suggests that we can think of Miguel as choosing payoffs for both of them from the set

$$U(b_F) = \{u_M(a_M, b_F), u_F(a_M, b_F)|a_M \in S_M\}$$

where S_M is the set of actions that he could choose.

Ignore from set $U(b_F)$ any payoff pairs that are not Pareto efficient and let $U_F^h(b_F)$ and $U_F^l(b_F)$ be the highest and lowest payoffs that Federica could get from set $U(b_F)$. We then call

$$U_F^e(b_F) = \frac{U_F^h(b_F) + U_F^l(b_F)}{2},$$

which is the payoff half-way between the highest and lowest, as the **equitable payoff**. We now come to the crux of the model, we say that Miguel's **kindness** to Federica if he chooses action a_M and believes that Federica will choose action b_F is:

$$k_{MF}(a_M, b_F) = u_F(a_M, b_F) - U_F^e(b_F).$$

So, Miguel is **kind** if he chooses an action that he believes will give Federica more than the equitable payoff. He is **unkind** if he chooses an action that he believes will give Federica less than the equitable payoff.

We next assume that Miguel wants to be kind to Federica if Federica is kind to him. The slight problem is that Miguel cannot know whether Federica is being kind to him, because he does not know Federica's beliefs. So, Miguel will need to form a belief about whether Federica is being kind. To do this, let c_M denote Miguel's belief about b_M. That is, Miguel believes that Federica believes that he will choose action c_M! Miguel's beliefs about how kind Federica is being to him are now:

$$\lambda_{MF}(c_M, b_F) = u_M(c_M, b_F) - U_M^e(c_M).$$

This expression, naturally extends kindness, to beliefs about kindness.

The utility function of Miguel can finally be written as:

$$U_M(a_M, b_F, c_M) = u_M(a_M, a_F) + \mu_M k_{MF}(a_M, b_F) \cdot \lambda_{MF}(c_M, b_F)$$

where μ_M is Miguel's desire to reciprocate. If Miguel does not care about fairness then $\mu_M = 0$ and his utility is his material payoff u_M. If he does care about fairness and believes that Federica is being kind, so, $\lambda_{MF}(c_M, b_F) > 0$, then he can increase his utility by also being kind, $k_{MF}(a_M, b_F) > 0$. If he believes that Federica is being unkind then he would also want to be unkind. A desire for reciprocity is, therefore, built into the utility function.

It is important that beliefs correspond to reality and so we say that there is a **fairness equilibrium** if $a_M = b_M = c_M$ and $a_F = b_F = c_F$.

This model may be a bit tricky to get one's head around but the basic idea is relatively simple. Miguel wants to be kind to Federica if Federica is kind to him, and vice versa. Where things get complicated is determining what is kind or not. This is why we needed to think about beliefs and beliefs about beliefs. To better understand what is going on I will work through the **ultimatum game**.

We can think of the proposer, Miguel, as proposing an amount $\$a_M$ to give while the receiver, Federica, simultaneously sets a minimum amount $\$a_F$ that she will accept. If $a_M \geq a_F$ then Federica accepts the offer. If Miguel believes that Federica will accept offers of b_F or more then he can offer $\$10 = U_F^h(b_F)$ or $\$b_F = U_F^l$ or anything in between and the outcome be Pareto efficient. The equitable payoff is, therefore:

$$U_F^e(b_F) = \frac{10 + b_F}{2}.$$

Miguel's kindness is:

$$k_{MF}(a_M, b_F) = a_M - \frac{10 + b_F}{2}.$$

This means that Miguel has to give quite a lot to be considered kind. For example, if $b_F = \$2$, then an offer of $6 or less is not kind!

If Federica believes Miguel will offer b_M she can either reject by setting $a_F > b_M$ or accept with $a_F \leq b_M$. Rejection can never, however, be Pareto efficient. This means that $\$10 - b_M = U_M^l(b_M) = U_M^h(b_M)$. If Federica accepts her kindness is zero, and if she rejects her kindness is $k_{FM} = -(10 - b_M)$. Federica can never be kind in this game!

Given that Federica cannot be kind, Miguel can never gain by being kind to Federica. Miguel does, however, still have to offer enough that Federica will not reject. If Federica accepts an offer of a_M her utility is a_M and if she rejects it is:

$$\mu_F k_{FM}(b_M, a_F) \cdot \lambda_{FM}(b_M, c_F) = -\mu_F(10 - b_M)\left(b_M - \frac{10 + c_F}{2}\right).$$

In equilibrium, therefore, where $b_M = c_F = a_M$ Federica will accept if $2a_M \geq \mu_F(10 - a_M)^2$. An offer of zero will, therefore, be rejected if $\mu_F > 0$, but a high enough offer will be accepted.

These results are similar to those obtained in the inequality aversion models. Can this model also capture the importance of intentions? The answer is a qualified yes. In the ultimatum game with qualified choice the model predicts that a responder may reject an $8, $2 split in the (5/5) and (2/8) game but should never reject an $8, $2 split in the (8/2) or (10/0) game. This is because the offered split is unkind in the first two games and kind or neutral in the last two games. So, the model does take account of intentions. It fails, however, to completely fit the data, because offers of an $8, $2 split were rejected some of the time in all the games.

7.3.2 *What is fair?*

The crux of the intentions-based model of fairness we have just been looking at is the equitable payoff, because kindness is judged by whether or not utility is above or below this equitable payoff. The equitable payoff can be thought of as an example of a **fair reference point** about which losses or gains are measured. A theme in chapters two, three and four was the potential arbitrariness of reference points; things are no different here. The equitable payoff is that payoff half-way between the highest and lowest possible (Pareto efficient) payoff, but why should the fair reference point be this and not something else?

The model is flexible to using any fair reference point, so we do not need to stick with the equitable payoff, but what reference point should we be using? We have looked at two candidates so far. In inequality aversion models, the fairness of a person's material payoff is judged relative to the payoff of others. So, the fair reference point is what others are earning, and the fairest outcome is one where everyone earns the same material payoff. In the intentions-based model we have just looked at, the fairness of a person's payoff is judged relative to the worst and best material payoff that she could have got. The fairest outcome is one where she gets at least half way between this worst and best.

In a symmetric game, like the ultimatum game with unconstrained choice, these two notions of a fair reference point will turn out the same. But in general they are not the same. For example, in the ultimatum game with constrained choice (10/0), a split of \$8, \$2 is unfair by the standards of inequality aversion because the proposer gets more than the receiver but is fair by the standards of the intentions based model because the receiver could have got less than she did.

The results that we have for the ultimatum game with constrained choice suggest that both notions of fair reference point are important. Is it possible to combine both elements in the same model? Falk and Fischbacher (2006) showed that it is if we use an intentions based model of fairness with a different definition of kindness.

In this revised model, the kindness of Miguel consists of two parts:

$$k_{MF}(a_M, b_F) = \Delta_{MF}(a_M, b_F) \bullet \vartheta_{MF}(a_M, b_F).$$

The first part, $\delta_{MF}(a_M, b_F)$, captures inequality aversion and is calculated as follows:

$$\delta_{MF}(a_M, b_F) = u_F(a_M, b_F) - u_M(a_M, b_F).$$

This means that Miguel is **kind** if he chooses an action that he expects to give Federica a higher material payoff than him. He is **unkind** if he chooses an action that he expects to give Federica a lower monetary payoff than him. The second part, $\vartheta_{MF}(a_M, b_F)$, of the kindness expression captures intentions and is called the **intention factor**. Letting $u_M = u_M(a_M, b_F)$ and $u_F = u_F(a_M, b_F)$, it is calculated using:

$$\vartheta_{MF}(a_M, b_F) = \begin{cases} 1 \text{ if } u_F > u_M \text{ and there exists } a \text{ such that } u_F(a, b_F) < u_M \\ \varepsilon \text{ if } u_F > u_M \text{ and there is no } a \text{ such that } u_F(a, b_F) < u_M \\ 1 \text{ if } u_F < u_M \text{ and there exists } a \text{ such that } u_F(a, b_F) > u_M \\ \varepsilon \text{ if } u_F < u_M \text{ and there is no } a \text{ such that } u_F(a, b_F) > u_M \end{cases}.$$

This might look complicated, but is not. The first two terms consider the case where Federica is earning a higher material payoff than Miguel. This appears kind, but we ask: did Miguel have any alternative but to be kind? If he did then the intention factor is one and Miguel is considered **intentionally kind**. If he did not then the intention factor is $\varepsilon < 1$ and so we consider Miguel **unintentionally kind**.

Similarly, the bottom two terms consider the case where Federica is earning less than Miguel. This looks unkind, but maybe Miguel had no choice? If he did the intention factor is one and if he did not the intention factor is $\varepsilon < 1$. For example, offering an $8, $2 split in the (10/0) game is considered **unintentional unkindness**, so is not as bad as offering an $8, $2 split in the (5/5) game which is **intentional unkindness**.

This model has both inequality aversion and intentions and can do a great job of fitting the data for the ultimatum game with and without constraints. It demonstrates, therefore, that intentions based models are flexible enough to consider any notion of what is fair or kind. That still leaves us asking, however, what we should consider kind. As with models of inequality aversion, the Falk and Fischbacher model proposes that fairness is primarily judged by comparing the relative material payoffs of people. Is there any situation where fairness should be judged relative to the best and worst payoff that a person could have got?

Yes. One issue we have not touched on yet is that of property rights. In all of the experiments we have discussed so far, subjects were randomly assigned roles in the game. In this case it seems natural that fairness should be judged by whether people earn the same material payoff. Now, suppose that people earn their material payoffs in some way and so have a stronger sense of ownership or **property rights** over their material payoff. Is it fair that a person who has earned more than another should give this away?

To start to answer that question we can look at a **dictator game with take and earnings**. Figure 7.11 provides some results from a study by List (2007). In the baseline treatment both proposer and receiver were given $5 (a show up fee) and the proposer was given an additional $5 he could split with the receiver. This corresponds to the standard ($5) game of Figure 7.1 (and the results are similar). In the 'take $1' and 'take $5' treatments the proposer could not only offer some of his or her $5 to the receiver but also take up to $1 or $5 from the receiver. In the earned $5 treatment the proposer and receiver 'earned' their money by completing a task including sorting and handling mailings for a charitable fund-raiser.

In the baseline treatment most proposers offer money, resulting in more equality between the proposer's and receiver's payoff. In the take $1 and take $5 experiments many fewer proposers give money. The fact that they can take money

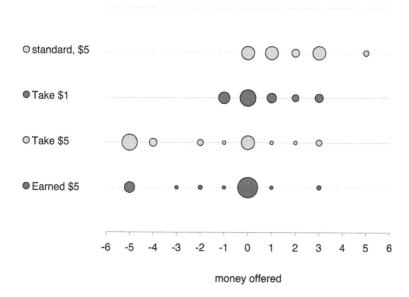

Figure 7.11 The amount shared by dictators in dictator games with take and earnings. Less is shared when there is the chance to take money, or money is earned.

Source: List (2007).

appears to excuse not giving money. This is consistent with an intentions based model of fairness (like that in section 7.3.1) where the kindness of a proposer is judged by the worst that he could have done to the receiver, and not one judged by how equal proposer and receiver payoffs are. In the earned $5 experiment we see that very few proposers take or offer money. Seemingly, money earned is money deserved.

What we learn from this study is that property rights and norms, or institutions, influence what people give and therefore presumably what is considered fair or kind. To take money is different to giving money. To have earned money is different to having been randomly given money. Other studies have similarly shown that perceptions of what is fair or kind will depend on how the problem is framed and the social norms that this brings to mind. Sometimes it is natural to judge kindness by equality of monetary payoffs. In others it is natural to judge kindness by whether a person could have done worse or better for another. There is, therefore, no set prescription for what the reference point should be. This though should come as no surprise given what we have seen in previous chapters.

7.4 Summary

We started by looking at a series of games and experimental studies that suggest people have social or interdependent preferences. The evidence suggested that many people are reciprocators in that they want to be kind to those who are kind and unkind to those who are unkind.

In our first attempt to formally model such reciprocation we looked at two models of inequality aversion. The basic idea behind both models is that a person dislikes earning less than others, and possibly dislikes earning more than others. The difference between the models we looked is the information a person is assumed to have. In the ERC model a person compares her payoff to the average payoff of others. In the Fehr-Scmidt model a person compares her payoff to the individual payoffs of others.

A great advantage of the ERC and Fehr-Schmidt models are that they are simple and easy to apply. We saw, however, that they only capture part of the story of social preferences. To try and fill the gap we considered models that take account of intentions. This meant we needed to think about what is a fair reference point, what is kind or unkind, and how we can model beliefs about kindness. We saw that the answer would depend on the context.

With intentions-based models we can account for much more of the behavior we observe, but that is primarily because the models are far more flexible. One symptom of this, which I did not mention, is that we can very easily end up with ambiguous outcomes: an equilibrium where everyone is unkind because everyone is being unkind, and an equilibrium where everyone is kind because everyone is being kind. Which of these is more plausible?

Intentions based models do, therefore, require us to answer some difficult questions, and the answers will likely depend on all sorts of context and framing effects. This means there never will be a perfect model of social preferences that we can just apply without much thought. What we do have, however, is a range of models and ways of thinking about social preferences that can allow us to capture behavior on a case-by-case basis.

Before we do get on to the applications, there is one last thing I want to mention. While we have seen clear evidence that many give to others we should probably not get too carried away. In all of the games we have looked at there are always some who behave 'as if selfish'. Even those who give only appear to give 'with strings attached'. Furthermore, in Figure 7.11, and a study I will look at in the next section, we see that many appear less likely to give if they have some excuse or wiggle room for not giving. The world is not full of altruists. But, it is full of people with very diverse social preferences.

7.5 Giving to charity

A lot of people give up time and money to charitable causes. For example, a survey by the Charities Aid Foundation in 2009, found that over 54 percent of UK adults gave to charity regularly, with donations averaging £31 per month. The Giving USA Foundation estimated giving in the USA in 2007 to be $306 billion. These are big numbers.

To understand why so many people give so much we surely need to think about social preferences. The story I have told so far seems, however, incomplete in understanding charitable giving. That's because the picture I have drawn is one of people helping and giving to others with strings attached. People help those who they see being kind or are earning less than them. Is there any role for pure altruism, people just helping others unconditionally? This seems plausible because many people give money and time to charity without knowing whether this will help people who are kind or not, or have more money than them.

So, why might a person give money or time to charity? There are three broad explanations: they might just want to help people, this would be **pure altruism**. They might feel good about themselves after giving, because of, say, prestige, respect or social approval. Call this a **warm glow** or **joy of giving**. Finally, they might feel bad about themselves if they do not give, because of, say, the social disapproval of others, or guilt. These last two reasons give rise to **impure altruism** in that the person directly benefits herself from giving, and so her motives for giving are not purely altruistic. But, does it matter whether a person gives for pure or impure reasons? Yes, for at least two reasons, which I shall look at in turn.

7.5.1 Crowding out

Suppose that Federica was planning to, say, contribute to a charity but then finds out that someone else has already done so. If Federica is motivated by pure altruism she would no longer want to give, because somebody else has done the good work for her. This is **crowding out**. If Federica is motivated by impure altruism she might still want to give, indeed she may feel more incentive to give in order to compete with the other giver. There will be less crowding out.

To illustrate the issues I will consider a special case of a **model of warm glow** developed by Andreoni (1990). Consider a group of individuals contributing to a charity or public good. The utility function of Federica is given by:

$$U_F(w_F - c_F, C, c_F) = w_F - c_F + \eta_F \sqrt{C} + \rho_F \sqrt{c_F}$$

where w_F is the Federica's wealth, c_F is how much she contributes to the public good, C are the total contributions (including hers) and η_F and ρ_F are parameters. If $\rho_F = 0$ then we can say that Federica is a pure altruist because all she cares about are her wealth after contributing and total contributions to the charity. If $\rho_F > 0$ then we can say that Federica is an impure altruist because she gets utility from having contributed. If $\eta_F = 0$ then Federica contributes only to get warm glow.

If we solve for the optimal contribution we get relation

$$1 = \frac{\eta_F}{2\sqrt{C}} + \frac{\rho_F}{2\sqrt{c_F}}.$$

If $\rho_F = 0$ then:

$$c_F = \frac{\eta_F^2}{4} - C_{-F}$$

where C_{-F} is total contributions of those other Federica. The pure altruist, therefore, wants $\eta_F^2/4$ to be contributed and does not care who contributes. If C_{-F} increases then she will decrease c_F and there will be complete crowding out. If $\eta_F = 0$ then:

$$c_F = \frac{\rho_F^2}{4}$$

and so the amount given is independent of the amount given by others. There will be zero crowding out. Whether or not giving is because of altruistic or impure altruistic reasons does, therefore, matter.

Testing whether or not there is crowding out can be done in the lab or with real data on charitable giving. In the lab the results suggest that there is sizeable but not complete crowding out. For example, Andrenoi (1993) and Bolton and Katok (1998) ran two very different experiments to test the extent of crowding out and found the remarkably similar results of 71.5 percent and 73.7 percent crowding out. That means a person reduces her giving by $0.715 or $0.737 for every $1 someone else gives. Real data on charitable giving shows far less crowding out. For example, Ribar and Wilhelm (2002) looked at private donations from the US to 125 international relief and development organizations between 1986 and 1992, and found that giving by the government and other organizations crowded out private donations by only 18 percent. The evidence consistently shows, therefore, that there is crowding out, but not complete crowding out. What it is hard to agree on is just how much crowding out there is.

Can we reconcile the differences between the experimental and empirical results? Ribar and Wilhelm (2002) suggest that we can by taking into account the number of other potential givers. To explain, suppose that Federica is an impure altruist who gets utility from both pure altruism and warm glow. Because of pure altruism she wants total donations to be sufficiently high, $\eta_F^2/4$ in the example. Because of the joy of giving she wants to give at least a certain amount herself, $\rho_F^2/4$ in the example. If there are few other potential givers, as is the experimental lab, total donations are likely to be lower so pure altruism will most influence her decision. If there are many other potential givers, as in real life, total donations will likely be high so joy of giving will most influence her decision. To see this in the model suppose that all contributors will contribute identical amounts. Then we can substitute in $C = nc$ and get:

$$c = \frac{1}{4}\left(\frac{\eta_F}{\sqrt{n}} + \rho_i\right)^2.$$

If n is large then η_F becomes irrelevant and only warm glow matters. If n is small then η_F is relevant and altruism will matter.

It seems, therefore, that we observe a mixture of both warm glow and altruistic reasons for giving; the extent of crowding out we observe depending on the number of other potential givers.

7.5.2 Who is watching?

A pure altruist will give irrespective of whether or not someone will know she has given. Someone motivated by impure altruism may give more if their giving will be observed. This is because giving can serve as a way for someone to signal something good about themselves. For example, giving may signal generosity or wealth. That people may want to give more if being observed offers a potentially important means to increase donations, and the evidence is that some people do indeed give in order to signal. But, before looking at that evidence I think it is useful to briefly look at a simple model to see how signaling interacts with altruism and warm glow.

Suppose that giving is seen as a signal of someone's generosity. For this to make sense we need there to actually be some variation in how generous people are. In the model of warm glow this would mean individuals vary in their values of η and ρ, with a high η and ρ being seen as generous. For simplicity suppose that there are only two types of individuals, the generous who have $\eta = 0$ and $\rho = 2$ and the not generous who have $\eta = \rho = 0$. If giving is not observed then the generous will give one and receive a warm glow, while the not generous will give zero. What happens if giving is observed?

A second ingredient of any model of signaling is that some individuals must want to appear like a different type of agent. In this case a not generous individual, say, Federica, will try to look like she is generous. She can do this by giving $c_F = 1$. Suppose that she receives a prestige bonus of P if she is perceived by others as generous, zero if she is perceived as not generous, and $0.5P$ if it is unclear whether she is generous or not. Contributing costs one but will gain a bonus of at least $0.5P$, so, if $0.5P > 1$ she will contribute. But what if a generous individual, called Miguel, also gets the prestige bonus? Miguel will want to contribute more in order to distinguish himself from Federica. By contribute a little bit more than $0.5P$ he does just enough to make sure Federica would not try to copy him and he can get the full bonus of P.

To summarize, if only the not generous get a bonus for being perceived as generous then both Federica and Miguel will give one, $c_M = c_F = 1$. If generous individuals do get the bonus then the Federica will give zero, $c_F = 0$, and Miguel will give more, $c_M = 0.5P$. Desires for appearing generous can thus increase the giving of either the not generous or the generous. In more general models the implications of signaling become more complicated but giving is always likely to increase. So, what of the evidence that people do give, at least partially, for signaling reasons?

In short, there is a lot of evidence that signaling is important for some. The most compelling evidence is that very few donors to charity choose to remain anonymous. In public good experiments we also see that giving is less the more anonymity there is. To illustrate this, and also make a slightly different point, I want to look at a study by Dana et al. (2007).

In the study subjects play variations of the dictator game in which proposers have reason or not to excuse not giving. The results are summarized in Table 7.7.

Table 7.7 Offers in a dictator game with varying amounts of moral anonymity

Treatment	Proportion choosing fair option	Other details
Baseline	74%	
Hidden	38%	56% of subjects chose to reveal the receivers payoff.
Two dictators	35%	
Possibly random	34%	76% of participants chose before the cut-off time.

Source: Dana et al. (2007).

In all the experiments proposers could, with some variations, offer a fair $5, $5 split, or an unfair $6, $1 split. In the baseline treatment we see what we would expect, given the evidence in section 7.1, in that most proposers chose the fair option. In all of the other treatments proposers had some plausible reason for not choosing the fair option. We see that the proportion choosing the fair option falls dramatically.

In the hidden information treatment a proposer knew their own payoff but had to choose to find out the payoff of the receiver. Even though this could be done without cost, nearly half of proposers chose not to find out the payoff of the receiver. A majority of those then chose the unfair option. In the two dictator treatments the offer sent was determined by two dictators simultaneously, either of which could enforce the sending of a fair offer. In the possibly random treatment the proposer's choice would be made randomly if he or she did not make their choice before some undisclosed cut-off time. Most did choose before the cut-off, but still chose the unfair option!

What this study nicely shows is how signaling is interrelated with intentions. In the baseline treatment a proposer's choice made his or her intentions very clear and so they could not hide, either from the receiver or themselves. This means that the proposer's actions would send a clear signal, so they had the incentive to send a good signal and receive a warm glow, avoid guilt etc. In the other three treatments a proposer's choice is much less revealing about their intentions. This lessens the incentive to send a good signal, and is enough for the majority of subjects to not choose the fair offer. We see, therefore, that a little bit of wiggle room to not give can be enough to significantly reduce the amount that is given. Signaling is the most plausible explanation for this.

7.5.3 Why do people give?

The picture we get is one of people giving for a variety of reasons. Giving does not appear to be solely due to pure altruism, but is likely a mixture of warm glow, guilt at not giving, signaling, and pure altruism. Understanding this can be useful in getting people to give more. To illustrate these points I shall wrap up this section by looking at a study by Alpizar et al. (2009).

Table 7.8 The proportion who contribute, the average contribution conditional on giving something and the average contribution to Poas National Park

Treatment	Proportion contribute	Conditional contribution	Average contribution
No gift	48	5.09	2.43
Gift	56	4.56	2.56
Anonymous	51	4.36	2.21
Non-anonymous	53	5.21	2.77
No reference	47	6.00	2.84
$2 reference	61	3.61	2.20
$5 reference	50	3.95	1.98
$10 reference	49	5.97	2.95

Souce: Alpizar et al. (2009).

They looked at giving by international visitors to Poas National Park in Costa Rica in 2006. A random sample of visitors was interviewed privately about their visit to the National Park, at the end of which they were asked to make a donation. Three things were varied: some were given a small gift of value $3, some were told that 'most common donations have been' $2, $5 or $10, and some made their donations without the interviewer knowing how much they gave.

The results are summarized in Table 7.8. A relatively high proportion did give but it is noticeable that the proportion who gave is increasing in the lowness of the reference point. The contribution, conditional on giving something, is 25 percent higher in the non-anonymous compared to anonymous treatments. We also see higher contributions the higher is the reference amount. Indeed many givers matched the reference amount. All of these findings are impossible to reconcile with a giver motivated solely by pure altruism or one who cares only about their own payoff. Instead they suggest the mix of motives for giving that we have looked at.

7.6 Price and wage rigidity

Take a look at the number of unemployed in just about any country and you will see some big numbers. The unemployment rate in the UK and US is typically above 5 percent of the workforce and in a few European countries the number can be as high as 20 percent. Some of this could be voluntary unemployment, but clearly not all of it. That means that labor markets are not clearing, at least in the short run. If there is an excess supply of labor then the standard story would say that the price of labor, or the wage rate, should fall until the market clears, or supply equals demand. If wages do not fall for some reason then we say there is **wage stickiness**. There are lots of reasons we might observe wage stickiness, such as regulation and unions, but the reason I want to focus on here is that of reciprocity and fairness.

Why should reciprocity matter? The relationship between that of an employer and a worker is a **principal–agent relationship**. The employer, or principal, hires a worker, or agent, to do a job for her. Given that the employer's profit will depend on how much effort and initiative the worker puts into her job, the employer needs to find a way to motivate the worker to work hard. Crucially, however, in most jobs the employer will not be able to tell for sure how hard the worker is working. At least, the worker may have ways to make it look as though she is working harder than she is. The employer, therefore, needs to think carefully about how to motivate the worker.

Now let's think about reciprocity. Positive reciprocity would imply that if the employer is kind to the worker the worker will be kind to the employer. Negative reciprocity would imply that if the employer is unkind to the worker the worker will be unkind to the employer. What is kind and unkind in this context? That will depend on the reference point. Given, however, what we have seen in chapters two and four and this chapter, the most obvious reference points would seem to be: the wage paid previously paid and/or the wage being paid to others. To cut wages or pay a lower wage than others would then be seen as unkind, while to increase wages or pay a higher wage than others would be seen as kind.

We might predict, therefore, that employers would pay high wages to motivate workers and appeal to positive reciprocity. They might be reluctant to cut wages and de-motivate workers because of negative reciprocity. Numerous surveys of employers have found both these effects, and particularly the latter, do happen. For example, Campbell III and Kamlani (1997) asked 184 firms why they do not cut wages as low as they could in a recession. The main concern of employers was that the most productive workers would leave (an adverse selection argument) but a close second was that worker effort would decrease (a reciprocity argument). Table 7.9, for instance, shows the percentage of employers who thought a

Table 7.9 The percentage of employers who thought that a 10 percent wage cut or increase would change worker effort, and change it by more than 10 percent. For example, after a 10 percent wage cut it is expected that 74.7 percent of blue collar workers will decrease effort by 10 percent or more.

Change in wages	Expected change in effort	Proportion of workers who will change effort		
		White collar workers	Blue collar workers	Less skilled workers
10% cut	Decrease	85.8%	92%	91.3%
	Decrease by 10% or more	61.7%	74.7%	78.8%
10% increase	Increase	55.8%	52.1%	53.2%
	Increase by 10% or more	19.4%	18.7%	22.5%

Source: Campbell III and Kamlani (1997)

10 percent pay cut or increase would have an effect, and a serious effect, on worker effort. A pay rise is predicted to have some benefit but it is clear that a wage cut is expected to have a significant negative effect.

If employers are reluctant to cut wages because it will cause negative reciprocity then we have a plausible reason for wage stickiness. But we should test this explanation out a bit more thoroughly. I will do so by formalizing the argument a bit more, using a model of fairness, and then looking at some experimental results.

7.6.1 A model of worker reciprocity

To formalize how reciprocity can result in sticky wages I shall work through the intentions-based model of fairness that we looked at in section 7.3.1. Figure 7.12 illustrates. To keep things simple imagine that a worker, Miguel, can put in either high or low effort $e \in \{H, L\}$ and high effort costs him some amount C. Suppose that if effort is high, $e = H$, the employer, Federica, gets revenue R and if effort is low, $e = L$, she gets zero revenue. Federica chooses a wage w and makes profit, or material payoff, of revenue $- w$. Miguel gets a material payoff of $w -$ effort cost.

Federica does not care about fairness and so simply wants to maximize her profit. Should she pay a high wage?

Miguel can be kind by putting in high effort and unkind by putting in low effort. The revenue of Federica is R in the first case and zero in the latter, so an equitable payoff is $0.5R - w$. The kindness of Miguel is thus $0.5R$ or $-0.5R$ depending on whether he puts in high effort or low effort. Federica can realistically offer any wage

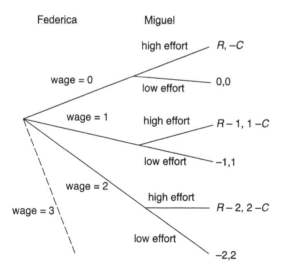

Figure 7.12 A simple model of worker reciprocity. Federica chooses a wage w and Miguel chooses effort. Federica's material payoff is revenue $- w$ and Miguel's is $w -$ effort cost.

between zero and R so the equitable payoff is also $0.5R$ and the kindness of Federica is, $w - 0.5R$.

This means that if Miguel puts in high effort his utility is:

$$w - C + \mu_M \left(w - \frac{R}{2} \right) \frac{R}{2}$$

and if he puts in low effort his utility is:

$$w - \mu_M \left(w - \frac{R}{2} \right) \frac{R}{2}$$

where recall that μ_M is his desire to reciprocate. Miguel will, therefore, put in high effort if:

$$w > \frac{R}{2} + \frac{C}{\mu_M R}.$$

We can see he may be willing to put in high effort if Federica is kind and offers a wage above the equitable payoff of $0.5R$.

Is Federica willing to pay this wage? If Miguel puts in high effort she gains R in revenue and so she will be willing to pay any wage less than R. Setting $w < R$ gives the condition $2C < \mu_M R^2$. Thus, provided the cost of effort is sufficiently small and/or Miguel has sufficient desire to reciprocate, Federica will be willing to pay a high enough wage that Miguel will be willing to put in high effort.

In this example we see that a worker may be willing to work hard if he believes the employer is being kind and offering a higher than equitable wage. We can also see how reciprocity can cause unemployment and wage stickiness. For instance, suppose that R were to subsequently fall but Miguel still equated kindness with his old wage, or the old value of w. We could get unemployment because Federica can no longer afford to pay the wage Miguel wants, or wage stickiness because Miguel will think a wage cut is unkind.

Do not, however, think of reciprocity as a bad thing that we could do without. Yes, it is the reason we might get wage stickiness and unemployment, but without it Miguel would never be willing to but in high effort and Federica would never make any profit! So, reciprocity is beneficial, but could have negative side effects.

7.6.2 *Wage stickiness in the lab*

The lab provides a controlled environment to try and better understand wage stickiness and has shown the importance of reciprocity. To illustrate I will look at the study of Fehr and Falk (1999). The basic design of the experiments was similar to that of the gift exchange game we already looked at in section 7.1. The main difference was a preliminary stage in which workers and employers were matched through a double auction. In this auction workers could say what wage they would accept, employers could say what wage they would pay, and if a worker and employer agreed on a wage they then played the gift exchange game. This procedure was repeated ten times but an employer could never know who the worker was, and so there was no opportunity for reputation building. The key to the experiment was that there was an excess supply of workers, eleven workers to seven employers, so unemployment was inevitable.

Figure 7.13 summarizes the main results. The reservation wage shows what wages the seven workers posting the lowest wages were willing to accept. This is, therefore, the wage that employers could have offered and got workers. We can compare this with the wage they did pay. First, look at the treatment where effort does not count, meaning that the employer's payoff did not depend on worker effort. In this treatment there was no incentive to pay a high wage and we consequently observe the average wage was low and similar to the reservation wage.

Now look at the treatment we are most interested in where effort did count. We see that wages are relatively high and most importantly above the reservation wage. So, employers could have hired cheaper workers but chose not to. They chose to hire workers who wanted a high wage! Was this a good decision? Around 34 percent of workers did not make effort conditional on wage but 66 percent did reciprocate a high wage with high effort. This was enough to mean that paying a high wage did pay back in higher profits.

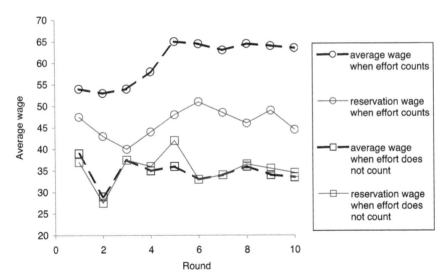

Figure 7.13 The average wage and reservation wage in experimental labor markets. In the treatment without effort the average wage is relatively low. When effort matters we see that employers pay relatively high wages, well above the minimum that some workers were willing to accept.

Source: Fehr and Falk (1999).

This experiment demonstrates nicely how positive reciprocity from workers can make it worthwhile to pay high wages. In a second part of their study Fehr and Falk (1999) show that negative reciprocity can also make it worthwhile to pay high wages. They do this by changing the workers effort costs so that it is least costly for a worker to put in maximum effort. Workers paid a low wage still on average lower their effort, but now at a cost to themselves. Workers are therefore willing to sacrifice own monetary payoff to punish a low paying employer.

7.6.3 How long to forget a wage change?

It seems clear that reciprocity is important in the labor market and is a causal factor in wage stickiness. But, before we move on, there is one final issue that I want to touch on, that of time. We have already talked in chapters two and four about how reference points can change over time. If an employer's wage changes then there reference point should also eventually change. That would suggest employers need to constantly increase the wage in order to motivate workers through positive reciprocity. This is consistent with the desire for an increasing wage profile that we talked about in chapter four. Do we have any idea how long it takes people to adjust to new wages?

A study by Gneezy and List (2006) suggested that it does not take long to forget a wage increase. They recruited people to do routine tasks, like data entry in the university library and door-to-door fundraising, and some were given an unexpected wage increase. Those given the increase did work harder for the first ninety minutes but after that their effort dropped to the level of those who did not receive an increase. Ultimately the wage increase did not pay for itself.

In a similar experiment, Kube et al. (2006) got a similar result to that of Kneezy and List when looking at a wage increase. They also, however, consider an unexpected cut in the wage and find that this has longer lasting consequences. Maybe people soon forget a wage increase but never forget a wage cut? This emphasizes the asymmetry that we had already seen in Table 7.9 where a decrease in wages was predicted to have stronger effects on worker effort than an increase in wages. This asymmetry is consistent with loss aversion and is key to explaining why reciprocity can lead to wage rigidity: Cutting wages is worse for worker effort than increasing wages is good for effort, so firms should avoid cutting wages.

7.6.4 Firm pricing

It is not only wages that can be sticky. If there is excess demand for a good then firms, according to a standard story, should push up prices until supply equals demand. Often, however, we observe large excess demand for goods. For example, tickets for major sporting events like the Superbowl or World Cup Final could be sold many times over. Similarly, ski resorts are bursting to capacity at Christmas and New Year. Why do prices not rise more?

There are good arguments to say that it is because of desires for fairness and reciprocity. The explanation is very similar to that for wage stickiness so I will not spend much time on this issue. But, I will talk through some of the results from a study by Kahneman et al. (1986) that help illustrate the key points. They conducted a household survey with questions like:

> A hardware store has been selling snow shovels for $15. The morning after a large snowstorm, they raise the price to $20. Please rate this action as: Completely fair, Acceptable, Unfair, Very unfair.

In times of excess demand firms have a rationale to increase prices, but 82 percent of respondents in the survey considered this price increase unfair. Reciprocity would suggest that this unfairness might be enough to stop people buying a show shovel.

As with wages, the most obvious reference price is probably the previous price or the price charged by others. This means that a price increase or relatively high price is unkind while a price decrease or relatively low price is kind. To get price stickiness we need the asymmetry whereby rising prices is considered worse than lowering prices is considered good. We do seem to observe it. For example, another survey question was:

> A shortage has developed for a popular model of automobile, and customers must now wait two months for delivery. A dealer has been selling these cars at list price. Now the dealer prices the model at $200 above list price.

Seventy-one percent considered this unfair. Other respondents were told:

> A dealer has been selling these cars at a discount of $200 below list price. Now the dealer sells this model only at list price.

Fifty-eight percent found this acceptable.

So, is it ever acceptable to raise prices? Most people surveyed did consider it fair for a firm to pass on increases in wholesale costs to consumers. They seemed to accept that firms need to make an acceptable level of profit and so are willing to accommodate this. What was considered unfair is for a firm to raise price because of increased market power. This is clear in the snow shovel question. As we might expect, therefore, the reference point is a little bit more subtle than the previous price.

You may disagree on what is fair or not, but the main thing is that firms do need to take account of customers' likely perceptions of a price rise. This is because we know that people do reject in ultimatum games and so presumably are willing to not buy a product they consider over-priced. Firms may, therefore be reluctant to increase prices, with the consequence that many markets may have excess demand.

Indeed, we can be more specific about which markets will have excess demand. Primarily it will be markets where there are large fluctuations in demand, but little change in costs, and where customer loyalty is important. This is because the

large fluctuations in demand will cause there to be excess demand but the importance of customer loyalty will make firms reluctant to increase prices. This is
often the case in sport and entertainment events. Prices do in fact vary for sporting
events and hotels according to demand but the evidence would suggest they do
not vary enough to stop excess demand at peak times. Kahneman et al. quote a
skiing industry explanation: 'If you gouge them at Christmas, they won't be back
in March'.

7.7 Further reading

The review articles by Thaler (1988), Camerer and Thaler (1995), and Fehr and
Gächter (2000b) provide a gentle introduction to the economics of social preferences, and the article by Sobel (2005) a more in-depth survey. A lot of the book
by Camerer (2003) is also relevant. For interesting insights on public goods a
classic book by Olson (1971) is recommended and I'll also recommend at this
point a great book by Frank (1991). The papers by Frank, Gilovich, and Regan
(1993) and Levitt and List (2007) raise some interesting issues. There's no review
article I know of on the economics of charitable giving so I will recommend Shang
and Croson (2009) as a recent, interesting paper that overviews relevant literature.
Bewley (2007) provides a survey on fairness in wage setting.

7.8 Review questions

7.1   What is the Nash equilibrium in a dictator game? What about the trust game
      and ultimatum game? Be careful to distinguish sub-game perfect Nash
      equilibria from other Nash equilibria.
7.2   Why might payoffs be lower in a public good game with punishment even
      if punishment increases contributions? Is it good to have the threat of
      punishment or not?
7.3   In section 7.1.5 I mentioned a study by Andreoni and Miller (2002). They
      asked subjects to play eleven different dictators game. In each game the
      proposer was given a number of tokens, from 40 to 100 and asked to divide
      the tokens between them and a receiver. Each token was worth $0.10 to
      $0.40 to the proposer and $0.10 to $0.40 to the receiver. For example, a
      token might be worth $0.40 to the proposer and $0.10 to the receiver, or
      $0.20 to the proposer and $0.30 to the receiver. How do you think the share
      given to receivers depended on the worth of tokens? How should it depend,
      to be consistent with utility maximization?
7.4   Should with equate material payoff with money?
7.5   Find the general conditions such that punishment can work in a linear public
      good game in the ERC model and the Fehr-Schmidt model. Hint: for the
      ERC model find the level of punishment such that after she has paid
      for punishing Anna will have exactly the social reference point. For the
      Fehr-Schmidt model find the level of punishment such that the free rider,
      Miguel, and punisher, Anna, will end up with the same material payoff.

7.6   Why can punishment work in a linear public good game according to the Fehr-Schmidt model if only one person is willing to punish, but in the ERC model only if two people are willing to punish?

7.7   How can an intentions based model of fairness be adapted to take account of earned versus unearned payoff, and social norms?

7.8   In the intentions based model of section 7.3.1 the equitable payoff was derived looking only at Pareto efficient outcomes. Why is this sensible?

7.9   Is it better to be in a firm where you earn $50,000 and the average salary is $80,000 or in a firm where you earn $45,000 and the average salary is $30,000?

7.10 Why can loss aversion help explain why a cut in wages is worse than a rise in wages is good? How is this related to wage stickiness and habit formation?

7.11 Should employers fine poorly performing workers, or give bonuses to well performing workers in order to provide the most effective incentives?

7.12 What can we learn from the ultimatum game about the interaction between a buyer and seller of a good?

Part III
Origins of behavior

8   Evolution and culture

It is not the strongest of the species that survives, nor the most intelligent, but rather the one most adaptable to change.

Clarence Darrow

In this, and the next, chapter our objective will shift away from trying to describe behavior to that of trying to understand the reasons for behavior. For example, we want to ask: Why are people risk averse? Why do people value fairness? Why is there reference dependence? Hopefully, you agree that these are fascinating questions. In answering them we can learn not only why people behave the way they do but can also get additional insight on how they behave. Potentially, therefore, we can learn a lot.

In this chapter I am going to take seriously the fact that anyone's behavior is shaped by our evolutionary history and the culture that we grow up and live in. I will begin by looking at the consequences of evolution and then turn to the role of culture. Note that the section on culture will make a lot more sense if you are familiar with the material in the last chapter.

8.1 Evolution and economic behavior

I shall not go deeply into the science of evolution, but it will be useful to know the basic idea. Evolution by natural selection relies on three things: **variation**, meaning that different individuals are different in their traits, abilities, characteristics, preferences, and so on; **inheritance**, meaning that offspring inherit similar traits to their parents; and **mutation**, meaning that with random chance the traits of the individual are altered during reproduction and slightly different to the traits of their parents. Over generations, the consequences of **natural selection** are twofold: (1) traits that result in an individual having relatively more offspring than others will become more common in the population, because of variation and inheritance; (2) traits that increase the relative number of offspring of an individual can emerge in the population, because of mutation and inheritance.

To illustrate, consider a very stylized example in which there are two types of people, some having green hair and some blue. Those with green hair find it easier to attack prey and catch food, so survive longer and have more children. On average greens have four offspring each and blues have two. Suppose there are ten greens and ten blues to start with. After one generation there are 40 greens and 20 blues; after two generations there are 160 greens and 40 blues; after three generations there are 640 greens and 80 blues. Clearly, the greens are becoming a larger proportion of the population, from 50 percent to 88 percent in three generations.

Now, suppose that because of some random mutation one person is born with yellow hair and another with red. A person with yellow hair finds it even easier to attack prey and so has on average six offspring, while someone with red hair is very poor at attacking prey and so has only one offspring. If you do the math you will find it is not many generations before those with yellow hair dominate the population.

This simple example avoids many complexities that we need to think about, but it will do for the moment and I shall provide a more nuanced picture as we proceed. What I want to begin talking about is what evolution has to do with modern economic behavior.

8.1.1 Looking for food and finding a utility function

Food and water is essential to survival and much time would have been spent in our evolutionary history trying to find enough of it. Indeed finding food is still the main preoccupation of many in the developing world today. Evolution should, therefore, favor those with good strategies for finding food and water. Can this shed light on how humans behave today?

Consider a person called Edward, looking for food. Every day he leaves his cave and can go either east or west in search of food. Suppose that on day t if he were to go west he would find f_t^W calories of food and if he were to go east he would find f_t^E. The more calories he finds the better. The problem is, Edward does not know f_t^W or f_t^E without going and looking, and he can only go one way per day. Which way should he go?

Let's suppose that the amount of food in either direction on any one day is random. The probability of finding f calories by going east is p_f^E and by going west is p_f^W. If:

$$\sum_{f=0}^{\infty} p_f^E f > \sum_{f=0}^{\infty} p_f^W f \tag{8.1}$$

then Edward will maximize his calorie intake by going east. Remember, however, that having children is the objective favored by natural selection, not eating a lot. Let $u(f)$ denote the expected number of extra children Edward (and his wife Anna) will have if Edward gets f calories of food on any one day. We do not need $u(f)$ to be an integer and, given that Edward will likely have far less children than meals, $u(f)$ will likely be a small fraction. If:

$$\sum_{f=0}^{\infty} p_f^E u(f) > \sum_{f=0}^{\infty} p_f^W u(f) \tag{8.2}$$

then Edward will maximize the expected number of children by going east.

Look at the difference between equations (8.1) and (8.2). In the first we calculate the expected number of calories, in the second the expected number of children. It may well be that going west gives the highest expected calories but going east the highest expected number of children. For instance, the amount of food to the east may always be a nice consistent amount, while that to the west is either very high or very low. Evolution will favor those who maximize the expected number of children, and so obey equation (8.2) rather than (8.1).

This means that Edward not only needs to work out how much food there is likely to be in each direction, he also needs to work out the relationship between the amount of food he eats and the number of children he will likely have! Given that Edward will have relatively few children, this looks like a hopeless task. Suppose, however, that Edward is born with the function u already hard-wired into his brain. What I mean is that when he sees and eats foods with a calorie content of f, he gets an enjoyment, satisfaction or utility of $u(f)$. Does Edward's problem become simpler?

Arthur Robson (2001b) showed that it does. Edward can now maximize his expected number of children with the following heuristic: today I go east, tomorrow I go west, the next day I go east, and so on; each day I keep a cumulative count of the difference in utility between going east versus west; if this difference reaches some critical threshold then from that moment on I always go east or west depending on which gave the highest utility. This is a simple solution to a complex problem and works because Edward is born with the utility function $u(f)$ and the heuristic of how to use it.

The utility function has two key benefits here. The first is that Edward only has to think about food. If he finds enough food to maximize his utility then, without knowing it, he will maximize his expected number of children. This is because evolution will favor those who have the correct utility function, i.e. get satisfaction from eating food proportional to the expected number of children that eating food provides. The utility function $u(f)$ thus encapsulates the **accumulated experience of past generations**.

The second benefit of the utility function is that Edward can adapt to novelty. Over generations it will likely change whether going east or west is best. It would, therefore, not be a good evolutionary strategy to follow the actions of one's ancestors, and say go west because a parent did. The utility function allows Edward to follow the strategies of his ancestors, as given by heuristics. Again, evolution will favor those with the best heuristic, meaning that Edward, and his children, will be very **adaptable to a changing environment**.

We have already seen in chapter three the distinction between expected utility, equations (8.2) and (3.1), and expected value, equations (8.1) and (3.2). Now we have an explanation for it, and a justification to assume people behave as if maximizing an expected utility function. Indeed, we see that evolution may have favored people with a cardinal utility function where satisfaction from goods comes in proportion to the expected number of children such goods give. We call such goods **intermediate goods** because they are anything that increases, or decreases, the expected number of children. Food and shelter are obvious examples of intermediate goods but status, generosity, esteem and a host of other things may be equally relevant, as we shall see.

Is this useful in understanding modern economic behavior? Yes. It gives us important clues as to what should give us utility and what probably will not. It also gives us clues as to what we should have good heuristics for, search being one of them. What I want to do now is add time and risk to the mix to see what else we can learn.

8.1.2 Choosing when to have children

I will start by adding time to the model by questioning when Edward (and Anna) should choose to have children. Let's suppose that Edward can have children up to T years of age. What he needs to do is to decide when to have children during those T years. In our story this choice is primarily determined by when he chooses to consume the intermediate goods such as food and shelter and not necessarily when he gets together with Anna. We represent his choice by a **reproductive profile** $x = \{x_1, \ldots, x_T\}$ that says how many children, x_t, he expects to have when age t. If all people, including Edward and his children, survive from one year to the next with probability s, what reproductive profile should Edward choose?

Again, this does not look a simple problem. It turns out, however, that if Edward has an inter-temporal utility function hard-wired into his brain then he can solve this problem relatively easily. Similar to before, he will not need to choose when to have children, but instead just consume intermediate goods in a way that maximizes his utility (and get together with Anna every so often). But what will the inter-temporal utility function look like? Robson and Samuelson (2009) show that evolution will favor people with the inter-temporal utility function:

$$u^T(x_1, \ldots, x_T) = \sum_{t=1}^{T} \delta^{t-1} x_t \tag{8.3}$$

where:

$$\delta = e^{-(\ln \phi - \ln s)}$$

and $\ln \phi$ is the population growth rate. The term $\ln \phi - \ln s$ is equal to the population growth rate plus the population death rate. You might want to refer back to chapter four to see in more detail what this means. But, basically it means evolution will favor people who use exponential discounting and have consistent, non-time varying preferences with a discount factor that depends on the population growth rate and death rate.

This gives us an explanation for exponential discounting and a prediction of what the discount factor should be. But why this specific discount factor? If Edward delays having children one year then he can expect to fall behind others because of population growth and the possibility he does not survive the year. So, a child next year needs to be discounted by the rate of population growth and death. The higher is population growth and the lower the chance of survival the more impatient Edward should be to consume intermediate goods and have children.

[Extra] For those curious how to derive equation (8.3), here are some of the details. Starting when Edward is zero years old we can roll forward time and keep track of how many descendants he has of each age. Let $N_a(t)$ denote the number of descendants of age a after t years. Things will evolve according to the equation:

$$[N_1(t+1), ..., N_T(t+1)] = [N_1(t), ..., N_T(t)] \begin{bmatrix} sx_1 & s & 0 & ... & 0 \\ sx_2 & 0 & s & ... & 0 \\ \vdots & \vdots & \vdots & & \vdots \\ sx_{T-1} & 0 & 0 & ... & s \\ sx_T & 0 & 0 & ... & 0 \end{bmatrix} \quad (8.4).$$

To explain, the number of one year olds after $t+1$ years is equal to the number of surviving offspring born to those who were one in year t, i.e. $N_1(t)sx_1$, plus the number born to those who were two in year t, i.e. $N_2(t)sx_2$, etc. The number of two year olds in year $t+1$ is equal to the number of one year olds who survive from year t to $t+1$, i.e. $N_1(t)s$, etc. The matrix in equation (8.4) is called the Leslie matrix and crucial to finding what reproductive profile evolution will favor. Technically, evolution will favor the profile that maximizes the dominant eigenvalue of the Leslie matrix. What this means in practice is that evolution will favor the utility function in equation (8.3).

8.1.3 Aggregate risk

So far we have described Edward as maximizing expected utility using exponential discounting. In chapters three and four we saw that people may not maximize expected utility or use exponential discounting, so how can we reconcile things a little? One way is to add aggregate risk to the story. To explain: an **idiosyncratic risk** is one that affects only one individual in the population while an **aggregate risk** is one that will likely affect all the population. For example, a cold winter or flood is an aggregate risk, while getting attacked by a predator is more likely to be idiosyncratic. I have focused on idiosyncratic risk so far, but in our evolutionary past aggregate risk was undoubtedly relevant. With the help of four examples, I shall illustrate that it likely had important consequences.

To guide us through the examples I shall immediately preview the main insights, and also point towards Table 8.1. In the presence of aggregate risk we find that evolution may favor people who: (i) diversify, (ii) avoid aggregate risk, (iii) have a relative high discount rate and so are impatient, and (iv) have a discount rate that decreases with age consistent with decreasing impatience. Clearly, aggregate risk makes a difference. Most interestingly, it offers an explanation for both risk aversion and hyperbolic discounting. So, let's work through the four examples.

Table 8.1 The four examples involving aggregate risk

Example	Brief description	Implication
Collecting food for winter	The extended family of types who randomly determine how much food to collect will be most able to prosper in good years and survive bad years.	Risk aversion and desire to diversify.
Live together or separately	It's better they live separately. If they live together there is a small probability of the population growing very large but a large probability the population will end up small.	Should avoid aggregate risk.
Surviving the winter	Aggregate risk should not affect how much people discount the future, because it is relative individual differences that matter and aggregate risk affects everyone equally.	The discount rate will be relatively high, suggesting impatience.
Something happens to 24-year-olds	Before they are 24 people should be relatively impatient because the aggregate shock at 24 lowers the expected growth rate of the population.	Hyperbolic discounting, and increasing patience with age.

In the first example, think about people collecting enough food to survive winter. Winters are either long or short and people are of two types, Long types who store enough food to survive any winter, and Short types who store enough to survive a short winter but not enough to survive a long winter. Because of the extra time spent collecting food, Long types have a 0.5 chance of surviving the summer while Short types have a 0.75 chance. What will happen? Despite being better at surviving summers, the Short types are doomed to extinction because they will all die in the first long winter! Evolution, thus, favors Long types.

Consider, now a new type of person who at the start of each summer randomly decides whether to store enough food for a long winter or short winter. The extended family of such Mixed types stand to do well because in any year some of them will collect enough for a long winter and some will not. That some of them do not collect enough for a long winter means the family can grow at a relatively quick rate. That some of them do collect enough for a long winter means the family will never be wiped out by one long winter. It turns out that evolution will favor people who store enough for a long winter with probability $3p$, where p is the probability of a long winter (see review question 8.2).

This example shows that in the presence of aggregate risk the optimal strategy may involve randomizing. This might look like an argument for risk loving behavior but actually it is more of an argument for risk aversion and diversification, because it shows that risks, like a long winter, should be guarded against.

Another way to interpret this first example is that in the presence of aggregate risk it may make sense to have idiosyncratic gambling. The next example takes this point one stage further by showing that idiosyncratic risk is preferred to aggregate risk.

A group of people are now deciding where to live and have two options. They could all live together in one big village or live separately. Every year each person has two children and, no matter where they live, there is a 0.5 chance that one child will not survive the winter because, say, there is an attack by a rival tribe. The difference is, that if everyone lives together this risk is aggregate, so there is a 0.5 chance that everyone in the group will have only one surviving child. If they all live separately the risk is idiosyncratic so each person independently has a 0.5 chance of having only one surviving child. Should they live together or separately?

It turns out that they should live separately (see below). The general lesson to take from this is that evolution will favor people who avoid aggregate risk. To give some intuition for why this is the case: After a few years aggregate risk leads to a small probability of there being a very large population but a large probability of there being a very small population. It is best to avoid such a gamble and people do that by avoiding aggregate risk. Interestingly, however, a person by himself may not be able to avoid aggregate risk because it depends what others do. For example, Edward and Anna cannot live alone if others follow them. This creates interdependence between individuals that we shall explore a bit more later on.

[Extra] Why should they live separately? For simplicity, suppose that no adult ever survives the winter. In both cases the expected population size by year t is $N(t) = 1.5^t N(0)$, where $N(0)$ is the original population size. In terms of expected utility, therefore, both options are equivalent. In an evolutionary sense, however, they are different. If they live separately, the number of people will be very close to $N(t) = 1.5^t N(0)$ because the risk is idiosyncratic. The growth rate of the population will, therefore, be:

$$\frac{\ln N(t) - \ln N(0)}{t} = \ln 1.5.$$

If everyone lives together the population size will be $N(t) = 2^{b(t)} N(0)$, where $b(t)$ is the number of years in which all children survived. The growth rate now is:

$$\frac{\ln N(t) - \ln N(0)}{t} = \frac{b(t)}{t} \ln 2 \to \frac{1}{2} \ln 2 = \ln \sqrt{2}.$$

The growth rate if they live separately exceeds that if they live together.

In the final two examples I want to return to the issue of when Edward should have children. First, imagine that the length of winter can be anything from $l = 100$ to 50 days long. The longer it is the less chance that a person survives the winter where the probability of survival is $s(l) \in (0,1)$. That the probability of survival $s(l)$ depends on the random length of the winter implies that there is aggregate risk. That each person survives independently with probability $s(l)$ means that there is also idiosyncratic risk. Does the aggregate risk make any difference to how Edward should discount the future?

Robson and Samuelson (2009) showed that Edward should maximize expected utility, discounting exponentially, with a discount rate equal to ln φ − ln s where ln φ and − ln s are the rate of population growth and death rate there would be without aggregate risk. This sounds like equation (8.3), but there is a difference. Aggregate risk, for the same reasons as in the previous example, will lower the actual population growth rate below what it would be without aggregate risk. Some numbers will help illustrate.

Suppose that in 'normal' conditions a population grows at 2 percent a year with a death rate of 4 percent a year, numbers plausible in human evolution. Also suppose that every so often a catastrophe occurs which decimates the population and means that, in the long run, population growth is around zero a year, which is also plausible in human evolution. Evolution will favor individuals who ignore the aggregate risk of the catastrophe and have a discount rate of 2 + 4 = 6 percent. If we had gone off equation (8.3) we would have expected a discount rate of 2 + 0 = 2 percent.

The catastrophe proves irrelevant, in an evolutionary sense, because it is an aggregate shock that affects all in the same way. This means that it will not alter the number of children Edward has relative to another and so he can ignore it. This makes people relatively impatient, because they should discount at, say, 6 percent rather than 2 percent a year. It also means we should not be surprised to see higher discount rates than might seem sensible given observed population growth and death rates.

In the final example, suppose, that for some reason, the average temperature has an effect on the survival rate of people who are 24 years old. To model this we say the probability of survival is $s(l) + d$(temp.) for anyone aged 24, for some function d(temp.), while the probability of survival for anyone not aged 24 remains $s(l)$. For instance, if $d(5) > 0$ and $d(-5) < 0$ then someone aged 24 has a higher probability of survival than others if the temperature is five, and a lower probability if it is minus five. This creates an aggregate shock that affects all 24-year-olds.

If Edward is not yet 24 the possibility of an aggregate shock when he is 24 should reduce the value he puts on children that he might have after he is 24. This is because aggregate risk, as we have seen, lowers the expected growth rate of the population. Edward should, therefore, be relatively impatient to consume intermediate goods and have children just before he is 24. Intriguingly, this is the case even if the aggregate shock at age 24 makes it more likely he will survive when he is 24 than any other age!

This shows that with age specific aggregate risk the discount rate will change with age. So, evolution need not necessarily favor individuals who use exponential discounting. In fact, provided the age specific effects are relatively small, the best thing is hyperbolic discounting where the discount rate decreases with age. Thus, evolution can help explain why we see the type of time preferences discussed in chapter four, although we have yet to see any explanation for time inconsistency.

8.1.4 Competing with others

The picture I have given so far is one of evolution as a struggle between Edward and the environment. This, however, is only half of the story because evolution is also a struggle between different people. A further two examples will help illustrate why this matters, Table 8.2 summarizes.

Suppose that some people are cooperative and some are non-cooperative. People randomly meet each other in pairs and collect food. Two cooperative people go together and share any food they collect. A non-cooperative person collects food with a cooperative person but then takes all the food. Finally, two non-cooperative people go off and steal the food from cooperative people! Payoffs are summarized in Table 8.3 (and see Research Methods 8.1 for how to interpret these payoffs).

Table 8.2 The two examples with inter-dependence

Example	Brief description	Implication
Cooperators and non-cooperators	If cooperators can find some way to interact more with each other than non-cooperators then they can prosper. The result is a signaling game of hide and seek, where cooperators try to distinguish themselves and non-cooperators try to copy them.	Seemingly irrelevant things can become important evolutionary signals.
Different ability at finding food	Women should prefer to mate with men who are better at finding food, which means men need to appear good at finding food.	People should be good at signaling their desirable attributes.

Table 8.3 The payoffs if people are cooperative or non-cooperative

		Person 2	
		Cooperative	Non-cooperative
Person 1	Cooperative	1, 1	0, 2
	Non cooperative	2, 0	0.5, 0.5

Research Methods 8.1

Evolutionary game theory

Once we recognize the importance of interactions between individuals it is natural to turn to game theory. Game theory has developed tools specific for modeling evolution which we can illustrate with a hawk-dove game introduced to model animal conflict.

Consider two animals competing for food with a value of V. Each animal can either attack or share. If they share each gets V/2. If one attacks and the other shares, the attacker takes all the food. If both attack there is a conflict that costs C and each has an equal chance of winning the food. The payoff matrix is given in Table 8.4. To put this in an evolutionary context we think of the strategy, attack or share, as a genetic trait or **phenotype** that is constant through the animal's lifetime and inherited by offspring. We also think of the payoffs as representing the net additional offspring the animal will get from consuming the food (in a similar way to in section 8.1.1).

Table 8.4 Payoffs in the hawk-dove game

		Person 2	
		Attack	Share
Person 1	Attack	$(V-C)/2, (V-C)/2$	$V, 0$
	Share	$0, V$	$V/2, V/2$

Imagine that the population was full of animals who share. If a mutation produces an animal with the attack strategy, this animal would have relatively many offspring. The strategy attack would, therefore, spread. Now imagine that the population was full of animals who attack. If $V < C$ an animal who shares would have relatively many offspring and the strategy share would spread. The population will be stable if the payoff from attacking is the same as sharing. If proportion p^* of animals attack this requires:

$$\left(\frac{V-C}{2}\right)p^* + (1-p^*)V = (1-p^*)\frac{V}{2}.$$

Which simplifies to $p^* = V/C$. This is known as the evolutionary stable strategy and means that we should expect to see a mix of animals who attack and share.

More generally, an **evolutionary stable strategy** details the proportion of the population that should be of each type if the population is to remain stable over time. Typically we would expect the population to converge to an evolutionary stable strategy and so these strategies tell us a lot about the likely consequences of evolution. Interestingly, an evolutionary stable strategy must be a Nash equilibrium. This, however, is by accident rather than design. A Nash equilibrium is such that anyone who deviates gets a lower payoff than if he did not deviate. An evolutionary stable strategy is such that anyone who deviates gets a lower payoff than those who do not deviate. There is, therefore, a subtle difference between the two, but one that turns out to not matter too much.

Unfortunately, evolution will favor non-cooperative people because they always have a higher payoff than cooperative people. Suppose, however, that cooperative people start to grow longer noses than non-cooperative people, meaning that people can tell who is cooperative and who is not. Now the odds swing back in favor of the people who are cooperative because they can make sure they only interact with each other. This means they can get a payoff of one, while non-cooperative people only get a payoff of 0.5. Evolution will now favor cooperative people. Unfortunately, though, the non-cooperative people might fight back by growing noses as long as the cooperative people.

This example illustrates how evolution can result in signaling games of hide and seek (not unlike that which we looked in chapter five and the last chapter). Evolution will favor cooperators who can signal that they are cooperators. But, it will also favor non-cooperators who can look like cooperators. This game of hide and seek can mean that seemingly irrelevant traits, like the length of nose, can become an important battleground of evolution.

What's going on here is something called assortative matching. We say that there is **assortative matching** if it is more likely certain types will meet than others. If a cooperator is more likely to interact with a cooperator than a non-cooperator is likely to interact with a cooperator, then there is assortative matching. This is crucial if cooperators are not to be exploited by non-cooperators, and so assortative matching is crucial if evolution is to favor cooperative people.

We see interesting evidence of assortative matching in human interaction, the 'lie detector' being one example. Experimental economists and psychologists have also shown that individuals have varying abilities to predict what an opponent will do in a game even if they only meet or see that person for a few seconds. For example, Pradel et al. (2009) did a study in which schoolchildren, aged ten to nineteen, were asked to predict what their classmates would do in a dictator game (see chapter seven for more on this game). As we would expect there was a split of children offering nothing (8 percent of children), half the amount (49 percent of children) or something in between.

Research Methods 8.2

Experimenting with children

The study by Pradel et al. involved children aged ten to nineteen as subjects and I am going to talk later about a study by Gneezy and Rustichini that involved children aged nine to ten. So, psychologists and behavioral economists do sometimes use children as subjects. This can be for convenience, because a school might provide a large group of willing volunteers. For the most part, though, it's because looking at how children behave can provide insight on the causes of behavior.

For instance, if we get children to play the ultimatum game and find they very rarely reject offers, then we can say that the desire to reject seems to develop later in life. Indeed, this might suggest it is a cultural thing (although care is needed because things can develop later in life because of genetic reasons, breasts being a fairly obvious example). To really exploit this opportunity we do need to experiment with very young children and that does pose some challenges. For example, young children need an incentive other than money and can more easily lose attention.

The most important thing for us is that the children were good, better than chance, at predicting what others would do, and were particularly good at knowing who would give nothing. This is illustrated in Figure 8.1, where we see that children were much better than chance at predicting the giving of friends and those they dislike. Furthermore, this was not just due to friends being like them but a genuine ability to predict giving.

If we are able to predict what others will do, then assortative matching becomes very relevant in understanding human cooperation. On a related note, the next thing I want to show is that evolution can lead to a desire for Edward to signal his good attributes.

Suppose that males differ in their skill at finding food and let $y \in (0,1)$ be an unobservable measure of a man's skill. The cost to a man of type y to find f calories of food is $c(f) = (y + 1 - f)^2$. More food improves the probability of children surviving, so let the benefit of finding f calories be $b(f) = 2f$. If mating is random a type y male will collect food until the marginal benefit of two, equals the marginal cost of $2(y + 1 - f)$, so he collects $f = y$ calories. As we might expect, a male collects more food if he has more skill.

This means, however, we should not expect to see random mating. Instead evolution will favor females who are fussy who they mate with, and search out those more skilled at finding food. But then males have an incentive to signal they are skilled at finding food, and they can do this by collecting lots of food. To

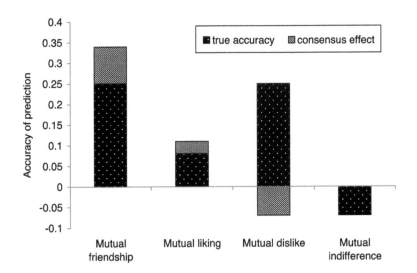

Figure 8.1 Accuracy of children's ability to predict the giving of fellow students in a dictator game, above that of guessing randomly. High accuracy could be because children expected those they like more to behave more like them, a consensus effect. Even taking this into account, however, children were good at predicting the giving of those they knew.

Source: Pradel et al. (2009).

illustrate, consider the most extreme case where females will only mate with the male who collects the most food. Then every male should collect as much food as he can. Basically the benefits of finding calories are now higher because the chances of mating and having children are higher.

In this case evolution will favor those who are good at signaling their ability to find food. More generally, we see another important evolutionary struggle, sometimes called **sexual selection**, between men and women. Evolution will favor people who are fussy who they mate with and look for the partner most likely to have healthy, well looked after children. This means that relative traits like strength, health and faithfulness become important. It also means that a person's ability to signal their desirable attributes becomes important. This provides an explanation why status and conspicuous consumption may be valid intermediate goods because those with higher status, who use conspicuous consumption to signal their status, may look more attractive to the opposite sex.

We have now started to touch on situations where culture will matter. This is because we have moved away from talking about intermediate goods, like food, that objectively do increase the probability of having children, to goods, like stylish hair or a new sports car, that increase the probability of having children if and only if they impress others. In different cultures different things might impress, in one place stylish hair and in another stylish clothes. So, now seems a good point to start adding culture to the mix.

8.2 Culture and multi-level selection

For the most part humans are very similar the world over. We all smile, laugh, cry and get angry in similar ways over similar things. This is a consequence of evolution. Behavior is not, however, solely determined by our genes. It is also shaped by the culture that we live in. Elsewhere in the book I have looked in some detail at how people can be influenced by what they see others doing and saying, and so I will not spend too much time here showing why culture matters. Instead, I want to focus on how culture can interact in interesting ways with evolution. To put this into some context it is useful to start by seeing if there are cross-cultural differences.

8.2.1 Cross-culture comparisons

I am going to look at three cross-culture comparisons. In each we compare how people behave in different cultures to see if there are systematic differences. You may want to look back on the last chapter for an explanation of the games we shall look at.

I'll start with a fascinating study by a group of economists and anthropologists, where the **ultimatum game** was played with members of 15 small-scale societies (Henrich et al. 2004). This can be coupled with a study by Roth et al. (1991), and the hundreds of other ultimatum game experiments performed around the world with university students, to give a picture of how behavior varies across cultures. Figure 8.2 shows proposer offers in a variety of different places.

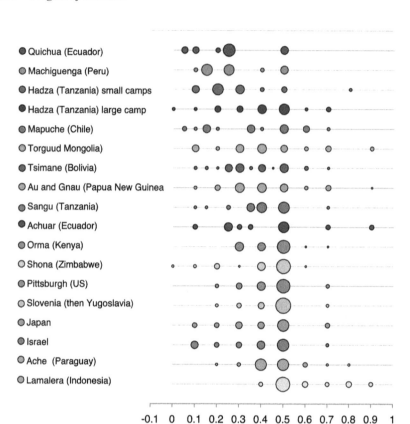

Figure 8.2 Ultimatum game offers across different cultures.

Source: Henrich et al. (2004), Roth et al. (1991).

In all cases we see that proposers do give something and so the picture we gave in chapter seven still holds true. There is, however, clearly a large variation in how much people do give. To see why, it's useful to look in a bit more detail at some of the societies.

The most giving was observed in Lamalera. This is a village located on an island in Indonesia where whale hunting is integral to village life. Whale hunting can only be done in groups and so cooperation and sharing is a big part of village life.

At the other extreme is the Machiguenga of the Peruvian Amazon. Here we observe least giving. The Machiguenga have traditionally lived in single family units and so sharing or cooperation outside of the family is rare.

The Achuar and Quichua are two ethnic/political groups in Conambo in the Ecuadorian Amazon. To look at the data it would seem that the Quichua give less than the Achuar. It turns out, however, that the differences can largely be put down to politics. High-status males in Conambo give meat in order to maintain strong alliances, and a strong correlation was observed between meat-giving and offers in the ultimatum game. The relatively low-status of the Quichua men can, therefore, explain the relatively low offers.

Finally, Au and Gnau are the languages spoken in two villages located near to each other in Papua New Guinea. The results in these villages were noticeable for the large rejection rates. The overall rejection rate was 32.8 percent, and three offers of a 0.7 share were rejected! When gifts are given by the Au and Gnau, it is understood by both the giver and receiver that the acceptor has incurred a debt that must be repaid at some future point. It can, therefore, be wise to not always accept a gift.

This gives only a snapshot of the differences across the different societies but does illustrate how behavior was influenced by everyday experience. People more used to sharing shared more, and people not used to sharing shared less, and so on. Henrich et al. take this one stage further by constructing two indices for each of the fifteen societies they considered: payoffs to cooperation, which depends on local ecology, and aggregate market integration, which depends on things such as social complexity and settlement size. There was a strong correlation between payoffs to cooperation, aggregate market integration and offers in the ultimatum game with those more used to cooperating, sharing and interacting with others offering more.

Research Methods 8.3

Statistics and lies: more, less or just different?

Comparing behavior in the ultimatum game across countries provides a good opportunity to illustrate what data and statistical tests tell us and what they do not. Figure 8.2 plots the distribution of offers. Why not just plot the mean, mode or median offers instead? This does not give such a complete picture of the data and can mislead. For example in the Ache the modal offer was 0.4, which is less than the 0.5 in most other societies, including the Mapuche, but the mean offer was higher than in many other societies, including the Mapuche.

While it is tempting to want to say that giving is higher in one society than another, in many cases this is simply impossibly to do. For example, were offers higher in the Achuar or Ache or Sangu? This also means that care is needed in interpreting statistical tests. Many tests, such as the Mann-Whitney, have a null hypothesis that two samples are drawn from the same distribution and an alternative, in this instance, that one sample stochastically dominates another. The primary thing learnt from a rejected test is that the samples are drawn from different distributions. A little care is needed in interpreting a rejected test as evidence for offers being higher or lower.

A more recent study by Gächter, Herrmann and Thöni (2010, 2008). provides a cross-cultural comparison of behavior in a **public good game with punishment**.

The most interesting thing to come out of this was differences in the use of punishment. Figure 8.3 plots the frequency of punishment relative to whether the subject contributed more than the average, the same as the average, or less than the average by varying amounts.

As we might expect, those who contributed less were punished, and the frequency of punishment did not vary too much across the locations. More surprising was the frequency of punishment for those who contributed more. In places such as Boston, Melbourne and Nottingham, there was little punishment of those contributing more. In Muscat, Athens and Riyadh, by contrast, those giving more were punished as much as those giving less. The best explanation for this is **anti-social punishment**, as a form of revenge. That's because there was a strong correlation between punishment received in one period and that given out in the next. So, those punished for giving less seemingly tried to punish those who had punished them!

The consequence of anti-social punishment was less cooperation. For example, mean contributions were 18 out of 20 in Boston and 17.7 in Copenhagen, but only 5.7 in Athens and 6.9 in Riyadh. The good news of the last chapter, therefore, that a threat of punishment can increase cooperation, needs to be toned down a little. The threat of punishment does not seem to work everywhere. So, why were there such differences in punishment?

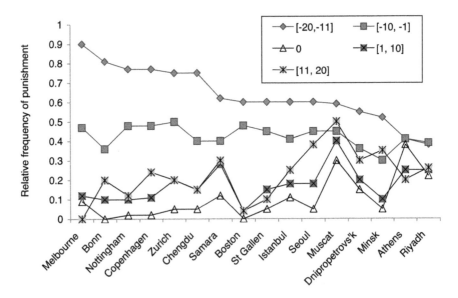

Figure 8.3 Punishment in a public good game in different locations. The proportion of times people were punished depended on whether they contributed a lot less [−20,−11], less [−10,−1], the same [0], more [1,10] or a lot more [11,20] than the person punishing.

Source: Herrmann et al. (2008).

One explanation is the strength of law and norms of civic cooperation in society. The stronger the rule of law, the less people might think that they need to rely on revenge, and the stronger the norms of cooperation the less people will want to punish those behaving in a socially desirable way. Consistent with this Herrmann et al. show that punishment of those who contributed less is positively correlated with stronger norms of civic cooperation, while punishment of those who contributed more is negatively correlated with the strength of both law and norms of civic cooperation. Again, we see local institutions and norms making a difference.

The final cross-cultural comparison I want to look at is that of **trust**. The World Values Survey is large scale survey of attitudes across a very broad selection of countries. The survey was first conducted in 1981 and has been done several times since. The survey is a fantastic source of information on how values and attitudes change across time and location. One question asked is: 'Generally speaking, would you say that most people can be trusted or that you need to be very careful in dealing with people?' The possible answers are 'Most people can be trusted' or 'Can't be too careful'. Figure 8.4 details by country what proportion did think most people can be trusted in the 1981 to 2000 data.

There is clearly large variation in what proportion say they can trust. Trust is relatively low in eastern Europe, South America and Africa, and relatively high in Scandinavia. But does this matter? In the last chapter we saw that trust can be beneficial in simple experimental games and it appears that this does transfer over to the real economy. Knack and Keefer (1997), for example, using data up to 1991, find that a 10 percent rise in the proportion who say they can trust

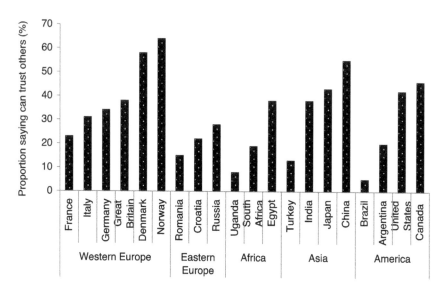

Figure 8.4 The proportion of respondents who said 'most people can be trusted'.

Source: World Value Survey.

is associated with a 0.8 percent increase in economic growth. This would suggest that the level of trust is potentially very important for the economy.

So what lessons can we take from these three cross-cultural comparisons? There seem to be two main ones. First, there is significant variation in how people behave across societies and cultures. In some places we see on average more giving, more cooperation, and more trust, than others. Second, this variation appears to come in large part from variation in institutions and norms. This does create a kind of chicken and egg problem of what comes first. Does behavior influence the norms and institutions that emerge, or do the institutions and norms that emerge influence behavior?

There are good reasons to think that it is at least partly the latter because of the environment that people live in. Some environments require cooperation for people to survive, like that of the Lamalera, while some environments allow people to be largely self-sufficient. The environment could, therefore, influence the norms and institutions that emerge which then influence behavior. The main thing, though, is that we do see cultural variation. What I want do now is see what implications this variation might have for evolution.

8.2.2 Group selection

That there are cultural differences implies that there must be distinct groups of people for different cultures to emerge and in our evolution past people will clearly have been separated into groups based on kinship and geography. This can give rise to something called **group selection** in which evolution acts on the level of the group rather than the level of the individual. We have already come across this in section 8.1, where we saw that evolution might favor groups who avoid aggregate risk. I now want to take things one stage further.

To do so I will look at a stylized model of group selection called the **haystack model**. It gets its name from thinking of mice living in haystacks but I will frame things in terms of people living in fields. So, imagine that nature provides fields with enough food that people can survive happily. The model then consists of three recurring stages, summarized in Table 8.5. In the first stage people randomly decide what field to live in. They then live together for T generations. After T generations all the fields are destroyed and everyone in the population is mixed together, before nature provides new fields and the process repeats. The key is the

Table 8.5 The three recurring stages of the haystack model. Natural selection takes place in stage two but group selection takes place overall

Stage	Description
1	People in the population randomly decide what field to live in.
2	People who chose the same field live together as a distinct colony for T generations.
3	The fields are destroyed and everyone in the population is mixed together.

periodic separation of people into distinct colonies and then mixing together when the fields are destroyed. This can lead to group selection.

To see why, suppose that there are cooperative people and free-riders. Cooperative people go out and collect food which is then shared amongst others. This costs c but benefits everyone in the colony by amount b/N where N is the number of people in the colony. Free-riders do not collect any food for others. So, if $q(t)$ is the proportion of cooperators in a colony at time t, we can assume that cooperators have $a + bq(t) - c$ children and free-riders have $a + bq(t)$ children, where a is some positive number.

Suppose that $b/N < c$ but $b > c$. Then we have a linear public good game where collecting food is the public good. Because $b > c$, the more cooperators a colony has, the more children will be produced in that colony. But, because $b/N < c$, a free-rider will always have more children than a cooperator. This latter effect means that if T is small, free-riders will have more children, and free-riders will eventually dominate the population. Fortunately, if T is large then colonies with more cooperators will have time to grow relatively large. This means that cooperators could be dominant in the population.

To illustrate, suppose that there are two fields. Field one starts with ten cooperators, and field two with nine cooperators and one defector. Figure 8.5 plots the proportion of each type over time. In the second field the number of free-riders exceeds the number of cooperators after eighteen generations. Eventually, free-riders will dominate this colony. The colony in field one, however, grows at a

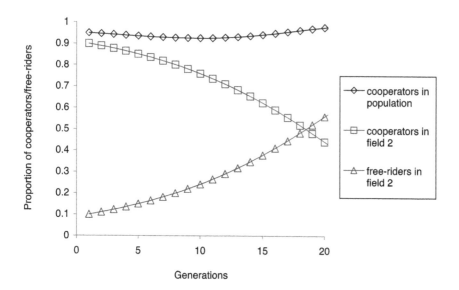

Figure 8.5 An example of the haystack model, where $a = 1$, $b = 3$, $c = 0.5$, field one starts with ten cooperators, and field two with nine cooperators and one defector. Field two becomes full of free-riders but the overall population is still full of cooperators.

higher rate because it is full of cooperators. This means that after ten generations the proportion of cooperators in the total population is increasing. Thus, cooperation can be sustained in the population if colonies with cooperators have long enough to benefit from being cooperative.

The haystack model shows that cooperative behavior can be sustained through group selection. As in section 8.1.3 this is possible because of **assortative matching**. A cooperator in a colony full of cooperators is more likely to meet a cooperator than is a free-rider in a colony full of free-riders. Thus, cooperators can do relatively well despite their apparent disadvantage relative to free-riders. For this to work we need the repeating process of reproduction in distinct colonies which then disperse and intermingle.

Some care, however, is needed not to read too much into group selection. Group selection does not mean that evolution will always favor what is good for the group and in reality it is typically a relatively weak force compared to individual selection. This is apparent in the haystack model where it is very unlikely that cooperation would emerge or spread. The best to hope for is that cooperation is not overtaken by free-riding. Even this only happens in ideal conditions!

The weakness of group selection should not though come as much surprise given what we saw in the previous chapter. There we saw that in social dilemmas most people behave either selfishly or reciprocate. We simply do not observe the cooperative, altruistic self-sacrifice that would be best for the group. That does not mean that group selection is not important. It just means we need to be realistic in what it can achieve. What it might be able to do is help explain reciprocal altruism, as I now shall explain.

When we looked at the haystack model we assumed a linear public good game without punishment. In this case, irrespective of $q(t)$, a cooperator always has c less offspring than a free-rider. Now suppose a third type emerges, willing to punish. A punisher will collect food and also at cost k lower the payoff of any free-rider by p. Now, if there are $q(t)$ cooperators, $l(t)$ punishers and $f(t)$ free-riders, cooperators will have $a + b(q(t) + l(t)) - c$ children, free-riders $a + b(q(t) + l(t)) - pl(t)$ and punishers $a + b(q(t) + l(t)) - c - kf(t)$. What difference does punishment make?

We can see that cooperators will have more children than free-riders if $c < pl(t)$. Thus cooperators will have more children than free-riders if the punishment given to free-riders is sufficiently high. Evolution could favor cooperation. There is, however, a second-order free-rider problem that we need to worry about. A punisher pays both the cost of collecting food and of punishing, so likely has the fewest offspring. Will, therefore, there be enough punishers to sustain cooperation, or will people free-ride on punishing?

To illustrate, suppose that women punish men who free-ride by not having children with them. In an evolutionary sense this is an extreme form of punishment that favors cooperation. But a woman who does not punish has a greater choice of men to mate with than one who does not, so will likely have more children. This means that evolution will favor women who do not punish. One partial solution is to punish women who have children with a free-rider. That is, to punish people who do not punish. But then it would be necessary to have someone to punish those who do not punish those who do not punish, and so on! This is the **second-order free-rider problem**.

The second-order free-rider problem means that punishing behavior could not have arisen by individual selection. Crucially, however, the numbers have now changed in a way that cooperation and punishment is easier to sustain by group selection. To explain: without punishment a cooperator always has c less offspring than a free-rider and, so a cooperator is always at a large disadvantage relative to a free-rider; group selection has lot to do to overcome this disadvantage. With punishment, a cooperator has more offspring than a free-rider and a punisher has $kf(t)$ less offspring than a cooperator. The crucial thing this means is that a punisher is only at a disadvantage if there are free-riders, so group selection has relatively less to do to help punishers overcome any disadvantage. This can tip the balance in a way that group selection can have a realistic role to play.

So, group selection is a plausible explanation for why we observe reciprocity. The story, however, is still a little incomplete. That's because while we now have a good story for why cooperation could be sustained through punishment we still do not have much of a story for why cooperation and punishment would emerge in the first place. For that we need to add culture.

8.2.3 Gene-cultural co-evolution

Group selection relies on people being separated into distinct groups or cultures. Behavior is still, however, determined by genetic evolution. So, Edward is, say, cooperative because he has a cooperative gene that he inherited from his parents. His payoff is influenced by those in his culture, but his behavior is not. This is consistent with cross-cultural variation but gives only a very minor role to culture itself. What happens if we start to add a bit more cultural influence?

Observing and learning from others can lead to cultural transmission, in which ideas are passed from one person to another. Ideas might be passed from parent to child, **vertical cultural transmission**, or between people of the same generation, **horizontal cultural transmission**. In the same way that good strategies or behaviors might be favored by genetic evolution, good ideas might be favored by **cultural evolution**. For example, Edward might copy or inherit the cooperative, trusting behavior he sees of a friend. Or, he might copy the latest fashion of the day.

The interaction between cultural and genetic evolution raises some fascinating questions. These are encapsulated in the **nature versus nurture debate** about whether a person's behavior is more shaped by their genes or the environment they grow up in. Is Edward more likely to be cooperative because he has a cooperative gene or grew up with cooperative people? I am not going to explore such questions here. But I think it is worth briefly thinking about how cultural evolution interacts with genetic evolution. Does cultural evolution, for example, overwhelm genetic evolution?

To me that seems unlikely. After all, genetic evolution gave us and shapes our ability to learn from others. Genetic evolution would also put a stop to certain types of cultural evolution, particularly by vertical cultural transmission. For example, a family passing from generation to generation the idea: 'use contraceptives and only have one child,' is probably not destined to last very long. Neither is a family with a norm to 'smoke, drink and exercise rarely'. Things, though can work the other way, and cultural evolution influence genetic evolution. For example, if there is a cultural norm to mate with tall people, then the average height of the population will likely rise over generations.

It seem most apt, therefore, to think of genetic and cultural evolution as part of one big process in which they complement each other rather than dominate each other. This interaction is termed **gene-culture co-evolution**. One interesting aspect of gene-culture co-evolution that I want pick up on here is how it can increase the possible strength of group selection. Let's see why.

Suppose that there is a **conformist bias**, whereby individuals copy the most prevalent behavior in the group or culture. We saw some evidence in chapter five that this is plausible. I now want to think through what consequence this has in the haystack model. A conformist bias means that colonies will become relatively homogenous, or at least, more homogenous than they would be without a conformist bias. For example, if most people in a colony are cooperative, then others will conform to that and so the colony as a whole becomes more cooperative.

This has two consequences. First, it means that the differences between colonies become more stark. We tend to get less colonies with a mixture of types, and more colonies dominated by one type, either cooperators or free-riders. The second thing it does is make colonies resistant to change. For example, a free-rider that joins a colony full of cooperators may conform and change his behavior, rather than having lots of children who subsequently turn the colony into one of free-riding.

Both of these things make the group selection explanation for reciprocation more plausible. Indeed, it may be enough for punishment and cooperation to emerge rather than just survive because cooperation, once established in one colony, can easily spread from colony to colony through cultural transmission. Also, in a group that has a cultural norm of cooperation, genetic evolution may favor individuals who do not free-ride. Cooperation in one colony may be enough, therefore, for cooperation to spread through the population.

The exact details of how reciprocation did emerge are still hotly debated, and there are certainly a lot of ifs and buts in the story that I have just told. We saw in the last chapter, however, that reciprocation is common in human behavior and so this must have an evolutionary explanation. Gene-culture co-evolution seems to offer the most promising explanation we have.

8.3 Summary

For most of us, finding food is now a simple task of going to the nearest supermarket, and we live well away from the savannahs of Africa. Hopefully, however, I have shown you that an evolutionary perspective is still useful in understanding modern economic behavior. Here's what we have seen.

We first saw that evolution will favor people who have good heuristics for maximizing expected utility. Intermediate goods that most increase the likelihood of having children will give most utility. We also saw that when risks are idiosyncratic evolution will favor people who use exponential discounting.

We also saw that the presence of aggregate risk and interdependence between people can have important implications. Aggregate risk can help explain risk aversion, impatience, and decreasing impatience with age. Interdependence between people can help explain why signaling and seemingly irrelevant traits become important; this, in turn, can help explain desires for things like status and esteem, and a keen ability to distinguish the motives or traits of others.

We next looked at the consequences of culture. Cross-cultural comparisons of behavior in the ultimatum game and public good game, and of trust provided evidence that important cultural differences do exist. These differences seem to depend a lot on local institutions and norms. We then questioned whether group selection can help explain reciprocation, and argued that it probably can if we take account of cultural transmission.

In sum, we have seen an evolutionary explanation for a cardinal utility function over intermediate goods, risk aversion, exponential and hyperbolic discounting, signaling and a desire for status and esteem, and reciprocity. That is by no means all the behaviors we have looked in this book but it is a pretty impressive list. For me, though, the most exciting thing about an evolutionary perspective is that it can suggest questions we may have ignored without it. For example, we have seen that an evolutionary perspective predicts a big difference between aggregate risk and idiosyncratic risk. We now need to go away and ask whether we do observe this, and whether it matters. An evolutionary perspective also gives different insight on what is likely to give people high utility and what not. This will prove useful when we look at happiness in chapter ten.

8.4 The gender gap

An issue that has always attracted much interest is the differences in opportunities and outcomes between men and women. I will not delve too deeply into how large and important these differences are, but Table 8.6 gives some figures from the World Economic Forum's Gender Gap Report 2008. Even in the highest-ranked country, Norway, we see that men participate more in the labor market, earn higher wages and are more represented in parliament. An important question is whether such differences are due to discrimination against women or due to different preferences and choices of women. In the former case the gender gap is a problem we need to solve, but in the latter case it is not.

Maybe we can learn something about the gender gap by looking at whether men and women behave differently when making economic decisions? Let's see. Before I do that, one point is worth making. Men and women generally do seem to behave in very similar ways. There is certainly far more heterogeneity in behavior within gender than there is variation in behavior between genders. That said there are some notable differences we do observe between the behavior of the

Table 8.6 Gender equality data

Country	Ranking	Labor force participation (%)		Wage for similar work	Estimated earned income (PPP $)		Members of parliament (%)	
		Men	Women	Men/Women	Men	Women	Men	Women
Norway	1	83	77	0.75	40,000	30,749	64	36
UK	13	82	70	0.62	40,000	26,242	80	20
US	27	81	70	0.69	40,000	25,005	83	17
Russia	42	76	67	0.68	13,581	8,476	86	14
China	57	88	75	0.74	8,213	5,220	79	21
Italy	67	74	51	0.54	39,163	18,501	79	21
Japan	98	85	61	0.59	40,000	17,802	91	9
India	113	84	36	0.67	5,194	1,620	91	9

Source: World Economic Forum. Gender Gap Report 2008.

average women and average man. It is these differences in the average that I want to look at.

8.4.1 Attitudes to risk

One difference we observe is in attitudes to risk. Women it seems are more risk averse than men. For example, several studies have shown that women are less likely than men to take risks in the economics laboratory. Other studies have shown women are less willing to speed, more likely to wear a seat belt, brush their teeth, and have regular blood pressure checks than men. To illustrate, I shall look at one study by Jianakoplos and Bernasek (1998).

They looked at a sample of 3,143 US households in 1989 to see whether women were less likely to invest in risky financial assets than men. The main findings are summarized in Table 8.7, which estimates the share of risky assets that a

Table 8.7 Predicted proportion of portfolio invested in risky assets. The baseline case is a 41–45-year-old white homeowner, employed, high school degree, $20,000 investment wealth and two children

	Single females	Single males	Married couples
Base case	43%	51%	48%
Wealth = $10,000	35%	39%	39%
= $20,000	43%	51%	48%
= $100,000	62%	79%	69%
= $500,000	81%	100%	89%
Age = 26–30	23%	63%	47%
= 31–35	32%	42%	37%
Education = 6 years or less	77%	79%	50%
Race = white	43%	51%	48%
= black	58%	49%	42%

Source: Jianakoplos and Bernasek (1998).

household held. Across the board, single females invest less in risky assets, than single men or couples. Also noteworthy is the effect of a change in wealth from $20,000 to $100,000. Both men and women are predicted to increase their share of risky assets, but men increase the share more than women. This is a sign of greater risk aversion in women.

Risky assets do in the long term give a higher rate of return and so differences in risk attitude can have large implications for investment return. For example, a return of 5 percent rather than 4.5 percent per year on a $1,000 investment will result in a $241 difference after 20 years. This can build up to a huge difference in wealth over a lifetime, suggesting that women will on average end up with less wealth than men.

Before moving on, I want to pick out three other notable things in Table 8.7. We see that young women are predicted to invest much less in risky assets than young men, while the less educated, and black women, are predicted to invest more in risky assets. This is interesting because it would suggest that differences in risk attitudes are due to culture rather than genes. There is, for instance, no genetic reason why black women would invest so much more in risky assets.

8.4.2 Attitudes to competition

A second difference we observe between men and women is how they respond to competition. Some studies have shown than men improve their performance when faced with competition while women do not. Other studies have shown that given the choice, men choose competitive environments while women do not. To illustrate, I shall look at two studies, the first by Gneezy and Rustichini (2004), the second by Niederle and Vesterlund (2007).

The Gneezy and Rustichini study was run in a school in Israel and involved nine- to ten-year-old children running a 40m track. First, each child ran by themselves and times were recorded. Next, pairs of children who recorded similar times were matched together and raced against each other. Finally, some children were just asked to run a second time by themselves. The results are summarized in Figure 8.6. In the first run, and when there was no competition, there are no differences between boys and girls. In a competitive environment, however, boys ran significantly faster and girls ran slower. Boys thus responded more to competition than girls. That this was observed in children maybe points more towards genes than culture?

The Niederle and Vesterlund study consisted of four parts. In the first three parts subjects had five minutes to add up as many five two-digit numbers as they could. In part one they were paid by a piece rate of $0.50 for each correct answer. In part two subjects were put in groups of four and payment was by tournament, the subject with the most correct answers getting $2 per correct answer. In part three participants could choose whether to be paid by piece rate or tournament. In part four subjects were asked to choose whether they wanted their part one performance paid by piece rate or tournament.

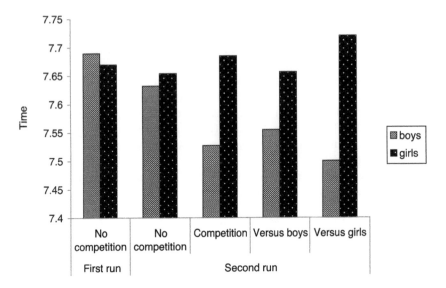

Figure 8.6 Running times of boys and girls. With no competition there is not much difference in times. With competition the boys get faster and the girls slower.

Source: Gneezy and Rustichini (2004).

This sounds a bit complicated so I will go through it step by step. In the first two
parts gender had no effect. Men and women were as good as each other with both
the piece rate, where there was no competition, and the tournament, where there
was competition. Interesting things start to happen in part three of the experiment
where subjects had to decide whether to be paid by piece rate or tournament.
Figure 8.7 illustrates what happened by plotting the proportion of subjects who
chose the tournament relative to how well they had performed. We see that men
were more likely to choose the tournament than women. Indeed, the best
performing women, on average, chose the tournament less often than the worst
performing men! The story is similar, if slightly less dramatic, in part four where
subjects were asked how they wanted to be paid for this part of the experiment.
Again, men were more likely to choose the tournament payment.

Research Methods 8.4

Incentives over time

If participants will play the same game a number of times issues arise about how to
pay them and maintain good incentives. An obvious solution is to pay participants
for every decision they make. If, however, a participant is going to make 25 decisions and be paid around $10 in total, then there is never going to be much incentive
to make good choices. Also, if participants have in mind some reservation amount

they want from participating in the experiment, then choices may change if they achieve that amount. This is a real concern in the Niederle and Vesterlund (2007) study where someone who does well in parts one and two may be more willing to take a risk in parts three and four. To avoid this it is typical to pay participants for one randomly selected round or part of an experiment. This should maintain good incentives but can lead to somewhat lucky and unlucky participants.

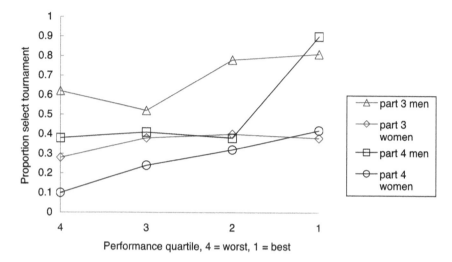

Figure 8.7 The proportion who choose competition conditional on how well they had performed.

Source: Niederle and Vesterlund (2007).

We see, therefore, that men appear to react differently to competition than do women. I shall shortly try to explain why this might be the case. For now, however, I want to point out that much is still unknown about how competition effects interact with gender. For example, the Gneezy and Rustichini study suggests women are less competitive with other women (see Figure 8.6). A complementary study by the same authors showed an opposite effect. We see similar complications when looking at social preferences.

8.4.3 Social preferences

In terms of social preferences there appears to be no simple relationship between gender and behavior. For example, in one set of experiments women might seem more altruistic, but then in another, men might seem more altruistic. In specific contexts, however, gender has been shown to matter. To illustrate these points I shall compare studies by Eckel and Grossman (2001) and Solnick (2001). In both studies the ultimatum game was played between a receiver and proposer of known gender. In both cases we see that gender has an effect on receiver behavior.

In the study by Eckel and Grossman (2001), subjects had to divide $5 and interacted in groups of four proposers and four receivers sitting opposite each other. A proposer could not know which of the four people sitting opposite would be the receiver to his or her offer, but one of them would be. Table 8.8 provides a snapshot of the results by looking at whether an offer of $1 is accepted or rejected (according to a model that fits the data). We see that a $1 offer from a female is more likely to be accepted than a similar offer from a male. We also see that females are more likely to accept than men. Eckel and Grossman call this chivalry and solidarity.

In the study by Solnick, subjects had to split $10 and were not sitting opposite each other. A further difference is that receivers wrote down minimal acceptable offers before seeing the actual offer they had received (see Research Methods 7.2). Table 8.9 details the minimal acceptable offers of receivers. This time things look very different. We see that both male and female receivers set a higher minimal acceptable offer when the proposer is a female rather than male. We also see females setting higher minimal acceptable offers than men. This means that if a male offers a $7, $3 split to another male, it is likely to be accepted, while between two females it is likely to be rejected. There are no signs of chivalry or solidarity here.

Table 8.8 The percentage of $1 offers accepted from a model fitted to the experimental data. For example, if the proposer was female, 36 per cent of males would accept the offer

		Responder	
		Male	Female
	Male	20%	39%
Proposer	Female	36%	78%
	Unknown	17%	42%

Source: Eckel and Grossman (2001).

Table 8.9 Minimal acceptable offers. For example, if the proposer was female, the average amount a male would accept was $3.39

		Responder	
		Male	Female
	Male	$2.45	$2.82
Proposer	Female	$3.39	$4.15
	Unknown	$2.71	$3.30

Source: Solnick (2001).

The results of these two studies come to very different conclusions about receiver behavior. These differences could arise from the strategic environment. Female offers were more likely to be accepted when subjects could see each other and when they were responding to an actual offer. Female offers were less likely to be accepted when subjects could not see each other and were deciding before an offer had actually been made. Gender does, therefore, matter, but seemingly in ways that are conditional on the strategic environment.

8.4.4 Why are men and women different?

We have seen that gender does seem to matter. Why? There are personality differences between men and women that could help explain the differences in economic behavior. Here are three of them.

First, women appear to experience stronger emotions than men. This could influence their behavior. For example, we saw in chapters two and three the importance of loss aversion and risk aversion. Both are these are partly emotional responses connected to the fear of losing money or something else. Stronger emotions may also explain why women were less likely to reject when face to face with an ultimatum game opponent.

Second, men appear to be more overconfident than women, at least in some situations. This could make men more willing to gamble and to prefer competition. For example, Niederle and Vesterlund found that 75 percent of men thought they would be the best in their group, compared to just 43 percent for women. Remember there were four in the group, so the number should have been 25 percent. Both men and women were overconfident, but men were far more overconfident!

Finally, men appear more stimulated by challenge than do women. Again this could account for less risk aversion and a preference for competition. In the Niederle and Vesterlund study, for instance, there was less difference between men and women in part four, which was about past behavior, than part three, which was about a task yet to be done.

But why do we see these personality differences? Is it genetic or cultural? The answer is probably a mix of both. There are good evolutionary reasons why we could see such differences. For example, there is far more possible variation in the number of offspring that a man can have relative to a women, so evolution could favor risk taking, competitive men. Also women differ from men in levels of testosterone and other hormones that are known to be correlated with things like aggression. Culture, however, can still play its part if boys and girls are raised and educated relative to stereotype. For instance, if women are expected to be less assertive then we should not be surprised that on average women might become less assertive.

So, what about the gender gap? If men are less risk averse and more competitive than women it is not hard to understand why a gender gap could arise. Whether the gender gap is a problem is a much more difficult question to answer. If genetic differences mean men and women want different things then maybe the gender gap is not such a problem? If the differences are cultural then arguably there is more to be worried about? These are not questions I can answer, so I leave them for you to think about.

8.5 The economics of family

It is typical in economics to focus on individuals. Occasionally we might talk about households, but it is only occasionally. Many economic decisions, however, are made as a family, or at least with the family in mind. For example, Edward and Anna might want to save money for their children's education, or save in order to bequeath something to them when they die. An evolutionary perspective is crucial to understanding such decisions.

One good reason to take account of evolution is kin selection. As a rough rule of thumb half of a child's genes are inherited from the father and half from the mother. This means that evolution should favor mothers and fathers who look after their children and make sure 'their genes' are passed on. More precisely, there is a **coefficient of relatedness** between a parent and child of 0.5, between a grandparent and child of 0.25, between brother and sister of 0.5, and so on. **Hamilton's rule** states that an individual who can, at cost C, benefit a relative by B should do so if $Br > C$ where r is the coefficient of relatedness between them. Put in its most extreme form Anna or Edward may be willing to sacrifice their own life to save two or more of their children.

Kin selection brings the unit of selection down to the level of the gene (compared to the individual and group selection we have seen so far) and is a form of assortative matching because it means an individual tries to interact with and help family rather than unrelated individuals. This makes it much easier to understand transfers between family members. For instance, it is not really altruistic for Edward and Anna to pay for their children's education, it is just good evolutionary sense.

Kin selection matters in all species, but humans have taken it to a relatively extreme level. To see why, it's interesting to compare humans with primates, our closest relatives. Humans are distinctive in at least five ways: (i) we have bigger brains, (ii) live longer, (iii) spend longer as infants being dependent on parents, (iv) spend time in a post-reproductive age looking after grandchildren, and (v) find men supporting women and their offspring.

To illustrate, Figure 8.8 compares human consumption and production of food in three hunter-gatherer societies (Ache, Hadza and Hiwi) and chimpanzees. In humans we see huge differences over a lifetime between production and consumption and between men and women. In chimpanzees we see hardly any difference between consumption and production. What this means is that chimpanzees are largely self-sufficient. Humans are far from self-sufficient. Indeed, the basic story with humans is that men aged twenty to sixty acquire enough food to support those under twenty, and women aged twenty to forty-five who are looking after children. This involves big transfers within the family.

The leading explanation for why we see such transfers is human's bigger brains. Bigger brains mean we need longer to develop, and that means we need the

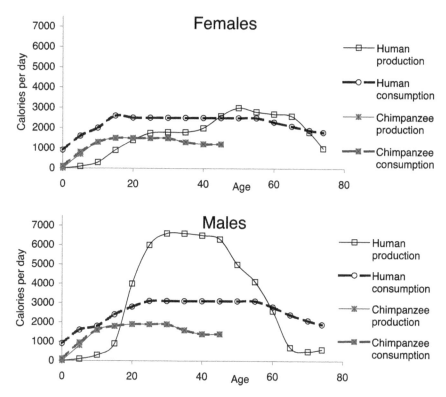

Figure 8.8 Food production and consumption by age in males and females, and in chimpanzees.

Source: Kaplan et al. (2000).

support of family when we are young. It also means that we need to leave longer in order to repay the debt that is accumulated in the early years of life. Luckily, a bigger brain also means that we have learnt more complicated ways to acquire food, and hence produce large amounts of food. It is a complicated mix, but everything holds together. What is not so clear is the catalyst that started the process. Did evolution favor big brains and we acquired ways to produce them? Or did evolution favor males who produced large amounts of food (see section 8.1.4) and big brains were a consequence?

What we can say for sure is that transfers within the family are an integral part of life. That is not going to stop just because food is more plentiful, for most of us, than in our evolutionary past. We should expect to see transfers between family members and this suggests we should more readily think of the household as most relevant in many economic decisions. It can also help us understand a bit better the transfers we do see whether that be bequests, paying for education, or supporting a poor relative.

To illustrate, one recent trend of family life is the growing importance of **remittances** from migrant workers to their families back in the native country. For example, in 2007, remittances to Honduras were equivalent to 21.5 percent of that country's GDP, 13.9 percent in Serbia, 6.6 percent in Kenya, 3.3 percent in India and 1 percent in China (figures from the World Bank). Put another way, over $45 billion was sent from the USA in 2007 in remittances. These are big numbers. Moreover, this possibility of sending back remittances has been a major motivation for individuals to seek work abroad, with the consequent increase in immigrant labor.

From an evolutionary point of view we should expect transfers to flow downwards from older to younger generations. This would suggest that remittances serve a 'helpers-at-the-nest' purpose whereby a worker abroad, say, sends money back to his parents so that they can support younger offspring. An alternative possibility is that children are supporting relatively poorer parents and so there is a transfer from younger to older generations. This is hard to justify with an evolutionary explanation but easier to support with cultural transmission if it becomes an accepted norm for children to go abroad and support poorer parents. It is not clear yet which way the flows typically go but a better understanding of the evolutionary and cultural forces at work may help provide the answers.

8.6 Further reading

For those eager to learn more: much of the material in section 8.1 was based on the work of Arthur Robson. Robson (2001a, 2001b, 2002) and Robson and Samuelson (2009) are useful references. For more on cultural differences I would suggest following up the references in the text, particularly the book by Henrich et al. (2004). Sobel (2002) provides an interesting review of the literature on trust and social capital. For more on group selection, and the evolution of cooperation, Bergstrom (2002) and the book by Gintis et al. (2005) are worth reading, while the 8 December 2006 issue of *Science*, with articles by Boyd, Bowles and Nowak, provides an interesting snapshot of research in this area. For more on the effects of gender see the excellent review article by Croson and Gneezy (2009) and for the economics of the family, Bergstrom (1996) is a good starting point. The fascinating article by Kaplan et al. (2000) explains the data on food production and consumption, while Robson and Kaplan (2003) offer an economic perspective. Webley (2004) provides interesting insights on children's understanding of economics. On a more general level the books by Frank (1985), Ridley (1997) and Laland and Brown (2005) are three I would pick out from the host of excellent, general readership books taking an evolutionary perspective.

8.7 Review questions

8.1   Give some examples of intermediate goods that may enter the utility function. Is money an intermediate good?

8.2   Let's go back to the first example of long and short winters. Suppose there are 1,600 adults of type L, 1,600 of type S, and 1,600 randomizer types. The randomizer types decide at the start of each summer whether to gather enough food for a long winter, and do gather enough with probability 0.4. Suppose we have the sequence summer, short winter, summer, short winter, summer short winter, summer, long winter, how many of each type will likely survive?

8.3 How can evolution explain reference dependence? How about loss aversion?

8.4 Is present bias and time inconsistency a good evolutionary strategy?

8.5 Design an experiment to find out whether people dislike aggregate risk compared to idiosyncratic risk.

8.6 Is natural selection relevant in understanding modern economic behavior or is it only culture that matters?

8.7 Why is it so hard to get cooperation to emerge in the haystack model?

8.8 Does maximizing utility mean maximizing happiness?

8.9 What do you think is the main cause of the gender gap?

8.10 How can confirmatory bias help explain the gender gap?

8.11 Why do many people save money all their life in order to bequeath to their children?

8.12 Why does it not make evolutionary sense for a young person to support an older parent? Why could it happen because of cultural influence?

9   Neuroeconomics

Giving up smoking is the easiest thing in the world. I know because I've done it
thousands of times.

Mark Twain

We use our brains to think and make decisions, whether consciously or uncon-
sciously, and so, if we understand how the brain works, we should be able to
better understand economic behavior. Clearly, things are not quite as simple as
this, because the brain is a very complicated thing. Over the last 20 years or so our
understanding of the brain, and our ability to measure brain activity, has, however,
improved a lot. It has improved so much that neuroscience is now a viable tool for
economists to use in interpreting economic behavior. The goal of this chapter is to
see what we have learnt so far.

9.1 An introduction to the brain

We will not get very far unless we know some basics of how the brain works. I am
not, though, going to go into very much depth on this subject; all we need is a
simple model of the brain that is not too far from reality. The model that economists typically work with assumes modularity. The idea behind **modularity**
is that the brain can be split into a number of distinct components or **brain
modules** that are each responsible for specific functions like breathing, seeing,
being altruistic or getting angry. We can think of these brain modules as distinct
areas of the brain, and so we can split the brain into areas that are responsible for
different things. This is schematically show in Figure 9.1. Controlling all of this is
the **interpreter** which monitors the output of the modules, interprets them, and
reacts.

Modularity is a fairly crude model of how the brain works. For instance, we
know that modules can work in parallel with other modules, and communicate
with each other while doing so. We also know that there is nothing anywhere near
as simple as an 'altruism module' or an 'anger module', and any classification is
inevitably one of judgment. To a rough approximation, however, modularity does
not seem too bad, and it is a very useful model for economists to work with.

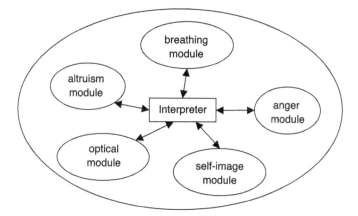

Figure 9.1 A schematic representation of modularity. The brain consists of modules that perform specific functions. An interpreter monitors and interacts with these modules.

It is useful because it potentially allows us to infer what causes a particular behavior. For example, suppose that someone called Rob has the chance to give Federica money, and does so. Furthermore, suppose that we know a brain module associated with altruism and another associated with self-image. If we monitor the brain and find that the altruism module is activated, but not the self-image module, when Rob gives money, then we could infer he gave to be kind to others and not to promote self-image.

For this to be useful we need to measure brain activity. Historically neuroscience has learnt a lot from people who for one reason or another, usually an accident, have brain damage in an area of the brain. If the person loses the ability to perform a function, such as get angry, then we can infer the anger module is where the brain damage is. More recent techniques such as EEG, PET and fMRI allow us to measure brain activity directly (see Research Methods 9.1). In principle these techniques allow us to see what parts of the brain are activated when Rob is, say, angry, and also measure the intensity of the brain activity, so we can say how angry he is.

Research Methods 9.1

Monitoring brain activity

There are three basic brain imaging methods: electro-encephalogram (EEG), positron emission topography (PET), and functional magnetic resonance imaging (fMRI). Each of these methods uses a different technique to measure brain activity in different parts of the brain. In an experiment, brain activity is measured during some baseline task and during some experimental events, such as the person being told they have won some money. It is the difference in brain activity between the baseline and experimental event that is important, because it gives us a clue to what parts of the brain are activated, and how much they are activated, by the experimental event.

EEG is the only one of the three methods that directly measures brain activity. It does so via electrodes attached to the scalp which pick up the electrical current that results when neurons fire.

PET and fMRI make use of the fact that active neurons need energy and they get this energy from glucose in blood. Neural activity, therefore, increases blood flow. It also, because the active neurons take glucose from the blood and not oxygen, relatively increases the oxygen content of the blood.

A **PET** scanner measures the blood flow in the brain. To do this, a radioactive tracer isotope is injected into the person's blood circulation. As this isotope decays it emits positrons which on meeting nearby electrons produce photons which can be detected. By counting the number of photons emitted it is possible to get an idea of how much blood and blood flow there is in different areas of the brain.

An **fMRI** scanner measures the oxygen content of blood. To do this, the head is put in a magnetic field. It so happens that the way blood interacts with this magnetic field depends on the oxygen content of the blood. This can be detected to show where in the brain the oxygen contains more or less oxygen and thus where there is more or less neural activity. This is the most widely used method in neuroeconomics today.

The technicalities of EEG, Pet and fMRI are interesting, but not ultimately our main concern. One thing, however, is worth mention: there is no perfect way, yet, of measuring brain activity. EEGs can record very accurately the time of brain activity (down to milliseconds), but are relatively inaccurate in saying where the activity was, or at picking up activity in some parts of the brain. PET and fMRI scanners can record much more accurately where the brain activity takes place (typically to within two to three millimeters) but are much less accurate on the time of activity (seconds rather than milliseconds). Also, none of the methods is very user friendly. EEG is relatively unobtrusive and portable compared to PET and fMRI but still a lot more involved than participating in a normal economic experiment.

The idea that we can measure the intensity of brain activity is exciting, because it suggests we can measure pleasure, pain and utility. Care is needed in pushing this idea too far, not least because of the crudeness of the modularity model of the brain. Even so, in principle, as Rob thinks about giving away money, we could measure activity in the altruism, self-image, and selfish modules, and see whether we can predict what he will choose from the intensity of activity. For instance, if the selfish module is activated a lot, we might be able to predict him keeping the money.

This already gives us two things to look at while we watch the brain: what areas of the brain are activated, and how much they are activated. Potentially, this can help us understand a bit better the behavior we observe, and we'll see how this works in practice soon enough. Before that, there are a couple of important things that I would like to do: introduce some of areas of the brain of most relevance to us, and talk a bit about different brain processes.

9.1.1 An economist's map of the brain

Neuroscience brings with it a load of terminology that is probably alien to many, at least it is me. An understanding of this terminology is, however, useful and so I will try to explain the main terms you are likely to come across. On the basis that this is an economics textbook and not a medical textbook, I shall only give the most basic introduction.

It is traditional to start with the big picture and progressively narrow things down. So, I should start with the nervous system. The **nervous system** transmits signals from one part of the body to another. In doing so it allows an individual to detect changes within themselves and their environment, analyze them, and respond to them. The latter two of these are of primary importance for us meaning we can focus on the central nervous system. The **central nervous system** consists of seven basic parts: the spinal cord, the cerebellum, the medulla, pons and midbrain, which are collectively called the **brainstem**, the **diencephalon** and the **cerebrum**. These are illustrated in Figure 9.2.

While the cerebellum, midbrain and diencephalon are of interest to economists (Table 9.1 outlines their main functions), most attention is usually given to the

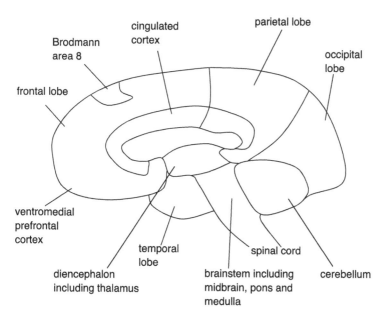

Figure 9.2 Some areas of the brain seen from the medial surface of the brain (i.e. by slicing the brain down the middle).

Table 9.1 Parts of the central nervous system and some of the main functions that go on in that part

Parts of the central nervous system	Functions include
Brainstem (including pons, medulla and midbrain)	Control of reflexes such as heart rate, breathing, and coughing. Basic aspects of reward and pleasure. Conduit of information in the system.
Cerebellum (little brain)	Sensory-motor skills necessary for smoothly coordinated movements.
Diencephalon (including thalamus)	Control of homeostatic and reproductive functions, such as body temperature, hunger and thirst.

cerebrum. This is the big part of the brain responsible for higher-level information processing and decision making. The cerebrum is more than big enough that we need to distinguish different parts of it, and there are various ways of doing this.

The one you are probably familiar with is the distinction between **left** and **right cerebal hemispheres,** corresponding to the left and right sides of the brain. Equally intuitive but probably less familiar is a distinction between the outside and inside of the cerebrum. The **cerebral cortex** is the distinctive outside layer of the cerebrum and is essentially a crumpled sheet of neurons around two to four millimeters thick. Within that we find something called the **basal ganglia**.

As well as distinguishing left and right and inside and outside, we need ways to pinpoint different areas of the cerebral cortex and basal ganglia. To get some intuition for how this is done, imagine a map of a country. There are natural features like mountains and rivers that we might use to pinpoint a specific location. There are also artificial features like county or city boundaries that we might want to use. Sometimes the natural and artificial features will coincide, but sometimes not. Something similar happens with mapping the cerebrum.

Let's start with the cerebral cortex and the artificial features: One classification splits it into four basic parts: the **frontal, parietal, temporal** and **occipital lobe**. These can be further distinguished into things like the **dorsolateral prefrontal cortex** and **ventromedial prefrontal cortex** (see Research Methods 9.2). If these names seem a bit unwieldy, then you may prefer a classification originally conceived by Brodmann. In this case the cerebral cortex is split into 52 areas known as **Brodmann areas**. Each area corresponds to a particular area of the cerebral cortex, area eight for instance is illustrated in Figure 9.2. These areas do not necessarily correspond to natural features of the brain but they do allow us to pinpoint specific locations of the cerebral cortex.

Research Methods 9.2

The terminology of neuroanatomy

Various terms are used to specify locations of the brain, some illustrated in Figure 9.3.

Simplest are: **anterior** and **posterior** which indicated front and back of the head; **inferior** and **superior** which indicate above and below; **medial** and **lateral** which indicate toward the centre or to the side.

Other terms come from drawing the axis of the body and brain. **Dorsal** refers to the back or upper half depending on whether the focus is the body or brain. **Ventral** refers to the front or lower half. **Rostral** indicates the direction towards the nose and **caudal** towards the back.

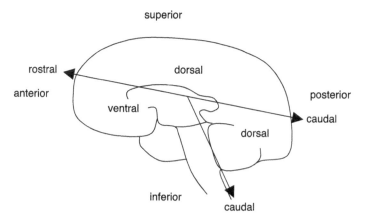

Figure 9.3 Terminology to describe location in the brain.

Source: Purves et al. (2008).

This is enough to understand terms like the posterior parietal cortex and anterior cingulated cortex. The only other thing you should need to know is that frontal lobe is commonly subdivided into the prefrontal cortex (corresponding to the frontal gyri at the front of the frontal lobe) and the precentral cortex (corresponding to the precentral gyrus at the back of the frontal lobe). Now you can understand terms like dorsolateral prefrontal cortex and ventromedial prefrontal cortex.

Now for the natural features: Recall that the cerebral cortex is like a crumpled sheet. The bits of the sheet that stick out are called **gyri** (singular, **gyrus**), while the concavities between are called **sulci** (singular, **sulcus**) or **fissures**. These are the mountains and rivers of the brain and provide a natural way to pinpoint specific locations of the cererbral cortex. For example, the cingulated cortex including the cingulate gyrus and cingulate sulcus runs along the bottom of the frontal and parietal lobes taking in Brodmann areas 23, 24, 26, 29, 30, 31 and 32.

Table 9.2 Parts of the cerebrum and some of the main functions that go on in that part

Parts of the cerebrum	Functions include
Frontal lobe	Controlling movement.
	Organizing, planning and decision making.
Parietal lobe	Bodily sensation including aspects of vision.
	Aspects of language.
	Attending to stimuli.
Temporal lobe	Hearing.
	Higher order visual tasks.
	Recognizing stimuli.
Occipital lobe	Initial processing of visual information.
Amygdala	Aspects of emotional processing.
Insula	Visceral and autonomic functions including taste.
Hippocampus	Certain kinds of memory.

Mixing both artificial and natural features gives us a further collection of names, some of which you may be familiar with, including the amygdala, hippocampus and insular. These tend to be towards the middle of the brain and not necessarily in the cerebral cortex. The **amygdala**, for instance, consists of a group of **nuclei** (where a nuclei is a compact collection of neurons) at the anterior pole of the temporal lobe. The **hippocampus** is a cortical structure lying inside the temporal lobe. The **insula** is a portion of the cerebral cortex folded deep between the frontal and temporal lobes.

The final thing we need to do is distinguish parts of the basal ganglia, the area inside the cerebral cortex. Most important are two nuclei called the **caudate** and **putamen** which are collectively referred to as the **striatum**.

Being able to pinpoint specific locations of the brain is critical in neuroscience and so understanding the above terminology is useful in following the literature of neuro-economics. It is not really necessary, however, for us to know exactly where, say, Brodmann area 41 is; we can leave that to the neuroscientists. More important for us is to know what different areas of the brain do. Tables 9.1 and 9.2 give you some idea as to basic functions. What I want to do now is introduce some functions of more specific interest to economists. In order to do that it's necessary to talk a bit more about brain processes.

9.1.2 Brain processes

Neuroscience is not just about filling in a map of the brain. It also helps us understand the processes by which decisions are made. To see why, it is useful to think of brain activities as fitting within a two-dimensional framework where we distinguish between controlled and automatic, and between cognitive and affective processes. This is summarized in Table 9.3.

We have already briefly come across the distinction between controlled and automatic processes in chapter two when comparing perception, intuition and

Table 9.3 Four different brain processes

	Cognitive processes	Affective processes
	Free of emotion	Involve emotion
Controlled processes Step-by-step conscious	e.g. thinking through a math problem.	e.g. an actor recalling being angry to better play his role in a play.
Automatic processes Parallel sub-conscious	e.g. playing a golf shot.	e.g. jumping when hearing a loud noise.

reasoning. **Controlled processes** involve step-by-step logic in which someone consciously thinks through some problem or about some event. **Automatic processes** are not accessible to consciousness and go on in parallel, allowing many tasks to be performed simultaneously. A person will typically have little conscious idea, during or after, how automatic processes work.

Affective processes involve emotions that typically result in a desire or drive to do something. For example, Rob feels fear and so runs away, or feels hungry so eats. We can simply think of **cognitive processes** as everything else, so thought processes that are free, or almost free, of emotion. For example, Rob driving his car or preparing his dinner.

Common sense tells us that most of what we do must involve automatic processes. As I write this, I am breathing, my heart is pumping, my fingers are pressing the keyboard, my eyes are watching the screen and the fields outside, I'm listening to the cars and birds, and thinking what to write, plus a lot of other things. There is clearly no way that this could all be done consciously and so most of it goes on at a sub-conscious level.

For this to work, we do need to learn how to do things automatically, because the more we can do automatically, the more we can do, and it is possible to do automatically quite complicated things, like hit a golf ball, or play a piano concerto. More interesting for our purpose is the reverse logic. We cannot possibly consciously decide what to do using controlled processes and so we must subconsciously decide what is 'important enough' to warrant conscious control. This leads to the idea of executive control.

In the absence of executive control we could imagine that behavior would be determined by a **default mode**. This is basically what would happen if we stopped to think consciously: life would go on with everything happening according to automatic processes. Young children and some adults with brain damage are thought to essentially be like this. Most of us though are not like that. Instead we have **executive control systems** that sometimes cut in and give us control to move away from default mode.

It's natural, therefore, to think of automatic processes as inevitable and the norm, while control processes are rarer and only happen when automatic processes let them happen. This is important because it goes a long way to justifying the important chain of reasoning that I highlighted in chapter two: framing and context influence intuition and perceptions which influence reasoning. On first encountering an event automatic processes, both cognitive and affective, get to work and it's only subsequently that controlled processes are given a role.

So, whether Rob feels a loss or a gain, feels happy or angry, or perceives something as kind or unkind will happen automatically and sub-consciously. This must then influence the starting point for any subsequent reasoning he does about how to behave. Hence we observe context and framing effects. Stylized though it is, this is a nice way to think about economic behavior, and one good thing about neuroscience is that it allows us to put some details to the idea. In particular, we can hope to understand a bit more about how automatic and controlled processes work and interact. For that we need to know more about executive control.

9.1.3 Executive control systems

To work well executive control systems need to perform a few intermediate processes. Most important is when to switch from automatic to control. Following that there is the need for inhibition and task switching. **Inhibition** is the suppression of automatic behavior no longer deemed appropriate while **task switching** involves starting any new behavior. An important part of this is likely to be **simulation** in which the possible consequences of different actions are worked through.

To illustrate, one test or means to measure executive control is the **Wisconsin card sorting task**. (You can find free versions of this test on the web, and it only takes around 20 minutes, so maybe you might want to have a go before reading on.) The task requires participants to sort a deck of cards according to some rule. The color, shape and number of symbols on the cards are different and determine the rule. For instance, the rule might be to sort cards according to color, or to sort according to number of symbols. Subjects are not told the rule but are told whether they are sorting the cards correctly so they can learn by trial and error what the rule is. The key to the test is that, without the subject being told, the rule periodically changes. For instance, it might go from sorting by color to sorting by shape. Of interest is whether, and how quickly, subjects adapt to the new rule.

This task means that subjects learn something well enough for it to become automatic, and then at some point have to realize that the default mode is no longer working, inhibit the old rule, and switch to a new one! Some of this might happen at a conscious level, but executive control need not be conscious. For instance, while driving along the highway, Rob might swerve to avoid something before he knows he's done it.

There are a few areas of the brain thought to be involved in executive control processes including the dorsolateral prefrontal cortex and ventromedial prefrontal cortex. These areas stand out as prime candidates because they are linked to many

Table 9.4 Main components of executive control systems

Parts of the brain	Functions include
Dorsolateral prefrontal cortex (DLPFC)	Initiating and shifting behavior, e.g. to switch task or change action. Inhibition, in the sense of getting rid of irrelevant information, e.g. forgetting the old rule in Wisconsin card sorting task. Simulating behavioral consequences and abstracting from reality.
Ventromedial prefrontal cortex (VMPFC)	Inhibition, in the sense of adhering to rules of behavior, e.g. behaving appropriately in social situations. Learning when things change by following the link between stimuli and reward.
Anterior cingulated cortex	Notices conflict and decides whether to run default mode or not.
Basal ganglia	Learning the connection between stimuli and reward.

other areas of the brain and so have the ability to control. Brain imaging allows us to confirm their role, as summarized in Table 9.4.

That these areas are important in executive control means they are going to be important areas of interest to economists, and while the functions might look a bit abstract at first sight, underlying them are things we need to think about. For example, simulating behavioral consequences and learning the connection between stimuli and reward are fundamental parts of making economic decisions.

In following this up there are three things that I now want to look at in turn, as we start to focus more on economic behavior: how outcomes are evaluated, how people learn about the value of outcomes, and finally, how people make decisions.

9.2 Valuing rewards and learning

In this section we are going to start looking directly at economic behavior but with a focus on automatic processes, primarily the valuation of rewards and learning. This will be a precursor to looking at the more involved controlled processes that are involved in economic decisions. The natural place to start is with the evaluation of rewards.

9.2.1 Reward evaluation

The basic question I want to start with is how people process rewards. For example, if Rob wins $10, or loses $10, what goes on in his brain? The action appears to start in the midbrain. The neurotransmitter **dopamine** is heavily involved in the evaluation of rewards, and there are two important structures in the midbrain that are associated with dopamine. These are called the **substantia nigra** and **ventral tegmental area (VTA)**. Most important for decision making is probably the VTA because this has pathways projecting into other important areas of the brain. In particular it has pathways to the frontal lobe, and pathways projecting to areas important for emotional and affective processing, such as the amygdala, hippocampus and other areas of basal ganglia. So, you might want to think of the VTA as the hub sending out messages to other areas of the brain about what has happened.

In principle, this means we should keep track of what happens in the VTA and all the areas that connect to the VTA. But, you may well have had enough of terminology by now and so I am going to make life a bit easier for us. In order that we can focus unencumbered on the economics I will primarily refer from here onwards to just two areas of the brain, summarized in Table 9.5. First is something called the nucleus accumbens, which I shall call the **NAcc**, and second is the ventromedial prefrontal cortex which I shall call **VMPFC**. Why these two areas? Both connect to the VTA; the nucleus accumbens is part of the basal ganglia, i.e. is inside the cerebrum, and is involved with reward evaluation while the VMPFC is part of the cortex, i.e. on the outside of the cerebrum, and is important in executive control. Keeping watch on these two areas will, therefore, give us a good idea what is going on.

(Just for the record, I am going to think of the nucleus accumbens and something called the ventral striatum as the same thing, and the VMPFC and something called the orbitofrontal cortex as the same thing. They are not quite the same things, but I don't think that matters much to us.)

Let's start looking at some data. I will begin with a study by Breiter et al. (2001). In each round of the study a subject was shown a circle split into three equally sized sectors labeled with an amount of money. For example, the circle might have one sector labeled $10, one labeled $2.50, and one labeled $0. An arrow would then spin and finally land on one of the sectors, with the subject winning the corresponding amount of money. So, if the arrow landed on the $10 sector the subject won $10. There were different circles used: a good one (with labels $10, $2.50 and $0), an intermediate one ($2.50, $0 and −$1.50) and a bad one ($0, −$1.50, −$6). Of interest is to see how subjects reacted to seeing which circle would be used and how they reacted to knowing how much they had won.

Figure 9.4 gives us some idea what happened in the NAcc and Figure 9.5 in the VMPFC. We are going to see a few of these types of figures so let me explain what they show. The vertical axis shows the change in signal from the relevant

Table 9.5 Two areas of the brain that connect with the VTA and are important in economic valuation and decision making

Area	Description
Nucleus accumbens (NAcc)	In the caudate nucleus, in the basal ganglia, that is on the inside of the cerebrum.
Ventromedial prefrontal cortex (VMPFC)	Part of the frontal lobe and part of the cortex, that is on the outside of the cerebrum.

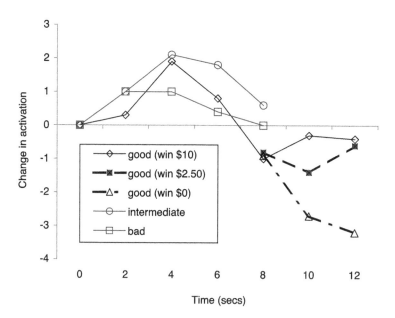

Figure 9.4 Activity in the nucleus accumbens on seeing the circle, around two seconds, and knowing how much is won, around eight seconds.

Source: Breiter et al. (2001).

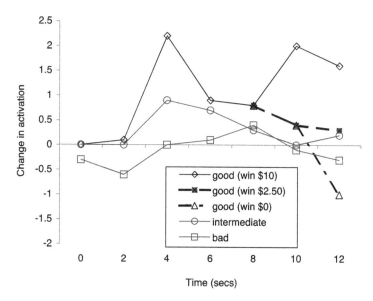

Figure 9.5 Activity in the ventromedial prefrontal cortex on seeing the circle, around two seconds, and knowing how much is won, around eight seconds.

Source: Breiter et al. (2001).

area of the brain relative to some baseline level. So, a positive suggests the area is more activated than normal, and a negative that it is less active than normal. The horizontal axis plots time relative to some start point. In this case the subject saw the circle being used after around two seconds and saw what they had won after eight seconds. We can, therefore, track changes in activation as things happen.

To keep the figures manageable I have only plotted outcomes for the good wheel, but in both the NAcc and VMPFC we see activation on seeing the circle and then also activation when the outcome is known. Further, the activation appears related to the desirability of the circle used and amount won. The better the circle the more activation observed, and the better the outcome the more activation observed. One thing to note for future reference is how the activation in the VMPFC on seeing the outcome is positive, while that in the NAcc is negative.

We need to be careful reading too much into one study (see Research Methods 9.3), but the results I have given above are representative of what is observed in other studies. Namely that the NAcc and VMPFC respond to rewards and might respond by an amount related to the size of the reward. (We shall see some more examples of this as we go on.) Maybe, therefore, we have found the utility function! That would be very premature to say, but it is an exciting possibility. For it to make sense, the brain would need to learn about rewards, so that's what I want to look at next.

Research Methods 9.3

Sample sizes and confidence intervals

One criticism with which neuroeconomics has been charged is the smallness of the sample sizes sometimes used. For example, the study by Breiter et al (2001) used twelve subjects, which is fairly typical in neuroscience. Is that enough? To answer that, we need to enter the murky world of statistical tests and confidence intervals.

To get us started think about an experiment, neuro or not, with the objective of finding what proportion of people use one heuristic or another. For example, we might be interested in what proportion of people use level one or level two reasoning (see chapter six). We invite subjects to the lab and get them to play games over a number of rounds. From this we need to: (i) estimate the heuristic used by individual subjects, and (ii) estimate what this tells us about the general population. Then we find out what we want to know.

The word 'estimate' here is important because we cannot know for sure the answer to either of these two questions, and that's why sample size matters. I am not going to go into the technicalities of confidence intervals but basically: (i) the more rounds a subject plays the more confident we can be in our estimate of what heuristic he is using, and (ii) the more subjects we ask to the experiment the more confident we can be in our estimate of what happens in the general population. So, we need lots of rounds and lots of subjects. Fortunately, the law of large numbers is on our side and so lots need not mean ridiculously many, but the more the better, and something like 100 is great, 50 not bad, but 10 too few.

In a normal experiment we can easily invite 100 subjects and have them play as much as we want. The cost involved in brain imaging makes that impractical in neuroscience. So, while we can confidently estimate what an individual subject is doing it is harder to confidently generalize any results to the wider population. It's not really clear at the moment whether this is a problem or not. Going on statistical logic it is a problem, but if we think that brains are fairly homogenous across the wider population it need not be.

You might be wondering how this relates to the more standard economic experiment involving treatments. For instance, we might have one treatment where subjects play an ultimatum game to split $10, and another where they play an ultimatum game to split $100, and we are interested if behavior is different in the two treatments. Some might say that we just need to have enough subjects to spot a difference, because if we observe a difference in, say, the 100 subjects we invite to the lab there must be a difference in the general population. Economists are prone to become fixated with such statistically significant differences, but of more interest is usually the magnitude of any difference. To estimate this with confidence the more subjects the better.

9.2.2 *Learning about rewards*

To get us started, imagine a sequence of events, like Rob putting a bet on a roulette wheel, seeing the roulette wheel stop on his number, getting the cash he won, buying a packet of chips with his winnings, and then eating the chips. Ultimately Rob should be happy. What I want us to think about now is when he feels happy. Is it when he bets, wins or eats the chips?

This brings us to the distinction between primary and secondary reinforcers. You can think of a **primary** or **unconditioned reinforcer** as something that has been 'hard wired' into Rob's brain, by evolution, to be important, like food, water and sex. You can think of a **secondary reinforcer** as something that Rob has learnt to indirectly associate with a primary or other secondary reinforcer, like money. In the previous chapter we saw that evolution could have favored lots of possible intermediate goods and so the distinction between primary and secondary reinforcer is not necessarily an easy one. The basic principle, however, is simple enough; Rob does not need to learn about a primary reinforcer, but he does about a secondary reinforcer.

For Rob, food is a primary reinforcer, while money is a secondary reinforcer, and seeing the roulette wheel stop, or start, are even more removed secondary reinforcers. So, when does he start to get excited at winning?

To illustrate what might happen, I will briefly mention a study by O'Doherty et al. (2002). The study involved subjects seeing a visual cue before getting 0.5ml of either a pleasant taste, an unpleasant taste, or a neutral taste. Some areas of the brain, including the VTA and NAcc, were activated when the subject saw the cue, rather than felt the taste. Other areas, however, including the VMPFC reacted more to the taste than to the cue. To take things one stage further, we can look at similar study by Knutson et al. (2001). This study involved money rather than taste, but the results are similar. On seeing the cue of a future payment, areas like the VTA and NAcc were activated but areas of the VMPFC reacted more on seeing the reward rather than the cue.

To put a few more details to this, Figure 9.6 plots the timeline as subjects see the visual cue at zero and then find out whether they won money or not. Focus first on what happens if they win money. Then we see activation of the NAcc when they are anticipating winning but not on knowing they have won. There is no such effect in the VMPFC. On finding out they have not won there is negative activity in both the NAcc and VMPFC. You might now want to check back and see what happens in Figures 9.4 and 9.5.

A stylized story of what is happening is that some areas of the brain, like the NAcc, learn to treat secondary reinforcers like primary reinforcers while other parts, like the VMPFC, keep a check on things and so react more to receiving the reward than expecting to receive it. This fits the story of executive control that I summarized in Table 9.4 with the NAcc, in the basal ganglia, and VMPFC updating ongoing predictions about how much reward can be expected in the future from a particular secondary reinforcer.

An interesting example of this is the **Iowa gambling task** (and again, free versions are available on the web if you want to try before reading further). This task involves four decks of cards which subjects are repeatedly asked to choose

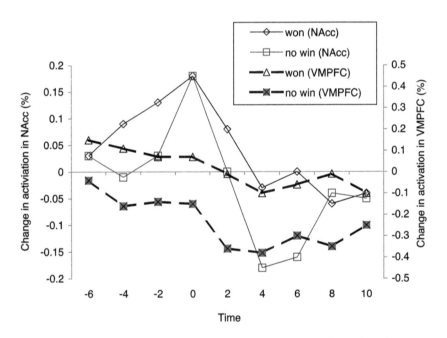

Figure 9.6 The response in the nucleus accumbens and ventromedial prefrontal cortex to anticipating and then winning or not winning money.

Source: Knutson et al. (2001).

from. Every card from decks A and B pays a large reward (e.g. $100) but some-times also entails a large loss (e.g. $1,250). Every card on decks C and D pays small reward (e.g. $50) and only sometimes entails a small loss. Overall, decks A and B have negative expected value, while decks C and D have positive expected value and most subjects soon choose only from decks C and D. Those, however, with damage to the VMPFC continue to choose from decks A and B. It's as though the VMPFC is not doing its job of checking whether decks A and B are the good choices that the NAcc thinks they are.

On a related theme, I next want to mention a study by O'Doherty et al. (2001). The task subjects did was partly like the Iowa gambling task, in that they had two choices: option A that gave large losses and small rewards, or option C that gave large rewards and small losses. Once, however, subjects had learnt that C was the best choice, the reward structure was reversed, similar to in the Wisconsin card sorting task. Figure 9.7 illustrates what happened in two areas of the VMPFC while the subjects were learning option C was best, and then after the change to option A being best.

The interesting thing here is how one area of the VMPFC (which I have labeled lateral) was activated following a loss and another (labeled medial) was activated

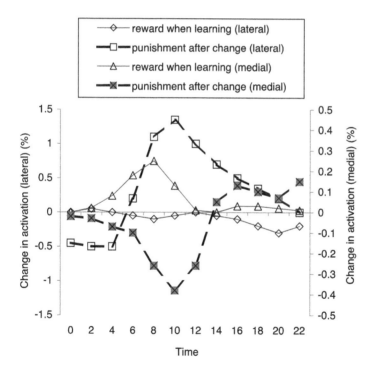

Figure 9.7 The change in activation in two areas of the VMPFC following a reward during a learning stage, or loss in a task reversal stage.

Source: O'Doherty et al. (2001).

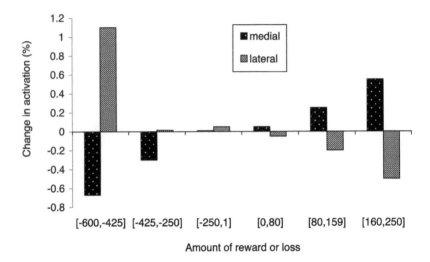

Figure 9.8 The change in activation in two areas of the VMPFC following a reward or loss of varying magnitudes.

Source: O'Doherty et al. (2001).

following a reward. Figure 9.8 takes this one stage further by showing how the activation correlates with the magnitude of the reward or loss. This is not only consistent with the VMPFC being involved in learning but also suggests that different areas of the VMPFC are activated for rewards and losses. If losses and gains do affect different areas of the brain then it's no surprise that this distinction matters when modeling economic behavior.

9.2.3 Risk and uncertainty

One important issue we need to address is that of risk. In most of the studies I have mentioned so far there has been risk. For instance, in the study by Breiter et al. (2001) subjects saw the arrow spin to decide what reward they would get. This raises the question of whether it's expected reward that matters, and how people learn when the outcome of an event is unknown. For example, what would be happening in Rob's brain between the roulette wheel starting to spin and stopping?

I will start by looking at a study by Preuschoff, Bossaerts and Quartz (2006). In the study, subjects were asked to bet whether the second of two cards would have a higher or lower number than the first, the numbers ranging from one to ten. They then saw the number on the first card, followed by the number on the second card. The gap between seeing the two numbers was long enough for subjects to realize their chance of winning. For example, if the subject said the second card would be lower, and the number on the first card was nine, then he or she had a good chance of winning. If the number was five, the chance of winning was less and the risk was higher.

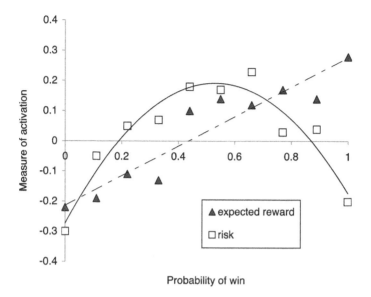

Figure 9.9 The fit between values and activity in three areas of the brain.

Source: Hare et al. (2008).

Figure 9.9 plots a measure of activation in the NAcc against the expected reward and the level of risk, where risk is highest if the probability of a win is 0.5. We see that activation is increasing in expected reward and is higher when there is more risk. A similar story has been told for the VMPFC. The brain it seems has no problem working with risk and expected values. What about uncertainty and ambiguity?

Recall that with a risky choice the probabilities of different outcomes are known, but with uncertainty they are not. For instance, suppose Rob is asked to bet on whether a red or blue card will be randomly drawn from a deck of 20 cards. If he knows that ten of the cards are red and ten blue, then he has a choice with risk. If he does not know how many are red or blue, then he has a choice with uncertainty. In a study by Hsu et al. (2005), subjects were given both risky and ambiguous choices like this in order to see whether uncertainty made a difference.

Figure 9.10 plots the timeline of activation in the NAcc and an area of the VMPFC. The subject would see the choices at zero seconds and the average decision what to choose was made at around six to seven seconds. Look first at what happens in the NAcc with a risky choice as compared to a choice with uncertainty. Clearly, once a decision has been made the NAcc is activated much less when there is uncertainty suggesting that the (expected or subjective) value put on an uncertain outcome is less than a risky outcome. Subjects, it appears, did not like uncertainty. Now look at what happens in the VMPFC. Here we see greater activation when there is uncertainty and when the subject is deciding what to choose.

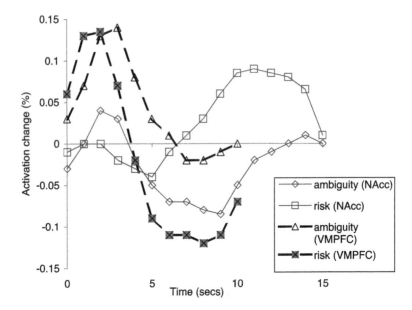

Figure 9.10 Activity in the NAcc (left ventral striatum) increases with expected value and risk.

Source: Preuschoff et al. (2006).

A similar pattern was observed in the amygdala, suggesting some of areas of the brain were activated to 'try and find the missing information'.

The picture we get, therefore, is that when there is uncertainty the brain is alerted to the fact information is missing and because of this a choice with uncertainty is not valued as much as a choice with risk. Indeed, it seemed that a choice with uncertainty was given a very low expected reward. That fits with what we looked at in chapter five and the suggestion that people are ambiguity averse. (We don't know yet what happens with compound lotteries.) I will come back to the differences between risk and uncertainty shortly, but I want to finish this section by looking at bit more at different types of reward.

9.2.4 Different types of reward

We have seen that brain activation can be nicely correlated with expected reward. An important concept in taking this idea further is **reward prediction error**. Basically, this is the difference between the reward expected and what was received. So, if Rob expected to win $5 and wins $0 or $10 then his prediction error is −$5 or $5. Reward prediction error is clearly important in determining how excited Rob should be and how he should learn for the future.

In the studies that we have looked at so far it is difficult to distinguish how the areas of the brain react to reward prediction error as opposed to expected reward.

It seems, however, that NAcc is activated in proportion to the reward prediction error. To illustrate, I will look at a study by Hare et al. (2008).

In the study, before going into the scanner, subjects stated a willingness to pay for 50 food items and were given some 'spending money'. Once, in the scanner they were given the chance to say yes or no to purchasing food items at a randomly determined price while also learning that their spending money had randomly been increased or decreased by some amount. For example, a subject might be presented with a screen displaying a candy bar, for sale at price $2, and something to say he or she had lost $1 of spending money.

The purpose of doing this was to distinguish three things that could influence the subject's reaction and choice. First, there is the willingness to pay for the good, second there is the difference between price and willingness to pay, and third there is the reward prediction error. You might recall that in chapter two I gave these first two things the name acquisition utility and transaction utility. Figure 9.11 illustrates how much activity in three different areas of the brain correlated with the three different values. The picture we get is again consistent with different areas of the brain reacting differently to these values. The NAcc is activated by the prediction error, and areas of the VMPFC by the willingness to pay and transaction utility.

I think we have already seen some exciting results. We have seen that the distinctions made earlier in the book, between losses and gains, risk and uncertainty, and acquisition and transaction utility, really do make sense, not only in trying to model choice, but as a description of how people think. The next step is to see if this translates into choice and decision making.

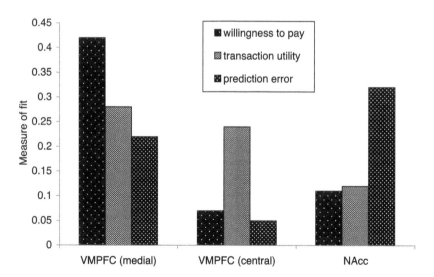

Figure 9.11 Activation in the NAcc (left striatum) and VMPFC (left orbitofrontal cortex) depended on whether the choice was with risk or uncertainty.

Source: Hsu et al. (2005).

9.3 Making decisions

So far the focus has been on people passively reacting to events largely out of their control. This firmly puts us in the domain of automatic processes, even if with some executive control. Now it's time to go up and gear and look at what happens when people have some choice, and so use reasoning and control processes.

To get us started, I want to look at a study by O'Doherty et al. (2004) that nicely illustrates the potential differences between passive learning and choice. In the study subjects were repeatedly exposed to two options before getting either a tasty juice or neutral reward. One of the options came with a 60 percent chance of getting the juice and the other with a 30 percent chance of getting the juice. So, subjects had to learn the correlation between option and reward. More interesting for our purpose was that sometimes subjects chose an option and sometimes the computer chose for them.

The main results of the study are summarized in Figure 9.12. Focus first on the left-hand side and the ventral striatum. For our purposes the ventral striatum and NAcc are the same and as we have now come to expect, this area was activated in proportion to the expected reward and reward prediction error. Now look at what happens in the dorsal striatum. This time there is activation when the subject has the chance to make a choice but not when the computer will decide. This relationship leads to the **actor-critic models** in which the ventral striatum is cast in the role of critic, evaluating rewards, while the dorsal striatum is cast in the role of actor, selecting what to choose.

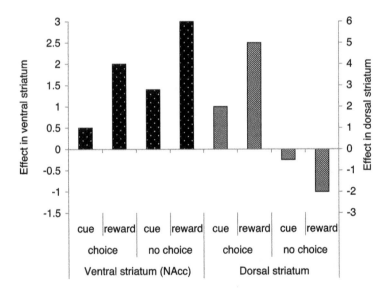

Figure 9.12 Activation in the dorsal and ventral striatum during a learning task on seeing the options or cue and getting the reward. Activation in the dorsal striatum depends on whether there is choice or not.

Source: O'Doherty et al. (2004).

Choice does, therefore, not unsurprisingly make a difference to what goes on in the brain as other areas are activated to seemingly help make the decision. An intriguing issue is whether we can use this to predict choice and strategy.

9.3.1 Choice and strategy

To show that this idea is not so crazy we can relate choice and strategy to brain activation, I want to look at two studies where subjects had to choose between risky and/or uncertain gambles.

I'll start with a study by Huettel et al. (2006). In this study subjects were presented with pairs of gambles or prospects of which some gambles involved risk and some uncertainty. For example, they might have to choose between a risky gamble that pays out $12 with probability 0.75 and $20 with probability 0.25, and an uncertain gamble that pays out $0 or $35 with unknown probability. We thus move away from asking how subjects respond to seeing risk or uncertainty to how they choose between the two.

For each subject, having seen what they choose, it is possible to construct indices of how much they seem to like (or not) ambiguity and risk. We can then see whether these preferences correlate with the brain activation observed while the subject was making choices. That is, we are trying to find a link between brain activation and choice. Figure 9.13 suggests we can find such a link, although we do have to temporally look at something other than the NAcc and VMPFC. This figure summarizes how ambiguity led to the greatest activation in the lateral prefrontal cortex for those whose choices suggest they like ambiguity. Similarly,

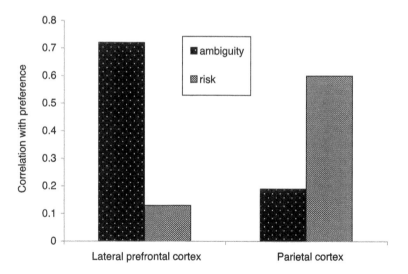

Figure 9.13 Areas of the lateral prefrontal cortex and parietal cortex are more activated in those with a preference for ambiguity and risk.

Source: Huettel et al. (2006).

risk led to the greatest activation in the parietal cortex for those whose choices suggest they are less risk averse.

We see, therefore, that not only do risk and ambiguity activate different areas of the brain but by seeing how much the brain is activated we can potentially predict choices. Can we go one stage further and predict strategy?

To see if we can I will look at a study by Venkatraman et al. (2009). In the study subjects were first presented with a risky prospect containing five possible outcomes, for example, to win $80 with probability 0.25, lose $75 with probability 0.2, and so on. They were then given two alternatives to improve the prospect and had to choose which they wanted. For example, the alternatives might be to make it a $100 win with probability 0.25, or a $55 loss with probability 0.2.

There are two basic types of strategy that one might employ in this scenario. The 'simple strategy' is to maximize the probability of making a difference, and so, for instance, to add $20 to the $80 outcome because this is more likely to matter than adding $20 to the the $75 loss. A more 'complex strategy' would be to maximize gains, by adding $20 to the $80, or minimize losses, by adding it to the $75 loss, or maximize expected utility in some other way.

In standard experiments, without brain imaging, most subjects were observed using the simple strategy but some did use a complex strategy. The main thing, though, was that subjects did seem to stick to a strategy through multiple rounds. We can, therefore, potentially disentangle choice from strategy.

Let's look first at choice. Figure 9.14 shows that choice was correlated with activation in different brain areas. For example, choosing the option that maximized the possible gain was associated with greater activity in the VMPFC, while choosing the option that minimized the possible loss was associated with greater activity in the insula. So far, so good.

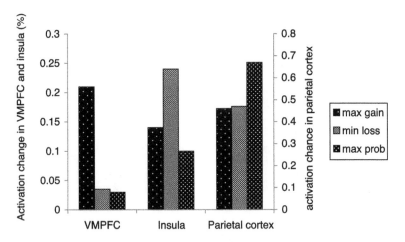

Figure 9.14 Different choices correlate with more activation in different areas of the brain.
Source: Venkatraman et al. (2009).

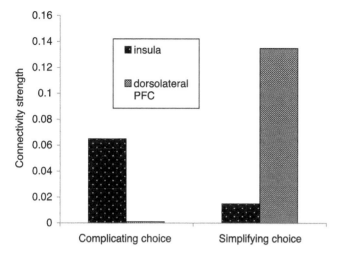

Figure 9.15 Increased connectivity is observed between the dorsomedial prefrontal cortex and the insula and parietal cortex when someone makes a choice inconsistent with their normal strategy.

Source: Venkatraman et al. (2009).

Now let's look at strategy. What we want to do here is see whether some areas of the brain are more activated when someone makes a choice not consistent with their usual strategy. That is, what happens when someone who usually uses a simple strategy decides to do something 'more complicated' like maximize the possible gain, or when someone who usually uses a complex strategy decides to do the 'simpler thing' of maximizing probability? When this happens the dorsomedial prefrontal cortex becomes more activated and what's more, as Figure 9.15 shows, we observe greater connectivity between this and the areas associated with choice.

So, greater activation of some areas correlates with choices made while greater activation in others correlates with strategy, or with the differences between choice and strategy. It looks, therefore, as though we can watch both choice and strategy being played out in the brain, which is fascinating stuff. What I want to do now is see how far this can take us in understanding social preferences, and then inter-temporal choice.

9.3.2 Fairness and norms

In getting us started with social preferences I want to talk about a study by Sanfey et al. (2003). The study basically involved subjects playing the ultimatum game (see chapter seven) to see how people react to unfair and fair offers. Subjects, in the role of receiver, were offered proposed splits of $5 and $5, of $9 and $1, of $8 and $2 and of $7 and $3. The main question of interest is how subjects responded to a fair offer, $5 and $5, as compared to unfair offers like $9 and $1.

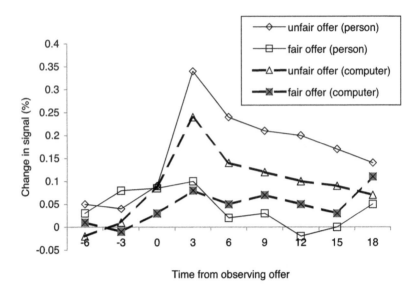

Figure 9.16 Timeline of activation in the (right anterior) insula depending on whether the offer was fair or unfair.

Source: Sanfey et al. (2003).

One area of the brain we have yet to talk about much is the insula, but now it does become relevant. As Figure 9.16 shows, the insula was activated more when a subject received an offer that was unfair rather than unfair, and more when the proposer making the unfair offer was known to be a human rather than a computer. There was also greater activation the more unfair the offer. Most interesting is probably Figure 9.17, which compares activation in the insula and dorsolateral prefrontal cortex (DLPFC) for offers that were subsequently rejected to those that were accepted. We see the rejection of an offer comes with relatively large activation of the insula. So, what is going on?

The only mention the insula has had so far is in Table 9.2 where I said it was involved in visceral and autonomic functions like taste. In fact, things that are consistently associated with the insula include negative emotional states like pain and distress, hunger, thirst, and disgust from taste or odor. This clearly fits with a story of receivers feeling a negative emotional response on receiving an unfair offer. By contrast, we know the DLPFC is usually associated with cognitive processes and executive control and so is possibly more focused on getting as much money as possible. This suggests a potential conflict between the insula, that wants to reject, and DLPFC, that wants to accept. Figure 9.17 is certainly consistent with this. Further credence to this idea comes from increased activation of the anterior cingulated cortex for unfair offers. Remember that this is thought to be involved in conflict resolution.

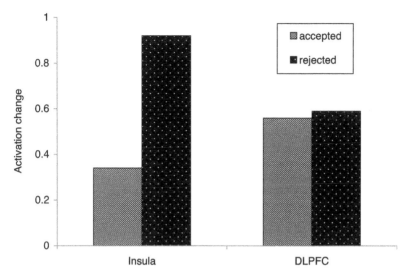

Figure 9.17 Activation in the (right) insula and (right) dorsolateral prefrontal cortex for offers that were subsequently rejected or accepted.

Source: Sanfey et al. (2003).

So, we get a neat story. The insula is upset by an unfair offer and wants to reject, while the DLPFC wants the money so is happy to accept. Sometimes the insula wins out and sometimes the DLPFC. Neat stories often have a catch, and this one is no exception. To see why I want to look at a study by Knoch et al. (2006). In this study low-frequency repetitive transcranial magnetic stimulation was applied to either the right or left DLPFC of subjects. This suppresses activity in that part of the brain. It basically switches off either the left or right DLPFC. So, what should happen if we switch off the DLPFC?

If the DLPFC wants to accept any offer, the insula wants to reject an unfair offer, and we switch of the DLPFC then we should see more rejection of unfair offers. Figure 9.18 shows that we observe the complete opposite! We see far less rejection of unfair offers when the right DLPFC is switched off than when the left is switched off, or when neither is switched off. This is despite the unfair offer still being perceived as unfair.

The story we get now, therefore, is one where the DLPFC wants to reject a low offer, because of fairness norms, and other areas of the brain want to accept, and get the money. Consistent with this, stimulation of the right DLPFC had less of an effect when the low offer was received from a computer rather than human proposer. So, it's not really very clear what's going on, but either way the (right) DLPFC does seem important for reciprocity.

To explore this further we can look at a study by Spitzer et al. (2007). In the study, subjects played two different games several times. One game was a

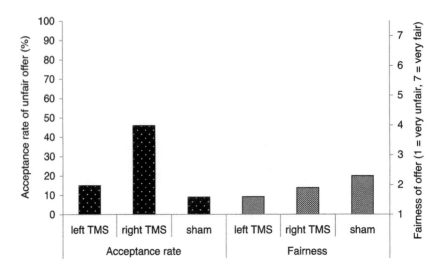

Figure 9.18 Acceptance rate and perceptions of an unfair offer in the ultimatum game. Those with stimulation (TMS) to the right DLPFC are more likely to accept despite still thinking the offer is unfair. In the sham treatment there is no stimulation.

Source: Knoch et al. (2006).

variation on the dictator game in that one subject, the proposer, was given 125 tokens and a second subject, the receiver, was given 25 tokens; the proposer could give up to 100 of his or her tokens to the receiver. The second game was a variation on the ultimatum game in that the receiver had the chance to punish the proposer after seeing how many tokens he or she had been given; for every one token the receiver spent punishing five tokens would be taken from the proposer. For example, if the proposer gave no tokens to the receiver and the receiver spent 25 tokens on punishing then both proposer and receiver would end up with zero tokens. Some subjects played the ultimatum game with another subject (and knew it) while some played against a pre-programmed computer (and knew it).

As discussed in chapter seven, the dictator game gives us an idea how much a subject would voluntarily give to another, while the ultimatum game gives us an idea how much he or she would give with the threat of punishment. The focus switches, therefore, more on the proposer than receiver. Comparing activation during the ultimatum game to that in the dictator game greater activation was observed in several areas including the DLPFC and VMPFC. Furthermore activation was higher when the receiver would be a person and not a computer in these same areas and the insula. There was also correlation between activation and the amount offered.

The task in the ultimatum game is already getting quite complex because the proposer needs to think through both how much they want to give and how much the receiver is likely to accept. It's no surprise therefore that various areas of the brain, including the DLPFC, VMPFC and insula are more activated. The story we get though, seems again to be one of the prefrontal cortex acting as a check on other areas that might want to take the money. To take this further it's interesting to look a bit more at preferences for punishment and equality.

9.3.3 Punishment and inequality aversion

A study by De Quervain et al. (2004) gives us interesting insights into preferences for punishment. They looked at a trust game (see chapter seven) in which an investor can invest zero or ten tokens with a proposer; if he or she does invest then the proposer has 50 tokens and must decide whether to return zero or 25 of those to the investor. The variation on this basic trust game is to allow the investor the option of punishing the proposer if the tokens were invested but not repaid.

Focusing solely on those cases where the investor invested but got no return, Figure 9.19 illustrates the activation in the striatum. There are four different conditions depending on whether the investor chose to punish (intentional) or the computer did, whether it was costly for the investor to punish (costly), and whether the punishment actually lowered the payoff of the proposer (costly and free versus symbolic). Recall that the striatum is involved in reward evaluation and so it's particularly interesting that this should be activated more in those conditions where the investor could meaningfully punish the proposer. Activation also correlated with the amount of punishment. So, do people get satisfaction from punishing?

One way to try and answer this is to compare what happens when punishment is free to when it is costly. Several subjects punished the maximum amount when

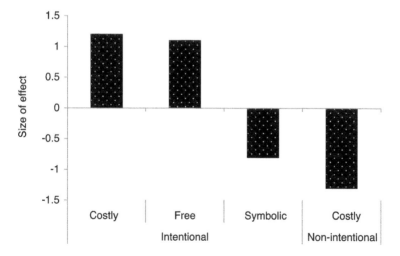

Figure 9.19 Activation in the striatum depends on the type of punishment.

Source: De Quervain et al. (2004).

punishment was free, and so we can say that any differences in activation between them were probably due to differences in a desire to punish. We then ask whether those who had higher activation when punishment was free punished more when it was costly and they did. This does suggest that people get satisfaction from punishing. One further piece of evidence is that the VMPFC was more activated when punishment was costly, suggesting that it was trading off the desire to punish with the cost of punishing.

If a preference for punishing seems a bit depressing then a study by Tricomi et al. (2010) gives a slightly more upbeat conclusion. In the study subjects participated in pairs. Having been given an initial $30 each, one subject was randomly given another $50 and the other nothing, creating a 'rich' and 'poor' subject. Subsequently, subjects were asked to evaluate future potential payments to them and the other subject. As we can see from the left-hand side of Figure 9.20, evaluations were consistent with inequality aversion: a rich subject valued a payment to them only slightly above a payment to the poor subject, while poor subjects rated relative highly payments to them and negatively payments to the rich subject. So, how did this inequality aversion translate into brain activity?

The right-hand side of Figure 9.20 shows a consistency between the valuations and activation in the NAcc and VMPFC. Most interesting is the NAcc which we have seen is activated by expected reward. Rich subjects seemed to be more activated by transfers to the poor subject, while poor subjects seemed to be more activated by transfers to the rich subject. This suggests that inequality aversion really does exist. The role of the VMPFC is again probably to trade off the desire to equalize payoffs with the desire to get money.

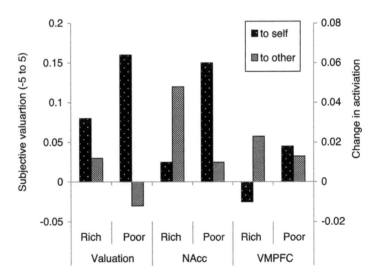

Figure 9.20 The effect of inequality on the valuation of subsequent transfers and activation in the NAcc and vmPFC.

Source: Tricomi et al. (2010).

It's fascinating to see that there potentially is pleasure in punishing and pleasure in redressing inequality. You might have noticed, however, that this brings us back full circle in trying to discern the competing incentives in the brain. If punishing and giving provide satisfaction, then it's not obvious whether the 'basic emotion' is to take the money or to punish. It's not exactly clear, therefore, what conflict the VMPFC and executive control systems have to sort out or inhibit. But, there's not much doubt that there are conflicting incentives and it's to this I now want to turn.

9.3.4 Present bias and a brain in conflict

If parallel processes are going on in the brain all the while then it is not surprising that these sometimes **conflict** in suggesting different behavior. Indeed, if the basic purpose of the executive control systems are to switch from automatic to control, and in so doing inhibit automatic processes, there is a clear potential for conflict. So, if it feels like one part of your brain is telling you one thing and another part something else, that may not be too far from reality.

We have already seen a potential tension between taking money offered or punishing in the ultimatum and trust game. It's not hard to find other examples. Someone falling asleep at the wheel despite trying to stay awake is a fairly extreme example. Another example you may be familiar with is the **Stroop task** where a person is asked to read color words very fast and some words are in the 'wrong' color, e.g. the word blue might be colored green. People take longer to reply when the word and color and incongruent because of the conflicting signals they get, the anterior cingulated cortex sorting the conflict out.

That someone could be 'of two minds' is potentially very important, particularly in thinking about present bias and time inconsistency (see chapter four). We could imagine, say, that Maria's automatic processes suggest she enjoys herself today, while her control processes say she should do her homework. If the automatic processes prove stronger than her control processes then she might want to do her homework, think it was best she did her homework, but still delay it for another day. We have a plausible explanation for time inconsistency.

To see if this story fits I will look first at a study by McClure et al. (2004). In the study subjects made a series of inter-temporal choices between an early or delayed monetary reward. Sometimes the early reward was available immediately but sometimes still only with some delay. This made it possible to distinguish brain areas more activated by choices involving an immediate outcome. To illustrate, Figure 9.21 compares activation in the NAcc and DLPFC. We can see that activation of the DLPFC is not influenced by the delay until getting the reward but the NAcc is. A reward today activates this area more than a delayed reward.

In chapter four I looked at a quasi-hyperbolic model of (β, δ) preferences where the δ captured exponential discounting and the β captured present bias. We can now see areas of the brain, like the NAcc, that possibly give us the β part while others, like the DLPFC, give us the δ part. If so, then choice should correlate with relative activation of areas associated with each part. Figure 9.22 shows that this is exactly what was seen; when a subject chose the early option areas of the brain we

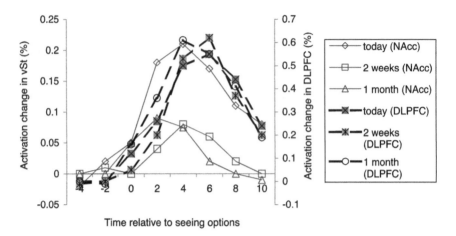

Figure 9.21 Activation in the NAcc and DLPFC depending on whether the reward was immediate or delayed.

Source: McClure et al. (2004).

might associate with the β part were more activated, and when they chose the delayed option areas of the brain we might associate with the δ part were activated.

To continue the story, I want to briefly mention a study by Diekhof and Gruber (2010). They ran experiments where in a first stage, subjects did a task in which they

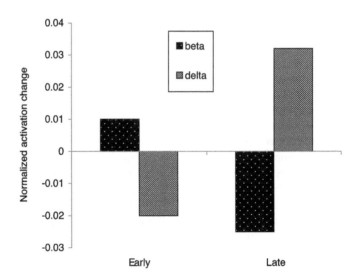

Figure 9.22 Areas associated with immediate reward (beta) are more activated when the subject chooses the early option and areas associated with delayed reward (delta) are more activated when choosing the later option.

Source: McClure et al. (2004).

learnt that choosing certain colors gave a reward. In a second stage they were give a task that involved choosing certain colors a fixed number of times. This created a conflict between the long-term goal of collecting the right number of each color and the impulse to choose a color that gives an immediate reward. As we would expect a color associated with a reward led to greater activation of the NAcc. The interesting thing comes during the second stage where a negative functional connectivity was observed between the NAcc and areas of the prefrontal cortex. In other words, the more the prefrontal cortex was activated, the less the NAcc. Furthermore the stronger this negative connectivity, the more likely the subject performed the task correctly.

I think these two studies are interesting to contrast in the way that conflict resolution appears to emerge. In the first we have the impression of two areas of the brain conflicting with the one activated the most winning. So impulsivity might win over patience, or a desire to punish might win over a desire to take the money (as in Figure 9.17). The second study gives more of an impression of areas of the prefrontal cortex overseeing and directing what is going on elsewhere in the brain. So, patience subdues impulsivity or the need for money subdues the desire to punish.

Both these ways of looking at things are really just part of the same executive control systems. On the one hand, controlled processes compete with automatic processes and on the other hand, controlled processes direct automatic processes. One interesting implication of this, which can have important economic consequences, is that behavior can depend on the cognitive load of the executive control systems. Basically if executive control is looking after one thing it might let slip something else.

An interesting example of this is provided in a study by Shiv and Fedorikhin (1999). The study involved subjects having to remember either a two-digit or seven-digit number while deciding whether to choose between chocolate cake or fruit salad. Figure 9.23 shows that subjects were significantly more likely to

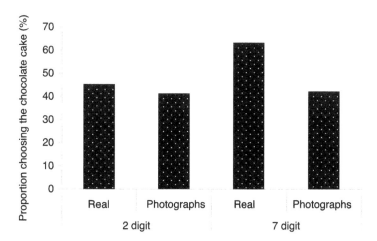

Figure 9.23   The proportion of subjects choosing chocolate cake is higher when the subject had to remember a seven-digit number and was shown the snacks for real.

Source: Shiv and Fedorikhin (1999).

choose the chocolate cake when the subject had to remember a seven-digit number and was shown the snacks for real. This is consistent with automatic processes being more likely to overpower the controlled processes if the controlled processes are busy doing something else.

9.3.5 Multiple self-models

This conflict being played out in the brain suggests why people have **self-control problems**. Recall, that in chapter four we saw that someone like Maria may want to pre-commit by, say, agreeing to meet with friends tomorrow, which means her homework has to be done today. Furthermore, she might want to pre-commit even if she does her homework today, because she still avoids the cost of overcoming temptation. This kind of thing is very hard for the standard economic model to cope with. Why would someone want to pre-commit and thereby reduce the options available to her? Now we have an explanation.

It's reassuring to have an explanation for self-control problems but can we go further? One possibility is to explicitly model the conflict going on in the brain. This leads to the idea of **multiple-self** or **dual-self** models. I will not go into too many details here because I will work through an example of such a model when looking at addiction, but the basic idea is simple. We can think of one self, whom Thaler and Shefrin (1981) suggest calling the **planner**, who wants to maximize lifetime utility, and another self, the **doer**, that wants to maximize utility today.

The easiest way to go is to think of the doer as being the one who always makes the decisions what to do now. This gives a lot of the power to automatic processes and is potentially quite worrying for the individual, because the doer will always sacrifice the future for today. Fortunately, the planner is given two main ways to constrain the doer. First, it could change the preferences or incentives of the doer. For example, Maria's planner might make it that the doer likes doing homework, or bets with a friend who will get the best homework mark. Second, it could impose rules that change the constraints of the doer. For example, Maria's planner might pre-commit to playing with friends tomorrow.

This type of model is very useful in understanding and modeling pre-commitment and self-control. It does give a big role to automatic processes, and for that reason is possibly most apt when thinking about something like addiction where the automatic processes will be a lot stronger, but that's not a big problem. So, should we be using dual-self models a lot more? Maybe it makes sense given the real conflict between automatic and controlled processes going on in the brain?

As ever, there can be a danger in taking an idea too far. The reason I say this is that conflict is already at the heart of the standard economic model. For example, when I wrote down Anna's utility function over breakfast cereals, $u(x, TQ, HQ)$, in chapter two, encapsulated within that is a conflict between her wanting money and wanting the cereal of the highest quality. Anna faces a potentially tough choice in trading off money for a tasty cereal, and so she may spend some time in the grocery store being in two minds what to buy. We do not need a multiple self model to capture that.

This is not an issue of whether there is or is not conflict between automatic and controlled processes. Indeed, I have made a point of saying that automatic processes will influence all decisions through perception and intuition. So Anna's choice will inevitably involve both controlled and automatic processes– we just have better ways to model this. For example, Anna might get angry at a price rise, an automatic process, and then be reluctant to buy despite knowing it's still a price she is willing to pay, a controlled process. In chapter two we saw how this can be captured by distinguishing between transaction utility and acquisition utility.

Dual-self models are probably not, therefore, as important in improving how well we can model economic behavior beyond self-control problems. We have also seen that when it comes to things such as fairness it is very hard to disentangle the automatic 'doer' behavior and the objectives of the controlled 'planner'. Indeed, in terms of modeling economic behavior it seems more natural to think of the dual self as a distinction between automatic processes that determine the reference point versus controlled processes that work around that reference point. That's the approach we have taken throughout most of the book.

9.4 Summary

I have only looked at a small selection of the many results from neuroscience and neuroeconomics, but I think there is already enough here to be impressed with what we can learn.

I started by describing the idea of modularity in which we think of different brain areas as performing different tasks. We then can potentially learn something from observing what areas are activated and by how much when a person observes something or makes a particular decision.

The second idea I talked about was that of different brain processes. We contrasted automatic processes with controlled processes and gave executive control the job of knowing when to switch from automatic to control. This suggests that there can potentially be conflict in the brain as one area wants to do one thing, another area something different, and executive control has to sort this conflict out.

In looking at economic behavior the focus to start with was on how people react to observing outcomes. We saw that some areas, like nucleus accumbens, are activated by the expectation of a reward and are potentially activated in proportion to the expected reward, or reward prediction error. We saw that other areas, like the ventromedial prefrontal cortex are more activated on getting the reward. While it may be a step too far to say that this is like seeing the utility function in the brain, it does allow us to see what types of outcome activate different reward areas and so learn something about preferences. We saw evidence consistent with ambiguity aversion, with present bias, with the distinction between transaction and acquisition utility, and with inequality aversion.

The next step was to add an element of choice to see how the brain is activated when making decisions. We saw that additional areas were activated suggesting the actor-critic distinction between areas of the brain primarily responsible for evaluation and those responsible for action. We saw that brain activation often does correlate with the action chosen and strategy used.

In looking at social preferences we saw that people appear to react negatively to an unfair offer and get a reward from punishing. Harder is to pull apart what are the automatic and controlled processes.

As I briefly mentioned in chapter one, neuroeconomics is a controversial topic, and so it seems natural, now that you have seen something of what it has to offer, to try and make sense of the controversy. The basic controversy is whether neuroeconomics can add anything useful to economics, and this is primarily a manifestation of the debates we looked at in chapter one. For instance, the main charge is that knowing how the brain works is neither necessary nor sufficient to understand, model and predict economic behavior.

I hope to have shown you in this chapter that knowing how the brain works can definitely help us to understand economic behavior a bit better. It's fascinating to see things like inequality aversion and present bias seemingly being acted out within the brain. Seeing such things should reassure that the models I have looked at earlier in the book, taking account of things like inequality aversion and present bias, make sense.

I also believe that knowing how the brain works can potentially help us model and predict economic behavior a bit better. For example, if we can distinguish automatic from controlled processes this could help us predict better how behavior will change as the context changes. To understand better, say, when people will want to punish unfair behavior and when they will not.

It is though slightly worrying to have to use the phrase 'potentially help us model and predict'. While neuroeconomics is undoubtedly fascinating in understanding economic behavior, it is much harder to see how it can significantly help us better model and predict economic behavior. It's hard to believe, for instance, that watching people's brains as they play the ultimatum game can make us any more able to predict what they will do than we have learnt from doing standard experiments. Given that economic theories are usually judged on their ability to predict behavior, this is where neuroeconomics loses out.

So, while neuroeconomics is clearly informative and worth doing, it's unlikely to revolutionize economics, as some of its proponents would have us believe. It's good – but not that good.

Where neuroeconomics can be more revolutionary is in neuroscience. While economists are unlikely to learn too much from watching people's brains as they play the ultimatum game, neuroscientists can potentially learn a lot, precisely because economists know so well how people do behave when playing such games. So, while we might debate just how good neuroeconomics is for economics, it is definitely good for neuroscience.

Turning around this logic I also think economics has a lot more to learn from neuroscience. In particular, the most depressing chapter for me to write in this book, was chapter six, on interaction and learning. Our ability to predict how people learn and behave in strategic situations is still quite poor. Given that learning, memory and social cognition are important components of neuroscience, maybe we can find some answers there?

9.5 Addiction

Addiction is a big social issue. For instance, the National Survey on Drug Use and Health suggests that in 2008, 14.2 percent of Americans aged 12 years or older had used illicit drugs during the past year. The National Drug Intelligence Center estimated the economic cost of this at nearly $215 billion, and summarized: 'The damage caused by drug abuse and addiction is reflected in an overburdened justice system, a strained healthcare system, lost productivity, and environmental destruction' (NDIC 2010). That's before we start on cigarettes and alcohol!

You might think that addiction is not a domain for economists but it is also a big economic issue. The UK government, for instance, raised an estimated $10.5 billion from cigarette taxation in 2009 to 2010. It's important, therefore, to know a bit about the issue.

In order to do that, we need to have a definition of what addiction is. One definition is to say that someone like Rob is **addicted** to a good if: (i) the more he consumes the good the more he wants to consume of the good – call this **reinforcement**; (ii) the more he consumes the good, the lower his utility from consuming the good in the future – call this **tolerance**.

This is a nice definition for economists because we can easily capture reinforcement and tolerance in simple models. It is, however, probably too broad definition for many. Indeed, according to this definition I am addicted to lots of things, including long distance running, and watching cricket. Given, however, I am an economist we will go with this definition for now, possibly thinking of it more as a definition of habit than addiction. We next need a model to capture this definition.

9.5.1 A model of rational addiction

To prove that I really am an economist I will start with a model of rational addiction (credit to Becker and Murphy 1988). It might seem strange to think of rational and addiction together, but this provides a natural starting point. Here is the model.

Rob can choose to consume an addictive good, called cigarettes, or a non-addictive good, called money. Let a_t denote the amount of cigarettes he consumes in period t and let c_t denote the amount of money he spends. We then assume that his utility from smoking will depend on his previous consumption of cigarettes. To do this we need to keep track of how much he has smoked in the past. We do that by letting:

$$S_t = d(S_{t-1} + a_{t-1})$$

denote the **stock of past consumption** where d measures the addictiveness of the good. The higher is d the more addictive cigarettes appear to be because the more past consumption is remembered. If $d = 1$, cigarettes are very addictive because past consumption is never forgotten.

We then assume that Rob's utility in period t will depend on present consumption and the stock of past consumption:

$$u_t = \begin{cases} c_t + 10\sqrt{a_t - S_t} & \text{if } a_t \geq S_t \\ c_t - 10(S_t - a_t) & \text{if } a_t < S_t \end{cases}.$$

We also assume that he uses exponential discounting (see chapter four) to find his inter-temporal utility:

$$u^T = u_1 + \delta u_2 + \delta^2 u_2 + \ldots + \delta^T u_T.$$

What Rob needs to do is plan his addiction. He knows that cigarettes are addictive, but he likes them none the less, and so needs to plan how many cigarettes to consume early in his life knowing that he will subsequently become addicted. The problem Rob faces is analogous to the faced by Maria in section 4.5.1 deciding when to consume goods, knowing she will become used to that level of consumption. One slight difference is that Maria could smooth consumption freely by saving for the future. To make things more interesting we are going to assume that Rob cannot save for the future, either cigarettes or money.

Working out Rob's optimal consumption of cigarettes is somewhat tedious exercise in math. So, I will just look at some addiction plans and see what Rob would think about them. Table 9.6 looks at three. For each one we can see what utility Rob

Table 9.6 The utility of several different addiction plans, assuming Rob has $10 per period and a pack of cigarettes costs $1 in periods one to three. In period four the amount of cigarettes that Rob can consume is constrained by his income. Unless stated, $d = 1$

Price in period 4	Cigarettes in period				Utility
	1	2	3	4	
$1	0	0	0	0	40.0
	1	2	4	10	70.3
	1	1	2	5	51.0
$2	0	0	0	0	40.0
	1	2	4	5	33.0
	1	1	2	5	46.0
$2.50	0	0	0	0	40.0
	1	2	4	4	23.0
	1	1	2	4	36
$2.50 and d = 0.5	0	0	0	0	40.0
	1	2	4	4	73.6
	1	1	2	4	70.5

would get depending on what happens to the price of cigarettes in period four. If the price of cigarettes is $1 in all four periods then Rob does best to consume a lot of cigarettes: he prefers to consume an increasing amount and in period four spends all his money on cigarettes. If the price of cigarettes increases to $2 in period four, then Rob does best to be a little restrained: he buys fewer cigarettes in periods one to three so that he does not become too addicted before cigarettes become expensive. If the price increases to $2.50 then he does best to abstain all together.

All this was assuming $d = 1$ and so cigarettes are highly addictive. If $d = 0.5$, so cigarettes are less addictive Rob still does best to consume a lot of cigarettes.

This example illustrates the main predictions that come out of a rational addiction model. Namely, that Rob should base his present consumption on how addictive cigarettes are, and what will likely happen to the future price of cigarettes. If cigarettes are addictive and the future price will increase then he should not consume now so as to not become trapped wanting something he cannot afford. If cigarettes are less addictive and/or he does not expect any increase in the price then he can consume more. We can call this **forward-looking behavior**.

Before we question the plausibility of forward-looking behavior I want to look at some data. The data is from a study by Gruber and Köszegi (2001) that looks at whether demand for cigarettes changes when taxes are announced. Given that there is often a delay of two months or more between a government announcing that taxes will increase and taxes actually increasing, it is possible to check for forward-looking behavior. We would expect consumption of cigarettes to fall when the tax increase is announced, not when prices actually rise. We might, however, expect demand for cigarettes to increase when the tax increase is announced, because it is a chance to hoard them before prices rise.

Gruber and Köszegi look at some data on both sales and consumption of cigarettes and find the predicted effects. In the sales data there is evidence of a hoarding effect with sales increasing after the announcement of a tax increase. For example, an increase in the tax from 10 to 35 cents in California was announced in November 1988 and become effective in January 1989. Cigarette sales jumped from an average of 6.68 packs per person in November to 8.71 packs in December, before falling back to around six packs. In the consumption data there is evidence of decreased consumption once the tax increase is announced. It seems, therefore, that consumers are using forward-looking behavior.

This suggests that Rob could be in control of his addiction, and the only rationale for policy intervention would be if Rob's smoking has a negative externality on others. Given the biases we have seen elsewhere in this book, this might seem a surprising conclusion. It is not, however, the end of the story. That's because we observe a lot of other behavior that is not so consistent with a rational model of addiction. To that I now turn.

9.5.2 Biases and addiction

The rational model of addiction suggests two important biases that we might observe. First, the rational model requires forward-looking behavior, and we have seen (in chapter four) that people like Rob may not be able to stick with a forward-looking plan because of a present bias. He might always plan to 'quit tomorrow' but never do so. Second, the rational model says Rob can smoke more if he thinks cigarettes are less addictive, and we have seen (in chapter five) that he may be biased in underestimating its addictiveness. For example, because of confirmatory bias and the law of large numbers he may ignore the scientific evidence on how addictive smoking is, because his friend was able to quit smoking.

Both these biases have the same basic prediction: Rob will become more addicted and consume more cigarettes than he planned to do. Evidence of this is not too hard to find. To demonstrate, we can look at some data from a report published in the UK about smoking-related attitudes and behavior (ONS 2004). Figure 9.24 summarizes how many people surveyed wanted to quit smoking. A lot of them did. Given this, we might expect they would try to quit. Figure 9.25 looks at how many smokers had tried to quit. Many had tried and failed. Finally, figure 9.26 summarizes the thoughts of those who planned to quit in the next twelve months. There was some realism about the difficulties of quitting, but overall people were more optimistic than they probably should have been about their chances of quitting.

There are lots more data I could have given, and all of it is hard to reconcile with a rational model of addiction. It looks, therefore, as though people are not forward-planning very well and are underestimating the difficulties of quitting smoking. More difficult is to say exactly why this is. Is it because of present bias, or an underestimation of the addictiveness of cigarettes? To try and answer this question let's look in a bit more detail how each bias would work.

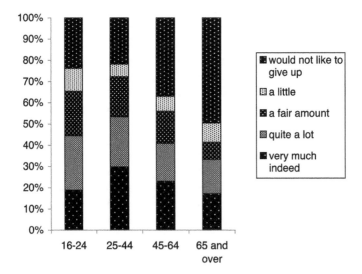

Figure 9.24 The proportion of people surveyed, by age group, who wanted to quit smoking.

Source: ONS (2004).

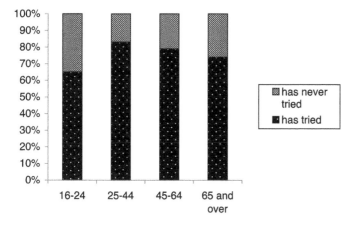

Figure 9.25 The proportion of current smokers who had tried quitting in the past.
Source: ONS (2004).

Table 9.7 illustrates the basic ideas. Imagine the price of cigarettes is expected to be $1 in periods one to three and to increase to $2.50 in period four. Also, imagine that $d = 1$ and so cigarettes are very addictive. Without any bias, of the profiles I am going to look at, Rob would do best to not smoke. What if he is biased?

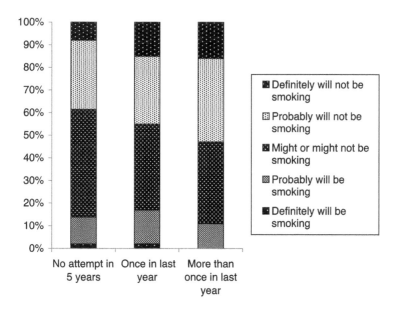

Figure 9.26 What smokers who were planning to quit in the next 12 months expected would happen after 12 months.
Source: ONS (2004).

Table 9.7 The consequences of underestimating the addictiveness of cigarettes, and present bias in the example

Bias	Cigarettes in period				Expected utility
	1	*2*	*3*	*4*	
None	0	0	0	0	40.0
	1	2	4	4	23.0
Thinks d = 0.5	0	0	0	0	40.0
	1	2	4	4	73.6
	1	3	4	4	73.4
	–	2	4	4	51.0
	–	3	4	4	51.2
Present bias β = 0.8	0	0	0	0	34.0
	1	2	4	4	22.2
Thinks d = 0.5 and has	0	0	0	0	34.0
present bias β = 0.8	1	2	4	4	62.6
	1	4	4	4	61.6
	–	2	4	4	44.4
	–	4	4	4	44.8

If he thinks cigarettes are less addictive than they are, then in period one he would prefer a plan with only two packs of cigarettes in period two. When he gets to period two, however, because he is more addicted than he thought he would be, he prefers having three packs of cigarettes rather than two. He will consume more cigarettes than he planned, and more than would maximize his utility.

If he has a present bias then not a lot happens in this example. We can see from the expected utility that consuming cigarettes has become slightly more attractive, but still not enough to warrant smoking. You can play around with the numbers yourself, but it turns out that present bias is not going to make much difference to what Rob will do unless he has a really strong present bias. I'll come back to why this is the case later.

It looks like underestimating the addictiveness of smoking is the real problem Rob needs to be wary of. Present bias can, however, make a difference if Rob underestimates the addictiveness of smoking. We see, for instance, that if Rob underestimates the addictiveness of cigarettes and has present bias he would be happy to smoke four packs of cigarettes rather than the two he planned when he is in period two. He will thus consume even more cigarettes than he planned and get an even lower utility. The less addictive Rob thinks smoking is, the more present bias is going to matter.

A combination of underestimating the addictiveness of smoking and present bias can, therefore, easily lead to Rob smoking more cigarettes than he planned and getting more addicted than he planned. It is no surprise, therefore, that he might end up wanting to quit but be unable to do so and the data we observe becomes a lot easier to explain. The role for government policy also changes because there becomes a clear rationale for more information on the addictiveness of smoking and it also makes sense to give people help in trying to quit. But, the story we have so far is primarily one of why Rob might become addicted. What we need to do now is look more at the potential difficulties of quitting.

9.5.3 Cues and addiction

One important factor in addiction can be **cue-elicited behavior**. The idea here is that some cue, such as a particular sound, smell or situation, makes someone crave something. For example, if Rob typically smokes a cigarette after dinner, or when he goes to the bar with friends, then his craving for a cigarette might be higher than normal at these times. We have seen how secondary reinforcers can have this effect, and such cue-elicited behavior is often cited as a reason for relapse in people trying to quit an addiction. For example, Laibson (2001) gives the story of a smoker who hadn't smoked for years, but on going to the beach one day had an intense craving to smoke. The craving was a consequence of smoking on the beach being common at one time in his life.

We can model cue-elicited behavior without too much change to the rational addiction model. All we need to add are the cues. Let's suppose that each day Rob either eats dinner at home or eats out. This will be the cue. At dinner he then decides to smoke or not. Instead of keeping stock of how many cigarettes Rob smokes, we now distinguish how many cigarettes he smokes during dinners at home and how many at dinners out.

To explain how we can do this, imagine that on day $t-1$ Rob decided to eat out. Then we let

$$S_t^{out} = d(S_{t-1}^{out} + a_{t-1})$$

denote the stock of past consumption of cigarettes when eating out, and keep

$$S_t^{in} = S_{t-1}^{in}$$

as the stock of past consumption of cigarettes when eating in. Similarly, if he had decided to eat in we would let

$$S_t^{in} = d(S_{t-1}^{in} + a_{t-1})$$

denote the stock of past consumption of cigarettes when eating in, and keep

$$S_t^{out} = S_{t-1}^{out}$$

as the stock of past consumption of cigarettes when eating out.

Rob's utility in period t then depends on where he eats and the difference between present consumption and the stock of past consumption. For instance if he eats out his utility is:

$$u_t = \begin{cases} c_t + 10\sqrt{a_t - S_t^{out}} & \text{if } a_t \geq S_t^{out} \\ c_t - 10(S_t - S_t^{out}) & \text{if } a_t < S_t^{out} \end{cases}.$$

If he eats in his utility is:

$$u_t = \begin{cases} c_t + 10\sqrt{a_t - S_t^{in}} & \text{if } a_t \geq S_t^{in} \\ c_t - 10(S_t - S_t^{in}) & \text{if } a_t < S_t^{in} \end{cases}.$$

We still assume that he uses exponential discounting to find his inter-temporal utility:

$$u^T = u_1 + \delta u_2 + \delta^2 u_2 + \ldots + \delta^T u_t.$$

To better understand the model, let's start by assuming that Rob eats out every day. Then the model is exactly the same as the rational model of addiction. But, whereas I previously assumed the discount factor was $\delta = 1$, meaning there was no discounting of the future, it is now going to be important to think a bit about the discount factor. Table 9.8 looks at what happens if the discount factor is $\delta = 0.7$ rather than $\delta = 1$. We can see that the decrease in the discount factor makes smoking look relatively more attractive. The reason for this is that the costs of smoking come primarily in period four, when Rob is very addicted. The lower the discount factor the less Rob worries about these costs.

Basically, the discount factor can matter a lot in Rob's choices. Incidentally this does not contradict me saying earlier that present bias may not have such a large effect. That's because the benefits of smoking come not just today but over the initial few periods, and so present bias discounts most of the benefits as well as the costs of smoking. The costs of smoking do, however, come after some time, and so something that discounts the future the further away it is will make a difference.

Why should we care about the discount factor? To see why the discount factor is important in understanding cues, imagine that Rob eats in six days a week and eats out on a Saturday. As Table 9.9 illustrates, when deciding whether to smoke on a Monday he knows that whether or not he smokes will affect his stock of past

Table 9.8 The effect of the discount factor on Rob's desire to smoke during dinner, assuming that $d = 1$ and a pack of cigarettes cost \$2 in all periods

Cigarettes on day				Utility	
1	*2*	*3*	*4*	$\delta = 1$	$\delta = 0.7$
0	0	0	0	40.0	25.33
1	2	3	5	28	27.73

Table 9.9 The discount factor matters if there are two cues

Day of week	Cue	If smoke when it will first matter
Monday	Eat in	Tuesday
Tuesday	Eat in	Wednesday
Wednesday	Eat in	Thursday
Thursday	Eat in	Friday
Friday	Eat in	Sunday
Saturday	Eat out	Next Saturday
Sunday	Eat in	Monday

consumption when eating in and so will affect his utility on the next day. By contrast, on a Saturday he knows that whether or not he smokes will affect his stock of past consumption when eating out and so will not affect his utility until one week. This means the effective discount factor for eating out is a lot lower than that for eating in. For example, if the discount factor is $\delta = 0.95$ then the effective discount factor for eating in is 0.95 but for eating out it is $0.95^7 = 0.7$.

We have already seen that a low discount factor makes it optimal for Rob to smoke more cigarettes. A probable outcome, therefore, is that he would not smoke when eating in but would smoke when eating out. This is why cues matter and why Rob may decide to smoke only when he gets certain cues. If we add present bias or an underestimation of the addictiveness of cigarettes to the story then we can see why addictiveness can become cue dependent and why Rob may become more addicted to smoking when eating out than he wanted to.

Cue dependence is interesting in thinking about how people can quit addiction. If addiction is cue dependent then people can avoid addiction by avoiding the cues that cause it. For example, if Rob does become too addicted to smoking when eating out then he can simply stop to eat out and solve the problem. This looks like good news for those wanting to quit because it provides a viable way to avoid addiction. It is not all good news, however, because Rob would have to sacrifice eating out, which he might like, and may remain vulnerable to reigniting his addiction if he ever does eat out. This last point may suggest why many people struggle to quit.

9.5.4 Addiction and neuroscience

Economists love simple models, and also love drawing analogies, but it's sometimes useful to check whether it all makes sense. That seems particularly pertinent in looking at addiction where economists are a long way from familiar ground. So, are the models we have just been looking at reasonable models of addiction, and how far can we generalize them in looking at habit and more mundane consumer purchases? Neuroscience can potentially guide us to an answer.

Fortunately, we do not need to delve too deeply into the complex neuroscience of addiction in order to learn some interesting things. In terms of hard drugs we know that on initial use such drugs increase dopamine transmission, which you might recall is usually associated with a positive reward. Users are, therefore, likely to associate the drug with pleasure, and begin to associate cues that might have proceeded using the drug with that pleasure. This is the same story as we looked at above in valuing rewards, and so there is little at this stage to distinguish drugs from anything else, i.e. money.

If, however, the person continues to use the drug then they go through various stages in which the neural circuitry appears to essentially be rewired by the drug use. This leads to addiction. In the final stage of addiction, the VMPFC seems to lead the way in demanding the drug, rather than passively responding to consumption of the drug. Potentially, this can become permanent, making it very hard for an addict to ever quit. It also means that addicts will be less responsive to 'normal' rewards, and less able to make decisions.

What do we learn from this? It lends strong support to a cue-based model of addiction, because it is cues that activate the VMPFC to crave the drug. It also lends support to the potential importance of underestimating the addictiveness of drugs, because drugs really are addictive and people may underestimate their effect. Present bias though starts to appear less relevant, because if a person really did know the consequences of drug addiction then any present bias would have to be very extreme for them to still use the drug. It's probably not present bias, therefore, that's at work, but a potential uncontrollable craving for the drug that is unrelated to present bias.

Knowing this gives us some idea what a model of addiction should look like (and actually points towards a model of addiction proposed by Bernheim and Rangel (2004) that I'm not going to look at here, but I suggest you do). It also gives us a better idea how to design policy to deal with the problems of addiction. For instance, it seems clear that conventional economic incentives, like increasing the price of a drug, are liable to be ineffective. More apt is probably to increase awareness of the problems of addiction and to help people avoid cues that trigger their addiction.

We can also see that addiction and habit are quite different things. So an analogy only gets us so far, and we probably will need different models to capture drug addiction versus a habit to watch cricket. Drawing the dividing line is not necessarily easy because drugs come in varying strength, from heroine to caffeine to chocolate, but a distinction does need to be made. We thus learn better how to model addiction, and also can be reassured that things like reference dependence and present bias are probably enough to capture habit.

9.6 Further reading

Textbooks on neuroscience and cognitive neuroscience, such as Purves et al. (2008) are a natural place to start. The book by Glimcher (2004) gives a more general introduction to the subject. Overlapping survey articles include Camerer (2007) and Camerer, Loewenstein and Prelec (2004, 2005). Fudenberg and Levine (2006) is a recent dual-self model of self-control. Schelling (1984) and Bernheim and Rangel (2007) provide interesting contrasts on the implications of multiple selves for measuring welfare. On addiction, the paper by Bernheim and Rangel (2004) is recommended, and Kalivas and Volkow (2005) provide more on the neuroscience of addiction. For more on the debate over whether neuroeconomics is a good or bad thing for economics, see Caplin and Schotter (2008).

9.7 Review questions

9.1   Why does the brain interpret money as a reward? Is it a primary or secondary reinforcer?

9.2   Do you think the brains reward systems react to expected value or 'expected utility'?

9.3   When does Rob feel the value of winning at roulette: when the wheel stops, when he collects his money, or when he eats the chips he buys with the money? Relate this to hedonic editing.

9.4   Why is reward prediction error relevant in interpreting Figures 9.4 to 9.7?

9.5   Relate reward prediction error to reference dependence.

9.6   Given that brain activation is constrained to fall within a fixed range, how can activation be in proportion to the reward? What does this suggest about our differing ability to distinguish relative from absolute magnitudes?

9.7   Why might it be consistent with forward-looking behavior that people want to quit smoking? What if I tell you that only 26 percent of people said they wanted to quit smoking because of financial reasons (ONS 2004), but 86 percent said they wanted to quit because of health reasons?

9.8   What policy should the government adopt to stop people doing drugs or smoking?

9.9   Is addiction different to habit?

9.10 Is a multiple-self model helpful in modeling economic behavior?

Part IV
Welfare and policy

10 Happiness and utility

> The great source of both the misery and disorders of human life seems to arise from overrating the difference between one permanent situation and another. Avarice overrates the difference between poverty and riches: ambition that between a private and a public station: vain-glory, that between obscurity and extensive reputation.
>
> Adam Smith, *The Theory of Moral Sentiments*

Having looked at how people do behave, and why, we shall now start to look at the welfare and policy implications of that behavior. The basic question I want us to look at in this chapter is whether people make the economic choices that will give them greatest satisfaction and happiness, and if not would they rather someone else make choices for them? To answer that question we need to know what makes people happy, whether people know what makes them happy, and how much people value choice. In the next chapter we shall make the logical next step in asking what role policy can play.

10.1 What makes us happy?

The story throughout the book has been one of people trying to maximize utility. For the most part we can think of utility as a measure of happiness, so, if people maximize utility, they maximize happiness. The standard economist's answer to the question 'What makes us happy?' is, therefore, simple: 'Whatever we do!' If we observe Emma going to the cinema, then we could infer that going to the cinema makes Emma happy; why else would she go? If we observe Alan buying car insurance then we infer this makes him happy; why else would he buy it? This is called **revealed preference**, because Emma's and Alan's actions reveal their preferences.

Can we be sure, however, that a person's choices truly reveal what makes them happy?

To answer that question we need to have an alternative measure of what makes people happy. One alternative is to ask people how happy they are, and see how their answer changes as things happen in their life. For example, if we observe Emma getting a job, then a revealed preference argument would suggest that having a job makes her happier. If we know how happy Emma said she was before she got the job, and how happy she says she is after getting the job, then we can check whether she really is happier.

Fortunately, there is a lot of data on how happy people say they are. For example, a question in the World Values Survey asks respondents: 'All things considered, how satisfied are you with your life as a whole these days?' Many other surveys ask similar questions. There are pertinent issues about how much we can rely on this data (see Research Methods 10.1 and 10.2) but the data does throw up some consistent results and so we'll assume it is reliable. This means we can check whether choices really do reveal what makes people happy. Before we do that, though, it is useful to have a look first at what people say does make them happy.

Research Methods 10.1

The law of large numbers: Can we trust happiness data?

Two ways we can measure happiness are to ask people questions like: 'How satisfied are you with your life as a whole these days?', or to ask them to look back at an event and try to recall the pleasure, pain or utility they felt during the event. Do people give a reliable answer to such questions?

We do know that people's answers to such questions can be affected by current mood and how the question is framed. This was amply demonstrated in an experiment by Norbert Schwarz where half those surveyed were 'lucky enough to find a dime' before being surveyed. Those who found the dime reported higher 'life satisfaction'. We also know that the same people can give quite different answers to how happy they are if they are asked two or more weeks apart. Clearly, therefore, we need to be a little skeptical of happiness measures.

So, should we be using happiness data at all? It probably will suffice for our purposes. That is because we will aggregate the data of many people. For example, we will be interested whether unemployed people are less happy than employed people. If we ask lots of unemployed and employed people whether they are happy and average out the responses, we should get a reliable measure of whether those who are employed are happier. If the data is a little unreliable or noisy, then we may have to ask more people, but we can still get reliable information.

Research Methods 10.2

An alternative measure of happiness

The **day reconstruction method** involves participants filling out a diary summarizing episodes that occurred the day before. They should describe what they did, how long they did it for, etc. and also how they felt during each event of the day. A study by Kahneman et al. (2004) used the method on a sample of 909 working women in Texas. Some of the data is given in Table 10.1. Net affect measures positive minus negative experience, and there are not too many surprises in what gives relatively high and low net affect.

Table 10.1 The day reconstruction method. Net affect is a measure of positive minus negative emotions. All responses were on a six-point scale, so six is the most positive and zero the most negative.

Activity	Time spent (hours)	Net affect	U-index
Intimate relations	0.23	4.83	0.040
Socializing after work	1.14	4.15	0.073
Relaxing	2.17	3.96	0.078
Dinner	0.81	3.94	0.074
Lunch	0.57	3.91	0.078
Exercising	0.22	3.85	0.088
Praying/worship	0.45	3.78	0.105
Socializing at work	1.12	3.78	0.100
Watching TV	2.19	3.65	0.095
Phone at home	0.93	3.52	0.126
Napping	0.89	3.35	0.131
Cooking	1.15	3.27	0.138
Shopping	0.41	3.23	0.157
Computer (non-work)	0.51	3.22	0.165
Housework	1.12	2.99	0.161
Childcare	1.10	2.99	0.199
Evening commute	0.61	2.77	0.209
Working	6.89	2.68	0.211
Morning commute	0.47	2.09	0.287

Source: Kahneman et al. (2004).

One way to use the day reconstruction method to measure happiness is the U-index. The **U-index** asks how much of the time a person spends doing unpleasant activities. There is no simple definition of when an activity is unpleasant, but one possibility is to count any event where the most intense feelings are negative. In Table 10.1 there is the U-index for the various day time activities. So, for example, 28 percent of the time spent commuting was unpleasant.

Figure 10.1 compares the U-index with the standard measure of happiness and household income and age and we see a strong correlation between the two measures. The U-index does, however, have one big advantage over the standard measure: interpersonal comparisons are more plausible. Interpersonal comparisons are hard to believe when focusing on satisfaction questions, because how people choose to rate themselves on, say, a ten-point satisfaction scale, can vary widely from person to person without any difference in their happiness. So, that Maria rates herself seven and Alan six does not convincingly tell you Maria is happier than Alan. The U-index is intuitively a more objective measure. People may more reliably remember whether or not an event is unpleasant, and the time spent doing unpleasant events is a readily understandable measure.

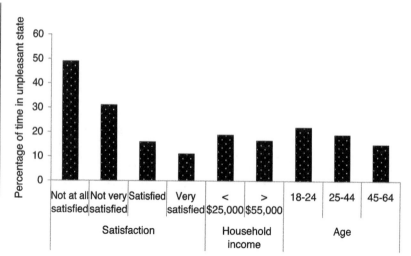

Figure 10.1 The U index compared to life satisfaction. The lower was life satisfaction, the less time people spent in an unpleasant state.

Source: Kahneman and Krueger (2006).

10.1.1 Happiness is relative

When we look at how happy people say they are, or how satisfied they say they are with their life, we get some surprises. Two studies in the 1970s, one in economics and one in psychology, first highlighted the issues, and it is interesting to look at both.

Brickman, Coates and Janoff-Bulman (1978) compared the happiness of lottery winners, accident victims, and a control group of people randomly selected from the phone book. The lottery winners had won between $50,000 and $1 million on the Illinois State Lottery. The accident victims were either paraplegic or quadriplegic as a result of their accidents.

The main results of the study are given in Figure 10.2. The first thing we see is very little difference in reported happiness between the lottery winners and control group. Winning the lottery does not seem to make people any happier. Being in an accident does have a more pronounced effect and, not surprisingly, lowers present happiness and increases the perception of past happiness. What is surprising is that the drop in happiness is not very large, and predictions of future happiness are no different to those of the lottery winners. Winning $1 million or becoming paraplegic is clearly a life-changing event, but this study suggests neither change life satisfaction as much as we might expect.

Easterlin (1974) looked at whether happiness correlates with income. Figure 10.3 reports data from a 1970 survey of the US population. As we might expect, those with higher income reported being happier. No surprises so far. If, however, increased income leads to increased happiness, then it seems logical

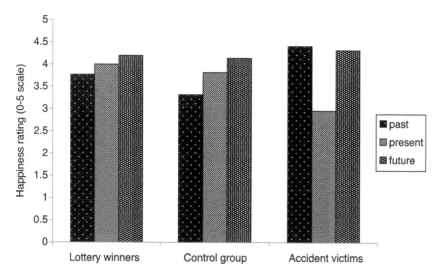

Figure 10.2 The change in reported life satisfaction following a life-changing event.

Source: Brickman, Coates and Janoff-Bulman (1978).

that: (i) people should be happier, on average, in countries with higher income, and (ii) people should become happier, on average, if incomes increase over time. The curious thing that Easterlin pointed out is that neither of these things happens! Figure 10.4 provides a recent cross-country comparison of reported happiness,

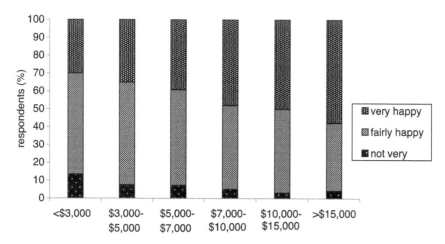

Figure 10.3 Life satisfaction and income. Those with higher income report higher life satisfaction.

Source: Easterlin (1974).

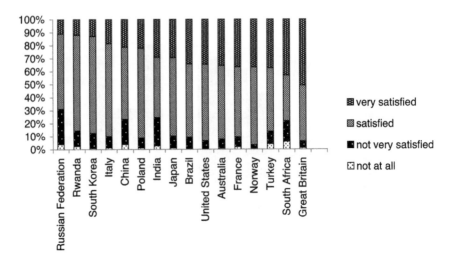

Figure 10.4 Life satisfaction in different countries. There is no apparent correlation between the average income in a country and satisfaction.

Source: World Values Survey 2005.

and we can see (compare the US with Great Britain, Rwanda, Turkey and South Africa, for example) that higher income does not translate into higher happiness. Figure 10.5 shows reported happiness in the US over time, and despite real income tripling over this period, reported happiness ultimately changed little.

Since these two studies there have been many more, some of which we shall look at below, and they all seem to confirm these early findings. Happiness, and unhappiness, it seems can be a little elusive. Before we start to look at the important implications of this, we need to ask why it happens. The leading explanation is reference dependence. If happiness depends on the relative rather than the absolute level of things like income and health, then changes in the absolute level need not change happiness. The two most likely reference points here are what others have, and what the person used to have. I will primarily focus on the latter of these two, and so let's briefly think about the implications of the first.

If people want to earn as much income as relatives and friends (and we saw evidence in chapters two and seven that they do) then those earning relatively more will be relatively happier than those earning relatively less. This is consistent with Figure 10.3. Logically, however, there must always be some in a society that are earning relatively more, and some earning relatively less. This can explain why we see no correlation between average happiness and income over time or between countries. That people judge their own income relative to others can, therefore, explain a lot. But it cannot explain everything, as we shall now see.

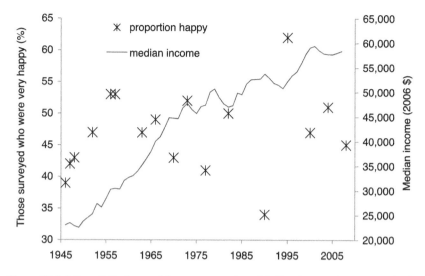

Figure 10.5 Life satisfaction and income over time. Median income increases a lot but
reported satisfaction does not.

Source: Easterlin (1974), Gallup and US Census Bureau.

10.1.2 Adaption and habituation

Looking back at Figure 10.2 we can see that happiness does not depend solely on
circumstances relative to others. The lottery winners should be relatively wealthy,
but are not happy. The accident victims should have relatively ill health, and were
less happy when asked, but did not expect to be less happy in the future. To
explain this we need to introduce the ideas of adaption and habituation.

To illustrate and motivate these concepts we can look at some data on how
peoples reported happiness or satisfaction changes in response to other 'life-
changing' events. Clark et al. (2003, 2008) analyze data from Germany that tracks
people's life satisfaction over the period 1984 to 1997. They use the first five or
seven years of the panel to obtain a person's baseline level of satisfaction and then
look at how satisfaction changes in the years leading up to and after events like
marriage, divorce, a first child and unemployment. Most of these events are
predictable, and so it is also useful to have some data on an event that is more
unpredictable. For that, we can look at data by Oswald and Powdthavee (2008)
from the UK on the consequences of disability.

I am not going to look at all of the data, but Figure 10.6 plots a representative
sample. In terms of marriage, the birth of first child and layoff, we appear to
see **anticipation**, in that happiness increases or decreases prior to the event.
Disability, as we might expect, causes a more sudden jump in happiness, because
it is less predictable. After the event, in the case of marriage and the birth of a
first child, we see **adaption** in that happiness returns to the baseline level. There

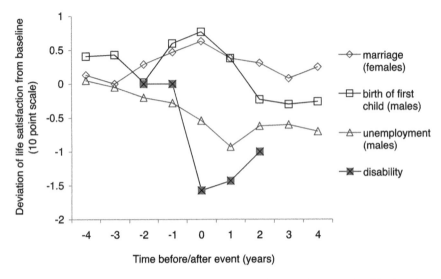

Figure 10.6 Changes in happiness relative to the baseline in, before and after life-changing events.

Sources: Clark et al. (2003), Oswald and Powdthavee (2008).

is some evidence of adaption in the case of disability, but not for being unemployed.

Adaption is a fascinating possibility because it implies that happiness will bounce back to baseline after a good or bad life event. This has profound implications for policy, and how we look at life. So, why does it happen? There are lots of interrelated possible causes, all with different interpretations, of which I will mention four.

We can distinguish two effects that result from a real change in utility. In terms of negative events there may be **readjustment** whereby the person finds new ways to fulfill their life. For example, someone who liked to play football but becomes paraplegic might learn to play wheelchair basketball. In this case the utility function or reference level has not changed but the person has had to relearn how to maximize utility. **Habituation** is where a person becomes accustomed to their new life. For example, the lottery winner becomes accustomed to buying expensive things, and the accident victim becomes accustomed to being in a wheelchair. This would imply a change in the reference level and/or a change in the utility function (similar to that we looked at in section 4.5.1).

We can next distinguish affects that focus more on how satisfied people feel they are. One is a **contrast effect** whereby an extreme good or bad event changes the scale by which all future events are judged. For example, nothing might seem 'as good' as winning the lottery or 'as bad' as being in an accident. Taking this

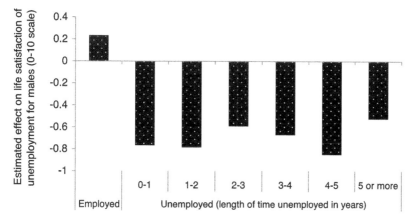

Figure 10.7 Estimated affect on life satisfaction of being employed versus unemployed. There is no evidence of adaption to being unemployed.

Source: Clark et al. (2008).

one stage further we get an **aspiration treadmill**, where a person adjusts aspirations to the satisfaction they normally experience. Consequently, the lottery winner is likely to downplay current satisfaction and the accident victim to overplay current satisfaction, given what they experienced before.

Readjustment and habituation suggest that utility regains its former level. The contrast effect and aspiration treadmill suggest that utility may not regain its former level but people's answer to the question how satisfied they feel does. This is a crucial distinction. Unfortunately we do not yet have good answers to what best explains adaption. It does not necessarily follow, therefore, that utility bounces back to the baseline.

What we do know is that adaption only seems to happen some of the time. For some types of event adaption can be incomplete and/or take a very long while. For instance, in Figure 10.6 we see little evidence of adaption after being unemployed. To illustrate this further Figure 10.7 plots the estimated effect of unemployment on life satisfaction for males. We see that being unemployed has long-run effects and so any adaption is very weak.

We will come back to the consequences of adaption soon enough, but I now want to return to the question of whether a person's choice reveals what makes them happy.

10.2 Do we know what makes us happy?

To illustrate some of the issues, imagine that someone called Ian has just come back from his annual summer holiday to Italy and we want to find out how happy he is and why he chose to go.

Thinking about things from a revealed preference perspective, we work back from the fact that Ian went on holiday. We would say that his decision utility for a holiday in Italy was greater than that for a holiday in France, or staying at home and not spending the $2,000 he spent on flights and hotels. We know that because we know that he decided to go for a holiday in Italy. More generally, **decision utility** is revealed by a person's behavior. Whenever I have referred to utility in this book up until now I was really talking about decision utility.

Thinking about things from a slightly different perspective, we can start with the concept of instant utility. **Instant utility** measures the pleasure or pain that Ian experienced at specific points in time. Figure 10.8 plots what this might look like over the course of his holiday. Like any good holiday we see some ups, a nice walk in the mountains, and some downs, mild food poisoning. From this we can calculate **total utility**, which is basically the sum of instant utilities. In the example, this would be the area under the instant utility curve, distinguishing between the positive area above the axis and negative area below the axis. The bigger the positive area and the smaller the negative area the greater is his total utility.

When we ask people how happy they are, we get a snapshot of their instant utility at that point in time. From this we could estimate total utility. Happiness data gives us, therefore, a means to measure total utility, and this looks like a good measure of happiness. The question we need to think about is whether total utility and decision utility coincide. If they do, then Ian's choice reveals what makes him happy, and so he must know consciously or subconsciously what makes him happy. Everything works nicely. But, what if decision utility and total utility are different? Then things become less simple, and there two good reasons that they can be different. I will look at each in turn.

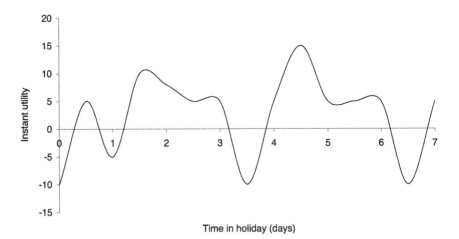

Time in holiday (days)

Figure 10.8 The instant utility over time of Ian on a holiday in Italy.

10.2.1 Remembered utility

When looking back on past experiences, it seems that people typically do not remember total utility. I shall illustrate this with a study by Daniel Kahneman et al. (1993). The study involved subjects experiencing and evaluating pain. Subjects were first asked to immerse their hand in cold water for 60 seconds. The water was kept at 14°C. Seven minutes later subjects were asked to put their other hand in cold water for 90 seconds. This time the water was kept at 14°C for 60 seconds and then gradually increased to 15°C. Seven minutes later each subject was told that they would be asked to put their hand in water a third time, but they could choose whether to repeat the first, 60-second trial, or the second, 90-second trial.

After all this was done, subjects were asked to plot their level of discomfort during the trials. If we convert this to instant utility we get something like Figure 10.9. The first thing to note is that the reported discomfort was the same in the 60-second trial as the first 60 seconds of the 90-second trial. This means that total utility had to be less for the 90-second than 60-second trial, because there is an extra 30 seconds of discomfort. Surely, therefore, people prefer to repeat the 60-second rather than the 90-second trial? In fact 69 percent of subjects said that they would prefer to repeat the 90-second trial!

Figure 10.10 looks at how subjects rated the 90-second trial relative to the 60-second trial on several criteria. We see that subjects did correctly realize the 90-second trial was longer, but otherwise remember it as less bad. Why would they do that? The only difference between the two trials, and the only thing that could explain it, is that the 90-second trial ends better. If people put extra weight on the last thing that they remember about an event, then we have a plausible explanation for why subjects preferred the 90-second trial.

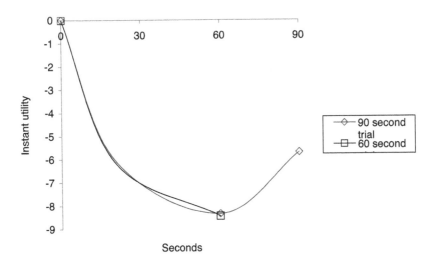

Figure 10.9 Instant utility while hand is immersed in cold water for 60 or 90 seconds.

Source: Kahneman et al. (1993).

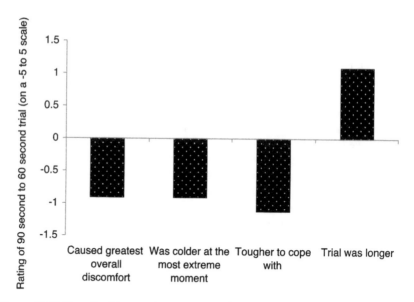

Figure 10.10 How the 90-second trial was rated compared to the 60-second trial. The 90-second trial was rated better on everything except length.

Source: Kahneman et al. (1993).

This study, and many others, suggest that people do not always make decisions based on total utility. It also suggests we need to take seriously the idea that people may not remember very well how much utility an event gave them. We can use the term **remembered utility** to measure the amount of utility a person thinks an event gave them. Evidence also suggests that the remembered utility of an event is accurately predicted by averaging the peak level of instant utility and end level of instant utility. This is called **peak-end evaluation**.

Ian's holiday will thus be remembered by the instant utility at the best and/or worst moment, and the instant utility at the end of the holiday. It is clear that this can mean a significant difference between remembered utility and total utility, or between decision utility and total utility. Do not necessarily expect, therefore, that people choose things that will give them highest total utility. Maybe Ian should have stayed at home and saved $2,000?

This raises some difficult but fascinating questions. For instance, peak-end evaluation implies there will be duration neglect. **Duration neglect** is where the duration of an event does not influence someone's memory of how good or bad the event was. This means that people can forget lots of good, or bad, moments and remember an event based on only a few instances. So, what is best: an event that gives higher total utility, or an event that will give higher remembered utility? Was the 60-second trial better because subjects suffered less total discomfort, or was the 90-second trial better because subjects remember less discomfort? What if we are talking about 60 or 90 days, months, or years, rather than seconds?

10.2.2 Projection bias

Having seen that people may not be accurate in looking back at their past, we next ask whether they are good at predicting the future. Adaption raises the possibility that people may not be good at this either, if they cannot predict how they will adapt to life events, and how their tastes and preferences will change. So, can people predict how their tastes and preferences will adapt? The simple answer seems to be that most people correctly predict the direction of change but not the magnitude. This leads to **projection bias** in which people overestimate how much future preferences and tastes will resemble current preferences and tastes. Projection bias can show up various different ways that I want to discuss and distinguish.

There is an **impact bias** if a person expects an event to have a bigger effect than it subsequently does. To illustrate, we can look at a study by Smith et al. (2008) that surveyed patients as they were waiting for a renal transplant, and again twelve months after they had had the transplant. Figure 10.11 summarizes the main results. An impact bias is shown by the patients predicting a greater increase in quality of life than actually occurred. We also see that patients remembered their quality of life as worse than it was. This could be because after the transplant we observe remembered utility, while beforehand we observe instant utility.

The opposite of the impact bias is when a person expects an event to have no effect but it subsequently does. One possible cause of this is the endowment effect we looked at in chapter two. Recall that the endowment effect causes people to

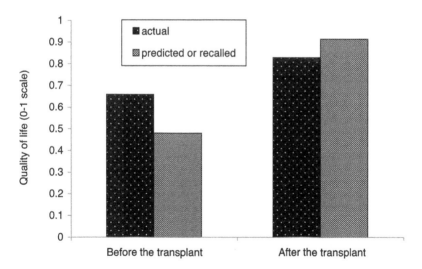

Figure 10.11 Predicted or recalled quality of life compared to actual before and after a renal transplant. Quality of life increases less than expected. People recalled quality of life being worse than it was.

Source: Smith et al. (2008).

value an item more when they own it. Do people predict this effect? Loewenstein and Adler (1995) asked this question in a study that involved subjects valuing a mug before and after they were given it. Figure 10.12 summarizes the results. We can see that before they got the mug, subjects said they would be willing to sell it for around $3.50 to $3.70. Having been given the mug, subjects increased their asking price. The control group, who were not influenced by giving a prediction before receiving the mug, provide a good measure of willingness to sell the mug once owned, and valued it at 50 to 100 percent more. This means that subjects under-estimated what effect ownership of the mug would have on their willingness to sell.

The impact bias and a failure to predict the endowment effect suggest that people are poor at predicting how they will adapt to events and how their reference level may change over time. The accident victim may overestimate the long-run affects of disability, and the lottery winner may underestimate how much his reference level will increase as he becomes accustomed to his new wealth. The final effect I want to look at shows that people can underestimate the effect of short-run mood.

I will illustrate with a study by Read and van Leeuwen (1998). They asked 200 office workers in Amsterdam to choose what, from a range of healthy and unhealthy snacks, they would want to get in one week's time. The workers were asked either after lunch or late afternoon and were told that they would be given the snack after lunch or late afternoon. The expectation was that people would be hungry late afternoon but satiated after lunch, and this would affect choice. The

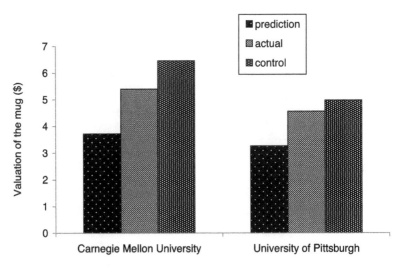

Figure 10.12 The endowment effect. Subjects failed to predict how ownership of a mug would increase their valuation of the mug.

Source: Loewenstein and Adler (1995).

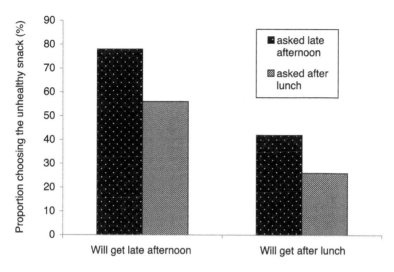

Figure 10.13 The proportion who chose an unhealthy snack for one week's time depends on current hunger.

Source: Read and van Leeuwen (1998).

results in Figure 10.13 suggest that it did. There is no good reason why current hunger should affect what the person will want in one week's time. For many, however, it seemed that current hunger affected what the person expected they would want in one week's time. Those who were relatively hungry when asked were relatively more likely to choose the unhealthy snack.

In summary, we observe a projection bias in which people overestimate how much future preferences and tastes will resemble current preferences and tastes, underestimate how much they will adapt to events, and are influenced by current mood.

10.3 Choice and commitment

Projection bias and the difference between decision and remembered utility suggest that people may not know what is best for them. We have already seen elsewhere in this book that even if people do know what is best for them, they may not make the best choices because of, say, present bias. Things do not look, therefore, very promising. But can people overcome projection bias and time-inconsistency? One way they might is by pre-commitment, either by pre-committing themselves to a plan of action or by allowing someone else to choose for them. What I want to do in this section is explore how well this could work.

To get us started on this question, let's stick with the subject of food a bit longer. After one week the workers in the study by Read and van Leeuwen were found and re-offered the choice of snacks. This time they got the snack they chose. As we can

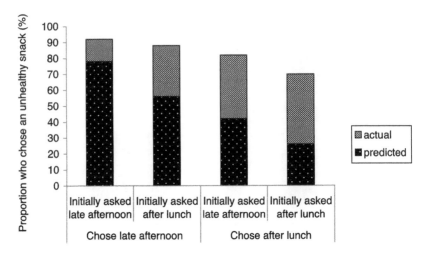

Figure 10.14 More chose an unhealthy snack than predicted they would, but fewer chose the unhealthy snack if they said they would choose a healthy snack.

Source: Read and van Leeuwen (1998).

see in Figure 10.14 a lot of those who said they would want the healthy snack actually chose an unhealthy snack. This looks like the dynamic time inconsistency problem we saw in chapter four. Interestingly, however, it seems that many stuck by the choice of a healthy snack they knew they made before. This would explain why the time they were initially asked affected subsequent choice.

We can follow this up with a study by Gilbert, Gill and Wilson (2002) that looked at the effect of hunger on grocery shopping. Shoppers in a grocery store were asked to take part in a survey in which they were asked to list their planned shopping. Some were given back the list and some were not, and some were given a muffin to try before shopping and some not. The number of unlisted items that the shopper subsequently bought was recorded. Figure 10.15 summarizes the main result. Not surprisingly shoppers purchased more items than they put on the list. Consistent with projection bias we see that those who were relatively hungry, because they did not eat the muffin, bought more unplanned items. Interestingly, however, those with the shopping list to hand were seemingly much less affected by their current mood.

In both these examples behavior seemed to be influenced by a loose precommitment. In the first case, knowing they said they would eat a healthy snack seemed enough to persuade some to stick with their choice. In the second case, having what they said written down, in the form of a shopping list, made people stick closer to what they planned. What we need to do is ask how useful pre-commitments can be generally.

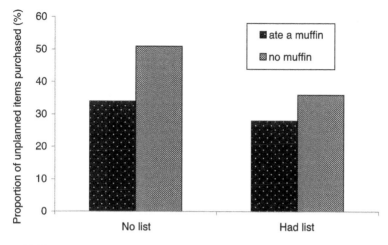

Figure 10.15 How many unplanned items shoppers bought depended on whether or not they ate a muffin and whether or not they had a shopping list to hand.

Source: Gilbert, Gill and Wilson (2002)

10.3.1 Does present bias matter?

Before we look in more detail at whether pre-commitment can work, it seems pertinent to take a step back and ask whether things like projection bias and present bias do really lower utility. In section 10.6.1 I will show you that projection bias can seriously lower utility. Here, I want to look at present bias and ask whether present bias lowers utility.

The first problem we have in answering this question is how to evaluate utility. The measure I am going to use takes a long run perspective in which we ignore any present bias, and say the total utility, if utility in periods one to T is u_1 to u_T, is

$$U^0(u_1, u_2, ..., u_T) = u_1 + \delta u_2 + ... + \delta^{T-1} u_T = \sum_{\tau=1}^{T} \delta^{\tau-1} u_\tau$$

where δ is the long-run discount factor. This definition has its problems, which you might want to think about, but it's as good as we have.

Now imagine that Ian, fresh from his holiday, is now deciding when to finish his dissertation. It's 1 April today and the work has to be handed in by 30 April. It plays on his mind that it is not done, and so his utility is 99 on every day it is not done and then 100 a day once it is finished. He knows that it would take just one day's work to finish it, and on that day his utility would be zero. Table 10.2 illustrates how things look on 1 April. It is clear that Ian gets the highest total utility if he does the dissertation immediately. But what if he has present bias?

Table 10.2 Ian's utility depends on when he finishes the dissertation. Total utility ignores any present bias, while decision utility takes into account present bias. Assuming that $\delta = 1$ and $\beta = 0.98$. Total utility is highest if he does the dissertation immediately, but present bias means he will constantly put it off until tomorrow and do it on 30 April

Plan	Utility on each day					Total utility	Decision utility	
	1st	2nd	3rd	4th	30th		Today	Tomorrow
Do it today	0	100	100	100	100	2900	2842	–
Do tomorrow	99	0	100	100	100	2899	2843	2744
Do on the 3rd	99	99	0	100	100	2898	2842	2745
Do on the 30th	99	99	99	99	0	2871	2816	2719

Recall (you might want to look back on chapter four to refresh your memory) we can write decision utility as:

$$U^T(u_1, u_2, \ldots, u_T) = u_1 + \beta\delta u_2 + \ldots, + \beta\delta^{T-1}u_T = u_1 + \beta\sum_{\tau=2}^{T}\delta^{\tau-1}u_\tau$$

where β measures the present bias. Let us assume $\beta = 0.98$, meaning Ian has only a very slight present bias. We can see that this present bias is enough that the decision utility is higher for doing the dissertation tomorrow. This, in itself, looks not too bad, because total utility is only one lower if he does it tomorrow. The problem is that tomorrow he will want to put it off until the next day, and so on. This means that, if he is naïve about his present bias, he will actually do it on 30 April and lose 29 in total utility.

Ian's naïve present bias will reduce his total utility by 1 percent. Nothing can be gained from arguing whether that is big or small, the main point we need to take from this is that a little bit of present bias can accumulate into a large loss in total utility. On any one day Ian is only willing to sacrifice one unit of total utility because of present bias. Unfortunately, he does not realize that he will end up sacrificing one unit every day, over lots of days, and so the total loss will be larger than he thought.

If Ian was sophisticated, and so knew about his present bias, he would do the dissertation straight away. Sophistication, however, does not mean he always avoids the welfare costs of present bias.

To illustrate, we can think about Emma who is sophisticated and eager to buy the latest book by her favorite author. As soon as she buys it she will read it and have utility 100. To complicate matters, the bookstore has a deal whereby the price of the book decreases by $1 every day starting at $29. Table 10.3 summarizes the choice Emma faces, again assuming $\beta = 0.98$. The best thing that Emma can do is wait until the price has gone down to $0. If she was naïve that is what she would do, but because she is sophisticated she will buy today! That's because she can predict that on the 29th she will buy, which means on the 28th she should

Table 10.3 Emma's utility depends on when she buys the book. Assuming that $\delta = 1$ and $\beta = 0.98$. Total utility is highest if she waits to buy the book. Present bias means she knows she will buy it earlier than that, so ultimately she buys it today

	Utility on each day					Total utility	Decision utility	
	1st	2nd	28th	29th	30th		on 28th	on 29th
Buy today	71	0	0	0	0	71	–	–
Buy on 28th	0	0	98	0	0	98	98	–
Buy on 29th	0	0	0	99	0	99	97	99
Buy on 30th	0	0	0	0	100	100	98	98

buy, and so on back to today. Again small day-to-day losses accumulate to a much bigger total loss.

It turns out that these examples are representative of what happens in general. If the costs are immediate and benefits later then there can be a big loss in total utility from present bias for someone who is naïve. If the benefits are immediate and the costs later then there can be a big loss in total utility from present bias for someone who is sophisticated.

Clearly, therefore, present bias is a potential problem. If someone keeps on putting something off, or bringing something forward, the losses will accumulate. And being sophisticated is not enough to avoid such losses, it can make them worse.

10.3.2 Pre-commitment

Now we know that present bias and projection bias really are a problem it becomes even more relevant to see whether pre-commitment can work. In principle it can. Ian might commit to doing the dissertation by say making a bet with his friend he will do it today. Emma might pre-commit by putting her money in a 'safe place' until the end of the month. In chapter four (see, for example, section 4.2.3) I already argued that people may want to pre-commit. Here, and the next chapter, I want to take that argument a bit further, and look at some data. I will start with a study by Ariely and Wertenbroch (2002).

In the study people were recruited to take part in a proof-reading task that involved reading three texts of around ten pages. Recruits were paid for every error they spotted, but had $1 deducted for each day of delay beyond a deadline. Recruits were randomly assigned to one of three conditions: an evenly spaced deadline condition where deadlines were set at seven-day intervals for each of the texts; an end day condition where all three texts were to be handed in at the end of 21 days; or a self-imposed deadline condition where recruits were invited to make their own deadlines for when to hand in the three texts over the next 21 days, with these deadlines then being enforced.

If a person has no present bias then they should prefer the end or self-imposed condition as this gives maximal flexibility when they do the task. If someone has a present bias and is sophisticated then they should prefer the self imposed

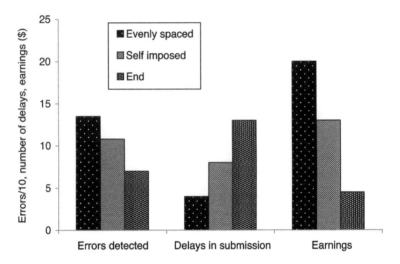

Figure 10.16 Performance in a proof-reading task. Performance depended on whether the deadlines were evenly spaced, self-imposed, or all at the end.

Source: Ariely and Wertenbroch (2002).

condition as they can commit to a plan that is optimal for them. Figure 10.16 illustrates what happened. We see that in terms of performance those in the evenly spaced condition do better than those in the self-imposed condition who do better than those in the end condition.

These results capture what we appear to see more generally. Namely, people do seem to want to pre-commit if possible. This suggests people are sophisticated to some extent about their present bias. Maybe, however, they do not choose the best plan when they do commit.

To illustrate the consequences of this recall the gym example in chapter four. Buying membership may be a way that Ian could try to overcome his present bias by pre-committing to going to the gym. They problem is, he might underestimate the strength of his present bias and so still not go to the gym. He has ended up paying a lot of money for a pre-commitment device that does not work! Pre-commitment, therefore, is not a panacea for present bias. It might work for some people in some situations. But, sometimes it might make matters worse, like for Ian going to the gym.

If people do not always make great choices, and others could potentially make better choices, it seems natural to let those others decide. Indeed, even if people can make great choices they might still prefer someone else to decide so they can avoid the psychological costs of temptation and the like. This seems to go partly against ideals of liberty and free choice, but if people would choose not to choose then the ideal of free choice becomes somewhat confused. To progress on this issue, it's useful to ask whether people like having choice or not.

10.3.3 Do people like having choice?

To illustrate how people respond to choice I am going to look at a study by Iyengar and Lepper (2000). In the study subjects were asked to select one chocolate from a selection of either six, a limited choice, or thirty, an extensive choice. Half the subjects then got to taste the chocolate they chose, and half got to taste a chocolate selected by the experimenter. On leaving the experiment, as payment for participation, subjects were given the choice of receiving $5 cash or a box of chocolates worth $5. The main result is clear from Figure 10.17, where we see that the proportion choosing chocolate over cash was far higher for subjects asked to choose from a limited number of chocolates and allowed to taste the one they selected.

Why is there such a difference? Figure 10.18 offers some clues. There are significant differences in perceptions of the participants depending on whether they had a limited or extensive choice. Interestingly, participants did appear to enjoy choosing more when there was a more extensive choice. On all other measures, however, participants seemed to benefit from a more limited choice: it was quicker, less difficult, less frustrating and they were more satisfied with their choice.

An experiment about chocolate seems a long way from us making conclusions on the benefits of free choice, but I like this study because it nicely illustrates two results observed much more generally. The first result is that more choice is not always a good thing. More choice can be bad because it complicates the decision and can lead to temptation and a need for self-control. This is consistent with what we saw in chapter two, where many preferred to delay a difficult decision, or seemed overwhelmed when there were too many choices on offer.

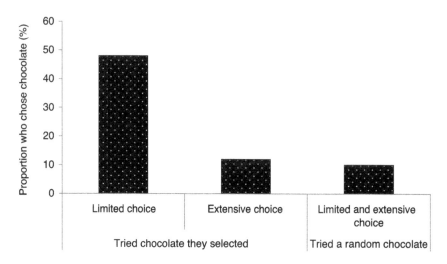

Figure 10.17 The proportion who chose chocolate rather than money depending on whether there was a limited or extensive choice, and whether they got to taste a chocolate they chose or the experimenter chose.

Source: Iyengar and Lepper (2000).

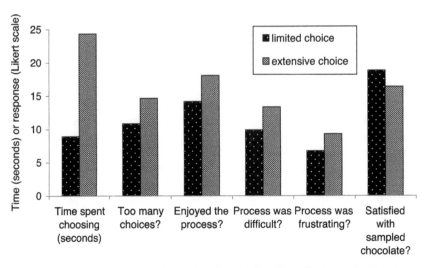

Figure 10.18 How opinions and behavior changed if subjects had a limited choice or extensive choice of chocolates.

Source: Iyengar and Lepper (2000).

Should we, therefore, be taking choice away from people? No, because the second result is that people like having a choice. We see this in the study by Iyengar and Lepper where subjects were more likely to want a box of chocolates rather than cash if they had tasted the chocolate they chose during the experiment, i.e. their choice mattered. More generally, the evidence is strong that people do like to make choices. One explanation is that people have a greater interest and motivation in things that they have **self-determined** through their own actions.

So, when faced with an increased choice of options, many people defer making a decision and/or feel less satisfied with the decision they make. This is called **choice overload**. People do, however, like to have some control and choice.

Putting these things together gives a somewhat bizarre conclusion. People like having choice, but do not like difficult choice. What people should like most, therefore, are easy choices! There's not much evidence to say whether this is a fair conclusion or not but what we do have is largely supportive. That's because choice seems to lead to the largest increases in motivation in experiments when the choice is largely irrelevant, such as choosing what color pen to use, or what name to give a game character. This raises some interesting policy implications that we can come back to in the next chapter.

10.4 Summary

Instant utility is how much utility a person gets at a specific point in time, and can be thought of as a measure of happiness. We saw that a person's instant utility, or level of happiness, appears to depend on their position relative to others and relative to what has happened to them in the past. In particular, we see varying degrees of adaption to life changing events.

We then distinguished between decision utility, total utility, and remembered utility. Roughly speaking, decision utility is how much utility a person thought they would get from doing something, when they decided to do it. Total utility is how much utility they actually got from doing it. Remembered utility is how much utility they think they got from doing it.

We saw that decision utility, total utility, and remembered utility can be different because of things like duration neglect and projection bias. This suggests that people may not know what things would make them happiest.

We then revisited the issue of present bias and showed it can cause a big drop in utility. This suggests that people may not choose the thing that would make them happiest even if they know what they should choose.

Given the suggestion that people may not always make good choices, we questioned whether people like having choice. We saw that many people do like to pre-commit and do not appear to like difficult choices. Generally, however, people do appear to enjoy some level of choice and self-determination.

We get, therefore, an interesting picture of people not always necessarily knowing what makes them happy, or will make them happy. We also see people willing to pre-commit or delegate choice to others, provided they retain some free choice. This seemingly provides a clear rationale for policy intervention, if, of course, we can trust policymakers to know any better what makes people happy!

10.5 Health and happiness

Health care is one context where it can be vital to understand what makes people happy, because the potential benefits or costs of being ill and getting treated can be so large. In this section I shall look at two possible applications of what we have learnt about the nature of happiness and utility.

10.5.1 Measuring the value of treatment

Valuing the costs and benefits of medical treatments is fundamental to allocating health care resources efficiently and most effectively. This is particularly the case in state-financed health care systems like the National Health Service in the UK. Given the limited resources available, priority should be given to treatments that have higher net benefits than others. This notion is often controversial, because it means the health service may not finance the treatment of one patient because there is a treatment for a different patient that has a higher net benefit. Such rationing is, however, inevitable, so should not be controversial. What can be controversial is how we go about measuring the net benefit of treatments, and that's what I want to look at in more detail.

To calculate the net benefit of a treatment we need some measure of its cost and benefits. The cost is a relatively objective thing to measure in principle. For example, the cost of a drug or the cost of a physician's time can easily be calculated. Much harder is to measure the benefits. There are two possible dimensions to any benefit: a treatment could improve the quality of life and/or prolong the length of life. How can we possibly measure the value of an improvement in quality of life, or an extra year of life?

One widely used way to do so is the QALY. Each year of perfect health is counted as one **quality adjusted life year** (QALY). A year of less than perfect health is given a QALY value of less than one. The lower the quality of life, the lower the value, with zero being equivalent to death. To get the overall value of a treatment we follow the QALY of a treatment over the subsequent life of the patient. To illustrate, Figure 10.19 tracks the quality of life of a patient if they have no treatment or two possible treatments, A and B. Without treatment the quality of life deteriorates. With treatment A the patient is stabilized and their life extended. With treatment B the patient's quality of life initially deteriorates, because of the side effects, but subsequently increases to a relatively high level.

Without treatment the patient gets 1.5 QALYs because there are 0.5 QALYs in the first year, 0.4 in the second year, and so on, adding up to 1.5. With treatment A the patient gets 2.4 QALYs and with treatment B they get 2.7. The net benefit of treatment A is, therefore, 2.4 − 1.5 = 0.9 QALYs, and that of treatment B is 1.2 QALYs.

In this example it looks like treatment B is better than treatment A. We do, however, need to take into account the cost. Suppose treatment A costs £10,000

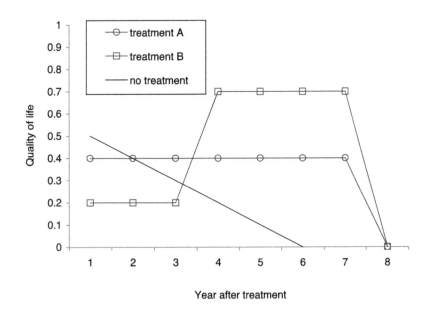

Figure 10.19 Changes in quality of life following two possible treatments A and B, or no treatment.

and treatment B costs £20,000. Then with treatment A each QALY costs £4,167 but with treatment B costs £7,407. In a publicly funded health service someone has to decide whether these amounts of money are worth paying. In the UK an organization called the National Institute for Health and Clinical Excellence (with the sometimes unfortunate acronym NICE) does that, and treatments below £30,000 a QALY are usually funded.

In order to get the data to calculate QALYs the EQ-5D system is often used. Patients are asked to fill out a questionnaire that asks five questions about mobility, pain, self-care, anxiety and ability to do normal activities. There are three possible answers to each question. A formula is then used to convert these answers into a QALY value. Table 10.4 gives some examples. If patients are tracked and fill in the EQ-5D questionnaire over time then we can obtain the data to draw Figure 10.19. So, everything looks in place to make things work. The whole process, however, hinges on the formula used to derive the numbers in Table 10.4, and this is where the things we have learned can start proving useful.

The formula used to calculate a QALY measure is derived using a **time trade-off valuation technique** or **visual analogue scale**. In both cases a random sample of people are asked to imagine a particular quality of life, like those in Table 10.4. The time trade-off technique then asks them to say what length of time in full health they consider to be equivalent to a longer period with this quality of life. The visual analogue scale directly asks them to rate the quality of life on a linear scale. Are people able to make accurate judgments of this sort?

Given what we know about adaption and habituation, the answer is probably no. People who are relatively healthy are likely to underestimate the quality of life of those in poorer health than them. Conversely, people who are relatively unhealthy are likely to overestimate the quality of life of those who are healthier than them. This matters if people find it easier to adapt to some states of ill health than others, and we have seen that adaption rates can vary. To illustrate the

Table 10.4 Examples of QALY measures using the EQ–5D system

Description	QALY
No problems.	1.000
No problems walking about; no problems with self-care; some problems with performing usual activities; some pain or discomfort; not anxious or depressed.	0.760
No problems walking about; some problems washing or dressing self; unable to perform usual activities; moderate pain or discomfort; extremely anxious or depressed.	0.222
Confined to bed; unable to wash or dress self; unable to perform usual activities; extreme pain or discomfort; moderately anxious or depressed.	−0.429

Source: Philips and Thompson (2009).

problem, Figure 10.20 plots how a person might adapt to treatment. We see that the person adapts very well to the health state resulting from treatment B and so would eventually report a quality of life near to full health. They adapt less well to the health state resulting from treatment A or no treatment.

If we ask non-patients to think what it would be like to have such treatments we are likely to get the low numbers that patients really do feel one year after treatment. This ignores the possibility of adaption and makes treatment A look better. If we ask patients after six or seven years of treatment, they would be more positive and feel particularly positive about treatment B. This forgets the fact that they have adapted. The key thing is we need to not only rate health states like those in Table 10.4 but also think how quickly patients will likely adapt to these health states. This should then enter the calculation for working out QALYs.

Unfortunately, it is not current practice to take into account adaption when calculating QALYs. One reason is probably that the notion of adaption can seem a little controversial because it raises the question: if people will adapt to ill-health then why do they need treatment? This looks a tricky question until we compare Figures 10.19 and 10.20. If we look at what happens with no treatment, then adaption does indeed improve the quality of life. The crucial thing is, however, that adaption increases the quality of life from having the treatment by even more. So, yes people may adapt to their poor health state but they might also adapt to the potentially less than perfect health state that treatment will result in. Adaption

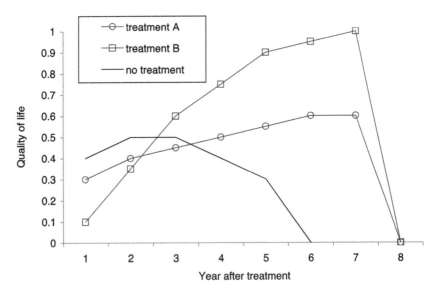

Figure 10.20 Changes in quality of life following two possible treatments, taking into account adaption.

does not, therefore, mean that we are any more or less likely to recommend treatment.

Valuing improvements in quality of life is controversial and difficult. But, if we are to make the best health choices we need these measures. I have only touched on the issue here but, hopefully, you have seen how the ideas we have looked at in this chapter, particularly adaption, can help inform the debate.

10.5.2 Improving the remembered utility of treatment

For effective prevention of health problems it is important that people turn up for relevant screening procedures. For example, colonoscopy is a screening procedure for colorectal cancer, one of the leading causes of cancer-related death. Colonoscopy saves lives, but only if patients are willing to undergo the fairly unpleasant procedure. Whether or not they are willing will depend to some extent on their recollections of previous treatments or procedures. Someone who remembers their last colonoscopy as painful and unpleasant may be less likely to turn up for a subsequent colonoscopy, and that could be very bad. This means that anything which can improve the remembered utility of the procedure should be a good thing. Redelmeier, Kahneman and Katz (1996, 2003) investigated whether this can be done.

In the study outpatients who were due for a colonoscopy were asked to take part. During the procedure patients were given a hand-held device with which they could indicate their discomfort on a scale of 0 to 10. Afterwards patients and physicians were asked questions about how much pain and discomfort was experienced during the procedure. The procedure can last anything from a few minutes to over an hour. The striking thing was, however, that patients' recollections of pain and discomfort did not depend on how long the procedure lasted. Instead they depended on the peak and end pain. This is further evidence of duration neglect.

Duration neglect and peak end evaluation suggests that extending the duration of a procedure while decreasing the end pain could make patients remember it less negatively. To test for this a randomized trial was done in which the colonoscopy procedure was extended by three minutes for selected patients (see Research Methods 10.3). During the extra three minutes there would have been discomfort, but less than during the main part of the procedure. Figure 10.21 summarizes some of the data. Consistent with peak-end evaluation, end pain is less with the prolonged procedure and the retrospective evaluation of pain is less. Patients were subsequently tracked to see whether they returned for a repeat colonoscopy, where the median follow-up time is around five years. Those who took part in the prolonged procedure were marginally more likely to return.

The effect on the proportion of patients who returned for a repeat colonoscopy was not huge in this study. But, if it comes from waiting just three extra minutes, and if it means one or two people suffer less from cancer, then that is a big gain. We do not know whether other more significant changes could have larger effects, but it is an intriguing possibility. This possibility arose from distinguishing between remembered and total utility.

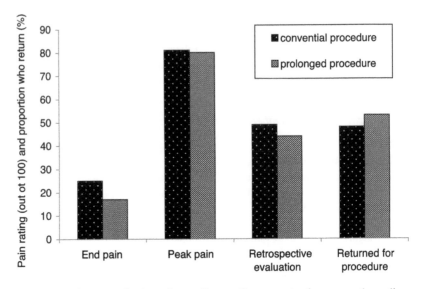

Figure 10.21 Measures of pain and rate of return for a repeat colonoscopy depending on whether the procedure was prolonged or not.

Source: Redelmeier et al. (2003).

Research Methods 10.3

Double blind experiments

In an experiment with multiple treatments it is sometimes a concern that the researcher knows what treatment a particular subject is in. This would be the case in the study of Redelmeier et al. (2003). If the physician knows that a particular patient is in the treatment with a prolonged procedure then he or she may treat the patient differently during the procedure. We need to avoid this.

A **double blind experiment** is one in which the researcher does not know what treatment is being run during an experimental session. Generally, this is not very simple, but there are ways to make it happen. In this particular study the treatment that a subject was assigned to was randomly determined and written down on a piece of paper in a sealed envelope. Only when the procedure was near to completion would the envelope be opened and the clinicians know whether to extend the procedure or not. A neat way to obtain double blindness.

10.6 Saving and retirement

In chapters two and four we spent some time looking at the implications of choice and time-inconsistency for saving, borrowing and the life cycle. It is natural to pick up these topics again in this chapter. I will start by looking at the implications of projection bias.

10.6.1 Projection bias in saving

In chapter four we looked at a model of habit formation in which Maria would become habituated to past levels of consumption. Such habituation is representative of adaption, and we showed that it could lead to an increase in saving following an increase in income. At that stage we did not need to assume any present bias. In the last chapter, when looking at addiction, we looked more at how present bias can matter once someone becomes habituated. What I want to do now is add projection bias to the story.

To see why projections bias matters we can work through an example. Suppose that Ian's utility in year t is:

$$u(c_t, h_t) = \begin{cases} \sqrt{c_t - h_t} & \text{if } c_t \geq h_t \\ -\sqrt{h_t - c_t} & \text{if } c_t < h_t \end{cases}$$

where c_t is his consumption and

$$h_t = c_{t-1}$$

is the reference level of consumption he is habituated too. So, Ian's reference level adapts every year to his consumption of the previous year. I leave you to think how this relates to the model we looked at in section 4.5.1.

Suppose that because of projection bias Ian underestimates how much his reference level will adapt. Specifically, suppose he believes that:

$$h_t = \alpha h_{t-1} + (1 - \alpha)c_{t-1}$$

where α is some parameter. If $\alpha = 0$, Ian does not have projection bias, but if $\alpha > 0$ he does.

Table 10.5 illustrates what consequences a projection bias could have. We see that Ian's income is going to increase in the next two years and then fall in year three. You could think of this as a condensed version of working and then retiring. How can Ian best smooth his consumption? The best he could do would be to increase his consumption slowly. This is what he will do if $\alpha = 0$ and so he has no projection bias. What if he does have a projection bias?

The easiest case to look at is where he has a very strong bias because $\alpha = 1$. In this case Ian completely fails to realize that he will adapt to increased consumption and so increases consumption as much as possible relative to his current reference level. This does not work very well because he does adapt, and so, while he is happy in year one, he is not so happy in years two and three.

Table 10.5 The consequences of projection bias in a simple example. Ian's income will fall in year three. If he has no projection bias he would choose a gradually increasing consumption profile and get total utility three. With projection bias he chooses a flatter consumption profile and gets less utility than he expects

	Time				Projected utility	Actual utility
	Year 0	Year 1	Year 2	Year 3		
Income	1	4	4	1	–	–
Planned consumption						
$\alpha = 0$	1	2	3	4	3.00	3.00
$\alpha = 1$	1	3	3	3	4.23	1.41
$\alpha = 0.5$ and in year 0	1	2.33	3	3.67	3.47	2.79
$\alpha = 0.5$ and in year 1	1	2.33	3.14	3.53	2.94	2.68

More realistic is the case where $\alpha = 0.5$ and so Ian knows that he adapts but underestimates how much he adapts. He would now choose a plan intermediate between those he would choose when $\alpha = 0$ and $\alpha = 1$. The consumption profile is increasing but flatter than optimal. The most interesting thing is what happens after one year. At this point Ian realizes that he underestimated how much he would adapt and so changes his plan. What's interesting is that the new plan he comes up with is worse than the original one! Basically, he knows that he needs to increase his consumption more now than he thought he would have to in order to be above his reference level.

Stylized though it is, this example illustrates two key implications of projection bias for saving and retirement. First, Ian saves less for retirement than he should have done. Second, he will be time-inconsistent and save less for retirement than he planned to do. We see this in the 0.14 difference between how much Ian thinks he will save in year two and how much he actually will save.

Both these implications are bad, and can accumulate over many years to a real shortfall in savings for retirement. Could we avoid this? In principle the second problem should, at least, be avoidable because Ian might be willing to pre-commit to a savings plan that does not allow him to change his mind. In the next chapter we shall see how such plans may work. The first problem could be avoided by 'forcing' Ian to save more, but this brings us back to the issue of choice and autonomy.

10.6.2 Investor autonomy

One way to 'push' people like Ian to save more for their retirement is to automatically enroll them in a savings plan. We are going to look at this in the next chapter, but you could probably guess from what we did in chapter four, that people usually stick to such plans. Even if they wanted to withdraw, present bias means they 'put if off until tomorrow' and never do get around to changing. So, let's imagine for now that automatic enrolment is like 'forcing' Ian to save.

This might be a good thing, but we encounter a problem. If we are going to automatically enroll Ian in a savings plan then we have to decide where to invest, how much to invest, and so on. Should we also decide that, or let Ian choose? This is a fascinating situation to question whether choice is good or not. Let's look at a study by Benartzi and Thaler (2002).

In the first part of the study they collected information about people enrolled in the UCLA retirement plan. There is no default option in this plan, so participants have to choose their own portfolio. Based on this information they predicted the retirement income a person could expect if invested in (a) the portfolio he or she was invested in, (b) the average portfolio, and (c) the median portfolio. (Just to clarify, the median portfolio will be significantly different to the average portfolio, because many invested a lot in cash and so the average portfolio is skewed towards investing more in cash.) Participants in the study were then asked to rate, on a scale of 1 to 5, how attractive a portfolio appeared, without knowing which one was theirs. As we can see in Figure 10.22 the median portfolio received a higher rating than their own portfolio. Indeed, only 21 percent of participants rated their own portfolio highest!

In the second part of the study Benartzi and Thaler surveyed employees at SwedishAmerican Health Systems. Employees at SwedishAmerican are automatically provided with an individual portfolio selected by an investment management firm, but have the possibility to opt out and choose their own portfolio. Focusing only on employees who had decided to opt out, they again predicted retirement income and asked participants how they would rank (a) his or her own portfolio, (b) the average portfolio, and (c) the default portfolio suggested by the

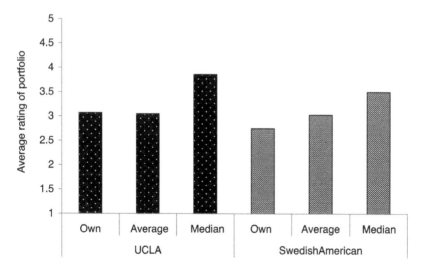

Figure 10.22 The average rating of portfolios at UCLA and SwedishAmerican.

Source: Benartzi and Thaler (2002).

investment management firm. This time we see in Figure 10.22 that the default portfolio gets the highest ranking. Only 20 percent preferred their own portfolio, and recall that participants had specifically opted out of the default option in order to choose their own portfolio!

These results suggest that investor autonomy is not worth much. In both cases participants rated higher a portfolio that was not chosen by them. We might be concerned that this is due to them having different expectations about what might happen to the stock market etc. When surveyed, however, most participants expressed no strong beliefs about what would be likely to happen. The more plausible explanation seems to be that participants did not have the skills and information to pick the best portfolio for their preferences.

So, should we be letting people choose where they invest? The simple answer given these results would seem to be no, but we do need to be careful. First, there is the problem of deciding where best the money should be invested and how. Twenty percent of those in the study were most happy with the portfolio they chose, and can we justify taking choice away from these to benefit the other 80 percent? Second, is the problem that people may like making a choice, even if they make a bad choice. The potential costs of investing unwisely are huge, so people would really have to like making a choice for this to matter much. Even so, it suggests that we might want to think about giving investors some choice.

10.7 Welfare trade-offs

In this final section I want to start talking more explicitly about policy. One fundamental issue in policymaking is to measure the welfare consequences of different policies. After all, the objective is to pursue policies that increase overall welfare and to do that we need to measure welfare. Here, I shall look at two very different examples of measuring the welfare consequences of policy. There are lots of other examples I could have given but I think these are two nice examples of what we have learnt that can be useful. The first example shows how we can fill in some of the blanks of existing theory. The second example shows how we can open up new issues not considered in existing theory.

10.7.1 The inflation, unemployment trade-off

It is common in macroeconomics to think of a government trying to maximize a social welfare function. Two things usually thrown into the welfare function are inflation and unemployment, with high inflation and unemployment associated with lower social welfare. The textbook story would be that a government wishes to reduce inflation, which will cause unemployment in the short run, and so wants to find the disinflationary path that minimizes the loss in social welfare. For this approach to make sense we need to have some idea of the relative loss in social welfare if there is unemployment or inflation.

A standard approach would be to assume a one-to-one trade-off, so the welfare function would look something like:

$$W = -(Y - \bar{Y})^2 - (\Pi - \bar{\Pi})^2$$

where $Y - \bar{Y}$ is the deviation of national income from the optimum and $\Pi - \bar{\Pi}$ is the deviation of inflation from the optimum. The reason to assume a one-to-one trade-off seems to be the lack of any better idea! Happiness data can potentially give us a better idea because we can estimate how much unemployment and inflation decrease reported happiness, and observe the trade-off.

Di Tella, MacCulloch and Oswald (2001) do this, looking at data from twelve European countries over the period 1975 to 1991. Table 10.6 summarizes some of the numbers they come up with. Unemployment causes two negative effects on happiness. There is a direct effect due to people who are unemployed being on average less happy. There is an additional indirect effect, what we could call 'the fear of unemployment', that lowers happiness of people still employed. Inflation has only an indirect effect.

With the numbers in Table 10.6 we can calculate the trade-off between inflation and unemployment. A 1 percent increase in the unemployment rate lowers the average satisfaction of everybody by 0.02 and lowers the satisfaction of the 1 percent who become unemployed by 0.33. Overall, therefore, average satisfaction decreases by $0.33 \times 0.01 + 0.02 = 0.0233$. To find the fall in inflation needed to compensate for this decrease in happiness we calculate $0.0233/0.014 = 1.66$. So, a 1.66 percent fall in inflation increases average satisfaction by as much as a 1 percent increase in unemployment decreases average satisfaction. Thus, the unemployment inflation trade-off is 1.66 and we might want a social welfare function

$$W = -1.66 (Y - \bar{Y})^2 - (\Pi - \bar{\Pi})^2.$$

This is not the end of the story, because, for example, unemployment and inflation may influence different parts of society differently and we might want to take account of that. We also know that being unemployed can have long-term effects on satisfaction, while a change in the inflation rate is unlikely to. The specific number 1.66 should not, therefore, be taken as definitive. But 1.66 does have more justification than the standard assumption of one. This illustrates how we can use measurements of happiness and life satisfaction to better inform on optimal policy. We have focused on the inflation and unemployment trade-off but a similar idea

Table 10.6 Changes in reported life satisfaction (on a 1–4 scale) if there is unemployment or inflation

	Change in life satisfaction
If unemployed	−0.33
If 1% rise in unemployment rate	−0.02
If 1% fall in inflation	+0.014

Source: Di Tella et al. (2001).

can be applied to a wide range of other policy questions such as the optimal level of unemployment benefit and optimal tax rates.

Before moving on I think it is interesting to briefly mention a study by Di Tella and MacCulloch (2005) that asked whether people on the political right had a different inflation-unemployment trade-off to those on the political left. Why would they? Typically we would associate right-wingers with policies that focus on reducing inflation rather than unemployment. By contrast, left-wingers would be associated with policies that focus on reducing unemployment rather than inflation. Figure 10.23 illustrates that those who rated themselves to the political right did have a relatively low trade-off and those to the left a relatively high trade-off. This is not due to them being rich or poor. Recall that these numbers are estimated by looking at how satisfied people say they are. So, these differences do not mean that those on the political right say they care more about inflation than those on the political left. It means that the life satisfaction of those on the political right really does depend more on inflation than those on the political left!

10.7.2 Tax saliency

One other thing it is important to have a welfare measure of is the deadweight loss caused by taxes. I will finish this chapter with an example of how a seemingly irrelevant change in the framing of a tax can potentially change the associated welfare loss.

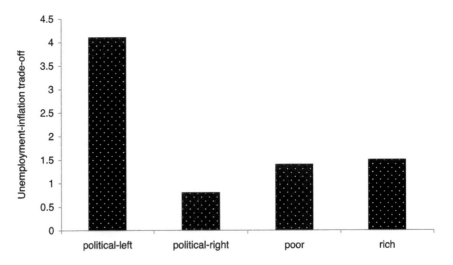

Figure 10.23 The inflation-unemployment trade-off of those on the political left is higher than those on the political right, and this is not because of differences in income.

Source: Di Tella and MacCulloch (2006).

In Europe the advertised price of a product includes any relevant taxes. In the US and Canada it is normal for the price of a product to not include the sales tax. To work out the full price of an item a customer would, therefore, have to calculate and add on the sales tax of 4 to 10 percent. Cognitively this is not an easy thing to do, even if he carries around a calculator to do the math, because some things are subject to sales tax, some not, etc. A study by Chetty, Looney and Kroft (2009) questioned the consequences of not including the sales tax in the advertised price.

The first part of the study involved an experiment carried out in a large grocery store in California. On some of the products they placed a label, in addition to the main label, giving the price of the good including the tax. This does not change the price of the good but does change the appearance of the price to the customer.

It may be that customers would be more likely to buy such a product because the label allows them to avoid the cognitive cost of working out the tax. On the other hand they may be less likely to buy the product because the label makes the product appear more expensive. What do you think happened?

By way of comparison the study looked at the change in demand on goods that did have the amount of sales tax displayed (treated goods in the treatment store) versus the change in demand for similar goods in a similar part of the store (control goods in the treatment store) and those same goods in a different store (control and treated goods in the control store). Figure 10.24 summarizes what happened. The story is fairly clear: demand fell on goods that did have the tax included in the price. This fall is also relatively large at 6 to 8 percent, depending on what is used as the comparator.

To check this result the second part of the study looked at demand for alcohol. Alcohol is subject to two taxes: an excise tax that is included in the price, and the sales tax that is not. This allows for a natural experiment in which we can track changes in the two tax rates and changes in demand. Chetty et al. do this with data

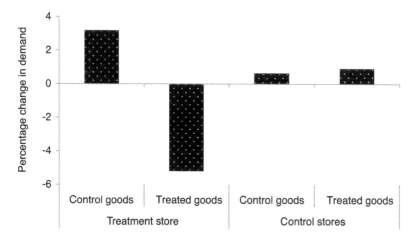

Figure 10.24 Change in demand if sales tax is displayed.

Source: Chetty et al. (2010).

from 1970 to 2003 and find that changes in the excise tax cause a much larger change in demand than changes in the sales tax. This is consistent with the story that customers focus on the price on the label, which includes excise tax, and largely ignore the sales tax that will be added at the till.

The clear suggestion is that the advertised price is salient. If the price on the label is higher then consumers buy less, even though the actual price is the same. What are the consequences of this? To answer that question I shall work through a model of consumer choice.

Suppose there are two goods, bananas and money. If Ian buys b bananas and has y left his utility is:

$$u(b, y) = 2\alpha\sqrt{b} + y$$

where α is some parameter. Further suppose that he has m to start with and the price of a banana is p ignoring the tax and $p(1 + t)$ taking into account the tax.

[Extra] If Ian takes into account the tax he would maximize his utility subject to the budget constraint $y = m - p(1 + t)b$. The optimum is where the marginal utility from consuming bananas equals the price and so where:

$$\frac{\alpha}{\sqrt{b}} = p(1+t) \quad \text{or} \quad b_T = \left(\frac{\alpha}{p(1+t)}\right)^2 \quad \text{and} \quad y_T = m - \frac{\alpha^2}{p(1+t)}.$$

If Ian does not take into account the sales tax he would maximize his utility subject to the budget constraint $y = m - pb$. The optimum in this case is where:

$$\frac{\alpha}{\sqrt{b}} = p \quad \text{or} \quad b_N = \left(\frac{\alpha}{p}\right)^2 \quad \text{and} \quad y_N = m - (1+t)\frac{\alpha^2}{p}.$$

In both cases Ian pays the sales tax, as seen when we calculate y. With this we can work out the difference in utility $\Delta = u(b_T, y_T) - u(b_N, y_N)$ whether Ian does or does not take into account the sales tax. It is:

$$\Delta = 2\alpha\left(\frac{\alpha}{p(1+t)}\right) + m - \frac{\alpha^2}{p(1+t)} - \left[2\alpha\left(\frac{\alpha}{p}\right) + m - (1+t)\frac{\alpha^2}{p}\right]$$

which we can simplify to:

$$\Delta = \frac{\alpha^2}{p(1+t)} - \frac{\alpha^2(1-t)}{p} = \frac{\alpha^2 t^2}{p(1+t)}. \tag{10.1}$$

Whether you followed the algebra or not, the main thing to know is that equation (10.1) tells us the amount Ian will lose if he does not take into account the sales tax. This difference will be small if t is small. For instance, if $t = 0.07375$, which is the relevant figure for California, we get:

$$\Delta = 0.0051 \frac{\alpha^2}{p}.$$

This is not going to be a big number unless α is big, meaning Ian really likes bananas. For example, if $\alpha = 10$, $m = 200$ and $p = 1$ then ignoring the sales tax, he will buy 100 bananas and spend \$107.38. If he was to take into account the sales tax his utility would be \$0.51 higher. That does not look like much of a gain, and so he does not lose much by ignoring the sales tax.

It turns out that this is quite a general result and not restricted to the functional form for utility I assumed. Primarily this is because by maximizing his utility, even if at slightly the wrong price, Ian reaches a point where he is relatively indifferent to changes in his consumption. So, if he were to take account of the tax it might change his behavior but would not much change his utility. If ignoring the tax means little welfare loss for the consumer, then it is no surprise we rarely see shoppers with calculators working out the tax on a good.

We can see the implications for the government with the help of Figure 10.25 and Table 10.7. These work through the consequences of a 5 and 10 percent tax. If there is no tax, Ian will buy 100 bananas, have \$100 left and have total

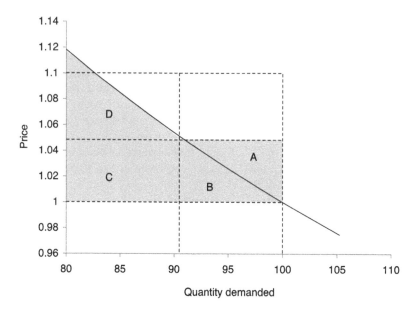

Figure 10.25 The consequences of ignoring the sales tax. If Ian takes account of the tax there is a deadweight loss of B and D + C + B. If he does not take account of the tax there is no deadweight loss but A + B is transferred from Ian to the government.

Table 10.7 The consequences of a 5 and 10 percent tax when $\alpha = 10$, $m = 200$ and $p = \$1$

	Is the tax salient?							
	No	Yes	No	Yes	No	Yes	No	Yes
Tax rate	Bananas bought		Money left		Utility		Tax revenue	
$t = 0$	100	100	$100.00	$100.00	300	300	$0.00	$0.00
$t = 0.05$	100	91	$95.00	$104.45	295	295	$5.00	$4.55
$t = 0.1$	100	83	$90.00	$108.70	290	291	$10.00	$8.30

utility 300. For a higher tax we can compare his utility and the tax revenue if he does or does not take account of the tax. Simplest is to measure welfare as utility plus the tax revenue, so it is $300 with no tax.

If the tax is 5 percent and Ian does take account of the tax then there is a deadweight welfare loss because some consumer surplus is lost. This is given by area B in Figure 10.25 and comes to $0.21. If the tax were 10 percent the deadweight loss would be equal to areas B + C + D and amount to $0.79. You might argue that these are not big numbers. If, however, there are a 1,000 or 10,000 consumers like this, then the overall welfare loss of the tax starts to add up.

What if Ian does not take account of the sales tax? He continues to buy 100 bananas. This means that if the tax is 5 percent we no longer loose area B. Instead area A + B gets transferred to the government in tax. We can see this by the fact consumer utility goes down by $5 but tax revenue goes up by $5. There is no deadweight loss of the tax, just a redistribution of welfare in which Ian becomes relatively worse off.

This is important because it suggests that taxes are not as bad as we might think in terms of efficiency but are possibly worse in terms of equity. Ultimately, however, it is good for overall welfare that Ian does not take account of the tax. This suggests that care is needed to not push the tax beyond the threshold that the consumer does take note of it. For example, if Ian ignores a 5 percent tax but does take note of a 10 percent tax, then increasing the tax from 5 to 10 percent would cause a big deadweight loss of B + C + D.

This example illustrates how it is important to take account of the likely behavior of people in designing policy. You might say that this is obvious, but the example shows that things can be a little subtle. In the next chapter I want to develop a more general framework with which to think through how behavioral economics can affectively inform policy.

10.8 Further reading

The literature on happiness gets ever larger and so you should not be short of places to find out more. Books include that by Frey (2008) and survey articles those by by Frey and Stutzer (2002), Di Tella and MacCulloch (2006) and

Kahneman and Krueger (2006). Two nice papers that did not get a mention, when talking about experience utility and projection bias, are Kahneman, Wakker and Sarin (1997) and Loewenstein, O'Donoghue and Rabin (2003). The implications for policy are discussed by Loewenstein and Ubel (2008) and a paper by Patall, Cooper and Robinson (2008) provides a comprehensive survey of the psychology literature on whether choice is good or not. I also want to mention a classic paper by Laibson (1997) that looks at savings, commitment and time-inconsistency. Finally, a useful source of information for more on how QALYs are measured and used is the website of the National Institute for Health and Clinical Excellence. The paper by Dolan and Kahneman (2008) provides a good overview of the issues.

One thing that I did not talk about, but is of current interest, is incorporating measures of happiness into measures of economic output. In February 2008, French President Nicolas Sarkozy asked Joseph Stiglitz to create a Commission, subsequently called 'The Commission on the Measurement of Economic Perform-ance and Social Progress', to identify the limits of GDP as an indicator of economic performance and social progress. The Commission website has a copy of the committee's report and videos of various speeches made.

10.9 Review Questions

10.1 Explain why peak-end evaluation causes duration neglect.

10.2 Should a person choose the thing that maximizes decision utility, total utility or remembered utility?

10.3 If a person has done something before, should we expect that remembered utility equals decision utility?

10.4 Why do you think a high national output does not translate to higher levels of life satisfaction? What are the implications of this for how we measure economic performance?

10.5 Suppose you are taking a course in behavioral economics that involves doing three assignments. Would you rather that the course organizer gives staggered deadlines for handing in the work, or that you merely need to hand in the work before the end of the course? Why?

10.6 How can we take account of adaption when calculating QALYs?

10.7 Given adaption and projection bias, are patients informed enough to decide what medical treatments are best for them?

10.8 Explain why projection bias is different to present bias. How does this show up in people's decisions to save for retirement?

10.9 Should we take account of adaption, or the lack of adaption to unemploy-ment, when calculating the unemployment inflation trade-off? What effect would this have?

10.10 Should Europe change policy, and not require firms to include the sales tax when advertising price?

11 Policy and behavior

A government agency will be set up to paint contour lines on to hills and colour roads the same as on maps. This will help people know where they are.

The Official Monster Raving Loony Party 2010
UK General Election Manifesto

In this final chapter I want to look at whether behavioral economics can be used by policymakers to help people make better choices. For instance, Maria might buy gym membership but then never go to the gym. Alan might not save enough for retirement. Can we change things so that they make better choices? This question raises some tricky issues, that I will get to, but has to be a major objective of behavioral economics. It allows us to apply what we know in trying to make the world a better place where people are a little bit (or a lot) happier.

In looking at how behavioral economics can inform policy, I think it's useful to distinguish two broad categories of economic policy. The first is about designing institutions so that good things happen. The second is about manipulating individual incentives so that good things happen. There is inevitably some overlap between the two. For example, in designing a good institution we need to provide good individual incentives. The distinction is, however, a useful one and so I will look at each category in turn, beginning with the design of institutions.

11.1 Designing good institutions

An economic **institution** is basically the means and rules by which people interact. We have already seen plenty of examples of institutions in this book, and seen plenty of examples of why institutions matter. For example, in chapter two we saw that whether the market is a double auction, posted offer, or negotiated price format will likely matter. In chapter six we saw that whether the auction is an English, Dutch, or first or second price format might matter. We also saw that whether there is leadership, communication and things like rebates or refunds can help people coordinate in providing, say, a threshold public good. Finally, in chapter seven we saw that the threat of punishment can help sustain cooperation.

What I want to do here is look at three very different examples of institution design. As well as further illustrating the importance of institutions, this will take us into the world of practical policy design and intervention. I'll briefly mention that institutions can be of two basic kinds, **formal institutions**, like markets, and **informal institutions**, like social norms. The first example, I want to look at is more about informal institutions and the latter two more about formal institutions.

11.1.1 The tragedy of the commons

To get us started, consider a lake used for fishing. Anyone who wants to go fishing is free to do so, and can fish as much as they want. What's going to happen? What might happen is **overuse** or **overexploitation** of the resource, whereby too many fishermen come along, catch too many fish, and leave the stock of fish too low to be sustainable. We don't want that to happen.

A fishing lake is one example of a common pool resource. A **common pool resource** is any good that it is difficult to exclude people from consuming but one person's consumption lowers the possible consumption of others. It might, for instance, be hard to stop people fishing in the lake, and one fisherman's catch cannot be another's. Other examples include forests, water systems for drinking or irrigation, and the global atmosphere. As this list suggests, common pool resources are immensely important in thinking about environmental issues.

The **tragedy of the commons** is that we should expect overuse of common pool resources. That is, we should expect the worst. To see why, we can look at a specific version of a common pool resource game, used in some experiments.

Suppose that there are eight people, including Anna, who each have ten tokens. They can invest their tokens in something that yields a 'safe return', or spend it on extracting goods from a common pool resource. I will think of people deciding whether to harvest food in their garden, for a safe return, or go fishing in the local lake, where the return will depend on what others do. Tokens could represent money, time, or a combination of both but I will think of time here. Table 11.1 summarizes some of the possible payoff combinations. For example, if

Table 11.1 Some of the possible payoff combinations in a common pool resource game involving Anna and seven others

Tokens spent in extracting goods from the common pool resource

Anna	The other seven					
	0	*14*	*28*	*42*	*56*	*70*
0	50	50	50	50	50	50
2	85	78	71	64	57	50
4	118	104	90	76	62	48
6	149	128	107	86	65	44
8	178	150	122	94	66	38
10	205	170	135	100	65	30

Anna spends four hours fishing and the others spend 14 hours fishing she gets a payoff of 104.

To make some sense of the numbers in Table 11.1, note that Anna gets 50 for sure if she spends all her time in the garden, that's why it's a safe return. If the others do relatively little fishing, then her payoff will be higher if she spends time fishing, because the lake is full of fish. By contrast, if the others do relatively a lot of fishing then her payoff will be lower if she spends time fishing, because the lake is already empty of fish. What is going to happen?

A good outcome is that each person spends four hours fishing to get a payoff of 90. If the others are going to fish a total of $7 \times 4 = 28$ hours, however, Anna does best to spend ten hours fishing. It looks unlikely, therefore, that people would stick to fishing for only four hours. More plausible is that they each spend eight hours fishing to get a payoff of 66. Why? If the others are going to fish a total of $7 \times 8 = 56$ hours then Anna does best to spend eight hours fishing, and so everything fits a bit better. This is all captured by the fact that 'everyone fish four hours' is the Pareto optimum while 'everyone fish eight hours' is the Nash equilibrium.

If everyone did fish for eight hours, then we would observe a version of the tragedy of the commons. People would be fishing too much and getting a lower payoff than they could do by fishing a bit less. This would not be good, but what happens in reality?

The evidence suggests that the tragedy of the commons can be avoided, sometimes. Indeed Elinor Ostrom won the Nobel Prize in Economics in 2009 because she: 'Challenged the conventional wisdom by demonstrating how local property can be successfully managed by local commons without any regulation by central authorities or privatization.' Examples of successful use of common pool resources include grazing land in the Swiss Alps and Japan, irrigation systems in Spain and the Philippines and use of the ground water basins around Los Angeles. In each of these cases, users of the resource found some way to maintain use of the resource at the efficient level, or, at least, below the level of overuse.

To give a specific example: in 1995 Alaska's halibut fisherman decided to use something called **individual fishing quotas**. The basic idea is that individuals are given ownership over a share of the total amount that can be fished. The change was dramatic. The length of season went from a dangerous, three-day race to get as many fish as possible, to an eight-month, demand-led, sustainable solution.

For every success story though there is an example where the new is not so good. For instance, the bluefin tuna has reached dangerously low levels in the Mediterranean but there is little consensus on how the decline could be halted, especially given that attempts to use individual fishing quotas in international waters have largely failed.

The pertinent question, therefore, is why the tragedy of the commons can be averted in some cases and not others. Ostrom addressed this question by looking at cases studies of common pool resources with the objective of seeing what distinguished the successes from the failures. An up-to-date list is given in Ostrom (2010) and includes things like: clear and locally understood boundaries between users and non-users, users of the resource have some say in how the resource is managed, and rules for using the resource are designed to include punishment for excessive use.

Such a list, providing as it does a neat dividing line between likely success and failure, is incredibly useful. For instance, it can help inform a policymaker when intervention is needed to avoid the tragedy of the commons, and when it is not. It can also help policymakers set things up so that users of the resource can help themselves, such as with individual fishing quotas. Clearly, however, this only works if the list is the right one, i.e. we have the right diving line between likely success and failure. And case studies necessarily involve some worrying comparisons, such as Alaskan and Spanish fisherman. One way to supplement case studies, and make sure we have things right, are lab experiments.

Lab experiments are useful because they allow specific elements to be varied one at a time. To illustrate I will look at a study by Ostrom, Walker and Gardener (1992). Subjects were involved in a common resource problem, like that in Table 11.1, for twenty rounds. In the first ten rounds subjects independently had to decide how much to spend extracting goods from the resource and in most cases there was overuse. Subjects were then given various means to try and avoid overuse in the ten subsequent rounds.

Figure 11.1 summarizes the results. It looks a bit messy so let's go through it slowly. In the baseline case subjects were not given any means to avoid overuse

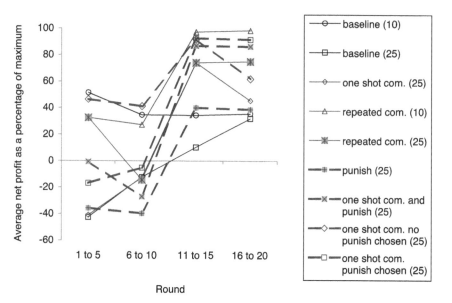

Figure 11.1 The average net profit as a percentage of the maximum over 20 rounds of a common resource problem. A negative percentage indicates subjects would have done better to invest in the asset with a safe return. 100 percent is the Pareto optimum. The (10) and (25) indicates whether subjects were given 10 or 25 tokens at the start of each round.

Source: Ostrom et al. (1992).

and profits remain well short of those possible. In some treatments subjects were given the chance to communicate with each other either once, one shot communication, or every round, repeated communication (see Research Methods 11.1); repeated communication definitely seemed to have a positive impact and lead to a sustained increase in profits. In another treatment subjects were given the chance to punish others (in a similar way to in the public good game of chapter seven); this seemed to have less of an impact. In the other treatments subjects were given the chance to both communicate and potentially punish others. This again seemed to help subjects avoid overuse.

Research Methods 11.1

Communication

As a general rule, experimental economists seem averse to letting subjects communicate with each other. There are good theoretical reasons for doing this because economic activity often takes place between people who simply cannot communicate with each other. There are also good practical reasons for doing this because it stops the experimenter losing control; for example one subject with a 'strong' personality could end up biasing a whole experiment. In theory, communication should not matter anyway, at least according to the standard economic model!

People do, though, often communicate, and intuitively it makes a difference, so we do need to take account of it. There are various different ways that subjects can be allowed to communicate in experiments.

The most restrictive way is to let a subject say what action he plans to take. So, before a subject chooses, say, an effort level in the weak link game he gets the chance to say to others what he plans to choose. This can be done in a way such that the experimenter loses no control of the experiment, and so is the preferred way of many.

A step up from this is to let subjects chat via computer. Now the experimenter starts to lose control because a subject is free to say anything. But, at least all that is said is recorded and relatively easy to analyze.

The final step, as in the experiment by Ostrom et al. (1992) is to let subjects talk to each other face to face. Now the experimenter loses a lot of control, and trying to record what happens is essentially impossible; we might be able to record what was said, but recording body language and the like is clearly difficult.

That latter type of experiment is very rare in economics, but I'm not sure that's a good thing.

The lesson from this study was that repeated communication in combination with some threat of punishment or sanction helped people avoid the tragedy of the commons. Other studies (such as one by Schmitt, Swope and Walker 2000) have shown that the benefits of communication are less if there are 'outsiders' who do not take part in the communication.

This is reassuringly similar to what we see in case studies. A combination of case studies and experiments can give us, therefore, important insights into when and how the tragedy of the commons can be avoided. The crucial things necessary to avoid the tragedy of the commons seem to be communication, a threat of sanctions, an ability to exclude outsiders, and a sense of ownership.

11.1.2 Matching markets

In chapter two when we looked at markets we contrasted double auction, posted offer and negotiated price institutions. The basic objective of these institutions is to **match** buyers and sellers so that they can do mutually beneficial deals. Recall that in a double auction market there is an auctioneer who accepts bids and asks and matches a seller to a buyer if the bid is higher than the ask. In a posted offer market sellers advertise their prices and buyers walk around and find a price they like. In a negotiated price market sellers and buyers walk around and ask each other what they are willing to sell or buy. What we hope to see is buyers being matched to sellers whenever the seller is willing to supply at a price a buyer is willing to buy.

In chapter two I suggested that double auction markets are typically efficient. What that basically means is that we get the best match of buyers and sellers. Great! Our focus, however, was on a market where each seller had the same thing to sell, the goods were **homogenous**. Often this seems appropriate, for instance, one share in a company, or one can of a particular brand of cola, is as good as any other, so a buyer should be relatively indifferent as to who they buy from. In many other cases, however, goods are not homogenous. For example, no two houses, restaurant meals, or used cars are exactly alike. This makes it much more difficult to match buyers and sellers efficiently.

To illustrate the problem, we can look at the problem of matching workers to employers. In many professions newly trained graduates simultaneously try to find entry level jobs with employers. What we hope to see is the best match between the worker or supplier of labor and the employer or demander of labor. Workers, however, will have different preferences over where they would rather work, and employers will have different preferences over who they would rather hire. It is very easy for this to become a bit of a mess with great candidates getting no offers, and great employers finding no one accepts their offers. Obtaining the best match is far from easy. One profession that has tried hard to tackle this problem is the medical profession.

The problem in the medical profession is to match newly trained doctors with hospitals willing to employ them. To demonstrate the problems there can be, we can look at the experience of the US. Before 1945 the market for new doctors was decentralized, like a negotiated price market. The outcome was an **unraveling of contract dates**, in which the best students were being hired earlier and earlier as hospitals tried to get the best candidates before anyone else did. In the end, students were being hired two years before graduation. This meant hospitals were hiring students before they had a chance to see how good they really were, or students had a chance to see what type of medicine they would most want to practice. This is inefficient.

In 1945 medical schools banded together to try and improve matters, but a new problem arose. This time candidates who had offers from one place would wait to see if they would get an offer at a preferred place. This might sound reasonable, but if everyone is doing it, then everyone is waiting for everyone else to make a decision. Nothing happens until the deadline for acceptance, and then there is a last-minute rush and decisions are being made with little time to think. This is also inefficient.

In 1952 the National Resident Matching Program was set up as a central clearinghouse for applications. They needed to find a way to match doctors with hospitals that would avoid the previous problems. Since 1998 the program has used a **matching algorithm** designed by economists, notably Alvin Roth, and the process is a lot more efficient. Let's look first at the algorithm used.

After a process of interviews and visits, doctors submit a ranking of their preferred hospitals, and hospitals submit a ranking of their preferred doctors. Table 11.2 gives an example to work through. Something like a **deferred acceptance algorithm** is then used. The algorithm is as follows: each doctor is assigned to his or her first choice of hospital. Table 11.3 keeps track of who is assigned where in the example. The posts at each hospital are then filled with the most preferred doctors assigned to them, and other doctors are rejected. In the example, Carol is rejected because Birmingham prefers to hire Bill. Any doctor rejected at this stage is assigned to his or her second choice of hospital. The posts of each

Table 11.2 An example of possible preferences of junior doctors looking for work and hospitals looking for junior doctors

		Preference		
		first	*second*	*third*
Doctors	Bill	Birmingham	New York	Boston
	Carol	Birmingham	Boston	New York
	Emma	Boston	New York	Birmingham
Hospitals	Birmingham	Bill	Carol	Emma
	New York	Bill	Carol	Emma
	Boston	Bill	Carol	Emma

Table 11.3 The deferred acceptance algorithm allocating doctors to hospitals for the example

	Doctors assigned			Doctors rejected
	Birmingham	*New York*	*Boston*	
Round 1	Bill and Carol	–	Emma	Carol
Round 2	Bill	–	Emma and Carol	Emma
Round 3	Bill	Emma	Carol	–

hospital are then re-filled with the most preferred doctors assigned to them, and other doctors rejected. This time it is Emma who is rejected because Boston prefers Carol. This process goes on until no doctors are rejected.

Things are a bit more complicated than this because, for example, there might be couples who want to work in a similar location, but this is the basic idea. The crucial thing about the deferred acceptance algorithm is that it leads to a **stable matching**, in the sense that no candidate or hospital can look back and wish they had done a different ranking.

Not all possible algorithms are stable. For example, consider a **priority matching algorithm** that works as follows: the priority of a match is measured by the product of the two rankings. For example, if a doctor ranks a hospital first and the hospital ranks the doctor third, the product is $1 \times 3 = 3$; if a doctor ranks a hospital fourth and the hospital ranks the doctor second the priority is $4 \times 2 = 8$. Posts are filled in order of priority. Thus, priority one matches are filled first, where both doctor and hospital ranked each other first, then priority two matches are filled, and so on, until all vacancies are filled. To see why this algorithm need not be stable we can look back at the example. The matching between Emma and Boston has priority three while the matching between Carol and Boston has priority four. This means that Emma will end up at Boston and Carol at New York. Once they know this, Boston can ring Carol and ask her to come, and she will accept. The assignment begins to unravel.

If the outcome of an algorithm is likely to not be stable then we can expect unraveling of contract times, because applicants and hospitals like Carol and Boston will be reluctant to trust the algorithm. The UK provides a nice field experiment, because different regions have over time used different algorithms. Table 11.4 summarizes what happened. I will not explain what the linear programming algorithm is but you can see that it provides something of a puzzle because it is, in principle, unstable yet did not lead to an unraveling of contract times.

One way to try and answer this puzzle is to replicate each matching algorithm in the experimental laboratory and see what happens. That is what Kagel and Roth (2000) and Unver (2005) did. The experiments they ran lasted for twenty-five rounds. In each round subjects, playing the role of worker and employer,

Table 11.4 Different methods used in the UK

Regional market	Algorithm	Stable	Unraveled
Edinburgh	Deferred acceptance	Yes	No
Cardiff	Deferred acceptance	Yes	No
Birmingham	Priority matching	No	Yes
Newcastle	Priority matching	No	Yes
Sheffield	Priority matching	No	Yes
Cambridge	Linear programming	No	No
London Hospital	Linear programming	No	No

Source: Kagel and Roth (2000).

tried to find a good match and were paid between $14 and $4 depending on who they matched with. To capture the possibility of unraveling, each round was split into three periods called −2, −1 and 0. If a worker and employer agreed a match in period −2 they each had to pay a fine of $2 and if they agreed in period −1 had to pay a fine of $1. What we want to see is whether things unravel in the sense that subjects agree matches in periods −2 and −1, despite the cost this entails.

Figure 11.2 summarizes what happened in the experiments. Start by focusing on the first ten rounds where matching was decentralized and so there was no matching algorithm used. We see that subjects paid the fine to get a good match early, and so there was an unraveling of contract time. From round 11 onwards the matching algorithm was used. It was used in period zero for those workers and employers who had not matched so far in periods −2 and −1. We see that the fine subjects were willing to pay fell quite dramatically and became almost zero with the deferred acceptance algorithm.

This shows that the deferred acceptance algorithm is working well. The priority and linear programming algorithm work less well in that the costs remain significant. The suggestion would be, therefore, that it is something of an accident that the linear programming algorithm worked for Cambridge and London Hospital.

The main thing, however, is that these experiments confirm the advantages of the deferred acceptance algorithm. The deferred acceptance algorithm looks like it does a good job both in theory and the experimental laboratory. This has translated into success in the real world. The algorithm has proved successful in

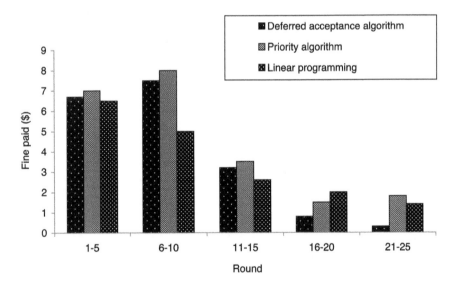

Figure 11.2 Matching algorithms compared.

Source: Unver (2005).

matching doctors to hospitals and is now being used in other areas as well, such as matching prospective students with schools. (The biggest mystery is why economists have not used it in their own profession to match junior faculty to departments!)

11.1.3 Spectrum auctions

The final example I want to look at is auction design. In particular I want to look at the so-called **spectrum auctions**. Before getting into the economics of these auctions, we need to know a bit about what is up for sale.

The electromagnetic spectrum is the name given to the range of electromagnetic frequencies that exist from gamma rays, with a relatively high frequency, to long waves, with a relatively low frequency. Towards the low frequency end of the spectrum are radio waves with a frequency of around 9 KHz to 300 GHz. Television, radio, mobile phones, wireless networking, emergency communications, the signal for the door to open when someone presses a car key fob, and lots of other things, are all transmitted via radio waves.

This creates a competition for a portion of electromagnetic spectrum. For example, if a television channel is transmitting its programs on a certain frequency, then it does not want anyone else transmitting on that same frequency, causing interference. Somehow, therefore, the spectrum needs to be split and allocated in such a way that television, radio, and everything else can work.

To illustrate, the frequencies between 470 MHz and 862 MHz are typically set aside for television. These are then split into 49 chunks, or frequency channels, of eight MHz each giving the frequency channels 21 to 69. A frequency channel is enough space to broadcast a television channel, or six to eight channels using digital television. Potential broadcasters who are allocated a frequency channel can broadcast without fear of interference. But how to decide which potential broadcaster gets allocated a frequency channel?

In many instances governments directly allocate portions of the spectrum to companies. For example, a government committee might decide who gets what after companies have applied for, or tendered for, the right to use a portion of the spectrum. An alternative, that has become increasingly common, is to auction portions of the spectrum. We saw in chapters two and six how auctions can work and the basic rationale behind auctioning spectrum is that the market, rather than the government, decides who gets what. This could be more efficient, and raise more revenue for the government.

Auctioning spectrum is, however, quite complicated, and much more complicated than the auctions I looked at in chapter six. That's why designing the spectrum auctions is no simple matter. To get some intuition for why things are so complicated, we can look at something called a chopstick auction.

I will start with a very simple version of the **chopstick auction**. Imagine that someone called Mathan goes to his favorite Chinese restaurant one evening and finds that the restaurant owners have come up with a game. At the start of the evening they are going to simultaneously auction ten sets of chopsticks. They will do so using a first price sealed bid auction. So, Mathan needs to write down how much he bids for the first set of chopsticks, how much for the second set, and so on. If he bids the highest amount for a set of chopsticks then he wins that set. If Mathan wins a set of chopsticks then he can enjoy his meal, but if he does not he will struggle to eat his meal. He wants, therefore, to win one and only one set of chopsticks, and does not care which one he wins.

The bidding for each set of chopsticks in isolation is very similar to the auctions we looked at in chapter six. The complication here is that there are ten sets being sold simultaneously. For this reason it is called a **multi-unit auction**. How much should Mathan bid for each set?

This turns out to be a difficult question to answer. To see why, first imagine there are ten diners in the restaurant. In principle this looks promising because there are ten sets of chopsticks available, and ten diners wanting chopsticks. If Mathan bids $1 for set one and $0 for the others, Emma bids $1 for set two and $0 for the others, and so on, they will all get a set of chopsticks for $1. Somehow, however, the diners need to coordinate. How can Mathan know he is supposed to bid $1 for set one and not sets two, or three? If the restaurant owners do not allow the diners to communicate with each other, there is no way he could know and so we will likely get coordination failure. This makes it hard to know how Mathan should bid. If there are twenty diners after the ten sets of chopsticks, or some chopsticks are more valuable than others, his task because ever more complicated.

We find these complications in auctioning spectrum. To demonstrate I will look at the spectrum auctions that have received most attention, namely those used to allocate spectrum to mobile phone companies. A mobile phone company needs a portion of spectrum in order to operate. For instance, around the year 2000, with the introduction of 3G or third generation mobile standards, phone companies needed a new portion of spectrum to start running these services. In most western countries governments ran auctions to allocate it.

To be specific, I will look in more detail at the UK auction. The UK government decided to offer five licenses, which you can think of as five portions of spectrum. Figure 11.3 illustrates that license A consisted of a total of 35 MHz. By comparison, license B consisted of a total of 30 MHz and the other three licenses a total of 25 MHz. It was decided that license A would only be available to a new entrant in the UK mobile phone market (which excluded BT, One2One, Orange and Vodafone). How does this compare to the chopstick auction?

There were five licenses or five sets of chopsticks up for sale. A company would want one and only one license but the more spectrum the better, so license A is better than license B which is better than licenses C to E. Overall there were thirteen companies who did bid, and so demand clearly exceeded supply, but remember four of these could not bid for license A. It is very hard to know how a company should bid in such circumstances. That makes it far from obvious whether auctions are a better way to allocate the spectrum than a government committee deciding. In order to work well, auctions need to be very well designed.

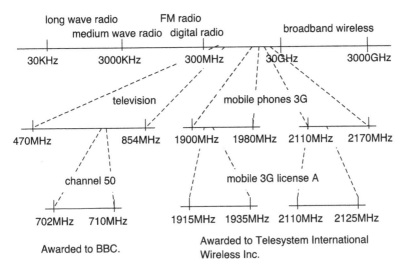

Figure 11.3 The radio wave portion of the electromagnetic spectrum and how it is allocated in the UK.

That is where economists can hopefully be of some use. The UK government employed a team of economists including Ken Binmore and Paul Klemperer to advise on the design of the UK 3G spectrum auction. The design eventually used was a simultaneous ascending auction, and I will go into the details of what that entails below when I look at the US example. What I want to highlight here is that the auction was a big success. The total raised from the five licenses was £22.5 billion, which was way in excess of what many had expected. It was also far more than was raised from auctions in other European countries, as Figure 11.4 shows.

Figure 11.4 illustrates quite starkly how the success of an auction can depend a lot on the design of that auction. The UK, German and Danish auctions were considered a success, others not so. The Netherlands, for example, used the same auction format as in the UK but had five incumbents compared to the UK's four. With five incumbents bidding for five licenses, other potential bidders stayed away and much less revenue was raised than expected. A similar thing happened in Switzerland. Things can, therefore, go badly wrong. An auction in 1990 in New Zealand of television spectrum is particularly notorious. A sealed bid second price auction was used, and only NZ$36 million was raised compared to a predicted NZ$250 million. One lucky company bid NZ$100,000 but only had to pay the second highest bid of NZ$6, and another bid NZ$7 million but only had to pay NZ$5,000!

If things can go so wrong, then it is clearly crucial to design the auction well. The most successful auctions have generally been simultaneous ascending auctions. The first significant use of an ascending auction was by the Federal Communications

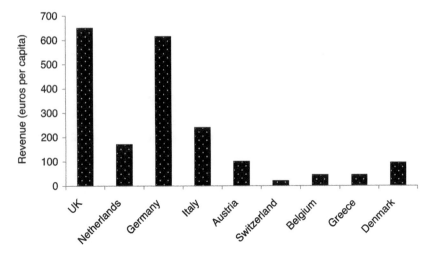

Figure 11.4 The revenue in euros per capita from the 3G spectrum auctions in different European countries in date order. The UK, German and Danish auctions were considered a success.

Source: Klemperer (2004).

Commission in the US in 1994, based on ideas of economists Paul Milgrom, Bob Wilson and Preston McAfee. The basic idea behind the **simultaneous ascending auction** is that there are a number of rounds in which bidders make sealed bids for any items, or portions of spectrum, that they want to bid on. At the end of each round the **standing high bid** for each item is posted as well as the minimum bid for the item in the next round. In order to give bidders an incentive to bid early an **activity rule** means that a bidder can only bid if they have bid in earlier rounds. Table 11.5 illustrates how the bidding progressed in the UK 3G spectrum auction.

The main benefit of an ascending auction is that bidders can coordinate over time by seeing how bids progress. This was particularly important in the auctions run in the US, and those in Germany. To see why, think back to the chopstick auction and imagine that instead of auctioning ten sets of chopsticks the restaurant owner auctions twenty chopsticks. Now Mathan wants to win two and only two chopsticks and his task seems even harder than before. Having the auction run over successive rounds can allow bidders to coordinate a little better. Mathan can be surer to get the two chopsticks he wants, rather than end up paying for one he does not want, or three which is excessive.

Splitting things up like this, and selling chopsticks rather than sets of chopsticks, might seem like an unnecessary complication. It can, however, make sense in spectrum auctions, because it lets the market decide how many firms there will be. For example, in Germany the 3G spectrum auctions involved twelve portions of spectrum (compared to the five in the UK) that in blocks of two or three were enough to operate a viable network. The number of firms in the market could therefore,

Table 11.5 Bidding over the rounds in the UK 3G spectrum auction. The standing high bid for each round is given in millions of pounds

Round	*License* A	B	C	D	E
1	TIW £170.0 m	Orange £107.4 m	–	Crescent £89.3 m	Epsilon £89.3 m
2	NTL Mobile £178.5 m	Telefonica £113.1 m	WorldCom £90.2 m	Crescent £89.3 m	Epsilon £89.3 m
3	NTL Mobile £178.5 m	TIW £176.5 m	Worldcom £90.2 m	3GUK £93.8 m	One2One £93.8 m
4	NTL Mobile £178.5 m	Orange £186.7 m	Telefonica £95.3 m	3GUK £93.8 m	One2One £93.8 m
5	Spectrumco £187.5 m	TIW £196.1 m	Telefonica £95.3 m	WoldCom £99.2 m	Epsilon £100.1 m
150	TIW £4,384.7 m	Vodafone £5,964.0 m	BT3G £4,030.1 m	One2One £4,003.6 m	Orange £4,095.0 m

Source: Ofcom.

have ended up as four, five or six. Designing auctions where bidders may want to win multiple items does, however, pose a new set of challenges. This has led to the use of **package** or **combinatorial auctions** in which bidders can bid on combinations of items. For example, Mathan might be able to bid $1 for chopstick one, $5 for chopsticks one and two, $3 for chopsticks four, five and six, and so on!

11.1.4 Behavioral economics and institution design

Hopefully you have seen that institutions matter, and designing good institutions is not easy. For example, avoiding the tragedy of the commons, matching doctors to hospitals, or designing an auction that will work efficiently when there are multiple items to sell is tricky. The tragedy of the commons is avoided in some situations and not others. Some matching markets and auctions have gone badly wrong and others have been very successful. The question I want to finish with is what institution design has to do with behavioral economics.

At first glance one might say, not too much. Auction design, for example, draws heavily on game theory and the economics of industrial organization. We would not need behavioral economics to predict the poor performance of the 3G spectrum auctions in the Netherlands and Switzerland; a bit of industrial organization theory would be enough. Look a little deeper, however, and behavioral economics does seem a vital tool in institution design.

This is easiest to see in designing institutions to solve things like the tragedy of the commons. There an understanding of social preferences and the ability to coordinate is crucial to understanding what will work and want will not. The case for behavioral economics is weaker in the design of auctions or matching markets, which are more like a combinatorial mathematical problem. Even here, though, behavioral economics can prove crucial. One reason it that the practicalities of institution design far exceed our theoretical ability, and so laboratory experiments can prove useful alongside theory, to give an idea of how different institutions will perform. We saw this in looking at designing matching markets. Both the teams designing the UK 3G spectrum auction and the first FCC auctions in the US also used laboratory experiments to test possible auction designs.

Behavioral economics is, and has proved to be, therefore, a useful tool in institutional design, both in informing how people can realistically be expected to behave, and as an important test bed for possible institutions. In many ways this seems inevitable, because institution design forces us to step outside the comfort of the standard economic model and recognize that it does not always work to assume people are like homo economicus. Behavioral economics gives us the tools and techniques to step with confidence beyond the standard economic model.

11.2 Nudge and behavior change

The second category of government policy I distinguished earlier was that of manipulating individual incentives. In recent years there has been much excitement that behavioral economics can change the way policy is viewed when it comes to individual incentives. To understand why there is such excitement it is worth pointing out first something obvious:

A policy focus on individual behavior is nothing new. For example, why would a central bank or government increase the interest rate? The answer might be that they want to reduce inflation, but for this to work they need individuals to respond to the change in interest rate. For instance, they need Mathan, who has a mortgage, to reduce his consumption because he knows he will have to pay more interest on his mortgage debt. To give a second example, why would a government give tax relief on saving for retirement? Presumably, they want to increase saving for retirement. Again, for this to work, they need people like Mathan to change his consumption plans and save more because the tax relief makes saving look a better deal.

So, how can behavioral economics change the way we look at policy? The traditional role for economics and policy has been about changing what I would call **incentives for homo economicus**. By this I primarily mean incentives that would matter to someone who maximizes utility without any mistakes or biases. A change in the interest rate or changes in tax relief are like this. Behavioral economics suggest that what I would call **incentives for homo sapiens** can also matter. By this I primarily mean incentives that can matter to someone who is biased in some way. It seems best to illustrate with some examples. I will look at two related to saving and time-inconsistency.

11.2.1 Savings accounts

If people are time inconsistent when it comes to saving decisions, then properly tailored saving plans may be able to influence behavior. A number of field experiments have now shown this to be the case. I shall illustrate with a study by Ashraf, Karlan and Yin (2006).

The study was done in partnership with the Green Bank of Caraga, a rural bank in the Philippines. In the first part of the study a household survey was done on 1,777 existing or former clients of the bank. One part of this survey involved hypothetical time preference questions (similar to those we looked at in section 4.1.2). This allowed respondents to be classified as time-consistent, time-inconsistent, or more patient now (meaning their discount factor decreased further into the future). In the second part of the study half of those surveyed were offered a new SEED (Save, Earn, Enjoy Deposits) account. Of the remaining people, half received no further contact (a control group) and half were encouraged to save more using existing accounts (a marketing group).

The SEED account was specifically designed so that a client had to specify a specific goal. This could be date based, such as to save for a birthday, or amount based, such as to save for a new roof. The client had complete flexibility in setting the goal, but having set the goal they had no access to their money until the goal was reached. This meant very restricted access to funds. Also, the interest rate of a SEED account was no higher than that of a normal savings account.

For a person who is time-consistent the SEED account looks like a bad deal because she has no access to her money and gets no higher interest rate. For someone who is time-inconsistent the SEED account may look attractive because it is a strong commitment device to save and overcome the short-term impulse to spend.

In all, 202 SEED accounts were opened, of which 147 were date-based. After 12 months, 116 of the accounts reached maturity or met the goal and all bar one opted to take out a new SEED account. Clearly, the SEED account proved relatively popular. The most fascinating thing is that a reliable predictor of who would take up a SEED account was time-inconsistent preferences. Women who exhibited time-inconsistent preferences were 15.8 percent more likely to take up the SEED product than those with time-consistent preferences. In men the figure was 4.6 percent. This is clearly consistent with the idea that the account would appeal to those who needed to commit to saving because of present bias.

The final thing we need to check is whether people saved more if they opened a SEED account. The simple answer seems to be yes. After twelve months, savings for those offered the SEED account was estimated to be 82 percent higher than those in the control group, and also much higher than those in the marketing group. This increase in saving seems to be because the SEED product offers consumers incentives to save. In particular, those who took up a SEED account saved a lot more than anyone else. This is clearly apparent in Figure 11.5.

The SEED account thus seemed to be popular and successful. It provided no incentives that would tempt homo economicus because there was no higher interest rate, or anything that should have appealed to someone who is unbiased. The account did, however, provide incentives for homo sapiens to save and seemingly did appeal to those with present bias who wanted a means to pre-commit to more saving.

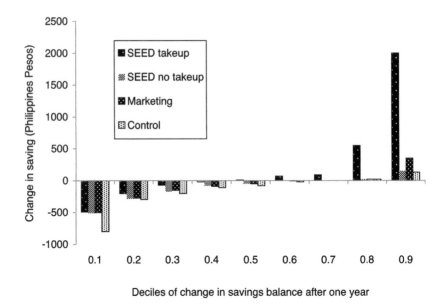

Figure 11.5 Changes in saving behavior after one year. The majority of those taking up the SEED account increased saving. For many, the increase in saving was very large.

Source: Ashraf et al. (2006).

11.2.2 A default to save

Accounts that restrict access to funds may help some overcome the urge to spend. They should work well for the consumer who is time-inconsistent but sophisticated and so looking for some way to commit for the long term. What about the consumer who is time-inconsistent and naïve? Such a consumer would never choose a restrictive savings account, so another solution is needed. One option is to automatically enroll him in a savings plans and thus put the emphasis on him to opt-out of saving rather than opt in. To see how this could work we can consider at a study by Madrian and Shea (2001).

The study looks at data from a large US company that changed enrolment and eligibility for the 401(k) retirement savings plan on 1 April 1998. Before this date, employees were only eligible to enroll in the plan after one year of employment, and did have to choose to enroll. After the change, all employees were immediately eligible to enroll, and new employees were automatically enrolled unless they chose to stay out. Figure 11.6 shows how dramatic the changes proved. The participation rate of employees hired after the change was above that of any subset of current employees. The most telling comparison is between new employees and those employed less than a year before the change (the window

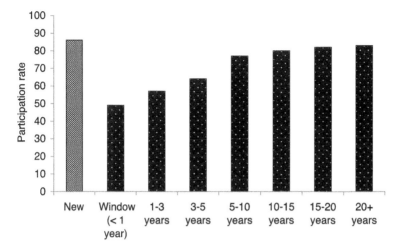

Tenure on 1st April 1998

Figure 11.6 Participation rate in 401(k) retirement savings plan. There was a dramatic increase in the participation rate once the default was to be enrolled in the savings plan.

Source: Madrian and Shea (2001).

group). The only substantive difference between these two groups is that enrolment was the default for one and non-enrolment the default for the other.

Clearly, making enrolment the default option increased participation, and we might consider this a good thing. There is, however, one problem. If employees are automatically enrolled then their investment choices also need to be set automatically. In this particular instance there were two choices to make: how much to contribute, and whether to invest in stocks, bonds or some other type of investment. The default chosen was a contribution rate of 3 percent of income invested in a money market fund. Basically, no one chose this combination before the change, but of those automatically enrolled, 71 percent stayed with this default option. Figure 11.7 illustrates the big contrast between the window group and the new group of employees.

Clearly, new employees tended to stick to the default, despite this probably not being the best thing they could do. This provides something of a conundrum. While the increased participation looks like a good thing, that people follow the default investment choices looks like a bad thing. Indeed, an employee who would have chosen to opt-in to the savings plan with different investment options may end up being worse off if he is enrolled in the plan by default.

I will come back to this conundrum shortly. For now, I want you to see again the distinction between incentives for homo economicus and those for homo sapiens. Changing the default option should make no difference to homo economicus. Whatever the default, he would have worked out his optimal savings

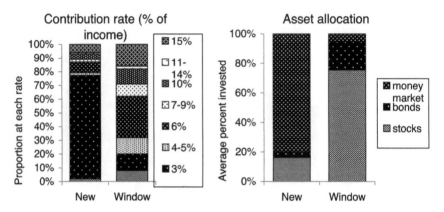

Figure 11.7 Contribution rate and asset allocation in the new and window groups.
Source: Madrian and Shea (2001).

plan and enacted it. For homo sapiens who are time-inconsistent or have other biases, the change can, and we see does, matter. Someone with present bias, for example, may procrastinate and never get around to changing their savings choices despite a desire to do so.

11.2.3 Nudge

In both the previous examples we see changes, the introduction of a new account and a default of enrollment in a savings plan, that made a big difference. To calm, calculating homo economicus they should not have made a difference, but it probably came as little surprise that they did make a difference for normal people. This opens up interesting new ways to think of economics and policy, informed by behavioral economics.

The two examples illustrate two different possibilities. In the first example, where a new account is created, something 'real' was changed in that people had different choices. Ideas from behavioral economics suggested that these different choices may prove popular and worthwhile. In the second example, where the default is changed, nothing really changes, in that everyone still has the same choices as before. The framing of those choices is, however, changed and ideas from behavioral economics suggest why this change in framing may matter.

So, behavioral economics can suggest changes to choices, and changes to the framing of choices that may make a difference. One of the reasons this has excited interest in policymaking is that both can come at relatively little cost! Changing the default, or administering a new account, are relatively cheap to do, particularly when compared with the things governments might normally do like change tax relief on savings. Basically, changing the incentives for homo sapiens is a lot cheaper than changing them for homo economicus.

But, to put behavioral economics to best use we need a framework to work with. The idea of nudge, made popular in a book by Richard Thaler and Cass Sunstein, is one way to go. To explain what a nudge is, we first need to explain the idea of a choice architect. A **choice architect** is anyone responsible for framing a decision that others will take. One example would be a sales assistant explaining to Emma the merits of different goods she might buy. The assistant has discretion to frame the choices in different ways by maybe emphasizing the good points of one good and the bad of another. A second example would be the way that share prices are listed when Alan looks up how well his investments are doing. Investments could be listed in alphabetical order, or performance order, declining stocks could be highlighted in bright red, or left in normal font, and so on.

This book has been full of examples where differences in framing have mattered. For instance, whether the sales tax is included or not in the price, and whether the default is to be enrolled or not enrolled in the savings plan are classic examples of where framing matters. We can be pretty confident that how the sales assistant talks to Emma, and how Alan's investments are displayed on the screen will also matter.

Now I want to move beyond saying framing matters, to asking whether we can change the framing of a decision in a way that helps people make better choices. This brings us to the idea of **nudge**. To quote from Thaler and Sunstein (2008), 'A nudge, as we will use the term, is any aspect of the choice architecture that alters people's behavior in a predictable way without forbidding any options or significantly changing their economic incentives. To count as a mere nudge, the intervention must be easy and cheap to avoid.'

So, something that changes the incentives of homo economicus cannot be a nudge. Something that changes the incentives of homo sapiens can. Changing the default option to that of being enrolled in a savings plan rather than being not enrolled is a fantastic example of a nudge. The options and economic incentives of the person are exactly the same whatever the default. All we have done is change the choice architecture or the framing of the choices in a seemingly small way. Even so, we get a predictable and big change in behavior.

Can policymakers harness the power of nudge and nudge people into making better choices? To answer that question it's useful to think about two subsidiary questions: when do people need a nudge? And how can people be most effectively given a nudge?

The first question is relatively easy for us to answer given what we have already covered in this book. We have seen that people are pretty clever, most of the time, and do learn with experience. So, nudges should only be needed sparingly, but there are four good reasons why we may need to nudge someone like Alan: (i) Alan may face a very complicated choice, and clever or not, can easily get it wrong. (ii) He has had very little experience or chance to learn what is best. (iii) He is relatively uninformed about what he should choose. (iv) He is biased and so may not make the choices he would have wanted himself to make.

If something ticks all four boxes then it looks a good place for a nudge. Saving for retirement is one clear example: it involves complicated choices; Alan is only going to get old once, so has no chance to go back and start again having learnt from experience; he may have no real idea what savings he will need in 30 or 40 years' time; present bias may also mean he puts off doing things he knows he should be doing. In the US, health care is another thing likely to tick all four boxes.

This gives us a framework to think when nudges might be needed. The next thing we need to think about is how to most effectively use nudges. This means it's time for our first mnemonic. Table 11.6 briefly describes the six principles Thaler and Sunstein suggest for a good choice architecture. Only the first of these would get much attention in thinking about pushing homo economicus. The basic idea, therefore, is to supplement incentives with things that take account of why the nudge is needed: to lessen the complexity (structure complex choices), create experience (give feedback), improve information (understand mappings), and work around biases (defaults, incentives and expect error).

This might look fine in principle, but can it work? Things are not necessarily so easy. For example, we have seen that making it the default option for people to be opted in to a savings plan may not be enough. We also need to encourage participants to choose the best contribution rate and stock options. Nudging people is, therefore, not simple, and can leave some worse off than they might have been. But there are some basic nudges that can move things in the right direction for most people. For example, most would probably agree that making it the default option for people to be opted into a savings plan is a good thing.

Thaler and Sunstein suggest various other nudges, and you can probably come up with some yourself. Before we move on, I want to look at one of these, which I think is pretty neat. It's called **save more tomorrow**. The idea is that a saver, like Mathan, can commit himself to save more tomorrow, in the sense that his contributions to a savings plan will automatically increase every time his pay

Table 11.6 Principles for good choice architecture, spell NUDGES

Principles	Brief description
iNcentives	People do respond to incentives like price and cost, but only if these are salient.
Understand mappings	People may need help understanding the mapping from the choices they may make to the outcomes they will get.
Defaults	Defaults matter a lot because of present bias and choice overload, so think carefully about them.
Give feedback	People do learn so give feedback on when things are going well or badly.
Expect error	People make mistakes, so we need something that is as forgiving as possible to mistakes they may make.
Structure complex choices	The more complex the choice the more problems a person has, and the more likely context effects will matter. So, keep things simple.

Source: Thaler and Sunstein (2008).

increases. Why does this make sense? Mathan might learn that he is saving too little but not want to increase his current savings, because that would lower his income, and we know from chapters two and four that people don't like that. If he says 'I will save more tomorrow', we also know that this is probably not going to happen, because of present bias. The save more tomorrow plan means Mathan commits to saving tomorrow.

If he knows he has a present bias then this looks like a great commitment device that helps Mathan to save and overcome any time-inconsistency. So, does it work? Thaler and Sunstein report what a great success it has been. In a pilot program many employees chose the save more tomorrow plan and stuck with it, and their savings rate almost quadrupled over the period. It's safe to say this would not have happened without the plan, and many large employers have now adopted the idea. So, this is one nudge that does look as though it worked.

11.2.4 Nudge and behavior change

One concern that many express about nudge is that it sounds a bit too much like big brother. It sounds a bit too much like the policymaker deciding on someone's behalf, and can we trust policymakers to know what is best?

An important aspect of nudge is that it should not involve sacrifice of liberty. This was clear in the quote I gave above from Thaler and Sunstein: 'without forbidding any options or significantly changing their economic incentives . . . the intervention must be easy and cheap to avoid'. In principle, therefore, a nudge should not impact on personal liberty. This, however, is a bit different to saying that a nudge is not about changing behavior in the way a policymaker thinks is best. Basically, a nudge should not change the set of options someone like Mathan has, but its very objective is to change the option that Mathan will choose.

There is no escaping the fact, therefore, that nudge does require us to think whether the policymaker knows best. It is about **behavior change**. That's one reason to think through, as we have done, when people will most need a nudge or behavior change. Is that enough? Well, we saw in the last chapter that most people might be comfortable with behavior change, and others making difficult decisions on their behalf, provided they retain some choice and self-determination. A nudge does retain choice and so does look reasonable enough.

Even so, you might be wondering whether we should be encouraging behavior change, and trusting that policymakers know what's best. The crucial point I want to make here is that we have no choice but to do this.

Recall, that in chapters two and nine I argued that framing and context effects are inevitable: context influences perceptions and intuition, which influence reasoning, which influence behavior. What that means is that behavior change is an inevitability of policy. To quote from a report published by the UKs Institute for Government (Dolan et al. 2010):

> We may not agree on how we would like policymakers to change our behaviour. But whether we like it or not, the actions of policy-makers, public service

professionals, markets and our fellow citizens around us have big, and often unintended, impacts on our behaviour. 'Doing nothing' is rarely a neutral option.

It's the lack of a neutral option that is key here. Is the neutral option that Mathan be not put in a savings plan, put in a savings plan, or put in a save more tomorrow plan? Quite simply, there is no neutral option, something has to be chosen. This means that policymakers have no choice but to change behavior. The key thing is to try and change behavior in the right direction.

That means it is time for our second mnemonic: The UK's Institute for Government came up with the idea of MINDSPACE. The basic idea is to provide a practical means to think about behavior change and apply insights from behavioral economics and psychology in policymaking. This is being used by policymakers in the UK and so gives one great example of policymakers using behavioral economics to try and change behavior in the right direction. Table 11.7 gives a brief overview of the main principles underlying MINDSPACE, and most of these are things we have looked at in this book.

The MINDSPACE principles are designed to help policymakers better understand how possible policies might change behavior; they are a kind of checklist of things to think about. The interesting thing that I want to finish with is how this checklist can serve different purposes. I will quote again from the report (Dolan et al. 2010):

Enhance. MINDSPACE can help policy-makers understand how current attempts to change behaviour could be improved.
Introduce. Some of the elements in MINDSPACE are not used extensively by policy-makers, yet may have considerable impact.
Reassess. Government needs to understand ways it may be changing the behaviour of citizens unintentionally. It is quite possible that the state is producing unintended – and possibly unwanted – changes in behaviour. The

Table 11.7 An overview of MINDSPACE

Principle	Description
Messenger	We are heavily influenced by who communicates information
Incentives	Our responses to incentives are shaped by predictable mental shortcuts, such as strongly avoiding losses.
Norms	We are strongly influenced by what others do.
Defaults	We 'go with the flow' of pre-set options.
Salience	Our attention is drawn to what is novel and seems relevant to us.
Priming	Our acts are often influenced by subconscious cues.
Affect	Our emotional associations can powerfully shape our actions.
Commitments	We seek to be consistent with our public promises, and reciprocate acts
Ego	We act in ways that make us feel better about ourselves.

Source: Dolan et al. (2010).

insights from MINDSPACE offer a rigorous way of assessing whether and how government is shaping the behaviour if its citizens.

The nice thing about this is that it illustrates the three different ways in which behavioral economics can have a positive impact on policy. It can help us come up with new ideas, like the save more tomorrow nudge; an example of 'introduce'. It can help us improve current policy, like changing the default to automatic enrollment; an example of 'enhance'. Finally, it can help us realize the problems with current policy, such as appreciating why a default of no automatic enrollment does not work; an example of reassess.

I would argue, therefore, that behavior change is not only inevitable, but is also something to be embraced as a positive means by which policymakers can design policies that work and avoid policies that do not.

11.3 Summary

I started by looking at how behavioral economics can help design good institutions, looking at the tragedy of the commons, matching markets, and auctions as examples. We saw that insights from behavioral economics can be useful in better predicting behavior. We also saw that experiments can be a useful testing ground to see how institutions will perform.

Next we looked at how behavioral economics can help inform on policies that are directed at changing individual behavior. Two examples showed that small changes could have big, and desirable consequences. This leads us to the concept of nudge and behavior change. We saw that behavioral economics can help us come up with new ideas, like the save more tomorrow program, and can also help us reassess why existing policies may not be working.

An important point in looking at both institution design and changing individual incentives is that context and framing will matter. This means that policymakers cannot be neutral. What they do is going to influence behavior and/or the success of the institution. They need, therefore, to come up with the policies that have the most positive impact and for that, they need behavioral economists to come up with the guiding principles, like those in Tables 11.6 and 11.7.

It's testament to the development of behavioral economics that it is now making an impact on policymaking. But, hopefully this is only the beginning. Behavioral economics has the power to completely change the way we think about all aspects of the economy and economic behavior. What's more, I believe it gives us a much better way to think about and understand economic behavior. That's why my hope is that behavioral economics will soon become something that all economists do some of the time, rather than something some economists do all of the time.

11.4 Further reading

The book by Ostrom (1990) and article (2010) are a good place to start for more on the tragedy of the commons. For more on matching markets see Roth (2002,

2008). On auction design there are lots of good resources. The books by Klemperer (2003) and Milgrom (2004) are good places to start. The web is also a great source of information. For more on the UK spectrum allocation see the Ofcom website and for more on the US spectrum allocation see the Federal Communications Commission (FCC) website. Thaler and Sunstein (2008) is the obvious place to read more about nudge, and there is a lot more about MIND-SPACE on the Institute for Government website, including the full report and interviews with the authors.

11.5 Review questions

11.1   What is the difference between a weak link game, threshold public good game, and common pool resource game?

11.2   Why is it easier to achieve sustainable fishing for national, inshore fishing than international, offshore fishing?

11.3   Do you think subjects should be allowed to communicate with each other during experiments?

11.4   Should the objective of a government running a spectrum auction be to raise as much money as possible?

11.5   Why is it useful to distinguish between policies about institutions and about individual behavior? You might want to contrast saving choices with interactive situations like a threshold public good game.

11.6   Why might people need a nudge in deciding what insurance to buy, or health care provider to use in the US? Where else might nudges make sense?

11.7   How could a charity or private firm exploit the save more tomorrow idea?

11.8   Is there any difference between a nudge that works at a conscious or subconscious level?

11.9   Should governments ask citizens whether they agree with behavior change, or just get on with it?

11.10 Come up with some nudges of your own.

Bibliography

Agarwal, S., Liu, C. and Souleles, N.S. (2007) 'The reaction of consumer spending and debt to tax rebates-evidence from consumer credit data', *Journal of Political Economy*, 115: 986–1019.

Alberti, F. and Cartwright, E. (2010) 'Does endowment size matter in threshold public good games', School of Economics, University of Kent working paper.

Alpizar, F., Carlsson, F. and Johansson-Stenman, O. (2008) 'Anonymity, reciprocity, and conformity: Evidence from voluntary contributions to a national park in Costa Rica,' *Journal of Public Economics*, 92: 1047–1060.

Anderson, L. R. and Holt, C. A. (1997) 'Information cascades in the laboratory', *American Economic Review*, 87: 847–862.

Andreoni, J. (1990) 'Impure altruism and donations to public goods: A Theory of Warm-Glow Giving', *Economic Journal*, 100: 464–477.

Andreoni, J. (1993) 'An experimental test of the public-goods crowding-out hypothesis', *American Economic Review*, 83: 1317–27.

Andreoni, J. and Miller, J. (2002) 'Giving according to GARP: An experimental test of the consistency of preferences for altruism', *Econometrica*, 70: 737–753.

Ariely, D. and Wertenbroch, K. (2002) 'Procrastination, deadlines, and performance: Self-control by precommitment', *Psychological Science*, 13: 219–224.

Ariely, D., Loewenstein, G. and Prelec, D. (2003) 'Coherent arbitrariness: Stable demand curves without stable preferences', *Quarterly Journal of Economics*, 118: 73–105.

Ashraf, M., Karlan, D. and Yin, W. (2006) 'Tying Odysseus to the mast: Evidence from a commitment savings product in the Philippines', *Quarterly Journal of Economics*, 121: 635–672.

Baicker, K., Buckles, K. S. and Chandra, A. (2006) 'Geographic variation in the appropriate use of cesarean delivery', *Health Affairs*, 25: w355–w367.

Barber, B. and T. Odean (2008) 'All that glitters: The effect of attention and news on the buying behaviour of individual and institutional investors', *Review of Financial Studies*, 21: 785–818.

Barberis, N. and Xiong, W. (2006) 'What drives the disposition effect? An analysis of a long standing preference-based explanation', NBER working paper no. 12397.

Barberis, N., Huang M. and Thaler, R. (2006) 'Individual preferences, monetary gambles, and stock market participation: A case for narrow framing', *American Economic Review*, 96: 1069–1113.

Bardsley, N., Cubitt, R., Loomes, G., Moffatt, P., Starmer, C. and Sugden, R. (2010) *Experimental Economics: Rethinking the Rules*, Princeton: Princeton University Press.

Bateman, I., Kahneman, D., Munro, A., Starmer, C. and Sugden, R. (2005) 'Testing competing models of loss aversion: an adversarial collaboration', *Journal of Public Economics*, 89: 1561–1580.

Becker, G. and Murphy, K. (1998) 'A theory of rational addiction', *Journal of Political Economy*, 46: 675–700.

Benartzi, S. and R. Thaler (1995) 'Myopic loss aversion and the equity premium puzzle', *Quarterly Journal of Economics*, 110: 73–92.

Benartzi, S. and R. Thaler (1999) 'Risk aversion or myopia? Choices in repeated gambles and retirement investments', *Management Science*, 45: 364–381.

Benartzi, S. and R. Thaler (2002) 'How much is investor autonomy worth', *Journal of Finance*, 57: 1593–1616.

Benartzi, S. and Thaler, R. (2007) 'Heuristics and biases in retirement savings behavior', *Journal of Economic Perspectives*, 21: 81–104.

Benzion, U., Rapoport, A. and Yagil, J. (1989) 'Discount rates inferred from decisions: An experimental study', *Management Science*, 35: 270–284.

Berg, J., Dickhaut, J. and McCabe, K. (1994) 'Trust, reciprocity, and social history', *Games and Economic Behavior*, 10: 122–142.

Berg, J., Dickhaut, J. and Rietz T. (2010) 'Preference reversals: The impact of truth-revealing monetary incentives', *Games and Economic Behavior*, 68: 443–468.

Bergstrom, T. (1996) 'Economics in a family way', *Journal of Economic Literature*, 34: 1903–1934.

Bergstrom, T. (2002) 'Evolution of social behaviour: Individual and group selection', *Journal of Economic Literature*, 16: 67–88.

Bernheim, D. and Rangel, A. (2004) 'Addiction and cue-triggered decision processes', *American Economic Review*, 94: 1558–1590.

Bernheim, D. and Rangel, A. (2007) 'Toward choice-theoretic foundations for behavioral welfare economics', *American Economic Review*, 97: 464–470.

Bewley, T. (2007) 'Fairness, reciprocity, and wage rigidity', in Diamond, P. and Vartiainen, H. (Eds.) *Behavioral Economics and its Applications*, Princeton: Princeton University Press.

Bikhchandani, S., Hirshleifer, D. and Welch, I. (1998) 'Learning from the behavior of others: Conformity, fads, and informational cascades', *Journal of Economic Perspectives*, 12: 151–170.

Binmore, K. (2008) 'Review of behavioral economics and its applications', *Economic Journal*, 118: F248–F251.

Bolton, G. and Katok, E. (1998) 'An experimental test of the crowding out hypothesis: The nature of beneficent behavior', *Journal of Economic Behavior and Organization*, 37: 315–331.

Bolton, G. and Ockenfels, A. (2000) 'ERC: A Theory of Equity, Reciprocity, and Competition', *The American Economic Review*, 90: 166–193.

Bowles, S. (2006) 'Group competition, reproductive leveling and the evolution of human altruism', *Science*, 314: 1555–1556.

Boyd, R. (2006) 'The puzzle of human sociality', *Science*, 314: 1560–1563.

Brandts, J. and Cooper, D. (2006) 'A change would do you good . . . An experimental study on how to overcome coordination failure in organizations', *American Economic Review*, 96: 669–693.

Brandts, J. and Cooper, D. (2007) 'It's what you say, not what you pay: An experimental study of manager-employee relationships in overcoming coordination failure', *Journal of the European Economic Association*, 5: 1223–1268.

Brandts, J. and Holt, C. A. (1992) 'An experimental test of equilibrium dominance in signaling games', *American Economic Review*, 82: 1350–1365.

Breiter, H., Aharon, I., Kahneman, D., Dale, A. and Shizgal, P. (2001) 'Functional imaging of neural responses to expectancy and experience of monetary gains and losses', *Neuron*, 30: 619–639.

Brickman, P., Coates, D. and Janoff-Bulman, R. (1978) 'Lottery winners and accident victims: Is happiness relative?', *Journal of Personality and Social Psychology*, 36: 917–927.

Brown, R. (1995) *Prejudice: It's Social Psychology*, Hoboken, NJ: Wiley-Blackwell.

Browning, M. and Crossley, T.F. (2001) 'The life-cycle model of consumption and saving', *Journal of Economic Perspectives*, 15: 3–22.

Bruni, L. and Sugden, R. (2007) 'The road not taken: How psychology was removed from economics, and how it might be brought back', *Economic Journal*, 117: 146–173.

Cadsby, C. and Maynes, E. (1999) 'Voluntary provision of threshold public goods with continuous contributions: experimental evidence', *Journal of Public Economics*, 71: 53–73

Caginalp, G., Porter, D. and Smith, V. L. (2000) 'Overreactions, momentum, liquidity, and price bubbles in laboratory and field asset markets', *Journal of Behavioral Finance*, 1: 24–48.

Camerer, C. (2003) *Behavioral Game Theory: Experiments in Strategic Interaction*, Princeton: Princeton University Press.

Camerer, C. (2006) 'Behavioral economics', in Blundell, R., Newey, W., and Persson, R. (Eds) *Advances in Economics and Econometrics: Theory and Applications, Ninth World Congress, Volume II*, New York: Cambridge University Press.

Camerer, C. (2007) 'Neuroeconomics: Using neuroscience to make economic predictions', *Economic Journal*, 117: C26–C42.

Camerer, C. and Ho, T-H. (1999) 'Experience-weighted attraction learning in normal form games', *Econometrica*, 67: 827–874.

Camerer, C. and Loewenstein, G. (2004) 'Behavioral economics: Past, present and future', in Camerer, C., Loewenstein, G. and Rabin, M. (Eds) *Advances in Behavioral Economics*, Princeton: Princeton University Press.

Camerer, C. and Thaler, R. (1995) 'Anomalies: Ultimatums, dictators and manners', *Journal of Economic Perspectives*, 9: 209–219.

Camerer, C. and Weber, M. (1992) 'Recent developments in modelling preferences: Uncertainty and ambiguity', *Journal of Risk and Uncertainty*, 5: 325–370.

Camerer, C., Ho, T-H. and Chong, J-K. (2004) 'A cognitive hierarchy model of games', *Quarterly Journal of Economics*, 119: 861–898.

Camerer, C., Loewenstein, G. and Prelec, D. (2004) 'Neuroeconomics: Why economics needs brains', *Scandinavian Journal of Economics*, 106: 555–579.

Camerer, C., Loewenstein, G. and Prelec, D. (2005) 'Neuroeconomics: How neuroscience can inform economics', *Journal of Economic Literature*, 43: 9–64.

Campbell III, C. and Kamlani, K. (1997) 'The reasons for wage rigidity: Evidence from a survey of firms', *Quarterly Journal of Economics*, 112: 759–789.

Caplin, A. and Schotter, A. (2008) *The Foundations of Positive and Normative Economics*, Oxford: Oxford University Press.

Carroll, C., Overland, J. and Weil, D. (2000) 'Saving and growth with habit formation', *American Economic Review*, 90: 341–355.

Cassar, A. and Friedman, D. (2004) *Economics Lab: An Introduction to Experimental Economics*, London: Routledge.

Chamberlin, E.H. (1948) 'An experimental imperfect market', *Journal of Political Economy*, 56: 95–108.

Chetty, R. (2006) 'A new method of estimating risk aversion', *American Economic Review*, 96: 1821–1834.

Chetty, R., Looney, A. and Kroft, K. (2009) 'Salience and taxation: Theory and evidence', *American Economic Review*, 99: 1145–77.

Cheung, Y-W. and Friedman, D. (1997) 'Individual learning in normal form games: Some laboratory results', *Games and Economic Behavior*, 19: 46–76.

Clark, A.E., Diener, E., Georgellis, Y. and Lucas, R.E. (2003) 'Lags and leads in life satisfaction: A test of the baseline hypothesis', DELTA working paper 2003–14.

Clark, A.E., Diener, E., Georgellis, Y. and Lucas, R.E. (2008) 'Lags and leads in life satisfaction: A test of the baseline hypothesis', *Economic Journal*, 118: F222–243.

Clotfelter, C. and Cook, P. (1991) 'Lotteries in the real world', *Journal of Risk and Uncertainty*, 4: 227–32.

Coats, J., Gronberg, T. and Grosskopf, B. (2009) 'Simultaneous versus sequential public good provision and the role of refunds – An experimental study', *Journal of Public Economics*, 93: 326–335.

Cohen, A. and Einav, L. (2007) 'Estimating risk preferences from deductible choice', *American Economic Review* 97: 745–788.

Conlisk, J. (1996) 'Why bounded rationality?', *Journal of Economic Literature*, 34: 669–700.

Cooper, D. (2006) 'Are experienced managers expert at overcoming coordination failure?' *Advances in Economic Analysis and Policy*, 6: 1–30.

Costa-Gomes, M. and Crawford, V. (2006) 'Cognition and behavior in two-person guessing games: An experimental study', *American Economic Review*, 96: 177–1768.

Costa-Gomes, M., Crawford, V. and Iriberri, N. (2009) 'Comparing models of strategic thinking in Van Huyck, Battalio, and Beil's coordination games', *Journal of the European Economic Association*, 7: 365–376.

Crawford, V. (1995) 'Adaptive dynamics in coordination games', *Econometrica*, 63: 103–43.

Crawford, V. and Iriberri, N. (2007) 'Level-k auctions: Can a non-equilibrium model of strategic thinking explain the winners curse and overbidding in private value auctions', *Econometrica*, 75: 1721–1770.

Croson, R. and Gneezy, U. (2009) 'Gender differences in preferences', *Journal of Economic Literature*, 47: 448–474.

Croson, R. and Marks, M. (2001) 'The effect of recommended contributions in the voluntary provision of public goods', *Economic Inquiry*, 39: 238–249.

Dana, J., Weber, R. and Xi Kuang, J. (2007) 'Exploiting moral wiggle room: Experiments demonstrating an illusory preference for fairness', *Economic Theory*, 33: 67–80.

Darley, J. M. and Gross, P. H. (1983) 'A hypothesis-confirming bias in labeling effects', *Journal of Personality and Social Psychology*, 44: 20–33.

DellaVigna, S. (2009) 'Psychology and economics: Evidence from the field', *Journal of Economic Literature*, 47: 315–372.

Della Vigna, S. and Malmendier, U. (2004) 'Contract design and self-control: Theory and evidence', *Quarterly Journal of Economics*, 119: 353–402.

DellaVigna, S. and Malmendier, U. (2006) 'Paying not to go to the gym', *American Economic Review*, 96: 694–719.

Di Tella, R. and MacCulloch, R.J. (2005) 'Partisan social happiness', *Review of Economic Studies*, 72: 367–393.

Di Tella, R. and MacCulloch, R.J. (2006) 'Some uses of happiness data in economics', *Journal of Economic Perspectives*, 20: 25–46.

Di Tella, R., MacCulloch, R.J. and Oswald, A.J. (2001) 'Preferences over inflation and unemployment: Evidence from surveys of happiness', *American Economic Review*, 91: 335–341.

Diamond, P. and Vartiainen, H. (2007) *Behavioral Economics and its Applications*, Princeton: Princeton University Press.

Diekhof, E. and Gruber, O. (2010) 'When desire collides with reason: Functional interactions between anteroventral prefrontal cortex and nucleus accumbens underlie the human ability to resist impulsive desires', *Journal of Neuroscience*, 30: 1488–1493.

Dolan, P. and Kahneman, D. (2008) 'Interpretations of utility and their implications for the valuation of health', *Economic Journal*, 118: 215–234.

Dolan, P., Hallsworth, M., Halpern, D., King, D. and Vlaev, I. (2010) 'MINDSPACE: Influencing behavior through public policy', Cabinet Office publication.

Dufwenberg, M. and Kirchsteiger, G. (2004) 'A theory of sequential reciprocity', *Games and Economic Behavior*, 47: 268–298.

Easterlin, R. (1974) 'Does economic growth improve the human lot? Some empirical evidence', in David, P.A. and Reder, M.W. (Eds) *Nations and Households in Economic Growth: Essays in Honour of Moses Abramovitz*, New York: Academic Press.

Eckel, C. and Grossman, P. (2001) 'Chivalry and solidarity in ultimatum games', *Economic Inquiry*, 30: 171–188.

Ellison, G. (2006) 'Bounded rationality in industrial organization', in Blundell, R., Newey, W., and Persson, R. (Eds) *Advances in Economics and Econometrics: Theory and Applications, Ninth World Congress, Volume II*, New York: Cambridge University Press.

Ellsberg, D. (1961) 'Risk, ambiguity, and the savage axioms', *Quarterly Journal of Economics*, 75: 643–669.

Engelmann, D. and Strobel, M. (2004) 'Inequality aversion, efficiency, and maximin preferences in simple distribution experiments', *The American Economic Review*, 94: 857–869.

Falk, A. and Fischbacher, U. (2006) 'A theory of reciprocity', *Games and Economic Behavior*, 54: 293–315.

Falk, A., Fehr, E. and Fischbacher, U. (2003) 'On the nature of fair behavior', *Economic Inquiry*, 41: 20–26.

Falk, A., Fehr, E. and Fischbacher, U. (2008) 'Testing theories of fairness – Intentions matter', *Games and Economic Behavior*, 62: 287–303.

Farber, H.S. (2005) 'Is tomorrow another day? The labour supply of New York City cabdrivers', *Journal of Political Economy*, 113: 46–82.

Farber, H.S. (2008) 'Reference-dependent preferences and labor supply: The case of New York City taxi drivers', *American Economic Revies*, 98: 1069–1082.

Fehr, E. and Falk, A. (1999) 'Wage rigidity in a competitive incomplete contract market', *Journal of Political Economy*, 107: 106–134.

Fehr, E. and Fischbacher, U. (2004) 'Third-party punishment and social norms', *Evolution and Human Behavior*, 25: 63–87.

Fehr, E. and Gächter, S. (2000a) 'Cooperation and punishment in public goods experiments', *American Economic Review*, 90: 980–994.

Fehr, E. and Gächter, S. (2000b) 'Fairness and retaliation: The economics of reciprocity', *Journal of Economic Perspectives*, 14: 159–181.

Fehr, E. and Schmidt, J. (1999) 'A theory of fairness, competition, and cooperation', *Quarterly Journal of Economics*, 114: 817–868.

Forsythe, R., Horowitz, J., Savin, N., and Sefton, M. (1994) 'Fairness in simple bargaining experiments', *Games and Economic Behavior*, 6: 347–369.

Frank, R. (1991) *Passions within Reason*, WW Norton and Co.

Frank, R. (2007) 'Behavioral economics and health economics', in Diamond, P. and Vartiainen, H. (Eds) *Behavioral Economics and its Applications*, Princeton: Princeton University Press.

Frank, R. and Hutchens, R. (1993) 'Wages, seniority, and the demand for rising consumption profiles', *Journal of Economic Behavior and Organization*, 3: 251–276.

Frank, R., Gilovich, T. and Regan, D. (1993) 'Does studying economics inhibit cooperation?', *The Journal of Economic Perspectives*, 7: 159–171.

Frederick, S., Loewenstein, G. and O'Donoghue, T. (2002) 'Time discounting and time preference: A critical review', *Journal of Economic Literature*, 40: 351–401.

Frey, B. (2008) *Happiness: A Revolution in Economics*, Cambridge, MA: MIT Press.

Frey, B. and Stutzer, A. (2002) 'What can economists learn from happiness research?' *Journal of Economic Literature*, 40: 402–435.

Friedman, M. (1953) *Essays in Positive Economics*, Chicago: University of Chicago Press.

Fudenberg, D. and Levine, D. (2006) 'A dual-self model of impulse control', *American Economic Review*, 96: 1449–1476.

Gabaix, X., Laibson, D., Moloche, G. and Weinberg, S. (2006) 'Costly information acquisition: Experimental analysis of a boundedly rational model', *American Economic Review*, 96: 1043–1068.

Gächter, S., and Falk, A. (2002) 'Reputation and reciprocity: Consequences for the labour relation,' *Scandinavian Journal of Economics*, 104: 1–26.

Gächter, S., Herrmann, B. and Thöni, C. (2010) 'Culture and Cooperation', *Philosophical Transactions of the Royal Society B – Biological Sciences*, 365: 2651–2661.

Genesove, D. and Mayer, C. (2001) 'Loss aversion and seller behaviour: Evidence from the housing market', *Quarterly Journal of Economics*, 116: 1233–1260.

Gilbert, D.T., Gill, M.J. and Wilson, T.D. (2002) 'The future is now: Temporal correction in affective forecasting', *Organizational Behavior and Human Decision Processes*, 88: 430–444.

Gilboa, I. and Schmeidler, D. (1995) 'Case-based decision theory', *Quarterly Journal of Economics*, 110: 605–639.

Gillet, J., Cartwright, E. and van-Vugt, M. (2010) 'Leadership in the weak link game', School of Economics, University of Kent working paper.

Gilovich, T., Vallone, R. and Tversky, A. (1985) 'The hot hand in basketball: On the misperception of random sequences', *Cognitive Psychology*, 17: 295–314.

Gintis, H., Bowles, S., Boyd, R. and Fehr, E. (2005) Moral *Sentiments and Material Interests*, Cambridge, MA: MIT Press.

Glimcher, P. (2004) *Decisions, Uncertainty, and the Brain: The Science of Neuroeconomics*, Cambridge, MA: MIT Press.

Gneezy, U and List, J. (2006) 'Putting behavioral economics to work: Field evidence on gift exchange,' *Econometrica*, 74: 1365–1384.

Gneezy, U. and Rustichini, A. (2004) 'Gender and competition at a young age', *American Economic Review*, 94: 377–381.

Gode, D.K. and Sunder, S. (1993) 'Allocative efficiency of markets with zer-intelligence traders: Market as a partial substitute for individual rationality', *Journal of Political Economy*, 101: 119–137.

Goeree, J. K., and Yariv, L. (2007) 'Conformity in the lab', working paper.

Grosskopf, B. (2003) 'Reinforcement and directional learning in the ultimatum game with responder competition', *Experimental Economics*, 6: 141–158.

Gruber, J. and Köszegi, B. (2001) 'Is addiction "rational"? Theory and evidence', *Quarterly Journal of Economics*, 116: 1261–1303.

Halevy, Y. (2007) Ellsberg revisited: An experimental study', *Econometrica*, 75: 503–536.

Hare, T., O'Doherty, J., Camerer, C., Schultz, W. and Rangel, A. (2008) 'Dissociating the role of the orbitofrontal cortex and the striatum in the computation of goal values and prediction errors', *Journal of Neuroscience*, 28: 5623–5630.

Harrison, G., List, J. and Towe, C. (2007) Naturally occurring preferences and exogenous laboratory experiments: A case study of risk aversion', *Econometrica*, 75: 433–458.

Heath, C. and Soll, J.B. (1996) 'Mental budgeting and consumer decisions', 23: 40–52.

Henker, J, and Owen, S. (2008) 'Bursting bubbles: Linking experimental financial market results to field market data', *Journal of Behavioral Finance*, 9: 5–14.

Henrich, J., Boyd, R., Bowles, S., Camerer, C., Fehr, E. and Gintis, H. (2004) *Foundations of Human Sociality*, Oxford: Oxford University Press.

Herrmann, B., Thöni, C. and Gächter, S. (2008) 'Antisocial punishment across societies', *Science*, 319: 1362–1367.

Ho, T-H., Camerer, C. and Weigelt, K. (1998) 'Iterated dominance and iterated best response in experimental "p-beauty contests"', *American Economic Review*, 88: 947–969.

Hoffman, E., McCabe, K., and Smith, V. (1996) 'Social distance and other-regarding behavior', *American Economic Review* 86: 653–660.

Hoffman, E., McCabe, K., Shachat, K., and Smith, V. (1994) 'Preferences, property rights and anonymity in bargaining games', *Games and Economic Behavior*, 7: 346–380.

Holt, C. and Laury, S. (2002) 'Risk aversion and incentive effects', *American Economic Review*, 92: 1644–1655.

Hsu, M., Bhatt, M., Adolphs, R., Tranel, D. and Camere, C. (2005) 'Neural systems responding to degrees of uncertainty in human decision-making', *Science*, 310: 1680–1683.

Huberman, G. and Jiang, W. (2006) 'Offering versus choice in 401(k) plans: Equity exposure and number of funds', *Journal of Finance*, 61: 763–80.

Huettel, S. Stowe, J., Gordon, E., Warner, B. and Platt, M. (2006) 'Neural signatures of economic preferences for risk and ambiguity', *Neuron*, 49: 765–775.

Hussam, R. N., Porter, D., and Smith, V. L. (2008) 'Thar she blows: Can bubbles be rekindled with experienced subjects?', *American Economic Review*, 93: 924–937.

Institute of Medicine (2001) *Crossing the Quality Chasm*, Washington, DC: NAS Press.

Iyengar, S.S. and Lepper, M.R. (2000) 'When choice is demotivating: Can one desire too much of a good thing', *Journal of Personality and Social Psychology*, 79: 995–1005.

Jehiel, P. (2005) 'Analogy-based expectation equilibrium', *Journal of Economic Theory*, 123: 81–104.

Jianakoplos, N. and Bernasek, A. (1998) 'Are women more risk averse?' *Economic Inquiry*, 36: 620–630.

Johnson, D.S., Parker, J.A. and Souleles, N.S. (2006) 'Household expenditure and the income tax rebates of 2001', *American Economic Review*, 96: 1589–1610.

Kagel, J. H. and Roth, A. E. (2000) 'The dynamics of reorganization in matching markets: A laboratory experiment motivated by a natural experiment', *Quarterly Journal of Economics*, 115: 201–235.

Kahneman, D. (2003) 'Maps of bounded rationality: Psychology for behavioural economics', *American Economic Review*, 93: 1449–1475.

Kahneman, D. and Dolan, P. (2008) 'Interpretations of utility and their implications for the valuation of health', *Economic Journal*, 118: 215–234.

Kahneman, D. and Krueger, A.B. (2006) 'Developments in the measurement of subjective well-being', *Journal of Economic Perspectives*, 20: 3–24.

Kahneman, D. and Tversky, A. (1973) 'On the psychology of prediction', *Psychological Review*, 80: 237–251.

Kahneman, D. and Tversky, A. (1979) 'Prospect theory: An analysis of decision under risk', *Econometrica*, 47: 263–291.

Kahneman, D. and Tversky, A. (1983) 'Choices, values, and frames', *American Psychologist*, 39: 341–350.

Kahneman, D., Knetsch, J. and Thaler, R.H. (1986) 'Fairness as a constraint on profit seeking: Entitlements in the market', *American Economic Review*, 76: 728–741.

Kahneman, D., Wakker, P. and Sarin, R. (1997) 'Back to Bentham? Explorations of experienced utility', *Quarterly Journal of Economics* 112: 375–405.

Kahneman, D., Fredrickson, D.L., Schreiber, C.A., and Redelmeier, D.A. (1993) 'When more pain is preferred to less: Adding a better end', *Psychological Science*, 4: 401–405.

Kaiser Family Foundation (2008) '2008 Update on Consumers' Views of Patient Safety and Quality Information', report no. 7819.

Kalivas, P. and Volkow, N. (2005) 'The neural basis of addication: A pathology of motivation and choice', *American Journal of Psychiatry*, 162: 1403–1413.

Kaplan, H. Hill, K., Lancaster, J. and Hurtado, A.M. (2000) 'A theory of human life history evolution: diet, intelligence, and longevity', *Evolutionary Anthropolgy*, 9: 156–185.

Karlsson, N., Loewenstein, G. and Seppi, D. (2009) 'The "ostrich effect": Selective attention to information about investments', *Journal of Risk and Uncertainty*, 38: 95–115.

Ketcham, J. Smith, V.L. and Williams, A.W. (1984) 'A comparison of posted-offer and double-auction pricing institutions', *Review of Economic Studies*, 51: 595–614.

Kilbanoff, P., Marinacci, M. and Mukerji, S. (2005) 'A smooth model of decision making under ambiguity', *Econometrica* 73: 1849–1892.

Klemperer, P. (2004) *Auctions: Theory and Practice*, Princeton: Princeton University Press.

Knack, S. and Keefer, P. (1997) 'Does social capital have an economic payoff? A cross-country investigation', *Quarterly Journal of Economics*, 112: 1251–1288.

Knoch, D., Pascual-Leone, A., Meyer, K., Treyer, K. and Fehr, E. (2006) 'Diminishing reciprocal fairness by disrupting the right prefrontal cortex', *Science*, 314: 829–832.

Knutson, B., Fong, G., Adams, C., Varner, J. and Hommer, D. (2001) 'Dissociation of reward anticipation and outcome with event-related fMRI', *NeuroReport*, 12: 3683–3687.

Kooreman, P. (2000) 'The labelling effect of a child benefit system', *American Economic Review*, 90: 571–583.

Kőszegi, B. and Rabin, M. (2006) 'A model of reference-dependent preferences', *Quarterly Journal of Economics*, 121: 1133–1165.

Kőszegi, B. and Rabin, M. (2007) 'Reference-dependent risk attitudes', *American Economic Review*, 97: 1047–1073.

Kube, S., André Maréchal, M. and Puppe, C. (2006) 'Putting reciprocity to work – Positive versus negative responses in the field,' University of St. Gallen Department of Economics working paper series 2006–27.

Laibson, D. (1997) 'Golden eggs and hyperbolic discounting', *Quarterly Journal of Economics*, 112: 443–447.

Laibson, D. (2001) 'A cue-theory of consumption', *Quarterly Journal of Economics*, 116: 81–119.

Laibson, D., Repetto, A. and Tobacman, J. (2007) 'Estimating discount functions with consumption choice over the lifecycle', NBER working paper 13314.

Laland, K. and Brown, G. (2005) *Sense and Nonsense*, Oxford: Oxford University Press.

Landsberger, M. (1966) 'Windfall income and consumption: comment', *American Economic Review*, 534–539.

Larrick, R. and Blount, S. (1997) 'The claiming effect: Why players are more generous in social dilemmas than in ultimatum games', *Journal of Personality and Social Psychology*, 72: 810–825.

Levitt, S. and List, J. (2007) 'What do laboratory experiments measuring social preferences reveal about the real world?', *The Journal of Economic Perspectives*, 21: 153–174.

Lichtenstein, S., Slovic, P., Fischhoff, B., Layman, M. and Combs, B. (1978) 'Judged frequency of lethal events', *Journal of Experimental Psychology: Human Learning and Memory*, 4: 551–78.

List, J. (2004) 'Neoclassical theory versus prospect theory: Evidence from the marketplace', *Econometrica*, 72: 615–625.

List, J. (2007) 'On the interpretation of giving in dictator games', *Journal of Political Economy*, 115: 482–493.

Loewenstein, G. and Adler, D. (1995) 'A bias in the prediction of tastes', *Economic Journal*, 105: 929–937.

Loewenstein G. and Prelec D. (1992) 'Anomalies in intertemporal choice: Evidence and an interpretation', *Quarterly Journal of Economics*, 107: 573–597.

Loewenstein, G. and Prelec, D. (1993) 'Preferences over sequences of outcomes', *Psychological Review*, 100: 91–108.

Loewenstein, G. and Ubel, P.A. (2008) 'Hedonic adaption and the role of decision and experience utility in public policy', *Journal of Public Economics*, 92: 1795–1810.

Loewenstein, G., O'Donoghue, T. and Rabin, M. (2003) 'Projection bias in predicting future utility', *Quarterly Journal of Economics*, 118: 1209–1248.

Loomes, G. and Sugden, R. (1982) 'An alternative theory of choice under uncertainty', *Economic Journal*, 92: 805–824.

Loomes, G. and Sugden, R. (1983) 'A rationale for preference reversal', *American Economic Review*, 73: 428–432.

Loomes, G. and Sugden, R. (1986) 'Disappointment and dynamic consistency in choice under uncertainty,' *Review of Economic Studies*, 53: 271–82.

Loomes, G., Starmer, C. and Sugden, R. (1991) 'Observing violations of transitivity by experimental methods', *Econometrica*, 59: 425–439.

Lord, C. G., Ross, L., and Lepper, M. R. (1979) 'Biased assimilation and attitude polarization: The effects of prior theories on subsequently considered evidence', *Journal of Personality and Social Psychology*, 37: 2098–2109.

Lucking-Reiley, D. (1999) 'Using field experiments to test equivalence between auction formats: Magic on the internet', *American Economic Review*, 89: 1063–1080.

McCall, T. B. (1996) *Examining your Doctor: A Patient's Guide to Avoiding Harmful Medical Care*, New York: Carol Publishing Corporation.

McClure, S., Laibson, D., Loewenstein, G. and Cohen, J. (2004) 'Separate neural systems value immediate and delayed monetary rewards', *Science*, 306: 503–507.

McKelvey, R. and Palfrey, T. (1995) 'Quantal response equilibria for normal form games', *Games and Economic Behavior*, 10: 6–38.

McKelvey, R., Palfrey, T. and Weber R. (2000) 'The effects of payoff magnitude and heterogeneity on behavior in 2x2 games with unique mixed strategy equilibria', *Journal of Economic Behavior and Organization* 42: 523–548.

Madrian, B.C. and Shea, D.F. (2001) 'The power of suggestion: Inertia in 401(k) participation and savings behavior', *Quarterly Journal of Economics*, 116: 1149–1187.

Marks, M. and Croson, R. (1998) 'Alternative rebate rules in the provision of a threshold public good: An experimental investigation', *Journal of Public Economics*, 67: 195–220.

Mehra, R. and Presccott, E. (2003) 'The equity premium puzzle in retrospect', in G.M. Constantinides, M. Harris and R. Stulz. *Handbook of the Economics of Finance*, Amsterdam: North Holland.

Mehta, J., Starmer, C. and Sugden, R. (1994) 'The nature of salience: An experimental investigation of pure coordination games', *American Economic Review*, 84: 658–73.

Milgrom, P. (2004) *Putting Auction Theory to Work*, Cambridge: Cambridge University Press.

Miravete, E. (2003) 'Choosing the wrong calling plan? Ignorance and learning', *American Economic Review*, 93: 297–310.

Mullainathan, S. and Thaler, R. H. (2000) 'Behavioral economics', in *International Encyclopedia of the Social and Behavioral Sciences*, Cambridge, MA: MIT Press.

Nagel, R. (1995) 'Unraveling in guessing games: An experimental study', *American Economic Review*, 85: 1313–1326.

National Drug Intelligence Center (2010) 'National Drug Threat Assessment 2010', report.

Neumark, D. and Postlewaite, A. (1998) 'Relative income concerns and the rise in married women's employment', *Journal of Public Economics*, 70: 157–183.

Niederle, M. and Vesterlund, L. (2007) 'Do women shy away from competition? Do men compete too much', *Quarterly Journal of Economics*, 122: 1067–1101.

Nowak, M. (2006) 'Five rules for the evolution of cooperation', *Science*, 314: 1569–1572.

Odean, T. (1998) 'Are investors reluctant to realize their losses?', *Journal of Finance*, 53: 1775–1798.

O'Doherty, J., Deichmann, R., Critchley, H. and Dolan, R. (2002) 'Neural responses during anticipation of a primary taste reward', *Neuron*, 33: 815–826.

O'Doherty, J., Kringelbach, M., Rolls, E., Hornak, J. and Andrews, C. (2001) 'Abstract reward and punishment representations in the human orbitofrontal cortex', *Nature Neuroscience*, 4: 95–102.

O'Doherty, J., Dayan, P., Schultz, J., Deichmann, R., Friston, R. and Dolan, R. (2004) 'Dissociable roles of ventral and dorsal striatum in instrumental conditioning', *Science*, 304: 452–454.

O'Donoghue, T. and Rabin, M. (1999) 'Doing it now or later', *American Economic Review*, 89: 103–124.

O'Donoghue, T. and Rabin, M. (2000) 'The economics of immediate gratification', *Journal of Behavioral Decision Making*, 13: 233–250.

O'Donoghue, T. and Rabin, M. (2006) 'Incentives and self control', in Blundell, R., Newey, W., and Persson, R. (Eds) *Advances in Economics and Econometrics: Theory and Applications, Ninth World Congress, Volume II*, New York: Cambridge University Press.

Office for National Statistics (2004) 'Smoking related behavior and attitudes', research report.

Olson, M. (1971) *The Logic of Collective Action: Public Goods and the Theory of Groups*, Cambridge, MA: Harvard University Press.

Oskarsson, A. T., Van Boven, L., McClelland, G., and Hastie, R. (2009) 'What's next? Judging sequences of binary events', *Psychological Bulletin*, 135: 262–285.

Ostrom, E. (1990) *Governing the Commons: The Evolution of Institutions for Collective Action*, New York: Cambridge University Press.

Ostrom, E. (2006) 'The value-added of laboratory experiments for the study of institutions and common-pool resources', *Journal of Economic Behavior and Organization*, 61: 149–163.

Ostrom, E. (2010) 'Beyond markets and states: Polycentric governance of complex economic systems', *American Economic Review*, 100: 641–672.

Ostrom, E., Walker, J. and Gardner, R. (1992) 'Covenants with and without a sword: Self-governance is possible', *American Political Science Review*, 86: 404–417.

Oswald, A. and Powdthavee, N. (2008) 'Does happiness adapt? A longitudinal study of disability with implications for economists and judges', *Journal of Public Economics*, 92: 1061–1077.

Patall, E.A., Cooper, H. and Robinson, J. C. (2008) 'The effects of choice on intrinsic motivation and related outcomes: A meta-analysis of research findings', *Psyhcological Bulletin*, 134: 270–300.

Phelps, C.E. and Mooney, C. (1993) 'Variations in medical practice: causes and consequences', in *Competitive Approaches to Health Care Reform* (eds Arnould, R., Rich, R. and White, W.) Washington, DC: Urban Institute Press.

Phillips, C. and Thompson, G. (2009) 'What is a QALY', Hayward Medical Communications.

Porter, D. P., and Smith, V. L. (2003) 'Stock market bubbles in the laboratory', *Journal of Behavioral Finance*, 4: 7–20.

Post, T., van den Assem, M.J., Baltussen, G. and Thaler, R.H. (2008) 'Deal or no deal? Decision making under risk in a large-payoff game show', *American Economic Review*, 98: 38–71.

Pradel, J., Euler, H. and Fetchenhauer, D. (2009) 'Spotting altruistic dictator game players and mingling with them: The elective assortation of classmates', *Evolution and Human Behavior*, 30: 103–113.

Pratt, J.W., Wise, D.A. and Zeckhauser, R. (1979) 'Price differences in almost competitive markets', *Quarterly Journal of Economics*, 93: 189–211.

Preuschoff, K., Bossaerts, P, and Quartz, S. (2006) 'Neural differentiation of expected reward and risk in human subcortical structures', *Neruon*, 51: 381–390.

Purves, D., Brannon, E., Cabeza, R., Huettel, S., LaBar, K., Platt, M. and Woldorff, M. (2008) *Principles of Cognitive Neuroscience*, Sunderland, Massachusetts: Sinauer Associates.

Rabin, M. (1993) 'Incorporating fairness into game theory and economics', *American Economic Review*, 83: 1281–1302.

Rabin, M. (1998) 'Psychology and economics', *Journal of Economic Literature*, 36: 11–46.

Rabin, M. (2000) 'Risk aversion and expected-utility theory: A calibration theorem', *Econometrica*, 68: 1281–1292.

Rabin, M. (2002) 'Inferences by believers in the law of small numbers', *Quarterly Journal of Economics*, 117: 775–816.

Rabin, M. and Schrag, J. (1999) 'First impressions matter: A model of confirmatory bias', *Quarterly Journal of Economics*, 114: 37–82.

Rapoport, A., and Budescu, D. V. (1997) 'Randomization in individual choice behavior', *Psychological Review*, 104: 603–617.

Read, D. and van Leeuwen, B. (1998) 'Predicting hunger: The effects of appetite and delay on choice', *Organizational behaviour and human decision processes*, 76: 189–205.

Redelmeier, D. and D. Kahneman (1996) 'Patients' memories of painful medical treatments: Real-time and retrospective evaluations of two minimally invasive procedures', *Pain* 66: 3–8.

Redelmeier, D., J. Katz and D. Kahneman (2003) 'Memories of colonoscopy: A randomized trial', *Pain* 104: 187–194.

Ribar, D. and Wilhelm, M. (2002) 'Altruistic and joy-of-giving motivations in charitable behavior', *Journal of Political Economy*, 110: 425–457.

Ridley, M. (1997) *The Origins of Virtue*, London: Penguin.

Robson, A. (2001a) 'The biological basis of economic behavior', *Journal of Economic Literature*, 39: 11–33.

Robson, A. (2001b) 'Why would nature give individuals utility functions', *Journal of Political Economy*, 109: 900–914.

Robson, A. (2002) 'Evolution and human nature', *Journal of Economic Perspectives*, 16: 89–106.

Robson, A. and Kaplan, H. (2003) 'The evolution of human life expectancy and inteliigence in hunter-gatherer economics', *American Economic Review*, 93: 150–169.

Robson, A. and Samuelson, L. (2009) 'The evolution of time preference with aggregate uncertainty', *American Economic Review*, 99: 1925–1953.

Roth, A. (1995) 'Introduction to experimental economics', in Kagel, J. and Roth, A. (Eds) *Handbook of Experimental Economics*, Princeton: Princeton University Press.

Roth, A. (2002) 'The economist as engineer: Game theory, experimentation, and computation as tools for design economics', *Econometrica*, 70: 1341–1378.

Roth, A. (2008) 'Deferred acceptance algorithms: History, theory, practice, and open questions', *International Journal of Game Theory*, 36: 537–569.

Roth, A. and Erev, I. (1995) 'Learning in extensive-form games: Experimental data and simple dynamic models in the intermediate term', *Games and Economic Behavior*, 8: 164–212.

Roth, A., Prasnikar, V., Okuno-Fujiwara, M. and Zamir, S. (1991) 'Bargaining and market behavior in Jerusalem, Ljubljana, Pittsburgh, and Tokyo: An experimental study', *American Economic Review*, 81: 1068–95.

Sanfey, A., Rilling, J., Aronson, J., Nystrom, L. and Cohen, J. (2003) 'The neural basis of economic decision-making in the ultimatum game', *Science*, 300: 1755–1759.

Schelling, T. (1984) 'Self-command in practice, in policy, and in a theory of rational choice', *American Economic Review*, 74: 1–11.

Schelling, T. (1990) *Strategy of Conflict*, Cambridge, MA: Harvard University Press.

Schmidt, U., Starmer, C. and Sugden, R. (2008) 'Third generation prospect theory', *Journal of Risk and Uncertainty*, 36: 203–223.

Schmitt, P. Swope, K. and Walker, J. (2000) 'Collective action with incomplete commitment: Experimental evidence', *Southern Economic Journal*, 66: 829–854.

Schunk, D. (2009) 'Behavioral heterogeneity in dynamic search situations: Theory and experimental evidence', *Journal of Dynamics and Control* 33: 1719–1738.

Selten, R. and Chmura, T. (2008) 'Stationary concepts for experimental 2x2 games', *American Economic Review* 98: 938–966.

Selten, R., Abbink, K. and Cox, R. (2005) 'Learning direction theory and the winner's curse', *Experimental Economics*, 8: 5–20.

Sent, E.-M. (2004) 'Behavioral economics: How psychology made its (limited) way back into economics', *History of Political Economy*, 36: 735–760.

Shafir, E. and R. Thaler (2006) 'Invest now, drink later, spend never: On the mental accounting of delayed consumption', *Journal of Economic Psychology*, 27: 694–712.

Shafir, E., I. Simonson and A. Tversky (1993) 'Reason-based choice', *Cognition*, 11–36.

Shang, J. and Croson, R. (2009) 'A field experiment in charitable contribution: The impact of social information on the voluntary provision of public goods', *Economic Journal*, 119: 1422–1439.

Shapiro, M.D. and Slemrod, J. (2003) 'Consumer response to tax rebates', *American Economic Review*, 93: 381–396.

Shefrin, H.M. and Thaler, R.H. (1988) 'The behavioural life-cycle hypothesis', *Economic Inquiry*, 26: 609–643.

Shiller, R. J. (2003) 'From efficient markets theory to behavioural finance', *Journal of Economic Perspectives*, 17: 83–104.

Shiv, B. and Fedorikhin, A. (1999) 'Heart and mind in conflict: The interplay of affect and cognition in consumer decision making', *Journal of Consumer Research*, 26: 278–292.

Siemens, J.C. (2007) 'When consumption benefits precede costs: Towards an understanding of "buy now, pay later" transactions', *Journal of Behavioral Decision Making*, 20: 521–531.

Simon, H. (1955) 'A behavioural model of rational choice', *Quarterly Journal of Economics*, 69: 99–118.

Simonsohn, U. and Loewenstein, G. (2006) 'Mistake #37: The effect of previously encountered prices on current housing demand', *Economic Journal*, 116: 175–199.

Simonson, I. and Tversky, A. (1992) 'Choice in context: Tradeoff contrast and extremeness aversion', *Journal of Marketing Research*, 29: 281–295.

Slonim, R. and Roth, A. (1998) 'Learning in high stakes ultimatum games: An experiment in the Slovak Republic', *Econometrica*, 66: 569–596.

Smith, D., Loewenstein, G., Jepson, C., Jankovich, A., Feldman, H. and Ubel, P. (2008) 'Mispredicting and misremembering: Patients with renal failure overestimate improvements in quality of life after a kidney transplant', *Health Psychology*, 27: 653–658.

Smith, V.L. (1962) 'An experimental study of competitive market behavior', *Journal of Political Economy*, 70: 111–137.

Smith, V.L. (2002) 'Markets, Institutions and Experiments', in L. Nadel (Ed.) *Encyclopedia of Cognitive Science*, London: John Wiley & Sons.

Smith, V.L. (2003) 'Constructivist and Ecological Rationality in Economics', *American Economic Review*, 93: 465–508,

Smith, V.L., Suchanek, G.L. and Williams, A.W. (1988) 'Bubbles, crashes, and endogenous expectations in experimental spot asset markets', *Econometrica*, 56: 1119–1151.

Sobel, J. (2002) 'Can we trust social capital', *Journal of Economic Literature*, 40: 139–154.

Sobel, J. (2005) 'Interdependent preferences and reciprocity', *Journal of Economic Literature*, 43: 392–436.

Solnick, S. (2001) 'Gender differences in the ultimatum game', *Economic Inquiry*, 39: 189–200.

Spitzer, M., Fischbacher, U., Herrnberger, B., Grön, G. and Fehr, E. (2007) 'The neural signature of social norm compliance', *Neuron*, 56: 185–196.

Starmer, C. (2000) 'Developments in non-expected utility theory: The hunt for a descriptive theory of choice under risk', *Journal of Economic Literature*, 2000: 332–382.

Strotz, R. H. (1956) 'Myopia and inconsistency in dynamic utility maximization', *Review of Economic Studies*, 23: 165–180.

Sugden, R. (1995) 'A theory of focal points', *Economic Journal*, 105: 533–50,

Sydnor, J. (2010) '(Over)insuring modest risks', *American Economic Journal: Applied Economics* forthcoming.

Terrell, D. (1994) 'A test of the gambler's fallacy: Evidence from pari-mutuel games', *Journal of Risk and Uncertainty*, 8: 309–317.

Thaler, R.H. (1981) 'Some empirical evidence on dynamic inconsistency', *Economics Letters*, 8: 201–207.

Thaler, R.H. (1988) 'Anomalies: The ultimatum game', *Journal of Economic Perspectives*, 2: 195–206.

Thaler, R.H. (1990) 'Anomalies: Saving, fungibility, and mental accounts', *Journal of Economic Perspectives*, 4: 193–205.

Thaler, R.H. (2008a) 'Mental accounting and consumer choice', *Marketing Science* 27: 15–25.

Thaler, R.H. (2008b) 'Mental accounting and consumer choice: Anatomy of a failure', *Marketing Science* 27: 1–14.

Thaler, R.H. and Shefrin, H.M. (1981) 'An economic theory of self-control', *Journal of Political Economy*, 89: 392–406.

Thaler, R.H. and Sunstein, C. R. (2008) *Nudge: Improving decisions about health, wealth, and happiness*, London: Yale University Press.

Tricomi, E., Rangel, A., Camerer, C. and O'Doherty, J. (2010) 'Neural evidence for inequality-averse social preferences', *Nature*, 463: 1089–1092.

Tversky, A. and Kahneman, D. (1974) 'Judgment under uncertainty: Heuristics and biases' *Science*, 185: 1124–1131.

Tversky, A. and Kahneman, D. (1981) 'The framing of decisions and the psychology of choice', *Science* 211: 453–458.

Tversky, A. and Kahneman, D. (1983) 'Extensional versus intuitive reasoning: The conjunction fallacy in probability judgment', *Psychological Review*, 90: 293–315.

Tversky, A. and Kahneman, D. (1986) 'Rational choice and the framing of decisions', *Journal of Business*, 59: S251–S278.

Tversky, A. and Kahneman, D. (1992) 'Advances in prospect theory: Cumulative representation of uncertainty', *Journal of Risk and Uncertainty*, 5: 297–323.

Tversky, A. and Shafir, E. (1992) 'Choice under conflict: The dynamics of deferred decision', *Psychological Science*, 3: 358–361.

Tversky, A., Slovic, P. and Kahneman, D. (1990) 'The causes of preference reversal', *American Economic Review*, 80: 204–217.

Unver, U. (2005) 'On the survival of some unstable two-sided matching mechanisms', *International Journal of Game Theory*, 33: 239–254.

Van Huyck, J., Battalio, R. and Beil, R. (1990) 'Tacit coordination games, strategic uncertainty, and coordination failure,' *American Economic Review*, 80: 234–48.

Venkatraman, V., Payne, J., Bettman, J., Frances Luce, M. and Huettel, S. (2009) 'Separate neural mechanisms underlie choices and strategic preferences in risky decision making', *Neuron*, 62: 593–602.

Walker, M. and Wooders, J. (2001) 'Minimax play at Wimbledon', *American Economic Review*, 91: 1521–1538.

Warner, J. and Pleeter, S. 'The personal discount rate: Evidence from military downsizing programs', *American Economic Review*, 91: 33–53.

Weber, R.A. (2003) ' "Learning" with no feedback in a competitive guessing game, *Games and Economic Behavior*, 44: 134–144.

Webley, P. (2004) 'Children's understanding of economics', in Barrett, M. and Buchanan-Barrow, E. *Children's Understanding of Society*, Hove: Psychology Press.

Weizsäcker, G. (2010) 'Do we follow others when we should? A simple test of rational expectations', *American Economic Review* forthcoming.

World Values Survey 1981–2008, Official Aggregate v.20090901, 2009. World Values Survey Association (www.worldvaluessurvey.org). Aggregate File Producer: ASEP/JDS, Madrid.

Index